MASTERING JAVASCRIPT PREMIUM EDITION

Mastering™ JavaScript® Premium Edition™

James Jaworski

SYBEX®

San Francisco • Paris • Düsseldorf • Soest • London

Associate Publisher: Cheryl Applewood
Acquisitions and Developmental Editor: Bonnie Bills
Editors: Brianne Agatep, Rebecca Rider, Nancy Sixsmith
Production Editor: Dennis Fitzgerald
Technical Editor: George Stones
Book Designer: Robin Kibby
Electronic Publishing Specialist: Nila Nichols
Proofreaders: Emily Hsuan, Nelson Kim, Dave Nash, Laurie
O'Connell, Yariv Rabinovitch, Amy J. Rasmussen, Nancy Riddiough
Indexer: Ted Laux
CD Coordinator: Christine Detlefs
CD Technician: Kevin Ly
Cover Designer: Design Site
Cover Illustrator/Photographer: Jack D. Myers

Library of Congress Card Number: 2001094595

ISBN: 0-7821-2819-X

To Manuel and Yvonne

ACKNOWLEDGMENTS

I'd like to thank everyone who helped to see this book to completion. In particular, I'd like to thank Margot Maley Hutchison of Waterside Productions for making it possible and all the great folks at Sybex for their terrific support—especially Cheryl Applewood, Bonnie Bills, Dennis Fitzgerald, Brianne Agatep, Nancy Sixsmith, Rebecca Rider, and Nila Nichols. Thanks to George Stones for his excellent technical support. I'd also like to thank my wife Lisa, for her patience, love, and understanding; my son Jason, for playing great music; and my daughter Emily, for her endless suggestions.

CONTENTS AT A GLANCE

CONTENTS

INTRODUCTION

With all of the available web development technologies (such as HTML, XHTML, XML, Java, and ActiveX), you are probably wondering why you should invest the time to learn JavaScript. The answer to this question is apparent when you compare the capabilities provided by the current set of web programming languages: HTML and XHTML are great for creating static web pages. However, they provide no capabilities to develop pages that dynamically respond to user inputs. JavaScript *does* provide these capabilities.

XML is a language for defining other markup languages and is a significant technology for creating advanced web applications. However, XML, like HTML, lacks JavaScript's dynamic programming capabilities.

Java and ActiveX are excellent languages for creating components that can be embedded in a web page. However, their output display is confined, for security reasons, to a limited area of the browser window. In addition, if you want to develop Java and ActiveX components, you'll be undertaking a significant programming investment. JavaScript, on the other hand, provides the capability to develop scripts that can access all aspects of the browser display and can do so in a secure and easy-to-develop manner.

JavaScript enables you to integrate HTML documents, web components (which may have been written in Java and ActiveX), and multimedia plug-ins so that you can develop web applications that are dynamic, respond to a variety of user inputs, and access advanced browser capabilities such as multimedia and style sheets. Further, the LiveConnect feature of Netscape and Microsoft browsers allows JavaScript to directly access the properties and methods of Java applets and to exercise a fine level of control over the operation of plug-ins. If these are not compelling enough reasons to learn JavaScript, read on.

JavaScript can also be used to develop server-side web applications. Both Netscape and Microsoft web servers support server-side JavaScript. In addition, many Java Server Pages (JSP) platform vendors support JavaScript as a programming language. You can use JavaScript to replace all of your CGI scripts that are written in Perl, C, and shell programming languages. Microsoft's Active Server Pages (ASP) lets you develop integrated client- and server-side applications using JScript, greatly simplifying browser-server communication and automatically making the output of server-side scripts available as HTML to browser clients. Netscape servers can be scripted with server-side JavaScript to develop similar applications.

Microsoft also integrates JScript with its Windows Scripting Host (WSH) and remote scripting host technologies. The Mozilla project provides an open source JavaScript programming environment named Rhino.

This book covers all aspects of JavaScript and JScript programming. You'll learn to program web browsers using client-side scripts and the Document Object Model (DOM). You'll learn how to program web servers using server-side scripts, ASP, JSP, and LiveWire. You'll also learn how to use both Rhino and WSH. More important, you'll learn how to combine all of these facets of JavaScript programming to develop integrated web applications that are attractive, informative, and easy to use.

Conventions Used in This Book

Certain conventions are used in this book to make it easier for you to work with:

Uppercase or lowercase?   Even though the case does not matter for HTML and JavaScript elements, to help keep them distinct, I use all uppercase letters for HTML elements and all lowercase letters for JavaScript elements. (Case *does* matter for Java elements; in my discussions of Java items I use whatever case is appropriate.)

Fonts   I use a `monospaced font` to display JavaScript objects, methods, functions, variables, and URLs. (The names of files and directories are also displayed in that font.) Words identifying program parameters or arguments within a syntax explanation (some books refer to these words as "descriptive placeholders") are also displayed in `monospaced font`.

↳   Within a script or code listing, you'll see this continuation arrow to indicate a line that is a continuation of the line above it and has been broken only to fit it into the book's margins. If you need to type that line of code into a text editor, you should neither break the line nor type a special arrow character. Simply enter both lines of code on a single long line.

Some Experience Required: HTML

This book is aimed at those who want to learn and master JavaScript. You do not require any previous programming experience or knowledge of JavaScript. However, you should have a basic familiarity with HTML (Hypertext Markup Language). If you are new to HTML, I recommend that you use one of the many online tutorials that are available on the Web to get up to speed. To find one of these tutorials, use your browser's search capabilities to search for the text "HTML tutorial." You can also check the URL `www.toolery.com/javascript/` for links to online tutorials and other information.

Hardware and Software Requirements

This book is oriented toward Windows users. However, the JavaScript that you will learn will run on any platform that supports Netscape Communicator, Microsoft Internet Explorer, or the Opera Software Opera browser (www.operasoftware.com). These include Windows, Macintosh, Linux, and Unix variations. To use this book with Windows and Netscape Communicator or Internet Explorer, I recommend that you have a Pentium or better processor with at least 32 megabytes of RAM. You can get away with 16 megabytes of RAM, but your browser will start and run very slowly.

To develop server-side JavaScript applications you will need a Netscape or Microsoft web server or a JSP platform.

What Browser Should You Use?

To make the best use of this book, I recommend that you use both Netscape Communicator 6 or later *and* Microsoft Internet Explorer 5.5 or later. This book covers JavaScript 1.5, which is supported by both browsers.

How This Book Is Organized

The chapters in this book have three basic elements: background information on a particular aspect of JavaScript, a discussion of how to apply that aspect of JavaScript to the development of web applications, and programming examples that show JavaScript in action.

This is a large book because there is a lot that you can do with JavaScript, and plenty to learn if you want to master all aspects of JavaScript programming. The book is organized into six parts, consisting of 31 chapters. A seventh part, consisting of five chapters, can be found on the CD. There are also six appendices.

Part I: Getting Started with JavaScript and JScript

In Part I (Chapters 1 through 6), you'll cover the elements of the JavaScript language and learn how to write simple scripts. Part I introduces you to JavaScript's syntax and gives you a feel for its use in browser programming. You learn about JavaScript's support of object-based programming, and you are introduced to JavaScript's predefined objects. These predefined objects enable your scripts to control the way information is displayed by your browser and also how your browser responds to user events. Mastery of these objects is critical to becoming a proficient JavaScript programmer.

Part II: Programming the Document Object Model

In Part II (Chapters 7 through 13), you'll learn the details of JavaScript's predefined objects and learn how to use the properties and methods of these objects in sample scripts. When you finish Part II, you will have been thoroughly introduced to JavaScript browser programming and you'll be prepared to go on in Part III to learning how to use JavaScript to create a number of very useful and entertaining scripts.

Part III: Developing Components and Applications

In Part III (Chapters 14 through 20), you'll learn how to use JavaScript to create some useful enhancements to your web pages. You'll develop several JavaScript components that you can use and reuse in your web pages. You'll integrate these components to develop an electronic commerce web application. You'll also develop some JavaScript-based games. When you finish Part III, you'll have mastered the basics of client-side JavaScript programming.

Part IV: Working with XML-Capable Browsers

Part IV (Chapters 21 through 26) shows how JavaScript can be combined with XML to develop advanced web applications. You'll learn how to style XML so that it can be displayed with Netscape Communicator and Microsoft Internet Explorer. You'll learn how to script XML in Communicator and Internet Explorer and how to use XSLT to transform XML files into JavaScript code. Then you'll learn how to develop XML-based web applications and work with browser-specific XML capabilities.

Part V: Communicating with Java, ActiveX, and Plug-Ins

In Part V (Chapters 27 through 29), you'll be introduced to Java applets, ActiveX components, and browser plug-ins and learn how to combine them with JavaScript. You'll learn how to use JavaScript to load, control, and communicate with Java applets and how a Java applet can invoke JavaScript functions. You'll be introduced to ActiveX and learn how JScript can be used to script ActiveX objects. You'll also learn how browser plug-ins work and how to use JavaScript to load and communicate with plug-ins.

Part VI: Shell Programming

In Part VI (Chapters 30 and 31), you'll learn how to use JavaScript to develop useful shell scripts. You'll learn about the open source Rhino scripting environment developed by Mozilla.org and use it to create an example shell script that transforms structured text files into JavaScript slide show presentations. You'll also learn to use Microsoft's Windows Scripting Host to develop Windows application scripts.

Appendices

This book contains six appendices that provide useful JavaScript reference information. Appendices A and B cover JavaScript's mathematical function library and its support for regular expressions. Appendices C, D, and E provide a language reference that describes the JavaScript objects, properties, methods, and event handlers defined by ECMAScript revision 3, the Document Object Model (DOM) Level 0, and the DOM Level 1.

What's on the CD

 On the CD are five chapters about server-side programming (CD Chapters 32-36) shows you how to use JavaScript to develop server-side applications. You'll learn about the Common Gateway Interface (CGI) and shows how server-side CGI scripts interact with client-side JavaScript scripts. You'll be introduced to LiveWire and LiveWire Database Services, and you'll learn how to use JavaScript to create server-side JavaScript applications on Netscape servers. In addition to learning how to script Microsoft servers and how to use JScript with Active Server Pages (ASP), you'll learn how JavaScript can be used with Java Active Server Pages (JSP). Finally, you'll learn what security issues you must consider when developing JavaScript-based web applications.

The CD also contains all of the code listings and support files used in all of the examples of this book.

PART I

Getting Started with JavaScript and JScript

CHAPTER 1

Learning the Fundamentals

- The Web

- Cascading style sheets

- Common gateway interface programs

- JavaScript, JScript, ECMAScript, and the Document Object Model

- XML and XSL

- Intranets, extranets, and distributed applications

Imagine being able to create interactive multimedia adventure games that anyone can play over the World Wide Web. Imagine being able to create animated product catalogs that not only help your customers find the products they want but enable them to purchase them using secure online payment systems. Imagine being able to create database applications for use by your company's sales force from one end of the country to another via the company's intranet. With JavaScript, you no longer have to imagine, you can do it all.

JavaScript is the powerful programming language for the World Wide Web that not only enables the development of truly interactive web pages, but it is also the essential glue that integrates *HTML, XML, Java applets, ActiveX Controls, browser plug-ins, server scripts,* and other web *objects,* permitting developers to create *distributed applications* for use over the Internet and over corporate *intranets* as well.

If all the terms in the preceding paragraphs are a bit confusing to you, you've come to the right place to begin your involvement with JavaScript and the world of interactive web page development. In this chapter, I will provide all the background information you need to begin mastering the JavaScript language. I'll start with the concepts that are essential to understanding the operation of the World Wide Web.

NOTE JavaScript is supported by Netscape Navigator, Microsoft Internet Explorer, Sun's HotJava, Opera Software's Opera Browser, and other browsers. As such, it is an important tool for both current and future web development. Throughout this book I will emphasize the scripting capabilities provided by Navigator 6 (JavaScript 1.5) and Internet Explorer 6 (JScript 5.5). The other JavaScript-capable browsers take their lead from Navigator and Internet Explorer.

The Web

The World Wide Web, or simply *the Web* for short, is one of the most popular services provided via the Internet. At its best, it combines the appeal of exploring exotic destinations with the excitement of playing a video game, listening to a music CD, or even directing a movie, and you can do it all by means of an intuitive, easy-to-use, graphical user interface. Probably the most appealing aspect of the Web, however, is the fact that it isn't just for spectators. Once you have some experience with web *authoring tools*, you can publish yourself—and offer over the Web anything you want to make available, from your company's latest research results to your own documentary on the lives of the rich and famous.

A little history: What exactly *is* the Web? The Web is the collection of all browsers, servers, files, and browser-accessible services available through the Internet. It was created in 1989 by a computer scientist named Tim Berners-Lee; its original purpose was to facilitate communication between research scientists. Berners-Lee, working at the *Conseil Européen pour la Recherche Nucléaire (CERN)*, the European Laboratory for Particle Physics, located in Geneva, Switzerland, designed the Web in such a way that documents located on one computer on the Internet could provide links to documents located on other computers on the Internet.

To many, the most familiar element of the Web is the *browser*. A browser is the user's window to the Web, providing the capability to view web documents and access web-based services and applications. The most popular browsers are Netscape's Navigator and Microsoft's Internet Explorer, the latest versions of which both support JavaScript. Both browsers are descendants of the *Mosaic* browser, which was developed by Marc Andreessen at the National Center for Supercomputing Applications (NCSA), located at the University of Illinois, Urbana-Champaign. Mosaic's slick graphical user interface (GUI, pronounced "gooey") transformed the Web from a research tool to the global publishing medium that it has become today.

Today's web browsers extend Mosaic's GUI features with multimedia capabilities and with *browser programming languages* such as Java and JavaScript. These programming languages make it possible to develop web documents that are highly interactive, meaning they do more than simply connect you to another web page elsewhere on the Internet. *Web documents created with JavaScript contain programs*—which you, as the user of a browser, run entirely within the context of the web pages that are currently displayed. This is a major advance in web publishing technology. It means, for one thing, that you can run web-based applications without having to install any additional software on your machine.

In order to publish a document on the Web, it must be made available to a web *server*. Web servers retrieve web documents in response to browser requests and forward the documents to the requesting browsers via the Internet. Web servers also provide gateways that enable browsers to access web-related applications, such as database searches and electronic payment system.

The earliest web servers were developed by CERN and NCSA. These servers were the mainstay of the Web throughout its early years. Lately, commercial web servers, developed by Netscape, Microsoft, and other companies, have become increasingly popular on the Web. These servers are designed for higher performance and to facilitate the development of complex web applications. They also support the development of server-based applications using JavaScript and Java. Code written in these languages can be integrated very tightly with the server, with the result that server-side programs are executed very efficiently.

Because the Web uses the Internet as its communication medium, it must follow Internet communication *protocols*. A protocol is a set of rules governing the procedures for exchanging information. The Internet's *Transmission Control Protocol (TCP)* and *Internet Protocol (IP)* enable worldwide connectivity between browsers and servers. In addition to using the TCP/IP protocols for communication across the Internet, the Web also uses its own protocol, called the *Hypertext Transfer Protocol (HTTP)*, for exchanges between browsers and servers. HTTP is used by browsers to request documents from servers and by servers to return requested documents to browsers. Figure 1.1 shows an analogy between the English language and telephony protocols over the phone system on the one hand, and HTTP and TCP/IP over the Internet, on the other hand. Browsers and servers communicate via HTTP over the Internet in the same way that an American and an Englishman would communicate via English over a phone system.

FIGURE 1.1:

An analogy. Browsers and servers communicate via HTTP over the Internet in the same way that an American writer and a British editor would communicate via English over a phone system.

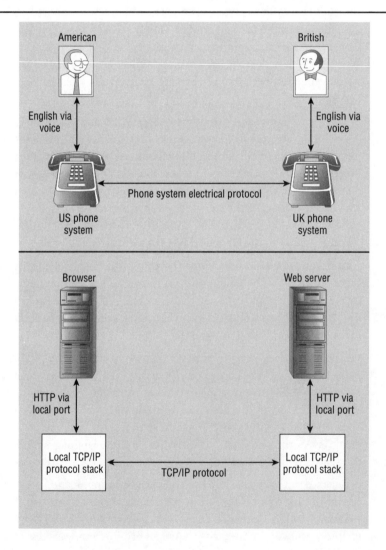

The Hypertext Markup Language

The Hypertext Markup Language (HTML) is the *lingua franca* of the Web. It is used to create web pages and is similar to the codes used by some word processing programs, notably WordPerfect.

HTML uses ordinary ASCII text files to represent web pages. The files consist of the text to be displayed and the *tags* that specify *how* the text is to be displayed. For example, the following line from an HTML file shows the text of a title between the appropriate title tags.

```
<TITLE>Mastering JavaScript</TITLE>
```

The use of tags to define the elements of a web document is referred to as *markup*. Some tags are used to specify the title of a document, others are used to identify headings, paragraphs, and hyperlinks. Still others are used to insert forms, images, multimedia objects, and other features in web documents.

NOTE   This book assumes that you already have a working knowledge of HTML. This section briefly reviews the important aspects of the language. If you have not used HTML, you should also check out the links to HTML tutorials and reference information located on this book's web page at www.jaworski.com/javascript/.

Tags always begin with a left angle bracket (<) and end with a right angle bracket (>). The name of the tag is placed between these two symbols. Usually, but not always, tags come in pairs, to surround the text that is marked up. Such tags are referred to as *surrounding* tags. For example, HTML documents begin with the <HTML> tag and end with the </HTML> tag. The first tag of a pair of tags is referred to as the *beginning* or *opening* tag and the second tag of the pair is referred to as the *ending* or *closing* tag. The ending tag has the same name as the beginning tag except that a / (a forward slash character) immediately follows the <.

Other tags, known as *separating* tags, do not come in pairs, and have no closing tags. These tags are used to insert such things as line breaks, images, and horizontal rules within marked-up text. An example of a separating tag is the <HR> tag, which is used to insert a horizontal rule (a line) across a web page.

Both surrounding and separating tags make use of *attributes* to specify properties of marked-up text. These attributes and their *attribute values*, if any, are included in the tag. For example, a horizontal rule 10 pixels wide may be specified using the following tag:

```
<HR SIZE="10">
```

The above HR tag contains a SIZE attribute that is assigned an attribute value of 10.

NOTE   Attributes and attribute values are placed in the opening tag of a pair of surrounding tags.

Listing 1.1 contains a sample HTML document that illustrates the use of tags in marking up a web page. Figure 1.2 shows how Netscape Navigator displays this HTML document. The <HTML> and </HTML> tags are used to identify the beginning and end of the HTML document. The document contains a head, identified by the <HEAD> and </HEAD> tags, and a body, identified by the <BODY> and </BODY> tags. The document's head contains a title which is marked by the <TITLE> and </TITLE> tags. (The title appears at the top of the Navigator window.)

NOTE   You can access the file for Listing 1.1, ch01-01.htm, on the CD that accompanies the book.

Listing 1.1:   Example HTML Document (ch01-01.htm)

```
<HTML>
<HEAD>
<TITLE>This text is the document's title.</TITLE>
</HEAD>
<BODY>
<H1 ALIGN="CENTER">This is a centered heading.</H1>
<P>This is the first paragraph.</P>
<P>This is the second paragraph.</P>
<HR SIZE="10">
<P ALIGN="CENTER">This paragraph is centered and below the horizontal rule.</P>
</BODY>
</HTML>
```

FIGURE 1.2:

A browser display of the HTML document shown in Listing 1.1

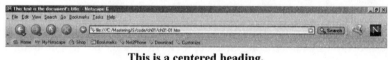

Here are a few items to notice within this listing:

- The document's body contains a Heading 1 that is marked by the `<H1>` and `</H1>` tags. The opening `<H1>` tag uses the ALIGN attribute to center the heading.

- Two paragraphs immediately follow the heading. These paragraphs are marked by the paragraph tags `<P>` and `</P>`.

- Following these two paragraphs is a horizontal rule with its SIZE attribute set to 10.

- The last element of the document's body is a paragraph that uses the ALIGN attribute to center the paragraph.

The Development of HTML and XHTML

HTML was originally developed by Tim Berners-Lee at CERN. Since then, it has evolved through several major revisions. Each revision adds new tags that increase the expressive power of the language. For example, HTML 2 added the capability to include forms within web documents, and HTML 3.2 added tags for tables and tags that support the use of JavaScript and Java.

 As of this writing (summer 2001), HTML 4.01 is the latest official version of the HTML language. HTML 4 adds support for international text, greater accessibility, more flexible tables, generic objects, printing, and advanced style sheets.

Although HTML is periodically standardized, the language continues to grow as the result of new tags, attributes, and attribute values that browser developers introduce. Because Netscape and Microsoft hold the largest share of the browser market, they have taken the lead in defining new additions to HTML. These additions are not part of the official HTML language, so they are referred to as *extensions*. Most extensions are eventually integrated into the official version of HTML.

While HTML 4 is the current standard, its days are numbered. The Extensible Hypertext Markup Language (XHTML) was released as a recommendation by the World Wide Web Consortium in January 2000. XHTML is essentially a reformulation of HTML to be more like XML. It's primary advantages over HTML are its simplicity and extensibility. XHTML removes the flexible coding supported by HTML. This makes XHTML simpler and easier to parse, allowing XHTML parsers to be quicker and smaller. Since XHTML is an XML application, it is easily extended. New tags and attributes can be defined and added to those that are defined in the standard.

Even though XHTML is the logical successor to HTML, there is no need to convert all of your web pages to the new standard. If you do, you'll find that some of your pages won't be rendered correctly by non-XHTML capable browsers. In addition, the document object models supported by current browsers are HTML-based. Even though Navigator 6 and

Internet Explorer 5 provide XML support, their primary capabilities and features still center around HTML.

Cascading Style Sheets

Style sheets provide the capability to control the way in which HTML elements are laid out and displayed. For example, you can use style sheets to control the color, font, and spacing used with different HTML elements. Support for cascading style sheets (CSS) was developed by the World Wide Web consortium and introduced with HTML 3.2, and additional CSS support was added in HTML 4. *Cascading* refers to the capability to use multiple levels of style sheets for a document where one level of style may be used to define another.

Two levels of cascading style sheets have been defined. CSS1 is a simple style sheet mechanism that allows basic styles (for example, fonts, colors, and spacing) to be associated with HTML elements. CSS1 is an outgrowth of HTML 3.2 and is supported by Internet Explorer 3 (and later), Navigator 4 (and later), as well as other browsers. CSS2 builds on CSS1 to add support for media-specific style sheets, content positioning, downloadable fonts, table layout, internationalization, automatic counters and numbering, and other capabilities.

In addition to CSS1 and CSS2, Navigator 4 introduced JavaScript style sheets (JSS). JSS is similar to CSS1 and makes styles available as JavaScript properties. Chapter 12, "Working with Styles and DHTML," introduces style sheets in more detail and shows how styles may be dynamically updated using JavaScript.

Helper Applications

Most graphical web browsers provide support for viewing images in common graphics formats, such as Graphics Interchange Format (GIF) and Joint Photographic Experts Group (JPEG). Some can even play audio files. However, most browsers do not provide much more than that in terms of multimedia features. Instead of building larger, more complicated browsers to handle many different file formats, browser developers use *helper applications*. When a browser encounters a file type that it does not know how to handle, it searches its list of helper applications to see if it has one that is capable of dealing with the file. If a suitable helper is found, then the browser executes the helper and passes it the name of the file to be run. If an appropriate helper cannot be found, then the browser prompts the user to identify which helper to use or to save the file for later display.

External Viewers and Plug-Ins

Early helper programs operated independently of the web browser. These programs, referred to as *external viewers*, were executed separate from the browser and created their own windows to display various types of files. Netscape and Microsoft developed the capability for their second-generation browsers to use *plug-in* or *add-in modules*, which not only execute automatically when needed but display their output in the browser window. Since then, numerous companies have developed plug-in modules to support everything from the three-dimensional worlds created by the Virtual Reality Modeling Language (VRML) to CD-quality audio.

Plug-in modules are generally quicker to load and more efficient than external viewers. Because they execute with the browser, they can be accessed from within the browser environment. Netscape provides the capability to control plug-in modules from Java and JavaScript code via its LiveConnect toolkit. Microsoft provides a similar capability through its Internet Explorer Object Model. You'll learn how to use JavaScript to control plug-ins in Chapter 29, "Scripting Plug-Ins."

Using MIME Types to Identify Helpers for File Formats

So far, I've described how browsers use helper applications to display different types of files, but how does a browser know which helpers to use for a given file? The answer lies in MIME types.

MIME stands for Multipurpose Internet Mail Extensions. MIME was originally developed as a standard for including different types of files in electronic mail. It was subsequently adopted for web servers and browsers to identify the types of files referenced in a web page.

MIME identifies file types using a *type/subtype* naming scheme. Examples of common MIME types are text/plain, text/html, image/gif, and video/quicktime. The first component of a MIME type identifies the general type of a file, while the second part identifies the specific type within the general category. For example, the text/plain and text/html types both belong to the text category, but they differ in their subtypes. Table 1.1 lists some common MIME types.

TABLE 1.1: Example MIME Types

MIME Type	Description
text/plain	Generic ASCII text file
text/html	Text file containing HTML
image/gif	Image in Graphics Interchange Format

Continued on next page

TABLE 1.1 CONTINUED: Example MIME Types

MIME Type	Description
image/jpeg	Image in Joint Photographic Experts Group format
audio/x-wav	File containing sounds stored in the Windows audio file format
video/mpeg	Video in the Moving Pictures Experts Group format
video/quicktime	Video in the Apple QuickTime format
application/octet-stream	Raw (unformatted) stream of bytes
application/x-javascript	File containing JavaScript source code

Web servers contain configuration files that match file extensions with their MIME types. For example, files that end with the extensions `.htm` or `.html` are associated with the text/html MIME type and files that end with `.jpg`, `.jpe`, or `.jpeg` are associated with the image/jpeg MIME type.

Browsers also contain configuration information about MIME types. This information is used to map MIME types to the helper application that displays files of that type.

When a browser requests a file from a web server, the server uses the file's extension to look up the file's MIME type. The server then identifies the file's MIME type to the browser. The browser uses the file's MIME type to determine which helper application, if any, is to be used to display the file. If the file is to be displayed by an external viewer, the browser waits until the file has been completely received before launching the viewer. If the file is to be displayed by a plug-in, the browser launches the plug-in and passes the file to the plug-in as the file is received. This enables the plug-in to begin displaying the file before it is fully loaded, which is an important capability of audio- and video-streaming applications.

Uniform Resource Locators (URLs)

A *uniform resource locator (URL)* is the notation used to specify the addresses of an Internet file or service. You have probably seen numerous examples of URLs. They are included in TV commercials, they're shown on billboards, and they appear in magazine ads. Examples of URLs include `http://home.netscape.com`, `http://www.microsoft.com`, and `ftp://ftp .cdrom.com`.

A URL always contains a *protocol identifier*, such as http or ftp, and a host name, such as `home.netscape.com`, `www.microsoft.com`, and `ftp.cdrom.com`, which appear in the previous examples. Commonly used protocol identifiers are `http`, `ftp`, and `gopher`. The protocol identifier is also referred to as a *scheme*. When writing a URL, the protocol identifier is followed by `://` and then the host name of the computer to which the protocol applies. (In URLs, path names are written using forward slash, /, characters rather than back slash, \, characters.) For example, to access the main home page of Microsoft on the host named www.microsoft.com, you would use the URL http://www.microsoft.com. To access the root directory of the File Transfer Protocol (FTP) server hosted by ftp.cdrom.com, you would use the URL ftp://ftp.cdrom.com.

In addition to the host name, the URL can specify the path and file name of a file to be accessed by adding a single / character followed by the name. For example, the home page for this book is located in the javascript subdirectory of my web server's root directory, in the file index.htm. The URL for this file is therefore

> http://www.jaworski.com/javascript/index.htm

(Actually, because my web server is set up to use the filename index.htm by default, it can be omitted from the URL. The URL http://www.jaworski.com/javascript would be sufficient to locate the file.)

NOTE   URLs may also contain additional addressing components, such as a port name before the path and filename and a file offset after the filename.

The "File" Protocol in URLs

Your browser can use the file protocol to access files located on your local machine. Suppose the file test.htm was located on your Windows desktop. The path to this file would be c:\windows\desktop\test.htm. To open the file with your browser, you would use the following URL: file://localhost/C|/WINDOWS/Desktop/test.htm.

The host name localhost in the previous URL is used to refer to the local file system and may be omitted safely. The slash following localhost, however, should be retained. The above URL could be thus be written as follows:

> file:///C|/WINDOWS/Desktop/test.htm

Note that in both examples above the C: drive designation that you are probably most familiar with from DOS conventions is written as C| instead.

The Hypertext Transfer Protocol (HTTP)

HTTP is the protocol used for communication between browsers and web servers. HTTP uses a request/response model of communication. A browser establishes a connection with a server and sends URL requests to the server. The server processes the browser's request and sends a response back to the browser.

A browser connects with a web server by establishing a TCP connection at port 80 of the server. This port is the address at which web servers "listen" for browser requests. Once a connection has been established, a browser sends a request to the server. This request specifies a request method, the URL of the document, program, or other resource being requested, the HTTP version being used by the browser, and other information related to the request.

Several request methods are available. GET, HEAD, and POST are the most commonly used ones:

- The GET method is used to retrieve the information contained at the specified URL. This method may also be used to *submit* data collected in an HTML *form* (the topic of Chapter 8, "Processing Forms") or to invoke a Common Gateway Interface program (a topic I discuss in the next section). When the server processes a GET request, it delivers the requested information (if it can be found). The server inserts at the front of the information an HTTP header that provides data about the server, identifies any errors that occurred in processing the request, and describes the type of information being returned as a result.

- The HEAD method is similar to the GET method except that when a web server processes a HEAD request, it only returns the HTTP header data and not the information that was the object of the request. The HEAD method is used to retrieve information about a URL without actually obtaining the information addressed by the URL.

- The POST method is used to inform the server that the information appended to the request is to be sent to the specified URL. The POST method is typically used to send form data and other information to Common Gateway Interface (CGI) programs. The web server responds to a POST request by sending back header data followed by any information generated by the CGI program as the result of processing the request.

 The current version of HTTP is HTTP 1.1. It incorporates performance, security, and other improvements to the original HTTP 1. A new version of HTTP, referred to as HTTP-NG, is currently being defined. (The NG stands for "next generation.") The goal of HTTP-NG is to simplify the HTTP protocol and make it more extensible.

Common Gateway Interface Programs

The *Common Gateway Interface* or CGI is a standard that specifies how external programs may be used by web servers. Programs that adhere to the CGI standard are referred to as CGI programs. CGI programs may be used to process data submitted with forms, to perform database searches and to support other types of web applications, such as clickable image maps.

A browser request for the URL of a CGI program comes about as the result of a user clicking a link or submitting a form. The browser uses HTTP to make the request. When a web server receives the request, the web server executes the CGI program and also passes it any data that was submitted by the browser. When the CGI program performs its processing, it usually generates data in the form of a web page, which it returns via the web server to the requesting browser.

The CGI standard specifies how data may be passed from web servers to CGI programs and how data should be returned from CGI programs to the web server. Table 1.2 summarizes these interfaces. In Chapter 8, "Processing Forms," and Chapter 32 on the CD, "Interfacing JavaScript with CGI Programs," you'll study CGI and learn how to create CGI programs.

TABLE 1.2: CGI Summary

Method of Communicating	Interface	Description
Command-line arguments	Web server to CGI program	Data is passed to the CGI program via the command line that is used to execute the program. Command-line arguments are passed to CGI programs as the result of ISINDEX queries.
Environment variables	Web server to CGI program	A web server passes data to the CGI program by setting special variables, referred to as environment variables, that are available to the CGI program via its environment.
Standard input stream	Web server to CGI program	A web server passes data to a CGI program by sending the data to the standard character input stream associated with the CGI program. The CGI program reads the data as if it were manually entered by a user at a character terminal.
Standard output stream	CGI program to web server	The CGI program passes data back to the web server by writing it to its standard output stream (for example, to a terminal). The web server intercepts this data and sends it back to the browser that made the CGI request.

Java Applets

The Java language, developed by Sun Microsystems, Inc., has realized tremendous popularity. Although it was originally developed as a language for programming consumer electronic devices, Java has increasingly been adopted as a hardware- and software-independent platform for developing advanced web applications. Java may be used to write stand-alone applications, but a major reason for its popularity is its ability to develop programs that can be executed by a web browser.

The Java programs that can be executed by the web browser are called *applets* rather than applications, because they cannot be run outside of the browser's own window. ("Application" usually implies a complete, stand-alone program.) Programmers create Java applets using built-in programming features of the Java Developer's Kit (JDK). Web pages, written in HTML, reference Java applets using the <APPLET> tag, in much the same way that images are referenced using the <IMAGE> tag. When a browser loads a web page that references a Java applet, the browser requests the applet code from the web server. When the browser receives the applet code, it executes the code and allocates a fixed area of the browser window. This area is identified by attributes specified with the applet tag. The applet is not allowed to update the browser display or handle events outside of its allocated window area.

By way of comparison, JavaScript provides access to the entire web page, but does not support many of the more advanced object-oriented programming features of Java.

Netscape Navigator and Microsoft Internet Explorer provide the capability for JavaScript scripts to load Java applets, access Java objects, and invoke their methods. Part V, "Communicating with Java, ActiveX, and Plug-Ins," shows how JavaScript and Java can be combined to produce advanced web applications.

ActiveX—Microsoft Objects

ActiveX is Microsoft's approach to executing objects other than Java applets in Internet Explorer. The name "ActiveX" was used to make it seem like a new and innovative technology. However, ActiveX is nothing more than Component Object Model (COM) objects that can be downloaded and executed by Internet Explorer. COM traces its origin back to the Object Linking and Embedding (OLE) technology of Microsoft Windows 3.1.

COM objects are instances of *classes* (object types) that are also organized into *interfaces*. Each interface consists of a collection of *methods* (functions). COM objects are implemented inside a *server* (dynamic-link libraries, operating system service, or independent process) and are accessed via their methods. The *COM library* provides a directory of available COM objects. Over the many years since Windows 3.1, many software components have been developed as COM objects.

ActiveX components are simply COM objects that implement a specific type of interface. They are important in that they provide a means for the large base of COM objects to be reused within Internet Explorer. They also allow older languages, such as C++ and C, to be used to build components for web applications.

While ActiveX components allow the use of legacy software in Internet Explorer, they also present some drawbacks. The most significant drawback is that ActiveX is only supported by Internet Explorer 4 and later. No other browser (including earlier versions of Internet Explorer) is able to use ActiveX. ActiveX has also been criticized for its poor security. An ActiveX component is not required to behave in a secure manner like a Java applet or JavaScript script. In fact, it has been demonstrated that ActiveX components can be used to steal or modify sensitive information or completely wipe out a user's system. Microsoft has countered this vulnerability by allowing ActiveX components to be digitally signed. This does not prevent ActiveX components from violating security, but, in some cases, it can be used to determine whether a particular website is responsible for causing damage.

ActiveX components are useful in intranet applications where all users of a particular company are required to use Internet Explorer and the components are signed by the company or a trusted developer. Because the Internet Explorer Object Model allows ActiveX components to be accessed from JavaScript, JavaScript scripts can be used to integrate the ActiveX components into the intranet applications. Chapter 28, "Scripting ActiveX Components," shows how to script ActiveX components using JavaScript.

A Brief History of JavaScript

Often, one programming language will evolve from another. For example, Java evolved from C++, which evolved from C, which evolved from other languages. This is also the case for JavaScript. Netscape originally developed a language called *LiveScript* to add a basic scripting capability to both Navigator and its web-server line of products; when it added support for Java applets in its release of Navigator 2, Netscape replaced LiveScript with JavaScript. Although the initial version of JavaScript was little more than LiveScript renamed, JavaScript has been subsequently updated with each new release of Navigator.

NOTE   Although JavaScript bears the name of Java, JavaScript is a very different language that is used for a very different purpose.

JavaScript supports both web browser and server scripting. Browser scripts are used to create dynamic web pages that are more interactive, more responsive, and more tightly integrated with plug-ins, ActiveX components, and Java applets. JavaScript supports these features by providing special programming capabilities, such as the ability to dynamically generate HTML and to define custom event-handling functions.

JavaScript scripts are included in HTML documents via the HTML <SCRIPT> tag. When a JavaScript-capable browser loads an HTML document containing scripts, it evaluates the scripts as they are encountered. The scripts may be used to create HTML elements that are added to the displayed document or to define functions, called *event handlers*, that respond to user actions, such as mouse clicks and keyboard entries. Scripts may also be used to control plug-ins, ActiveX components, and Java applets.

Microsoft implemented their version of JavaScript, named JScript, in its Internet Explorer 3. The scripting capability of Internet Explorer 3 is roughly equivalent to Navigator 2. Netscape introduced JavaScript 1.1 with Navigator 3 and JavaScript 1.2 with Navigator 4. JavaScript 1.1 added a number of new features, including support for more browser objects and user-defined functions. JavaScript 1.2 added new objects, methods, properties, and support for style sheets, layers, regular expressions, and signed scripts.

Netscape also supported server-side scripting with its LiveWire and LiveWire Pro (renamed to LiveWire Database Service) features of its Enterprise and FastTrack web servers. On the server side, JavaScript is used to more easily develop scripts that process form data, perform database searches, and implement custom web applications. Server-side scripts are more tightly integrated with the web server than CGI programs.

Microsoft introduced its ECMAScript-compliant version of JScript, in Internet Explorer 4. JScript is tightly coupled to Internet Explorer and allows almost all HTML elements to be scripted. Microsoft also included server-side JavaScript support with its Internet Information Server (IIS). It later developed a more general approach to server-side scripting with its Windows Scripting Host and Remote Scripting technologies. Remote scripting allows Internet Explorer to remotely execute scripts on a server and receive the server script outputs within the context of a single web page. You'll learn server-side programming in Chapters 32–36 on the CD.

Netscape and Microsoft submitted their scripting languages to the European Computer Manufacturers Association (ECMA) for standardization. ECMA released the Standard ECMA-262 in June of 1997. This standard describes the ECMAScript language, which is a compilation of the best features of JavaScript and JScript. Updated versions of this standard were released in June 1998 (Revision 2) and December 1999 (Revision 3). ECMA also released ECMA-290 in June 1999. ECMA-290 covers the development of reusable components in ECMAScript.

Microsoft worked closely with ECMA and updated Internet Explorer 4 and JScript (JScript 3.1) to achieve ECMAScript compliance. Navigator achieved ECMAScript compliance with JavaScript 1.3, which is supported in Navigator 4.06 through 4.7.

Internet Explorer 5 introduced JScript 5, which provides additional scripting capabilities, such as the `try - catch` statement. This statement provides advanced error handling support and is included in ECMAScript Revision 3. Internet Explorer 5.5 was introduced after ECMAScript Revision 3 and provides full Revision 3 support. Navigator 6.0 supports JavaScript 1.5, which is fully compliant with ECMAScript Revision 3.

While Netscape and Microsoft were busy introducing new versions of their browsers and scripting languages, another JavaScript-compatible browser was launched by Opera Software (`www.operasoftware.com`). In addition, Sun jumped into the JavaScript field with its HotJava browser. HotJava 3.0 is ECMAScript compliant. Other browser developers followed by developing JavaScript-capable browsers of their own.

Another JavaScript-related standardization effort was initiated by the World Wide Web Consortium to standardize the basic objects that are made available by browsers when processing HTML and XML documents. This effort resulted in a specification known as the Document Object Model (DOM) Level 1. It provides a standard set of objects for representing HTML and XML documents, a standard model of how these objects can be combined, and a standard interface for accessing and manipulating them. The DOM is like an application programming interface (API) for HTML and XML documents. However, the DOM is not a complete API in that it does not specify the events that occur when a user interacts with an HTML or XML document (and methods for handling them). Version 6 of Navigator and version 5 of Internet Explorer support the DOM.

LiveWire and LiveWire Database Service

LiveWire is a graphical environment for developing and managing websites. Netscape created it for use with its servers. One of LiveWire's features is that it supports the development of server-side programs using the JavaScript language. These programs are used in the same way as CGI programs, but they are more closely integrated with web servers and the HTML pages that reference them. The LiveWire Database Service provides the capability to connect server scripts to databases. Server scripts access databases using the industry-standard Structured Query Language (SQL).

Server-based JavaScript programs are compiled with HTML documents into a platform-independent bytecode format. When a web browser requests a compiled document, it is translated back into HTML format and sent out to the browser. The server-based scripts remain with the server and are loaded to perform any server-side processing. The HTML document loaded by the browser communicates with the server-side scripts to implement advanced web applications that are distributed between the browser, server, and other server-side programs, such as database and electronic commerce applications.

 LiveWire provides a number of programming objects that JavaScript scripts can use to implement CGI-style programs. These objects simplify the communication between browsers, web servers, and server-side scripts. Chapter 33 on the CD, "Scripting Netscape Servers," introduces LiveWire and shows how it is used to develop server-side scripts.

Active Server Pages, Windows Scripting Host, and Remote Scripting

Microsoft's Active Server Pages (ASP) is a server-side scripting environment that is similar to LiveWire. You can use it to include server-side scripts and ActiveX components with HTML pages. The combined HTML and script file is stored as an ASP file. When a browser requests the ASP file from your web server, the server invokes the ASP processor. The ASP processor reads through the requested file, executes any script commands, and sends the processing results as a web page to the browser. ASP pages can also invoke ActiveX components to perform tasks, such as accessing a database or performing an electronic commerce transaction. Because ASP scripts run on the web server and send standard HTML to the browser, ASP is browser independent.

Microsoft introduced ASP with IIS version 3. It also works with later versions of IIS, Personal Web Server for Windows 95, and Peer Web Server for Windows NT Workstation.

NOTE   Chapter 34 on the CD, "Scripting Microsoft Servers," and Chapter 31, "Working with Windows Scripting Host," cover ASP and WSH.

As a result of the success of ASP, Microsoft developed Windows Scripting Host (WSH), a technology that allows scripts to be run on Windows 95, 98, ME, NT 4, 2000, and Windows XP. WSH is language independent and supports JScript, VBScript, and other languages. It allows scripts to be executed from the Windows desktop or a console (MS-DOS) window. WSH scripts are complete in themselves and do need to be embedded in an HTML document. WSH is an exciting technology in that it extends the capabilities of JScript beyond the Web to the Windows desktop and operating system. WSH scripts can be used to replace MS-DOS scripts and provide the capability to take full advantage of the Windows GUI, ActiveX, and operating system functions in JScript scripts.

NOTE   A platform-independent JavaScript scripting environment known as Rhino is available from the Mozilla website at `www.mozilla.org`. Rhino is covered in Chapter 30, "Programming Rhino."

NOTE   WSH can be freely downloaded from Microsoft's website at `http://msdn.microsoft.com/scripting/`.

Microsoft's latest addition to scripting technology is referred to as *Remote Scripting*. Remote Scripting enables client-side scripts, running on Internet Explorer, to execute server-side scripts, running on IIS. This lets Internet Explorer and IIS perform simultaneous processing and communicate with each other within the context of a web page, allowing the page to be dynamically updated with server information without having to be reloaded. This frees the user from having to reload a web page during the execution of a web application and provides for a higher degree of interaction between the browser and web server. For example, with Remote Scripting, a web server can validate form data and provide the user with feedback while the user is still filling out the form.

Remote scripting allows browser/server communication to be accomplished in either a synchronous or asynchronous manner. When synchronous communication is used, a client-side script executes a server-side script and waits for the server-side script to return its result. When asynchronous communication is used, the client-side script executes the server-side script and then continues with its processing without waiting for the server-side script to finish.

NOTE Remote Scripting can be freely downloaded from Microsoft's website at `http://msdn.microsoft.com/scripting/`.

XML and XSL

One of the most powerful features of Navigator 6 and Internet Explorer 5 is their support for the Extensible Markup Language (XML). These browsers can display XML files directly. Moreover, they allow XML files to be scripted using JavaScript and JScript in much the same way as HTML files are scripted. This is a very powerful capability as you'll learn in Part IV, "Working with XML-Capable Browsers."

XML documents are similar to HTML documents in their use of tags and attributes to mark up text. However, XML differs from HTML in that it does not define a fixed set of markup tags. Instead, XML provides the capability to define the tags and attributes of customized markup languages. For example, you could use XML to define a product catalog and then display the catalog directly with an XML-capable browser. You could customize the way the catalog is displayed using CSS or the Extensible Style Language (XSL). You could also translate the XML to HTML in a format specified by an XSL style sheet.

NOTE The XML 1.0 specification is available at `www.w3.org/TR/REC-xml`. The XSL specification is available at `www.w3.org/TR/xsl/`. The XSL Transformations specification is available at `www.w3.org/TR/xslt`.

XSL is to XML as CSS is to HTML. XSL is a language for expressing style sheets. It is organized into two parts: the XSL Transformations language (XSLT) and a vocabulary (expressed in XML) for specifying formatting semantics. XSLT provides the capability to specify how an XML document of one type may be transformed into a document of another set of markup tags. XSLT may also be used to specify how XML documents should be translated into HTML. The second part of XSL, the formatting language, provides the capability to specify how XML documents should be rendered for a variety of display media, such as the Web and printed documents.

NOTE   XML documents may also be formatted using CSS.

Intranets, Extranets, and Distributed Applications

In the last couple of years, corporations have begun to look at ways of deploying TCP/IP networks inside of their companies to take advantage of the full range of standards-based services provided by the Internet. These "company-internal internets" have become known as *intranets*. Intranets may be private networks that are physically separate from the Internet, internal networks that are separated from the Internet by a firewall, or simply a company's internal extension of the Internet.

Companies deploy intranets so that they can make Internet services available to their workers. E-mail, web browsing, and web publishing are the most popular of these services. Many companies make web servers available for their employees' intranet publishing needs. These intranet web servers allow departments, groups, and individuals within a company to conveniently share information while usually limiting access to the information published on the intranet to company employees.

The popularity of intranets as a way of communicating and of sharing information within a company has brought about a demand for more powerful and sophisticated intranet applications. The eventual goal is for the intranet to provide a common application framework from which a company's core information processing functions can be implemented and accessed. Netscape, Sun, Microsoft, and other web software providers are focusing on the intranet as the primary application framework for the development of business software.

Because of its client/server architecture and user-friendly browser software, the Web is the perfect model for implementing these common intranet application frameworks. The approach taken by Netscape, Microsoft, and other web software developers is to use the web browser as the primary interface by which users connect to the intranet and run intranet and extranet applications. These applications are referred to as *distributed applications*, because their execution is distributed in part on the browser (via JavaScript, Java, ActiveX, XML, and other languages), in part on the server (via CGI programs and JavaScript and Java server-side programs), and in part on database and other enterprise servers.

Distributed intranet and extranet applications use HTML, JavaScript, Java, XML, and other languages for programming the browser-based user interface portion of the distributed application. They also use JavaScript and Java to perform server-side programming. "Server-Side Programming" on the CD covers the use of JavaScript in developing distributed applications.

In many distributed application development approaches, Java is seen as a key technology for developing the components of distributed applications and JavaScript is seen as the essential glue that combines these components into fully distributed web-based intranet and extranet applications.

Summary

This chapter covered the concepts that are essential to understanding the operation of the Web. You learned about web development languages, such as HTML, XML, Java, and JavaScript. You also covered related web technologies, such as HTTP, CGI, LiveWire, ASP, and Remote Scripting. You should have a basic understanding of how these elements work together to develop web applications. In the next chapter, you'll begin the exciting process of learning to use JavaScript to write some sample scripts.

CHAPTER 2

Introducing JavaScript and JScript

- JavaScript and browsers; JavaScript and servers

- Embedding JavaScript in HTML

- Telling non-JavaScript browsers to ignore your code

- JavaScript comments

- Generating HTML

- Types and variables

This chapter introduces you to the JavaScript language. I'll show you how JavaScript works with both the Netscape and Microsoft browsers and web servers and how to embed JavaScript statements in HTML documents. I'll then cover JavaScript's use of *types* and *variables*, and show you how to use *arrays*. By the time you have finished this chapter, you'll be able to write simple scripts and include them in your web pages.

JavaScript with Browsers and Servers

JavaScript is a script-based programming language that supports the development of both client and server components of web-based applications. On the client side, it can be used to write programs that are executed by a web browser within the context of a web page. On the server side, it can be used to write web server programs that can process information submitted by a web browser and then update the browser's display accordingly. Figure 2.1 provides an overview of how JavaScript supports both client and server web programming.

FIGURE 2.1:

JavaScript supports both client and server web applications.

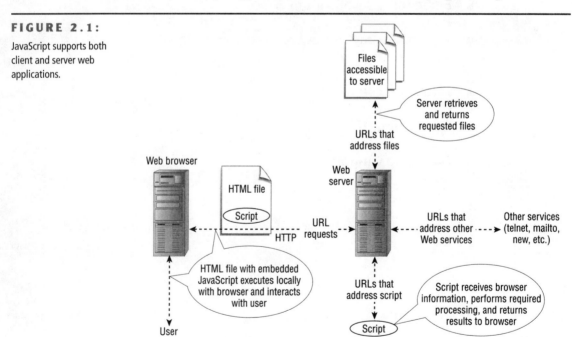

Microsoft's version of JavaScript is named JScript. I use "JavaScript" to refer to both JavaScript and JScript unless I'm referring to one but not the other. In these cases, I'll refer to "Netscape's JavaScript" and "Microsoft's JScript."

On the left side of the figure, a web browser displays a web page. As I mentioned in Chapter 1, "Learning the Fundamentals," this is a result of the browser acting on the instructions contained in an HTML file. The browser reads the HTML file and displays elements of the file as they are encountered. In this case, the HTML file (which the browser has retrieved from a web server, seen on the right) contains embedded JavaScript code. The process of reading the HTML file and identifying the elements contained in the file is referred to as *parsing*. When a script is encountered during parsing, the browser executes the script before continuing with further parsing.

The script can perform actions, such as generating HTML code that affects the display of the browser window. It can perform actions that affect the operation of plug-ins, Java applets, or ActiveX components. The script can also define JavaScript language elements that are used by other scripts. Figure 2.2 summarizes the parsing of HTML files that contain JavaScript scripts.

FIGURE 2.2:

HTML files are parsed and displayed one element at a time.

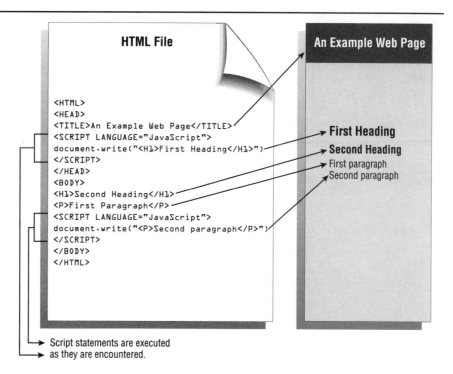

HTML File

```
<HTML>
<HEAD>
<TITLE>An Example Web Page</TITLE>
<SCRIPT LANGUAGE="JavaScript">
document.write("<H1>First Heading</H1>")
</SCRIPT>
</HEAD>
<BODY>
<H1>Second Heading</H1>
<P>First Paragraph</P>
<SCRIPT LANGUAGE="JavaScript">
document.write("<P>Second paragraph</P>")
</SCRIPT>
</BODY>
</HTML>
```

An Example Web Page

First Heading

Second Heading

First paragraph
Second paragraph

Script statements are executed
as they are encountered.

Some scripts may define functions for handling *events* that are generated by user actions. For example, you might write a script to define a function for handling the event "submitting a form" or "clicking a link." The event handlers can then perform actions such as validating the form's data, generating a custom URL for the link, or loading a new web page.

JavaScript's event-handling capabilities provide greater control over the user interface than HTML alone. For example, when a user submits an HTML form, a browser that isn't implementing JavaScript handles the "submit form" event by sending the form data to a CGI program for further processing. The CGI program processes the form data and returns the results to the web browser, which displays the results to the user. By comparison, when a user submits an HTML form using a browser that *does* implement JavaScript, a JavaScript event-handling function may be called to process the form data. This processing may vary from validating the data (that is, checking to see that the data entered by the user is appropriate for the fields contained in the form) to performing all of the required form processing, eliminating the need for a CGI program. In other words, JavaScript's event-handling capabilities allow the *browser* to perform some, if not all, of the form processing. Figure 2.3 compares JavaScript's event-handling capabilities to those provided by HTML. Besides providing greater control over the user interface, these event-handling capabilities help to reduce network traffic, the need for CGI programs, and the load on the web server.

FIGURE 2.3:

Event-handling functions enable scripts to respond to user actions.

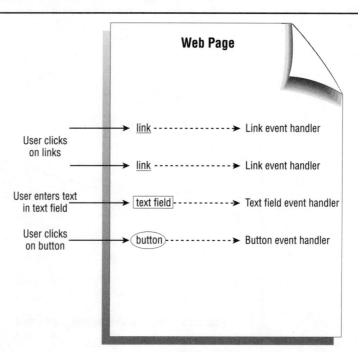

TIP   I'll cover JavaScript's event-handling capabilities more fully in Chapter 4, "Handling Events."

While JavaScript's browser programming capabilities can eliminate the need for *some* server-side programs, others are still required to support more advanced web applications, such as those that access database information, support electronic commerce, or perform specialized processing. Server-side JavaScript scripts are used to replace traditional CGI programs. Instead of a web server calling a CGI program to process form data, perform searches, or implement customized web applications, a JavaScript-enabled web server can invoke a precompiled JavaScript script to perform this processing. The web server automatically creates JavaScript objects that tell the script how it was invoked and the type of browser requesting its services; it also automatically communicates any data supplied by the browser. The script processes the data provided by the browser and returns information to the browser, via the server. The browser then uses this information to update the user's display. Figure 2.4 illustrates how server-side scripts are used.

FIGURE 2.4:

Server-side scripts are used to replace CGI programs.

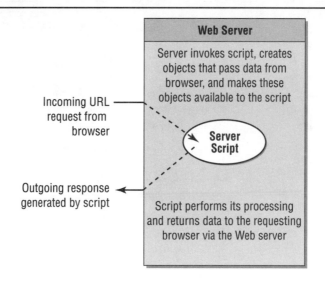

There are several advantages to using server-side JavaScript scripts on Netscape and Microsoft web servers:

- Because these web servers have been specially designed for executing JavaScript scripts, they are able to minimize the processing overhead that is usually associated with invoking the script, passing data, and returning the results of script processing.

- You can use JavaScript to replace CGI scripts written in other languages. This eliminates the problems that are usually associated with managing multiple CGI programs, which may have been written in an OS shell language, Perl, tcl, C, and other languages. It also provides tighter control over the security of these server-side applications.

- The database extensions integrated within these servers provide a powerful capability for accessing information contained in compatible external databases. These database extensions may be used by server-side scripts.

The database connectivity supported by these servers enables even beginning programmers to create server-side JavaScript programs to update databases with information provided by browsers (usually through forms) and to provide web users with web pages that are dynamically generated from database queries. You can imagine how exciting this is for researchers gathering and reporting information over the Web and for entrepreneurs who have catalogs full of products and services to sell over the Web. Figure 2.5 illustrates the use of JavaScript to provide database connectivity to web applications.

FIGURE 2.5:

Netscape and Microsoft web servers provide database connectivity to server-side scripts.

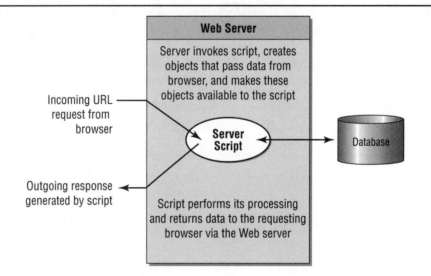

Web Server

Server invokes script, creates objects that pass data from browser, and makes these objects available to the script

Incoming URL request from browser

Server Script

Database

Outgoing response generated by script

Script performs its processing and returns data to the requesting browser via the Web server

NOTE   In this section, I've provided an overview of the different ways in which JavaScript can be used for browser and server-side web applications. JavaScript's syntax is the same for both client (browser) *and* server programming; however, the examples I will be using in this chapter mainly reflect how JavaScript relates to browser programming. For examples of JavaScript *server* programming, see the five chapters that make up Part VI, "Programming Servers."

Embedding JavaScript in HTML

JavaScript statements can be included in HTML documents by enclosing the statements between an opening <script> tag and a closing </script> tag. Within the opening tag, the LANGUAGE attribute is set to "JavaScript" to identify the script as being JavaScript as opposed to some other scripting language, such as Visual Basic Script (VBScript). The script tag is typically used as follows:

```
<script language="JavaScript">
 JavaScript statements
</script>
```

The script tag may be placed in either the *head* or the *body* of an HTML document. In many cases, it is better to place the script tag in the head of a document to ensure that all JavaScript definitions have been made before the body of the document is displayed. You'll learn more about this in the "Use of the Document Head" section later in this chapter.

The traditional first exercise with any programming language is to write a program to display the text *Hello World!* This teaches the programmer to display output, a necessary feature of most programs. A JavaScript script that displays this text is shown in Listing 2.1.

NOTE You can access the file for Listing 2.1, ch02-01.htm, and all of the code listings in this chapter on the CD that accompanies this book.

Listing 2.1:   **Hello World! (ch02-01.htm)**

```
<html>
<head>
<title>Hello World!</title>
</head>
<body>
<script language="JavaScript">
document.write("Hello World!")
</script>
</body>
</html>
```

The body of our example document (the lines between the <body> and the </body> tags) contains a single element: a script, identified by the <script> and </script> tags. The opening script tag has the attribute language="JavaScript" to identify the script as JavaScript. The script has a single statement, document.write("Hello World!"), that writes the text *Hello World!* to the body of the current document object. Figure 2.6 shows how the HTML document is displayed by a JavaScript-enabled browser—Netscape Navigator. The text written by the script becomes part of the HTML document displayed by the browser.

FIGURE 2.6:

The very simple result of
Listing 2.1, *Hello
World!*, displayed by
Netscape Navigator

Other Language Attributes

All JavaScript-capable browsers will process JavaScript code if the LANGUAGE attribute is set to
JavaScript. However, the LANGUAGE attribute can also be set to the following other values in
order to limit the browsers that are able to process JavaScript code:

JavaScript1.1   Used to limit execution of a script to browsers that support JavaScript 1.1.
These browsers are Navigator 3 and later, Internet Explorer 4 and later, HotJava 2.0 and
later, and Opera 3.5 and later.

JavaScript1.2   Used to limit execution of a script to browsers that support JavaScript 1.2.
These browsers are Navigator 4 and later, Internet Explorer 4 and later, Opera 4 and later,
and HotJava 3.0 and later.

JavaScript1.3   Used to limit execution of a script to browsers that support JavaScript 1.3.
These browsers are limited to Navigator 4.06 and later, Internet Explorer 5.0, and later,
Opera 5 and later, and HotJava 3.0 and later.

    JavaScript1.5   Used to limit execution of a script to browsers that support JavaScript 1.5.
These browsers are limited to Navigator 6.0 and later, Internet Explorer 5.5 and later, and
Opera 5 and later.

JScript   Used to limit execution of a script to browsers that support JScript. These browsers are limited to Internet Explorer 3 and later. The Opera browser may be configured to support JScript by setting it to Internet Explorer mode. Table 2.1 identifies which of the above attributes are supported by popular browsers. If a browser does not support an attribute, it will simply ignore the <SCRIPT> tags.

TABLE 2.1: Browser Support of the LANGUAGE Attribute

Browser	JavaScript	JavaScript1.1	JavaScript1.2	JavaScript1.3	JavaScript 1.5	JScript
Navigator 2	X					
Navigator 3	X	X				
Navigator 4	X	X	X			
Navigator 4.06	X	X	X	X		
Navigator 6.0, 6.1, and later	X	X	X	X	X	
Internet Explorer 3	X					X
Internet Explorer 4	X	X	X			X
Internet Explorer 5	X	X	X	X		X
Internet Explorer 5.5	X	X	X	X	X	X
Internet Explorer 6 and later	X	X	X	X	X	X
Opera 3.62	X	X	X	X	X	X
Opera 4	X	X	X	X	X	X
Opera 5	X	X	X	X	X	X
HotJava 3.0	X	X	X	X		

You may wonder whatever happened to JavaScript 1.4? JavaScript 1.4 corresponds to ECMAScript Revision 2. The only browser that recognizes and supports the JavaScript1.4 attribute value is HotJava 3.0. The Opera browser recognizes the JavaScript1.4 attribute value, but it does not support the language features.

NOTE   The Opera browser reports that it supports all **LANGUAGE** attribute values.

TIP   To ensure that more browsers are able to execute your scripts, set the **LANGUAGE** attribute to **JavaScript**. Your JavaScript code can then perform checks to detect which type and version of browser is currently executing a script. Chapter 5, "Working with Objects," covers browser detection techniques.

NOTE   In addition to the LANGUAGE attribute, Internet Explorer 4 and later support the use of conditional compilation directives. These directives are used to limit script execution to selected portions of scripts.

Telling Non-JavaScript Browsers to Ignore Your Code

Not all browsers support JavaScript. Older browsers, such as Netscape Navigator 1, Internet Explorer 2, and the character-based Lynx browser, do not recognize the script tag and, as a consequence, display as text all the JavaScript statements that are enclosed between <script> and </script>. Figures 2.7 and 2.8 show how the preceding JavaScript script is displayed by Internet Explorer 2 and by DosLynx.

FIGURE 2.7:

Internet Explorer 2 displays the Hello World! script of Listing 2.1 instead of executing it.

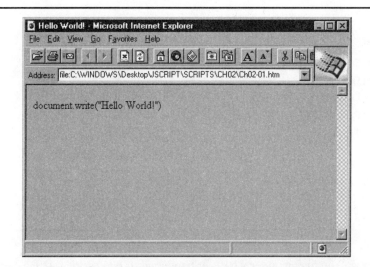

FIGURE 2.8:

DosLynx displays the Hello World! script of Listing 2.1 instead of executing it.

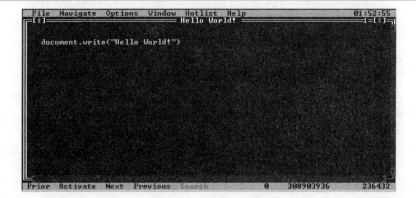

Fortunately, HTML provides a method to conceal JavaScript statements from such JavaScript-challenged browsers. The trick is to use HTML *comment* tags to *surround* the JavaScript statements. Because HTML comments are displayed only within the code used to create a web page, they do not show up as part of the browser's display. The use of HTML comment tags is as follows:

```
<!- Begin hiding JavaScript
JavaScript statements
// End hiding JavaScript ->
```

The `<!-` tag begins the HTML comment and the `->` tag ends the comment. The `//` string identifies a JavaScript comment, as you'll learn later in this chapter in the "JavaScript Comments" section.

The comment tags cause the JavaScript statements to be treated as comments by JavaScript-challenged browsers. JavaScript-enabled browsers, on the other hand, know to ignore the comment tags and process the enclosed statements as JavaScript. Listing 2.2 shows how HTML comments are used to hide JavaScript statements. Figure 2.9 shows how Internet Explorer 2 displays the HTML document shown in Listing 2.2.

Listing 2.2:   **Using HTML Comments to Hide JavaScript Code (ch02-02.htm)**

```html
<html>
<head>
<title>Using HTML comments to hide JavaScript code</title>
</head>
<body>
<script language="JavaScript">
<!-- Begin hiding JavaScript
document.write("Hello World!")
// End hiding JavaScript -->
</script>
</body>
</html>
```

FIGURE 2.9:

Result of using HTML comments (Listing 2.2) with Internet Explorer 2. Compare to Figures 2.7 and 2.8.

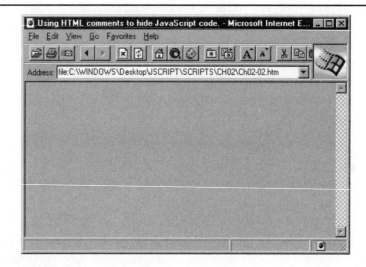

The noscript Tag

Versions 2 and later of Netscape Navigator and versions 3 and later of Microsoft Internet Explorer support JavaScript. These browsers account for nearly 90 percent of browser use on the Web and their percentage of use is increasing. This means that most browser requests come from JavaScript-capable browsers. However, there are still popular browsers, such as Lynx, that do not support JavaScript. In addition, both Navigator and Internet Explorer provide users with the option of *disabling* JavaScript. The noscript tag was created for those browsers that can't or won't process JavaScript. It is used to display markup that is an alternative to executing a script. The HTML instructions contained inside the tag are displayed by JavaScript-challenged browsers (as well as by JavaScript-capable browsers that have JavaScript disabled). The script shown in Listing 2.3 illustrates the use of the noscript tag. Figure 2.10 shows the web page of Listing 2.3 as displayed by a JavaScript-capable browser. Compare that display to Figure 2.11, which shows how it is displayed by Internet Explorer 2, a non-JavaScript browser.

Listing 2.3:   Using the noscript Tag (ch02-03.htm)

```
<html>
<head>
<title>Using the noscript tag.</title>
</head>
<body>
```

```
<script language="JavaScript">
<!-- Begin hiding JavaScript
document.write("Hello World!")
// End hiding Javascript -->
</script>
<NOSCRIPT>
[JavaScript]
</NOSCRIPT>
</body>
</html>
```

FIGURE 2.10:

Using the noscript tag
with Navigator, a
JavaScript-capable browser
(Listing 2.3)

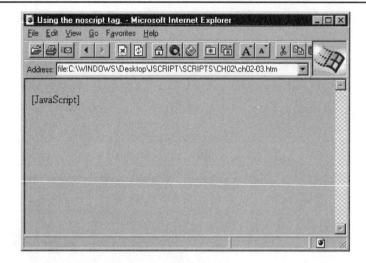

FIGURE 2.11:

Using the noscript tag
with Internet Explorer 2, a
non-JavaScript browser
(Listing 2.3)

The Script Tag's SRC Attribute

The script tag itself provides another way to include JavaScript code in an HTML document, via the tag's SRC attribute, which may be used to specify a *file* containing JavaScript statements. Here's an example of the use of the SRC attribute:

```
<script language="JavaScript" SRC="src.js">
</script>
```

In this example, the file src.js is a file containing JavaScript statements. (The file could have been named anything, but it should end with the .js extension; I just chose src.js to help you remember the SRC attribute.) Note that the closing </script> tag is still required.

If the file src.js contains the following code, then the HTML document shown in Listing 2.4 would produce the browser display shown in Figure 2.12.

```
<!- Begin hiding JavaScript
document.write("This text was generated by code in the src.js file.")
// End hiding JavaScript ->
```

Listing 2.4:   Inserting Source JavaScript Files (ch02-04.htm)

```
<html>
<head>
<title>Using the SRC attribute of the script tag.</title>
</head>
<body>
<script language="JavaScript" SRC="src.js">
</script>
</body>
</html>
```

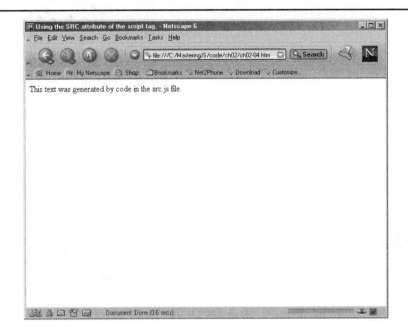

FIGURE 2.12:

Using the SRC attribute of
the script tag to include
JavaScript code (Listing 2.4)

NOTE   The SRC attribute may have a URL as its attribute value. Web servers that provide the source
file, however, *must* report the file's MIME type as `application/x-javascript`; otherwise,
browsers will not load the source file.

JavaScript Entities

JavaScript entities allow the value of an HTML attribute to be provided by a JavaScript
expression. This allows attribute values to be dynamically calculated during the loading of a
web page.

A JavaScript entity begins with &{ and ends with };. The following example shows how the
HREF attribute of a link may be specified by the JavaScript linkTo variable:

```
<A HREF="&{linkTo};">Click here.</A>
```

The value of linkTo, which must be calculated earlier in the script, must be a valid URL.

NOTE   You'll learn about variables in the "Variables—Value Storehouses" section in this chapter.

Listing 2.5 shows how the linkTo tag can be used to create a link to this book's web page.

Listing 2.5:   Using JavaScript Entities (ch02-05.htm)

```
<html>
<head>
<title>Using the JavaScript entities.</title>
<script language="JavaScript"><!--
linkTo="http://www.jaworski.com/javascript"
// -->
</script>
</head>
<body>
<A HREF="&{linkTo};">Click here.</A>
</body>
</html>
```

WARNING   Microsoft Internet Explorer does not support JavaScript entities. Use of entities with Internet Explorer may lead to scripting errors.

JavaScript Comments

The JavaScript language provides comments of its own. These comments are used to insert notes and processing descriptions into scripts. The comments are ignored (as intended) when the statements of a script are parsed by JavaScript-enabled browsers.

JavaScript comments use the syntax of C++ and Java. The // string identifies a comment that continues to the end of a line. An example of a single line comment follows:

```
// This JavaScript comment continues to the end of the line.
```

The /* and */ strings are used to identify comments that may span multiple lines. The comment begins with /* and continues up to */. An example of a multiple line comment follows:

```
/* This is
an example
of a multiple
line comment */
```

The script shown in Listing 2.6 illustrates the use of JavaScript comments. The script contains four statements that, if they weren't ignored, would write various capitalizations of the text *Hello World!* to the current document. However, since the first three of these statements are contained in comments, and since browsers ignore comments, these statements have no effect on the web page generated by the script. Figure 2.13 shows how the JavaScript comments in Listing 2.6 are handled by a JavaScript-capable browser.

Listing 2.6:   Using JavaScript Comments (ch02-06.htm)

```html
<html>
<head>
<title>Using JavaScript comments</title>
</head>
<body>
<script language="JavaScript">
<!-- Begin hiding JavaScript
// document.write("hello world!")
/* document.write("Hello world!")
document.write("Hello World!") */
document.write("HELLO WORLD!")
// End hiding Javascript -->
</script>
</body>
</html>
```

FIGURE 2.13:

How JavaScript comments are handled by a JavaScript-capable browser (Listing 2.6)

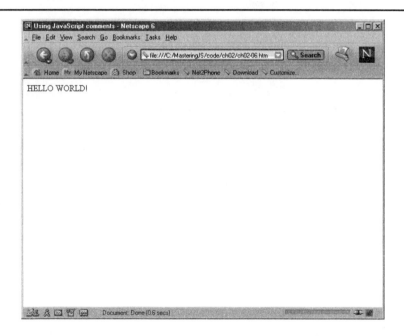

NOTE Throughout the rest of the book, all browser references will be to JavaScript-capable browsers, unless otherwise specified.

Use of the Document Head

The head of an HTML document provides a great place to include JavaScript definitions. Because the head of a document is processed before its body, placing definitions in the head will cause them to be defined before they are used. This is important, because any attempt to use a variable before it is defined results in an error. Listing 2.7 shows how JavaScript definitions can be placed in the head of an HTML document. The script contained in the document head defines a variable named `greeting` and sets its value to the string `Hi Web surfers!` (You'll learn all about variables in the "Variables–Value Storehouses" section later in this chapter.) The script contained in the document's body then writes the value of the `greeting` variable to the current document. Figure 2.14 shows how this document is displayed.

Listing 2.7:   Using the Head for Definitions (ch02-07.htm)

```
<HTML>
<HEAD>
<TITLE>Using the HEAD for definitions</TITLE>
<SCRIPT language="JavaScript">
<!--
greeting = "Hi Web surfers!"
// -->
</SCRIPT>
</HEAD>
<BODY>
<SCRIPT language="JavaScript">
<!--
document.write(greeting)
// -->
</SCRIPT>
</BODY>
</HTML>
```

It is important to make sure that all definitions occur before they are used; otherwise an error will be displayed when your HTML document is loaded by a browser. Listing 2.8 contains an HTML document that will generate a "use before definition" error. In this listing, the head contains a JavaScript statement that writes the value of the `greeting` variable to the current document; however, the `greeting` variable is not defined until the body of the document. Figure 2.15 shows how this error is displayed by a browser.

FIGURE 2.14:

How the greeting variable is displayed (Listing 2.7)

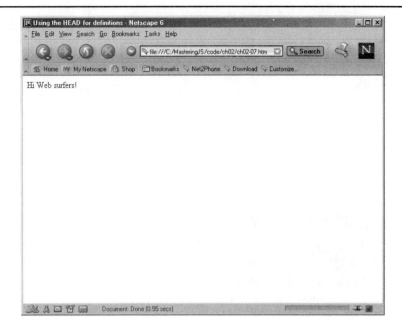

Listing 2.8:   Example of Use before Definition (ch02-08.htm)

```html
<HTML>
<HEAD>
<TITLE>Use before definition</TITLE>
<SCRIPT language="JavaScript">
<!--
document.write(greeting)
// -->
</SCRIPT>
</HEAD>
<BODY>
<SCRIPT language="JavaScript">
<!--
greeting = "Hi Web surfers!"
// -->
</SCRIPT>
</BODY>
</HTML>
```

FIGURE 2.15:

JavaScript generates an
error when a variable is
used before it is defined
(Listing 2.8)

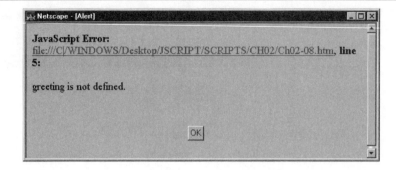

Generating HTML

The examples presented so far have shown how you can use JavaScript to write simple text to the document object. By including HTML tags in your JavaScript script, you can also use JavaScript to generate HTML elements that will be displayed in the current document. The example shown in Listing 2.9 illustrates this concept. Figure 2.16 shows how the web page generated by this script is displayed.

Listing 2.9:   Using JavaScript to Create HTML Tags (ch02-09.htm)

```
<HTML>
<HEAD>
<TITLE>Using JavaScript to create HTML tags</TITLE>
<SCRIPT LANGUAGE="JavaScript">
<!--
greeting = "<H1>Hi Web surfers!</H1>"
welcome = "<P>Welcome to <CITE>Mastering JavaScript and JScript</CITE>.</P>"
// -->
</SCRIPT>
</HEAD>
<BODY>
<SCRIPT LANGUAGE="JavaScript">
<!--
document.write(greeting)
document.write(welcome)
// -->
</SCRIPT>
</BODY>
</HTML>
```

FIGURE 2.16:

Generating HTML from
JavaScript (Listing 2.9)

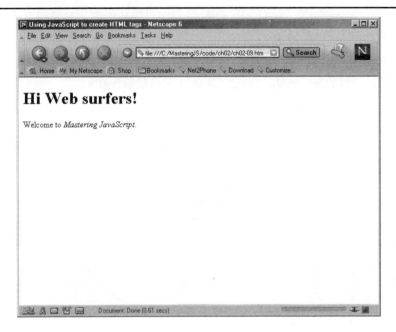

In the script contained in the head of the HTML document, the variables `greeting` and `welcome` are assigned text strings containing embedded HTML tags. These text strings are displayed by the script contained in the body of the HTML document:

- The `greeting` variable contains the heading *Hi Web surfers!*, which is surrounded by the HTML heading tags `<H1>` and `</H1>`.

- The `welcome` variable is assigned the string *Welcome to Mastering JavaScript*.

  - The citation tags, `<CITE>` and `</CITE>`, cause the `welcome` variable's string to be cited as a literary reference (which means it shows up in italic).

  - The paragraph tags, `<P>` and `</P>`, which surround the `welcome` text, are used to mark it as a separate paragraph.

The resulting HTML document generated by the script is equivalent to the following:

```
<HTML>
<HEAD>
<TITLE>Using JavaScript to create HTML tags</TITLE>
</HEAD>
<BODY>
<H1>Hi Web surfers!</H1>
<P>Welcome to <CITE>Mastering JavaScript</CITE>.</P>
</BODY>
</HTML>
```

So far, I've been making use of variables, such as greeting and welcome, without having explicitly defined what they are. In the next section, I formally introduce variables.

Variables—Value Storehouses

JavaScript, like other programming languages, uses variables to store values so they can be used in other parts of a program. Variables are names that are associated with these stored values. For example, the variable imageName may be used to refer to the name of an image file to be displayed and the variable totalAmount may be used to display the total amount of a user's purchase.

Variable names can begin with an uppercase letter (*A* through *Z*), lowercase letter (*a* through *z*), an underscore character (_), or dollar sign character ($). The remaining characters can consist of letters, the underscore character, the dollar sign character, or digits (0 through 9). Examples of variable names are as follows:

- orderNumber2
- _123
- SUM
- Image7
- Previous_Document

Variable names are case sensitive. This means that a variable named sum refers to a different value than one named Sum, sUm, or SUM.

WARNING   Because variable names are case sensitive, it is important to make sure that you use the same capitalization each time you use a variable.

WARNING   The dollar sign ($) character is reserved for machine-generated code and should not be used in your scripts. In particular, it should not be used for scripts that will be run by earlier browsers that are not fully ECMAScript-compatible.

Types and Variables

Unlike Java and some other programming languages, JavaScript does not require you to specify the *type* of data contained in a variable. (It doesn't even allow it.) In fact, the same variable may be used to contain a variety of different values, such as the text string *Hello World!*, the integer *13*, the floating-point value *3.14*, or the logical value *true*. The JavaScript interpreter keeps track of and converts the type of data contained in a variable.

JavaScript's automatic handling of different types of values is a double-edged sword. On one side, it frees you from having to explicitly specify the type of data contained in a variable and from having to convert from one data type to another. On the other side, because JavaScript automatically converts values of one type to another, it is important to keep track of what types of values should be contained in a variable and how they are converted in expressions involving variables of other types. The next section, "Types and Literal Values," identifies the types of values that JavaScript supports. The "Conversion between Types" section later in the chapter covers important issues related to type conversion.

Types and Literal Values

JavaScript supports five primitive types of values, and supports complex types, such as arrays and objects. *Primitive types* are types that can be assigned a single literal value, such as a number, string, or Boolean value. Here are the primitive types that JavaScript supports:

Number   Consists of integer and floating-point numbers and the special NaN (not a number) value. Numbers use a 64-bit IEEE 754 format.

Boolean   Consists of the logical values true and false.

String   Consists of string values that are enclosed in single or double quotes.

The Null type   Consists of a single value, null, which identifies a null, empty, or nonexistent reference.

 The Undefined type   Consists of a single value, undefined, which is used to indicate that a variable has not been assigned a value.

> **WARNING**   The undefined value was introduced with the ECMAScript specification and is not supported by browsers that are not fully ECMAScript compatible. This includes Navigator 4.05 and earlier and Internet Explorer 3 and earlier.

> **NOTE**   You'll learn about the Object type later in the "The Object Type and Arrays" section later this chapter.

In JavaScript, you do not declare the type of a variable as you do in other languages, such as Java and C++. Instead, the type of a variable is implicitly defined based on the literal values that you assign to it. For example, if you assign the integer *123* to the variable total, then total will support number operations. If you assign the string value *The sum of all accounts* to total, then total will support string operations. Similarly, if you assign the logical value *true* to total, then it will support Boolean operations.

It is also possible for a variable to be assigned a value of one type and then, later in the script's execution, be assigned a value of another type. For example, the variable total could be assigned 123, then The sum of all accounts, and then true. The type of the variable would change with the type of value assigned to it. The different types of literal values that can be assigned to a variable are covered in the following subsections.

Number Types—Integers and Floating-Point Numbers

When working with numbers, JavaScript supports both integer and floating-point values. It transparently converts from one type to another as values of one type are combined with values of other types in numerical expressions. For example, integer values are converted to floating-point values when they are used in floating-point expressions.

Integer Literals

Integers can be represented in JavaScript in decimal, hexadecimal, or octal form:

- A *decimal* (base 10) integer is what nonprogrammers are used to seeing—the digits 0 through 9, with each new column representing a higher power of 10.

- A *hexadecimal* (base sixteen) integer in JavaScript must always begin with the characters 0x or 0X in the two leftmost columns. Hexadecimal uses the numbers 0 through 9 to represent the values zero through nine and the letters *A* through *F* to represent the values normal people know as 10 through 15.

- An *octal* (base 8) integer in JavaScript must always begin with the character 0 in the leftmost column. Octal uses only the digits 0 through 7.

Examples of decimal, hexadecimal, and octal integers are provided in Table 2.2.

TABLE 2.2. Examples of Decimal, Hexadecimal, and Octal Integers for the Same Values

Decimal Number	Hexadecimal Equivalent	Octal Equivalent
19	0x13	023
255	0xff	0377
513	0x201	01001
1024	0x400	02000
12345	0x3039	030071

The program shown in Listing 2.10 illustrates the use of JavaScript hexadecimal and octal integers. Figure 2.17 shows how the web page generated by this program is displayed. Note that the hexadecimal and octal integers are converted to decimal before they are displayed.

Listing 2.10:   Using JavaScript Integers (ch02-10.htm)

```html
<HTML>
<HEAD>
<TITLE>Using JavaScript integers</TITLE>
</HEAD>
<BODY>
<SCRIPT LANGUAGE="JavaScript">
<!--
document.write("0xab00 + 0xcd = ")
document.write(0xab00 + 0xcd)
document.write("<BR>")
document.write("0xff - 0123 = ")
document.write(0xff - 0123)
document.write("<BR>")
document.write("-0x12 = ")
document.write(-0x12)
// -->
</SCRIPT>
</BODY>
</HTML>
```

FIGURE 2.17:

Using hexadecimal and octal integers (Listing 2.10)

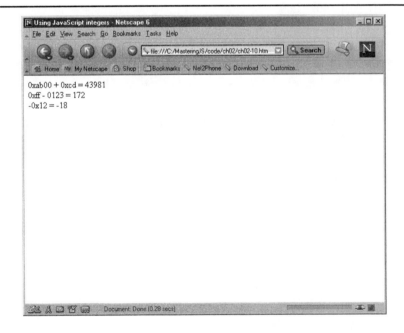

Floating-Point Literals

Floating-point literals are used to represent numbers that require the use of a decimal point, or very large or small numbers that must be written using exponential notation.

A floating-point number must consist of either a number containing a decimal point or an integer followed by an exponent. The following are valid floating-point numbers:

-4.321

55.

12e2

1e-2

7e1

-4e-4

.5

As you can see in these examples, floating-point literals may contain an initial integer, followed by an optional decimal point and fraction, followed by an optional exponent ("e" or "E") and its integer exponent value. For example, 4e6 equals 4×10 to the sixth power, which equals 4,000,000. Also, the initial integer and integer exponent value may be signed as positive or negative (+ or –). Up to 20 significant digits may be used to represent floating-point values.

The script shown in Listing 2.11 and Figure 2.18 illustrates how JavaScript displays these values. Notice that JavaScript simplifies the display of these numbers whenever possible.

Listing 2.11:   Using Floating-Point Numbers (ch02-11.htm)

```
<HTML>
<HEAD>
<TITLE>Using floating-point numbers</TITLE>
</HEAD>
<BODY>
<SCRIPT LANGUAGE="JavaScript">
<!--
document.write(-4.321)
document.write("<BR>")
document.write(55.)
document.write("<BR>")
document.write(12e2)
document.write("<BR>")
document.write(1e-2)
document.write("<BR>")
document.write(7e1)
```

```
document.write("<BR>")
document.write(-4e-4)
document.write("<BR>")
document.write(.5)
// -->
</SCRIPT>
</BODY>
</HTML>
```

FIGURE 2.18:

How JavaScript displays
floating-point numbers
(Listing 2.11)

Boolean Values

JavaScript, like Java, supports a pure Boolean type that consists of the two values true and
false. Several logical operators may be used in Boolean expressions, as you'll learn in the
"Logical Operators" section in Chapter 3. JavaScript automatically converts the Boolean values true and false into 1 and 0 when they are used in numerical expressions. The script
shown in Listing 2.12 illustrates this automatic conversion. Figure 2.19 shows the results of
this conversion as displayed by Navigator.

NOTE   A *Boolean value* is a value that is either true or false. The word *Boolean* is taken from the
name of the mathematician George Boole, who developed much of the fundamental theory
of mathematical logic.

Listing 2.12:   Conversion of Logical Values to Numeric Values (ch02-12.htm)

```
<HTML>
<HEAD>
<TITLE>Conversion of logical values to numeric values</TITLE>
</HEAD>
<BODY>
<SCRIPT LANGUAGE="JavaScript">
<!--
document.write("true*5 + false*7 = ")
document.write(true*5 +false*7)
// -->
</SCRIPT>
</BODY>
</HTML>
```

FIGURE 2.19:

How logical values are
converted to other types
(Listing 2.12)

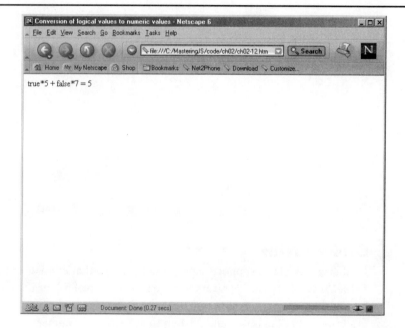

String Values

JavaScript provides built-in support for strings of characters. A *string* is a sequence of zero or more characters that are enclosed by double (") or single quotes ('). If a string begins with a double quote, then it must end with a double quote. Likewise, if a string begins with a single quote, then it must end in a single quote.

To insert a single or double quote character in a string, you must precede it by the backslash (\) escape character. The following are examples of the use of the escape character to insert quotes into strings:

```
"He asked, \"Who owns this book?\""
'It\'s Bill\'s book.'
```

The script shown in Listing 2.13 illustrates the use of quotes within strings. Figure 2.20 shows how the strings are displayed. Note that single quotes do not need to be coded with escape characters when they are used within double-quoted strings. Similarly, double quotes do not need to be coded when they are used within single-quoted strings.

Listing 2.13:   Using Quotes within Strings (ch02-13.htm)

```
<HTML>
<HEAD>
<TITLE>Using quotes within strings</TITLE>
</HEAD>
<BODY>
<SCRIPT LANGUAGE="JavaScript">
<!--
document.write("He said, \"That's mine!\"<BR>")
document.write('She said, "No it\'s not."<BR>')
document.write('That\'s all folks!')
// -->
</SCRIPT>
</BODY>
</HTML>
```

FIGURE 2.20:

How quotes are inserted
into strings (Listing 2.13)

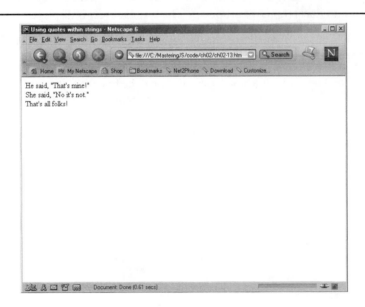

JavaScript defines special formatting characters for use in strings. These characters are identified in Table 2.3.

TABLE 2.3. SPECIAL FORMATTING CHARACTERS

Character	Meaning
\'	Single quote
\"	Double quote
\\	Backslash
\n	New line
\r	Carriage return
\f	Form feed
\t	Horizontal tab
\b	Backspace
\v	Vertical tab

The script shown in Listing 2.14 shows how these formatting characters are used. Figure 2.21 displays the web page generated by this script. The web page uses the HTML *pre-formatted text* tags to prevent the formatting characters from being treated as HTML white space characters. Notice that the backspace character is incorrectly displayed, the form feed character is incorrectly displayed, and that the carriage return character is displayed in the same manner as the new line character. Even though these characters are not fully supported in the display of web pages, they may still be used to insert formatting codes within data and files that JavaScript produces. The way that text is displayed is also dependent upon how the user has configured the browser's default font and language settings.

NOTE   Any Unicode character may be encoded using a special escape sequence consisting of \u*xxxx* where each *x* is a hexadecimal digit and the four digits provide the Unicode value for the character. For example, \u0041 is the escape sequence for the letter *A*.

Listing 2.14:   Using Special Formatting Characters (ch02-14.htm)

```
<HTML>
<HEAD>
<TITLE>Using special formatting characters</TITLE>
</HEAD>
<BODY>
<PRE>
<SCRIPT LANGUAGE="JavaScript">
<!--
```

```
document.write("This shows how the \bbackspace character works.\n")
document.write("This shows how the \ttab character works.\n")
document.write("This shows how the \rcarriage return character works.\n")
document.write("This shows how the \fform feed character works.\n")
document.write("This shows how the \nnew line character works.\n")
// -->
</SCRIPT>
</PRE>
</BODY>
</HTML>
```

FIGURE 2.21:

This is how formatting characters are handled (Listing 2.14). Note that your web browser does not process all characters.

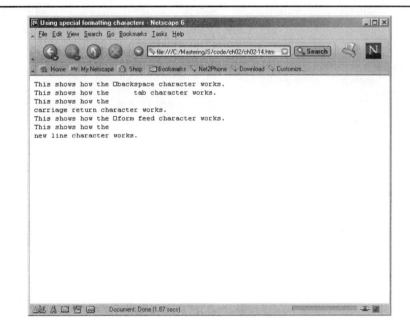

The null Value

The null value is common to all JavaScript types. It is used to set a variable to an initial value that is different from other valid values. Use of the null value prevents the sort of errors that result from using uninitialized variables. The null value is automatically converted to default values of other types when used in an expression, as you'll see in the "Conversion between Types" section shortly.

The undefined Value

The undefined value indicates that a variable has been created but not assigned a value. Like the null value, the undefined value is common to all JavaScript types and is automatically converted to default values of these types. The undefined value is converted to NaN for numeric types, false for Boolean, and undefined for strings.

Conversion between Types

JavaScript automatically converts values from one type to another when they are used in an expression. This means that you can combine different types in an expression and JavaScript will try to perform the type conversions that are necessary for the expression to make sense. For example, the expression, "test" + 5 will convert the numeric 5 to a string 5 and append it to the string test, producing test5. JavaScript's automatic type conversion also allows you to assign a value of one type to a variable and then later assign a value of a different type to the same variable.

How does JavaScript convert from one type to another? The process of determining when a conversion should occur and what type of conversion should be made is fairly complex. JavaScript converts values when it evaluates an expression or assigns a value to a variable. When JavaScript assigns a value to a variable it changes the type associated with the variable to the type of the value that is assigned.

When JavaScript evaluates an expression, it parses the expression into its component unary and binary expressions based upon the order of precedence of the operators it contains. It then evaluates the component unary and binary expressions of the parse tree. Figure 2.22 illustrates this process. Each expression is evaluated according to the operators involved. If an operator takes a value of a type that is different than the type of an operand, then the operand is converted to a type that is valid for the operator.

Some operators, such as the + operator, may be used for more than one type. For example, "a"+"b" results in the string "ab" when the + operator is used with string values, but it assumes its typical arithmetic meaning when used with numeric operands. What happens when JavaScript attempts to evaluate "a"+3? JavaScript converts the integer 3 into the string "3" and yields "a3" for the expression. In general, JavaScript will favor string operators over all others, followed by floating-point, integer, and logical operators.

FIGURE 2.22:

Expressions are evaluated
based on the types of
operators involved.

Expression   Parse Tree

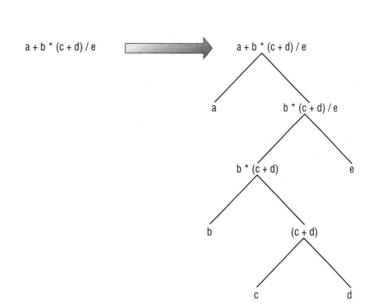

NOTE   Expressions are covered in the "Operators and Expressions" section in Chapter 3.

The script shown in Listing 2.15 illustrates JavaScript conversion between types when the + operator is used. Figure 2.23 shows how the web page resulting from this script is displayed.

Listing 2.15:   Automatic Conversion between Types (ch02-15.htm)

```
<HTML>
<HEAD>
<TITLE>Implicit conversion between types</TITLE>
<SCRIPT LANGUAGE="JavaScript">
<!--
s1="test"
s2="12.34"
i=123
r=.123
lt=true
lf=false
n=null
// -->
</SCRIPT>
```

```
</HEAD>
<BODY>
<H1>Implicit conversion between types</H1>
<TABLE BORDER=2>
<SCRIPT LANGUAGE="JavaScript">
<!--
// Column headings for table
document.write("<TR>")
document.write("<TH>row + column</TH>")
document.write("<TH>string \"12.34\"</TH>")
document.write("<TH>integer 123</TH>")
document.write("<TH>float .123</TH>")
document.write("<TH>logical true</TH>")
document.write("<TH>logical false</TH>")
document.write("<TH>null</TH>")
document.write("</TR>")
// First operand is a string
document.write("<TR>")
document.write("<TH>string \"test\"</TH>")
document.write("<TD>")
document.write(s1+s2)
document.write("</TD><TD>")
document.write(s1+i)
document.write("</TD><TD>")
document.write(s1+r)
document.write("</TD><TD>")
document.write(s1+lt)
document.write("</TD><TD>")
document.write(s1+lf)
document.write("</TD><TD>")
document.write(s1+n)
document.write("</TD>")
document.write("</TR>")
// First operand is an integer
document.write("<TR>")
document.write("<TH>integer 123</TH>")
document.write("<TD>")
document.write(i+s2)
document.write("</TD><TD>")
document.write(i+i)
document.write("</TD><TD>")
document.write(i+r)
document.write("</TD><TD>")
document.write(i+lt)
document.write("</TD><TD>")
document.write(i+lf)
document.write("</TD><TD>")
document.write(i+n)
document.write("</TD>")
document.write("</TR>")
// First operand is a float
```

```
document.write("<TR>")
document.write("<TH>float .123</TH>")
document.write("<TD>")
document.write(r+s2)
document.write("</TD><TD>")
document.write(r+i)
document.write("</TD><TD>")
document.write(r+r)
document.write("</TD><TD>")
document.write(r+lt)
document.write("</TD><TD>")
document.write(r+lf)
document.write("</TD><TD>")
document.write(r+n)
document.write("</TD>")
document.write("</TR>")
// First operand is a logical true
document.write("<TR>")
document.write("<TH>logical true</TH>")
document.write("<TD>")
document.write(lt+s2)
document.write("</TD><TD>")
document.write(lt+i)
document.write("</TD><TD>")
document.write(lt+r)
document.write("</TD><TD>")
document.write(lt+lt)
document.write("</TD><TD>")
document.write(lt+lf)
document.write("</TD><TD>")
document.write(lt+n)
document.write("</TD>")
document.write("</TR>")
// First operand is a logical false
document.write("<TR>")
document.write("<TH>logical false</TH>")
document.write("<TD>")
document.write(lf+s2)
document.write("</TD><TD>")
document.write(lf+i)
document.write("</TD><TD>")
document.write(lf+r)
document.write("</TD><TD>")
document.write(lf+lt)
document.write("</TD><TD>")
document.write(lf+lf)
document.write("</TD><TD>")
document.write(lf+n)
document.write("</TD>")
document.write("</TR>")
// First operand is null
```

```
document.write("<TR>")
document.write("<TH>null</TH>")
document.write("<TD>")
document.write(n+s2)
document.write("</TD><TD>")
document.write(n+i)
document.write("</TD><TD>")
document.write(n+r)
document.write("</TD><TD>")
document.write(n+lt)
document.write("</TD><TD>")
document.write(n+lf)
document.write("</TD><TD>")
document.write(n+n)
document.write("</TD>")
document.write("</TR>")
// -->
</SCRIPT>
</TABLE>
</BODY>
</HTML>
```

FIGURE 2.23:

Conversion table for the + operator (Listing 2.15)

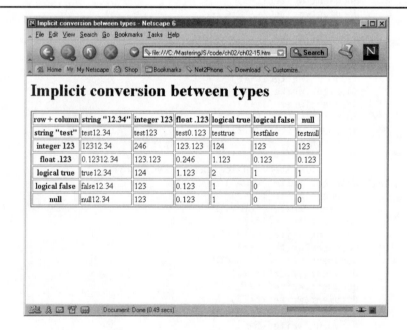

Implicit conversion between types

row + column	string "12.34"	integer 123	float .123	logical true	logical false	null
string "test"	test12.34	test123	test0.123	testtrue	testfalse	testnull
integer 123	12312.34	246	123.123	124	123	123
float .123	0.12312.34	123.123	0.246	1.123	0.123	0.123
logical true	true12.34	124	1.123	2	1	1
logical false	false12.34	123	0.123	1	0	0
null	null12.34	123	0.123	1	0	0

Note that in all cases where string operands are used with a non-string operator, JavaScript converts the other operator into a string:

- Numeric values are converted to their appropriate string value.

- Boolean values are converted to 1 and 0 to support numerical operations.

- The null value is converted to *"null"* for string operations, false for logical operations, and 0 for numerical operations.

Let's take a look at Listing 2.15. The script in the document head defines the variables to be used in the table's operations. The s1 and s2 variables are assigned string values. The i and r variables are assigned integer and floating-point values. The lt and lf variables are assigned logical values. The n variable is assigned the null value.

The script in the document body is fairly long. However, most of the script is used to generate the HTML tags for the cells of the conversion table. The script is surrounded by the tags <TABLE BORDER=2> and </TABLE>. The script then generates the cells of the table one row at a time. The <TR> and </TR> tags mark a row of the table. The <TH> and </TH> tags mark header cells. The <TD> and </TD> tags identify normal non-header table cells.

First, the column header row is displayed. Then each row of the table shown in Figure 2.23 is generated by combining the operand at the row heading with the operand at the table heading using the + operator.

NOTE Internet Explorer displays Figure 2.23 slightly differently. If a decimal number has a magnitude less than 1, then Internet Explorer inserts a zero at the beginning of the number when displaying the number or converting it to a string value. For example, .123 is displayed as 0.123.

Conversion Functions

Functions are collections of JavaScript code that perform a particular task, and often return a value. A function may take zero or more parameters. These parameters are used to specify the data to be processed by the function. You'll learn more about functions in the "Function Call Statements" section of Chapter 3.

JavaScript provides three functions that are used to perform explicit type conversion. These are eval(), parseInt(), and parseFloat().

NOTE Functions are referenced by their name with the empty parameter list—()—appended. This makes it easier to differentiate between functions and variables in the discussion of scripts.

The eval() function can be used to convert a string expression to a numeric value. For example, the statement total = eval("432.1*10"), results in the value *4321* being assigned to the total variable. The eval() function takes the string value "*432.1*10*" as a parameter and returns the numeric value 4321 as the result of the function call. When using the eval() function to convert a string expression to a numeric value, if the string value passed as a parameter to the eval() function does not represent a numeric value, then use of eval() results in an error being generated.

The parseInt() function is used to convert a string value into an integer. Unlike eval(), parseInt() returns the first integer contained in the string or *0* if the string does not begin with an integer. For example, parseInt("123xyz") returns *123* and parseInt("xyz") returns *0*. The parseInt() function also parses hexadecimal and decimal integers.

The parseFloat() function is similar to the parseInt() function. It returns the first floating-point number contained in a string or *0* if the string does not begin with a valid floating-point number. For example, parseFloat("2.1e4xyz") returns *21000* and parseFloat("xyz") returns *0*.

The script shown in Listing 2.16 illustrates the use of JavaScript's explicit conversion functions. Figure 2.24 shows how the web page that this script generates is displayed.

Listing 2.16:   Explicit Conversion Functions (ch02-16.htm)

```
<HTML>
<HEAD>
<TITLE>Using Explicit Conversion Functions</TITLE>
</HEAD>
<BODY>
<H1 ALIGN="CENTER">Using Explicit Conversion Functions</H1>
<SCRIPT LANGUAGE="JavaScript"><!--
document.write('eval("12.34*10") = ')
document.write(eval("12.34*10"))
document.write("<BR>")
document.write('parseInt("0x10") = ')
document.write(parseInt("0x10"))
document.write("<BR>")
document.write('parseFloat("5.4321e6") = ')
document.write(parseFloat("5.4321e6"))
// --></SCRIPT>
</BODY>
</HTML>
```

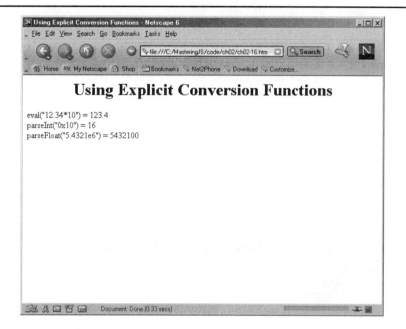

The Object Type and Arrays

In addition to the primitive types discussed in the previous sections, JavaScript supports the Object type. This type is referred to as a complex data type because it is built from the primitive types. I'll address objects in general and the Object type in Chapter 5, "Working with Objects." In this chapter, I'll cover a special JavaScript object—the array.

NOTE   Arrays are a special type of JavaScript object.

Arrays—Accessing Indexed Values

Arrays are objects that are capable of storing a sequence of values. These values are stored in indexed locations within the array. For example, suppose you have a company with five employees and you want to display the names of your employees on a web page. You could keep track of their names in an array variable named `employee`. You would construct the array using the following statement:

```
employee = new Array(5)
```

And you would store the names of your employees in the array using the following statements:

```
employee[0] = "Bill"
employee[1] = "Bob"
```

```
employee[2] = "Ted"
employee[3] = "Alice"
employee[4] = "Sue"
```

You could then access the names of the individual employees by referring to the individual elements of the array. For example, you could display the names of your employees using statements such as the following:

```
document.write(employee[0])
document.write(employee[1])
document.write(employee[2])
document.write(employee[3])
document.write(employee[4])
```

The script shown in Listing 2.17 illustrates the use of arrays. Figure 2.25 shows how the web page this script generates is displayed.

Listing 2.17:   Using JavaScript Arrays (ch02-17.htm)

```
<HTML>
<HEAD>
<TITLE>Using Arrays</TITLE>
</HEAD>
<BODY>
<H1 ALIGN="CENTER">Using Arrays</H1>
<SCRIPT LANGUAGE="JavaScript"><!--
employee = new Array(5)
employee[0] = "Bill"
employee[1] = "Bob"
employee[2] = "Ted"
employee[3] = "Alice"
employee[4] = "Sue"
document.write(employee[0]+"<BR>")
document.write(employee[1]+"<BR>")
document.write(employee[2]+"<BR>")
document.write(employee[3]+"<BR>")
document.write(employee[4])
// --></SCRIPT>
</BODY>
</HTML>
```

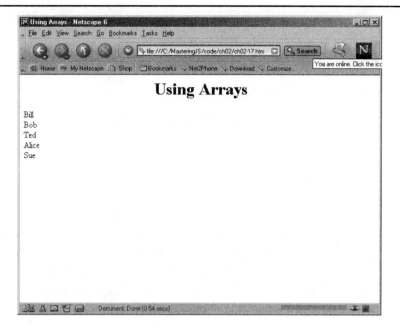

FIGURE 2.25:

Arrays allow multiple values to be stored with a single variable (Listing 2.17).

The *length* of an array is the number of elements that it contains. In the example script of Listing 2.17, the length of the employee array is 5. The individual elements of an array are referenced using the name of the array followed by the index of the array element enclosed in brackets. Because the first index is 0, the last index is one less than the length of the array. For example, suppose that you have an array named day that has a length of 7 and contains the names of the days of the week. The individual elements of this array would be accessed as day[0], day[1], ..., day[6].

Constructing Arrays

An array object must be constructed before it is used. An array may be constructed using either of the following two statement forms:

- ```
  arrayName = new Array(arrayLength)
  ```

- ```
  arrayName = new Array()
  ```

NOTE   A third form of array construction is discussed in the following "Constructing Dense Arrays" section.

In the first form, the length of the array is explicitly specified. An example of this form is the following:

```
days = new Array(7)
```

In this example, days corresponds to the array name and 7 corresponds to the array length.

In the second array construction form, the length of the array is not specified and results in the creation of an array of length 0. An example of using this type of array construction follows:

```
order = new Array()
```

This constructs an array of length 0 that is used to keep track of customer orders. JavaScript automatically extends the length of an array when new array elements are initialized. For example, the following statements create an order array of length 0 and then subsequently extend the length of the array to 100 and then 1,000.

```
order = new Array()
order[99] = "Widget #457"
order[999] = "Delux Widget Set #10"
```

When JavaScript encounters the reference to order[99], in the above example, it extends the length of the array to 100 and initializes order[99] to "*Widget #457*". When JavaScript encounters the reference to order[999] in the third statement, it extends the length of order to 1,000 and initializes order[999] to "*Delux Widget Set #10*".

Even if an array is initially created with a fixed initial length, it still may be extended by referencing elements that are outside the current size of the array. This is accomplished in the same manner as with zero-length arrays. Listing 2.18 shows how fixed-length arrays are expanded as new array elements are referenced. Figure 2.26 shows the how the web page that this script generates is displayed.

Listing 2.18: **Extending the Length of an Array (ch02-18.htm)**

```
<HTML>
<HEAD>
<TITLE>Extending Arrays</TITLE>
</HEAD>
<BODY>
<H1 ALIGN="CENTER">Extending Arrays</H1>
<SCRIPT LANGUAGE="JavaScript"><!--
order = new Array()
document.write("order.length = "+order.length+"<BR>")
order[99] = "Widget #457"
document.write("order.length = "+order.length+"<BR>")
order[999] = "Delux Widget Set #10"
document.write("order.length = "+order.length+"<BR>")
// --></SCRIPT>
</BODY>
</HTML>
```

FIGURE 2.26:

An array's length dynamically expands as new elements are referenced (Listing 2.18).

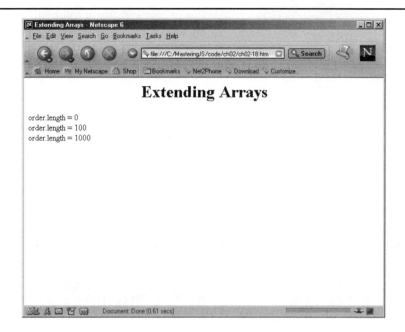

Constructing Dense Arrays

A *dense array* is an array that is initially constructed with each element being assigned a specified value. Dense arrays are used in the same manner as other arrays. They are just constructed and initialized in a more efficient manner. Dense arrays are specified by *listing* the values of the array elements in place of the array length. Dense array declarations take the following form:

```
arrayName = new Array(value0, value1, ... , valuen)
```

In the previous statement, because we start counting at zero, the length of the array is n+1.

When creating short length arrays, the dense array declaration is very efficient. For example, an array containing the three-letter abbreviations for the days of the week may be constructed using the following statement:

```
day = new Array('Sun','Mon','Tue','Wed','Thu','Fri','Sat')
```

The Elements of an Array

JavaScript does not place any restrictions on the values of the elements of an array. These values could be of different types or could refer to other arrays or objects. For example, you could create an array as follows:

```
junk = new Array("s1",'s2',4,3.5,true,false,null,new Array(5,6,7))
```

The junk array has length 8 and its elements are as follows:

```
junk[0]="s1"
junk[1]='s2'
junk[2]=4
junk[3]=3.5
junk[4]=true
junk[5]=false
junk[6]=null
junk[7]=a new dense array consisting of the values 5, 6, & 7
```

The last element of the array, junk[7], contains an array as its value. The three elements of junk[7] can be accessed using *a second set of subscripts*, as follows:

```
junk[7][0]=5
junk[7][1]=6
junk[7][2]=7
```

The script shown in Listing 2.19 illustrates the use of arrays within arrays. Figure 2.27 shows the web page that results from execution of this script.

Listing 2.19:   An Array within an Array (ch02-19.htm)

```
<HTML>
<HEAD>
<TITLE>Arrays within Arrays</TITLE>
</HEAD>
<BODY>
<H1 ALIGN="CENTER">Arrays within Arrays</H1>
<SCRIPT LANGUAGE="JavaScript"><!--
junk = new Array("s1",'s2',4,3.5,true,false,null,new Array(5,6,7))
document.write("junk[0] = "+junk[0]+"<BR>")
document.write("junk[1] = "+junk[1]+"<BR>")
document.write("junk[2] = "+junk[2]+"<BR>")
document.write("junk[3] = "+junk[3]+"<BR>")
document.write("junk[4] = "+junk[4]+"<BR>")
document.write("junk[5] = "+junk[5]+"<BR>")
document.write("junk[6] = "+junk[6]+"<BR>")
document.write("junk[7][0] = "+junk[7][0]+"<BR>")
document.write("junk[7][1] = "+junk[7][1]+"<BR>")
document.write("junk[7][2] = "+junk[7][2])
// --></SCRIPT>
</BODY>
</HTML>
```

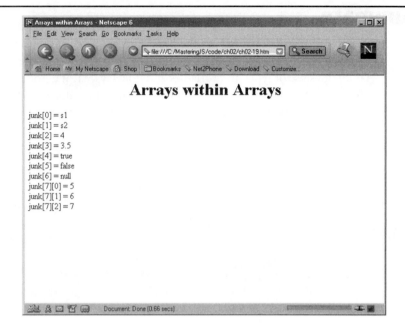

Objects and the `length` Property

JavaScript arrays are implemented as objects. *Objects* are named collections of data that have properties and may be accessed via methods. A *property* returns a value that identifies some aspect of the state of an object. *Methods* are used to read or modify the data contained in an object.

The length of an array is a property of an array. You can access the property of any object in JavaScript by appending a period (.) plus the name of the property to the name of the object, as shown here:

```
objectName.propertyName
```

For example, the length of an array is determined as follows:

```
arrayName.length
```

Now, consider the following array:

```
a = new Array(2,4,6,8,10)
```

The value returned by `a.length` is 5.

In addition to the `length` property, arrays also support several methods. These methods and the process of creating and using JavaScript objects are covered in Chapter 5, "Working with Objects."

Summary

This chapter introduced you to the JavaScript language. You learned how JavaScript works and how JavaScript statements are embedded in HTML documents. You learned about JavaScript's use of types and variables and how JavaScript automatically converts values of one type to another. In the next chapter, you'll be introduced to JavaScript's operators and programming statements, and you'll learn how functions are created and invoked.

CHAPTER 3

Using Operators, Statements, and Functions

- Operators and expressions

- Operator precedence

- Statements and declarations

- Functions and function calls

- Local and global variables

- Accessing objects in statements

$\mathbf{T}$his chapter continues your introduction to the JavaScript language. You'll cover all of the operators provided by JavaScript and learn how expressions are evaluated. You'll learn to use JavaScript's programming statements and develop sample scripts that demonstrate the use of each statement. You'll also learn how to create and invoke *functions*. When you have finished this chapter, you'll be able to write JavaScript scripts that use JavaScript's operators and statements to perform a variety of computations.

Operators and Expressions

In the previous chapter, you used some of the basic operators provided by JavaScript. These include the + operators used with string and numeric types and the = assignment operator. In this section, you'll be introduced to all of the operators provided by JavaScript. These operators are organized into the following categories:

- Arithmetic
- Logical
- Comparison
- String
- Bit manipulation
- Assignment
- Conditional

Let's start with a little terminology. An *operator* is used to transform one or more values into a single resultant value. The values to which the operator applies are referred to as *operands*. The combination of an operator and its operands is referred to as an *expression*.

Expressions are *evaluated* to determine the value of the expression. This value is the value that results when the operator is applied to the operands. Some operators, like the = (assignment) operator, result in a value being assigned to a *variable*. Others produce a value that may be used in other expressions.

NOTE   For some operators, such as the * multiplication operator, the *order* of the operands does not matter—for example, x * y = y * x is true for all integers and floating-point numbers. Other operators, such as the + (string concatenation) operator, yield different results for different orderings of their operands. For example, "ab" + "cd" does not equal "cd" + "ab".

Unary operators are operators that are used with only one operand. For example, the unary operator ! is applied to a logical value and returns the *logical not* of that value. Most

JavaScript operators are *binary* operators, operators that have two operands. An example of a binary operator is the * (multiplication) operator, which is used to calculate the product of two numbers. For example, the expression 7 * 6 is evaluated as 42 by applying the * operator to the operands 7 and 6.

So far we've only been dealing with simple expressions. More complex expressions can be constructed by combining simple unary and binary expressions. In order to evaluate complex expressions we must *parse* them into their component unary and binary expressions, applying the rules of order or *precedence* (for example, evaluating groups before adding or multiplying them). You'll learn more about parsing expressions later in this chapter in the "Operator Precedence" section.

NOTE   JavaScript also supports *regular expressions* through the **RegExp** object. You'll learn how to use this object in Appendix B, "Working with Regular Expressions."

Arithmetic Operators

Arithmetic operators are the most familiar operators because we use them every day to perform common mathematical calculations. The mathematical operators supported by JavaScript are listed in Table 3.1.

TABLE 3.1: Arithmetic Operators

Operator	Description
+	Addition
-	Subtraction or unary negation
*	Multiplication
/	Division
%	Modulus
++	Increment and then return value (or return value and then increment)
—	Decrement and then return value (or return value and then decrement)

NOTE   The % (modulus) operator calculates the *remainder* of dividing two integers. For example, 17 % 3 = 2 because 17/3 = 5 with a remainder of 2.

Logical Operators

Logical operators are used to perform Boolean operations on Boolean operands, such as *logical and*, *logical or*, and *logical not*. The logical operators supported by JavaScript are listed in Table 3.2.

TABLE 3.2: Logical Operators

Operator	Description
&&	logical and
‖	logical or
!	logical not

Comparison Operators

Comparison operators are used to determine whether two values are equal or to compare numerical values to determine which value is greater than the other. The comparison operators supported by JavaScript are listed in Table 3.3.

TABLE 3.3: Comparison Operators

Operator	Description
==	Equal
===	Strictly equal
!=	Not equal
!==	Strictly not equal
<	Less than
<=	Less than or equal
>	Greater than
>=	Greater than or equal

The equal (==) and not equal (!=) operators perform type conversions before testing for equality. For example, "5" == 5 evaluates to true. The strictly equal (===) and strictly not equal (!==) operators do not perform type conversions before testing for equality. For example, "5" === 5 evaluates to false and "5" !== 5 returns true. The strictly equal (===) and strictly not equal (!==) operators are part of the ECMAScript 1 standard. They were only introduced to Navigator in JavaScript 1.3 and are only supported by Navigator 4.06 and later. They are also supported by Internet Explorer 4 and later.

WARNING If the <SCRIPT> tag's LANGUAGE attribute is set to "JavaScript1.2" Navigator 4 (and later) treats the equality operator (==) as the strict equality operator. For example, "5" == 5 evaluates to false. This is a Navigator flaw.

String Operators

String operators are used to perform operations on strings. JavaScript currently supports only the + *string concatenation* operator. It is used to join two strings together. For example, "ab" + "cd" produces "abcd".

Bit Manipulation Operators

Bit manipulation operators perform operations on the bit representation of a value, such as shifting the bits to the right or the left. The bit manipulation operators supported by JavaScript are listed in Table 3.4.

TABLE 3.4: Bit Manipulation Operators

Operator	Description
&	And
|	Or
~	Bitwise complement
^	Exclusive or
<<	Left shift
>>	Sign-propagating right shift
>>>	Zero-fill right shift

Assignment Operators

Assignment operators are used to update the value of a variable. Some assignment operators are combined with other operators to perform a computation on the value contained in a variable and then update the variable with the new value. The assignment operators supported by JavaScript are listed in Table 3.5.

TABLE 3.5: Assignment Operators

Operator	Description
=	Sets the variable on the left of the = operator to the value of the expression on its right.
+=	Increments the variable on the left of the += operator by the value of the expression on its right. When used with strings, the value to the right of the += operator is appended to the value of the variable on the left of the += operator.
-=	Decrements the variable on the left of the -= operator by the value of the expression on its right.
*=	Multiplies the variable on the left of the *= operator by the value of the expression on its right.
/=	Divides the variable on the left of the /= operator by the value of the expression on its right.
%=	Takes the modulus of the variable on the left of the %= operator using the value of the expression on its right.
<<=	Left shifts the variable on the left of the <<= operator using the value of the expression on its right.
>>=	Takes the sign-propagating right shift of the variable on the left of the >>= operator using the value of the expression on its right.
>>>=	Takes the zero-filled right shift of the variable on the left of the >>>= operator using the value of the expression on its right.
&=	Takes the bitwise *and* of the variable on the left of the &= operator using the value of the expression on its right.
!=	Takes the bitwise *or* of the variable on the left of the != operator using the value of the expression on its right.
^=	Takes the bitwise *exclusive or* of the variable on the left of the ^= operator using the value of the expression on its right.

The Conditional Expression Ternary Operator

JavaScript supports the conditional expression operator ? : found in Java, C, and C++. This operator is a *ternary* operator since it takes three operands—a condition to be evaluated and two alternative values to be returned based on the truth or falsity of the condition. The format for a conditional expression is as follows:

```
condition ? value1 : value2
```

NOTE   A *condition* is an expression that results in a logical value—for example, `true` or `false`.

If the condition is `true`, *value1* is the result of the expression. Otherwise, *value2* is the result. An example of using this expression follows:

```
(x > y) ? 5 : 7
```

If the value stored in variable x is greater than the value contained in variable y, then 5 is the result of the expression. If the value stored in x is less than or equal to the value of y, then 7 is the result of the expression.

Special Operators

JavaScript supports a number of special operators that don't fit into the operator categories covered in the preceding sections:

The comma (,) operator   This operator evaluates two expressions and returns the value of the second expression. Consider the statement a = (5+6) , (2*20). Both expressions (5+6) and (2*20) are evaluated and the value of the second expression (40) is assigned to a.

The *delete* operator   The delete operator is used to delete a property of an object or an element at an array index. For example, delete myArray[5] deletes the sixth element of myArray. You'll learn how to use delete with object properties in Chapter 5, "Working with Objects." The delete operator always returns the *undefined* value as of JavaScript 1.2.

The *new* operator   The new operator is used to create an instance of an object type. You'll learn how it is used in Chapter 5.

The *typeof* operator   The typeof operator returns a string value that identifies the type of an operand. Consider the statement, a = typeof 17. The value assigned to a is number. Try using typeof with different expressions to see the values that it returns. You can also use it with objects and functions.

The *instanceof* operator   The instanceof operator returns a Boolean value that identifies whether an object belongs to a particular class (object type). For example, you can check whether the variable today refers to a Date object using the expression today instanceof Date.

The *in* operator   The in operator returns a Boolean value that indicates whether an object has a particular property. For example, the expression "appName" in navigator evaluates to true.

The *void* operator   The void operator does not return a value. It is typically used with the *javascript:* protocol to return a URL with no value. Chapter 10, "Working with Links," provides examples of its use.

Operator Summary Table

The script shown in Listing 3.1 illustrates the use of many of the JavaScript operators introduced in the preceding subsections. It generates the HTML table shown in Figure 3.1.

NOTE   You can access the file for Listing 3.1, `ch03-01.htm`, and all of the code listings in this chapter on the CD that accompanies the book.

Listing 3.1:   JavaScript Operators (ch03-01.htm)

```
<html>
<head>
<title>JavaScript Operators</title>
</head>
<body>
<h1>JavaScript Operators</h1>
<table BORDER="2" CELLPADDING="4" ALIGN="CENTER">
<tr><td>Category</td>
<td>Operator</td>
<td>Description</td>
<td>Usage Example</td>
<td>Value/Result</td></tr>
<tr><td>String</td>
<td>+</td>
<td>concatenation</td>
<td>&quot;Java&quot; + &quot;Script&quot;</td>
<td><script><!--
document.write("Java"+"Script")
// --></script>
</td></tr>
<tr><td ROWSPAN="10">Arithmetic</td>
<td>+</td>
<td>addition</td>
<td>2 + 3</td>
<td><script><!--
document.write(2+3)
// --></script>
</td></tr>
<tr><td ROWSPAN="2">-</td>
<td>subtraction</td>
<td>6 - 4</td>
<td><script><!--
document.write(6-4)
// --></script>
</td></tr>
<tr><td>unary negation</td>
<td>-9</td>
<td><script><!--
document.write(-9)
// --></script>
</td></tr>
<tr><td>*</td>
<td>multiplication</td>
```

```
<td>3 * 4</td>
<td><script><!--
document.write(3*4)
// --></script>
</td></tr>
<tr><td>/</td>
<td>division</td>
<td>15/3</td>
<td><script><!--
document.write(15/3)
// --></script>
</td></tr>
<tr><td>%</td>
<td>modulus</td>
<td>15%7</td>
<td><script><!--
document.write(15%7)
// --></script>
</td></tr>
<tr><td ROWSPAN="2">++</td>
<td>increment and then return value</td>
<td>x=3; ++x</td>
<td><script><!--
x=3
document.write(++x)
// --></script>
</td></tr>
<tr><td>return value and then increment</td>
<td>x=3; x++</td>
<td><script><!--
x=3
document.write(x++)
// --></script>
</td></tr>
<tr><td ROWSPAN="2">--</td>
<td>decrement and then return value</td>
<td>x=3; --x</td>
<td><script><!--
x=3
document.write(--x)
// --></script>
</td></tr>
<tr><td>return value and then decrement</td>
<td>x=3; x--</td>
<td><script><!--
x=3
document.write(x--)
// --></script>
</td></tr>
<tr><td ROWSPAN="6">Bit Manipulation</td>
<td>&amp;</td>
```

```
<td>and</td>
<td>10 &amp; 7</td>
<td><script><!--
document.write(10&7)
// --></script>
</td></tr>
<tr><td>|</td>
<td>or</td>
<td>10 | 7</td>
<td><script><!--
document.write(10|7)
// --></script>
</td></tr>
<tr><td>^</td>
<td>exclusive or</td>
<td>10 ^ 7</td>
<td><script><!--
document.write(10^7)
// --></script>
</td></tr>
<tr><td>&lt;&lt;</td>
<td>left shift</td>
<td>7 &lt;&lt; 3</td>
<td><script><!--
document.write(7<<3)
// --></script>
</td></tr>
<tr><td>&gt;&gt;</td>
<td>sign-propagating right shift</td>
<td>-7 &gt;&gt; 2</td>
<td><script><!--
document.write(-7>>2)
// --></script>
</td></tr>
<tr><td>&gt;&gt;&gt;</td>
<td>zero-fill right shift</td>
<td>-7 &gt;&gt;&gt; 2</td>
<td><script><!--
document.write(-7>>>2)
// --></script>
</td></tr>
<tr><td ROWSPAN="3">Logical</td>
<td>&amp;&amp;</td>
<td>logical and</td>
<td>true &amp;&amp; false</td>
<td><script><!--
document.write(true&&false)
// --></script>
</td></tr>
<tr><td>||</td>
<td>logical or</td>
```

```
<td>true || false</td>
<td><script><!--
document.write(true||false)
// --></script>
</td></tr>
<tr><td>!</td>
<td>not</td>
<td>!true</td>
<td><script><!--
document.write(!true)
// --></script>
</td></tr>
<tr><td ROWSPAN="6">Comparison</td>
<td>==</td>
<td>equal</td>
<td>3 == 7</td>
<td><script><!--
document.write(3==7)
// --></script>
</td></tr>
<tr><td>!=</td>
<td>not equal</td>
<td>3 != 7</td>
<td><script><!--
document.write(3!=7)
// --></script>
</td></tr>
<tr><td>&lt;</td>
<td>less than</td>
<td>3 &lt; 7</td>
<td><script><!--
document.write(3<7)
// --></script>
</td></tr>
<tr><td>&lt;=</td>
<td>less than or equal</td>
<td>3 &lt;= 7</td>
<td><script><!--
document.write(3<=7)
// --></script>
</td></tr>
<tr><td>&gt;</td>
<td>greater than</td>
<td>3 &gt; 7</td>
<td><script><!--
document.write(3>7)
// --></script>
</td></tr>
<tr><td>&gt;=</td>
<td>greater than or equal</td>
<td>3 &gt;= 7</td>
```

```
<td><script><!--
document.write(3>7)
// --></script>
</td></tr>
<tr><td>Conditional Expression</td>
<td>(condition) ? value1 : value2</td>
<td>if condition is true then value1 else value2</td>
<td>true ? 3 : 7</td>
<td><script><!--
document.write(true?3:7)
// --></script>
</td></tr>
</table>
</body>
</html>
```

FIGURE 3.1:

JavaScript operator
reference (Listing 3.1)

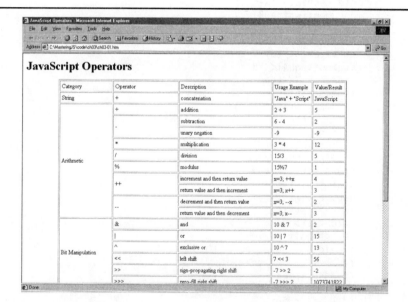

Operator Precedence

The *precedence* of the operator determines which operations are evaluated before others during the parsing and execution of complex expressions. For example, when you evaluate the expression 3 + 4 * 5, you should come up with *23* as your answer, not *35*. This is because the multiplication operator (*) has a higher precedence than the addition operator (+).

JavaScript defines the precedence and, therefore, the order of evaluation of all it operators. Table 3.6 summarizes the precedence of the JavaScript operators.

TABLE 3.6: Operator Precedence

Precedence	Operator
1	Parentheses, function call, or array subscript
2	`!, ~, - (unary), ++, --, typeof, new, void, delete` (see note)
3	`*, /, %` (see note)
4	`+, - (binary)` (see note)
5	`<<, >>, >>>` (see note)
6	`<, <=, >, >=, instanceof, in` (see note)
7	`==, != , ===. !==` (see note)
8	`&`
9	`^`
10	`|`
11	`&&`
12	`||`
13	`?:`
14	`=, +=, -=, *=, /=, %=, <<=, >>=, >>>=, &=, ^=, |=` (see note)
15	The comma (`,`) operator

NOTE: Where more than one operator is listed at a given level, those operators are all of equal priority—I don't mean to imply that `=`, for example, has a slightly higher priority than `+=` or `-=` in level 14. Rather, it means that as JavaScript reads an expression from left to right at that level of precedence, it will evaluate any of those operators as it comes across them.

To see how you would use Table 3.6 to determine the order of evaluation, consider the following complex expression:

```
a = 3 * (9 % 2) - !true >>> 2 - 1
```

Because parentheses surround 9 % 2 ("nine modulo two"), we evaluate that term first, resulting in the following:

```
a = 3 * 1 - !true >>> 2 - 1
```

NOTE   As mentioned previously, the % (modulus) operator calculates the remainder of dividing two integers. For example, 9 % 2 = 1, because 9/2 = 4 with a remainder of 1.

The highest precedence operator is now the ! negation operator. After evaluation of !true we get the following:

```
a = 3 * 1 - false >>> 2 - 1
```

The * operator is the next to be evaluated, resulting in the following:

```
a = 3 - false >>> 2 - 1
```

The two - operators now have the highest precedence. The logical value `false` is converted to *0*, and the simple expression 2 - 1 is evaluated to *1*, yielding the following:

```
a = 3 >>> 1
```

Then, because >>> has a higher precedence than =, the expression is evaluated to the following:

```
a = 3
```

Finally, the = assignment operator assigns the integer value *3* to variable a.

JavaScript Programming Statements

The *statements* of any programming language are the instructions from which programs are written. Most programming languages support a common core set of statements, such as assignment statements, if statements, loop statements, and others. These languages differ only in the syntax used for their statements and the degree to which the languages support software development paradigms and programming features such as object-oriented programming, abstract data definition, inference rules, and list processing.

JavaScript provides a complete range of basic programming statements. While it is not an object-oriented programming language, it *is* an object-*based* language and supports objects, object properties, and methods. You'll learn more about these object-based programming features in Chapter 5, "Working with Objects."

The statements provided by JavaScript are summarized in Table 3.7 and covered in the following subsections.

TABLE 3.7: JavaScript Statement Summary

Statement	Purpose	Example
assignment	Assigns the value of an expression to a variable	x = y + z
variable declaration	Declares a variable (and optionally assigns a value to it)	var card = new Array(52)

if	Alters program execution based on the value of a condition	if (x>y) {
		  z = x
		}

TABLE 3.7 CONTINUED: JavaScript Statement Summary

Statement	Purpose	Example
switch	Selects from a number of alternatives	```switch (val) {\n case 1:\n // First alternative\n break;\n case 2:\n // Second alternative\n break;\n default:\n // Default action\n}```
while	Repeatedly executes a set of statements until a condition becomes false	```while (x!=7) {\n x %= n\n --n\n}```
for	Repeatedly executes a set of statements until a condition becomes false	```for(i=0;i<7;++i){\n document.write(x[i])\n}```
do while	Repeatedly executes a set of statements while a condition is true	```do {\n // Statements\n} while (i>0)```
label	Associates a label with a statement	```labelName :\n statement```
break	Immediately terminates a do, while, or for statement	`if(x>y) break`
continue	Immediately terminates the current iteration of a do, while, or for statement	`if(x>y) continue`
function call	Invokes a function	`x=abs(y)`
return	Returns a value from a function call	`return x*y`
with	Identifies the default object	```with (Math) {\n d = PI * 2 * r;\n}```
for in	Iterates over an object's properties	```for (prop in employee) {\n document.write(prop+" ")\n}```
throw	Throws an exception	`throw "My Error"`
try	Checks for and processes exceptions	```try {\n // Tricky code\n}\ncatch (excpetion) {\n // Handle exception\n}\nfinally {\n // Post processing\n}```

TABLE 3.7 CONTINUED: JavaScript Statement Summary

Statement	Purpose	Example
delete	Deletes an object property or an array element	delete a[5]
method invocation	Invokes a method of an object	document.write("Hello!")
import	Imports objects, properties, and functions that have been exported by a signed script	import myObject.propertyX
export	Exports objects, properties, and functions so that they can be imported by another script	export myObject.propertyX

NOTE   The throw, try, and catch statements are only supported by Internet Explorer 5, Navigator 6.0, and later. The import and export statements (see Chapter 34 on the CD, "Securing Your Scripts") are used with signed scripts and are only supported by Navigator 4 and later.

Here are a few things to keep in mind when writing a series of statements:

- More than one statement may occur on a single line of text, provided that each statement is separated by a semicolon (;). The semicolon is the JavaScript "line separator" indicator.

- No semicolon is needed between statements that occur on separate lines.

- A long JavaScript statement may be written using multiple lines of text. No line-continuation identifier is required for such multiline statements. (In this book, however, I *will* show a continuation arrow, at least in the early chapters when I feel it's helpful for clarifying the extent of long statements that might be unfamiliar to you.)

- A semicolon appearing by itself on a line is referred to as an *empty statement*.

Assignment Statements

The most basic statement found in almost any programming language is the *assignment* statement. The assignment statement updates the value of a variable based upon an assignment operator and an expression (and, optionally, the current value of the variable being updated). You have seen numerous examples of assignment statements in the earlier sections of this chapter and in Chapter 2, "Introducing JavaScript and JScript." For example, the following statement assigns the value of x plus 10 to the y variable:

    y = x + 10

Variable Declarations

Variable declarations identify a variable to the JavaScript interpreter. So far you have been declaring simple variables through assignment statements. For example, the statement

```
a = 25
```

causes a to be implicitly declared as an integer variable and initialized to 25. The variable a is referred to as a *global* variable. This means that it can be accessed by all subsequent scripts defined in an HTML document. Later in this chapter, in the section titled "Local Variable Declarations," you'll learn how to declare variables that are *local* to a function definition.

Array declarations are another example of variable declaration statements. For example, the following array declarations declare array variables:

```
// Declares an array of zero elements
customerNum = new Array()

// Declares an array of 100 null valued elements
productCode = new Array(100)
```

Dense array declarations provide the capability to declare an array and assign initial values to all of the elements of the array. Here are two examples of these declaration statements:

```
// Declares and initializes a seven-element array
day = new Array("Sun","Mon","Tue","Wed","Thu","Fri","Sat")

// Declares and initializes a four-element array
name = new Array("Bob","Sybil","Ricky","Mad Dog")
```

Another type of variable declaration involves the creation of an instance of an object. You'll learn about objects and their creation in Chapter 5, "Working with Objects." For now, instances of objects are created using statements of the following form:

```
variableName = new objectConstructor(p1,p2,...,pn)
```

The variableName is the name of a variable that is assigned the newly created object, new is the new object creator, objectConstructor() is a function that is used to create the object, and p1 through pn are an optional list of arguments that are used in the object's creation.

The *if* Statement

The if statement provides the capability to alter the course of a program's execution based on an expression that yields a logical value. If the logical value is true, a specified set of statements is executed. If the logical value is false, the set of statements is skipped (and, optionally, a second set of statements is executed). The if statement comes in two forms. The syntax of the first form is as follows:

```
if ( condition ) {
 statements
 }
```

If the specified condition is `true`, then the statements identified within the braces { and } are executed. Execution then continues with the statement following the `if` statement. If the specified condition is `false`, then the statements enclosed by braces are skipped and execution continues with the statement following the `if` statement. For example, the following statement writes the text *Good morning* to the current web document when the value of the hour variable is less than 12.

```
if(hour<12){
  document.write("Good morning")
}
```

The syntax of the second form of the `if` statement is similar to the first form except that an `else` clause is added. The syntax of the second form is as follows:

```
if ( condition ) {
  first set of statements
} else {
  second set of statements
}
```

If the specified condition is `true`, then the first set of statements is executed. If the specified condition is `false`, then the second set of statements is executed. In both cases, execution continues with the statement following the `if` statement.

An example of the second form of the `if` statement follows:

```
if(hour<12){
  document.write("Good morning")
}else{
  document.write("Hello")
}
```

The `if` statement results in the current document being updated with the text *Good morning* if the value of the hour variable is less than 12 or with the text *Hello* if hour is greater than or equal to 12.

NOTE   The braces enclosing the statements in the `if` and `else` clauses can be omitted if only one statement is enclosed.

Loop Statements

Loop statements are used to repeat the execution of a set of statements while a particular condition is `true`. JavaScript supports three types of loop statements: the `while` statement, the do `while` statement, and the `for` statement. JavaScript also provides the `label`, `break`, and `continue` statements. The `break` statement is used to terminate all loop iteration. The `continue` statement is used to cause a single loop iteration to end immediately and proceed to the next loop iteration. The `label` statement labels a statement for use with the `break` and `continue` statements. These statements are covered in the following subsections.

The *while* Statement

The `while` statement is a basic loop statement, used to repeat the execution of a set of statements while a specified condition is true. The syntax of the `while` statement is as follows:

```
while ( condition ) {
  statements
}
```

The `while` statement evaluates the condition and, if the condition evaluates to `true`, executes the statements enclosed within braces. When the condition evaluates to `false`, it transfers control to the statement following the `while` statement.

Listing 3.2 provides an example of how the `while` statement can be used to generate the content of an HTML document. Figure 3.2 shows how the document generated by this script is displayed by a web browser. The script iterates from 1 to 6, generating six levels of HTML headings. The index variable is incremented each time it passes through the loop.

Listing 3.2:   The *while* Statement (ch03-02.htm)

```
<HTML>
<HEAD>
<TITLE>Using the While Statement</TITLE>
</HEAD>
<BODY>
<SCRIPT><!--
i=1
while(i<7){
  document.write("<H"+i+">This is a level "+i+" heading." +"</H"+i+">")
  ++i
}
// --></SCRIPT>
</BODY>
</HTML>
```

FIGURE 3.2:

Using the while
statement to generate an
HTML document
(Listing 3.2)

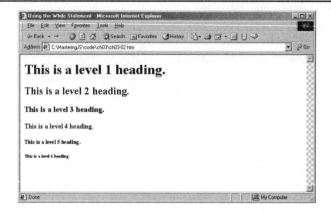

The *do while* Statement

The do while statement, introduced in JavaScript 1.2, is similar to the while statement. The only difference is that the looping condition is checked at the end of the loop, instead of at the beginning. This ensures that the enclosed statements are executed at least once. The syntax of the do while statement is as follows:

```
do {
  statements
while (condition);
```

For example, the following statements display the integers 1 through 10:

```
i = 0
do {
  ++i
  document.writeln(i+"<BR>")
} while (i < 10);
```

The *for* Statement

The for statement is similar to the while statement in that it repeatedly executes a set of statements while a condition is true. It is different from the while statement in that it is designed to update a variable after each loop iteration. The following is the syntax of the for statement:

```
for ( initializationStatement; condition; updateStatement ) {
  statements
}
```

The initialization statement is executed only at the beginning of the for statement's execution. The condition is then tested, and if it is true, the statements enclosed within braces are executed. If the condition is false, the loop is terminated and the statement following the for statement is executed.

If the statements enclosed within the braces of the for statement are executed, the update statement is executed, and then the condition is retested. The enclosed statements and update statement are repeatedly executed until the condition becomes false.

NOTE   The initialization statement, condition, and update statement are optional and may be omitted. For example, you could create a loop just using for(;;) {}.

An example for statement follows:

```
a = new Array(2,4,6,8,10)
sum = 0
for (i = 0;i < a.length;++i) {
  sum += a[i]
}
```

The first statement of the above example creates a five-element array with the values 2, 4, 6, 8, and 10. The second statement initializes the variable sum to 0. The for statement begins by initializing the variable i to 0 and tests the length of a to see if it is greater than i. Because i is 0 and a.length is 5, the statement enclosed within the braces is executed and the value of sum is incremented by a[i], which is 2.

The update statement, ++i, is then executed. This causes i to be incremented to 1. The condition is retested and because i is less than 5 the statement enclosed within braces is then re-executed. This time sum is incremented by 4 and its value becomes 6.

The update statement, ++i, is executed a second time and the condition is retested. At this point, you should be able to follow the remainder of the for statement's execution. The for loop continues to iterate until i < a.length is no longer true. This happens when i becomes 5. At this point, sum has become the sum of all the elements of a and its value is 30.

Listing 3.3 shows how the script shown in Listing 3.2 can be updated to use a for statement instead of a while statement. The web page resulting from the execution of this script is the same as that displayed in Figure 3.2.

Listing 3.3:   **Use of the *for* Statement (ch03-03.htm)**

```
<HTML>
<HEAD>
<TITLE>Using the For Statement</TITLE>
</HEAD>
<BODY>
<SCRIPT><!--
for(i=1;i<7;++i)
  document.write("<H"+i+">This is a level "+i+" heading." +"</H"+i+">")
// --></SCRIPT>
</BODY>
</HTML>
```

NOTE   The braces enclosing the statements in the `for` and `while` statements can be omitted if only one statement is enclosed.

The *label* Statement

Any statement may be labeled, by placing `labelName :` before the statement. For example,

```
MyLabel :
  a = 2 * b
```

causes the previous statement to be labeled `MyLabel`. Labels are used to identify statements. They are typically used to label `loop`, `switch`, or `if` statements. You can reference labeled statements via the `break` and `continue` statements, as discussed in the following sections.

The *break* Statement

The `break` statement is used to terminate execution of a loop and transfer control to the statement following the loop. The `break` statement consists of the word `break`, followed by an optional label. When the `break` statement is encountered, the loop is immediately terminated. An example of its use follows:

```
a = new Array(5,4,3,2,1)
sum = 0
for (i = 0;i < a.length;++i) {
  if (i == 3) break;
  sum += a[i]
}
```

The above `for` statement executes for i equal to 0, 1, 2, and 3. When i equals 3 the condition of the `if` statement is true and the `break` statement is executed. This causes the `for` statement to immediately terminate. The value of `sum` is 12 upon termination of the `for` statement.

Listing 3.4 provides a script that illustrates the use of the `break` statement. Figure 3.3 shows the web page generated by this script. The script loops to test the integers from 100 to 1 until it finds one that is evenly divisible by 17. When it finds such a number, it terminates the loop.

Listing 3.4:   The *break* Statement (ch03-04.htm)

```
<HTML>
<HEAD>
<TITLE>Using the Break Statement</TITLE>
</HEAD>
<BODY>
<SCRIPT><!--
```

```
for(i=100;i>0;--i){
 document.write(i+"<BR>")
 if(i%17==0) break
}
// --></SCRIPT>
</BODY>
</HTML>
```

FIGURE 3.3:

Using the break
statement (Listing 3.4)

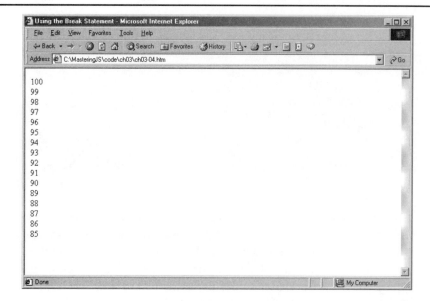

If the break statement is used with a label, then control is transferred to the first statement following the labeled statement. The labeled statement does not need to be a loop statement. Consider the following example:

```
test1 :
   if (val > 0) {
       document.write("Greater than zero: ")
       test2 :
         if (val == 2) {
             document.write(val)
             break test1
         }
       // Other code
   }
```

The break statement causes control to transfer to the first statement following the outer if statement (test1).

The *continue* Statement

The continue statement is similar to the break statement in that it affects the execution of the for, do while, or while statement in which it is contained. It differs from the break statement in that it does not completely terminate the loop's execution, but only terminates the execution of the statements in the loop's current iteration.

When a continue statement is encountered in a while, do while, or for loop, the rest of the statements being iterated are skipped and control of execution returns to the condition of the loop.

Consider the following while loop as an example:

```
i = 1
sum = 0
while(i<10) {
  i *= 2;
  if (i == 4) continue
  sum += i + 1
}
```

The while loop iterates for i equal to 1, 2, 4, and 8 at the beginning of each loop. However, sum is only updated when i equals 1, 4, and 8 at the time the loop is begun. When i equals 2 at the beginning of the loop, it is doubled to 4 as the result of the first statement of the loop's execution. This causes the condition of the if statement to be true and the continue statement to be executed. Execution of the continue statement causes the last statement in the loop to be skipped and control to return to the evaluation of the condition of the while statement. The final value of sum is 29. The continue statement may also be used with a label. The label specifies the loop statement to which the continue statement applies. For example, a label could have been used with the while statement in the previous code.

Listing 3.5 provides a script that illustrates the use of the continue statement. Figure 3.4 shows the web page generated by this script. The script iterates the for loop using the integers 1 through 9 (inclusive), but uses the continue statement to skip printing out all odd integers.

Listing 3.5:   The *continue* Statement (ch03-05.htm)

```
<HTML>
<HEAD>
<TITLE>Using the Continue Statement</TITLE>
</HEAD>
<BODY>
<SCRIPT><!--
for(i=1;i<10;++i){
  if(i%2!=0) continue
  document.write(i+"<BR>")
```

```
    }
    // --></SCRIPT>
    </BODY>
    </HTML>
```

FIGURE 3.4:

Using the `continue` statement (Listing 3.5)

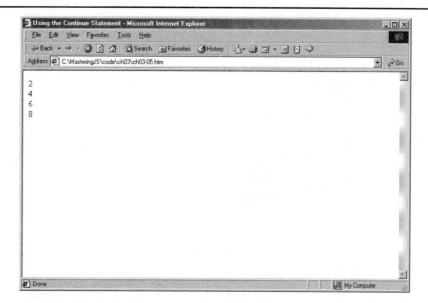

The *switch* Statement

JavaScript 1.2 added the `switch` statement. Its syntax is the same as in Java and C++:

```
switch (expression) {
  case value1:
    statements
    break
        .
        .
        .
  case valuen:
    statements
    break
  default:
    statements
}
```

The `switch` statement evaluates the expression and determines if any of the values (`value1` through `valuen`) match the expression's value. If one of them matches, the statements for that particular case are executed, and then statement execution continues after the `switch` statement. If there is no matching value, then the statements for the `default` case are executed.

The break statements may be omitted. However, if they are omitted, execution continues with the next case (if any).

The following `switch` statement prints the string value of the number corresponding to 1, 2, or 3, or prints *I don't know* otherwise.

```
switch (i) {
  case 1:
    document.writeln("one")
    break
  case 2:
    document.writeln("two")
    break
  case 3:
    document.writeln("three")
    break
  default:
    document.writeln("I don't know")
}
```

Listing 3.6 provides a script that illustrates the use of the `switch` statement. Figure 3.5 shows the web page generated by this script. The script displays the names of the numbers 1 through 10.

Listing 3.6:   **The *switch* Statement (ch03-06.htm)**

```
<HTML>
<HEAD>
<TITLE>Using the switch Statement</TITLE>
</HEAD>
<BODY>
<SCRIPT LANGUAGE="JavaScript"><!--
for(i=1; i<=10; ++i) {
 switch (i) {
  case 1:
   val = "one"
   break;
  case 2:
   val = "two"
   break;
  case 3:
   val = "three"
   break;
  case 4:
   val = "four"
   break;
```

```
      case 5:
       val = "five"
       break;
      case 6:
       val = "six"
       break;
      case 7:
       val = "seven"
       break;
      case 8:
       val = "eight"
       break;
      case 9:
       val = "nine"
       break;
      case 10:
       val = "ten"
       break;
      default:
       val = "unknown"
     }
     document.writeln(val+"<BR>");
    }
    // -->
    </SCRIPT>
    </BODY>
    </HTML>
```

FIGURE 3.5:

Using the switch
statement (Listing 3.6)

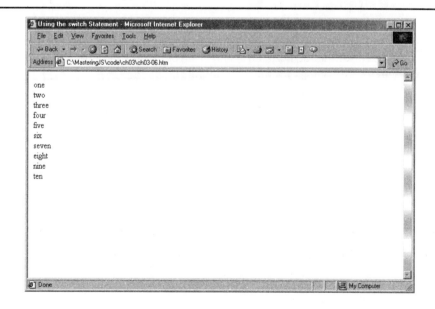

Function Call Statements

Most programming languages support function calls. *Functions* are named blocks of statements that are referenced and executed as a unit. Data that is required for the execution of a function may be passed as *arguments* to the function. Functions may return a value, but are not required to do so. When a function returns a value, the invocation of the function is usually part of an expression. For example, the following statement invokes the `factorial()` function, passing it the integer value 5 as an argument:

```
n = factorial(5)
```

In the previous example, the function call, `factorial(5)`, returns a value that is assigned to the variable n. The `factorial()` function is a hypothetical function and is not defined by JavaScript.

When a function does not return a value, it is usually used to perform an operation that updates a variable or an object that is external to JavaScript. The invocation of a non-value returning function is a complete statement, not merely part of a larger expression. For example, consider the function invocation in the following statement:

```
notifyUser("Product code is invalid")
```

Here, the function `notifyUser()` takes the string `"Product code is invalid"` as an argument. It then displays this string to the user. The function does not return a value and, therefore, is not on the right side of an assignment statement.

Defining Functions

A function must be defined before it can be used. Function definitions are usually placed in the head of an HTML document, although it is not mandatory to do so. Placing function definitions in the head, however, ensures that the definition occurs before the function is used. The syntax of a function definition is as follows:

```
function functionName(p1, p2, ..., pn) {
  statements
}
```

The function name is the name used to refer to the function in function calls. The arguments are the names of variables that receive the values passed to the function when the function is invoked. The statements enclosed in braces are executed as the result of a function call.

For example, consider the following function definition:

```
function display(text) {
  document.write(text)
}
```

If the above function is invoked with the statement display("xyz"), the text *xyz* is written to the current web document. The display("xyz") function call is thus equivalent to the statement document.write("xyz").

Listing 3.7 provides an example of a function definition. Figure 3.6 shows the web page that this script generates.

Listing 3.7:   A Function Definition (ch03-07.htm)

```
<HTML>
<HEAD>
<TITLE>A function definition</TITLE>
<SCRIPT LANGUAGE="JavaScript"><!--
function displayTaggedText(tag, text) {
 document.write("<"+tag+">")
 document.write(text)
 document.write("</"+tag+">")
}
// -->
</SCRIPT>
</HEAD>
<BODY>
<SCRIPT LANGUAGE="JavaScript"><!--
displayTaggedText("H1","This is a level 1 heading")
displayTaggedText("P","This text is the first paragraph of the document.")
// -->
</SCRIPT>
</BODY>
</HTML>
```

FIGURE 3.6:

Defining and using a
function (Listing 3.7)

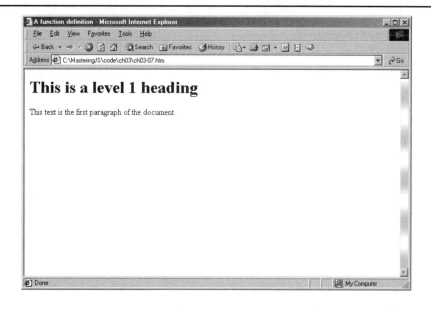

The script in the document head defines the function `displayTaggedText()`, which takes two arguments: `tag` and `text`. Actual values for `tag` and `text` are passed to the function via these arguments when the function is invoked. The function consists of three statements. The first statement writes the left angle bracket, followed by the value of the `tag` argument plus a right angle bracket to the current document. The second `write` statement writes the value of the `text` variable to the current document. The third statement writes the string </, followed by the value of the `tag` variable followed by the right angle bracket to the current document. The `displayTaggedText()` function does not return a value.

The script in the body of the document executes two function call statements that invoke the `displayTaggedText()` function to write a level-1 HTML heading and a paragraph of text to the current document. The arguments passed in the first invocation are `H1` and `This is a level 1 heading`. The `H1` string is passed to the `displayTaggedText()` function via the `tag` variable. The `This is a level 1 heading` string is passed via the `text` variable. The second invocation of `displayTaggedText()` is handled in the same manner. The string `P` is passed via `tag` and `This is a level 1 heading` is passed via `text`.

Defining Functions with a Variable Number of Arguments

JavaScript provides the capability to define functions that take a variable number of arguments, using the `arguments` array. The `arguments` array is automatically created by JavaScript for each function invocation. Suppose function `f` is invoked with the arguments `"test"`, `true`, and `77` as in the following statement:

```
f("test",true,77)
```

The array `f.arguments` contains the values of these arguments. In this case, the variables are as follows:

```
f.arguments.length = 3
f.arguments[0] = "test"
f.arguments[1] = true
f.arguments[2] = 77
```

The following function definition illustrates the use of the `arguments` array.

```
function sum() {
 n = sum.arguments.length
 total = 0
 for(i=0;i<n;++i) {
  total += sum.arguments[i]
 }
 return total
}
```

The sum() function is designed to add an arbitrary list of arguments. The variable n is assigned the length of the sum.arguments array. The total variable is used to add the elements of sum.arguments.

Local Variable Declarations

When defining a function, it is often necessary to define variables that will be used to store values calculated by the function. You could declare variables using the declaration statements that you studied in the "Variable Declarations" section earlier in the chapter. However, this causes the function definition to be dependent on these global variables and, as a result, less modular and more difficult to debug. Instead, it is better to declare variables that are used only within the function. These variables, referred to as *local variables*, are accessible only within the function that they are declared. Figure 3.7 illustrates the difficulties inherent with using global variables within functions.

FIGURE 3.7:

Using global variables within functions

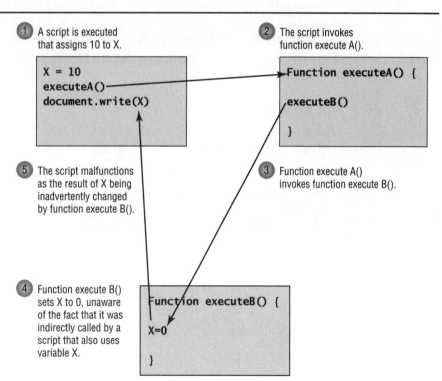

1. A script is executed that assigns 10 to X.

2. The script invokes function execute A().

```
X = 10
executeA()
document.write(X)
```

```
Function executeA() {

    executeB()

}
```

5. The script malfunctions as the result of X being inadvertently changed by function execute B().

3. Function execute A() invokes function execute B().

4. Function execute B() sets X to 0, unaware of the fact that it was indirectly called by a script that also uses variable X.

```
Function executeB() {

    X=0

}
```

Local variables are declared in the same manner as global variables, except that local variable declarations are made within the body of the function and are preceded by the keyword var. The following are examples of local variable declarations:

```
// Declares temp as a local variable
var temp

// Declares index as a local variable and initializes it to 1
var index = 1

/* Declares the product array with an initial
    capacity of 100 elements */
var product = new Array(100)
```

Local variables may have the same name as global variables. In the case that a local variable and global variable have the same name, all references to the variable name within the function that the local variable is defined refer to the local variable of that function and not to the global variable. All references to the variable name outside of the function that defines the local variable are to the global variable. Listing 3.8 provides a script that illustrates the use of global and local variables with the same names. Figure 3.8 displays the web page that this script generates. The variable x is a local variable in the displaySquared() function and a global variable in the script contained in the document body. Note that the local and global x variables may be updated independently.

Listing 3.8:   Use of Global and Local Variables (ch03-08.htm)

```
<HTML>
<HEAD>
<TITLE>Global and Local Variables</TITLE>
<SCRIPT LANGUAGE="JavaScript"><!--
function displaySquared(y) {
var x = y * y
document.write(x+"<BR>")
}
// -->
</SCRIPT>
</HEAD>
<BODY>
<SCRIPT LANGUAGE="JavaScript"><!--
for(x=0;x<10;++x)
 displaySquared(x)
// -->
</SCRIPT>
</BODY>
</HTML>
```

FIGURE 3.8:

An example of using global
and local variables
(Listing 3.8)

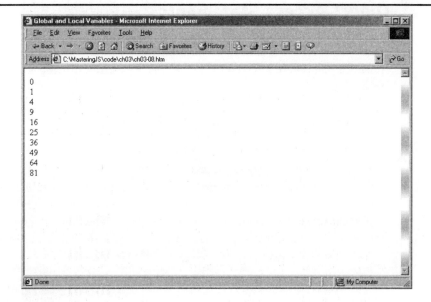

The *return* Statement

The return statement is used to return a value as the result of the processing performed by a function. This value is returned to the statement that invoked the function. The following is the syntax of the return statement:

```
return expression
```

The expression evaluates to the value to be returned by the function. When the return statement is encountered, the expression is evaluated and the value to which the expression evaluates is immediately returned by the function. No subsequent statements of the function are processed.

An example of the use of the return statement is shown in the following function definition:

```
function factorial(n) {
 var sum = 1
 for(i=1;i<=n;++i)
  sum *= i
 return sum
 }
```

In this example, sum is calculated as the product of all integers from 1 through n. This value is then returned via the return statement.

Object-Access Statements

Objects are JavaScript data structures that both contain data and provide functions, referred to as *methods*, that are used to perform operations on this data. The individual variables comprising an object are referred to as *properties*. Properties provide access to the data contained in an object.

NOTE   JavaScript objects are covered in Chapter 5. This section focuses on programming statements that use object properties and methods.

Because properties provide access to the values contained in the variables comprising an object, they are usually used in expressions that appear in the right or left side of an assignment statement. For example, suppose the `employee` variable refers to an object of type `employeeRecord` that has the `employeeID` property. The following assignment statement retrieves the value of the `employeeID` property and assigns it to the `id` variable.

```
id = employee.employeeID
```

The following is the general syntax used to access the property of an object:

```
variableName.propertyName
```

The variable name is the name of a variable that refers to an object and the property name is the name of the property to be retrieved.

When a property reference appears in the left side of an assignment statement, the property of the referenced object is updated. In the following example, the `employeeID` property of the object referred to by the `employee` variable is updated with the value stored in the `id` variable.

```
employee.employeeID = id
```

The methods of an object are functions that are used to perform operations on the object. These methods are invoked in a similar manner as properties. However, since methods are functions, they must include the method's argument list. An empty argument list is specified in the same manner as for function calls. The general syntax of a method invocation is shown here:

```
variableName.methodName(p1,p2,...,pn)
```

The variable name is the name of a variable that refers to an object and the method name is the name of the method to be invoked. The arguments `p1` through `pn` are an optional list of method arguments.

Some methods do not return a value. Their invocation is a complete statement in itself. A common example that you've been using so far is the `write()` method of the `document` object:

```
document.write("text to be displayed")
```

Some methods return a value. In this case, the method invocation may appear as part of a larger expression, as in the following example:

```
payroll=0
for(i=0;i<employee.length;++i)
  payroll += employee[i].netPay()
```

In the above example, `employee` is an array of `employeeRecord` objects. The `netPay()` method calculates the net pay of each employee based on data contained in the properties of the `employeeRecord` objects.

The *with* Statement

The `with` statement is provided as a convenience to eliminate retyping the name of an object that is to be referenced in a series of property references and method invocations. The syntax of the `with` statement is as follows:

```
with(variableName){
  statements
}
```

The variable name identifies the default object to be used with the statements enclosed in braces. An example of the `with` statement follows:

```
with(document) {
  write("<H1>With It</H1>")
  write("<P>")
  write("Eliminate object name references with with")
  write("</P>")
}
```

In this example, the need to prefix each `write()` method invocation with the `document` object is eliminated because `document` is identified in the `with` statement. Without the `with` statement, the preceding code would need to be written as follows:

```
document.write("<H1>With It</H1>")
document.write("<P>")
document.write("Eliminate object name references with with")
document.write("</P>")
```

The *for in* Statement

You learned how the `for` statement is used to iterate a set of statements based on a loop condition and an update statement. The `for in` statement is similar to a `for` statement in that it repeatedly executes a set of statements. However, instead of iterating the statements based on the loop condition, it executes the statements for all properties that are defined for an object.

The syntax of the for in statement is as follows:

```
for (variableName in objectName) {
  statements
}
```

The for in loop executes the statements enclosed in braces one time for each property defined for objectName. Each time the statements are executed, the variable specified by variableName is assigned a string identifying the current property name. For example, consider the execution of the following for in statement in the case of the employee object having the properties employeeID, employeeName, and employeeLocation:

```
for(prop in employee)
    document.write(prop+"<BR>")
```

The previous for in statement would cause the following text to be written to the current document:

```
employeeID
employeeName
employeeLocation
```

These are the three properties that are defined for the employee object.

The *throw, try,* and *catch* Statements

One of the nicest features of ECMAScript revision 3 is its support for the throw, try, and catch statements. These statements work together to give you advanced control over any errors and exceptions that may arise in your code. If you are a Java programmer, these statements will be familiar to you. JavaScript uses the same syntax for these statements as Java.

NOTE   The throw, try, and catch statements only work with Internet Explorer 5, Navigator 6, and later browsers.

An *exception* is an error that is generated by your script to call attention to a problem that is discovered during the script's execution. Your script generates an exception so that the error may be handled and resolved. In the parlance of exceptions, you generate an exception by *throwing* it. The code that handles exceptions thrown by your scripts (or the JavaScript interpreter) is referred to as an *exception handler*. Exception handlers are said to *catch* exceptions. Figure 3.9 provides an overview of the exception handling process.

FIGURE 3.9:

How exception handling works

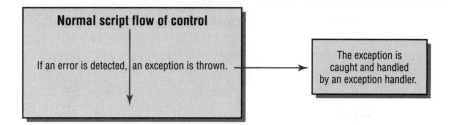

The `throw` statement is used to throw an exception. Its syntax follows:

```
throw expression
```

The value of `expression` is used to identify the type of error that occurred. For example, the following statement throws an exception named `BadInputFromUser`.

```
throw "BadInputFromUser"
```

TIP   While it isn't mandatory, it's a good idea to throw string values. This will make your code easier to understand and debug.

The `try` statement and the `catch` statement work together to support exception handling. Their syntax follows:

```
try {
  statement(s) where an exception may be thrown
}
catch(errorVariable) {
  statement(s) that handle the exception
}
```

The `try` statement surrounds the statements for which exception handling is to be performed. It is immediately followed by a `catch` statement that performs the exception handling. The `errorVariable` is used to reference any exception that occurs. It is assigned an instance of the `error` object. If an exception is thrown during the processing of the statements contained within the `try` statement, then the `errorVariable` is assigned an `error` object that identifies the exception, and control immediately transfers to the statements contained within the `catch` statement. If no exception is thrown during the processing of the statements contained within the `try` statement, then the `catch` statement is skipped and control transfers to the statement following the `catch` statement.

Let's work an example to get a feel for how this all works. Listing 3.9 shows a simple HTML file that contains two scripts, one in the document's head and the other in its body. The script in the document's body iterates i between 0 and 21, passing it as an argument to the `primeTest()` function. The script in the document's head defines the `primeTest()` function.

This function checks the argument n to determine if it is prime. It contains a try statement in which the prime testing is performed. The first if statement checks to see if n is between 1 and 20. If it is not, then the It's out of range exception is thrown and control passes to the catch statement. If n is between 1 and 20 the control passes to the for statement.

Listing 3.9:   **An Exception Handling Example (ch03-09.htm).**

```
<HTML>
<HEAD><TITLE>Exception Test</TITLE></HEAD>
<SCRIPT LANGUAGE="JavaScript"><!--
function primeTest(n) {
 document.write("Testing "+n+": ")
 try {
  if(n < 1 || n > 20) throw "It's out of range"
   for(var i = 2; i < n; ++i)
    if(n % i == 0) throw "It's divisible by " + i
   document.writeln("It's prime.<BR>")
 }
 catch (exception) {
  document.writeln(exception+".<BR>")
 }
}
--></SCRIPT>
<BODY>
<P>This script only works with Internet Explorer 5, Navigator 6, or later
browsers.</P>
<SCRIPT LANGUAGE="JavaScript"><!--
for(i = 0; i <= 21; ++i) {
 primeTest(i)
}
--></SCRIPT>
</BODY>
</HTML>
```

The for statement iterates i between 2 and n-1. If n modulous i is zero, then n is not prime, the It's divisible by exception is thrown, and control passes to the catch statement. Otherwise, It's prime is written to the document window and the function returns.

The catch statement simply writes the exception to the document window.

Figure 3.10 shows the output that is displayed by primeTest() as the result of the script's processing.

FIGURE 3.10:

The results of the exception processing (Listing 3.9)

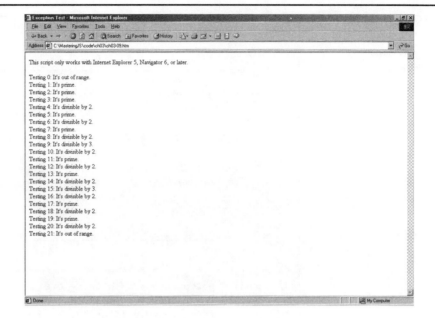

Nesting *try* Statements and Rethrowing Exceptions

JavaScript allows you to nest try statements within each other. By doing so, you can implement multiple levels of exception handling. Figure 3.11 provides an overview of this approach. The try and catch statements of a lower-level exception handler are enclosed in a higher-level try statement. If an exception occurs in the lower-level try statement, it is caught by the lower-level catch statement. If the lower-level catch statement encounters an error in handling the exception, it can throw a new exception that is handled by the higher-level catch statement. The lower-level catch statement can also rethrow any exception that requires higher-level processing.

FIGURE 3.11:

Nested exception handling
allows exceptions to be
rethrown.

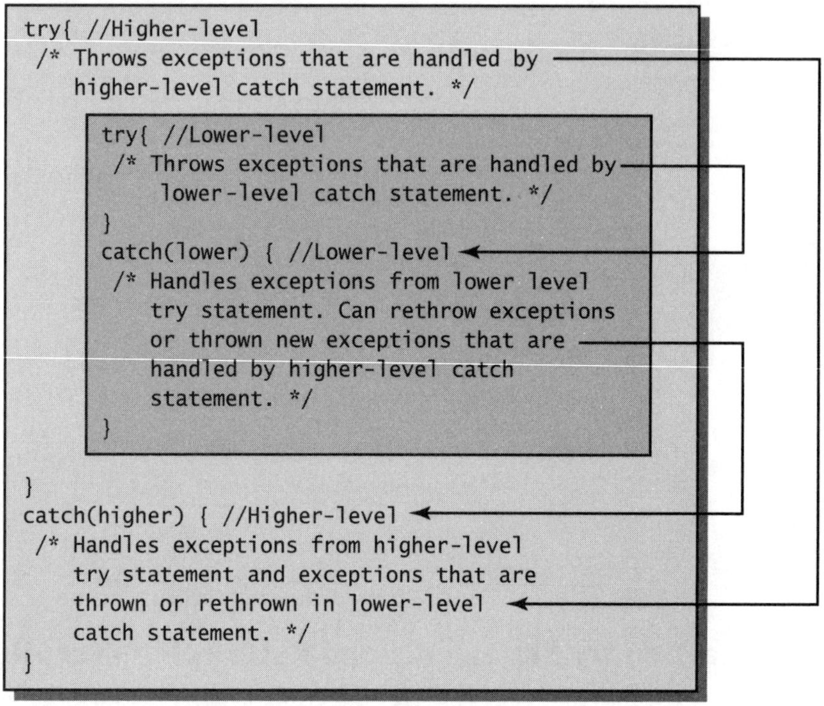

```
try{ //Higher-level
  /* Throws exceptions that are handled by
     higher-level catch statement. */

     try{ //Lower-level
       /* Throws exceptions that are handled by
          lower-level catch statement. */
     }
     catch(lower) { //Lower-level
       /* Handles exceptions from lower level
          try statement. Can rethrow exceptions
          or thrown new exceptions that are
          handled by higher-level catch
          statement. */
     }

}
catch(higher) { //Higher-level
  /* Handles exceptions from higher-level
     try statement and exceptions that are
     thrown or rethrown in lower-level
     catch statement. */
}
```

Listing 3.10 provides an example of nested exception handling and the rethrowing of
exceptions. It consists of two scripts, one in the document head and the other in the document body. The script in the document body iterates i from 1 to 100 and invokes the
selected() function to determine if the value of i should be displayed. If the selected()
function returns true then i is displayed.

Listing 3.10:   Nested Exception Handling (ch03-10.htm)

```
<HTML>
<HEAD><TITLE>Exception Test</TITLE></HEAD>
<SCRIPT LANGUAGE="JavaScript"><!--
function selected(n) {
 try {
  try {
   if (n % 3 == 2) throw "No way"
   if (n % 3 == 1) throw "Try again"
  }
  catch (ex1) {
   if(ex1 == "Try again")
    if (n % 5 == 0) throw "Try again"
```

```
   return false
  }
  if (n % 7 == 3) throw "Try again"
  if (n % 7 != 0) throw "No way"
 }
 catch (ex2) {
  if(ex2 != "Try again") return false
  if(n % 11 != 0) return false
 }
 return true
}
--></SCRIPT>
<BODY>
<P>This script only works with Internet Explorer 5, Navigator 6, or later
browsers.</P>
<SCRIPT LANGUAGE="JavaScript"><!--
for(i = 1; i <= 100; ++i) {
 if (selected(i)) document.writeln(i+"<BR>")
}
--></SCRIPT>
</BODY>
</HTML>
```

The processing of interest occurs in the selected() function. This function takes an argument n and performs a series of tests on it to determine whether it should return true or false. The selected() function contains two sets of try/catch statements with one set nested within the other. The inner try statement checks the value of n % 3. If this value is 2, then the No way exception is thrown. If it is 1, then the Try again exception is thrown. The catch statement processes the Try again exception by checking to see if n is divisible by 5. In this case the Try again exception is rethrown. Otherwise, the catch statement returns a value of false.

Two if statements appear after the inner try statement but before the end of the outer try statement. If n % 7 is 3, then the Try again exception is thrown. Otherwise, if n % 7 is not 0, then the No way exception is thrown.

The outer catch statement returns a value of false for the No way exception and for the Try again exception when n is not divisible by 11. If the value of n manages to get through the gauntlet of exceptions, then selected() returns a value of true.

Figure 3.11 shows the output generated by Listing 3.10. The reason that I put together such a complicated set of exceptions is so that you can trace through the scripts code to see how the output of Figure 3.12 is generated. By doing so, you'll have a firm understanding of how nested exception handling and exception rethrowing work.

FIGURE 3.12:

The output generated by nested exception handlers (Listing 3.10)

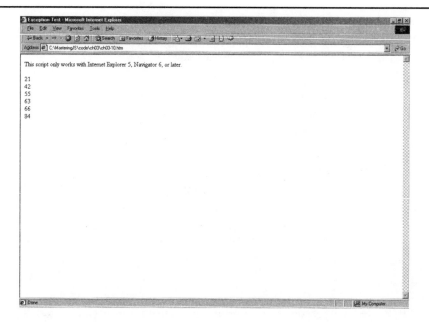

Summary

This chapter introduced you to more elements of the JavaScript language. You covered all of the operators provided by JavaScript and learned how expressions are evaluated using operator precedence. You learned to use JavaScript's programming statements and developed sample scripts that demonstrated the use of these statements. You also learned how to create and invoke functions. In the next chapter, you'll extend your JavaScript programming expertise by learning how JavaScript supports the handling of user-generated events.

CHAPTER 4

Handling Events

- How JavaScript handles events

- Types of events

- Setting event handlers from within JavaScript

- The event object

- Event capturing

- Error handling

Events are the mechanism by which browsers respond to user actions. JavaScript's event-handling features give you the ability to alter the standard way in which a browser reacts to these actions. This enables you to develop web pages that are more interactive, more responsive, and easier to use.

This chapter illustrates the use of JavaScript's event-handling features. It describes JavaScript's approach to event handling and identifies the event handlers that are predefined by JavaScript. It shows you how to write your own event-handling functions and how to associate them with user interface actions. By the time you finish this chapter, you'll be able to use event-handling functions to develop highly interactive web pages.

What Are Events?

Events describe actions that occur as the result of user interaction with a web page or other browser-related activities. For example, when a user clicks on a hyperlink or a button, or enters data in a form, an event is generated informing the browser that an action has occurred and that further processing is required. The browser waits for events to occur, and when they do, it performs whatever processing is assigned to those events. The processing that is performed in response to the occurrence of an event is known as *event handling*. The code that performs this processing is called an *event handler*. Figure 4.1 illustrates the notion of an event and the process of event handling.

FIGURE 4.1:

Events and event handling

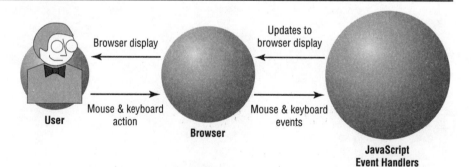

For a simple example of event processing, consider what normally happens when a user clicks on a hyperlink that is displayed on a web page. The default HTML action arising from such an event is that the browser loads and displays the page associated with that URL. With JavaScript, however, you can change that default action by writing a different event handler. Here are just a few things you can do with events using JavaScript event handlers:

• Display a dialog box when a user moves the mouse over a link.

- Validate the data a user has just entered into a form.

- Load and display an animation sequence when a user clicks a button.

- Interact with Java applets and browser plug-ins.

JavaScript's event-handling features are what enables JavaScript to create web pages that come alive and interact with web users.

How JavaScript Handles Events

JavaScript's approach to event handling is a two-step process: First it defines the events that can be handled by scripts, and then it provides a standard method of connecting these events to the user-supplied JavaScript code.

JavaScript-enabled browsers define events for most of the major objects found in web pages including links, images, image maps, form elements, and windows. These browsers also define special attributes for the tags corresponding to these HTML elements. These attributes are used to identify event-handling JavaScript code. The values of these attributes are text strings that identify the event-handling code.

Table 4.1 summarizes the events that are common to Navigator and Internet Explorer. The first two columns identify the name and tags associated with the HTML element. The third and fourth columns identify and describe the events that JavaScript defines for the HTML element. I'll provide examples of these events throughout this chapter. For now, just try to get a feel for the kinds of events that can be handled through JavaScript.

TABLE 4.1: Events Defined by Both Navigator and Internet Explorer

HTML Element	HTML Tags	Event	Description
Link or anchor	`<A> ... </A>`	`click`	The mouse is clicked on a link (link only).
		`dblClick`	The mouse is double-clicked on a link or anchor.
		`mouseDown`	The mouse button is pressed (link only).
		`mouseUp`	The mouse button is released (link only).
		`mouseOver`	The mouse is moved over a link or anchor.
		`mouseOut`	The mouse is moved from within a link (or anchor) to outside of that link (or anchor).
		`keyDown`	The user presses a key (link only).
		`keyUp`	The user releases a key (link only).
		`keyPress`	The user presses and releases a key (link only).

TABLE 4.1 CONTINUED: Events Defined by Both Navigator and Internet Explorer

HTML Element	HTML Tags	Event	Description
Image	`<IMG>`	abort	The loading of an image is aborted as the result of a user action.
		error	An error occurs during the loading of an image.
		load	An image is loaded and displayed.
		keyDown	The user presses a key.
		keyUp	The user releases a key.
		keyPress	The user presses and releases a key.
Area	`<AREA>`	mouseOver	The mouse is moved over an area of a client-side image map.
		mouseOut	The mouse is moved from within an image map area to outside of that area.
		dblClick	The user double-clicks an area of an image map.
Document body	`<BODY> … </BODY>`	click	The user clicks in the body of a document.
		dblClick	The user double-clicks in the body of a document.
		keyDown	The user presses a key.
		keyUp	The user releases a key.
		keyPress	The user presses and releases a key.
		mouseDown	The user presses the mouse button.
		mouseUp	The user releases the mouse button.
Window, frame set, frame	`<BODY> ... </BODY>`	blur	A window loses the current input focus.
	`<FRAMESET> ... </FRAMESET>`		
	`<FRAME> ... </FRAME>`	error	An error occurs when a window is loaded.
		focus	A window receives the current input focus.
		load	The loading of a window is completed.
		unload	The user exits a window.
		resize	A window is resized.
Form	`<FORM> … </FORM>`	submit	A form is submitted by the user.
		reset	A form is reset by the user.

Continued on next page

TABLE 4.1 CONTINUED: Events Defined by Both Navigator and Internet Explorer

HTML Element	HTML Tags	Event	Description
Text field	`<INPUT TYPE = "text">`	`blur`	A text field loses the current input focus.
		`focus`	A text field receives the current input focus.
		`change`	A text field is modified and loses the current input focus.
		`select`	Text is selected within a text field.
Password field	`<INPUT TYPE = "password">`	`blur`	A password field loses the input focus.
		`focus`	A password field gains the input focus.
Text area	`<TEXTAREA> … </TEXTAREA>`	`blur`	A text area loses the current input focus.
		`focus`	A text area receives the current input focus.
		`change`	A text area is modified and loses the current input focus.
		`select`	Text is selected within a text area.
		`keyDown`	The user presses a key.
		`keyUp`	The user releases a key.
		`keyPress`	The user presses and releases a key.
Button	`<INPUT TYPE = "button">`	`click`	A button is clicked.
		`blur`	A button loses the input focus.
		`focus`	A button gains the input focus.
		`mouseDown`	A user presses the left mouse button over a button.
		`mouseUp`	A user releases the left mouse button over a button.
Submit	`<INPUT TYPE = "submit">`	`click`	A submit button is clicked.
		`blur`	A submit button loses the input focus.
		`focus`	A submit button gains the input focus.
Reset	`<INPUT TYPE = "reset">`	`click`	A reset button is clicked.
		`blur`	A reset button loses the input focus.
		`focus`	A reset button gains the input focus.
Radio button	`<INPUT TYPE = "radio">`	`click`	A radio button is clicked.
		`blur`	A radio button loses the input focus.
		`focus`	A radio button gains the input focus.
Check box	`<INPUT TYPE = "checkbox">`	`click`	A check box is clicked.
		`blur`	A check box loses the input focus.
		`focus`	A check box gains the input focus.

Continued on next page

TABLE 4.1 CONTINUED: Events Defined by Both Navigator and Internet Explorer

HTML Element	HTML Tags	Event	Description
File upload	`<INPUT TYPE = "file">`	blur	A file upload form element loses the input focus.
		change	A user selects a file to be uploaded.
		focus	A file upload form element gains the input focus.
Selection	`<SELECT> ... </SELECT>`	blur	A selection element loses the current input focus.
		focus	A selection element receives the current input focus.
		change	A selection element is modified and loses the current input focus.

NOTE Navigator and Internet Explorer define many events besides those identified in Table 4.1. However, if you use those events, your scripts will not work correctly under both browsers. Throughout this book, I focus on showing you how to write scripts that work with both browsers.

NOTE Some events can be a combination of other events. For example, the `click` event involves `mouseDown` and `mouseUp` events.

JavaScript recognizes special event-handling attributes for each of the HTML elements identified in Table 4.1. These attributes are used to specify the JavaScript code to be executed in response to a particular event. For example, suppose you wanted to handle the event associated with a user moving the mouse over a particular link. You would connect the link to the event-handling code as follows:

```
<A HREF="http://www.jaworski.com" onMouseOver="event-handling code">
text associated with link</A>
```

The onMouseOver attribute identifies the event handler to be associated with the mouseOver event. The actual code is placed between the quotes. Listing 4.1 provides an example of using the onMouseOver attribute.

NOTE You can access the file for Listing 4.1, `ch04-01.htm`, and all of the code listings in this chapter on the CD that accompanies the book.

○ **Listing 4.1:** **Example Event Handler (ch04-01.htm)**

```
<HTML>
<HEAD>
<TITLE>Example Event Handler</TITLE>
</HEAD>
<BODY>
<H1>Example Event Handler</H1>
<P><A HREF="http://www.jaworski.com/javascript"
onMouseOver=
  "alert('Link to the Mastering JavaScript Home Page.')">Move your mouse over
this link and a popup window is displayed.</A></P>
</BODY>
</HTML>
```

In Listing 4.1, the JavaScript event-handling code is the following:

```
alert('Link to the Mastering JavaScript Home Page.')
```

This code consists of a call to the `alert()` method of the window object with the string `'Link to the Mastering JavaScript Home Page.'` passed as a parameter. The `alert()` method displays a pop-up window with the specified text. Figure 4.2 shows the web page that is displayed before the mouse is moved over the link. Figure 4.3 shows the pop-up window that is displayed as the result of handling the `mouseOver` event. Note that if you click on the link, the pop-up window is not displayed. The `click` event is handled by a different event handler. This event handler is specified by the `onClick` attribute.

FIGURE 4.2:

Initial display of the event-handling example from Listing 4.1

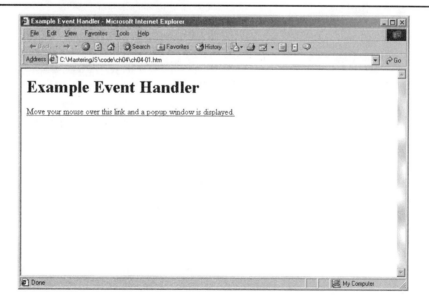

FIGURE 4.3:

Pop-up window resulting
from mouseOver event of
Listing 4.1

The attribute for the mouseOver event is onMouseOver. The JavaScript code that is executed as the result of the event is provided as the attribute value of the onMouseOver attribute. In general, the name of the event-handling attribute is the name of the event prefixed by on. The attributes are case insensitive, which means that you can use onMouseOver, onmouseover, ONMOUSEOVER, or any other upper- and lowercase character combinations.

WARNING   In some rare cases, Internet Explorer only handles an event if the event attribute is uppercase. This is an Internet Explorer bug.

Table 4.2 lists and describes the event-handling attributes of the HTML elements that were presented in Table 4.1. In the following section, you'll learn how to write event handlers for each of these attributes.

TABLE 4.2: Event-Handling Attributes

Event-Handling Attribute	Identifies Code to Execute under These circumstances
onAbort	The loading of an image is aborted as the result of a user action.
onBlur	A document, window, frame set, or form element loses the current input focus.
onChange	A text field, text area, file upload field, or selection is modified and loses the current input focus.
onClick	A link, client-side image map area, or form element is clicked.
onDblClick	A link, client-side image map area, or document is clicked.
onError	An error occurs during the loading of an image, window, or frame.
onFocus	A document, window, frame set, or form element receives the current input focus.
onKeyDown	The user presses a key.
onKeyPress	The user presses and releases a key.
onKeyUp	The user releases a key.
onLoad	An image, document, or frame set is loaded.
onMouseDown	The user presses a mouse button.
onMouseOut	The mouse is moved out of a link or an area of a client-side image map.
onMouseOver	The mouse is moved over a link or an area of a client-side image map.

Continued on next page

TABLE 4.2 CONTINUED: Event-Handling Attributes

Event-Handling Attribute	Identifies Code to Execute under These circumstances
onMouseUp	The user releases a mouse button.
onReset	A user resets a form by clicking on the form's reset button.
onResize	The user resizes a window or frame.
onSelect	Text is selected in a text field or text area.
onSubmit	A form is submitted.
onUnload	The user exits a document or frame set.

NOTE   From now on, I'll follow Netscape's approach and refer to events by the names of their event-handling attributes.

Handling JavaScript Events

To handle any of the JavaScript events identified in Table 4.1, all you have to do is include the event-handling attribute for that event in an appropriate HTML tag and then specify the event-handling JavaScript code as the attribute's value. This usually takes the form of a call to an event-handling function. You've seen an example of this in Listing 4.1. In the following subsections, you'll encounter many more examples of JavaScript event handling. Before I go off to develop these examples, I'll spend a short time discussing the best way to insert code for the value of an event-handling attribute.

In general, you can insert any JavaScript code for the value of an event-handling attribute. However, if you surround the attribute value with double quotes ("), you must use single quotes (') within your event-handling code. Likewise, if you use single quotes to surround the attribute value, you must use double quotes within your event-handling code. Multiple JavaScript statements must be separated by semicolons (;). Listing 4.2 provides an example of an event handler that inserts multiple statements within the event-handling attribute.

Listing 4.2:   **Event Handler with Multiple Statements in Attribute Value (ch04-02.htm)**

```
<HTML>
<HEAD>
<TITLE>Event Handler With Multiple Statements</TITLE>
<SCRIPT LANGUAGE="JavaScript">
<!--
count=0
```

```
//-->
</SCRIPT>
</HEAD>
<BODY>
<H1>Event Handler With Multiple Statements</H1>
<P><A HREF="http://www.jaworski.com" ONMOUSEOVER='++count;
alert("You moved your mouse here "+count+" times!")'>Displays
the number of times you move your mouse over this link.</A></P>
</BODY>
</HTML>
```

In this example, the variable count is initialized to 0 in the document's head. The onMouseOver event handler consists of the following statements:

```
++count; alert("You moved your mouse here "+count+" times!")
```

The semicolon is needed to separate the two statements. The first statement, ++count, increments count each time the mouse passes over the link. The second statement creates a pop-up window that displays this information to the user. Figure 4.4 shows how this information is displayed.

FIGURE 4.4:

Pop-up window that displays the number of times a link was passed over (Listing 4.2)

As a matter of good style, it is best to have a single function call as the value of an event-handling attribute. This makes the event-handling code easier to debug, more modular, and more capable of being reused in other web pages. Listing 4.3 shows a more complex event handler that is accessed via a single function call.

Listing 4.3:   Using Functions as Event Handlers (ch04-03.htm)

```
<HTML>
<HEAD>
<TITLE>Using functions as event handlers</TITLE>
<SCRIPT LANGUAGE="JavaScript">
<!--
function confirmLink() {
 alert("The contents of this link may be objectionable to anyone over the age of
ten.")
 if(confirm("Are you ten years old or younger?")) {
  window.location="http://www.jaworski.com"
 }
}
```

```
//-->
</SCRIPT>
</HEAD>
<BODY>
<H1>Using functions as event handlers</H1>
<P><A HREF="somewhere" onClick="return false"
onMouseOver="confirmLink()">Confirms
whether you want to connect via this link.</A></P>
</BODY>
</HTML>
```

The confirmLink() function is defined in the head of the document. This function is the event handler for the onMouseOver event of the link defined in the body of the document. The confirmLink() function invokes the alert() method of the current window to display a warning to the user. This message is shown in Figure 4.5. It then uses the current window's confirm() method to determine the user's age (see Figure 4.6). If the user presses Cancel in the confirm dialog box, then the confirm() method returns false and no further action is performed. If the user presses OK in the confirm dialog box, then the confirm() method returns true and the location property of the current window is set to a new URL. This causes the new document to be loaded without the user ever clicking on a link to that document. In fact, the destination of the link in the body of the web document is just the dummy URL somewhere. However, the clicking of this link is disabled by setting the onClick event handler to return false. Whenever a false value is returned, the action associated with a click event is canceled. You'll learn more about this feature in later examples.

FIGURE 4.5:

Age warning pop-up window (Listing 4.3)

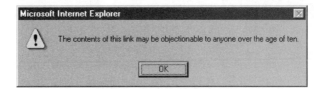

FIGURE 4.6:

Confirming the user's age (Listing 4.3)

The important point about Listing 4.3 is that the onMouseOver event handling is performed via a single function call to confirmLink(). This allows confirmLink() to be developed without having to worry about quoting or trying to fit all of its statements in a single attribute value. The result is a much cleaner implementation of the event handler.

NOTE   The event-handling examples in this chapter are geared to provide a simple explanation of the mechanics of event handling. I'll develop more sophisticated examples throughout the course of the book after I've covered JavaScript objects beginning in the next chapter.

Handling Link Events

So far, you've seen several examples of handling events associated with links. Let's explore link event handling further before moving on to handling events associated with other HTML elements.

There are nine events that are associated with links, as shown in Table 4.1. In Listings 4.1 through 4.3, I already covered the handling of the onMouseOver event. These examples showed how the onMouseOver event can be used to provide the user with warnings or other information about a link before the user clicks on it. Besides onMouseOver, two other link-related attributes, onMouseOut and onClick, are frequently used with link events.

The onMouseOut event is similar to the onMouseOver event, except that it is triggered when the user *leaves* a link, not when the mouse approaches the link. As such, onMouseOut event handlers generally try to provide information to a user after they have left a link. Listing 4.4 provides an example of an onMouseOut event handler.

Listing 4.4:   Handling *onMouseOut* or Links (ch04-04.htm)

```
<HTML>
<HEAD>
<TITLE>Handling onMouseOut for links</TITLE>
<SCRIPT LANGUAGE="JavaScript">
<!--
function advertiseLink() {
 alert("The ACME Widget Company is having a 50% off sale on their best
widgets.")
 if(confirm("Would you like to visit them and save 50% on an ACME widget?")) {
   window.location="http://www.jaworski.com/javascript/acme.htm"
 }
}
//-->
</SCRIPT>
</HEAD>
<BODY>
<H1>Handling onMouseOut for links</H1>
<P><A HREF="somewhere" ONMOUSEOUT="advertiseLink()">Tells you why you
should connect to this link.</A></P>
</BODY>
</HTML>
```

In Listing 4.4, an advertiseLink() function is defined in the document head. This function is set up to be the event handler for onMouseOut events and is set in the link defined in the body of the HTML document. When a user moves the mouse away from the link, the advertiseLink() function is invoked. The advertiseLink() function first notifies the user via the alert() method that the ACME Widget Company is having a 50-percent-off sale (Figure 4.7). It then uses a confirm() method to ask the user if they want to visit the ACME Widget Company (Figure 4.8). If the user responds by clicking OK, then advertiseLink() sets the location property of the window to cause the ACME web page to be loaded (Figure 4.9). If the user clicks Cancel, then the event handling is terminated.

FIGURE 4.7:

Alerting the user to ACME Widget Company (Listing 4.4)

FIGURE 4.8:

Asking the user to link to ACME Widget Company (Listing 4.4)

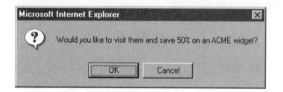

FIGURE 4.9:

The ACME Widget Company home page is loaded (Listing 4.4).

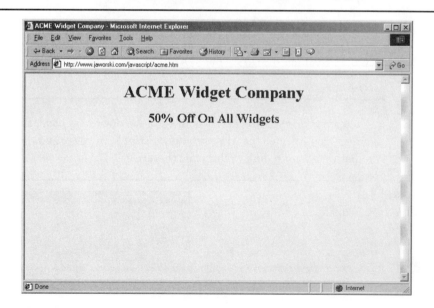

The advertiseLink() function presented above is just one example of how the onMouseOut event can be handled. Of course, it may be an annoying nuisance to your web users if you badger them with an advertisement every time they refrain from following a link, so exercise a little creativity when you use anything similar to this example.

Another link event handling attribute, onClick, allows the clicking of a hyperlink to be handled in a custom manner. If the onClick event handler returns the value false, then the action associated with the click—in this case, the linking to a new document—is canceled. This capability lets the onClick event handler query the user to confirm or deny whether they want to proceed with a link. Listing 4.5 provides an example of this type of onClick event handling.

Listing 4.5:   Handling *onClick* or Links (ch04-05.htm)

```
<HTML>
<HEAD>
<TITLE>Handling onClick for links</TITLE>
<SCRIPT LANGUAGE="JavaScript">
<!--
function confirmLink() {

 alert("This is the Mastering JavaScript Home Page.")
 return confirm("Are you sure you want to load this document?")
}
//-->
</SCRIPT>
</HEAD>
<BODY>
<H1>Handling onClick for links</H1>
<P><A HREF="http://www.jaworski.com/javascript"
ONCLICK="return confirmLink()">Asks you to confirm
your selection of this link.</A></P>
</BODY>
</HTML>
```

The confirmLink() function is defined in the document head. It alerts the user to the fact that they have selected the Mastering JavaScript home page and then asks the user to confirm whether they want to link to this page (Figure 4.10).

FIGURE 4.10:

Confirming a user selection
(Listing 4.5)

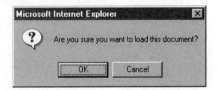

The results of the `confirm()` method are then returned. Notice that in the `onClick` event handler, the `confirmLink()` method is not invoked directly, but rather is invoked as part of a `return` statement:

```
return confirmLink()
```

This is because the value returned by `confirm()` and `confirmLink()` must be propagated to the point where the event handler was invoked in order for a `false` value to cancel the action associated with the clicking of the link. Try removing the return statement and calling `confirmLink()` directly. You will find that canceling the link is no longer an option.

Handling Window Events

Window events apply to normal HTML documents that contain a body and produce a display; they also apply to layout documents that replace the document body with a frame set. (*Layout documents* are used to organize the display of other documents via frames. If you're unfamiliar with these objects, turn to Chapter 7, "Creating Frames and Windows," for more information.) In this section, I'll look at the event handling associated with both types of documents. Table 4.1 lists the events that are associated with these window objects. Listing 4.6 illustrates the handling of the `onLoad` and `onUnload` events for a normal displayable HTML document. When the document is first loaded, the alert message shown in Figure 4.11 is displayed. As you leave the document to go to another location or to reload that same document, the alert message shown in Figure 4.12 is displayed.

Listing 4.6:   Handling Load Events in a Content Document (ch04-06.htm)

```
<HTML>
<HEAD>
<TITLE>Handling load events in a content document</TITLE>
</HEAD>
<BODY onLoad="alert('Hello!')" onUnload="alert('Bye Bye!')">
<H1>Handling load events in a content document</H1>
<P>This document has a body and is displayed in typical fashion.</P>
</BODY>
</HTML>
```

FIGURE 4.11:

The `onLoad` message
(Listing 4.6)

The onLoad event handler is typically used to perform any necessary initialization for web pages that use Java or plug-ins, or it is used to make a grand entrance by playing an audio file or an animation sequence. You can use it to determine whether all required resources, such as image files, are present before beginning a script's execution. The onUnload event handler performs a similar function—terminating Java applets and plug-ins or enabling a dramatic exit. You'll see examples of using onLoad and onUnload for these uses in later chapters. Listing 4.7 shows how onLoad and onUnload can be used with layout documents.

Listing 4.7:   Handling Load Events in a Layout Document (ch04-07.htm)

```
<HTML>
<HEAD>
<TITLE>Handling load events in a layout document</TITLE>
<SCRIPT LANGUAGE="JavaScript"><!--
function selectFrames(){
 base="frames/"
 newFrames=new Array("red.htm","yellow.htm","blue.htm","green.htm","white.htm")
 window.firstFrame.location=base+newFrames[Math.round(5*Math.random())%5]
 window.secondFrame.location=base+newFrames[Math.round(5*Math.random())%5]
}
//-->
</SCRIPT>
</HEAD>
<FRAMESET
COLS="*,*" ONLOAD="selectFrames()" ONUNLOAD="alert('Thanks for stopping by!')">
<FRAME SRC="frames/grey.htm" NAME="firstFrame">
<FRAME SRC="frames/grey.htm" NAME="secondFrame">
</FRAMESET>
</HTML>
```

NOTE   If you are not familiar with Netscape frames, refer to Chapter 7.

The HTML document shown in Listing 4.7 defines the selectFrames() function to handle the onLoad event. Before I describe the processing performed by the setFrames() function, I'll discuss what's going on in the frame set part of the document. The frame set tags specify that two frames are to be contained in the document. The frames are to be organized into columns with the first frame named firstName and the second named second-Frame. Initially, both frames display the document at the relative URL frames/grey.htm. The onLoad attribute of the frame set tag specifies that the selectFrames() function should handle the event associated with the frame's loading. The onUnload event just displays the pop-up window with the text *Thanks for stopping by!* when the frame set is unloaded to either reload the page or load a new page.

The selectFrames() function randomly loads two new documents into firstFrame and secondFrame. The newFrames array contains the names of five documents. A document is randomly selected from the list using the random() and round() methods of the Math object to calculate an index into the newFrames array. The location property of firstFrame and secondFrame are set to the randomly selected documents. (You'll learn all about the Math and window objects in the next chapter.)

When you load Listing 4.7, it opens a two-frame document with both the left and right frames initially set to gray. As soon as the document is loaded, the onLoad event is generated and selectFrames() is invoked to load new frame documents as shown in Figure 4.13. When you leave the document to go to another location, the message shown in Figure 4.14 is displayed.

FIGURE 4.13:

The onLoad event causes new frames to be loaded (Listing 4.7).

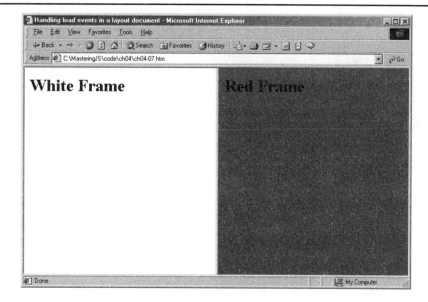

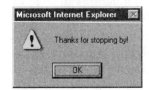

FIGURE 4.14:

The onUnload message
displayed when the frame
set is exited (Listing 4.7).

While the onLoad and onUnload events are generated at the beginning and end of a document's existence, the onFocus and onBlur events can be triggered several times while a document is loaded. The onFocus event is generally used to restore a document to a default starting state or to continue previously interrupted processing. The onBlur event is used to interrupt the processing being performed on a page, such as the playing of an audio file or an animation, before a new page or area within the current page is activated. Listings 4.8 through 4.10 present examples of the use of onLoad and onUnload event handlers. The frames are organized in column order.

Listing 4.8:   Defining the Frame Set (ch04-08.htm)

```
<!-- ch04-08.htm -->
<HTML>
<HEAD>
<TITLE>Handling onFocus and onBlur events in a frame</TITLE>
</HEAD>
<FRAMESET COLS="*,*">
<FRAME SRC="frames/doc1.htm">
<FRAME SRC="frames/doc2.htm">
</FRAMESET>
</HTML>
```

Listing 4.9:   Handling *onBlur* and *onFocus* in Frames (doc1.htm)

```
<!-- doc1.htm -->
<HTML>
<HEAD>
<TITLE>Document 1</TITLE>
<SCRIPT LANGUAGE="JavaScript">
function gotFocus() {
 document.bgColor="#FFFFFF"
}
function lostFocus() {
 document.bgColor="#FF0000";
}
</SCRIPT>
</HEAD>
<BODY onFocus="gotFocus()" onBlur="lostFocus()" BGCOLOR="#FF0000">
```

```
<H1>Document 1</H1>
</BODY>
</HTML>
```

Listing 4.10:   Displaying an Alternative Background Color (doc2.htm)

```
<!-- doc2.htm -->
<HTML>
<HEAD>
<TITLE>Document 2</TITLE>
</HEAD>
<BODY BGCOLOR="#FF0080">
<H1>Document 2</H1>
</BODY>
</HTML>
```

The file doc1.htm is the heart of this example. When it is loaded, it displays a reddish-orange color and lists a simple heading. The body tag specifies that the event handlers, got-Focus() and lostFocus(), are used for the onFocus and onBlur events. The document head defines these functions. The gotFocus() function sets the background color of the frame occupied by the document to white. The lostFocus() function resets the color of the frame back to its original color.

Figure 4.15 shows the original state of the frame set. Figure 4.16 shows how the background of the first frame changes to white when it receives the input focus.

FIGURE 4.15:

The frame set in its initial state (Listings 4.8 through 4.10)

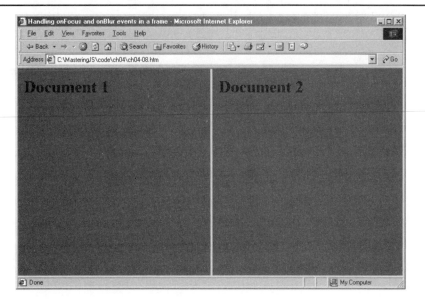

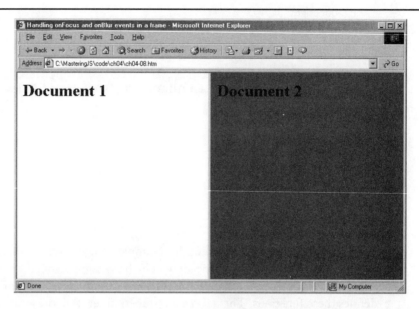

The file doc2.htm is a simple document that merely displays a heading and dark pink background color. It is used to provide contrast for doc1.htm.

Handling Image Events

Image events are used to monitor the progress of image loading. Usually, images are the elements in a web document that take the longest to load. In many applications, it is important to know whether they have been loaded, are in the process of loading, or have had their loading interrupted. The image events provide this capability. They are summarized in Table 4.1. The onLoad event occurs when an image's loading and display has been completed. In many cases, such as in an image map application, it may be important to wait for the onLoad event to occur before further processing is allowed. The onAbort and onError events are used to respond to any exceptions that may occur in the loading process. Listing 4.11 illustrates the use of these event-handling capabilities.

Listing 4.11:   Image Event Handling (ch04-11.htm)

```
<HTML>
<HEAD>
<TITLE>Image Event Handling</TITLE>
<SCRIPT LANGUAGE="JavaScript"><!--
function imageLoaded() {
 document.bgColor="#FFFFFF"
 alert(document.images[0].src+" has been loaded.")
```

```
}
function imageAborted() {
 alert("Hey! You just aborted the loading of the last image!")
}
function imageError() {
 alert("Error loading image!")
}
//-->
</SCRIPT>
</HEAD>
<BODY>
<H1>Image Event Handling</H1>
<P>An image is loaded after this paragraph.</P>
<IMG SRC="image1.gif"
 onLoad="imageLoaded()"
 onAbort="imageAborted()"
 onError="imageError()">
</BODY>
</HTML>
```

The document shown in Listing 4.11 displays a heading, a one-line paragraph, and an image. The image has event handlers that respond to the onLoad, onAbort, and onError events. The onLoad event is handled by the imageLoaded() function. When an image has been loaded, the imageLoaded() function changes the document background color to green and displays an alert dialog box that identifies the name of the image and the fact that it has been loaded. Figure 4.17 shows the document window after the onLoad event has been handled.

FIGURE 4.17:

Handling the onLoad event for images (Listing 4.11)

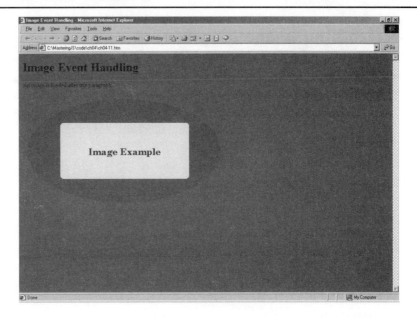

The onAbort event occurs as the result of a user action that causes image loading to be aborted, such as clicking the Stop button or changing to a new document. It is handled by the imageAborted() function, which simply notifies the user that they have caused the image's loading to be aborted. Figure 4.18 shows the result of processing the onAbort event.

FIGURE 4.18:

Handling the onAbort event for images (Listing 4.11)

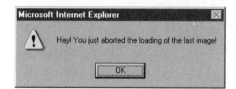

The onError event occurs as the result of an error that prevents an image from loading. A common example of this type of an error is the failure of a web browser to locate the image. The imageError() function handles the onError event by displaying a notification to the user. Figure 4.19 shows how the onError event is handled as the result of the image file being moved from its specified location.

FIGURE 4.19:

Handling the onError event for images (Listing 4.11)

Handling Image Map Events

Image maps are a popular feature found on many web pages. An image map consists of an image that is divided into different areas or regions. When the user clicks on a particular location within the image, a connection is made to the URL associated with that location. This allows the image map to exhibit different responses based on the area clicked by the user. Figure 4.20 summarizes the basic mechanics of image maps.

FIGURE 4.20:

How image maps work

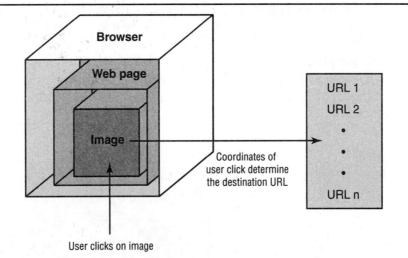

JavaScript supports two types of image maps: *server-side image maps* and *client-side image maps*. Server-side image maps were developed first. As their name implies, most of the processing is performed on the server. The server contains a map file that defines the various regions of the image and associates these regions with specific URLs. When a user clicks on a location in the image, the coordinates of the location are passed to the web server. The server determines which region was selected and returns the URL associated with that region. The user's browser then connects to this URL. Figure 4.21 summarizes server-side image map processing.

FIGURE 4.21:

How server-side image maps work

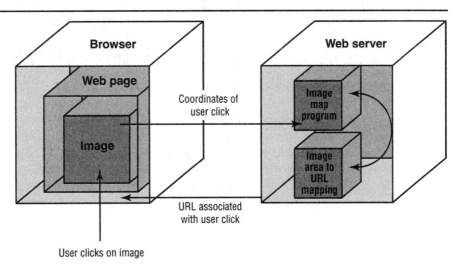

Client-side image maps are a very efficient improvement over server-side image maps. Instead of the map file being maintained on the server, it is embedded in the map element of the HTML file being browsed. This allows the browser to perform all of the processing required to determine which map area the user selected and to choose the destination URL. Figure 4.22 summarizes client-side image map processing.

FIGURE 4.22:

How client-side image maps work

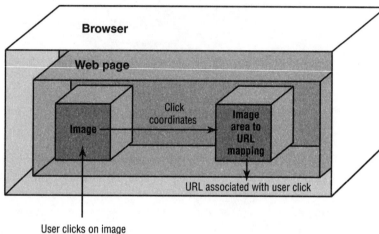

User clicks on image

JavaScript provides event-handling capabilities that support the processing of client-side image maps. The events supported for image maps are a subset of those that were covered for links, which are summarized in Table 4.1. These events enable custom handling of user image-map clicks and mouse movements around a particular map area.

TIP

In order to use the onMouseOver, onMouseOut, and onDblClick events with the AREA tag, you may have to set the HREF attribute of the AREA tag. If the NOHREF attribute is present, these events may not function properly.

Listing 4.12 presents an example of the handling of onMouseOver and onMouseOut events. The document displays a heading and an image that is used as a client-side image map. Note that the image sets the USEMAP attribute to #blockman, which is the name of the image map described by the map tags. The image used in the image map is blockman.gif. It is shown in Figure 4.23 along with the coordinates of various points within the image. These coordinates are used to create the parameters for the area tags that are enclosed by the map tags.

Listing 4.12:   Image Map Event Handling (ch04-12.htm)

```html
<HTML>
<HEAD>
<TITLE>Image Map Event Handling</TITLE>
<SCRIPT LANGUAGE="JavaScript"><!--
firstTimeOnHead=true
function onHead() {
 if(firstTimeOnHead) {
  alert("You're on my head!")
  firstTimeOnHead=false
 }
}
function myEye() {
 alert("Be careful or you'll poke out my eye!")
}
function myNose() {
 alert("Aaacchhooo!")
}
function myMouth() {
 alert("Get out of my mouth!")
}
//-->
</SCRIPT>
</HEAD>
<BODY>
<H1>Image Map Event Handling</H1>
<IMG SRC="blockman.gif" USEMAP="#blockman">
<MAP NAME="blockman">
<AREA COORDS="80,88,120,125" HREF="ch04-10.htm"
onMouseOver="myEye()">
<AREA COORDS="169,88,208,125" HREF="ch04-10.htm"
onMouseOver="myEye()">
<AREA COORDS="124,147,165,181" HREF="ch04-10.htm"
onMouseOut="myNose()">
<AREA COORDS="92,210,192,228" HREF="ch04-10.htm"
onMouseOut="myMouth()">
<AREA COORDS="6,4,292,266" HREF="ch04-10.htm"
onMouseOver="onHead()">
</MAP>
</BODY>
</HTML>
```

FIGURE 4.23:

Coordinates within
`blockman.gif`
(Listing 4.12)

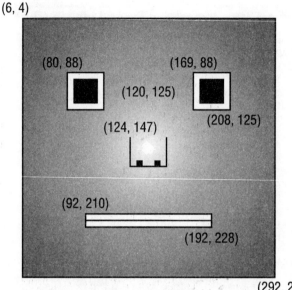

The first and second <AREA> tags (and corresponding area objects) describe rectangles that enclose block man's eyes. Both tags specify that the myEye() function should be called to handle the onMouseOver event. The third area tag describes the rectangle formed by block man's nose. It specifies that the myNose() function should handle the onMouseOut event. The fourth area tag describes the rectangle formed by block man's mouth. It specifies that the onMouseOut event should be handled by the myMouth() function. Finally, the fifth area tag describes the larger rectangle that handles block man's head. This tag handles the onMouseOver event via the onHead() function.

The area tags are processed in a first-come, first-handled order. The browser checks the location of a mouse action with each area tag in the order that the tags appear in the map tag. If the browser gets to the last tag, it is processing a mouse action that occurred outside the other area tags but within the outline of block man's head.

The event-handling functions in this listing are quite simple. The myEye(), myNose(), and myMouth() functions display cute messages using the alert() method. The onHead() function is just a tad more sophisticated. The firstTimeOnHead variable is initialized to true when the HTML document is first loaded. The onHead() function displays a message when firstTimeOnHead is true and then sets firstTimeOnHead to false. This causes the alert message to be displayed only once. Figure 4.24 shows the web page displayed by a browser as the result of handling the initial onMouseOver event for block man's head.

FIGURE 4.24:

Handling onMouseOver
for AREA tags
(Listing 4.12)

Handling Form Events

So far, you have learned to handle events associated with links, windows, images, and image maps. However, in most practical JavaScript applications the event handling will be associated with forms. Forms provide a number of sophisticated graphical user interface (GUI) controls such as buttons, check boxes, and text fields. These controls are associated with a number of events that reflect user actions, such as clicking on a button or check box or selecting text in a text field. These events are summarized in Table 4.3.

TABLE 4.3: Form Events

Event	Form element	Event-handling Attribute
The form is submitted by the user.	Overall form	onSubmit
The form is reset by the user.	Overall form	onReset
A form element loses the input focus.	All form elements	onBlur
A form element receives the input focus.	All form elements	onFocus
A form element is modified and loses the current input focus.	File upload field, select field, text field, or text area	onChange
Text is selected within the text field or text area.	Text field or text area	onSelect
A button or check box is clicked.	Button, submit button, reset button, radio button, or check box	onClick
A mouse button is pressed or released.	Button	onMouseDown, onMouseUp
A key is pressed, released, or pressed and released.	Text area	onKeyDown, onKeyUp, onKeyPress

I'll present three examples that cover many of the events in Table 4.3. Other examples will be presented in subsequent chapters. The first example, shown in Listing 4.13, illustrates events associated with text field and text area buttons and the onSubmit form event. The second example is presented in Listing 4.14. It illustrates the onClick event used with different types of buttons and check boxes. The third example is shown in Listing 4.15 and shows how the onChange selection element event is handled.

Listing 4.13:   Text Field and Text Area Event Handling (ch04-13.htm)

```html
<HTML>
<HEAD>
<TITLE>Text Field and Text Area Events</TITLE>
<SCRIPT LANGUAGE="JavaScript"><!--
function nameSelect() {
 if(isBlank(""+document.contest.last.value)) {
  document.contest.last.value="Surname"
  document.contest.last.focus()
  document.contest.last.select()
 }
}
function isBlank(s) {
 var len=s.length
 var i
 for(i=0;i<len;++i) {
  if(s.charAt(i)!=" ") return false
 }
 return true
}
function validate(fieldName,fieldValue) {
 if(isBlank(fieldValue)) {
  alert(fieldName+" cannot be left blank.")
  return false
 }
 return true
}
function validateEmail() {

 validate("The e-mail field",document.contest.email.value)
}
function validateEssay() {
 validate("The essay field",document.contest.essay.value)
}
function validateForm() {
 if(!validate("The last name field",document.contest.last.value))
  return false
 if(!validate("The e-mail field",document.contest.email.value))
  return false
 if(!validate("The essay field",document.contest.essay.value))
  return false
}
//--></SCRIPT>
</HEAD>
<BODY>
<FORM NAME="contest" ONSUBMIT="return validateForm()">
<H2 ALIGN="CENTER">Contest Application</H2>
<P>Last name:
<INPUT TYPE="TEXT" NAME="last" SIZE="16"
```

```
 ONCHANGE="nameSelect()">
First name:
<INPUT TYPE="TEXT" NAME="first" SIZE="12">
Middle Initial:
<INPUT TYPE="TEXT" NAME="initial" SIZE="2"></P>
<P>E-mail address:
<INPUT TYPE="TEXT" NAME="email" SIZE="32"
 ONCHANGE="validateEmail()"></P>
<P>In 50 words or less, state why you should win the contest:</P>
<TEXTAREA NAME="essay" ROWS="5" COLS="40"
 ONCHANGE="validateEssay()"></TEXTAREA>
<P>Submit your winning entry:
<INPUT TYPE="SUBMIT" NAME="go" VALUE="Make me a winner!"></P>
</FORM>
</BODY>
</HTML>
```

The previous listing presents the contest application form shown in Figure 4.25. Event handlers are associated with the last, email, and essay fields of the form as well as with the form as a whole. The last and email fields are text fields and the essay field is a text area field. The onChange event of the last field uses the nameSelect() function to handle the event associated with the changes to the field's contents. The nameSelect() function uses the isBlank() function to determine if the user made changes to the field that resulted in it becoming blank. If the field is left blank, then the field's value is set to Surname, the current focus is set to the field, and the text is selected. Figure 4.26 shows the result of the name-Select() processing.

FIGURE 4.25:

Contest application form
(Listing 4.13)

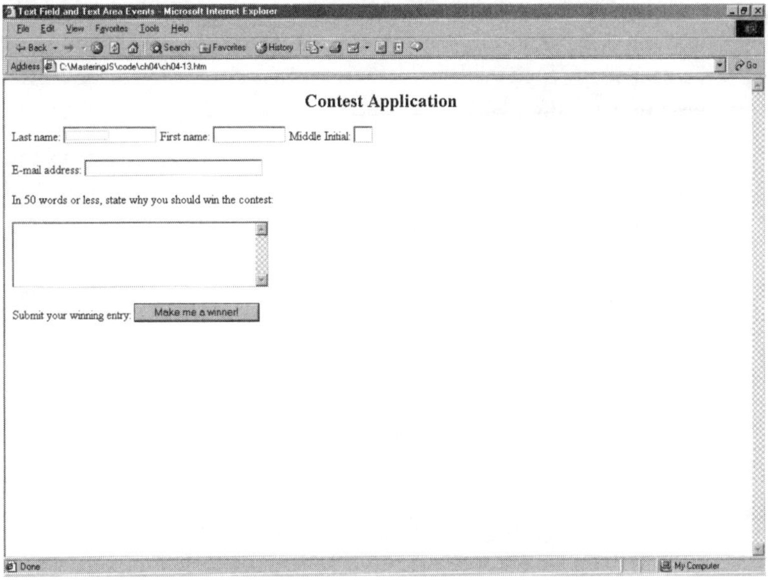

FIGURE 4.26:

Result of nameSelect() processing (Listing 4.13)

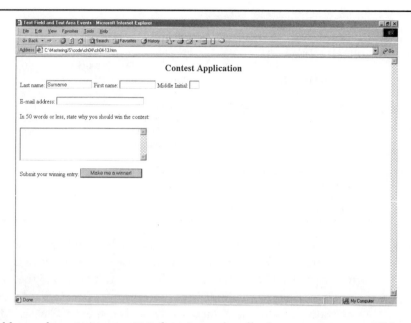

The email field uses the validateEmail() function to handle the onChange event. This function invokes the validate() function to check whether the field had been left blank and uses the alert() function to send a notification to the user that the field cannot be blank. The validateEssay() function is used in the same manner by the essay field. The form tag specifies that the onSubmit event should be handled by the statement return validate-Form(). When the user clicks on the button labeled Make Me a Winner!, the validateForm() function is invoked to check whether the last, email, or essay fields are blank and to notify the user if any field is blank. It returns false to prevent the form from being submitted with these fields being blank.

The script shown in Listing 4.14 presents the survey form shown in Figure 4.27. This form illustrates the handling of the onClick event for buttons and check boxes. When any of the radio buttons or check boxes are selected, the results text field displays the checked fields. When the button labeled To Upper Case is clicked, the results field is converted to uppercase. When the Submit or Reset button is clicked, a confirmation window is displayed. Note that the effect of the Submit button may be canceled—with the result that the form is not submitted.

Listing 4.14:   Button and Check Box Event Handling (ch04-14.htm)

```
<HTML>
<HEAD>
<TITLE>Button and Check Box Events</TITLE>
<SCRIPT LANGUAGE="JavaScript"><!--
```

```
    function showResults() {
     var resultMsg=""
     if(document.survey.age[0].checked) resultMsg+="under 30, "
     if(document.survey.age[1].checked) resultMsg+="between 30 and 60, "
     if(document.survey.age[2].checked) resultMsg+="over 60, "
     if(document.survey.sex[0].checked) resultMsg+="male, "
     if(document.survey.sex[1].checked) resultMsg+="female, "
     if(document.survey.reading.checked) resultMsg+="reading, "
     if(document.survey.eating.checked) resultMsg+="eating, "
     if(document.survey.sleeping.checked) resultMsg+="sleeping, "
     document.survey.results.value=resultMsg
    }
    function upperCaseResults() {
     var newResults=document.survey.results.value
     document.survey.results.value=newResults.toUpperCase()
    }
    //--></SCRIPT>
    </HEAD>
    <BODY>
    <FORM NAME="survey">
    <H2 ALIGN="CENTER">Survey Form</H2>
    <P><B>Age:</B>
    <INPUT TYPE="RADIO" NAME="age" VALUE="under30"
     ONCLICK="showResults()">Under 30
    <INPUT TYPE="RADIO" NAME="age" VALUE="30to60"
     ONCLICK="showResults()">30 - 60
    <INPUT TYPE="RADIO" NAME="age" VALUE="over60"
     ONCLICK="showResults()">Over 60</P>
    <P><B>Sex: </B>
    <INPUT TYPE="RADIO" NAME="sex" VALUE="male"
     ONCLICK="showResults()">Male
    <INPUT TYPE="RADIO" NAME="sex" VALUE="female"
     ONCLICK="showResults()">Female</P>
    <P><B>Interests: </B>
    <INPUT TYPE="CHECKBOX" NAME="reading"
     ONCLICK="showResults()"> Reading
    <INPUT TYPE="CHECKBOX" NAME="eating"
     ONCLICK="showResults()"> Eating
    <INPUT TYPE="CHECKBOX" NAME="sleeping"
     ONCLICK="showResults()"> Sleeping</P>
    <P>
    <INPUT TYPE="BUTTON" NAME="makeUpper"
     VALUE="To Upper Case" ONCLICK="upperCaseResults()"></P>
    <P><B>Results: </B><INPUT TYPE="TEXT" NAME="results" SIZE="50"></P>
    <INPUT TYPE="SUBMIT" NAME="submit" VALUE="Submit"
     ONCLICK='return confirm("Sure?")'>
    <INPUT TYPE="RESET" NAME="reset"
     ONCLICK='return confirm("Sure?")'>
    </FORM>
    </BODY>
    </HTML>
```

FIGURE 4.27:

Survey form (Listing 4.14)

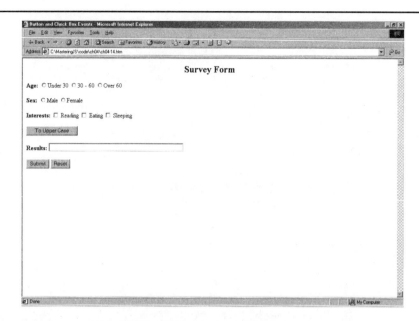

The radio and check boxes in Listing 4.14 use a single event-handling function— showResults(). This function checks the status of these fields and creates a text message, which it displays in the results field. The upperCaseResults() function handles the onClick event of the makeUpper button by converting the contents of the results field to uppercase. You'll learn more about the mechanics of how this happens in the next chapter on JavaScript objects.

The script in Listing 4.15 presents a menu for The Web Diner page, as shown in Figure 4.28. This form consists of a multiple selection list, from which fast-food items are selected, and a text area field, which displays the results of the user's selection. The update-Order() function handles the onChange event associated with the selection list. It checks through all of the options in the selection list to see which have been selected and displays a formatted text string in the text area field which summarizes the user's selection.

Listing 4.15:   Selection List Event Handling (ch04-15.htm)

```
<HTML>
<HEAD>
<TITLE>Handling Selection List Events</TITLE>
<SCRIPT LANGUAGE="JavaScript"><!--
function updateOrder() {
 var orderString=""
 var n=document.diner.entries.length
```

```
  for(i=0;i<n;++i) {
   if(document.diner.entries.options[i].selected) {
    orderString+=document.diner.entries.options[i].value+"\n"
   }
  }
  document.diner.summary.value=orderString
}
//--></SCRIPT>
</HEAD>
<BODY>
<FORM NAME="diner">
<H2 ALIGN="CENTER">The Web Diner</H2>
<P><B>Place your order:</B></P>
<SELECT NAME="entries" SIZE="4" MULTIPLE="MULTIPLE"
 ONCHANGE="updateOrder()">
<OPTION VALUE="Hamburger">Hamburger</OPTION>
<OPTION VALUE="Hot Dog">Hot Dog</OPTION>
<OPTION VALUE="Chicken Sandwich">Chicken Sandwich</OPTION>
<OPTION VALUE="French Fries">French Fries</OPTION>
<OPTION VALUE="Onion Rings">Onion Rings</OPTION>
<OPTION VALUE="Soda">Soda</OPTION>
<OPTION VALUE="Milk Shake">Milk Shake</OPTION>
<OPTION VALUE="Coffee">Coffee</OPTION></SELECT>
<P><B>You ordered: </B></P>
<P>
<TEXTAREA NAME="summary" ROWS="4" COLS="20"></TEXTAREA></P>
<P><INPUT TYPE="SUBMIT" NAME="order" VALUE="Let me have it!"></P>
</FORM>
</BODY>
</HTML>
```

FIGURE 4.28:

The Web Diner menu
(Listing 4.15)

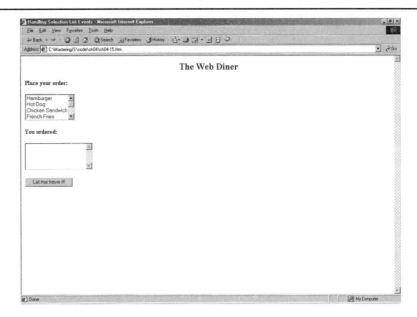

Setting Event Handlers from within JavaScript

Until now, I have been explicitly identifying event handlers using the event attribute of the tag to which the event handlers apply. You can also identify event handlers from within JavaScript. This capability adds greater flexibility in specifying event handlers.

NOTE   The capability to set event handlers from within JavaScript was introduced with JavaScript 1.1.

As you'll learn in Chapter 5, "Working with Objects," most of the individual elements of an HTML document can be accessed as objects that are automatically created by JavaScript. These objects have properties that specify the values of data items associated with the object. For example, in Listing 4.15, the entries selection list is identified by the following object:

```
document.diner.entries
```

The number of options in the selection list is a property of the list and is identified by the following:

```
document.diner.entries.length
```

Objects that are associated with events, such as links and form elements, have properties that identify the functions used to handle these events. For example, in Listing 4.15, the onChange event handler associated with the entries selection list is identified by the following property:

```
document.diner.entries.onchange
```

Instead of specifying updateOrder() as the event handler for entries in its input tag definition, we could have used the following JavaScript statement:

```
document.diner.entries.onchange=updateOrder
```

If we used this approach, the above statement would need to be placed in a script that is executed *after* the entries input tag is defined or else a JavaScript error would result.

When an event-handling function is explicitly assigned to the event property of an object, the trailing parentheses () are omitted. It is important that both the object and the function be defined prior to the assignment statement.

TIP   Use all lowercase letters for the event property. Some older browsers will not recognize the property if it is mixed case.

Listing 4.16 illustrates the process of setting event handlers from within JavaScript, and Figure 4.29 shows the web page that is generated. It consists of a single clickMe button that, when clicked, causes the text *Set by handler1* or *Set by handler2* to be alternately displayed in a text field. The input tag of the Click Me! button does not identify a event handler via the onClick attribute. Instead, a script follows the form definition that assigns handler1 to document.test.clickMe.onclick. This script causes the initial event handler for the onClick event of the Click Me! button to be handler1().

Listing 4.16:   Setting Event Handlers from within JavaScript (ch04-16.htm)

```
<HTML>
<HEAD>
<TITLE>Setting event handlers from within JavaScript</TITLE>
<SCRIPT LANGUAGE="JavaScript"><!--
function handler1() {
 document.test.result.value="Set by handler1"
 document.test.clickMe.onclick=handler2
}
function handler2() {
 document.test.result.value="Set by handler2"
 document.test.clickMe.onclick=handler1
}
//--></SCRIPT>
</HEAD>
<BODY>
<FORM NAME="test">
<INPUT TYPE="BUTTON" NAME="clickMe" VALUE="Click Me!">
<P><INPUT TYPE="TEXT" NAME="result" SIZE="20"></P>
</FORM>
<SCRIPT LANGUAGE="JavaScript"><!--
 document.test.clickMe.onclick=handler1
//--></SCRIPT>
</BODY>
</HTML>
```

When handler1() is invoked to handle the onClick event, it sets the result text field to Set by handler1 and then changes the onClick event handler to handler2(). The next time the Click Me! button is clicked, handler2() handles the onClick event. The handler2() function sets the result field to Set by handler2 and changes the onClick event handler back to handler1().

This simple example illustrates the flexibility and power of explicitly assigning event handlers from within JavaScript. There is an additional benefit to assigning event handlers from within JavaScript. If you set the LANGUAGE attribute of the SCRIPT tag to anything other than JavaScript, then earlier browsers, such as Navigator 2, will not be able to see your scripts. If you also use an event-handling attribute to set an event handler, then older browsers will look for an event-handling function and not be able to find it (because it is hidden by the LANGUAGE attribute). This results in a scripting error. On the other hand, if you specify event handlers from within your scripts, then you can avoid this type of error.

FIGURE 4.29:

Setting event handlers from
within JavaScript
(Listing 4.16)

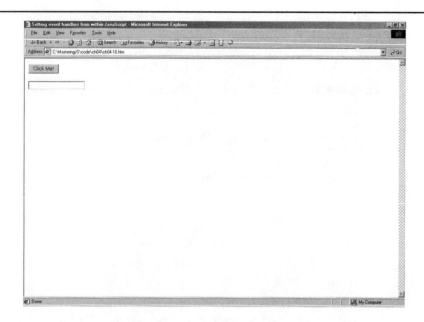

Event Simulation Methods

In the previous section, you learned how HTML elements are represented by JavaScript objects and how certain properties of these objects can be used to assign event handlers. In addition to these properties, some objects have methods that can be used to *simulate* the occurrence of events. When an event simulation method is invoked, the object to which it refers acts as if the event is taking place. For example, button objects have the `click()` method that, when invoked, causes the button's event handler to be invoked.

Listing 4.17 provides an example of event simulation. Figure 4.30 shows the web page displayed by this document. It consists of two buttons—Button 1 and Button 2.

Listing 4.17:   Emulating Events (ch04-17.htm)

```
<HTML>
<HEAD>
<TITLE>Simulating Events</TITLE>
<SCRIPT><!--
function button1Clicked() {
 document.test.button2.click()
}
function button2Clicked() {
 alert("Button 2 was clicked!")
```

```
}
//--></SCRIPT>
</HEAD>
<BODY>
<FORM NAME="test">
<INPUT TYPE="BUTTON" NAME="button1" VALUE="Button 1"
 ONCLICK="button1Clicked()">
<INPUT TYPE="BUTTON" NAME="button2" VALUE="Button 2"
 ONCLICK="button2Clicked()">
</FORM>
</BODY>
</HTML>
```

FIGURE 4.30:

An event simulation
example (Listing 4.17)

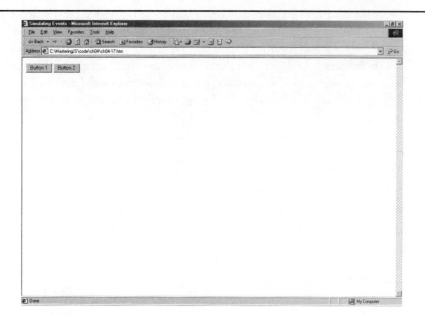

When you click on Button 1, the function button1Clicked () is invoked; it executes the following statement:

```
document.test.button2.click()
```

This statement then causes Button 2 to act as if it is being clicked. This results in Button 2's event handler, button2Clicked(), being invoked. The button2Clicked() function then displays the alert message shown in Figure 4.31.

The *event* Object

The event object was introduced in JavaScript 1.2 as a mechanism to provide additional information about events. This information is provided through the object's properties (refer to Table 4.4). As you can see from Table 4.4, the event object is implemented differently by Navigator and Internet Explorer. The properties that are available to a particular event object instance depend on the type of event that occurs and the type of browser that is executing the script. For example, a mouseDown event will have the pageX and pageY properties under Navigator and the x and y properties under Internet Explorer.

TABLE 4.4: Properties of the event Object

Property	Browser	Description
data	Navigator	An array of strings containing the URLs of objects dropped as the result of a DragDrop event. (The Drag-Drop event is a Navigator-specific event).
height and width	Navigator	The height and width of a window or frame (in pixels).
pageX and pageY	Navigator	The cursor's horizontal and vertical position in pixels, relative to the page.
screenX and screenY	Navigator Internet Explorer	The cursor's horizontal and vertical position in pixels, relative to the screen.
layerX and layerY	Navigator	The cursor's horizontal and vertical position in pixels, relative to the layer in which the event occurred. When used with the resize event, layerX and layerY specify the width and height of the object to which the event is targeted.
clientX and clientY	Internet Explorer	The cursor's horizontal and vertical position in pixels, relative to the web page in which the event occurred.
offsetX and offsetY	Internet Explorer	The cursor's horizontal and vertical position in pixels, relative to the container in which the event occurred.
x and y	Internet Explorer	The cursor.s horizontal and vertical position in pixels, relative to the document in which the event occurred.

Continued on next page

TABLE 4.4 CONTINUED: Properties of the event Object

Property	Browser	Description
target	Navigator	The object to which the event was originally sent.
srcElement	Internet Explorer	The object to which the event was originally sent.
type	Navigator Internet Explorer	The type of event that occurred.
which	Navigator	Either the mouse button (left = 1, middle = 2, and right = 3) that was pressed or the ASCII value of a pressed key
keyCode	Internet Explorer	Identifies the Unicode key code associated with a key press.
button	Internet Explorer	Identifies the mouse button that was pressed when the event occurred Values are the following: 0 No button 1 Left button 2 Right button 4 Middle button
modifiers	Navigator	Identifies the modifier keys (ALT_MASK, CONTROL_MASK, SHIFT_MASK, and META_MASK) associated with a mouse or key event.
altKey, ctrlKey, and shiftKey	Internet Explorer	Set to **true** or **false** to indicate whether the Alt, Control, or Shift keys were pressed when the event occurred.
cancelBubble	Internet Explorer	Set to **true** or **false** to cancel or enable event bubbling (see the "Event Bubbling" section later in this chapter).
fromElement and toElement	Internet Explorer	Specifies the HTML element being moved from or to.
reason	Internet Explorer	Used to indicate the status of data transfer for data source objects.
returnValue	Internet Explorer	Set to **true** or **false** to indicate the event handler's return value. Same as returning **true** or **false** from the event handler.
srcFilter	Internet Explorer	Specifies the **filter** object that caused an **onfilterchange** event. (The **onfilterchange** event is an Internet Explorer–specific event.)

NOTE   JavaScript objects, properties, and methods are covered in Chapter 5.

Whenever an event occurs, an event object is automatically generated. This object is made available to event handlers in one of two different ways, depending on the browser (Navigator or Internet Explorer) you are using. Internet Explorer defines a global object, named event, that can be accessed from your event handling function. For example, the following code accesses the global event object in an event handler:

```
function myEventHandler() {
  // Access the Internet Explorer event object
  // to display the mouse's x and y position when the
  // event occurred.
  alert(event.screenX+","+event.screenY)
}
```

Navigator does not define a global event object. Instead, it implicitly passes an event object to event-handling functions. To use this extra parameter, you can simply rewrite the above function to take an eventObject parameter:

```
function myEventHandler(eventObject) {
  // Access the Navigator event object
  // to display the mouse's x and y position when the
  // event occurred.
  alert(eventObject.screenX+","+ eventObject.screenY)
}
```

You can combine both approaches by explicitly passing the event object to the event-handling function in your event-handling attributes. This will ensure compatibility between Internet Explorer and Navigator. Listing 4.18 provides an example. When you open ch04-18.htm in your browser (Navigator or Internet Explorer) it displays the web page shown in Figure 4.32. Click on the link and an alert displays the coordinates of your mouse's position at the time of the click. Refer to Figure 4.33.

Listing 4.18:   Using the Event Object with Navigator and Internet Explorer (ch04-18.htm)

```
<HTML>
<HEAD>
<TITLE>Using the event Object</TITLE>
<SCRIPT><!--
function clickHandler(eventObject) {
  alert(eventObject.screenX+","+ eventObject.screenY)
}
//--></SCRIPT>
</HEAD>
<BODY>
<H1>Using the event Object</H1>
<A HREF="javascript:void(0)" onClick="clickHandler(event)">Click this link.</A>
</BODY>
</HTML>
```

FIGURE 4.32:

Click on the link to invoke
the event handler
(Listing 4.18).

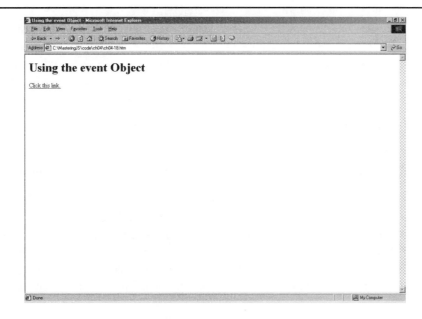

FIGURE 4.33:

The event object allows
you to determine the coordinates of the mouse when
the event occurred
(Listing 4.18).

NOTE   The event object is only supported by version 4 (Navigator or Internet Explorer) or later
browsers.

The key to supporting compatibility with Navigator and Internet Explorer is to pass the
event object as a parameter to the event-handling function. This is done in the onClick
attribute of the document's link. The clickHandler() function takes the object as a parameter and then processes the event independent of the browser type.

Event Capturing

Navigator 4 and later provide the capability for window, document, and layer objects to capture the events of lower-level objects that are displayed in the window, document, and layer.

For example, all the events associated with a form can be captured and processed by a document's event handlers. This is a useful capability if you want to centralize all the event handling that occurs in a document. (I generally avoid this approach because it relies on Navigator-specific code.) In order to set up a `window`, `document`, or `layer` to capture events, you simply invoke the object's `captureEvents()` method and pass it the type of event that you want to capture. For example, to capture all of a document's click events, you simply invoke `captureEvents()` as follows:

```
document.captureEvents(Event.CLICK)
```

NOTE   The `window` and `document` objects are covered in Chapter 5. The `layer` object is a Navigator-specific object that is covered in Chapter 12, "Working with Styles and DHTML."

The `Event.CLICK` parameter that you pass to `captureEvents()` is unique to Navigator. The Event object (different from the lowercase `event` object) specifies constants for event types and special keys. It is defined by Navigator as a distinct object from the `event` object. To identify a particular event type, use `Event.NAME` where `NAME` is the name of the event in uppercase without the preceding `ON`. Some examples of this convention are as follows:

```
Event.CLICK
Event.DBLCLICK
Event.MOUSEDOWN
Event.MOUSESUP
```

The Event object is also used to specify constants for special keys. These constants are as follows:

```
Event.ALT_MASK
Event.CONTROL_MASK
Event.META_MASK
Event.SHIFT_MASK
```

NOTE   The Meta key corresponds to the Command key on the Macintosh.

In addition to the `captureEvents()` method, the `window`, `document`, and `layer` objects also support the `releaseEvent()` and `routeEvent()` methods. The `releaseEvents()` method is used to turn off event capturing. The `routeEvent()` method passes a captured event to its normal destination. Both methods take the same argument as the `captureEvents()` method. The `handleEvent()` method may be used to directly invoke an object's event handler. It is used as follows:

```
object.handleEvent(Event.TYPE)
```

The `TYPE` is the type of event to be handled, such as `CLICK` or `MOUSEDOWN`.

The example provided in Listing 4.19 shows how to use event capturing and the Event object. Remember, these capabilities are unique to Netscape Navigator 4 or later. When you open ch04-19.htm with Navigator, it displays the web page shown in Figure 4.34. Click anywhere in the document while holding down a combination of the Alt, Control, and Shift keys. The document captures the mouseDown event and displays an alert dialog that identifies which of the special keys were pressed. Refer to Figure 4.35.

Listing 4.19:   Using Event Capturing and the Event Object (ch04-19.htm)

```
<HTML>
<HEAD>
<TITLE>Event Capturing and the Event Object</TITLE>
<SCRIPT><!--
function mouseDownHandler(eventObject) {
  specialKeys = "Special keys: "
  if(eventObject.modifiers & Event.ALT_MASK) specialKeys += "ALT "

if(eventObject.modifiers & Event.CONTROL_MASK) specialKeys += "CONTROL "
  if(eventObject.modifiers & Event.META_MASK) specialKeys += "META "
  if(eventObject.modifiers & Event.SHIFT_MASK) specialKeys += "SHIFT "
  alert(specialKeys)
}
//--></SCRIPT>
</HEAD>
<BODY>
<H1>Event Capturing</H1>
<P>This only works with Navigator 4 or later.</P>
<P>Click anywhere in the document.</P>
<SCRIPT><!--
document.captureEvents(Event.MOUSEDOWN)
document.onmousedown = mouseDownHandler
//--></SCRIPT>
</BODY>
</HTML>
```

Note that in the mouseDownHandler() function of Listing 4.19, the constants, Event.ALT_MASK, Event.CONTROL_MASK, Event.META_MASK, and Event.SHIFT_MASK are *anded* with the eventObject.modifiers value. The modifiers property contains a string of bits that identify which of the special keys were pressed. By *anding* the special key event constants to modifiers, you can obtain a boolean value identifying whether a particular key was pressed.

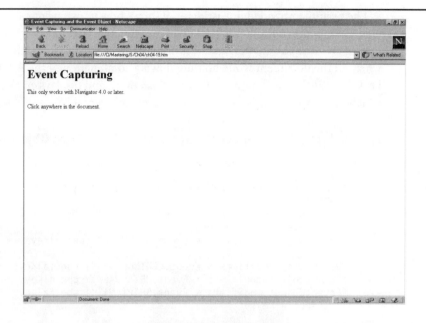

The *onMouseMove* Event

The onMouseMove event must be captured when used with Navigator. This event is not associated with any particular object. Listing 4.20 shows how to use event capturing with the onMouseMove event. Because the example uses event capturing, it will only work with Navigator 4 or later. Figure 4.36 shows the web page displayed by this script. When you move your mouse around the web page, the coordinates of the mouse's position are shown in the default status location. Refer to the bottom of Figure 4.36.

Listing 4.20:   **Using Event Capturing with the *onMouseMove* Event (ch04-20.htm)**

```
<HTML>
<HEAD>
<TITLE>Using the onMouseMove Event</TITLE>
```

```
<SCRIPT><!--
function mouseMoveHandler(eventObject) {
 window.defaultStatus =
   "(" + eventObject.screenX + "," + eventObject.screenY + ")"
}
//--></SCRIPT>
</HEAD>
<BODY>
<H1>Capturing the onMouseMove Event</H1>
<P>This only works with Navigator 4 or later.</P>
<P>Move your mouse around the document.</P>
<SCRIPT><!--
document.captureEvents(Event.MOUSEMOVE)
document.onmousemove = mouseMoveHandler
//--></SCRIPT>
</BODY>
</HTML>
```

FIGURE 4.36:

The onMouseMove event can be used to track the mouse's movement and location (Listing 4.20).

Event Bubbling

Internet Explorer does not support Navigator's event-capturing approach. Instead, it uses an approach called *event bubbling*, which can be used to achieve the same results. In Internet Explorer, when an event occurs, it is directed toward the lowest-level object to which the event applies. For example, suppose a user clicks on a button contained in a form. The button's onClick event handler is invoked to handle the event. When the button's event handler is finished processing the event, the event *bubbles* up to the form's onClick event handler. The form's onClick event handler handles the event and then the event bubbles up to the document's onClick handler. The document's onClick handler then handles the event. If any of the button, form or document event handlers are omitted, the event just bubbles up to the next higher event handler. If you keep the document's object hierarchy in mind, you should visualize events bubbling up from lower-level objects to the higher-level objects in which they are contained.

Listing 4.21 provides an example of event bubbling. Figure 4.37 shows the web page it displays. Click on the button and three alert boxes are displayed, one from each event handler. Figures 4.38 through 4.40 show these dialog boxes.

Listing 4.21:   Using Event Bubbling with the *onClick* Event (ch04-21.htm)

```
<HTML>
<HEAD>
<TITLE>Using Event Bubbling</TITLE>
<SCRIPT><!--
function buttonClickHandler() {
 alert("The onClick event was handled by buttonClickHandler()")
}
function formClickHandler() {
 alert("The onClick event was handled by formClickHandler()")
}
function documentClickHandler() {
 alert("The onClick event was handled by documentClickHandler()")
}
//--></SCRIPT>
</HEAD>
<BODY ONCLICK="documentClickHandler()">
<H1>Using Event Bubbling</H1>
<P>This only works with Internet Explorer 4 or later.</P>
<FORM ONCLICK="formClickHandler()">
<INPUT TYPE="BUTTON" ONCLICK="buttonClickHandler()"
VALUE="Click here!">
</FORM>
</BODY>
</HTML>
```

FIGURE 4.37:

The onClick event is
bubbled from the button's
onClick event handler to
the onClick event
handler of the form and
document (Listing 4.21).

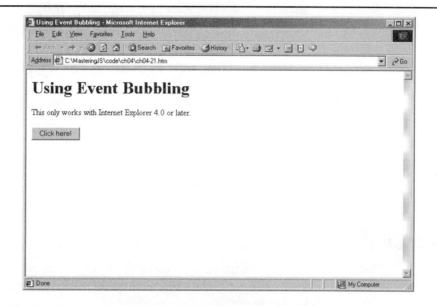

FIGURE 4.38:

The onClick event is
handled by the button's
onClick event handler
(Listing 4.21).

FIGURE 4.39:

The onClick event is
handled by the form's
onClick event handler
(Listing 4.21).

FIGURE 4.40:

The onClick event is
handled by the document's
onClick event handler
(Listing 4.21).

In order to cancel event bubbling for a particular event, set the following in the event's handler:

```
event.cancelBubble = true
```

For example, the following code cancels the bubbling of onClick events in Listing 4.21.

```
function buttonClickHandler() {
  alert("The onClick event was handled by buttonClickHandler()")
  event.cancelBubble = true
}
```

NOTE   Setting the event.cancelBubble property to true only affects bubbling for the current event. It has no impact on subsequent events.

Error Handling

There is nothing more frustrating for a user than loading a web page and receiving an endless sequence of scripting errors. As script writers, our goal should be to create scripts that are error free. Unfortunately, due to the subtle incompatibilities between Navigator and Internet Explorer, it is likely that some errors will eventually find their way into our scripts. On the positive side, JavaScript and JScript both provide the capability to handle errors during a script's execution. JavaScript 1.1 and later provide error-handling support through the error event and the onError event handling attribute.

The *onError* Event Handler

The error event was introduced in JavaScript 1.1 to provide the capability to handle errors associated with the loading of images or documents. The onError event handler of the image object (refer to the " Handling Image Events" section earlier in this chapter) is used to handle image-related loading errors. The onError event handler of the window object is used to handle errors that occur during the loading and processing (syntax and runtime errors) of a document.

The function that you use to handle onError differs from other event handling functions in that it is automatically passed three parameters by the browser (both Internet Explorer and Navigator):

errorMessage   The error message associated with the error.

url   The URL of the document in which the error occurred.

line   The line number at which the error occurred.

You can use these parameters to provide custom error information to your users. In addition, the value returned by your onError event handler determines whether standard error messages are displayed to the user. A true return value causes the standard error message to be suppressed. A false return value causes the standard error message to be displayed.

To use onError in a way that works with both Navigator and Internet Explorer, set the window.onerror property to your event handling function. Internet Explorer does not handle the onError attribute of the <BODY> tag correctly.

NOTE   Setting the window.onerror property to null prevents runtime errors from being displayed to users of Navigator (but not Internet Explorer).

Listing 4.22 provides an example of using onError that works with both Internet Explorer and Navigator. Figure 4.41 shows the web page that is displayed. When you click the Click Here to Generate an Error button, the button's onClick event handler tries to invoke the nonexistent createAnError() function. This results in a runtime error. The errorHandler() function handles the error by displaying the error message shown in Figure 4.42.

Listing 4.22:   Using the *onError* Event Handler (ch04-22.htm)

```
<HTML>
<HEAD>
<TITLE>Handling Errors with onError</TITLE>
<SCRIPT><!--
function errorHandler(errorMessage,url,line) {
  document.write("<P><B>Error message:</B> "+errorMessage+"<BR>")
  document.write("<B>URL:</B> "+url+"<BR>")
  document.write("<B>Line number:</B> "+line+"</P>")
  return true
}

onerror = errorHandler
// --></SCRIPT>
</HEAD>
<BODY>
<H1>Handling Errors with onError</H1>
<FORM>
<INPUT TYPE="BUTTON" ONCLICK="createAnError()"
VALUE="Click here to generate an error.">
</FORM>
</BODY>
</HTML>
```

FIGURE 4.41:

Click on the button to generate a runtime error (Listing 4.22).

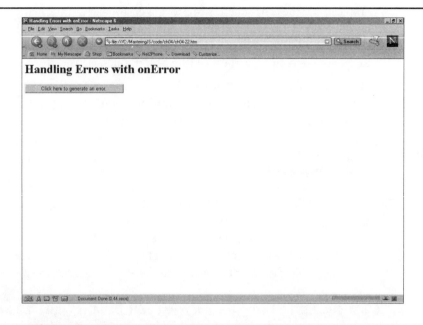

FIGURE 4.42:

The runtime error is handled and an error message is displayed (Listing 4.22).

Summary

This chapter illustrated the use of JavaScript's event-handling capabilities. It described JavaScript's approach to event handling and identified the event handlers that are predefined by both Navigator and Internet Explorer. You learned how to write your own event-handling functions and how to associate them with user interface actions. In the next chapter, you'll learn about JavaScript's support of objects and how to create your own objects and methods in JavaScript.

CHAPTER 5

Working with Objects

- What are objects?

- What is object-oriented programming?

- The JavaScript object model

- Color constants

- Defining object types

- Extending object types

- Deleting properties and methods

One of the most important features of JavaScript is that it is an object-based language. This simplifies the design of JavaScript programs and enables them to be developed in a more intuitive, modular, and reusable manner.

This chapter describes JavaScript's support of objects and object-based programming. It introduces the JavaScript object model and summarizes the predefined JavaScript objects that are supported by both Internet Explorer and Netscape Navigator. It also shows how to create your own object types. When you finish this chapter, you'll be able to define and use objects in your web pages.

TIP   Part II, "Programming the Document Object Model," provides detailed descriptions and examples of JavaScript's predefined objects.

What Are Objects?

Most people know that objects are entities that exist in the real world of people, places, and things. But they also exist in the cyber world of computers and networking. Examples of real-world objects include you, the book you are reading, and the lamp that you use to provide you with light. Examples of cyber-world objects are the web pages that you create and the individual HTML elements they contain. It is these types of objects that I will be discussing in relation to JavaScript.

An object consists of two things:

- A collection of *properties* that contain data
- *Methods* that enable operations on the data contained in those properties

When you view something as an object, then you look at it in terms of its properties and methods. Table 5.1 identifies some of the properties and methods that could apply to the example objects mentioned in the previous paragraph.

TABLE 5.1: Examples of Objects, Properties, and Methods

Object	Properties	Methods
You	height	eat()
(real-world object)	weight	exercise()
	hairColor	grow()
This book	pages	turnPageForward()
(real-world object)	currentPage	turnPageBackward()
		goToPage()

Continued on next page

TABLE 5.1 CONTINUED: Examples of Objects, Properties, and Methods

Object	Properties	Methods
A lamp	`onOffState`	`turnOn()`
(real-world object)		`turnOff()`
A web page	`title`	`open()`
(cyber-world object)	`bgColor`	`close()`
	`links`	`write()`
An HTML button	`name`	`setLabel()`
(cyber-world object)	`value`	

You've already seen several examples of JavaScript objects. You've used the `document` object and its `write()` method in many of the scripts in previous chapters. You've also used the `alert()` method of the `window` object to display messages to the user. The fields of a form are also objects. You've seen how the `value` property of a field can be used to test and set the field's value. By the time you finish this chapter, you will have encountered all of the predefined JavaScript objects supported by both Internet Explorer and Navigator and learned how to create objects of your own.

What Is Object-Oriented Programming?

The field of software engineering has evolved over the 50 or so years of the computer's existence. This evolution has brought about different approaches and strategies to the task of creating high-quality software while minimizing development time and costs. The most successful development approach currently in use is the object-oriented approach. This approach *models* the elements of a software application as objects—by modeling I mean object types are named, their properties are identified, and their methods are described. Once an object type is defined, it can then be used to create specific instances of other objects of that type and to construct other, more complex object types.

NOTE   Object-oriented programming is sometimes referred to by the acronym OOP.

NOTE   An object type is referred to as a *class* in object-oriented languages such as Java and C++.

Object Types and Instances

An *object type* is a template from which specific objects of that type are created. It defines the properties and methods that are common to all objects of that type. For example, let's consider a person's mailing address as an object type. I'll name it `MailAddress` and give it the properties of `streetAddress`, `city`, `state`, and `postalCode`. In addition to these properties, I'll define `changeAddress()` as a method for changing one person's address and `findAddress()` as a method for finding out another person's address. Don't worry about how I'm doing this—you'll learn that later—for this explanation just focus on what's being done.

When I define the `MailAddress` object type, I haven't specified anyone's address. I've only developed a template for the creation of an address—kind of like a blank Rolodex card. The address type can be *instantiated*, which is the programming term for creating a specific *instance* of that type of object; in this case, it would mean creating a specific person's address record. This is similar to producing a Rolodex card, filling it in, and sticking it in the Rolodex.

The capability to define an object type from which specific object instances can then be created is a very basic but important feature of object-oriented software development.

Creating Object Types

While the definition and instantiation of object types is a basic feature of object-oriented languages, it is not the only feature these languages provide. The ability to use object types to define *other* object types is what really gives object-oriented programming its power. There are two major ways in which this is accomplished: through *object composition* and *inheritance*.

Object Composition

One approach to developing object types is to define primitive object types that serve as simple building blocks from which more complex types may be composed. This approach is referred to as *object composition*. Consider the process of building a house. At some point, somebody must construct the boards, nails, and glass panes that are used as the basic building blocks for constructing most homes. These building objects are assembled into more complex objects such as doors, windows, and prefabricated walls. These more complex objects are then, in turn, assembled into larger objects that eventually are integrated into a finished home. In the same way that boards, nails, glass panes, and other simple objects are used to construct a wide variety of different homes, simple object types are used in programming to create more complex object types which are eventually integrated into a final software application. For example, the `MailAddress` object may be used to create an employment application form, which is itself used to create a personnel database system.

Object composition is closely related to and depends on the capability to support *object re-use*. When an object type is defined, it is often very desirable that it be defined in such a way that it can be reused in other software applications. This simplifies the development of other applications, and naturally leads to cost and schedule savings. The reuse of software objects is just as important as the reuse of technology in other engineering disciplines. Imagine the state of the automotive industry if the wheel had to be reinvented for every new type of car that's been developed.

Encapsulation–Packaging Objects

Software objects are reusable when they follow certain design principles. One of the most important of these principles is *encapsulation*. Encapsulation is the packaging of the properties and methods of an object into a container with an appropriately defined interface. The object's interface must provide the methods and properties that enable the object to be used in the manner that is intended and must do it without providing methods or properties that would allow the object to be misused. If this abstract description is difficult to fathom, con-sider the interface of an automobile. Auto designers provide standardized steering, braking, and throttling capabilities in all cars, since these capabilities are basic to driving. However, no automobile manufacturer provides drivers with the capability to manually control the firing of spark plugs from the dashboard. Even if drivers were provided with this capability, they more than likely could not use it to any advantage.

Modularity and Information Hiding

Encapsulation depends upon two important concepts for its success. The first concept, *modu-larity*, refers to an object's being complete in and of itself and not accessing other objects out-side their defined interfaces. Modular objects are said to be "loosely coupled," which means that dependencies between objects are minimized, and internal changes to an object do not require changes in other objects that make use of the object. The second concept, *information hiding*, refers to the practice of limiting information about an object to that which is required to use the object's interface. It is accomplished by removing information about the internal operation of an object from the object's interface.

Inheritance—A Hierarchical Approach to Object Design

The second major way of constructing object types from other object types is through *inheri-tance*. In this approach, higher-level, more abstract object types are defined, and from these defined objects, lower-level, more concrete object types are derived. When a lower-level object type is created, it identifies one or more higher-level object type as its *parent* type. The *child* type inherits all of the properties and methods of its parents. This eliminates the need to redefine these properties and methods. The child type is free to redefine any of the methods that it inherits or to add new properties and methods. This enables the child type to tailor its inherited characteristics to new situations.

As an example, consider the various types of objects that may be constructed to implement a scrolling marquee. At the highest level, a `GenericMarquee` may be constructed that has the basic properties `scrolledText` and `scrollRate`. It may provide basic methods, such as `startScrolling()` and `stopScrolling()`. From this generic marquee, more complex marquees may be created. For example, `HorizontalMarquee` and `VerticalMarquee` object types may be constructed that add the property `scrollDirection` to those inherited from `Generic-Marquee`. These, in turn, may be further refined into marquees which use colored text and backgrounds. The properties `textColor` and `backgroundColor` and the methods `randomText-Color()` and `randomBackgroundColor()` could be added.

Using inheritance, more sophisticated, tailored object types can be created from those that are already defined. This is done by just adding the properties and methods needed to differentiate the new objects from their parents. Once a useful object type is created, it can then be re-used many times to create several child objects and numerous generations of offspring.

Classification and Inheritance

Object-oriented programming languages, such as Java and C++ (but not JavaScript), refer to an object's type as its "class," and provide the capability to develop child classes from parent classes using inheritance. The resulting class structure is referred to as a *classification scheme*. The classification schemes that result from object-oriented development mimic those that are fundamental to the way we as human beings acquire and organize knowledge. For example, we develop general class names, such as "animal," that we use to refer to large groups of real-world objects. We then develop names of subclasses, such as "mammal," "bird," and "insect," which we use to refine our concept of animal. We continue to develop more detailed classes that differentiate between objects of the same class. The same sort of classification process is carried out by developers of object-oriented programs.

Single and Multiple Inheritance

Part of the reason that inheritance is a successful approach to object development is that it mimics the way we acquire and organize knowledge—it is therefore *intuitive* to us. In addition to this, inheritance is *efficient*, because it only requires you to define the properties and methods that are unique for an object's type.

Some languages, notably Java, enforce a more restricted form of inheritance, known as *single inheritance*. Single inheritance requires that a child class have only one parent. However, a parent may have multiple children. Since a child class inherits its properties and methods from a single parent, it is an exact duplicate of its parent before it adds its own unique properties and methods.

Other languages, notably C++, support *multiple inheritance*. As you might expect, multiple inheritance allows child classes to inherit their properties and methods from more than one parent class. Multiple inheritance is much more powerful than single inheritance, because it allows independent, but complementary, branches of the class structure to be fused together into a single branch.

Multiple inheritance does, however, introduce some difficulties with respect to name resolution. Suppose that class C is the child of both class A and class B. Suppose also that both class A and B define different `save()` methods. Which of these two methods is inherited by class C? How does the compiler determine which method to use for objects of class C? Although it is certainly possible to develop naming schemes and compilers that resolve naming difficulties resulting from multiple inheritance, these solutions often require a significant amount of additional compilation and runtime processing.

Polymorphism—Many Methods with the Same Name

While at first it may appear to be undesirable to have many methods of the same name, the capability to do so is actually a feature of object-oriented programming. *Polymorphism* is the capability to take on different forms. It allows an object type to define several different implementations of a method. These methods are differentiated by the types and number of parameters they accept. For example, several different `print()` methods may be defined, each of which is used to print objects of different object types. Other `print()` methods may be defined which take a different number of parameters. The interpreter, compiler, or runtime system selects the particular `print()` method that is most appropriate for the object being printed. Polymorphism allows the programmer to use a standard method, such as `print()`, to perform a particular operation and to define different forms of the method to be used with different parameters. This promotes standardization and reusable software and eliminates the need to come up with many slightly different names to distinguish the same operation being performed with different parameters.

JavaScript's Object-Based Programming Features

In the previous section, you learned about the capabilities that are common to object-oriented programming languages. JavaScript does not support several of the capabilities described, but Java does support them. You won't be studying Java until Part V, "Communicating with Java, ActiveX, and Plug-Ins," but it is worth your while to become familiar with the object-oriented programming capabilities described in the previous section. That way, when you do get to Part V, you'll be ready to start learning how Java applets can be integrated with JavaScript scripts.

In this section, you'll learn which object-oriented programming capabilities JavaScript supports and how they are used to develop object-based JavaScript programs.

JavaScript does not support the basic object-oriented programming capabilities of encapsulation and information hiding. However, this is not as bad as it first appears. JavaScript is a scripting language, not a full programming language. The features that it does provide are geared toward providing a capability to quickly and easily generate scripts that execute in the context of a web page or a server-side application.

JavaScript supports the development of object types and the instantiation of these types to create object instances. It provides great support for object composition, but only fair support for modularity and object reuse. Table 5.2 summarizes JavaScript's object-based programming capabilities.

TABLE 5.2: JavaScript's Object-Based Programming Capabilities

Capability	Description
Object types	JavaScript supports both predefined and user-defined object types. However, JavaScript does not provide capabilities for type enforcement. An object of any type may be assigned to any variable.
Object instantiation	Object types are instantiated using the `new operator` to create specific object instances.
Object composition	Object types may be defined in terms of other predefined or user-defined object types.
Modularity	JavaScript code may be defined in a modular fashion, but JavaScript does not provide any features that enforce modular software development.
Object reuse	JavaScript software may be reused via the `SRC` attribute of the `SCRIPT` tag. Software may be made available for reuse via the Internet.
Information hiding	JavaScript does not provide any capabilities to support information hiding.
Encapsulation	Because JavaScript lacks information hiding capabilities, it cannot be used to develop encapsulated object types. Any method or property that is defined for a type is always directly accessible.
Inheritance	An object type may extend and inherit the properties and methods of another object type.
Classification	Because JavaScript supports inheritance, it can be used to develop a hierarchy of object types.
Polymorphism	JavaScript supports polymorphism using the `arguments` array for function definitions.

Although JavaScript does not provide all of the features of full object-oriented programming languages, such as Java, it does provide a suite of object-based features that are specially tailored to browser and server scripting. These features include a number of predefined browser and server objects and the capability to access related objects through the properties and methods of other objects. If this seems very abstract at this point, don't worry—you'll see several concrete examples of these features throughout this chapter as well as in Part II, "Programming the Document Object Model."

The JavaScript Object Model

JavaScript supports a simple object model that is supported by a number of predefined objects. The *JavaScript object model* centers around the specification of object types that are used to create specific object instances. Object types under this model are defined in terms of properties and methods:

- *Properties* are used to access the data values contained in an object. Properties, by default, can be updated as well as read, although some properties of the predefined JavaScript objects are read-only.

- *Methods* are functions that are used to perform operations on an object. Methods may use the object's properties to perform these operations.

> **NOTE** This chapter describes the JavaScript object model as implemented by both Navigator and Internet Explorer. Each of these browsers also provide browser-specific objects, methods, and properties.

Using Properties

An object's properties are accessed by combining the object's name and its property name as follows:

```
objectName.propertyName
```

For example, the background color of the current web document is identified by the `bgColor` property of the predefined `document` object. If you wanted to change the background color to white, you could use the following JavaScript statement:

```
document.bgColor="white"
```

This statement assigns the string `"white"` to the `bgColor` property of the predefined document object. Listing 5.1 shows how this statement can be used in an example script. Figure 5.1 shows the web page that it produces. Several buttons are displayed with the names of different colors. When a button is clicked, the button's `onClick` event handler changes the background of the document by setting the `document.bgColor` property.

> **NOTE** You can access the file for Listing 5.1, `ch05-01.htm`, and all of the code listings in this chapter on the CD that accompanies the book.

Listing 5.1:   Using JavaScript Properties (ch05-01.htm)

```
<HTML>
<HEAD>
<TITLE>Using Properties</TITLE></HEAD>
<BODY>
<H1>Using Properties</H1>
<FORM>
<P><INPUT TYPE="BUTTON" NAME="red" VALUE="Red"
 ONCLICK='document.bgColor="red"'></P>
<P><INPUT TYPE="BUTTON" NAME="white" VALUE="White"
 ONCLICK='document.bgColor="white"'></P>
<P><INPUT TYPE="BUTTON" NAME="blue" VALUE="Blue"
 ONCLICK='document.bgColor="blue"'></P>
</FORM>
</BODY>
</HTML>
```

FIGURE 5.1:

Using properties to change
background colors
(Listing 5.1)

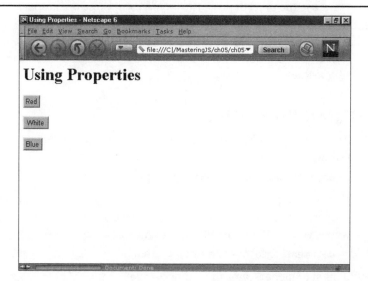

Using Methods

An object's methods are accessed in the same manner as its properties:

objectName.methodName(parameterList)

The parameters, if any, are separated by commas. The parentheses must be used even if no parameters are specified. The following is an example of a method invocation:

```
r=Math.random()
```

The `random()` method of the predefined `Math` object is invoked. This method returns a random floating-point number between 0 and 1. The number is then assigned to the r variable.

You have been using the methods of predefined JavaScript objects since your first script in Chapter 2, "Introducing JavaScript and JScript." You've used the `write()` method of the document object to generate HTML entities that are written to the current document. You've also used the `alert()` method of the `window` object to display pop-up dialog boxes. In the next section, you'll be introduced to some of the objects that are automatically created by JavaScript-capable browsers. Later in this chapter, all of the predefined JavaScript objects will be introduced in summary form. Part II of this book will show you how to use each of these predefined objects in your web pages.

Creating Instances of Objects

Instances of objects of a particular object type are created using the new operator. You've previously used the new operator to create array objects. The same syntax is used to create objects of other types:

```
variable = new objectType(parameters)
```

The `objectType(parameters)` portion of the previous statement is referred to as the *constructor*. Some object types have more than one constructor. Constructors differ in the number of parameters that they allow.

For example, `Date` is a predefined JavaScript object type. To create an instance of `Date` with the current date and time and assign it to the `currentDate` variable, you would use the following statement:

```
currentDate = new Date()
```

In this statement, the `Date()` constructor does not take any parameters. The `Date` object type also allows object instances to be created for a specified date. For example, the following statement creates an instance of `Date` for January 1, 2005:

```
currentDate = new Date(2005,1,1)
```

The constructor used in the previous statement, `Date(2005,1,1)`, takes three parameters. The `Date` object type provides other constructors in addition to the ones described in this section. (The `Date` object type is formally introduced later in this chapter in the "The `Date` Object Type" section.)

Browser Objects

When a web page is loaded by a JavaScript-capable browser, the browser creates a number of JavaScript objects that provide access to the web page and the HTML elements it contains. These objects are used to update and interact with the loaded web page. Table 5.3 identifies these objects and summarizes their use.

TABLE 5.3: Browser Objects

Object	Use
window	To access a browser window or a frame within a window. The window object is assumed to exist and does not require the "window." prefix when referring to its properties and methods.
document	To access the document that is currently loaded into a window. A document refers to an HTML document that provides content, that is, one that has HEAD and BODY tags.
location	To represent a URL. It can be used to create a URL object, access parts of a URL, or modify an existing URL.
history	To maintain a history of the URLs accessed within a window.
frame object	To access an HTML frame. The frames array is used to access all frames within a window.
frames array	
link object	To access a text- or image-based source anchor of a hypertext link. The links array is used to access all link objects within a document. Internet Explorer combines the link object with the anchor object.
links array	
anchor object	To access the target of a hypertext link. The anchors array is used to access all anchor objects within a document.
anchors array	
image object	To access an image that is embedded in an HTML document. The images array is used to access all image objects within a document.
images array	
area	To access an area within a client-side image map.
applet object	To access a Java applet. The applets array is used to access all applets in a document.
applets array	
event object	To access information about the occurrence of an event. The event object provides information about a specific event. The Event (capitalized) object provides constants that are used to identify events.
Event object	
form object	To access an HTML form. The forms array is used to access all forms within a document.
forms array	
elements array	To access all form elements (fields or buttons) contained within a form.
text	To access a text field of a form.

Continued on next page

TABLE 5.3 CONTINUED: Browser Objects

Object	Use
textarea	To access a text area field of a form.
radio	To access a set of radio buttons of a form or to access an individual button within the set.
checkbox	To access a check box of a form.
button	To access a form button that is not a Submit or Reset button.
submit	To access a Submit button of a form.
reset	To access a Reset button of a form.
select option	To access a select list of a form. The option object is used to access the elements of a select list.
password	To access a password field of a form.
hidden	To access a hidden field of a form.
fileupload	To access a file upload element of a form.
navigator	To access information about the browser that is executing a script.
screen	To access information about the size and color depth of a user's screen.
embed object	To access an embedded object. The embeds array provides access to all embedded objects in a document.
embeds array	
mimeType object	To access information about a particular MIME type supported by a browser. The mimeTypes array is an array of all mimeType objects supported by a browser. Internet Explorer provides tacit support for mimeTypes, returning an empty array.
mimeTypes array	
plugin object	To access information about a particular browser plug-in. The plugins array is an array of all plug-ins supported by a browser. Internet Explorer provides tacit support for plugins, returning an empty array.
plugins array	

Table 5.3 summarizes the predefined objects that are created by a JavaScript-capable browser when a web page is loaded. JavaScript also supports object types that are independent of the web page that is loaded. These objects are described in the "Other Predefined Object Types" section later in this chapter.

The Browser Object Hierarchy

Your browser creates the objects presented in Table 5.3 as the results of web pages that you design. For example, if you create a web page with three forms, then the forms array will contain three form objects corresponding to the forms that you have defined. Similarly, if you define a document with seven links, then the links array will contain seven link objects that correspond to your links.

The browser objects are organized into a hierarchy that corresponds to the structure of loaded web documents and the current state of the browser. This hierarchy is referred to as an *instance hierarchy*. The window and navigator objects are the highest-level objects in this hierarchy.

The *Window* Object

The window object represents a browser window, and it has properties that are used to identify the objects of the HTML elements that comprise that window. For example, the frames array is a property of a window object. If the window uses the FRAMESET tag to define multiple frames, then the frames array contains the frame object associated with each frame. The window's location property refers to the location object that contains the URL associated with the window. The window's screen property may be used to obtain the user's screen dimensions and color depth.

If a window contains displayable content, as opposed to a FRAMESET tag, then the window object's document property refers to the document object associated with the window. The document object contains properties that reference objects that are displayed in the window. These properties include the links, anchors, images, and forms arrays. The links array identifies all link objects contained in a document. The anchors array identifies all named anchors. Link objects refer to the source of a hyperlink, while anchor objects refer to the named destinations of a link. The images, applets, and forms arrays identify all image, applet, and form objects contained in a document. A document's area property refers to an area within a client-side image map that is defined in the document. A document's history property refers to a history object that contains a list of URLs that the user has visited within a particular window.

NOTE   Internet Explorer combines the link and anchor objects. Both links and anchors can be accessed via the anchors array.

    A document object's forms array identifies all form objects that are defined in the document. Although a document may define any number of forms, usually only one form is defined. The form object provides access to the individual elements defined for a particular form via the elements array. The elements array refers to text, textarea, radio, checkbox, button, submit, reset, select, password, hidden, and fileupload form fields. These fields may also be individually accessed by their names. You'll learn how to use form-related objects in Chapter 8, "Processing Forms," and Chapter 32 on the CD, "Interfacing JavaScript with CGI Programs."

The *Navigator* Object

The `navigator` object, like the `window` object, is a top-level object in the browser hierarchy. The `navigator` object is used to describe the configuration of the browser being used to display a window. Two of its properties, `mimeTypes` and `plugins`, contain the list of all MIME types and plug-ins supported by the browser. Internet Explorer returns empty arrays for the `mime-Types` and `plugins` properties. Instead, it uses the `embeds` property to access the objects that have been embedded using the HTML `EMBED` tag. Navigator does not support the `embeds` property.

Hierarchical Object Identifiers

Because your browser organizes the various objects of a web page according to the instance hierarchy described in the previous section, a hierarchical naming scheme is used to identify these objects. For example, suppose an HTML document defines three forms, and the second form has seven elements. Also suppose the fifth element of the second form is a radio button. You can access the name of this radio button using the following identifier:

```
document.forms[1].element[4].name
```

This identifier refers to the name of the fifth element of the second form of the current document. (Remember that array indices begin at 0.) You could display this name using the following statement:

```
document.write(document.forms[1].element[4].name)
```

NOTE   You do not have to identify the `window` object when you refer to the current window's properties and methods—your browser will assume the current window object by default. There is one exception, however: in event-handling code, it is the current **document** object that is assumed by default.

In most cases, you can refer to a property or method of a browser-created object by starting with `document` and using the property names of the objects that contain the object (such as `links`, `anchors`, `images`, and `forms`) to identify the object within the instance hierarchy. When you have named the object in this fashion, you can then use the object's property or method name to access the data and functions defined for that object.

Listing 5.2 provides an example of using hierarchical names to access the elements defined within a web document. The document defines a number of functions in the document head. It begins by invoking the `open()` method of the `window` object to open a second browser window. This second window is assigned to the `outputWindow` variable and is used to write the description of the objects defined for the HTML document shown in Listing 5.2. The `open()` method takes two parameters—the URL of the document to be loaded in the window and a window name. Because you don't want to load a document at another URL, set the URL parameter to a blank string.

Listing 5.2:   Using Hierarchical Object Identifiers

```
<HTML>
<HEAD>
<TITLE>Using Hierarchical Object Identifiers</TITLE>
<SCRIPT LANGUAGE="JavaScript"><!--
outputWindow = open("","output")
function setupWindow() {
 outputWindow.document.write("<HTML><HEAD><TITLE>Output
  Window</TITLE></HEAD><BODY>")
}
function describeBrowser() {
 outputWindow.document.write("<H2>Browser Properties</H2>")
 outputWindow.document.write(navigator.appCodeName+" ")
 outputWindow.document.write(navigator.appName+" ")
 outputWindow.document.write(navigator.appVersion+"<BR>")
 outputWindow.document.write(navigator.mimeTypes.length+" MIME
  types are defined. ")
 outputWindow.document.write(navigator.plugins.length+"
  plug-ins are installed.")
}
function describeWindow() {
 outputWindow.document.write("<H2>Window Properties</H2>")
 outputWindow.document.write("Frames: "+frames.length+"<BR>")
 outputWindow.document.write("URL: "+location.href+"<BR>")
}
function describeDocument() {
 outputWindow.document.write("<H2>Document Properties</H2>")
 describeLinks()
 describeForms()
}
function describeLinks(){
 outputWindow.document.write("<H3>Links</H3>")
 outputWindow.document.write("This document contains "
  +document.links.length+" links:<BR>")
 for(i=0;i<document.links.length;++i)
  outputWindow.document.write(document.links[i].href+"<BR>")
}
function describeForms() {
 outputWindow.document.write("<H3>Forms</H3>")
 for(i=0;i<document.forms.length;++i) describeForm(i)
}
function describeForm(n) {
 outputWindow.document.write("Form "+n+" has "
  +document.forms[n].elements.length+" elements:")
 for(j=0;j<document.forms[n].elements.length;++j)
  outputWindow.document.write(" "
```

```
    + document.forms[n].elements[j].name)
  outputWindow.document.write("<BR>")
}
function finishWindow() {
  outputWindow.document.write("<FORM><INPUT Type='button'
  Value='Close Window' onClick='window.close()'></FORM>")
  outputWindow.document.write("</BODY></HTML>")
}
// --></SCRIPT></HEAD>
<BODY>
<H1>Using Hierarchical Object Identifiers</H1>
<P><A HREF="http://www.jaworski.com/javascript">Link to
  Mastering JavaScript home page.</A></P>
<P><A HREF="http://home.netscape.com/">Link to Netscape's home
  page.</A></P>
<FORM>
<P><INPUT TYPE="TEXT" NAME="textField1"
  VALUE="Enter text here!"></P>
<P><INPUT TYPE="CHECKBOX" NAME="checkbox1"
  CHECKED="CHECKED">I'm checkbox1.</P>
<P><INPUT TYPE="CHECKBOX" NAME="checkbox2"> I'm checkbox2.</P>
<INPUT TYPE="SUBMIT" NAME="submitButton" VALUE="Click here!">
</FORM>
<SCRIPT LANGUAGE="JavaScript"><!--
setupWindow()
describeBrowser()
describeWindow()
describeDocument()
finishWindow()
// --></SCRIPT>
</BODY>
</HTML>
```

The `setupWindow()` function is used to generate the head of the second document and its opening `BODY` tag. It uses the `outputWindow` variable to select the second window as the target for writing. This function and other functions in the script write their output using statements of the form:

```
outputWindow.document.write()
```

These statements tell JavaScript to write to the `document` object of the `window` object identified by the `outputWindow` variable.

The `describeBrowser()` function displays some of the `navigator` object's properties to the second window. It also uses the `outputWindow` variable to select this window. It displays the `appCodeName`, `appName`, `appVersion`, and uses the `length` property of the `mimeTypes` and `plug-ins` arrays to determine the number of MIME types and plug-ins supported by the browser.

The describeWindow() function displays some properties of the original (first) window. It displays the number of frames defined by the window and the URL of the document loaded into the window. Since the window does not define any frames, the length of the frames array is 0. The href property of the window's location object is used to get the text string corresponding to the URL. The URL displayed when you execute the script will be different depending on the directory from which you run the files of this chapter.

The describeDocument() function displays some of the properties associated with the current document in the second window. It invokes the describeLinks() and describeForms() functions to perform this processing.

The describeLinks() function uses the length property of the links array to identify the number of links contained in the document. It then executes a for loop to display the URL associated with each of these links. The href attribute of the link object is used to get the text string corresponding to the URL.

The describeForms() function uses the length property of the forms array to iterate through the document's links and display each one. The displayForm() function is used to display each form.

The displayForm() function uses the length property of the elements array of each form object to identify the number of elements contained in a form. It takes a single parameter, identified by the n variable. This parameter identifies the index into the forms array of the form object being displayed. The name of each field element is displayed by referencing the name property of each object contained in the elements array of each form object identified in the forms array. This is a good example of using hierarchical object naming to access the low-level elements of an HTML document.

The finishWindow() function appends the following HTML to the body of the document displayed in the second window:

```
<FORM>
<INPUT Type='button' Value='Close Window'
  onClick='window.close()'>
</FORM>
</BODY>
</HTML>
```

The form is used to create a button, labeled Close Window, that is used to close the second window. The onClick attribute of the INPUT tag is assigned the event handling code, window.close(), which is used to close the window upon clicking of the button. The window object should be explicitly referenced in event handlers to ensure that the current window is closed and not the current document. The </BODY> and </HTML> tags are used to end the displayed document.

The main body of the HTML document defines two links—one to the *Mastering JavaScript* home page and one to Netscape's home page. The document then defines a form with four elements—a text field, two check boxes, and a Submit button.

The script contained in the main body of the document invokes the `setupWindow()`, `describeBrowser()`, `describeWindow()`, `describeDocument()`, and `finishWindow()` functions to display the contents of the first window in the second window referenced by the `output-Window` object. This script is placed at the end of the document so that the various HTML elements of the document are defined when the script is invoked.

A second window is created to display the various properties of the document. The web browser displays this second window as shown in Figure 5.2. When the user clicks the Close Window button, the original document, shown in Figure 5.3, is displayed. You can also use your browser's Window pull-down menu to switch between the two windows.

FIGURE 5.2:

The output window
(Listing 5.2)

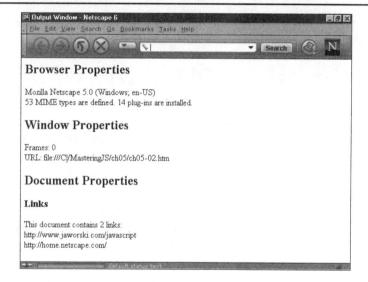

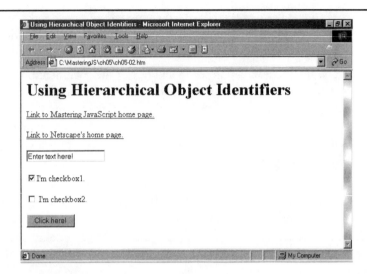

Other Predefined Object Types

In addition to the predefined browser objects discussed in earlier sections, JavaScript also provides general-purpose object types that support common operations. These object types are defined by the ECMAScript specification and are described in the following sections. Some earlier browsers do not support all of the properties and methods of these objects.

The *Array* Object

The Array object allows arrays to be accessed as objects. The ECMAScript specification defines two properties for the Array object: length and prototype. The length property identifies the length of an array. The prototype property is a property that is supported by all object types. It allows additional properties and methods to be defined for an object type. It is covered in the "Adding Properties and Methods to an Object Type" section later in this chapter.

ECMAScript defines the following Array methods:

toString()   Returns a string version of an array. Array elements are separated by commas.

toLocaleString()   Returns a string version of an array. Array elements are separated by locale-specific separators.

concat(item1, …, itemn)   Appends the specified items to the array and returns the modified array. If an item is an array, then the elements of the item array are appended.

join(separator)   Returns a string version of an array. Array elements are separated by the *separator* string. If no separator is specified, a comma is used.

pop()   Removes the last element from the array and returns it.

push(item1, ..., itemn)   Appends the specified items to the array. If an item is an array, then the elements of the item array are appended.

reverse()   Reverses the elements of an array—that is, the last element appears first and the first element appears last.

shift()   Removes the first element from the array and returns it.

slice(start, end)   Returns an array consisting of all elements beginning with the index start and ending at the index end. If end is omitted, then all elements from start to the end of the array are returned.

sort(comparisonFunction)   Sorts the elements of an array according to a comparison function. If no comparison function is specified, the array elements are sorted in dictionary order. If a comparison function is specified, it should take two parameters, p1 and p2, and return a negative integer if p1 is less than p2, zero if p1 equals p2, and a positive integer if p1 is greater than p2.

splice(start, deleteCount, item1, ..., itemn)   The deleteCount elements of the array starting at array index start are replaced by item1, ..., itemn.

unshift(item1, ..., itemn)   The items are prepended (in order) to the front of the array.

Listing 5.3 illustrates the use of some of the listed methods. It creates an array of integers 0 through 10 and applies the toString(), join(':'), reverse(), and sort() methods to it. Figure 5.4 shows the results it displays.

Listing 5.3:   Using the Methods of the *Array* object

```
<HTML>
<HEAD>
<TITLE>Using Arrays</TITLE>
<SCRIPT LANGUAGE="JavaScript"><!--
// --></SCRIPT></HEAD>
<BODY>
<H1>Using Arrays</H1>
<SCRIPT LANGUAGE="JavaScript"><!--
myArray = [0, 1, 2, 3, 4, 5, 6, 7, 8, 9, 10]
document.write("myArray: "+myArray+"<P>")
document.write("myArray.toString(): "+myArray.toString()+"<P>")
document.write("myArray.join(':'): "+myArray.join(':')+"<P>")
document.write("myArray.reverse(): "+myArray.reverse()+"<P>")
document.write("myArray.sort: "+myArray.sort())
// --></SCRIPT>
</BODY>
</HTML>
```

FIGURE 5.4:

The results of applying array methods (Listing 5.3)

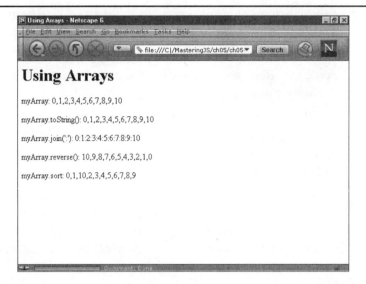

> **NOTE**   Internet Explorer and Navigator provide browser-specific `Array` methods in addition to those of the ECMAScript specification.

The *Boolean* Object

The `Boolean` object allows Boolean values to be accessed as objects. It supports the prototype property and the `toString()` and `valueOf()` methods. The `toString()` method returns the string-equivalent of a Boolean value. The `valueOf()` method returns `true` or `false` depending on the value of the underlying object.

Boolean objects are created by identifying their value as an argument to the constructor:

```
myBoolean  = new Boolean(false)
yourBoolean = new Boolean(true)
```

Why would you want to create a `Boolean` object instead of just setting a variable to `true` or `false`? By creating a `Boolean` object, you can use the `toString()` and `valueOf()` methods. While this may not seem to be much of an added capability, when you get to the `Date` object, you'll be able to appreciate the advantages of working with objects instead of primitive values.

The *Date* Object

The `Date` object type provides a common set of methods for working with dates and times. These methods are summarized in Table 5.4. The methods with UTC in their name refer to Universal Coordinated Time, which is the time set by the World Time Standard. The `Date` object type supports the `prototype` property. Instances of the `Date` object type may be created with any of the constructors shown in Table 5.5. Listing 5.4 illustrates the use of the `Date` object type.

TABLE 5.4: Methods of the `Date` Object

Method	Description
getDate() getUTCDate() setDate(date) setUTCDate(date)	Returns or sets the day of the month of the **Date** object.
getDay() getUTCDay()	Returns the day of the week of the **Date** object.
getHours() getUTCHours() setHours(hours [, min, sec, ms]) setUTCHours(hours [, min, sec, ms])	Returns or sets the hour of the **Date** object.
getMilliseconds() getUTCMilliseconds() setMilliseconds(ms) setUTCMilliseconds(ms)	Returns or sets the milliseconds value of the **Date** object.
getMinutes() getUTCMinutes() setMinutes(min [, sec, ms]) setUTCMinutes(min [, sec, ms])	Returns or sets the minutes of the **Date** object.
getMonth() getUTCMonth() setMonth(month [, date]) setUTCMonth(month [, date])	Returns or sets the month of the **Date** object.
getSeconds() getUTCSeconds() setSeconds(sec [, ms]) setUTCSeconds(sec [, ms])	Returns or sets the seconds of the **Date** object.
getTime() setTime(time)	Returns or sets the time of the **Date** object.
getTimeZoneOffset()	Returns the time zone offset (in minutes) of the **Date** object.

Continued on next page

TABLE 5.4 CONTINUED: Methods of the Date Object

Method	Description
getYear()	Returns or sets the year of the **Date** object. The full year methods use four-digit year values.
getFullYear() getUTCFullYear() setYear(year) setFullYear(year [,month, date]) setUTCFullYear(year [,month, date])	
toGMTString()	Converts a date to a string in Internet GMT (Greenwich Mean Time) format.
toLocaleString()	Converts a date to a string in *locale* format, which means the format commonly used in the geographical region in which the user is located.
toLocaleDateString() toLocaleTimeString()	
toString() toDateString() toTimeString()	Returns a string value of a **Date** object.
valueOf()	Returns the number of milliseconds since midnight on January 1, 1970.
toUTCString()	Returns a string that represents the time in UTC.

TABLE 5.5: Date Constructors

Constructor	Description
Date()	Creates a **Date** instance with the current date and time.
Date(dateString)	Creates a **Date** instance with the date specified in the **dateString** parameter. The format of the **dateString** is **month day, year hours:minutes:seconds**.
Date(milliseconds)	Creates a **Date** instance with the specified number of milliseconds since midnight January 1, 1970.
Date(year, month, day, hours, minutes, seconds, milliseconds)	Creates a **Date** instance with the date specified by the year, month, day, hours, minutes, seconds, and milliseconds integers. The year and month parameters must be supplied. If other parameters are included, then all preceding parameters must be supplied.

Listing 5.4:   **Using the *Date* Object**

```
<HTML>
<HEAD>
<TITLE>Using the Date Object Type</TITLE>
</HEAD>
<BODY>
<H1>Using the Date Object Type</H1>
<SCRIPT LANGUAGE="JavaScript"><!--
currentDate = new Date()
with (currentDate) {
 document.write("Date: "+(getMonth()+1)+"/"+getDate()+"/"+getFullYear()
  +"<BR>")
 document.write("Time: "+getHours()+":"+getMinutes()+":"
  +getSeconds())
}
// --></SCRIPT>
</BODY>
</HTML>
```

The previous document uses the methods of the Date object type to write the current date and time to the current document object. The currentDate variable is assigned a new Date object that is created using the new operator and the Date() constructor. A with statement is used to make the object stored with currentDate the default object for object references. The two write() method invocations use the getMonth(), getDate(), getFullYear(), getHours(), getMinutes(), and getSeconds() methods to access the various components of a Date object. Figure 5.5 shows the web page generated by Listing 5.4.

FIGURE 5.5:

Using the Date object type (Listing 5.4)

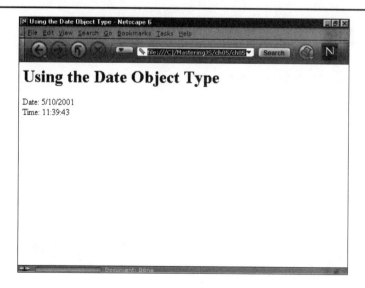

The *Function* Object

The Function object allows functions to be accessed as objects. It can be used to dynamically create and invoke a function during a script's execution. The ECMAScript specification identifies the length and prototype properties. The length property identifies the number of parameters defined for a function. Navigator and Internet Explorer define the arguments property and the caller property. The arguments property is an array that identifies the arguments that are passed to a function when it is invoked. The caller property identifies the function that invoked a particular function. Navigator also defines the arity property, which is identical to the length property.

The ECMAScript specification defines the toString(), apply(thisArg, argArray), and call(thisArg, arg1, ..., argn)() methods. The toString() method returns a string representation of the function. The apply() method invokes the function on the object specified by thisArg with the arguments contained in argArray. The call() method is similar to the apply() method, but it passes the arguments individually.

Function objects are created by supplying the function's parameters and body to the Function() constructor:

```
variable = new Function("p1", "p2", ..., "pn", "body")
```

The opening and closing brackets ({ and }) of the function body are not specified. The following function returns $x^2 + y^2$:

```
myFunction = new Function("x", "y", "return x*x + y*y")
```

Listing 5.5 illustrates the use of the Function object. It creates a function that surrounds a string with braces ([and]). Figure 5.6 shows the results that are displayed by Listing 5.5.

Listing 5.5: **Using the *Function* Object**

```
<HTML>
<HEAD>
<TITLE>Using the Function Object</TITLE>
<BODY><H1>
<SCRIPT LANGUAGE="JavaScript"><!--
addBraces = new Function("s","return '['+s+']'")
document.write(addBraces("This"))
document.write(addBraces("is"))
document.write(addBraces("a"))
document.write(addBraces("test."))
// --></SCRIPT>
</H1></BODY>
</HTML>
```

FIGURE 5.6:

The results of the
dynamically created
function (Listing 5.5)

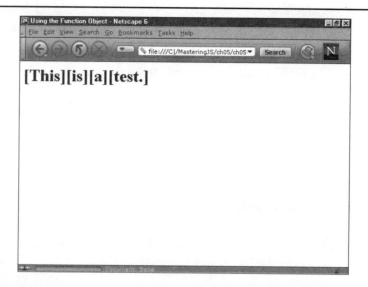

FIGURE 5.6:

The results of the dynamically created function (Listing 5.5)

The *Global* Object

The ECMAScript specification defines the Global object to associate an object with the globally accessible variables and functions defined in earlier versions of JavaScript. Navigator and Internet Explorer implement the Global object, but do not allow it to be explicitly created (via new Global()) or referenced (via "Global."). Instead, its properties and methods are referenced directly as global variables and functions.

The ECMAScript specification defines three constant properties: undefined, NaN, and Infinity. The undefined constant is used to identify a variable that does not have a defined value. The NaN constant means *not a number*. The Infinity property represents positive infinity. Methods defined for the Global object are as follows:

eval(x)   Evaluates and returns the value of the expression *x*.

isFinite(number)   Returns true if *number* is finite and false otherwise.

isNaN(number)   Returns true if *number* is not a number and false, otherwise.

parseFloat(string)   Parses the *string* as a floating-point value.

parseInt(string, radix)   Parses the *string* as an integer of base *radix*.

escape(string)   Converts the *string* into a new string where certain characters are converted into escape sequences in accordance with RFC 1738.

unescape(string)   Converts strings encoded by escape() back to their original value.

encodeURI(uri)   Converts the *uri* into an encoded URI using UTF-8 encoding.

decodeURI(uri)   Performs the opposite transformation of the `encodeURI()` function.

encodeURIComponent(uriComponent)   Converts the *uriComponent* into an encoded URI using UTF-8 encoding. Assumes that the argument is a component of a URI rather than a complete URI.

decodeURIComponent(uriComponent)   Performs the opposite transformation of the `encodeURIComponent()` function.

The above methods can be used to support numerical tests and URI encoding/decoding in accordance with RFC 1738 and RFC 2396.

The *Math* Object

The `Math` object provides a standard library of mathematical constants and functions. The constants are defined as properties of `Math` and are listed in Table 5.6. The functions are defined as methods of `Math` and are summarized in Table 5.7. Specific instances of `Math` are not created because `Math` is a built-in object and not an object type. Listing 5.6 illustrates the use of the `Math` object; Figure 5.7 shows the web page it generates.

TABLE 5.6: Math Properties

Property	Description
E	Euler's constant
LN2	The natural logarithm of 2
LN10	The natural logarithm of 10
LOG2E	The base 2 logarithm of e
LOG10E	The base 10 logarithm of e
PI	The constant π
SQRT1_2	The square root of _
SQRT2	The square root of 2

TABLE 5.7: Math Methods

Method	Description
abs(x)	Returns the absolute value of *x*.
acos(x)	Returns the arc cosine of *x* in radians.
asin(x)	Returns the arc sine of *x* in radians.

Continued on next page

TABLE 5.7: Math Methods

Method	Description
atan(x)	Returns the arc tangent of *x* in radians.
atan2(x,y)	Returns the angle of the polar coordinate corresponding to (*x*,*y*).
ceil(x)	Returns the least integer that is greater than or equal to *x*.
cos(x)	Returns the cosine of *x*.
exp(x)	Returns e^x.
floor(x)	Returns the greatest integer that is less than or equal to *x*.
log(x)	Returns the natural logarithm of *x*.
max(x,y)	Returns the greater of *x* and *y*. If more than two arguments are supplied, the method returns the greatest of all the arguments.
min(x,y)	Returns the lesser of *x* and *y*. If more than two arguments are supplied, the method returns the least of all the arguments.
pow(x,y)	Returns «Xtags error: No such font: tag f»x^y.
random()	Returns a random number between 0 and 1.
round(x)	Returns *x* rounded to the closest integer.
sin(x)	Returns the sine of *x*.
sqrt(x)	Returns the square root of *x*.
tan(x)	Returns the tangent of *x*.

Listing 5.6: **Using the *Math* Object**

```
<HTML>
<HEAD>
<TITLE>Using the Math Object</TITLE>
</HEAD>
<BODY>
<H1>Using the Math Object</H1>
<SCRIPT LANGUAGE="JavaScript"><!--
document.write(Math.PI+"<BR>")
document.write(Math.E+"<BR>")
document.write(Math.ceil(1.234)+"<BR>")
document.write(Math.random()+"<BR>")
document.write(Math.sin(Math.PI/2)+"<BR>")
document.write(Math.min(100,1000)+"<BR>")
// --></SCRIPT>
</BODY>
</HTML>
```

FIGURE 5.7:

Example of using the
Math object (Listing 5.6)

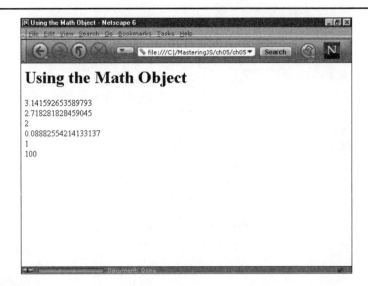

The *Number* Object

The Number object type allows numbers to be treated as objects. The ECMAScript specification defines the following Number properties:

MAX_VALUE   The number is the maximum possible numeric value.

MIN_VALUE   The number is the minimum possible numeric value.

NaN   The number is not a number.

NEGATIVE_INFINITY   The number is negative infinity.

POSITIVE_INFINITY   The number is positive infinity.

prototype   The prototype property that is supported by all object types.

The previous properties are used to identify numbers as having special characteristics. They are not normally used in scripts. Instead, use the properties and methods of the Global object.

The ECMAScript specification defines the following Number methods:

toString(radix)   Returns a string that represents the number in base *radix*.

toLocaleString()   Returns a string that represents the number in a locale-specific format.

toFixed(fractionDigits)   Converts the number into a string representation with the specified fixed number of fraction digits.

toExponential(fractionDigits)   Converts the number into an exponential string representation with the specified number of fraction digits.

toPrecision(precision)   Converts the number into a string representation with the specified numerical precision.

valueOf()   Returns the numeric value of the Number object.

Instances of the Number object are created by supplying a numeric value to the Number() constructor:

```
myNumber = new Number(123.456)
```

The *Object* Object

The Object object is the base object from which all other objects are derived. Its properties and methods are available to other object types.

The Object object supports the prototype and constructor properties. The constructor property identifies the name of the object's constructor.

The Object object supports the following methods:

toString()   Returns a string representation of the object.

toLocaleString()   Returns a string representation of the object in a locale-specific format.

valueOf()   Returns the object upon which the method is invoked.

hasOwnProperty(propertyName)   Returns a Boolean value indicating whether or not the object has the specified property.

isPrototypeOf(object)   Returns a Boolean value indicating whether or not the object is a prototype of the other object.

propertyIsEnumerable(precision)   Returns a Boolean value indicating whether or not the object has the specified property and the property is enumerable.

Object objects can be created by supplying a number, string, Boolean value, or function in the Object() constructor. However, this is rarely done. Instead, it is better to use the constructor of the specific object type (that is, Number(), String(), Boolean(), or Function()).

The *String* Object

The String object type allows strings to be accessed as objects. It supports the length and prototype properties. The length property identifies the string's length in characters.

The String object type provides a set of methods for manipulating strings. The methods defined in the ECMAScript specification are summarized in Table 5.8. Any JavaScript string value or variable containing a string value is able to use these methods. Both Netscape and Internet Explorer define String methods in addition to those contained in Table 5.8.

TABLE 5.8: String Methods

Method	Description
charAt(index)	Returns a string that consists of the character at the specified index of the string to which the method is applied.
charCodeAt(index)	Returns the Unicode encoding of the character at the specified index.
concat(s1, …, sn)	Concatenates the specified strings to the string upon which the method is invoked and returns the new string.
fromCharCode(codes)	Creates a string from a comma-separated sequence of character codes.
indexOf(pattern)	Returns the index of the first string specified by the pattern parameter that is contained in a string. Returns –1 if the pattern is not contained in the string.
indexOf(pattern, startIndex)	Same as the previous method except that searching starts at the position specified by startIndex.
lastIndexOf(pattern)	Returns the index of the last string specified by the pattern parameter that is contained in a string. Returns –1 if the pattern is not contained in the string.
lastIndexOf(pattern, startIndex)	Same as the previous method except that searching starts at the position specified by startIndex.
localeCompare(s)	Compares the string with the string s using a locale-specific comparison. It returns 0 if the strings are equivalent and a non-zero numeric value if the strings are not equivalent.
match(regExp)	Matches the string against the specified regular expression. Refer to Appendix B, "Working with Regular Expressions."
replace(searchValue, replaceValue)	Replaces searchValue with replaceValue and returns the result. Refer to Appendix B.
search(regExp)	Searches the string for the specified regular expression and returns the index of where it is found. Refer to Appendix B.
slice(start, end)	Returns a substring starting from character position *start* and running to, but not including character position *end* (or through the end of the string if *end* is undefined).
split(separator, limit)	Separates a string into an array of substrings based upon the *separator*. If limit is specified, then the array is limited to the number of elements given by limit.
substring(startIndex)	Returns the substring of a string beginning at startIndex.
substring(startIndex, endIndex)	Returns the substring of a string beginning at startIndex and ending at endIndex.

Continued on next page

TABLE 5.8 CONTINUED: String Methods

Method	Description
toLowerCase()	
toLocaleLowerCase()	Returns a copy of the string converted to lowercase.
toString()	Returns the string value of the object.
toUpperCase()	
toLocaleUpperCase()	Returns a copy of the string converted to uppercase.
valueOf()	Returns the string value of the object.

Listing 5.7 illustrates the use of the String object type. The script in the document body begins by defining the function displayLine(), which displays text followed by the BR tag. The displayLine() function is used to display several text strings which are modified using sample string methods. Figure 5.8 shows the web page generated by Listing 5.7.

Listing 5.7:   Using the *String* Object

```
<HTML>
<HEAD>
<TITLE>Using the String Object Type</TITLE>
</HEAD>
<BODY>
<SCRIPT LANGUAGE="JavaScript"><!--
function displayLine(text) {
 document.write(text+"<BR>")
}
s = new String("This is a test of the JavaScript String methods.")
displayLine('s = '+s)
displayLine('s.charAt(1) = '+s.charAt(1))
displayLine('s.charCodeAt(1) = '+s.charCodeAt(1))
displayLine('s.indexOf("is") = '+s.indexOf("is"))
displayLine('s.lastIndexOf("is") = '+s.lastIndexOf("is"))
displayLine('s.substring(22,32) = '+s.substring(22,32))
displayLine('s.toLowerCase() = '+s.toLowerCase())
displayLine('s.toUpperCase() = '+s.toUpperCase())
split = s.split(" ")
for(i=0; i<split.length; ++i)
 displayLine('split['+i+'] = '+split[i])
// --></SCRIPT>
</BODY>
</HTML>
```

FIGURE 5.8:

Using the `String` object
(Listing 5.7)

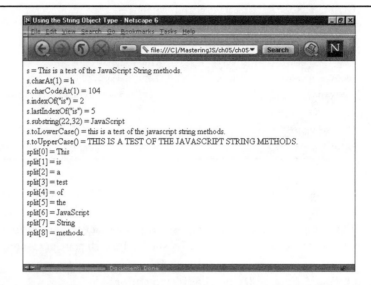

```
s = This is a test of the JavaScript String methods.
s.charAt(1) = h
s.charCodeAt(1) = 104
s.indexOf("is") = 2
s.lastIndexOf("is") = 5
s.substring(22,32) = JavaScript
s.toLowerCase() = this is a test of the javascript string methods.
s.toUpperCase() = THIS IS A TEST OF THE JAVASCRIPT STRING METHODS.
split[0] = This
split[1] = is
split[2] = a
split[3] = test
split[4] = of
split[5] = the
split[6] = JavaScript
split[7] = String
split[8] = methods.
```

Creating *String* Objects

`String` objects may be created in the same manner as other JavaScript objects using the new operator. For example, the variable `text` may be assigned the string `"I am a string"` using the following statement:

```
text = new String("I am a string")
```

This statement is equivalent to the following:

```
text = "I am a string"
```

Regular Expressions and the *RegExp* Object

Support for *regular expressions* was introduced in JavaScript 1.2. Regular expressions are string expressions that describe a pattern of characters. They provide a powerful capability for finding patterns in text strings and performing search and replace operations on text. Regular expressions make use of a very compact, powerful, but somewhat arcane syntax that is covered in detail in Appendix B, "Regular Expressions." In JavaScript, regular expressions are implemented using the `RegExp` object. The `RegExp` object is also covered in Appendix B.

NOTE   Although regular expressions were not included in the ECMAScript specification, they will be included in ECMAScript 2.

Color Constants

JavaScript defines a number of color constants that can be used with methods and functions that take color parameters. Some of these color constants are `"red"`, `"orange"`, `"yellow"`, `"green"`, `"blue"`, `"white"`, `"black"`, and `"brown"`.

Defining Object Types

JavaScript provides the capability for you to define your own object types and create specific object instances. To create a new object type, you simply define a function that is used to construct specific instances of the object type. Essentially, this constructor function does two things:

- It assigns values to the object type's properties.

- It identifies other functions to be used as the object type's methods.

As an example of defining a new object type, we'll create the `Table` object type. This object type will be used to create simple tables using JavaScript and write them to the current document.

NOTE   The function used as a constructor of an object type must have the same name as the object type.

Identifying and Assigning Properties

The first thing that we'll do is identify the properties of the `Table` object type. The number of rows and columns of the table are obvious properties with which to start. Let's name these properties `Table.rows` and `Table.columns`. We'll also need to define a property to store the elements of the Table. Let's call this property `Table.data` and let it be an array of the following length:

```
Table.rows * Table.columns
```

Because HTML allows some table cells to be designated as header cells, let's also define the property `Table.header` as an array of the same length as above, `Table.rows * Table.columns`, where each element is a Boolean value indicating whether a table cell is a header cell. Finally, let's define a property, `Table.border`, that identifies the border width of the table. The following code shows how the table constructor would be defined using the items we just identified:

```
function Table(rows,columns) {
  this.rows = rows
  this.columns = columns
```

```
this.border = 0
this.data = new Array(rows*columns)
this.header = new Array(rows*columns)
}
```

As you can see, the `Table()` constructor takes the parameters `rows` and `columns`, and assigns them to `this.rows` and `this.columns`. The `this` prefix is a special keyword that is used to refer to the current object. For example, the statement `this.rows = rows` assigns the value stored in the `rows` parameter to the `rows` property of the current object. Similarly, `this.columns = columns` assigns the `columns` parameter to the `columns` property of the current object. The parameters to the `Table()` constructor do not have to be named rows and columns—they could have been named x and y. However, it is common to see parameters named after the object type properties to which they are assigned.

The `border` property of the current object is set to the default value of 0. This results in the creation of a borderless table. As mentioned earlier, the `data` and `header` properties are each assigned an array of size `rows * columns`.

In order to create an object that is an instance of the `Table` object type, you use the `new` operator in conjunction with the `Table` constructor. For example, the following statement creates a table of three rows by four columns and assigns it to the `t` variable:

```
t = new Table(3,4)
```

Defining Methods

So far, we've defined the properties of the `Table` object type. However, we'll need to define some methods to update the values of the `data`, `header`, and `border` properties and to write the `Table` object to a `document` object.

Methods are defined by assigning the name of an already defined function to a method name in an object type constructor. For example, suppose the `Table_setValue()` function is defined as follows. This function sets the value of the table cell at the specified `row` and `column` parameters to the `value` parameter.

```
function Table_setValue(row,col,value) {
  this.data[row*this.columns+col]=value
}
```

We can use the previously defined `Table_setValue()` function as the `setValue()` method of the `Table` object type by including the following statement in the `Table` constructor:

```
this.setValue = Table_setValue
```

Note that trailing parentheses are not used in the previous statement. The new `Table` constructor is as follows:

```
function Table(rows,columns) {
  this.rows = rows
```

```
  this.columns = columns
  this.border = 0
  this.data = new Array(rows*columns)
  this.header = new Array(rows*columns)
  this.setValue = Table_setValue
  }
```

An example of invoking the setValue() method for the Table object stored in the t variable follows:

```
  t.setValue(2,3,"Hello")
```

This statement sets the table data value at row 2 and column 3 to "Hello".

Definition of the *Table* Object

Listing 5.8 provides a complete definition of the Table object. Note that functions must be defined before they can be assigned to a method name.

Listing 5.8:   Definition of the *Table* Object (table.js)

```
function Table_getValue(row,col) {
 return this.data[row*this.columns+col]
}
function Table_setValue(row,col,value) {
 this.data[row*this.columns+col]=value
}
function Table_set(contents) {
 var n = contents.length
 for(var j=0;j<n;++j) this.data[j]=contents[j]
}
function Table_isHeader(row,col) {
 return this.header[row*this.columns+col]
}
function Table_makeHeader(row,col) {
 this.header[row*this.columns+col]=true
}
function Table_makeNormal(row,col) {
 this.header[row*this.columns+col]=false
}
function Table_makeHeaderRow(row) {
 for(var j=0;j<this.columns;++j)
   this.header[row*this.columns+j]=true
}
function Table_makeHeaderColumn(col) {
 for(var i=0;i<this.rows;++i)
   this.header[i*this.columns+col]=true
}
function Table_write(doc) {
```

```
 doc.write("<TABLE BORDER="+this.border+">")
 for(var i=0;i<this.rows;++i) {
  doc.write("<TR>")
  for(var j=0;j<this.columns;++j) {
   if(this.header[i*this.columns+j]) {
    doc.write("<TH>")
    doc.write(this.data[i*this.columns+j])
    doc.write("</TH>")
   }else{
    doc.write("<TD>")
    doc.write(this.data[i*this.columns+j])
    doc.write("</TD>")
   }
  }
  doc.writeln("</TR>")
 }
 doc.writeln("</TABLE>")
}
function Table(rows,columns) {
 this.rows = rows
 this.columns = columns
 this.border = 0
 if(rows * columns > 0) {
  this.data = new Array(rows*columns)
  this.header = new Array(rows*columns)
 }else{
  this.data = new Array(1)
  this.header = new Array(1)
 }
 this.getValue = Table_getValue
 this.setValue = Table_setValue
 this.set = Table_set
 this.isHeader = Table_isHeader
 this.makeHeader = Table_makeHeader
 this.makeNormal = Table_makeNormal
 this.makeHeaderRow = Table_makeHeaderRow
 this.makeHeaderColumn = Table_makeHeaderColumn
 this.write = Table_write
}
```

Listing 5.8 adds the getValue(), set(), isHeader(), makeHeader(), makeNormal(), make-HeaderRow(), makeHeaderColumn(), and write() methods to the table definition introduced in the previous section.

The getValue() method returns the data value stored at a specified row and column. The set() method stores an array of values as the contents of a table. The makeHeader() and makeNormal() methods are used to identify whether a cell should or should not be a header cell. The makeHeaderRow() and makeHeaderColumn() methods are used to designate an entire row or column as consisting of header cells. The write() method is used to write a table to a document object.

Using the *Table* Object

Listing 5.9 provides an example of the use of the Table object. The document's body contains a script that creates, initializes, and displays a three-row by four-column Table object. Using the SRC attribute of the SCRIPT tag, it includes the table.js file presented in the previous section. It begins by creating a Table object and assigning it to the t variable. It then creates an array, named contents, that contains a list of values. The set() method is invoked to assign the contents array to the cells of the table stored at t. The table's border property is set to four pixels, and the cells of column 0 are designated as header cells. Finally, the write() method is used to write the table to the current document object. Figure 5.9 shows the web page resulting from the script of Listing 5.9.

Listing 5.9:   **Using the *Table* Object**

```
<HTML>
<HEAD>
<TITLE>Defining Object Types</TITLE>
<SCRIPT LANGUAGE="JavaScript" SRC="table.js"><!--
// --></SCRIPT>
</HEAD>
<BODY>
<H1>Defining Object Types</H1>
<SCRIPT LANGUAGE="JavaScript"><!--
t = new Table(3,4)
contents = new Array("This","is","a","test","of","the","table","object.",
 "Let's","see","it","work.")
t.set(contents)
t.border=4
t.makeHeaderColumn(0)
t.write(document)
// --></SCRIPT>
</BODY>
</HTML>
```

FIGURE 5.9:

An example table
(Listing 5.9)

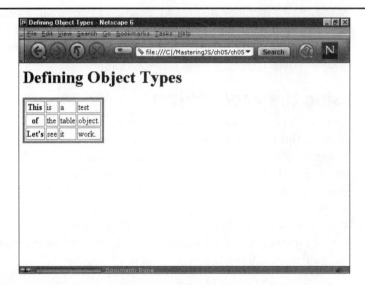

Adding Properties and Methods to an Object Type

Object types that can be instantiated with the new operator are referred to as *instantiable* object types. They include all user-defined object types and most of the predefined object types. Examples of object types that are not instantiable are Math and Global. JavaScript provides the capability to add properties and methods to already defined instantiable object types via the prototype property.

For example, suppose we wanted to add a background color attribute to the Table object type defined in the previous section. We could add the new attribute with the following statement:

```
Table.prototype.bgColor = "cyan"
```

The previous statement uses the prototype property of the Table object type to create a new property called bgColor to represent the background color of the table.

Now that we've defined the bgColor property, we should create an additional method called colorWrite() that writes a table using the bgColor property. The following function performs this processing:

```
function Table_colorWrite(doc) {
  doc.write("<TABLE BORDER="+this.border+" BGCOLOR="+this.bgColor+">")
  for(var i=0;i<this.rows;++i) {
   doc.write("<TR>")
   for(var j=0;j<this.columns;++j) {
    if(this.header[i*this.columns+j]) {
```

```
      doc.write("<TH>")
      doc.write(this.data[i*this.columns+j])
      doc.write("</TH>")
    }else{
      doc.write("<TD>")
      doc.write(this.data[i*this.columns+j])
      doc.write("</TD>")
    }
   }
   doc.writeln("</TR>")
  }
  doc.writeln("</TABLE>")
}
```

We can use the `Table_colorWrite()` function in the previous listing as the `colorWrite()` method by including the following statement in our script:

```
Table.prototype.colorWrite=Table_colorWrite
```

Listing 5.10 updates the script shown in Listing 5.9 to make use of the new `bgColor` property and the `colorWrite()` method. Figure 5.10 shows the web page that results from Listing 5.10. Note that we did not have to modify the original `table.js` file that is included via the SRC attribute.

TIP   Always create an object of the object type being modified before using the object type's prototype property. This will ensure that any new properties and methods are correctly added.

Listing 5.10:   Updating an Object Type Definition

```
<HTML>
<HEAD>
<TITLE>Updating Object Types</TITLE>
<SCRIPT LANGUAGE="JavaScript" SRC="table.js"><!--
// --></SCRIPT>
</HEAD>
<BODY>
<H1>Updating Object Types</H1>
<SCRIPT LANGUAGE="JavaScript"><!--
function Table_colorWrite(doc) {
 doc.write("<TABLE BORDER="+this.border+" BGCOLOR="+this.bgColor+">")
 for(var i=0;i<this.rows;++i) {
  doc.write("<TR>")
  for(var j=0;j<this.columns;++j) {
   if(this.header[i*this.columns+j]) {
    doc.write("<TH>")
    doc.write(this.data[i*this.columns+j])
    doc.write("</TH>")
   }else{
```

```
      doc.write("<TD>")
      doc.write(this.data[i*this.columns+j])
      doc.write("</TD>")
     }
    }
   doc.writeln("</TR>")
  }
  doc.writeln("</TABLE>")
}

t = new Table(3,4)
Table.prototype.bgColor="cyan"
Table.prototype.colorWrite=Table_colorWrite
contents = new Array("This","is","a","test","of","the","table","object.",
 "Let's","see","it","work.")
t.set(contents)
t.border=4
t.makeHeaderColumn(0)
t.colorWrite(document)
// --></SCRIPT>
</BODY>
</HTML>
```

FIGURE 5.10:

Tables with a background
color (Listing 5.10)

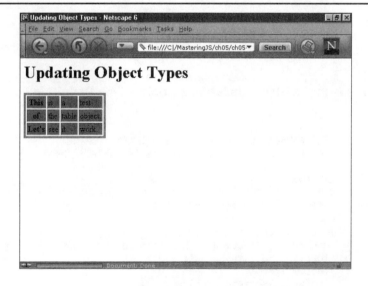

Extending Object Types

In the previous example, we customized the Table object by adding a new method to its prototype. JavaScript also provides the capability to extend an object type and create a new object type that has all of the properties and methods of the extended object type in addition to new properties and methods of its own.

Extending object types is easy with JavaScript. For example, suppose we've defined an object type A and we want to extend it with object type B. All we have to do is insert the following statement after B's definition:

```
B.prototype = new A;
```

This statement tells JavaScript that the A object type is to be used as the prototype for defining the B object type.

Extending Table with *ColoredTable*

To see how easy it is to extend an object type, let's extend the `Table` object type with a new object type named `ColoredTable`. The `ColoredTable` object type will add a `bgColor` property and redefine the `write()` method to display the table's background color. Listing 5.11 shows the `ColoredTable` object's definition. The `ColoredTable` constructor is redefined to add the `bgColor` argument. Note that the `write()` method is redefined as the `Table_colorWrite()` function from Listing 5.10. The `ColoredTable` is identified as extending `Table` via the following line:

```
ColoredTable.prototype = new Table;
```

This line is placed after the `ColoredTable` constructor.

Listing 5.12 shows how to use the `ColoredTable` object. Note that `table.js` and `colored-table.js` must be included in the document. The page that it generates is similar to that shown in Figure 5.10.

Listing 5.11:   Extending an Object Type Definition (coloredtable.js)

```
function ColoredTable(rows,columns,bgColor) {
  this.rows = rows
  this.columns = columns
  this.bgColor = bgColor
  this.data = new Array(rows*columns)
  this.header = new Array(rows*columns)
  this.write = Table_colorWrite
}

ColoredTable.prototype = new Table;
```

```
function Table_colorWrite(doc) {
 doc.write("<TABLE BORDER="+this.border+" BGCOLOR="+this.bgColor+">")
 for(var i=0;i<this.rows;++i) {
  doc.write("<TR>")
  for(var j=0;j<this.columns;++j) {
   if(this.header[i*this.columns+j]) {
    doc.write("<TH>")
    doc.write(this.data[i*this.columns+j])
    doc.write("</TH>")
   }else{
    doc.write("<TD>")
    doc.write(this.data[i*this.columns+j])
    doc.write("</TD>")
   }
  }
  doc.writeln("</TR>")
 }
 doc.writeln("</TABLE>")
}
```

Listing 5.12:   Extending an Object Type Definition (ch05-12.htm)

```
<HTML>
<HEAD>
<TITLE>Extending Object Types</TITLE>
<SCRIPT LANGUAGE="JavaScript" SRC="table.js"><!--
// --></SCRIPT>
<SCRIPT LANGUAGE="JavaScript" SRC="coloredtable.js"><!--
// --></SCRIPT>
</HEAD>
<BODY>
<H1>Extending Object Types</H1>

<SCRIPT LANGUAGE="JavaScript"><!--
t = new ColoredTable(3,4,"yellow")
contents = new Array("This","is","a","test","of","the","table","object.",
 "Let's","see","it","work.")
t.set(contents)
t.border=4
t.makeHeaderColumn(0)
t.write(document)
// --></SCRIPT>
</BODY>
</HTML>
```

Deleting Properties and Methods

The delete operator was introduced in Chapter 3, "Using Operators, Statements, and Functions," where you learned how it can be used to delete an element of an array. The delete operator can also be used to delete a property or method of a user-defined object. Its syntax is as follows:

```
delete objectName.propertyName
delete objectName.methodName
```

For example, suppose the myTable variable refers to a Table object. The following statement deletes the header property of the object referenced by myTable:

```
delete myTable.header
```

There are few occasions in which it is desirable to delete a property or method of an existing object. As such, the delete operator is rarely used.

The *event* Object

In Chapter 4, "Handling Events," you learned how to handle events and errors. Now that you know what objects are, we'll go over the properties and methods of the event object. An instance of the event object is created whenever an event occurs during the execution of a script. Navigator and Internet Explorer each define a different set of properties for the event object. Both browsers use the type property to identify the type of event that occurred and the screenX and screenY properties to identify the screen location at which the event occurred. Navigator and Internet Explorer also implement some similar properties with different names as summarized in Table 5.9.

TABLE 5.9: Similar Navigator and Internet Explorer Event Properties

Navigator Property	Internet Explorer Property	Description
pageX, pageY	clientX, clientY	The location of the event relative to the web page
target	srcElement	The event source
which	button	The mouse button associated with the event
key	keyCode	The Unicode character code of the character corresponding to the key press
modifiers	altKey, ctrlKey, shiftKey	The state of the Alt, Control, or Shift keys

Summary

This chapter described JavaScript's support of objects and object-based programming. It introduced the JavaScript object model and summarized the predefined JavaScript objects. It also showed you how to create your own objects and methods. In the next chapter, you'll learn how to debug your scripts.

CHAPTER 6

Debugging Your Scripts

- Discovering the sources of errors

- Resolving errors

- Using the Microsoft Script Debugger

I t's sad but true: as a JavaScript programmer, you'll encounter bugs in many, if not most, of the scripts that you write. Hopefully, you'll be able to find these bugs before you publish your scripts. If you don't, your users certainly will.

This chapter is about JavaScript debugging. It describes the types of errors that are found in JavaScript scripts, shows you how to find errors in your scripts, and shows you how to avoid the errors in the first place. It also shows how to use the Navigator JavaScript Console and the Microsoft Script Debugger. When you finish this chapter, you should be better able to find and eliminate the bugs in your scripts.

Sources of Errors

If you think that JavaScript scripts are more error-prone than Perl scripts, Java, or C++ programs, you are probably right. The JavaScript programmer is faced with a number of obstacles that prevent writing error-free code:

Users   If there is an error in your script, then some user will find it. Users are ingenious in the ways that they make your scripts fail. They enter bad data in forms, fail to enter required data, and copy and paste URLs from one type of browser to another. They also configure their browsers to disable Java and refuse cookies. An error-free script must be able to stand up to all these obstacles and more.

Browsers   Browsers themselves have bugs—lots of them—and different object models, too. Your scripts must be able to work with several different types and versions of browsers, including betas and prereleases.

Server-side resources   Your script may fail to obtain the resources (such as images, applets, and ActiveX components) that it needs to perform its processing. These resources may be filtered by firewalls, delayed by servers, or lost due to connection timeouts.

Scripts   Your scripts can contain syntax errors, runtime errors, and other types of errors.

The following sections identify different categories of JavaScript errors. By knowing the types of errors that can occur, you'll be better prepared to avoid them.

Syntax Errors

The most noticeable scripting errors are syntax errors. Fortunately, these errors follow patterns and are easy to deal with. The most common of these errors follow.

Variable and Function Definition

A common error is to use variables and functions that have not been defined or whose definition occurs later in the document than that use of it. Both generally result in syntax errors. Listing 6.1 (novar.htm) provides an example of the use of an undefined variable (myVar). Listing 6.2 provides an example of an undefined function (myFun()).

Listing 6.1:   An Undefined Variable (novar.htm)

```
<html>
<head>
<title>Variable Not Defined</title>
</head>
<body>
<script language="JavaScript">
 document.writeln(myVar+1)
</script>
</body>
</html>
```

When Internet Explorer encounters an error, it may, depending on how it is configured, display an error icon in the lower-left of the status bar, as shown in Figure 6.1. Double-click the icon to see the corresponding error message(s).

FIGURE 6.1:

Internet Explorer identifies an error with the error icon shown in the lower left part of the status bar.

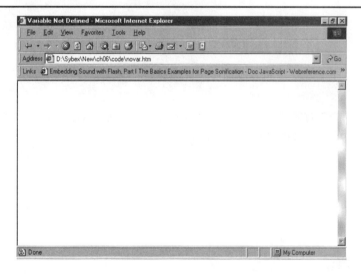

Figure 6.2 shows the error message that is generated by Internet Explorer as the result of running novar.htm. The message is helpful in identifying the cause of the error. Figure 6.3 shows the error message that it generates for nofun.htm. This message is misleading at best.

Internet Explorer identifies
an undefined variable.

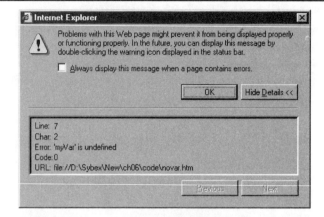

The error message
displayed by Internet
Explorer when it encoun-
ters an undefined function

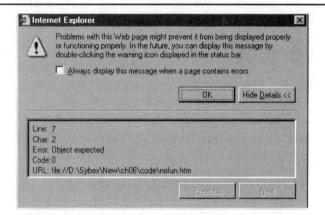

Navigator 6.1 does not indicate that an error has occurred when you open Listing 6.1. You
need to open the JavaScript console to see the error shown in Figure 6.4. You can open the
JavaScript console by selecting Tasks ➢ Tools and then selecting JavaScript Console.
Figure 6.5 shows the error message that is displayed when you run Listing 6.1 in Navigator. I
generally find Navigator's error messages and JavaScript Console easier to work with. However, when it comes to more complex bugs, Microsoft's Script Debugger is more powerful.

FIGURE 6.4:

Navigator identifies the undefined variable in the JavaScript console window.

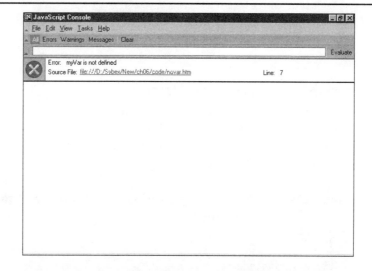

FIGURE 6.5:

Navigator correctly identifies the undefined function reference.

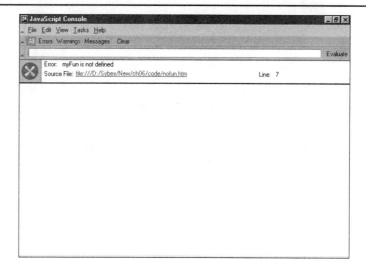

Listing 6.2:   An Undefined Function (nofun.htm)

```html
<html>
<head>
<title>Function Not Defined</title>
</head>
<body>
<script language="JavaScript">
```

```
    document.writeln(myFun())
  </script>
  </body>
  </html>
```

Variable and Function Names

Another source of syntax errors comes from incorrectly referencing variables and functions. Remember that JavaScript is case sensitive. Listings 6.3 and 6.4 provide examples of syntax errors that occur when you reference a variable (S) or function (myfunction()) with the right name but the wrong case.

Listing 6.3.   **Referencing a Variable with a Name of the Wrong Case (varcase.htm)**

```
<html>
<head>
<title>Variable case</title>
</head>
<body>
<script language="JavaScript">
 var s = "Text"
 document.writeln(S)
</script>
</body>
</html>
```

Listing 6.4.   **Referencing a Function with a Name of the Wrong Case (funcase.htm)**

```
<html>
<head>
<title>Function case</title>
<script language="JavaScript">
function myFunction() {
 document.write("Text")
}
</script>
</head>
<body>
<script language="JavaScript">
myfunction()
</script>
</body>
</html>
```

Statement Case

Statement names (if, for, switch, etc.) are also case sensitive. If you are a Visual Basic programmer, you may see a lot of syntax errors related to using statement names of the wrong case. Listing 6.5 provides an example of a for statement that is mistakenly capitalized.

Listing 6.5:   Capitalized for Statement (for.htm)

```
<html>
<head>
<title>Statement case</title>
</head>
<body>
<script language="JavaScript">
For(var i=0; i<5; ++i)
  document.writeln(i+"<br>")
</script>
</body>
</html>
```

Parentheses and Braces

Missing or mismatched parentheses and braces are always a problem—even more so because browsers often report them as errors of a different kind. It's a good idea to use a text editor with syntax-highlighting or brace-matching functions so that you can more easily catch these types of errors. Listing 6.6 provides an example of a missing brace in a function definition.

Listing 6.6:   A Missing Right Brace (braces.htm)

```
<html>
<head>
<title>Mismatched Braces</title>
<script language="JavaScript">
function writeHeading(s, n) {
  if(s != "") {
    document.writeln("<h"+n+">"+s+"</h"+n+">")
}
</script>
</head>
<body>
<script language="JavaScript">
 writeHeading("This is a level 1 heading.", 1)
</script>
</body>
</html>
```

Single and Double Quotes

Another source of syntax errors comes from the use of single and double quotes. Failure to close a string with a matching quote character can lead to subsequent code being treated as part of the string.

Another type of syntax error occurs when you nest quotes of the same kind within a string. Listing 6.7 provides an example. To avoid this type of error, nest single quotes within double quotes, and vice versa, as shown in Listing 6.8.

Listing 6.7·   **A Quoting Error (quotes.htm)**

```
<html>
<head>
<title>Quotes</title>
</head>
<body>
<script language="JavaScript">
 document.writeln("<h1 align="center">This is a centered heading</h1>")
</script>
</body>
</html>
```

Listing 6.8:   **A Fix for the Quoting Error (quotes.htm)**

```
<html>
<head>
<title>Quotes</title>
</head>
<body>
<script language="JavaScript">
 document.writeln("<h1 align='center'>This is a centered heading</h1>")
</script>
</body>
</html>
```

Coding Errors

Coding errors consist of errors that use correct syntax but make mistakes in language usage. Coding errors are generally more difficult to find than syntax errors because they may not always immediately manifest themselves in a script's execution. Examples of errors are provided in the following sections.

Comparisons

A very common coding error occurs when you use the assignment operator (=) instead of the comparison operator (==) in an if statement. Listing 6.9 provides an example. The script runs to completion but displays the wrong result, as shown in Figure 6.6.

Listing 6.9:   Using an Assignment Operator Instead of a Comparison Operator (comparisons.htm)

```
<html>
<head>
<title>Comparisons</title>
</head>
<body>
<script language="JavaScript">
var i = 0
if(i = 0) document.write("i is 0")
else document.write("i is not 0")
</script>
</body>
</html>
```

FIGURE 6.6:

The script displays the wrong result.

Variable Scopes

A variable may be defined in a global scope, as an argument to a function or method, as a local variable of a function or method, or as a property of an object. If you redefine a variable in a more-specific scope, it will mask a variable of the same name that is defined in a more general scope. This can often lead to hard-to-find errors. Listing 6.10 provides an example of a scoping error. Figure 6.7 shows the output it generates.

Listing 6.10:   The *s* Variable Defined in Different Scopes (scopes.htm)

```
<html>
<head>
<title>Scopes</title>
<script language="JavaScript">
var s = 1
function myFunction(s) {
 var s = 3
 document.write(s)
}
</script>
</head>
<body>
<script language="JavaScript">
myFunction(2)
document.write("<br>"+s)
</script>
</body>
</html>
```

FIGURE 6.7:

The output generated by
scopes.htm

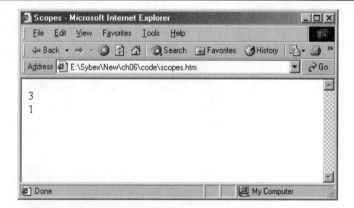

Loops and Loop Indices

A common kind of coding error happens when we mix up the loop indices of nested loops. I tend to use i as my loop index and j for a first-level nested loop. However, I sometimes refer to the wrong loop index (i instead of j) in my nested for loop. Listing 6.11 provides an example that results in an infinitely executing loop.

Listing 6.11:   Mixing Up Loop Indices (loops.htm)

```
<html>
<head>
<title>Loops</title>
</head>
<body>
<script language="JavaScript">
for(var i=0; i<5; ++i) {
  for(var j=0; j<3; ++i) {
    document.write(i+j+"<br>")
  }
}
</script>
</body>
</html>
```

Array Errors

JavaScript arrays are indexed from 0 to the length of the array minus one. It's a common error to refer to the element at the index of the array's length. Of course, this element is undefined. Listing 6.12 provides an example of this kind of error.

Listing 6.12:   Accessing an Undefined Element of an Array (arrays.htm)

```
<html>
<head>
<title>Arrays</title>
</head>
<body>
<script language="JavaScript">
var a = new Array("A", "B", "C")
for(var i=0; i<=a.length; ++i) {
  document.writeln(a[i]+"<br>")
}
</script>
</body>
</html>
```

Conversions

One nice feature of JavaScript is that it automatically converts between one type and another. For example, numbers are automatically converted to strings when appended to the string. However, strings are not always converted to numbers. Listing 6.13 provides an example of a coding error that results when you rely on JavaScript's type conversion. Figure 6.8 shows the output it generates.

Listing 6.13:   **A Type Conversion Gone Bad (conversions.htm)**

```html
<html>
<head>
<title>Conversions</title>
</head>
<body>
<script language="JavaScript">
var version = navigator.appVersion
if(version > 3) document.write("Browser version is greater than 3.")
else document.write("Browser version is 3 or less.")
</script>
</body>
</html>
```

FIGURE 6.8:

The output generated by conversions.htm

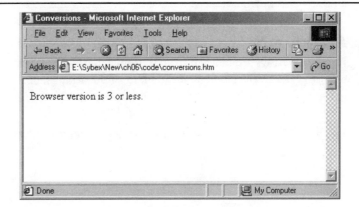

The + Operator

The + operator is used for both numeric addition and string concatenation. When using a mix of numeric and string operands it is sometimes hard to tell which operator will be used. The rule of thumb is that is when one operand is a string, the concatenation operator will be used. Listing 6.14 provides an example of several uses of the + operator. Can you predict what output will be displayed? Refer to Figure 6.9.

Listing 6.14:   **Sample Expressions Using the + Operator (plus.htm)**

```html
<html>
<head>
<title>Plus</title>
</head>
<body>
```

```
<script language="JavaScript">
var x = 0
var y = 3
var s = "1"
document.writeln(x + s + "<br>")
document.writeln(x + y + s + "<br>")
document.writeln(s + x + y + "<br>")
</script>
</body>
</html>
```

FIGURE 6.9:

The output generated by plus.htm

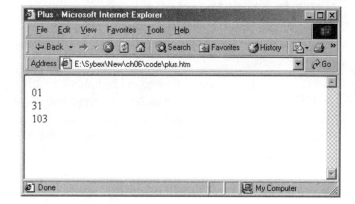

Bad Design

Syntax and coding errors are easy to fix in comparison to design errors. If you design your scripts poorly, you may have to rewrite a significant portion of them in order to make them work right. The following sections cover different types of errors that occur at the design level and show you how to avoid these errors.

Bad Structure

When writing very small prototype scripts, it's often convenient to write HTML and JavaScript off the top of your head. Your scripts may contain several lines of JavaScript code that are embedded in HTML and are not organized into functions or objects.

This approach to designing your scripts is a recipe for disaster when writing more complicated scripts. They fail to take advantage of JavaScript's object-oriented nature and tend to be more difficult to debug and maintain.

When designing your scripts, you should try to abide by the following guidelines. Failure to do so can result in scripts that are structurally unsound.

- Minimize the use of global variables.

- Organize related code into functions.

- Identify the basic types of objects that are used in your scripts and write them as JavaScript object types.

- Provide properties and methods for accessing objects of these types.

- Organize the object types into separate .js files.

The value of the above approach increases with the size and complexity of your web applications.

Failure to Validate Data

When writing your scripts, it's important to validate data received from users. Failure to do so can lead to errors that can cause your scripts to fail unexpectedly, or worse, corrupt your server-side databases.

Some data, such as credit card numbers and phone numbers, can be more easily validated than other types of data, such as names and street addresses. However, you can use the user as part of the validation process. For example, if a user is purchasing a product from your website, it's in the user's best interest to make sure that it goes to the right person at the right address. However, the user might not care if someone else's credit card gets charged.

In general, you should validate any data input that has even one of the following characteristics:

- Is part of a calculation

- Identifies the user

- Is essential to your application's processing

The best time to validate data is when it is first received by a form's onsubmit or onclick event handler.

 Data that is validated via JavaScript may need to be revalidated on the server. That's because it's possible for malicious users to circumvent your scripts and send data directly to your server-side scripts.

Unavailable Resources

Sometimes a web application may require that a resource (such as an image, an applet, or an ActiveX control) be available in order to perform its processing. Since these objects may be delayed or lost in the transmission between your server and the user's browser, it is important to check for their availability before attempting to access them. Listing 6.15 provides an example of a script that generates an error when it attempts to access an unavailable image.

This type of an error can be avoided by checking to make sure that the image has been loaded, as shown in Listing 6.16.

Listing 6.15:   An Image Loading Error (resources.htm)

```
<html>
<head>
<title>Resource Unavailability</title>
<script language="JavaScript">
function displayImageProperties() {
 alert(document.images[2].x)
}
</script>
</head>
<body onload="displayImageProperties()">
<img src="none.jpg">
<img src="none.jpg">
<img src="none.jpg">
</body>
</html>
```

Listing 6.16:   Fixing the Loading Error (resourcefix.htm)

```
<html>
<head>
<title>Resource Availability Fix</title>
<script language="JavaScript">
function displayImageProperties() {
 if(document.images.length >= 2) {
  for(var i=0; i<=2; ++i) {
   if(!document.images[i].complete) break
   if(i==2) alert(document.images[2].x)
  }
 }
}
</script>
</head>
<body onload="displayImageProperties()">
<img src="none.jpg">
<img src="none.jpg">
<img src="none.jpg">
</body>
</html>
```

Unexpected Events

Error-free scripts must be able to respond to events that occur as the result of user actions. For example, a user may open up a frame in a separate, new window. A user may close a window that was previously opened by a script. There are two complementary ways to handle these types of events: you can write event handlers that detect the occurrence of the event (e.g., using a window's unload event handler) and you can check for the effect of the event (e.g., window not available) before performing any processing that is affected by the event.

Browser Incompatibilities

Incompatibilities between browsers are a major source of errors for JavaScript programmers. Not only do your scripts have to deal with incompatibilities between Internet Explorer and Navigator, but they also have to address incompatibilities between different versions of the same browser. The most notorious incompatibility is between Navigator 6 and Navigator 4, where Navigator 6 abandons some of the objects of the old Navigator object model. The introduction of Navigator 6 caused many scripts to be rewritten.

Another example of a Netscape incompatibility is the == operator. In JavaScript 1.1, the expression "5" == 5 evaluates to true. In JavaScript 1.2, it evaluates to false. In JavaScript 1.3, it evaluates to true again. In JavaScript 1.3, Netscape introduced the === operator to mean strict equality (i.e., no conversion).

A programmer must be aware of these incompatibilities in order to avoid them. The best way to do this is to test your scripts with multiple browser versions and learn from the errors that you encounter.

Browser Bugs

Just when you've finally worked out all the bugs in your scripts, Microsoft or Netscape will release a beta version of their latest browser that will contain new bugs. What's worse, it's not always obvious whether the bugs are in the browser or your script. Its very frustrating to try to find and eliminate a bug that has nothing to do with your script. Anyway, when a user encounters the bug while surfing your website, he or she will just assume that it came from your web pages.

The best solution to this type of problem is to stay on top of the bug lists that are maintained by Microsoft and Netscape. The good news is that most bugs are fixed in the next browser release. The bad news is that some of your users won't upgrade—at least not for a while. Of course, you can always use JavaScript to detect the browser version and inform your users that they are running a defective browser.

Resolving Errors

How does one go about locating and resolving errors in one's scripts? The answer is testing, testing, and more testing. You must thoroughly exercise your script's logic on a variety of browsers, browser versions, and operating systems. For example, the same version of Internet Explorer may behave differently depending on whether it is running on Windows or MacOS. The only way to find these types of errors is to run your scripts on all of the platforms that you intend to support.

NOTE   Peer review may be used in addition to testing to identify design-level problems in scripts and to ensure that the scripts of different programmers adhere to a common set of coding standards.

Once you've located an anomaly that appears to be a bug, there are two approaches to locating and resolving the bug: inserting debugging code in your scripts and running your scripts in a script debugger. In some cases, you may have to do both, because there might not be a script debugger that runs on the platform in which you are encountering errors.

When you insert debugging code into your scripts you typically insert statements that provide feedback as to whether your script is executing a particular branch of code and what the values of certain variables are when your script is in that branch. You can use the `alert()` method of the `window` object to generate this output. However, it can be pretty annoying to have to close a lot of alert dialog boxes, particularly when they are generated from within a loop.

Another technique is to use the `defaultStatus` property of the `window` object to display output. This works for small amounts of data that change slowly, but it is impractical for displaying a lot of data or data that changes rapidly.

The `try-catch` statement may be used to locate errors that cause exceptions. By carefully inserting `try-catch` statements in your code you may be able to hone in on an elusive syntax or runtime error. The `try-catch` statement is also a way to ensure that any unknown errors that remain in your code (after it has been published) are handled gracefully when they are encountered by users. For example, a `catch` statement may be used to display a nicely formatted message that notifies the user that a problem has been detected and to request that the user inform you of the problem (so you can fix it).

Using the Microsoft Script Debugger

There are times when it's very difficult to determine the reason for a particular problem using code analysis and simple debugging. That's when debuggers are invaluable. The

Microsoft Script Debugger is a free debugger that comes with later versions of Windows (Windows 2000, Windows Me, and Windows XP) and is a great tool for resolving bugs. It is very flexible and provides a number of ways in which it can be used. For example, you can use it to debug both client- and server-side scripts in JScript, Java, and VBScript.

The script debugger enables you to monitor a script's execution and to observe and interact with the script in a number of ways:

- View the script's code
- View and modify the values of variables
- Start and stop the script's execution
- Alter the course of the script's execution

These capabilities enable you to determine where your script is working correctly, where it is not, and why it is not.

NOTE   The Microsoft Script Debugger is available for download from Microsoft's website. It can be found at http://msdn.microsoft.com/scripting/.

You can check to see if the script debugger is installed by clicking on the View menu in Internet Explorer. Refer to Figure 6.10. If it is installed, you will see a menu item named Script Debugger. If the menu item is not shown, check your browser configuration options to make sure that it hasn't been disabled, as shown in Figure 6.11.

FIGURE 6.10:

Checking to see if the script debugger is installed

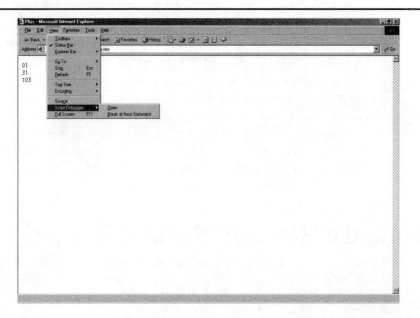

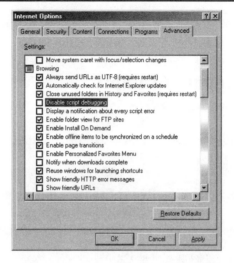

> **NOTE** There are two versions of the script debugger: a simple version (which we'll cover here) and a more advanced version that comes with Personal Web Server and Microsoft's programming tools.

Running the Debugger

You can start the debugger in four different ways depending on your needs:

From Internet Explorer   Simply select Script Debugger from the View menu. This is the most common way to start the debugger when debugging client-side scripts.

As a Windows program   Run Script Debugger by selecting Start ➤ Programs ➤ Script Debugger. This is the approach taken to debug server-side scripts.

Via the debugger statement   If you place the debugger statement within a script, the script's execution will stop and the debugger will run and load the script. Remember to take it out before you publish your script!

As the result of a syntax or runtime error   Internet Explorer presents you with the option to run the debugger when it encounters an error during a script's execution. This is a very common way to deal with syntax and runtime errors.

Depending on how the debugger was invoked, it may or may not load a document when it starts up. If the debugger does not have the document you want loaded, you can open the document using the debugger's File menu.

TIP   When debugging client-side scripts, your best option is to start the debugger from Internet Explorer.

A Debugging Example

The best way to get a feel for how the debugger works is to use it to debug a buggy script. Listing 6.17 provides an example of a buggy script. The purpose of the script is to display a user-specified message in a user-specified number of HTML headings, with the headings descending in size, h1, h2, h3, etc.

Listing 6.17:   The Buggy Example (bugsy.htm)

```html
<html>
<head>
<title>Debugging Example</title>
<script language="JavaScript">
function setMessage() {
 var msg =
  window.prompt("What message do you want to display?", "My message")
 var n = window.prompt("How many do you want to display?", "4")
 return n
}
function createHTMLString(n) {
 var s = "<"+"n"+">"+msg+"</"+n+">"
 return s
}
function displayOutput(n) {
 var s
 for(i = 0; i<n; ++i) {
  s += createHTMLString(i)
  document.write(s)
 }
}
</script>
</head>
<body>
<script language="JavaScript">
var n = setMessage()
displayOutput(n)
</script>
</body>
</html>
```

Once you have the debugger installed and enabled, open `bugsy.htm` in Internet Explorer. You will be asked to enter a message that will be displayed in your document and the number of messages to display. Refer to Figures 6.12 and 6.13.

FIGURE 6.12:

Enter the message to be displayed.

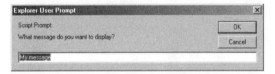

FIGURE 6.13:

Enter the number of messages to be displayed.

Once you enter these values, you will be confronted with the error dialog shown in Figure 6.14. Click Yes to enter the debugger.

FIGURE 6.14:

Internet Explorer informs you of an error and provides you with the option of starting the debugger.

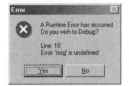

The debugger will display the window shown in Figure 6.15. Line 11 of the script is highlighted in yellow, indicating this is the line for which `msg` is not defined. If you look in the `setMessage()` method, you can see that `msg` is defined as a local variable. You'll need to update `bugsy.htm` so that `msg` is defined as a global variable:

```
var msg
function setMessage() {
 msg = window.prompt("What message do you want to display?", "My message")
 var n = window.prompt("How many do you want to display?", "4")
 return n
}
```

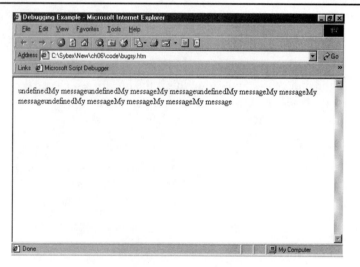

Close the debugger, make the change, and then reopen bugsy.htm. This time it displays
the weird output shown in Figure 6.16. Select View ➢ Script Debugger ➢ Break at Next
Statement from the Internet Explorer menu bar and then reload the document. The debugger will be opened as shown in Figure 6.17.

FIGURE 6.17:

The debugger is reopened.

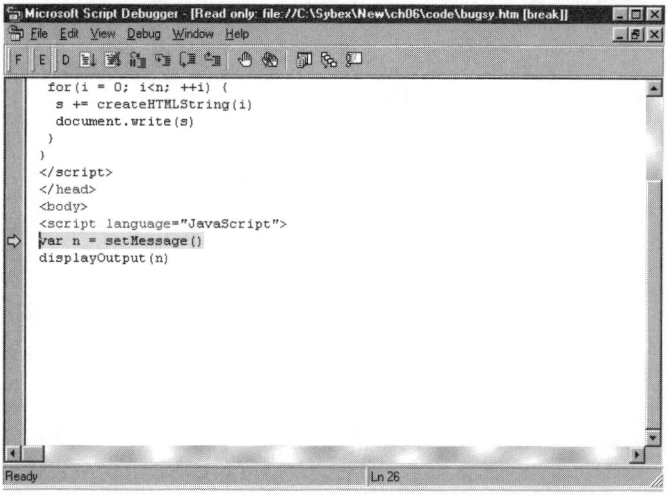

Since there is no syntax error to highlight, the debugger will highlight line 26, which is the first JavaScript statement that it executes. The line number is displayed in the lower-right debugger status bar.

Select the `displayOutput(n)` line by double-clicking it. Then select Toggle Breakpoint from the Debug menu. A red circle appears next to the line as shown in Figure 6.18. The circle indicates that a breakpoint has been set. A breakpoint is a place in the script where the script will stop execution and the debugger will run.

FIGURE 6.18:

The red circle identifies a breakpoint.

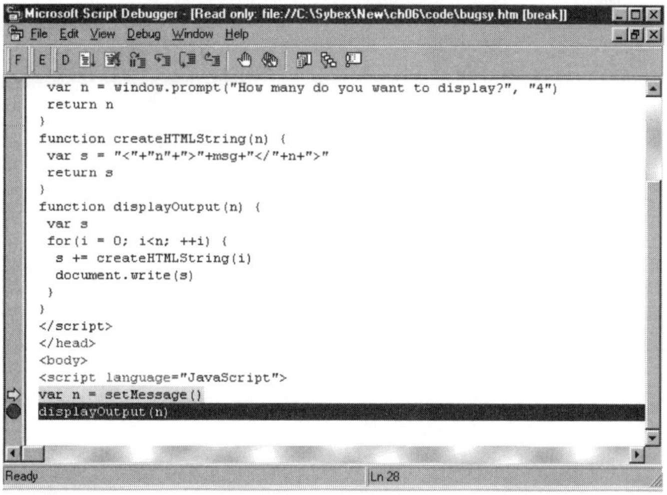

Now select Run from the debugger menu and go back to Internet Explorer to respond to the prompts shown in Figures 6.12 and 6.13. Once you've entered the message and number of messages, switch back to the debugger. It will display the script as shown in Figure 6.19. The yellow arrow over the breakpoint indicates that the debugger has stopped at the breakpoint.

FIGURE 6.19:

The breakpoint has been reached.

```
   var n = window.prompt("How many do you want to display?", "4")
   return n
   }
function createHTMLString(n) {
   var s = "<"+"n"+">"+msg+"</"+n+">"
   return s
   }
function displayOutput(n) {
   var s
   for(i = 0; i<n; ++i) {
     s += createHTMLString(i)
     document.write(s)
   }
}
</script>
</head>
<body>
<script language="JavaScript">
var n = setMessage()
displayOutput(n)
```

Let's find out what the values are for n and msg. Select Command Window from the View menu. The window shown in Figure 6.20 is displayed.

FIGURE 6.20:

The Command Window is opened.

You can enter JavaScript expressions in this window and their values will be displayed. Enter n and the value of n is displayed. Enter msg and you'll see that it is set to the message you entered. Refer to Figure 6.21.

FIGURE 6.21:

The values of n and msg are displayed.

Close the Command Window and then select Step Into from the Debug menu. The debugger displays the output shown in Figure 6.22.

FIGURE 6.22:

The Step Into command steps into a function.

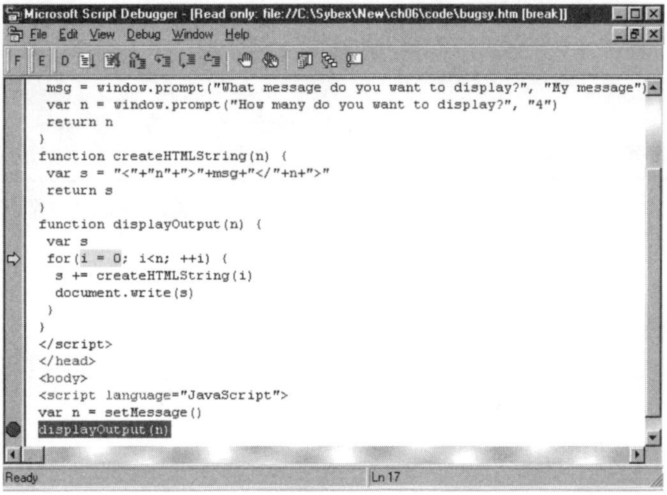

```
msg = window.prompt("What message do you want to display?", "My message")
var n = window.prompt("How many do you want to display?", "4")
return n
}
function createHTMLString(n) {
var s = "<"+"n"+">"+msg+"</"+n+">"
return s
}
function displayOutput(n) {
var s
for(i = 0; i<n; ++i) {
s += createHTMLString(i)
document.write(s)
}
}
</script>
</head>
<body>
<script language="JavaScript">
var n = setMessage()
displayOutput(n)
```

The Step Into command tells the debugger to step into a function, method, or statement block and then stop at the first statement within the function, method, or block. The Step Over command tells the debugger to stop after the function, method, or block has been executed. The Step Out command tells the debugger to stop after it has returned from a function or method.

Select Step Into two more times to step into the for statement, as shown in Figure 6.23. Select Step Over to get to the line shown in Figure 6.24.

FIGURE 6.23:

Stepping into the for statement

FIGURE 6.24:

Stepping over a statement

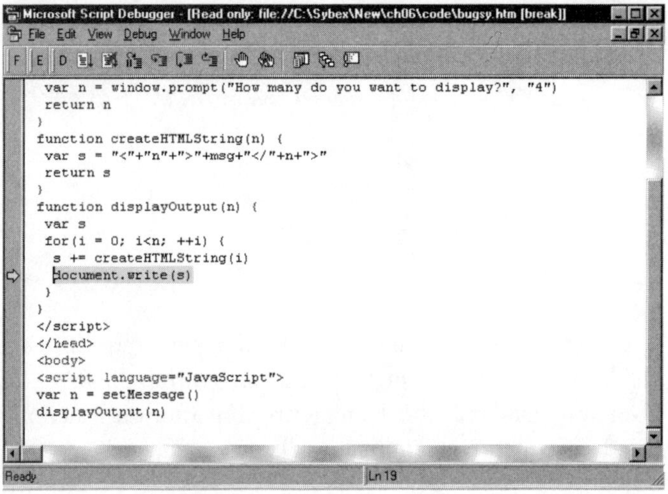

Now, let's see what the value of s is. Open the command window and enter s, as shown in Figure 6.25. We can see that the value of s is messed up. This is our clue to identifying and fixing the bugs.

FIGURE 6.25:

Viewing the value of s

By the fact that s begins with undefined we can see that we need to initialize it to a blank string. Make the following fix:

```
function displayOutput(n) {
  var s = ""
  for(i = 0; i<n; ++i) {
    s += createHTMLString(i)
    document.write(s)
  }
}
```

The other thing that we can see is that the tags around msg are wrong—there is no such thing as an <hn> tag. Edit createHTMLString() as follows:

```
function createHTMLString(n) {
  var s = "<h"+n+">"+msg+"</h"+n+">"
  return s
}
```

Now stop the debugger, and rerun the script in Internet Explorer. You should see the output shown in Figure 6.26. We've made progress but we're still not finished. Select View ➤ Script Debugger ➤ Break at Next Statement, and then reload the document. The debugger will stop at line 26 again (refer to Figure 6.17). Set a break point for line 20 (document.write(s)) as shown in Figure 6.27. Then select Run from the Debug menu.

FIGURE 6.26:

The output is still incorrect.

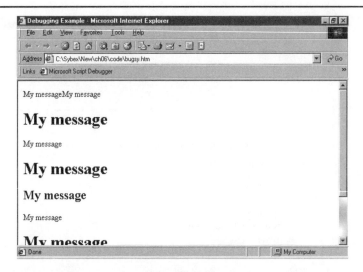

FIGURE 6.27:

Setting a breakpoint

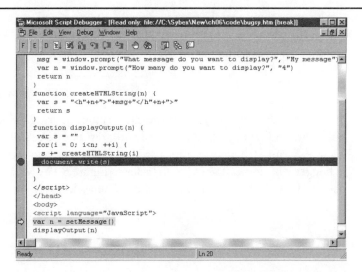

You'll need to go back to Internet Explorer to fill in the prompt dialog boxes. When you've finished, the debugger will display the output shown in Figure 6.28. Open the Command Window and enter s, as shown in Figure 6.29. The loop statement should begin with an index of 1, not 0. Fix it as follows:

```
function displayOutput(n) {
 var s
 for(i = 1; i<=n; ++i) {
```

```
    s += createHTMLString(i)
   document.write(s)
    }
  }
```

Back in the debugger

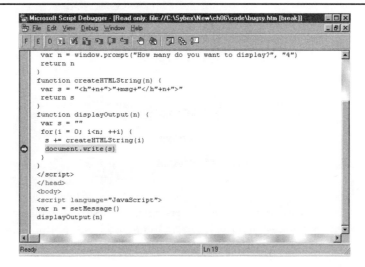

FIGURE 6.29:

The value of s

When you load the file again in Internet Explorer, you'll see that it still has problems. Refer to Figure 6.30.

FIGURE 6.30:

Getting closer

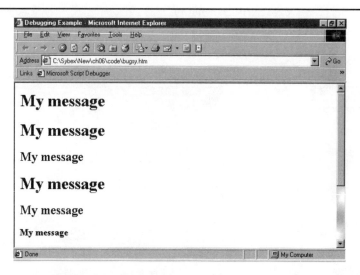

Select View ➤ Script Debugger ➤ Break at Next Statement, and then reload the document. Set a breakpoint as shown in Figure 6.27. Select Run from the debug window and then fill in the prompt dialog boxes. Use the Command Window to display the value of s (refer to Figure 6.31).

FIGURE 6.31:

So far, so good.

Select Run from the Debug window to advance to the next loop iteration. Then display the new value of s in the Command Window (refer to Figure 6.32).

FIGURE 6.32:

We have a clue.

We've found the problem: the `document.write(s)` statement should be outside of the `for` statement. Fix it as follows:

```
function displayOutput(n) {
  var s
  for(i = 1; i<=n; ++i) {
   s += createHTMLString(i)
  }
  document.write(s)
}
```

When you load the file again, you'll notice that it works as intended, as shown in Figure 6.33.

FIGURE 6.33:

It worked!

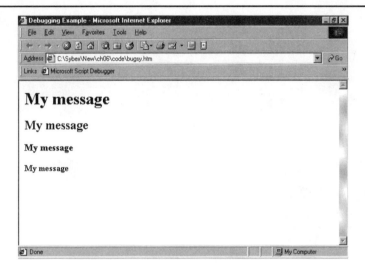

Summary

In this chapter, you learned about the types of errors that are found in JavaScript scripts. You learned how to find errors in your scripts and how to avoid them in the first place. You also learned how to use the Navigator JavaScript Console and the Microsoft Script Debugger. In the next chapter, you'll learn how to use JavaScript to work with frames and windows.

PART II

Programming the Document Object Model

CHAPTER **7**

Creating Frames and Windows

- Opening and closing windows

- Simple communication windows—messages, prompts, and status bars

- Using the window "synonyms"

- Frames and frame sets

- Generating document contents

- Browser identification

- Working with colors

This chapter shows you how to use five important JavaScript objects: the window, frame, document, navigator, and screen objects. It describes how to use them to create and manage multiple frames and windows in your web pages. It also shows how to obtain version information about the browsers that execute your scripts. When you have finished this chapter, you'll be able to use frames and windows to effectively organize your web pages.

The *window* Object

The window object is basic to all browser scripts. Like the navigator object, the window object is a top-level object that is automatically defined by your browser. A separate window object is defined for each window that is opened. If you use Netscape Navigator, these windows are listed under the Window menu item from the Communicator pull-down menu, as shown in Figure 7.1. Internet Explorer does not have a similar capability.

FIGURE 7.1:

Your browser's Window pull-down menu lists all of the windows that are currently opened.

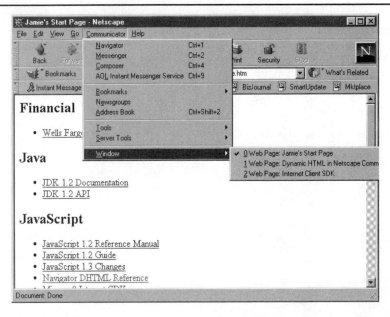

The window object is so important to writing browser scripts that the current window object is assumed by default in many cases and may be omitted. For example, when you use the following statement in a script, JavaScript assumes that you are referring to the current window object:

```
document.write("Write this text to the current window.")
```

JavaScript then executes the following statement:

```
window.document.write("Write this text to the current window.")
```

In addition, the `window` object has several *synonyms* that let you refer to the current `window` object being displayed by your browser, as well as to other related `window` objects. These synonyms are implemented as properties of the `window` object. You'll learn about these synonyms in the section, "Using the Window Synonyms," later in this chapter.

Tables 7.1 and 7.2 summarize the properties and methods of the `window` object that both Navigator and Internet Explorer support. These properties and methods are described in the following sections. Appendix D, "DOM 0 Object Reference," identifies properties and methods that are unique to either Navigator or Internet Explorer.

TABLE 7.1: Properties of the *window* Object

Property	Description
closed	Identifies whether the window is closed.
defaultStatus	Specifies the default status message that appears on the status bar on the bottom of the browser window.
document	An object that refers to the current document being displayed in a window.
frames	An array that consists of all `frame` objects contained in a `window` object.
history	Refers to the window's `history` object, which contains a list of URLs last loaded into the window.
length	Identifies the number of frames contained in a `window`.
location	An object that identifies the URL associated with a `window` object.
name	Identifies the name of the window.
offscreenBuffering	Boolean value that specifies whether offscreen buffering of window information should be used. *Offscreen buffering* is used to load all of a window's elements before displaying the window.
opener	Identifies the `window` object that caused a window to be created and opened.
parent	A synonym that identifies the window containing a particular window.
self	A synonym that identifies the current window being referenced.
status	Specifies a temporary message that appears on the status bar on the bottom of the browser window.
top	A synonym that refers to the topmost browser window in a series of nested windows.
window	A synonym that identifies the current window being referenced.

TABLE 7.2: Methods of the *window* Object

Method	Description
alert(*text*)	Displays an alert dialog box.
blur()	Removes focus from a window.
clearInterval(*interval*)	Clears a previously set interval timer.
clearTimeout(*timer*)	Clears a previously set timeout.
close()	Closes the specified window.
confirm(*text*)	Displays a confirm dialog box.
focus()	Gives focus to a window.
open(*url*,*name*,*[options]*)	Opens a new window and creates a new window object.
prompt(*text*,*defaultInput*)	Displays a prompt dialog box.
scroll(*x*,*y*)	Scrolls a window to the specific location.
setInterval(*expression, milliseconds*) setInterval(*function, milliseconds, [arguments]*)	Repeatedly evaluates an expression or invokes a function after the elapse of a specified time interval. The *arguments* are a possibly empty comma-separated list of arguments to the function to be invoked. Returns an interval reference that can be cleared by clearInterval().
setTimeout(*expression, milliseconds*) setTimeout(*function, milliseconds, [arguments]*)	Evaluates an expression or invokes a function after a timeout period has elapsed. The *arguments* are possibly an empty comma-separated list of arguments to the function to be invoked. Returns a timer reference that can be cleared by clearTimeout().

Opening and Closing Windows

When you launch your browser, it creates and opens a window to display your startup page. This is the most common way that a window object is created. In most cases, the window that you open during browser startup stays open until you exit your browser. When you open a new web document or a local file with your browser, you usually *replace* the document contained in the opened window, and do not create or open a new window. In Netscape Navigator, new windows are created and opened when you select New ➤ Navigator Window from the File menu. In Microsoft Internet Explorer, you use the New Window menu item to create a new window. When a new window is created, it can be accessed from the browser's Window pull-down menu, as shown in Figure 7.1.

The `open()` and `close()` methods may be used from within JavaScript to open and close browser windows. The `open()` method opens a new web browser window at a specified URL with a given set of options. A newly created object is returned as the result of invoking `open()`. This object is usually assigned to a variable, which is used to keep track of the window. The syntax of the `open()` method is as follows:

```
variable = open(url, name, [options])
```

where *variable* is the name of the variable to which the `window` object is assigned, *url* is the URL of the document to open in the window, *name* is the name to be associated with the window, and *options* can be used to specify different characteristics of the window. The name may be used in the target attribute of a `<form>` tag or an `<a>` tag.

The options, if supplied, consist of a set of comma-separated *option=value* pairs. The options that both Navigator and Internet Explorer support are shown in Table 7.3. Browser-specific options are covered in Appendix D.

TABLE 7.3:   Options of the *open()* Method

Option	Values	Description
toolbar	yes no	The window has a toolbar.
location	yes no	The window displays the location field.
directories	yes no	The window provides directory buttons.
status	yes no	The window has a status bar.
menubar	yes no	The window has a menu bar.
scrollbars	yes no	The window provides scroll bars.
resizable	yes no	The window is resizable.
width	*integer*	The width of the window in pixels.
height	*integer*	The height of the window in pixels.

NOTE: The values 1 and 0 may be used instead of yes and no.

An example of the use of the `open()` method follows:

```
win = open("http://www.sybex.com","sybex")
```

The previous statement opens a new window and loads the Sybex home page, located at www.sybex.com, into the window. The window is given the name *sybex* and is assigned to the `win` variable.

The `close()` method is used to close a window that has been opened. For example, `win.close()` can be used to close the window opened above.

Listings 7.1 and 7.2 provide a colorful example of how the open() and close() methods are used in an example web page. Listing 7.1 creates a web page that announces a New Year's Eve party. Listing 7.2 provides a map. Figure 7.2 shows the party invitation that is generated by Listing 7.1. You can access the file for Listing 7.1, ch07-01.htm, and all the code listings in this chapter on the CD-ROM that accompanies the book.

Listing 7.1:   Opening a New Window (ch07-01.htm)

```
<HTML>
<HEAD>
<TITLE>Party</TITLE>
<SCRIPT LANGUAGE="JavaScript"><!--
function directions() {
 open("ch07-02.htm","map")
}
// --></SCRIPT>
</HEAD>
<BODY>
<H1>New Years Eve Party!</H1>
<P><B>When:</B> December 31, 2003 8pm</P>
<P><B>Where:</B> 613 Beyer Way #504</P>
<P><B>Dress:</B> Casual </P>
<FORM>
<INPUT TYPE="BUTTON" VALUE="Click for directions"
 ONCLICK="directions()">
</FORM>
<P>RSVP by December 28th.
<A HREF="mailto:jamie@jaworski.com">
 <I>jamie@jaworski.com</I></A></P>
</BODY>
</HTML>
```

Listing 7.2:   Closing a Window (ch07-02.htm)

```
<HTML>
<HEAD>
<TITLE>Directions</TITLE>
</HEAD>
<BODY ONLOAD="defaultStatus='It\'s at the big star!'">
<FORM>
<INPUT TYPE="BUTTON" VALUE="Close window"
 ONCLICK="window.close()">
</FORM>
<IMG SRC="map.gif">
</BODY>
</HTML>
```

FIGURE 7.2:

A party invitation
(Listing 7.1)

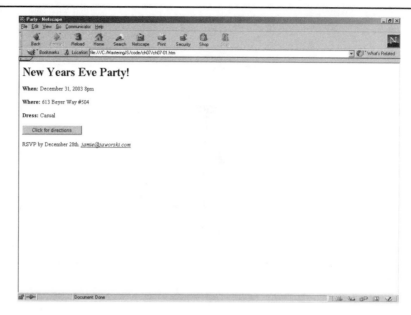

When a user clicks the Click for Directions button shown in Figure 7.2, a new window is created and opened using the document of Listing 7.2. This window is shown in Figure 7.3. (If you select the Window menu item from the Communicator pull-down menu, you can verify that a new window has been created—see Figure 7.4.) Clicking the Close window button closes the second window.

FIGURE 7.3:

Directions to the party
(Listing 7.2)

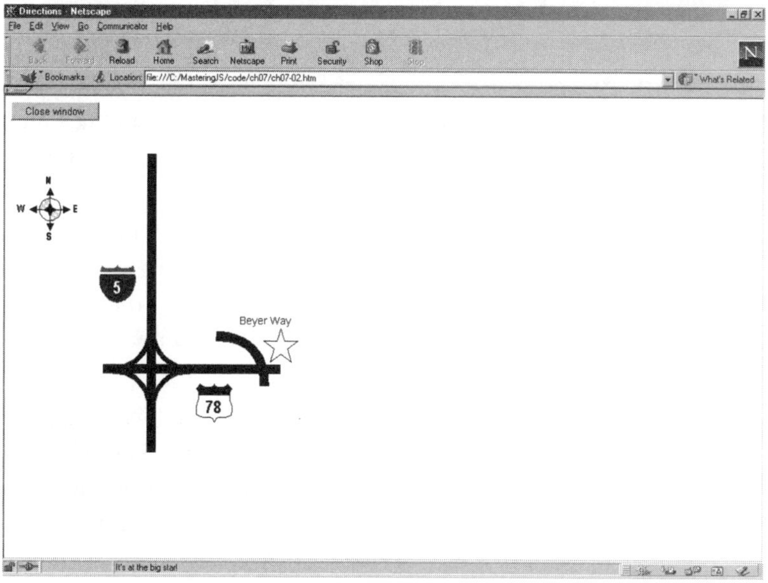

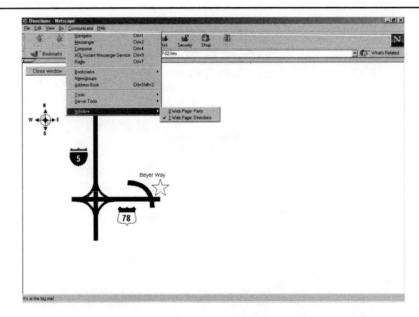

The directions() function of Listing 7.1 uses the open() method to open the file
ch07-02.htm (see Listing 7.2). It assigns the name "map" to the newly created window.

As shown in Listing 7.2, the onClick event handler of the Close window button invokes
the close() method to close and dispose of the second window.

Communicating with the User

Some of the most useful methods provided by the window object are those that support dialog
with the user. These methods are as follows:

- The alert() method displays a dialog box containing a message and an OK button.
  You use the alert() method to provide the user with critical information that must be
  acknowledged, by means of an OK button.

- The confirm() method is similar to the alert() method, except that it produces a dialog box with a message, an OK button, and a Cancel button. The confirm() method
  returns *true* if the user clicks OK, and *false* if the user clicks Cancel. You use the con-
  firm() method to inform the user and ask him to confirm whether he wants to perform
  a particular action.

- The prompt() method displays a message to the user, and prompts the user to type
  information into a text field. It provides the capability to display default text in the text
  field. You use the prompt() method to obtain text input from the user such as a name
  or a URL. The value entered by the user is the return value of the prompt method.

You used these methods in Chapter 4, "Handling Events," and Chapter 5, "Working with Objects."

Listing 7.3 provides an example of the use of each of these three methods. Figure 7.5 shows the initial page displayed by this script. When you open this script in your browser, you can click the buttons provided to see an example of each type of dialog box.

Listing 7.3:   Dialog Box Demo (ch07-03.htm)

```
<HTML>
<HEAD>
<TITLE>Dialog box demo</TITLE>
</HEAD>
<BODY>
<FORM>
<INPUT TYPE="BUTTON" VALUE="Alert"
 ONCLICK="alert('An alert dialog box.')">
<INPUT TYPE="BUTTON" VALUE="Confirm"
 ONCLICK="confirm('A confirm dialog box.')">
<INPUT TYPE="BUTTON" VALUE="Prompt"
 ONCLICK="prompt('A prompt dialog box.','Type something!')">
</FORM>
</BODY>
</HTML>
```

FIGURE 7.5:

Dialog box demo opening display (Listing 7.3)

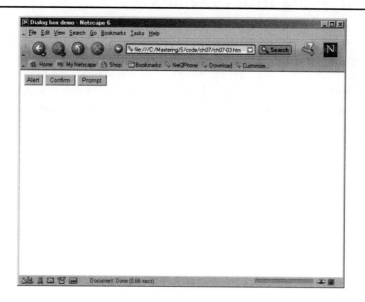

Displaying Status Information

The window object provides two properties that can be used to display status information in the browser's status bar:

- The defaultStatus property specifies a permanent default status message.

- The status property specifies a transient status message that appears as the result of a user action such as moving a mouse to a particular window location.

Use the defaultStatus property to show any messages that you want permanently displayed.

Using the Window Synonyms

As mentioned earlier in the section, "The *window* Object," the window object provides several properties that are used as synonyms to identify the current window object as well as related objects. The window and self properties both refer to the current window being referenced. The parent property is used in multiframe windows, and refers to the window that contains a particular window. The opener property refers to the window from which a particular window was opened. The top property is used with framed windows. It refers to the topmost window containing a particular window.

Working with Timeouts

The setTimeout() and clearTimeout() methods provide a clever way to wait a specified amount of time for a user to perform a particular action and, if the action does not occur within the specified time, perform timeout processing. The setTimeout() method identifies an expression to be evaluated after a specified number of milliseconds; it is this expression that performs the timeout processing. The setTimeout() method returns a value that is used to identify the timeout. It is usually assigned to a variable, as shown in the following example:

```
timVar = setTimeout("timeoutProcessing()",10000)
```

In the previous statement, the setTimeout() method is invoked to perform the timeout processing specified by the timeoutProcessing() function after 10,000 milliseconds (10 seconds) have elapsed. The setTimeout() method returns a value that identifies the timeout. This value is assigned to the timVar variable.

The clearTimeout() method is used to cancel a timeout before it occurs and prevent the timeout processing from being performed. It takes the value of the timeout as an argument. For example, to clear the timeout created above, use the following statement:

```
clearTimeout(timVar)
```

The previous statement clears the timeout identified by `timVar`. When called before the timeout period has occurred, this prevents the `timeoutProcessing()` function from being invoked.

Listing 7.4 provides a more concrete example of performing timeout processing. It generates the web page shown in Figure 7.6, and sets a 10-second timeout for the user to click on the provided button. If the user does not click on the button within 10 seconds, the alert dialog box shown in Figure 7.7 is displayed. If the user does click on the button within 10 seconds, the button's `onClick` event handler clears the timeout and congratulates the user.

Listing 7.4:   A Timeout Processing Example (ch07-04.htm)

```
<HTML>
<HEAD>
<TITLE>Timeout Program</TITLE>
<SCRIPT LANGUAGE="JavaScript"><!--
function setTimer() {
 timer=setTimeout("alert('Too slow!')",10000)
}
function clearTimer() {
 clearTimeout(timer)
 alert("Congratulations!")
}
// --></SCRIPT>
</HEAD>
<BODY>
<SCRIPT LANGUAGE="JavaScript"><!--
setTimer()
// --></SCRIPT>
<FORM>
<INPUT TYPE="BUTTON" VALUE="Click here within ten seconds."
 ONCLICK="clearTimer()">
</FORM>
</BODY>
</HTML>
```

FIGURE 7.6:

Opening window for time-out processing example (Listing 7.4)

FIGURE 7.7:

This is what happens when a timeout occurs (Listing 7.4).

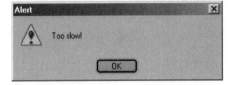

Working with Intervals

The setInterval() and clearInterval() methods were introduced in JavaScript 1.2. These methods are used to repeatedly execute a function or expression every so many milliseconds. This capability is very useful in performing animation, as you'll learn in Chapter 15, "Developing Animations and Slide Shows." The setInterval() method is similar to setTimeout(). The difference is that setTimeout() executes a function or expression once, whereas setInterval() executes it repeatedly. Listing 7.5 provides an example of using setInterval(). It changes the document background color every three seconds. Figure 7.8 provides a snapshot of its output.

Listing 7.5:   Using setInterval () to Repeatedly Change the Document Background Color (ch07-05.htm)

```html
<HTML>
<HEAD>

<TITLE>Using setInterval()</TITLE>
<SCRIPT LANGUAGE="JavaScript1.2"><!--
colors = new Array("red","orange","green","blue","brown","purple",
  "gray","white")
colorIndex = 0
function changeColor() {
 document.bgColor = colors[colorIndex]
 colorIndex = (colorIndex + 1) % colors.length
}
function startColorChange() {
 setInterval("changeColor()",3000)
}
window.onload = startColorChange
// --></SCRIPT>
</HEAD>
<BODY BGCOLOR="white">
<H1>Changing Background Colors</H1>
<P>The <CODE>setInterval()</CODE> method is used to repeatedly change the
document background color every three seconds.</P>
</BODY>
</HTML>
```

FIGURE 7.8:

The document background color changes every three seconds (Listing 7.5).

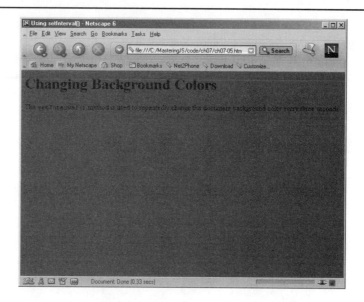

The *frame* Object

Frames are an HTML innovation developed by Netscape. They enable you to partition a window into independent display areas and organize and control the information displayed in these areas in powerful ways. You've already been exposed to frames in Chapter 4. Their use is summarized in this section in preparation for introducing the *frame* object.

An HTML file can contain either a document body or a *frame set*. You already know what a document body is, but what is a frame set? Frame sets are used to organize frames. If a file contains a document body, it uses the <body> tags to specify the document's contents. If a file contains a frame set, it uses the <frameset> tags instead of the <body> tags to enclose one or more <frame> tags, which are used to identify the individual frames contained in the frame set. Frame sets can also be nested within each other. The <frame> tags identify other HTML files to be loaded in the frame. These files can contain a document body or another (nested) frame set.

The <frameset> tag supports the ROWS and COLS attributes. These attributes are used to lay out the frames contained in the frame set. By default, they specify the dimensions of the frame set, in pixels.

Frame objects are automatically created by your browser, and they enable your scripts to control how frames are used. These frame objects allow you to load new documents into frames, based on user-generated or other events. For example, a common use of frames is to use one frame as a clickable table of contents, and use another frame to display the sections the user has selected.

The properties and methods of the frame object are the same as the window object with one exception—the frame object does not support the close() method. Navigator and Internet Explorer actually implement frame objects as window objects. That's because frame objects are also windows in the sense that a frame can contain a document body or a frame set. This important characteristic of frames allows multiple nested frame sets to be displayed in a single browser window.

Tic-Tac-Toe

In order to learn how to use frames and have some fun at the same time, you will use frames in this section to create a tic-tac-toe game. Several HTML and JavaScript files work together to implement this game.

Listing 7.6 shows the contents of the ttt.htm file, which provides the main entry point into the game. When you open the ttt.htm file with your browser, it displays the window shown in Figure 7.9. It displays a 3X3 tic-tac-toe grid in the upper-left corner and a Restart button in the lower-right corner.

Listing 7.6:   The Main Tic-Tac-Toe File (ttt.htm)

```
<HTML>
<HEAD>
<TITLE>Tic Tac Toe</TITLE></HEAD>
<FRAMESET ROWS="300,*" COLS="300,*" BORDER=0>
<FRAME SRC="board.htm">
<FRAME SRC="values.htm">
<FRAME SRC="blank.htm">
<FRAME SRC="control.htm">
</FRAMESET>
</HTML>
```

FIGURE 7.9:

The initial tic-tac-toe
display (Listing 7.6).

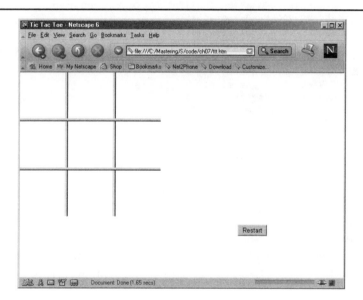

The Top-Level Frame Set

The ttt.htm file is the top-level frame set. This file creates a frame set that has two rows and two columns. The first row and first column are 300 pixels wide, and the second row and column use the rest of the window. The frame set does not have a border.

The four frames making up the frame set load the HTML files: board.htm, values.htm, blank.htm, and control.htm. The tic-tac-toe grid is created by the board.htm file that is loaded into the first frame. The Restart button is created by the control.htm file that is loaded in the fourth frame. The files values.htm and blank.htm do not display information in their respective frames.

The *board.htm* File

Listing 7.7 shows the contents of board.htm. This file creates a second-level nested frame set, which is displayed in the first frame of the top-level frame set; this is itself defined in ttt.htm. The frame set defined by board.htm is organized into a 3X3 grid of 100-pixelX100-pixel squares. The documents loaded into these squares are contained in the files square0.htm through square8.htm.

Listing 7.7:   The Frames of the Tic-Tac-Toe Board (board.htm)

```
<HTML>
<HEAD>
<TITLE>Tic Tac Toe</TITLE></HEAD>
<FRAMESET ROWS="100,100,100" COLS="100,100,100">
<FRAME SRC="square0.htm">
<FRAME SRC="square1.htm">
<FRAME SRC="square2.htm">
<FRAME SRC="square3.htm">
<FRAME SRC="square4.htm">
<FRAME SRC="square5.htm">
<FRAME SRC="square6.htm">
<FRAME SRC="square7.htm">
<FRAME SRC="square8.htm">
</FRAMESET>
</HTML>
```

Before going on to see what's in the square files, let's look at the remaining three frames defined in ttt.htm.

The *values.htm* File

The values.htm file is shown in Listing 7.8. It contains a single form with nine hidden fields; each is assigned the value of *no one*. Later on in the discussion, I'll show how this hidden form is used.

Listing 7.8:   A Hidden Form (values.htm)

```
<HTML>
<HEAD>
<TITLE>Values</TITLE>
</HEAD>
<BODY>
<FORM NAME="hiddenform">
<INPUT NAME="f0" TYPE="HIDDEN" VALUE="no one">
<INPUT NAME="f1" TYPE="HIDDEN" VALUE="no one">
<INPUT NAME="f2" TYPE="HIDDEN" VALUE="no one">
<INPUT NAME="f3" TYPE="HIDDEN" VALUE="no one">
<INPUT NAME="f4" TYPE="HIDDEN" VALUE="no one">
```

```
<INPUT NAME="f5" TYPE="HIDDEN" VALUE="no one">
<INPUT NAME="f6" TYPE="HIDDEN" VALUE="no one">
<INPUT NAME="f7" TYPE="HIDDEN" VALUE="no one">
<INPUT NAME="f8" TYPE="HIDDEN" VALUE="no one">
</FORM>
</BODY>
</HTML>
```

The *blank.htm* File

The file blank.htm, shown in Listing 7.9, contains a blank HTML file that is used as a dummy placeholder to fill up the third frame defined in ttt.htm. It does not display any information in the browser window.

Listing 7.9:   A Blank Document (blank.htm)

```
<HTML>
<HEAD>
<TITLE>Blank</TITLE>
</HEAD>
<BODY>
</BODY>
</HTML>
```

The *control.htm* File

Listing 7.10 shows the contents of the control.htm file. It implements the Restart button by invoking the restart() function. This function restarts the tic-tac-toe game to its original state using the following statement:

```
parent.location.href="ttt.htm"
```

This statement uses the parent property of the current window to access the window containing the frame set defined by ttt.htm. It then sets the href property of the window's location, causing the ttt.htm file to be reloaded.

Listing 7.10:   Implementing the Restart Button (control.htm)

```
<HTML>
<HEAD>
<TITLE>Blank</TITLE>
<SCRIPT LANGUAGE="JavaScript"><!--
function restart() {
 parent.location.href="ttt.htm"
}
// --></SCRIPT>
</HEAD>
```

```
<BODY>
<FORM>
<P ALIGN="CENTER">
<INPUT TYPE="Button" VALUE="Restart" onClick="restart()">
</P>
</FORM>
</BODY>
</HTML>
```

The Second-Level Frame Set

Now that we've covered the top-level frame set defined by ttt.htm, let's look into the second-level frame set defined by board.htm. As shown in Listing 7.7, this frame set defines nine
frames containing the files square0.htm through square8.htm. Listing 7.11 shows the contents of the square4.htm file as an example. All nine files are identical, except that the fourth
line of each file sets the cell variable to a value that indicates which grid cell is occupied by a
square. For instance, square0.htm sets cell to 0, square1.htm sets cell to 1, and
square8.htm sets cell to 8.

Listing 7.11:   A Sample Square (square4.htm)

```
<HTML>
<HEAD>
<TITLE>Blank</TITLE>
<SCRIPT LANGUAGE="JavaScript"><!--
cell=4
// --></SCRIPT>
</HEAD>
<SCRIPT LANGUAGE="JavaScript" SRC="ttt.js"><!--
// --></SCRIPT>
</HEAD>
<BODY onFocus="playerMoves()">
</BODY>
</HTML>
```

The important point to notice about the square files is that the onFocus event of each file
invokes the playerMoves() function. You may wonder where this function is defined. It's
defined in the ttt.js file, which is included in each square file via the SRC attribute of the
<script> tag included in each file's head. The ttt.js file provides the JavaScript code that is
at the heart of the tic-tac-toe game's operation. This file is shown in Listing 7.12.

Listing 7.12:   The JavaScript Code that Implements the Tic-Tac-Toe Game (ttt.js)

```
function isBlank(n) {
```

```
  if(owns("player",n) || owns("computer",n)) return false
  return true
}
function owns(who,i) {
 var fr = parent.parent.frames[1]
 var doc = fr.document
 var field = doc.forms[0].elements["f"+i]
 if(field==null || field.value==who) return true
 return false
}function setOwner(who,n) {
 var fr = parent.parent.frames[1]
 var doc = fr.document
 var field = doc.forms[0].elements[n]
 field.value=who
}
function ticTacToe(who,n1,n2,n3) {
 if(owns(who,n1) && owns(who,n2) && owns(who,n3)) {
  parent.parent.frames[3].focus()
  return true
 }
 return false
}
function isTicTacToe(who) {
 if(ticTacToe(who,0,1,2)) return true
 if(ticTacToe(who,3,4,5)) return true
 if(ticTacToe(who,6,7,8)) return true
 if(ticTacToe(who,0,3,6)) return true
 if(ticTacToe(who,1,4,7)) return true
 if(ticTacToe(who,2,5,8)) return true
 if(ticTacToe(who,0,4,8)) return true
 if(ticTacToe(who,2,4,6)) return true
 return false
}
function gameOver() {
 numMoves = 0
 for(i=0;i<9;++i) {
  if(!isBlank(i)) ++numMoves
 }
 if(numMoves==9) return true
 if(isTicTacToe("player")) return true
 if(isTicTacToe("computer")) return true
 return false
}
function computerMoves() {
 if(gameOver()) return -1
 var newMove = Math.round(9*Math.random())
 while(!isBlank(newMove)) {
  newMove = (newMove + 1) % 9
 }
 setOwner("computer",newMove)
 return newMove
```

```
}
function playerMoves() {
 if(!gameOver() && isBlank(cell)) {
  setOwner("player",cell)
  var move = computerMoves()
  location.href="o.htm"
  if(move!=-1) parent.frames[move].location.href="x.htm"
 }
}
function showWinner() {
 if(isTicTacToe("player")) alert("Congratulations! You win.")
}
function showLoser() {
 if(isTicTacToe("computer")) alert("Sorry. You Lose.")
}
```

In order to understand just what `ttt.js` does, open `ttt.htm` with your browser, and click one of the tic-tac-toe squares after the document has been loaded, as shown in Figure 7.10. An O appears in the square that you click; the computer responds by marking an X in another square.

FIGURE 7.10:

Playing tic-tac-toe

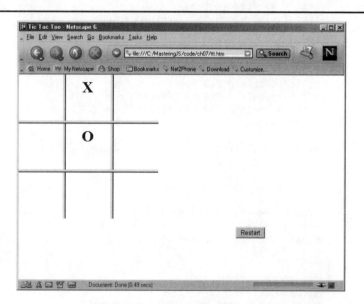

Click once more, and the computer responds again; continue clicking on blank squares until the game is over. The computer plays randomly, so you *should* win at least once in awhile. If you or the computer wins, an alert dialog box pops up to inform you of the result. If neither of you wins, all of the squares are filled in, as in the paper version of the game.

Investigating *ttt.js*

Now that you know how the game works, let's analyze ttt.js. It defines 10 functions: isBlank(), owns(), setOwner(), ticTacToe(), isTicTacToe(), gameOver(), computerMoves(), playerMoves(), showWinner(), and showLoser().The playerMoves() function is invoked when you click on a square in the tic-tac-toe grid. It uses the isBlank() function to determine whether the square is empty. The cell variable identifies which square has been clicked on. If the game is not over and the cell is blank, the setOwner() function is invoked to set the owner of the cell as the player. The computerMoves() function is invoked to get the program's next move. The playerMoves() function then loads the o.htm file into the frame by setting the href property of the document's location. This marks the frame with an O to indicate that it belongs to the player. The o.htm file also notifies the user if and when he or she has won the tic-tac-toe game. If the program is unable to make a move, it returns a value of -1. The if statement checks to see whether the computer has moved; if it has, it loads the x.htm file into the frame. This file marks the frame with an X, and notifies the user if the computer has won the game.

The isBlank() function uses the owns() function to determine whether the player or the computer currently owns a cell. If either owns a cell, it returns *false*. Otherwise, it returns *true*.

The owns() function performs some fairly intricate processing. It sets the doc variable to the document loaded in the second frame of the top-level frame set. This is the document created when the values.htm file is loaded. I could have used the top property instead of parent.parent to access the top-level frame set. The frames array contains all the frame objects in the frame set. The element frames[1] refers to the second frame. The document property of the frame object refers to the document that is loaded in the second frame. The field variable is assigned the corresponding element of form contained in the values.htm document. The value of this field is checked to see if it equals the value passed via the who argument. If the values match, *true* is returned; otherwise, *false* is returned. The values of the hidden fields of the form contained in the document generated by values.htm are used to maintain the state of the tic-tac-toe game. You'll learn more about using hidden fields in Chapter 9, "Using Hidden Fields and Cookies."

The setOwner() function updates the ownership of a cell by setting the *n*th cell's owner to the value of the who parameter. It uses parent.parent to access the top-level frame set, frames[1].document to access the frame containing the values.htm document, and elements[n].value to access the value of the *n*th hidden field in this document. It then assigns the value of who to this field.

The ticTacToe() function checks to see if the player identified by who owns all three of the cells specified by n1, n2, and n3. If tic-tac-toe has occurred, it sets the tic-tac-toe input focus to the frame containing the Restart button, and returns a value of *true*. The isTicTacToe()

function uses the `ticTacToe()` function to check each of the eight possible tic-tac-toe combinations.

The `gameOver()` function checks to see if all squares have been played, or if either the player or computer has made tic-tac-toe. If any of these occur, the game is over, and *true* is returned. Otherwise, *false* is returned.

The `computerMoves()` function makes a random move for the computer. If the game is over, it returns -1. Otherwise, it uses the `random()` and `round()` methods of the `Math` object to generate a random integer between 0 and 8. It uses the randomly generated integer and a `while` statement to look for the next blank cell. When it finds a blank cell, it sets the owner of the cell to the computer and returns the frame number associated with the cell. The `showWinner()` and `showLoser()` functions are used by the `o.htm` and `x.htm` files (Listings 7.13 and 7.14) to check to see whether the player (`showWinner()`) or the computer (`showLoser()`) won. These functions are invoked when the `o.htm` and `x.htm` files are loaded.

Listing 7.13:   Displaying an O (o.htm)

```
<HTML>
<HEAD>
<TITLE>O</TITLE>
<SCRIPT LANGUAGE="JavaScript" SRC="ttt.js"><!--
// --></SCRIPT>
</HEAD>
<BODY onLoad="showWinner()">
<H1 ALIGN="CENTER">O</H1>
</BODY>
</HTML>
```

Listing 7.14:   Displaying an X (x.htm)

```
<HTML>
<HEAD>
<TITLE>X</TITLE>
<SCRIPT LANGUAGE="JavaScript" SRC="ttt.js"><!--
// --></SCRIPT>
</HEAD>
<BODY onLoad="showLoser()">
<H1 ALIGN="CENTER">X</H1>
</BODY>
</HTML>
```

The *document* Object

The document object is a very important JavaScript object. It allows you to update a document that is being loaded and to access the HTML elements contained in a loaded document. It provides many properties that help you to access these elements, as shown in Table 7.4. Many of these properties are objects that we'll be studying in subsequent chapters. Table 7.5 identifies the methods of the document object that are supported by Navigator and Internet Explorer.

TABLE 7.4: Properties of the *document* Object

Property	Description
alinkColor	Identifies the value of the alink attribute of the <body> tag.
anchor	An object that refers to an array contained in a document. See Chapter 10, "Working with Links."
anchors	An array of all the anchors contained in a document. See Chapter 10.
applet	An object that refers to an applet that is contained in a document. See Chapter 27, "Communicating with Java Applets."
applets	An array of all the applets contained in a document. See Chapter 27.
area	An object that refers to an image map area contained in a document. See Chapter 11, "Using Images."
bgColor	Identifies the value of the bgcolor attribute of the <body> tag.
cookie	Identifies the value of a cookie. See Chapter 9.
embeds	An array of all the plug-ins contained in a document. See Chapter 29, "Scripting Plug-Ins."
fgColor	Identifies the value of the text attribute of the <body> tag.
form	An object that refers to a form contained in a document. See Chapter 8, "Processing Forms."
Forms[]	An array of all the forms contained in a document. See Chapter 8.
image	An object that refers to an image contained in a document. See Chapter 11.
Images[]	An array of all the images contained in a document. See Chapter 11.
lastModified	The date that a document was last modified.
link	An object that refers to a link contained in a document. See Chapter 10.
links	An array of all the links contained in a document. See Chapter 10.
linkColor	Identifies the value of the link attribute of the <body> tag.
plugin	An object that refers to a plug-in contained in a document. See Chapter 29.
Plugins[]	An array of objects that describe the plug-ins supported by a browser.
referrer	The URL of the document that provided the link to a document. See Chapter 10.
title	The document's title.
URL	The URL of a document. See Chapter 10.
vlinkColor	Identifies the value of the vlink attribute of the <body> tag.

TABLE 7.5: Methods of the *document* Object

Method	Description
close()	Closes a stream (see note nearby) used to create a document object.
open([*mimeType*][,"replace"])	Opens a stream used to create a document object with the optional MIME type. The "replace" parameter is used with the text/html MIME type to replace the current document in the history list.
write(*expr1[,expr2,...,exprN]*)	Writes the values of the expressions to a document.
writeln(*expr1[,expr2,...,exprN]*)	Writes the values of the expressions to a document followed by a newline character.

NOTE   The term *stream* refers to a sequence of input or output characters. In the case of the open() and close() methods, it refers to the sequence of characters that constitute the document being created.

Generating Document Contents

You already know how to use the methods of the document object to generate HTML. For instance, you've used write() and writeln() extensively to write HTML code to a document as it is loaded in a window. The document object also provides two additional methods—open() and close()—that can help you to generate the contents of a document. Both of these additional methods work with the write() and writeln() methods.

The open() method allows you to update a document that is in a window other than the current window. For example, suppose that the variable win2 refers to a window that you have created. You can use open() to generate the document loaded into win2 as follows:

```
win2.document.open()
.
.
.
win2.document.write()
win2.document.writeln()
.
.
.
win2.document.close()
```

In the preceding example, the open() method opens the document for writing, the write() and writeln() methods are used to write to the document, and the close() method is used to close the document after writing has been completed. The vertical dots indicate code lines that were omitted.

The open() method takes two optional string parameters that specify the MIME type of the document being generated and whether the document should replace the current document in the history list. If the MIME type parameter is omitted, the *text/html* MIME type is assumed. If the MIME type parameter is supplied, the `"replace"` parameter may also be used.

Your browser will display the document according to its MIME type. For example, if you open a document with the image/gif MIME type, it will display the document as a GIF image. However, in order to create the GIF image, you must write the GIF header and pixel data to the document.

If you use `open()` with a MIME type that is not supported directly by your browser, it will look to see if it has a plug-in that supports the MIME type. If a suitable plug-in exists, your browser will load the plug-in and pass the contents of the document to the plug-in as the document is written. You'll learn more about using `open()` and `close()` with plug-ins in Chapter 29.

NOTE   If `open()` cannot open a document for any reason, it returns the value `null`. If `open()` can open a document, it will return a value other than `null`.

Accessing Document Contents

The `document` object provides several properties that can be used to access the contents of an HTML document. These properties were listed in Table 7.4 earlier in the chapter. In many cases, the document properties refer to objects that are contained within the displayed document. You'll learn how to use these objects in subsequent chapters.

Listing 7.15 provides an example of using the properties of the `document` object to summarize the objects that are contained in a document. (That is, it lists the objects that are contained in the document, and displays a count of how many of each type are contained.) This example also shows how to use the `open()` method to generate the contents of a document that is contained in another window.

Listing 7.15:   Accessing Document Contents (ch07-15.htm)

```
<HTML>
<HEAD>
<TITLE>Accessing Document Contents</TITLE>
<SCRIPT LANGUAGE="JavaScript"><!--
function createSummary() {
 win2 = open("","window2")
 win2.document.open("text/plain")
 win2.document.writeln("Title: "+document.title)
 win2.document.writeln("Links: "+document.links.length)
 win2.document.writeln("Anchors: "+document.anchors.length)
 win2.document.writeln("Forms: "+document.forms.length)
 win2.document.writeln("Images: "+document.images.length)
 win2.document.writeln("Applets: "+document.applets.length)
 win2.document.writeln("Embeds: "+document.embeds.length)
```

```
  win2.document.close()
}
// --></SCRIPT>
</HEAD>
<BODY>
<A NAME="#top"></A>
<P><A HREF="http://www.jaworski.com/javascript <IMG SRC="master.gif"></A>
<A HREF="http://www.sybex.com/"><IMG SRC="sybex.gif"></A></P>
<FORM>
<INPUT TYPE="BUTTON" NAME="Help" VALUE="Help"
  ONCLICK="alert('Click one of the above images.')">
</FORM>
<SCRIPT LANGUAGE="JavaScript"><!--
setTimeout("createSummary()",5000)
// --></SCRIPT>
</BODY>
</HTML>
```

When you open the file shown in Listing 7.15, it generates the web page shown in Figure 7.11. This web page has two images that are used as the source of links. It also contains a form with one button and an internal anchor (not visible) that names the top of the document. After five seconds, your browser creates a new window and displays the document shown in Figure 7.12. This action is caused by the script contained in the body of Listing 7.15. It contains a single statement that sets a five-second timeout before invoking the createSummary() function.

FIGURE 7.11:

The opening window
(Listing 7.15)

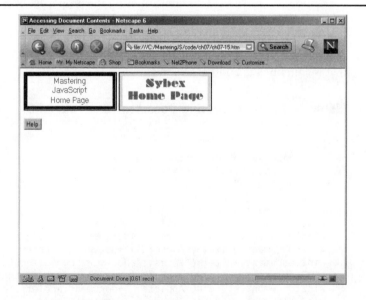

FIGURE 7.12:

The document summary window (Listing 7.15)

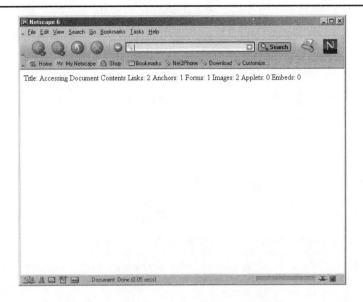

The `createSummary()` function is defined in the document's head. It creates a new window using the `open()` method of the `window` object. This new window is blank; it is assigned to the `win2` variable. The document contained in the new window is opened using the text/plain MIME type. A series of writes to the document are performed and then the document is closed. The write statements access the properties of the document that is displayed in the first window, and summarize these properties in the second window. These properties describe the document title and identify the number of links, anchors, forms, images, applets, and plug-ins contained in the document.

Working with Colors

The `document` object provides several properties that allow you to change the colors used to display web pages. Unfortunately, most of these properties must be specified before the body of a document has been laid out. This means that the properties must be set by scripts that execute when the document's header is processed. An exception to this is the `bgColor` property. It can be used to change a document's background color at any time.

The `fgColor` property allows you to change the color of text that is displayed in a document. It applies to all text that is not part of a link. The `linkColor` property specifies the color for links that have not been visited (that is, ones not clicked on), and the `vlinkColor` property specifies the color of visited links. Finally, the `alinkColor` property specifies the color of a link as it is to appear while it is being clicked.

Listing 7.16 provides an example of using the bgColor, fgColor, and linkColor attributes. It generates the document display shown in Figure 7.13. Note that the fgColor and link-Color attributes are set in the document header so that they can go into effect when the document body is laid out. The bgColor attribute is set in the document body.

Listing 7.16: **Using Color Attributes (ch07-16.htm).**

```
<HTML>
<HEAD>
<TITLE>Changing Colors</TITLE>
<SCRIPT LANGUAGE="JavaScript"><!--
document.fgColor="white"
document.linkColor="yellow"
// --></SCRIPT>
</HEAD>
<BODY>
<H1>Changing Colors</H1>
<P>This Web page shows how document colors can be changed.</P>
<P>Here is a <A HREF="nowhere">sample link</A>.</P>
<SCRIPT LANGUAGE="JavaScript"><!--
document.bgColor="black"
// --></SCRIPT>
</BODY>
</HTML>
```

FIGURE 7.13:

The document generated by Listing 7.16

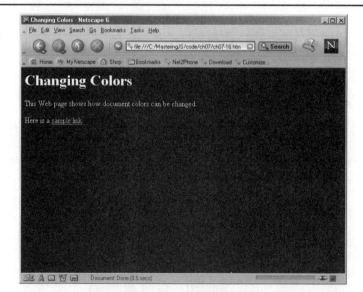

The *navigator* Object

The navigator object provides information about the type and version of the browser that is used to run a script. You can use this object to determine the capabilities of a user's browser and run code that is supported by that browser. Navigator and Internet Explorer both support the navigator object (even if it was named after Netscape's browser). The navigator properties supported by both Navigator and Internet Explorer are identified in Table 7.6.

TABLE 7.6: Properties of the *navigator* Object

Property	Earliest Browser Support	Description
appCodeName	Navigator 2 Internet Explorer 3	The code name of the browser.
appName	Navigator 2 Internet Explorer 3	The name of the browser.
appVersion	Navigator 2 Internet Explorer 3	The version of the browser.
mimeTypes	Navigator 3 Internet Explorer 4	An array of all MIME types currently supported by the browser.
platform	Navigator 4 Internet Explorer 4	The operating system platform on which the browser executes.
plugins	Navigator 3 Internet Explorer 4	An array of all plug-ins currently installed on the browser.
userAgent	Navigator 2 Internet Explorer 3	The user-agent header sent in the HTTP protocol from the browser to the server.

Both Navigator and Internet Explorer support the javaEnabled() and taintEnabled() methods. The javaEnabled() method returns a Boolean value that indicates whether the user has enabled the use of Java on his browser. The taintEnabled() method returns a Boolean value that indicates whether the user has enabled data tainting. *Data tainting* is a security mechanism implemented in JavaScript 1.1. It is covered in Chapter 34, "Securing Your Scripts." Internet Explorer always returns *false* when taintEnabled() is invoked.

The navigator object, like the window object, is a top-level object in the browser object model in that it is not a property of some other higher-level object. Listing 7.17 shows how it is used to acquire information about the user's browser. Figure 7.14 shows the output it displays for Navigator. Figure 7.15 shows the output it displays for Internet Explorer.

Listing 7.17:   Using Navigator Properties (browser.htm).

```
<HTML>
<HEAD>
<TITLE>Detecting Browser Capabilities</TITLE>
<SCRIPT LANGUAGE="JavaScript">
function displayNavigatorProperties() {
 with(document) {
  write("<B>appName: </B>")
  writeln(navigator.appName+"<BR>")
  write("<B>appVersion: </B>")
  writeln(navigator.appVersion+"<BR>")
  write("<B>appCodeName: </B>")
  writeln(navigator.appCodeName+"<BR>")
  write("<B>platform: </B>")
  writeln(navigator.platform+"<BR>")
  write("<B>userAgent: </B>")
  writeln(navigator.userAgent+"<BR>")
  write("<B>language: </B>")
  writeln(navigator.language+"<BR>")
  write("<B>Number of mimeTypes: </B>")
  writeln(navigator.mimeTypes.length+"<BR>")
  write("<B>Number of plugins: </B>")
  writeln(navigator.plugins.length)
 }
}
function displayExplorerProperties() {
 with(document) {
  write("<B>appName: </B>")
  writeln(navigator.appName+"<BR>")
  write("<B>appVersion: </B>")
  writeln(navigator.appVersion+"<BR>")
  write("<B>appMinorVersion: </B>")
  writeln(navigator.appMinorVersion+"<BR>")
  write("<B>appCodeName: </B>")
  writeln(navigator.appCodeName+"<BR>")
  write("<B>platform: </B>")
  writeln(navigator.platform+"<BR>")
  write("<B>cpuClass: </B>")
  writeln(navigator.cpuClass+"<BR>")
  write("<B>userAgent: </B>")
  writeln(navigator.userAgent+"<BR>")
  write("<B>cookieEnabled: </B>")
  writeln(navigator.cookieEnabled+"<BR>")
  write("<B>browserLanguage: </B>")
  writeln(navigator.browserLanguage+"<BR>")
  write("<B>userLanguage: </B>")
  writeln(navigator.userLanguage+"<BR>")
  write("<B>systemLanguage: </B>")
  writeln(navigator.systemLanguage+"<BR>")
```

```
    write("<B>onLine: </B>")
    writeln(navigator.onLine+"<BR>")
    write("<B>Number of mimeTypes: </B>")
    writeln(navigator.mimeTypes.length+"<BR>")
    write("<B>Number of plugins: </B>")
    writeln(navigator.plugins.length+"<BR>")
    write("<B>userProfile: </B>")
    writeln(navigator.userProfile)
   }
  }
  function displayBrowserProperties() {
   if(navigator.appName=="Netscape")
    displayNavigatorProperties()
   else
    if(navigator.appName=="Microsoft Internet Explorer")
      displayExplorerProperties()
  }
  displayBrowserProperties()
 </SCRIPT>
 </HEAD>
 <BODY>
 </BODY>
 </HTML>
```

FIGURE 7.14

The navigator properties
displayed by Navigator 6.1
(Listing 7.17)

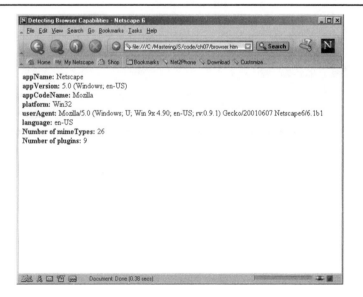

FIGURE 7.15:

The navigator properties
displayed by Internet
Explorer 6 (Listing 7.17)

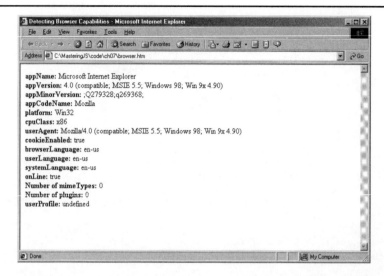

The script contains three functions: displayBrowserProperties(), displayNavigator-
Properties(), and displayExplorerProperties(). The displayBrowserProperties() function uses the navigator.appName property to determine the browser type, and invokes either
displayNavigatorProperties() or displayExplorerProperties(), depending on the value
of navigator.appName.

The *screen* Object

The screen object is an object that is a property of the window object. It provides information about the dimensions and color depth of the user's screen. The screen properties supported by both Navigator and Internet Explorer are the following:

- height is the current height of the user's screen (in pixels).

- width is the current width of the user's screen (in pixels).

- colorDepth is the number of bits per color currently supported by the user's
  screen/video card. For example, 8-bits of color depth corresponds to 256 colors
  because 2 raised to the eighth power is 256.

You can use this information to determine how to organize the information you display to
the user. In addition, both Navigator and Internet Explorer support browser-specific screen
properties. These additional properties are covered in Appendix D. Listing 7.18 contains a
script that displays the height, width, and colorDepth properties supported by a browser.
Figure 7.16 shows the results it displays when I run it on my notebook computer.

Listing 7.18:   Displaying the Properties of the Screen Object (screen.htm)

```
<HTML>
<HEAD>
<TITLE>Test</TITLE>
<SCRIPT LANGUAGE="JavaScript">
function displayScreenProperties() {
 with(document) {
  write("<B>height: </B>")
  writeln(screen.height+"<BR>")
  write("<B>width: </B>")
  writeln(screen.width+"<BR>")
  write("<B>colorDepth: </B>")
  writeln(screen.colorDepth+"<BR>")
 }
}
displayScreenProperties()
</SCRIPT>
</HEAD>
<BODY>
</BODY>
</HTML>
```

FIGURE 7.16:

The screen properties
displayed by my browser
(Listing 7.18)

Summary

This chapter showed you how to use the predefined `window`, `frame`, `document`, `navigator`, and `screen` objects to create and manage web pages with multiple windows and frames. It also provided several examples of using windows and frames to organize your web pages. In the next chapter, you'll learn how to use predefined JavaScript objects to implement local form-processing functions.

CHAPTER 8

Processing Forms

- The *form* object

- Accessing forms within JavaScript

- Accessing form elements

- Using form event handlers

- Performing local form processing

- Working with CGI scripts

Forms provide you with an important capability for web page development—they allow you to gather information from individuals who browse your web pages. This is especially important if you use your website to advertise or sell your products. Forms make it easy to collect information from your web page users. They provide a full range of graphical user interface (GUI) controls, and they automatically submit the data they collect to your web server. This data can then be processed by CGI programs, server-side JavaScript scripts built upon Netscape's LiveWire, server-side JScript scripts written as Microsoft's Active Server Pages, or other types of server-side scripts.

JavaScript provides a number of features that can be used to enhance the forms that you develop for your particular web applications. These features allow you to validate form data before it is submitted to your server and to exercise greater control of the interaction between your forms and web users.

This chapter introduces the form object, and discusses the JavaScript objects that are associated with form fields and GUI controls. It shows how to use the properties and methods of these objects, and how to handle form-related events. When you finish this chapter, you will know how to use JavaScript to create forms that perform local processing, and you will be able to use these forms to communicate with CGI programs.

NOTE   If you are unfamiliar with the HTML tags used to create forms, consult www.jaworski.com/ javascript/ for links to HTML tutorials and reference documents.

The *form* Object

JavaScript provides the form object to enable your scripts to interact with and exercise control over HTML forms. The form object is accessed as a property of the document object. Your browser creates a unique form object for every form that is contained in a document. These objects can be accessed via the document.forms[] array.

The form object is important because it provides you with access to the forms contained in your documents, and allows you to respond to form-related events. Table 8.1 lists the properties of the form object that are supported by both Internet Explorer and Navigator. These properties provide access to a form's attributes, and allow you to work with a form's fields and GUI controls. The form object provides two common methods, submit(), and reset(). The submit() and reset() methods are used to submit a form or reset a form's entries to their default values. (The events that forms handle are covered in Chapter 4, "Handling Events," and in the section, "Using Form Event Handlers," later in this chapter.)

TABLE 8.1: Properties of the *form* Object

Property	Description
action	Provides access to the HTML ACTION attribute of the <form> tag
button	An object representing a button GUI control
checkbox	An object representing a check box field
elements	An array containing all the fields and GUI controls included in a form
encoding	Provides access to the HTML ENCTYPE attribute of the <form> tag
FileUpload	An object representing a file-upload form field
hidden	An object representing a hidden form field
length	Provides access to the length of the elements array
method	Provides access to the HTML METHOD attribute of the <form> tag
name	Identifies the name of the form (from the NAME attribute of the <form>tag)
password	An object representing a password field
radio	An object representing a radio button field
reset	An object representing a reset button
select	An object representing a selection list
submit	An object representing a submit button
target	Provides access to the HTML TARGET attribute of the <form> tag
text	An object representing a text field
textarea	An object representing a text area field

Accessing Forms within JavaScript

Because form objects are properties of documents, they are accessed by referencing the documents in which they are contained. If you name a form when you create it, you can access the form by its name. Forms are named using the form's NAME attribute. For example, if you create a form named employeeData you can access the form's method property using employee-Data.method.

You can also use the forms property of the document object to access the forms contained in a particular document. The forms property is an array that contains an entry for each form contained in a document. Suppose that the employeeData form is the third form contained in the document loaded into the current window. You can access the form's method property using document.forms[2].method or document.forms["employeeData"].method.

Accessing Form Elements

A form may contain a wide variety of fields and GUI controls. These form components are referred to as *elements* of the form, and are objects in their own right. Table 8.2 lists and summarizes the objects that may be contained in a form.

TABLE 8.2: Objects that May Be Contained in a Form

Object	Description
button	A general-purpose button for implementing GUI controls
checkbox	A clickable field that allows multiple selections from within a group
FileUpload	A field that allows a user to specify a file to be submitted as part of the form
hidden	A field that may contain a value, but is not displayed within a form
password	A text field in which the values that a user enters are hidden via mask characters
radio	A clickable field that allows only a single selection from within a group
reset	A button that is used to reset the contents of a form to its default state
select	A list from which individual list items may be selected
submit	A button that is used to submit the data entered into a field
text	A single-line field for entering text
textarea	A multiline field for entering text

If the elements of a form are named using an HTML name attribute, the element can be accessed using this name. For example, suppose that you have a form named form1 that contains a text field named ssn. You can access the value of this field using form1.ssn.value.

In most cases, you will access the elements of a form using the elements array property of the form object. This array contains an object for each element of a form. Suppose that the ssn field of the form1 form is the seventh element defined in the form. You can access the value of the ssn field using form1.elements[6].value.

The objects described in Table 8.2 reference the elements of a form, and have properties and methods of their own, as summarized in Tables 8.3 and 8.4.

TABLE 8.3: Properties of Form Elements

Object	Property	Description
button	name	Provides access to the button's NAME attribute
	type	Identifies the object's type
	value	Identifies the object's value

Continued on next page

TABLE 8.3 CONTINUED: Properties of Form Elements

Object	Property	Description
checkbox	checked	Identifies whether the check box is currently checked
	defaultChecked	Identifies whether the check box is checked by default
	name	Provides access to the check box's HTML NAME attribute
	type	Identifies the object's type
	value	Identifies the object's value
FileUpload	name	Provides access to the object's NAME attribute
	type	Identifies the object's TYPE attribute
	value	Identifies the object's value
hidden	name	Provides access to the object's NAME attribute
	type	Identifies the object's type
	value	Identifies the object's value
password	defaultValue	Identifies the object's default value
	name	Provides access to the object's NAME attribute
	type	Identifies the object's type
	value	Identifies the object's value
radio	checked	Identifies whether the radio button is currently checked
	defaultChecked	Identifies whether the radio button is checked by default
	name	Provides access to the object's NAME attribute
	type	Identifies the object's type
	value	Identifies the object's value
reset	name	Provides access to the object's NAME attribute
	type	Identifies the object's type
	value	Identifies the object's value
select	length	Identifies the length of the select list
	name	Provides access to the object's NAME attribute
	options	An array that identifies the options supported by the select list
	selectedIndex	Identifies the first selected option within the select list
	type	Identifies the object's type
submit	name	Provides access to the object's NAME attribute
	type	Identifies the object's type
	value	Identifies the object's value
text	defaultValue	Identifies the default text to be displayed in the text field
	name	Provides access to the object's NAME attribute
	type	Identifies the object's type
	value	Identifies the object's value

Continued on next page

TABLE 8.3 CONTINUED: Properties of Form Elements

Object	Property	Description
textarea	defaultValue	Identifies the default text to be displayed in the text area field
	name	Provides access to the object's NAME attribute
	type	Identifies the object's type
	value	Identifies the object's value

NOTE   All form elements have the **form** property. This property references the form in which the element is contained. All form elements except the **hidden** element provide the **handleEvent()** method for directly invoking the element's event handlers.

TABLE 8.4: Methods of Form Elements

Object	Method	Description
button	click()	Simulates the button being clicked
	blur()	Removes focus from the button
	focus()	Gives focus to the button
checkbox	click()	Simulates the check box being clicked
	blur()	Removes focus from the check box
	focus()	Gives focus to the check box
FileUpload	blur()	Removes focus from the file upload field
	focus()	Gives focus to the file upload field
	select()	Selects the input area of the file upload field
hidden	None	
password	blur()	Removes input focus from the password field
	focus()	Gives input focus to the password field
	select()	Highlights the text displayed in the password field
radio	click()	Simulates the clicking of the radio button
	blur()	Removes focus from the radio button
	focus()	Gives focus to the radio button
reset	click()	Simulates the clicking of the reset button
	blur()	Removes focus from the reset button
	focus()	Gives focus to the reset button
select	blur()	Removes focus from the selection list
	focus()	Gives focus to the selection list

Continued on next page

TABLE 8.4 CONTINUED: Methods of Form Elements

Object	Method	Description
submit	click()	Simulates the clicking of the submit button
	blur()	Removes focus from the submit button
	focus()	Gives focus to the submit button
text	blur()	Removes focus from the text field
	focus()	Gives focus to the text field
	select()	Highlights the text in the text field
textarea	blur()	Removes focus from the text area
	focus()	Gives focus to the text area
	select()	Highlights the text in the text area

Listing 8.1 shows how the individual forms and form elements can be accessed in multi-form documents. It creates the three-form document shown in Figure 8.1. When you click the Submit button of the first form, the onSubmit() handler invokes the displayFormData() function. Note that it does this in the context of a return statement. This causes the form submission to be aborted when displayFormData() returns a *false* value. This is always the case because displayFormData() always returns *false*.

NOTE   You can access the file for Listing 8.1, formacc.htm, and all of the code listings in this chapter on the CD-ROM that accompanies the book.

Listing 8.1   Accessing the Elements of a Form (formacc.htm)

```
<HTML>
<HEAD>
<TITLE>Multiform Document Example</TITLE>
<SCRIPT LANGUAGE="JavaScript"><!--
function displayFormData() {
 win2=open("","window2")
 win2.document.open("text/plain")
 win2.document.writeln("This document has "+
  document.forms.length+" forms.")
 for(i=0;i<document.forms.length;++i) {
  win2.document.writeln("Form "+i+" has "+
   document.forms[i].elements.length+" elements.")
  for(j=0;j<document.forms[i].elements.length;++j) {
   win2.document.writeln((j+1)+" A "+
    document.forms[i].elements[j].type+" element.")
  }
 }
```

```
    win2.document.close()
    return false
}
// --></SCRIPT>
</HEAD>
<BODY>
<H1>Multiform Document Example</H1>
<FORM ACTION="nothing" onSubmit="return displayFormData()">
<H2>Form 1</H2>
<P>Text field: <INPUT TYPE="TEXT" NAME="f1-1"
 VALUE="Sample text"></P>
<P>Password field: <INPUT TYPE="PASSWORD" NAME="f1-2"></P>
<P>Text area field:
<TEXTAREA ROWS="4" COLS="30"
  NAME="f1-3">Write your novel here.</TEXTAREA></P>
<P><INPUT TYPE="SUBMIT" NAME="f1-4" VALUE="Submit">
<INPUT TYPE="RESET" NAME="f1-5"></P>
</FORM>
<HR>
<FORM>
<H2>Form 2</H2>
<P><INPUT TYPE="CHECKBOX" NAME="f2-1" VALUE="1"
 CHECKED> Check me!</P>
<P><INPUT TYPE="CHECKBOX" NAME="f2-1" VALUE="2"> No.
 Check me!</P>
<P><INPUT TYPE="CHECKBOX" NAME="f2-1" VALUE="3"> Check all of
 us!</P>
<P><INPUT TYPE="RADIO" NAME="f2-2" VALUE="1"> AM</P>
<P><INPUT TYPE="RADIO" NAME="f2-2" VALUE="2" CHECKED> PM</P>
<P><INPUT TYPE="RADIO" NAME="f2-2" VALUE="3"> FM</P>
<INPUT TYPE="FILE" NAME="f2-3">
</FORM>
<HR>
<FORM>
<H2>Form 3</H2>
<INPUT TYPE="HIDDEN" NAME="f3-1">
<SELECT NAME="f3-2" SIZE="4">
<OPTION VALUE="">Item 1</OPTION>
<OPTION VALUE="">Item 2</OPTION>
<OPTION VALUE="" SELECTED>Item 3</OPTION>
<OPTION VALUE="">Item 4</OPTION>
<OPTION VALUE="">Item 5</OPTION>
</SELECT>
</FORM>
</BODY>
</HTML>
```

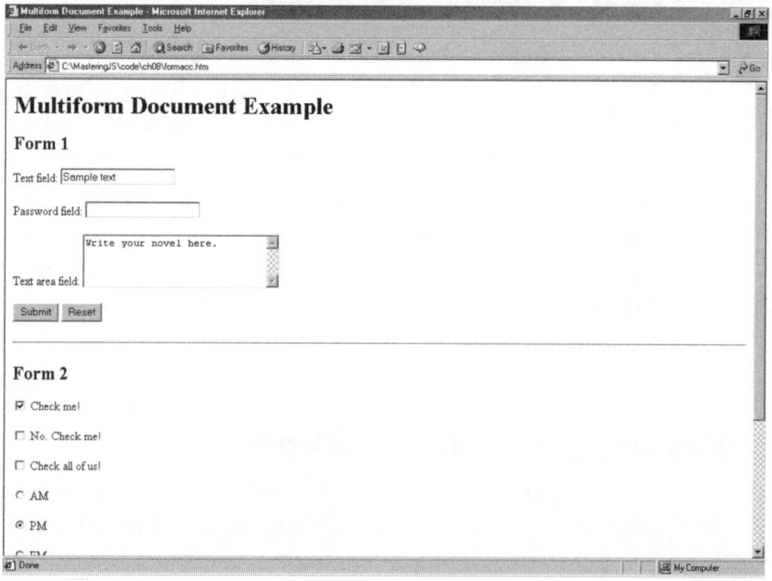

FIGURE 8.1:

A multiform document
(Listing 8.1)

FIGURE 8.1:

A multiform document
(Listing 8.1)

The displayFormData() function creates and opens a separate window, and assigns the window object to the win2 variable. It then opens the window's document with a text/plain MIME type. It uses the forms array of the document object of the first window to determine how many forms are contained in the document. It then writes this information to the document contained in win2. Next, it identifies the number of elements in each form using the length property of the form's elements array. Finally, it displays the type property of each form element via win2, as shown in Figure 8.2.

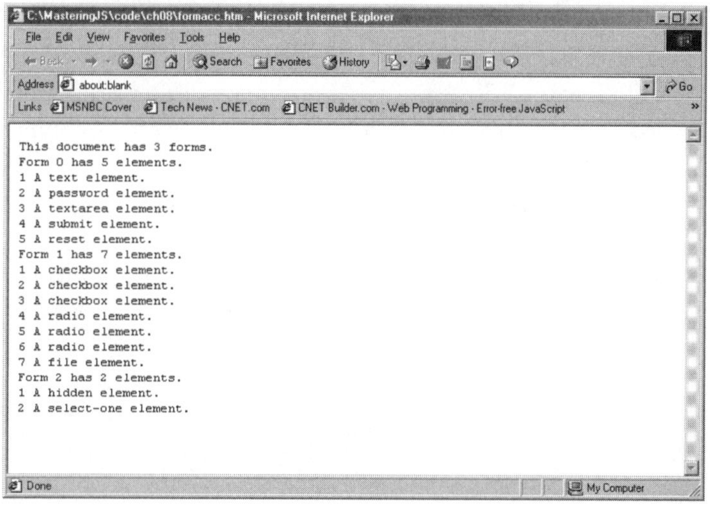

FIGURE 8.2:

A summary of the contents
of the multiform document
(Listing 8.1)

Using Form Event Handlers

JavaScript's capability to handle form-related events is a very powerful tool for customizing form behavior. It allows you to control the user's interaction with your forms and to process form data as the user enters it. It also allows you to process form data locally at the user's browser, reducing the load on your communication bandwidth and on your web server.

Form event handlers respond to events that indicate the user has performed an input action, such as filling in a text field, clicking a button, or submitting an entire form. These event handlers check the data entered by the user and then either prompt the user to correct any errors or provide the user with other feedback on the data that was entered. Form event handlers may also be used to adaptively present new forms to a user based upon the user's response to prior forms.

Responding to User Actions

Event handling in general, and form event handling in particular, are introduced in Chapter 4. If you have not already read Chapter 4, you should do so before continuing on in this chapter.

Within Chapter 4, Table 4.2 identifies all of the JavaScript event-handling attributes, and Table 4.7 identifies which event-handling attributes apply to forms and form elements. From Table 4.7, you can see that most form events fall into the following categories:

Clicks and checks   These are the most common types of form events. A user clicks a button or checks a check box to provide information or to perform an action. These events are handled by event-handling functions that provide feedback to the user on the results of the actions taken in response to the click or check.

Text changes   Text changes are another common type of form event. The user enters data into a text field or text area, an event is generated, and the event handler validates the user's entry and performs further processing based on the user's input.

List selection   When a user selects an item from a selection list, event-handling code is used to verify that the selection is consistent with other inputs and to perform any processing indicated by the selection.

Change of focus   Change-of-focus events occur when a form element, such as a text field or selection list, receives or loses the current input focus. These events usually do not require special event handing. However, JavaScript provides the capability to do so when required.

Form submission and reset   These events are generated when a user clicks a submit or reset button. Form-submission events are typically handled by validating all the data entered by the user, performing any local processing on that data, and then forwarding the data to a CGI program or other server-side script.

Because you have already covered form event handling in Chapter 4, I'm not going to bore you with any more trivial examples. Instead, we'll use JavaScript's event-handling capabilities to create a form-based Hangman game—something that is impossible to do in HTML alone.

If you're not already familiar with Hangman, here's a short description of the game. Hangman is a game in which you try to guess a word, one letter at a time. You are initially presented with a word pattern in which each letter of the word to be guessed is represented by an underscore (_) character. This tells you how many letters are in the word, but nothing more. When you guess a letter that is in the word, the underscore that represents that letter is replaced by the letter you guessed correctly. This tells you that you guessed the correct letter, and shows you where the letter appears in the word. You continue to guess until you run out of guesses or until you guess all of the letters of the word.

Your status in terms of guesses is depicted in a gallows—that's why it's called Hangman. Each time you guess incorrectly, a "body part" is added to the victim being hanged. You are allowed only seven incorrect guesses (head, upper and lower torso, two arms, two legs) before the game is over. The purpose of the game is not to be morbid, but to improve your word-recognition skills.

Before going on to learn how the game is implemented using form event handling, you should play a few games. Start the game by opening `hangman.htm` from your browser. The file is located on the CD in the ch08 folder. At startup, it presents the display shown in Figure 8.3. Play the game by clicking any of the buttons labeled A through Z. If you guess correctly, the game will display the position of the letter in the Word to Guess text field, as shown in Figure 8.4. If you guess incorrectly, a part of your body will be hung in the gallows, as shown in Figure 8.5. If you continue to guess incorrectly, your complete effigy will be hung (see Figure 8.6), an alert dialog box will tell you that you lost, and the game will start again. If you are clever enough to guess the word before you are hung, an alert dialog box will tell you that you won, and the game will start over. Clicking the Start Again button will immediately restart the game with a new word to guess.

NOTE   If you try to modify any of the form's text fields, an alert message will be displayed that tells you not to mess with that field.

FIGURE 8.3:

The Hangman opening display (Listing 8.2)

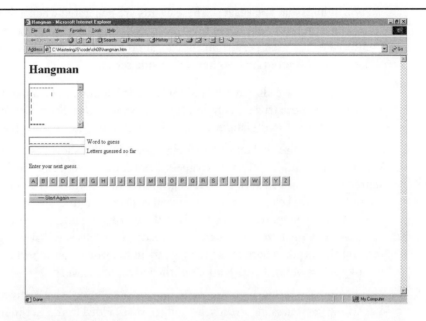

FIGURE 8.4:

You guessed correctly (Listing 8.2).

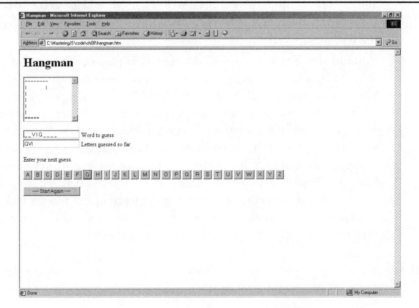

FIGURE 8.5:

You guessed incorrectly
(Listing 8.2).

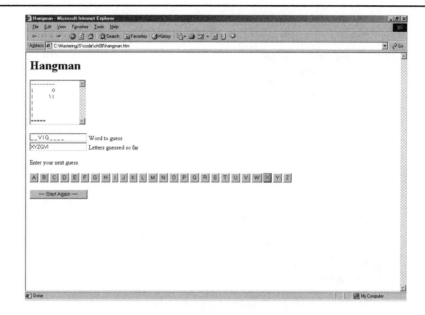

FIGURE 8.6:

You're hung (Listing 8.2).

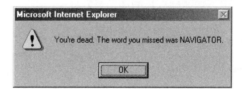

Listing 8.2 shows the contents of the hangman.htm file. This file is fairly long, but don't worry; I'll go over it one small piece at a time. The file contains two scripts: one in the document head and one in the document body. I'll start with the script in the document head because that's the part your browser processes first.

Listing 8.2   A JavaScript Hangman Game (hangman.htm)

```
<HTML>
<HEAD>
<TITLE>Hangman</TITLE>
<SCRIPT LANGUAGE="JavaScript"><!--
gallows = new Array("--------\n|        |\n|\n|\n|\n|\n\n=====",
"--------\n|        O\n|\n|\n|\n|\n\n=====",
"--------\n|        O\n|        |\n|\n|\n|\n\n=====",
"--------\n|        O\n|       \\|\n|\n|\n|\n\n=====",
"--------\n|        O\n|       \\|/\n|\n|\n|\n\n=====",
```

```
"--------\n|        O\n|      \\|/\n|       |\n|\n|\n\n=====",
"--------\n|        O\n|      \\|/\n|       |\n|      /\n|\n\n=====",
"--------\n|        O\n|      \\|/\n|       |\n|      / \\\n|\n\n=====")
guessChoices = new
Array("JavaScript","Navigator","LiveConnect","LiveWire")
function startAgain() {
 guesses = 0
 max = gallows.length-1
 guessed = " "
 len = guessChoices.length - 1
 toGuess = guessChoices[Math.round(len*Math.random())].toUpperCase()
 displayHangman()
 displayToGuess()
 displayGuessed()
}
function stayAway() {
 document.game.elements[3].focus()
 alert("Don't mess with this form element!")
}
function displayHangman() {
 document.game.status.value=gallows[guesses]
}
function displayToGuess() {
 pattern=""
 for(i=0;i<toGuess.length;++i) {
  if(guessed.indexOf(toGuess.charAt(i)) != -1)
    pattern += (toGuess.charAt(i)+" ")
  else pattern += "_ "
 }
 document.game.toGuess.value=pattern
}
function displayGuessed() {
 document.game.guessed.value=guessed
}
function badGuess(s) {
 if(toGuess.indexOf(s) == -1) return true
 return false
}
function winner() {
 for(i=0;i<toGuess.length;++i) {
  if(guessed.indexOf(toGuess.charAt(i)) == -1) return false
 }
 return true
}
function guess(s){
 if(guessed.indexOf(s) == -1) guessed = s + guessed
 if(badGuess(s)) ++guesses
 displayHangman()
 displayToGuess()
 displayGuessed()
 if(guesses >= max){
```

```
  alert("You're dead. The word you missed was "+toGuess+".")
  startAgain()
 }
 if(winner()) {
  alert("You won!")
  startAgain()
 }
}
// --></SCRIPT>
</HEAD>
<BODY>
<H1>Hangman</H1>
<FORM NAME="game">
<PRE>
<TEXTAREA NAME="status" ROWS="7" COLS="16"
 ONFOCUS="stayAway()"></TEXTAREA>
</PRE><P>
<INPUT TYPE="TEXT" NAME="toGuess"
 ONFOCUS="stayAway()"> Word to guess<BR>
<INPUT TYPE="TEXT" NAME="guessed"
 ONFOCUS="stayAway()"> Letters guessed so far<BR>
<P>Enter your next guess.</P>
<INPUT TYPE="BUTTON" VALUE=" A " ONCLICK="guess('A')">
<INPUT TYPE="BUTTON" VALUE=" B " ONCLICK="guess('B')">
<INPUT TYPE="BUTTON" VALUE=" C " ONCLICK="guess('C')">
<INPUT TYPE="BUTTON" VALUE=" D " ONCLICK="guess('D')">
<INPUT TYPE="BUTTON" VALUE=" E " ONCLICK="guess('E')">
<INPUT TYPE="BUTTON" VALUE=" F " ONCLICK="guess('F')">
<INPUT TYPE="BUTTON" VALUE=" G " ONCLICK="guess('G')">
<INPUT TYPE="BUTTON" VALUE=" H " ONCLICK="guess('H')">
<INPUT TYPE="BUTTON" VALUE=" I " ONCLICK="guess('I')">
<INPUT TYPE="BUTTON" VALUE=" J " ONCLICK="guess('J')">
<INPUT TYPE="BUTTON" VALUE=" K " ONCLICK="guess('K')">
<INPUT TYPE="BUTTON" VALUE=" L " ONCLICK="guess('L')">
<INPUT TYPE="BUTTON" VALUE=" M " ONCLICK="guess('M')">
<INPUT TYPE="BUTTON" VALUE=" N " ONCLICK="guess('N')">
<INPUT TYPE="BUTTON" VALUE=" O " ONCLICK="guess('O')">
<INPUT TYPE="BUTTON" VALUE=" P " ONCLICK="guess('P')">
<INPUT TYPE="BUTTON" VALUE=" Q " ONCLICK="guess('Q')">
<INPUT TYPE="BUTTON" VALUE=" R " ONCLICK="guess('R')">
<INPUT TYPE="BUTTON" VALUE=" S " ONCLICK="guess('S')">
<INPUT TYPE="BUTTON" VALUE=" T " ONCLICK="guess('T')">
<INPUT TYPE="BUTTON" VALUE=" U " ONCLICK="guess('U')">
<INPUT TYPE="BUTTON" VALUE=" V " ONCLICK="guess('V')">
<INPUT TYPE="BUTTON" VALUE=" W " ONCLICK="guess('W')">
<INPUT TYPE="BUTTON" VALUE=" X " ONCLICK="guess('X')">
<INPUT TYPE="BUTTON" VALUE=" Y " ONCLICK="guess('Y')">
<INPUT TYPE="BUTTON" VALUE=" Z " ONCLICK="guess('Z')"><P>
<INPUT TYPE="BUTTON" NAME="restart" VALUE="---- Start Again ----"
 ONCLICK="startAgain()">
<SCRIPT LANGUAGE="JavaScript"><!--
```

```
startAgain()
// --></SCRIPT>
</FORM>
</BODY>
</HTML>
```

The script defines two arrays: gallows and guessChoices; and eight functions: startAgain(), stayAway(), displayHangman(), displayToGuess(), displayGuessed(), badGuess(), winner(), and guess(). Each of these is discussed in the following paragraphs.

The *gallows* Array

This array contains eight string entries that correspond to the eight states that the gallows pole may be in: empty, head hanging, head and upper torso hanging, and so on. The strings may look very cryptic. That's because new lines are represented by the newline character (\n), and backslashes are represented by a pair of backslashes (\\). These are the standard escape characters used by JavaScript, Java, C, and C++. Try decoding and drawing each of the strings in the gallows array to get a better feel for how these escape characters are used.

The *guessChoices* Array

This array contains four words, which are the words that the user is required to guess. One word from this array is randomly selected for each play of the game. You can add or replace the words contained in this array to tailor Hangman to your own word list.

The *startAgain()* Function

This function starts and restarts the Hangman game. It initializes variables used by the program and then invokes the functions required to display the hangman, show the word to be guessed, and display the letters that the user has already guessed. The guesses variable keeps track of how many incorrect guesses the user has made. It is used to select which element of the gallows array is to be displayed. The max variable determines how many guesses the user can make before he or she is hung. The guessed variable is initialized to " " (one space) to indicate that the user has not yet guessed any letters.

NOTE   The value " " is used instead of "" (no space) because the indexOf() method of the string object does not work correctly for the value "".

The len variable is used to calculate the maximum array subscript of the guessChoices array. The toGuess variable is set to a randomly selected word in the guessChoices array. This word is then converted to uppercase. The displayHangman() function displays the hangman figure in the status text area. The displayToGuess() function displays the word being guessed in the toGuess text field. The displayGuessed() function displays the letters guessed by the user in the guessed text field. When the game is first started or restarted, the displayGuessed() function is used to blank out the guessed text field.

The *stayAway()* Function

This function is called by the onFocus event handlers of the form's text fields to warn the user not to mess around with these fields. This is to discourage the user from trying to change the content of these fields. Note that it moves the input focus to the "A" button before it displays the alert box.

The *displayHangman()* Function

This function displays the hangman character figure in the status text area. It does this by setting the value property of the status field of the game form of the current document to the gallows array entry corresponding to the number of incorrect guesses.

The *displayToGuess()* Function

This function displays a word pattern based on the word to be guessed and the letters the user has currently guessed. If a user has guessed a letter of the word, that letter is displayed. Otherwise, an underscore character is displayed in place of the letter. It loops through each letter of the word contained in toGuess, and uses the indexOf() method of the string object to determine whether that letter is contained in the guessed string. The word pattern is then written to the toGuessed text field.

The *displayGuessed()* Function

This function writes the value of the guessed variable to the guessed text field to inform the user of the letters that he or she has already tried. The guessed variable is updated each time a user makes a new letter guess.

The *badGuess()* Function

This function returns *true* if the letter represented by the s parameter is not in the word contained in the toGuess variable. It returns *false*, otherwise. It is used to determine whether the user has guessed incorrectly.

The *winner()* Function

This function checks each letter in the word contained in the toGuess variable, and returns *false* if any letter is not in the string contained in the guessed variable. It returns *true* otherwise. It is used to determine whether the user has correctly guessed all letters of the toGuess word.

The *guess()* Function

This function is invoked whenever the user clicks a button with the letters A through Z. It is invoked by the button's onClick event handler, and passes the letter associated with the button via the s parameter. Here's how it works:

1. The guess() function first checks to see if the letter is currently in the list of letters the user has already guessed, and adds the letter to the list if it is not.

2. It then checks to see if the letter is an incorrect guess, and increments the guesses variable accordingly.

3. Next, it invokes the appropriate functions to redisplay the form's text fields.

4. It then checks to see if the user has run out of guesses; if so, it alerts the user that they have been hung.

5. Finally, it invokes the winner() function to determine if the user has correctly guessed all letters of the toGuess word; if so, it tells the user that they have won.

The form displayed by the browser is named game. It contains the text area named status, the text fields named toGuess and guessed, the buttons labeled A through Z, and the Start Again button. Each of these form elements performs event handling that supports the processing of the Hangman game. This event handling is as follows:

status, toGuess, and guessed   These fields handle the onFocus event by invoking the stayAway() function to tell the user to not mess with the field's contents.

A through Z   These buttons handle the onClick event by invoking the guess() function and passing as a parameter the letter associated with the button.

Start Again   This button invokes the startAgain() function to reinitialize the game's variables and restart the game.

The script contained in the document body contains the single statement startAgain(), which initializes the variables used in the game and displays the contents of the form's text fields.

Client-Side Form Processing

The Hangman game of the previous section is a great example of the power of local form processing. However, unless your sole purpose in web programming is to entertain those who browse your web page, you'll probably want to use forms to return some data to your web server. This brings up the very important question of which processing should be performed locally via browser-side scripts and which should be performed on the server? For the most part, this question is easy to answer: "If it can be performed on the browser, do it." It's a pretty good rule of thumb. However, as with most rules of thumb, there are cases that create exceptions to the rule. For example, if you don't want anyone to know how you process the form data, don't do it locally on the browser. Anyone can figure out your processing approach by examining your JavaScript code. Another consideration is performance. If your web application requires a time- or resource-intensive computation, you can avoid upsetting your user by having the data sent back to your high-performance server for processing. However, forms processing is short and quick in most cases, and no noticeable impact is made on browser performance.

Working with CGI Scripts

Before the advent of JavaScript, the data the forms collected from users was submitted to Common Gateway Interface (CGI) programs. The CGI programs performed all processing on the form data, and sent the results of that processing back to the browser so that it could be displayed to users. The "The Hypertext Transfer Protocol (HTTP)" and "Common Gateway Interface Programs" sections of Chapter 1 provide a summary of the methods by which browsers communicate with CGI programs. In this section, I'll show how to use JavaScript scripts to communicate with CGI programs. More importantly, I'll show how to use JavaScript to perform local processing of form data before sending the data to CGI programs.

Sending Form Data to a CGI Program

When a form sends data to a CGI program, it uses either the GET or POST method. This method is specified by setting the METHOD attribute of the form to either "GET" or "POST". If the GET method is used, the form encodes and appends its data to the URL of the CGI program. When a web server receives the encoded URL, it passes the form data to the CGI program via a program variable known as an *environment* variable. If the POST method is used, the web server passes the form's data to the CGI program via the program's standard input. The POST method is preferred over the GET method because of data-size limitations associated with environment variables. The method property of the form object allows a form's method to be set within JavaScript.

A form's ACTION attribute specifies the URL of the CGI program to which a form's data is to be sent. The action property of the form object allows this URL to be set or changed within JavaScript. This allows a script to send a form's data to one of several CGI programs, depending upon the form's contents as entered by a user. For example, you can have a general-purpose form that collects information on users interested in your product line and then process that data in different ways, depending upon the demographic data supplied by the user.

In most cases, form data is encoded using the URL encoding scheme identified by the following MIME type: application/x-www-form-urlencoded.

However, it is likely that another scheme will become popular because of its support for file uploads:

```
multipart/form-data encoding
```

This encoding scheme is discussed in RFC 1867, which can be found at the URL www .jaworski.com/javascript/rfc1867.txt. The encoding property of the form object identifies what encoding scheme was specified by the form's ENCTYPE attribute. The encoding property may also be used to change this attribute.

NOTE   An RFC (literally a Request for Comments) is a document that is used to describe a particular aspect of the Internet, such as a protocol standard or a coding scheme.

Performing Local Form Processing

Having covered the basic form properties that control a form's interaction with a CGI program, let's investigate how JavaScript can be used to locally process a form's data and then send the processed data to the web server.

When a form is submitted, either as the result of a user clicking a submit button or the invocation of a form's SUBMIT() method, all the data contained in the form's fields are sent to the web server. This is both inefficient and undesirable because we can use JavaScript to preprocess a form's data.

The secret to using JavaScript to send processed form data to CGI programs is to use a *summary form* to hold the data that is the result of any local form processing. Once a form's data has been initially processed, it is put into a summary form and then the summary form is sent to the CGI program for any additional processing that is required. Listing 8.3 illustrates this concept. A web page is designed with two forms. The first form is visible to the user and is the form used to collect raw input data. This form is shown in Figure 8.7. It provides the user with four selection lists from which the user can select a particular type of automobile.

Listing 8.3   **Using a Summary Form to Support Local Processing (orderform.htm)**

```
<HTML>
<HEAD>
<TITLE>Submitting the results of local form processing</TITLE>
<SCRIPT LANGUAGE="JavaScript"><!--
```

```
function processOrder() {
 order = ""
 order += document.orderForm.model.selectedIndex
 order += document.orderForm.doors.selectedIndex
 order += document.orderForm.color.selectedIndex
 sel = document.orderForm.accessories
 for(i=0;i<sel.length;++i)
  if(sel.options[i].selected) order += i
 document.submitForm.result.value = order
 document.submitForm.submit()
 return false
}
// --></SCRIPT>
</HEAD>
<BODY>
<H1>Select your next car:</H1>
<PRE>Model          Doors      Color    Accessories</PRE>
<FORM ACTION="" NAME="orderForm"ONSUBMIT="return processOrder()">
<SELECT NAME="model" SIZE="3">
<OPTION>Big Blob</OPTION>
<OPTION>Wild Thing</OPTION>
<OPTION>Penny Pincher</OPTION>
<OPTION>Class Act</OPTION>
</SELECT>
<SELECT NAME="doors" SIZE="3">
<OPTION>2 doors</OPTION>
<OPTION>4 doors</OPTION>
</SELECT>
<SELECT NAME="color" SIZE="3">
<OPTION>red</OPTION>
<OPTION>white</OPTION>
<OPTION>blue</OPTION>
<OPTION>black</OPTION>
<OPTION>brown</OPTION>
<OPTION>silver</OPTION>
<OPTION>pink</OPTION>
</SELECT>
<SELECT NAME="accessories" SIZE="3" MULTIPLE="MULTIPLE">
<OPTION>air conditioning</OPTION>
<OPTION>CD player</OPTION>
<OPTION>bigger engine</OPTION>
<OPTION>fancy dashboard</OPTION>
<OPTION>leather seats</OPTION>
</SELECT>
<P><INPUT TYPE="SUBMIT" NAME="order" VALUE="I'll take it!"></P>
</FORM>
<FORM ACTION="http://www.jaworski.com/javascript/echo.cgi"
      METHOD="GET" NAME="submitForm">
<INPUT TYPE="HIDDEN" NAME="result">
</FORM>
</BODY>
</HTML>
```

FIGURE 8.7:

The form that is presented to the user (Listing 8.3).

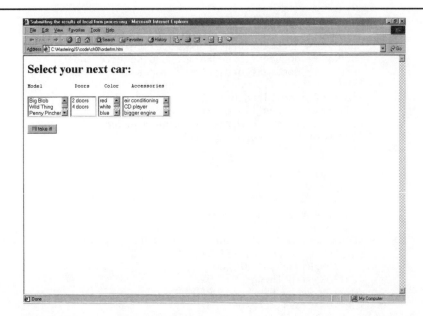

When the first form is submitted, the onSubmit event handler invokes the processOrder() function as the argument of a return statement. If the return statement returns *false*, the form is not submitted. If the return statement returns *true*, the form *is* submitted. Because processOrder() *always* returns *false*, the form will never be submitted. Instead, process-Order() fills in the invisible field in the second form, and submits the second form to a CGI program located on my web server. This CGI program is located at the URL www.jaworski.com/javascript/echo.cgi. It merely echoes back any form fields that it has received from the browser. Figure 8.8 provides an example of the CGI program's output.

FIGURE 8.8:

The form data that is echoed by the web server (Listing 8.3)

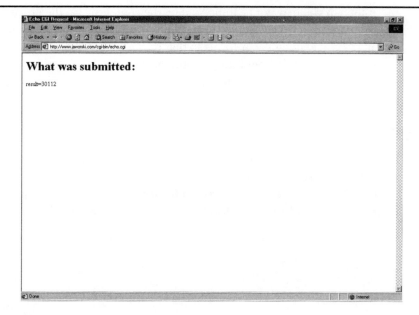

I'll summarize what I've covered so far. The first form is used to gather automobile selection data from the user. When the first form is submitted, processOrder() is invoked to process this data locally on the user's browser. processOrder() then inserts the processed data into the second form (named submitForm), and submits the second form to my web server. The web server then echoes the form fields back to the browser.

The processing performed by processOrder() is quite simple, but it illustrates how locally processed form data can be sent to a web server. Here are the steps:

1. processOrder() begins by setting the order variable to a string that contains the indices of the list items selected in the model, doors, and colors selection lists. Each of these three lists is a single-selection list.

2. For each item in the multiple-selection accessories list, processOrder() checks to see if the item has been selected, and appends the index of each selected accessories item to the string stored in the order variable.

3. The processOrder() function then sets the invisible results field of submitForm to the value stored in order. By doing so, it has placed all of the first form's results into a single field in submitForm.

4. The processOrder() function then invokes the submit() method of submitForm to send the result field to my web server.

Although you may not be impressed by the complexity of the processing performed by processOrder(), you should realize the value of the approach that it takes. This approach allows you to design your forms so that they are most appealing to your end users. When the user submits a filled-out form, you can process the form's results and send the results to your web server in whatever format is most efficient for your CGI or other server-side programs.

Summary

This chapter introduced the form object, and discussed the JavaScript objects that are associated with form fields and GUI controls. It showed you how to use the properties and methods of these objects, and how to handle form-related events. In the next chapter, you will learn how to enhance your forms by using hidden form fields and cookies.

CHAPTER 9

Using Hidden Fields and Cookies

- Maintaining state information

- Using hidden form fields

- Using cookies

- How is information stored in a cookie?

- Comparison—cookies versus hidden form fields

The Web was originally designed to be *stateless*, in the sense that all web servers would process URL requests in the same manner, independent of any previous requests. This enabled the first web servers to be fast and efficient by not requiring them to maintain information about the browsers requesting URLs. Browsers also operated in a stateless fashion, processing new URL requests independently of previous requests.

The stateless design of the Web works well in most cases. When a browser requests a particular web page, the web server that provides that page will serve it up to the browser in the same way every time. Similarly, all web browsers requesting a particular web page always request that page in the same way. However, there are situations in which you *want* the processing of one web page to be dependent on the processing of previous pages. For example, you may want to enable a user to complete a series of forms in which the user's responses to the first form determine which forms are provided next. For example, you may want to create a form that collects general information about the user, such as name and address, and link it to subsequent forms to collect more information. However, those forms will vary, depending on what country the user has entered in the first form.

A number of capabilities have been successively introduced to enable web applications to be built upon the stateless design of the Web. *Hidden form fields* were introduced first, followed by HTTP "cookies." These capabilities were introduced to allow CGI programs to maintain information about individual web browsers. With JavaScript's support of browser-side scripting, the use of hidden fields and cookies can be taken to new levels.

In this chapter, you'll learn how to use hidden fields and cookies to maintain browser state information and how you can use this information in your scripts to develop more capable and powerful web applications. When you've finished this chapter, you'll be able to read and update hidden fields and cookies using JavaScript, and locally implement on the browser side much of the complex state-related processing that would otherwise be performed by server-side CGI programs.

Maintaining State Information

To gain a greater understanding of the problem of maintaining state information, let's explore the example discussed in this chapter's introduction. Suppose that you want to develop a web page that presents a related series of forms to a user as follows:

Form one   Collects the user's name, address, phone number, and e-mail address.

Form two   Asks the user which of your products he or she currently uses.

Form three   Asks the user to evaluate the products that he or she uses.

Say the user receives the first form, fills it out, and submits it. It goes to a CGI program located on your web server. This CGI program processes the form's data, and sends the second form to the user. The user fills out the second form and submits it. It goes to the same or perhaps a different CGI program on your server. When this CGI program receives the second form's data, it has no way of knowing that the second form's data is related to the data of the first form. Therefore, it cannot combine the results of the two forms in its database. The same problem occurs with the CGI program that receives the third form's data.

There is a work around to this problem. You can have the user enter some small piece of common information, such as his e-mail address, in all three forms. When the second and third forms are submitted to your web server, a CGI program can combine their data based upon the common e-mail address. This work-around allows your CGI programs to continue to operate in a stateless manner. However, your users suffer by having to re-enter their e-mail address in all three forms. Although this may not seem to be much of an inconvenience, it is noticeable, and it detracts from the appeal of your forms.

What would be even better is if somehow your CGI program could remember the e-mail address that was entered into the first form, and attach it to the second and third forms that it sends to your browser. *Hidden form fields* (discussed next) were invented to provide CGI programs with this specific capability.

Using Hidden Form Fields

Hidden form fields are text fields that are not displayed and cannot be modified by a user. Forms with hidden fields are dynamically generated by CGI programs as the result of processing data submitted by other forms.

A CGI program sets a hidden field to a particular value when the server sends a form to a browser. When a user fills out and submits a form containing a hidden field, the value originally stored in the field is returned to the server. The server uses the information stored in the hidden field to maintain state information about the user's browser. To see how this works, let's examine how hidden fields can be used in the three-form example discussed in the previous section.

When a user fills out the name and address information and submits form 1, the CGI program on your server processes the form data by creating a record in a database and sending form 2 back to the user. However, instead of sending a static form 2, it dynamically *generates* a form 2 that contains a hidden field, with the field's value set to the e-mail address that was submitted in the first form.

When the user fills out and submits form 2, the hidden field (still with the user's e-mail address) is sent to your CGI program. Your CGI program can now relate the data of the second form with that of the first because they both have the same value in the e-mail address field. (This is true even if the user did not have to retype his or her e-mail address in the second form.) The same process is carried out for the third form, after which the CGI program sends back a web page to the user, thanking him or her for filling out the forms.

JavaScript and Hidden Form Fields

At this point, you are probably wondering what any of this has to do with JavaScript. JavaScript's browser-side programming features take full advantage of and enhance the capabilities provided by hidden fields. With JavaScript, you can eliminate the need to send three forms back and forth between the user's browser and your CGI programs. A JavaScript script can perform the processing of all three forms locally on the user's browser and then consolidate the forms' results before sending them to a CGI program.

To see how JavaScript can use hidden fields to implement our three-form customer survey, open the `survey.htm` file (Listing 9.1) with your browser. This file uses the hidden form, `control.htm`, shown in Listing 9.2. Your browser will display the first form of a three-form series, as shown in Figure 9.1. Fill out this form and click the Next button. Make sure that you fill in the *E-mail address* field; otherwise, you will receive the alert message shown in Figure 9.2.

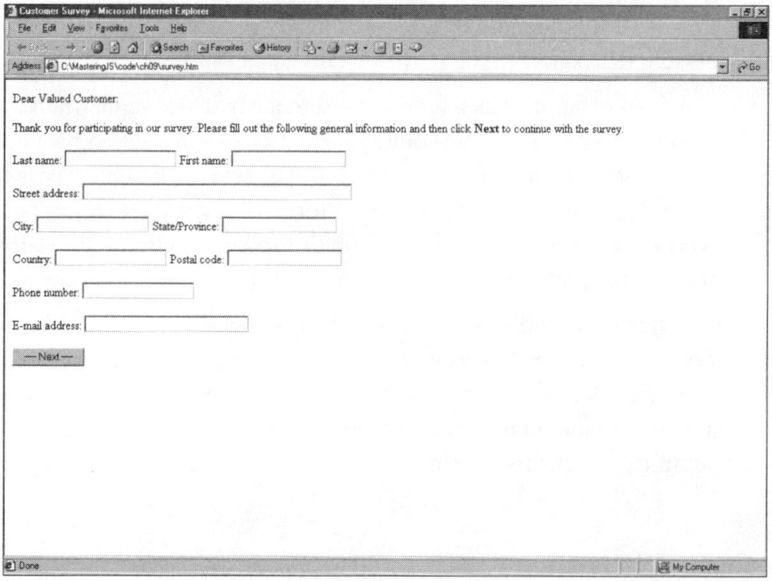

FIGURE 9.1:

The first form of the customer survey asks the user to enter general name and address information.
(Listing 9.3)

FIGURE 9.2:

If the user skips the *E-mail address* field, the form validation alert notifies the user that this information is necessary. (Listing 9.3)

After you click the Next button, the form shown in Figure 9.3 is displayed. This form asks you to identify which products you use. Click the check box of at least one of these fictitious products.

FIGURE 9.3:

The second form of the customer survey asks users what products they use. (Listing 9.4)

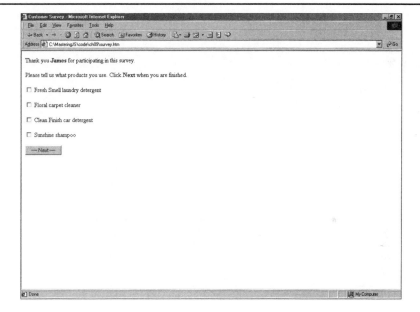

NOTE   If you do not select at least one of the four products, the third part of the form will be skipped.

After you click the Next button of the second form, the third form is displayed, as shown in Figure 9.4. The third form asks you to evaluate the products that you selected in the second form. Use the radio buttons to perform your product evaluation.

FIGURE 9.4:

The third form of the customer survey asks customers how they like the products. (Listing 9.5)

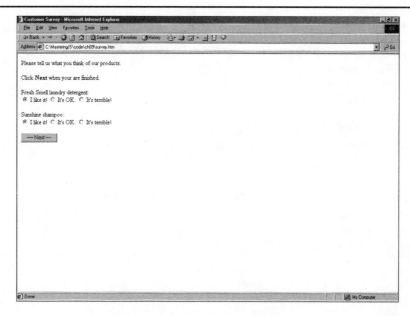

When you click the Next button on the third form, all of the values of the three forms are collectively sent to the CGI program located at www.jaworski.com/cgi-bin/thanks.cgi. This CGI program reads these values and then sends back the thank-you message shown in Figure 9.5.

FIGURE 9.5:

The thank-you message is displayed after the user completes the survey.

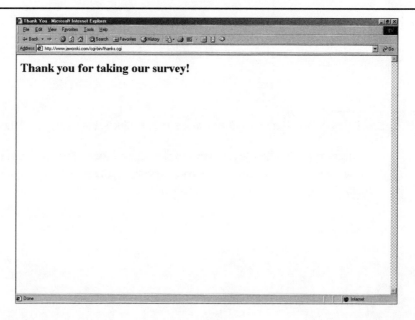

The processing performed in the example all takes place on the user's browser. A CGI program is not required until after all three forms have been filled out. The values of these forms are stored in a separate invisible form that consists entirely of hidden fields. As the user completes each form, the values of the current form are stored in the hidden fields of the invisible form. When the user has completed the third form (or completed the second form without checking any products), the invisible form is submitted to the CGI program. This is much more efficient than having a CGI program process the results of each form separately.

TIP   If you were creating a real survey, you would dress up the form with graphics and a catchier layout.

The survey.htm file shown in Listing 9.1 defines a two-frame set. The first frame loads the file form1.htm (Listing 9.3) and the second frame loads control.htm (Listing 9.2). The border attribute of the frame set is set to 0 to avoid displaying a distracting border between frames.

Listing 9.1:   Defining the Survey's Frame Set (survey.htm)

```
<HTML>
<HEAD>
<TITLE>Customer Survey</TITLE>
</HEAD>
<FRAMESET COLS="*,10" BORDER=0>
<FRAME SRC="form1.htm">
<FRAME SRC="control.htm">
</FRAMESET>
</HTML>
```

Listing 9.2:   The Survey's Hidden Form (control.htm)

```
<HTML>
<HEAD>
<SCRIPT LANGUAGE="JavaScript"><!--
// --></SCRIPT>
</HEAD>
<BODY>
<FORM ACTION="http://www.jaworski.com/cgi-bin/thanks.cgi"
 NAME="controlForm"
 METHOD="post" TARGET="_top">
<INPUT TYPE="HIDDEN" NAME="lastName" VALUE="">
<INPUT TYPE="HIDDEN" NAME="firstName" VALUE="">
<INPUT TYPE="HIDDEN" NAME="street" VALUE="">
<INPUT TYPE="HIDDEN" NAME="city" VALUE="">
<INPUT TYPE="HIDDEN" NAME="state" VALUE="">
<INPUT TYPE="HIDDEN" NAME="country" VALUE="">
```

```
<INPUT TYPE="HIDDEN" NAME="zip" VALUE="">
<INPUT TYPE="HIDDEN" NAME="phone" VALUE="">
<INPUT TYPE="HIDDEN" NAME="email" VALUE="">
<INPUT TYPE="HIDDEN" NAME="products" VALUE="">
<INPUT TYPE="HIDDEN" NAME="evaluation" VALUE="">
</FORM>
</BODY>
</HTML>
```

The control.htm file defines a form with 11 hidden fields. Because all of the form's fields are hidden, the form is not displayed. These fields are filled in with the data collected by the three visible forms that are displayed to the user.

The form's NAME attribute is set to "controlForm". This allows the form to be referenced by name by the JavaScript code that executes with the forms contained in the first frame.

The form's ACTION attribute is set to the URL of my CGI program and its METHOD attribute is set to "post". When the form is submitted, this CGI program receives the data that has been stored in the hidden fields, and returns a thank-you message to the user. The form's TARGET attribute is "_top". This causes the thank-you message to be displayed in the full window occupied by survey.htm rather than in the frame occupied by control.htm.

The form1.htm file displays the form shown in Figure 9.1 in the first frame of the frame set. It contains a single script that defines the processForm1() function. This function handles the onClick event that is generated when the user clicks on the Next button. It sets the form1 variable to document.forms["formOne"] so that it can be used as a shortcut (to avoid having to retype the document prefix). It then checks to see if the email field is blank. If it is blank, it displays an alert dialog box to the user; otherwise, it continues on with its processing. The controlForm variable is used as a shortcut to the hidden form stored in the second frame. All the fields from form1 are then copied into the hidden fields of controlForm. Finally, the form2.htm (Listing 9.4) file is loaded into the first frame, and formTwo replaces formOne.

Listing 9.3:   The First Form of the Survey (form1.htm)

```
<HTML>
<HEAD>
<TITLE>Customer Survey: General Information</TITLE>
<SCRIPT LANGUAGE="JavaScript"><!--
function processForm1() {
 form1 = document.forms["formOne"]
 if(form1.email.value=="")
  alert("You must fill in your e-mail address!")
 else {
  controlForm = parent.frames[1].document.controlForm
```

```
      controlForm.lastName.value=form1.lastName.value
      controlForm.firstName.value=form1.firstName.value
      controlForm.street.value=form1.street.value
      controlForm.city.value=form1.city.value
      controlForm.state.value=form1.state.value
      controlForm.country.value=form1.country.value
      controlForm.zip.value=form1.zip.value
      controlForm.phone.value=form1.phone.value
      controlForm.email.value=form1.email.value
      location.href="form2.htm"
  }
}
// --></SCRIPT>
</HEAD>
<BODY>
<P>Dear Valued Customer:</P>
<P>Thank you for participating in our survey. Please fill out
 the following general information and then click <B>Next</B> to
 continue with the survey.</P>
<FORM ACTION="" NAME="formOne">
<P>Last name: <INPUT TYPE="TEXT" NAME="lastName">
 First name: <INPUT TYPE="TEXT" NAME="firstName"></P>
<P>Street address: <INPUT TYPE="TEXT" SIZE="50" NAME="street">
 </P>
<P>City: <INPUT TYPE="TEXT" NAME="city">
 State/Province: <INPUT TYPE="TEXT" NAME="state"></P>
<P>Country: <INPUT TYPE="TEXT" NAME="country">
 Postal code: <INPUT TYPE="TEXT" NAME="zip"></P>
<P>Phone number: <INPUT TYPE="TEXT" NAME="phone"></P>
<P>E-mail address: <INPUT TYPE="TEXT" SIZE="30" NAME="email">
 </P>
<P></P>
<INPUT TYPE="BUTTON" NAME="next" VALUE="---- Next ----"
 onClick="processForm1()">
</FORM>
</BODY>
</HTML>
```

The form2.htm file displays the form shown in Figure 9.3. It contains two scripts—one in the document head and the other in the document body. The script in the document body is executed when the web page is generated. This script is used to insert the first name of the user into the text that is displayed above the form.

Listing 9.4:   The Second Form of the Survey (form2.htm)

```
<HTML>
<HEAD>
<TITLE>Customer Survey: Product Usage</TITLE>
<SCRIPT LANGUAGE="JavaScript"><!--
```

```
function processForm2() {
 controlForm = parent.frames[1].document.controlForm
 form2 = document.forms["formTwo"]
 products = ""
 if(form2.laundry.checked) products += "1"
 else products += "0"
 if(form2.carpet.checked) products += "1"
 else products += "0"
 if(form2.car.checked) products += "1"
 else products += "0"
 if(form2.shampoo.checked) products += "1"
 else products += "0"
 controlForm.products.value=products
 location.href="form3.htm"
}
// --></SCRIPT>
</HEAD>
<BODY>
<SCRIPT LANGUAGE="JavaScript"><!--
var s = "<P>Thank you <B>"
s += parent.frames[1].document.controlForm.firstName.value
s += "</B>"
document.write(s)+
document.writeln("for participating in this survey.</P>")
// --></SCRIPT>
<P>Please tell us what products you use. Click <B>Next</B> when you are
finished.</P>
<FORM NAME="formTwo">
<P><INPUT TYPE="CHECKBOX" NAME="laundry"> Fresh Smell laundry detergent</P>
<P><INPUT TYPE="CHECKBOX" NAME="carpet"> Floral carpet cleaner</P>
<P><INPUT TYPE="CHECKBOX" NAME="car"> Clean Finish car detergent</P>
<P><INPUT TYPE="CHECKBOX" NAME="shampoo"> Sunshine shampoo</P>
<P></P>
<P><INPUT TYPE="BUTTON" NAME="next" VALUE="---- Next ----"
onClick="processForm2()"></P>
</FORM>
</BODY>
</HTML>
```

The script in the document head defines the processForm2() function. This function handles the onClick event that is generated when the user clicks the Next button. It sets the hidden products field of controlForm based upon the products the user has checked off. It then loads form3.htm (Listing 9.5) as the replacement for form2.htm in the first frame.

Listing 9.5:   The Third Form of the Survey (form3.htm)

```
<HTML>
<HEAD>
<TITLE>Customer Survey: Product Evaluation</TITLE>
```

```
<SCRIPT LANGUAGE="JavaScript"><!--
function usesProducts() {
 productsUsed = parent.frames[1].document.controlForm.products.value
 usage = new Array(productsUsed.length)
 productsInUse=false
 for(i=0;i<usage.length;++i) {
  if(productsUsed.charAt(i)=="0") usage[i]=false
  else{
   usage[i]=true
   productsInUse=true
  }
 }
 return productsInUse
}
function askAboutProducts() {
 document.writeln('<P>Please tell us what you think of our products.</P>')
 document.writeln('<P>Click <B>Next</B> when your are finished.</P>')
 document.writeln('<FORM NAME="formThree">')
 if(usage[0]){
  document.writeln('<P>Fresh Smell laundry detergent:<BR>')
  document.writeln('<INPUT TYPE="RADIO" NAME="laundry"')
  document.writeln('VALUE="like" CHECKED> I like it!')
  document.writeln('<INPUT TYPE="RADIO" NAME="laundry"')
  document.writeln('VALUE="ok"> It\'s OK.')
  document.writeln('<INPUT TYPE="RADIO" NAME="laundry"')
  document.writeln('VALUE="dislike"> It\'s terrible!')
  document.writeln('</P>')
 }
 if(usage[1]){
  document.writeln('<P>Floral carpet cleaner:<BR>')
  document.writeln('<INPUT TYPE="RADIO" NAME="carpet"')
  document.writeln('VALUE="like" CHECKED> I like it!')
  document.writeln('<INPUT TYPE="RADIO" NAME="carpet"')
  document.writeln('VALUE="ok"> It\'s OK.')
  document.writeln('<INPUT TYPE="RADIO" NAME="carpet"')
  document.writeln('VALUE="dislike"> It\'s terrible!')
  document.writeln('</P>')
 }
 if(usage[2]){
  document.writeln('<P>Clean Finish car detergent:<BR>')
  document.writeln('<INPUT TYPE="RADIO" NAME="car"')
  document.writeln('VALUE="like" CHECKED> I like it!')
  document.writeln('<INPUT TYPE="RADIO" NAME="car"')
  document.writeln('VALUE="ok"> It\'s OK.')
  document.writeln('<INPUT TYPE="RADIO" NAME="car"')
  document.writeln('VALUE="dislike"> It\'s terrible!')
  document.writeln('</P>')
 }
 if(usage[3]){
  document.writeln('<P>Sunshine shampoo:<BR>')
  document.writeln('<INPUT TYPE="RADIO" NAME="shampoo"')
```

```
   document.writeln('VALUE="like" CHECKED> I like it!')
   document.writeln('<INPUT TYPE="RADIO" NAME="shampoo"')
   document.writeln('VALUE="ok"> It\'s OK.')
   document.writeln('<INPUT TYPE="RADIO" NAME="shampoo"')
   document.writeln('VALUE="dislike"> It\'s terrible!')
   document.writeln('</P>')
  }
 document.writeln('<P></P><P>')
 document.writeln('<INPUT TYPE="BUTTON" NAME="next"')
 document.writeln('VALUE="---- Next ----" ')
 document.writeln(' onClick="processForm3()"></P>')
 document.writeln('</FORM>')
 }
function processForm3() {
 controlForm = parent.frames[1].document.controlForm
 form3 = document.forms["formThree"]
 evaluation = ""
 for(i=0;i<form3.elements.length-1;++i)
  if(form3.elements[i].checked)
    evaluation += form3.elements[i].value + " "
 controlForm.evaluation.value=evaluation
 controlForm.submit()
 }
// --></SCRIPT>
</HEAD>
<BODY>
<SCRIPT LANGUAGE="JavaScript"><!--
if(usesProducts()) askAboutProducts()
else parent.frames[1].document.controlForm.submit()
// --></SCRIPT>
</BODY>
</HTML>
```

The form3.htm file, unlike form1.htm and form2.htm, consists almost entirely of JavaScript code. Most of the code is contained in the script located in the document's head. A small script is contained in the document's body. This script invokes the usesProducts() function to determine whether the user had checked any products when he filled out formTwo. If the user had checked at least one product, the askAboutProducts() function is invoked to generate formThree. Otherwise, the controlForm is submitted as is, without the user having to fill in formThree.

• The script in the document head defines three functions: usesProducts(), askAbout-Products(), and processForm3.

These functions are discussed in the following subsections.

The *usesProducts()* Function

This function checks the hidden products field of controlForm to determine what products the user checked off when filling in formTwo. It initializes the usage array based upon this information. It sets productsInUse to *true* if the user has checked off any products in formTwo, and to *false* otherwise. It then returns this value as a result.

The *askAboutProducts()* Function

This function generates the HTML content of formThree. It creates a short text introduction to the form, generates the <form> tag, and then generates a set of three radio buttons for each product the user selected in formTwo. It then generates a Next button for the form, setting the form's onClick event handler to processForm3(). Finally, it generates the closing </form> tag.

The *processForm3()* Function

This function handles the onClick event generated when the user clicks on the Next button after filling out formThree. It summarizes the radio buttons checked by the user and stores this summary in the hidden evaluation field of controlForm. It then submits the data contained in controlForm.

Using Cookies

Hidden form fields were introduced to enable CGI programs to maintain state information about web browsers. They work well in situations in which the state information is to be maintained for a short period of time, as is the case when a user fills out a series of forms. However, hidden fields do not allow state information to be maintained in a *persistent* manner. That is, hidden fields can only be used within a single browser session. When a user exits the browser, the information contained in a hidden form field is lost forever.

Netscape developed the *cookie* as a means to store state-related and other information in a persistent manner. The information stored in a cookie is maintained between browser sessions; it survives when the user turns off their machine. Cookies allow CGI and other programs to store information on web browsers for significantly longer time periods.

NOTE   Cookies are supported by Netscape Navigator, Internet Explorer, and most other major browsers.

A cookie often consists of information sent by a server-side program in response to a URL request by the browser. The browser stores the information in the local cookie file ("the cookie jar") according to the URL of the CGI program sending the cookie. This URL may be generalized, based upon additional information contained in the cookie. Different browsers will store the cookie in different files. For example, Netscape Navigator stores cookies in a file named `cookies.txt`. Internet Explorer stores cookies in multiple files in the `\windows\cookies` directory.

WARNING   Internet Explorer 3 correctly processes cookies only when a document is read from the Web via an HTTP connection. In particular, it does not support cookies when a document is read from the local file system.

When a browser requests a URL from a web server, the browser first searches the local cookie files to see if the URL of any of its cookies matches the URL that is being requested. The browser then sends the information contained in the matching cookie or cookies to the web server as part of the URL request. Cookies provide CGI programs with the capability to store information on browsers. Browsers return this information to CGI programs when they request the URL of the CGI program. CGI programs update cookies when they respond to browser URL requests. In this manner, a CGI program can use browsers to maintain state information and have the browsers return this information whenever they invoke the CGI program.

To get a better feel for how cookies work, let's revisit the three-form example introduced in the beginning of this chapter. The goal is to implement a sequence of forms in which each form expands upon the information gathered in previous forms. In order to do this, a CGI program must be able to relate the data received in later forms with that received in earlier forms. The solution is for the CGI program to identify related forms using data that is common to these forms. A person's e-mail address is a common example of this identifying data.

Cookies provide a persistent mechanism for storing identifying data. When a browser submits formOne to a CGI program, the CGI program responds by sending formTwo to the browser. A cookie containing the user's e-mail address accompanies this second form. When the browser submits formTwo, it returns any cookies that match the CGI program to which the form is submitted. This causes the user's e-mail address to be returned with the submitted formTwo data. The CGI program then sends formThree to the browser. When the user submits formThree, the browser again checks the local cookie file and sends any related cookies.

Cookies are obviously more powerful than hidden form fields. Because cookies can persist between browser sessions, they may be used to store permanent user data, such as identification information (e-mail address) and preferences (frames, background colors, and so on), as well as state information (the current page in an online book).

How Is Information Stored in a Cookie?

A cookie is created when a CGI program includes a Set-Cookie header as part of an HTTP response. This response is generated when a browser requests the URL of the CGI program. The syntax of the Set-Cookie header is the following:

```
Set-Cookie: NAME=VALUE
[; expires=DATE][; path=PATH][; domain=DOMAIN_NAME][; secure]
```

The `NAME=VALUE` field (discussed next) is required. The other fields are optional; however, they should all appear on the same line as the Set-Cookie header.

NOTE   More than one Set-Cookie header may be sent in a single HTTP response.

The *NAME=VALUE* Field

This field contains the essential data being stored in a cookie. For example, when used to store my e-mail address, it could appear as `email=jamie@jaworski.com`. A semicolon, comma, or white-space character is not allowed in the `NAME=VALUE` string per the cookie specification. Applications are free to develop their own encoding schemes for these strings.

The expires=*DATE* Field

This field specifies the expiration date of a cookie. If it is omitted, the cookie expires at the end of the current browser session. The date is specified in the following format:

```
Weekday, DD-Mon-YY HH:MM:SS GMT
```

Weekday is the day of the week. *DD* is the day of the month. *Mon* is the first three letters of the month. *YY* is the year (for example, 02). *HH* is hours. *MM* is minutes. *SS* is seconds. The GMT time zone is always used. An example date is the following:

```
Monday, 20-Sep-10 12:00:00 GMT
```

The previous date is noon GMT on September 20th, 2010. Although cookies store the year in a two-digit year format, there is no year 2000 (Y2K) problem associated with them. Browsers accept the year 10 as the year 2010. If cookies are still around in the middle of the twenty-first century, browsers of that era will need to be updated to support dates in the later part of that century. Cookies that specify long-term user preferences should specify an expiration date of several years to help ensure that the cookies will be available as needed in the future. Cookies that specify short-term state information should expire in days, at which point the expired (stale) cookies are automatically destroyed.

The domain=*DOMAIN_NAME* Field

When a cookie is stored in the local file system, it is organized by the URL of the CGI program that sent the cookie. The domain field is used to specify a more general domain name to which the cookie should apply. For example, suppose that the URL of the CGI program that sends a cookie has the domain *athome.jaworski.com*. A domain=jaworski.com field in a cookie would associate that cookie with all hosts in the *jaworski.com* domain, not just the single host *athome.jaworski.com*. The domain field cannot be used to associate cookies with top-level domains *.com*, *.mil*, *.edu*, *.net*, *.org*, *.gov*, and *.int*. Any domain name that is not part of the top-level domains (for example, *ca.us*) must include an extra subdomain. For example, *sd.ca.us* is allowed, but *ca.us* is not.

The path=*PATH* Field

This field is used to specify a more general path for the URL associated with a cookie. For example, suppose that the URL of a CGI program is www.courseone.com/mastering-javascript/js-examples/ch09/test.asp. The *path* of that CGI program is /mastering-javascript/js-examples/ch09/. In order to associate a cookie with all of my CGI programs in this example, I could set path=/masteringjavascript.

The *secure* Field

If the secure field is specified, a cookie is sent over only a secure communication channel (HTTPS servers).

When a browser sends matching cookies back to a web server, it sends an HTTP request header in the following format:

```
Cookie: NAME1=VALUE1; NAME2=VALUE2; ... NAMEN=VALUEN
```

NAME1 through NAMEN identify the cookie names, and VALUE1 through VALUEN identify their values.

NOTE   You can find Netscape's original documentation on cookies at www.netscape.com/newsref/std/cookie_spec.html.

Using JavaScript with Cookies

Cookies provide a powerful feature for web application development, but using them with CGI programs can be somewhat messy. You have to design your programs to send cookies via the HTTP response header and to receive cookies via the HTTP request header.

Although this is not difficult to implement, it means that more processing is performed on the server and not on the browser.

JavaScript, on the other hand, can take full advantage of cookies by reading and setting them locally on the browser, eliminating the need for the cookies to be processed by CGI programs. A JavaScript script can then forward any information the CGI program requires to perform its processing. By using JavaScript to maintain cookies and perform as much processing as possible on the browser, CGI programs can be greatly simplified, and in most cases, eliminated.

The cookie associated with a document is set using the document's `cookie` property. When you set a cookie, you must provide the same cookie fields that would be provided by a CGI program. For example, consider the following statements:

```
email="jamie@jaworski.com"
expirationDate="Thursday, 01-Dec-11 12:00:00 GMT"
document.cookie="email="+email+";expires="+expirationDate
```

These statements set the value of the `cookie` property of the current document to the string `"email=jamie@jaworski.com; expires=Thursday, 01-Dec-11 12:00:00 GMT"`. Note that the `expires` field is required to keep the cookie from expiring after the current browser session. `Domain`, `path` and `secure` fields can also be used when a `cookie` property is set.

When the value of the cookie is retrieved using the following statement, the `cookieString` variable will be assigned the value "`email=jamie@jaworski.com`":

```
cookieString=document.cookie
```

If multiple cookies had been set for the current document, `cookieString` would contain a list of semicolon-separated `name=value` pairs. For example, consider the following statements:

```
email="jamie@jaworski.com"
firstName="Jamie"
lastName="Jaworski"
expirationDate="Thursday, 01-Dec-11 12:00:00 GMT"
document.cookie="email="+email+";expires="+expirationDate
document.cookie="firstName="+firstName
 +";expires="+expirationDate
document.cookie="lastName="+lastName+";expires="+expirationDate
cookieString=document.cookie
```

The value of `cookieString` includes the `name=value` pairs of the `email`, `firstName`, and `lastName` cookies. This value is `"email=jamie@jaworski.com; firstName=Jamie; lastName=Jaworski"`.

NOTE   Bill Dortch provides a number of reusable cookie-processing functions at `www.hidaho .com/cookies/cookie.txt`.

In order to get a feel for how cookies are accessed via JavaScript, run the file cooktest.htm shown in Listing 9.6. It will display the form shown in Figure 9.6. This form allows you to enter the text of a cookie and then set the cookie by clicking the Set Cookie button. The new value of the cookie is displayed at the top of the web page.

Listing 9.6:   A Cookie Test Program (cooktest.htm)

```
<HTML>
<HEAD>
<TITLE>Cookie Test</TITLE>
<SCRIPT LANGUAGE="JavaScript"><!--
function updateCookie() {
 document.cookie=document.form1.cookie.value
 location.reload(true)
}
// --></SCRIPT>
</HEAD>
<BODY>
<SCRIPT LANGUAGE="JavaScript">
 document.write("Your current cookie value is: '"+
   document.cookie+"'")
</SCRIPT>
<FORM ACTION="" NAME="form1">
<P>Enter new cookie: <INPUT TYPE="TEXT" SIZE="60"
 NAME="cookie"></P>
<INPUT TYPE="BUTTON" NAME="setCookie" VALUE="Set Cookie"
 onClick="updateCookie()">
</FORM>
</BODY>
</HTML>
```

To see how this script works, enter the cookie shown in Figure 9.7, and click the Set Cookie button. The new cookie is displayed, as shown in Figure 9.8. Experiment with this program by entering cookies with different or no expiration dates, terminating your browser, and restarting it to see what cookies have persisted between browser sessions.

FIGURE 9.6:

The cookie test program's opening screen tells the user what the current cookie value is, and prompts them to enter a new cookie. (Listing 9.6)

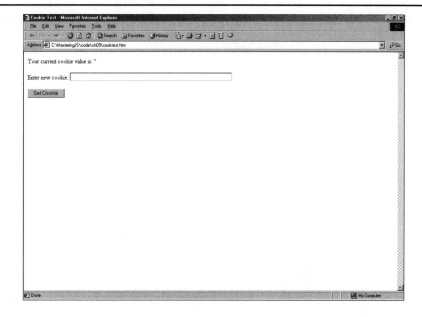

FIGURE 9.7:

An example of how to enter the text of a cookie. (Listing 9.6)

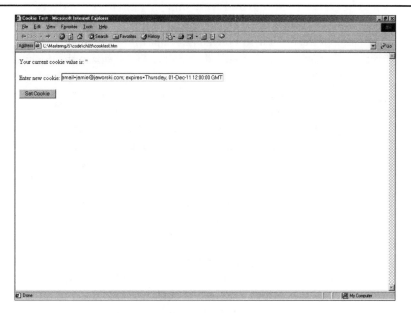

FIGURE 9.8:

When the page reloads, the
new cookie is displayed.
(Listing 9.6)

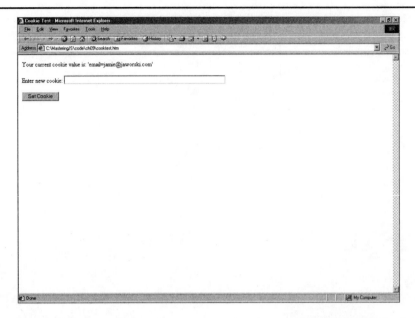

The cookie test program is very simple. This attests to the power and flexibility with which JavaScript supports cookies. The program consists of two scripts—one in the document head and one in the document body. The script in the document body displays the current cookie values that are available to the document. The script in the document head handles the onClick event associated with the Next Cookie button by setting a cookie with the value entered by the user. It then reloads the current cooktest.htm document so that the updated cookie value is displayed. Note that the cookie test program runs locally without the need for a CGI program. For web applications that do not require you to collect information from users, the combination of JavaScript and cookies can, in many cases, eliminate the need to develop CGI programs.

As another example of how JavaScript and cookies can be combined to build web applications that execute entirely on the browser, we'll develop a JavaScript application that quizzes users about their understanding of historical facts.

Open quiz.htm with your browser; it displays the web page shown in Figure 9.9. Click the radio button corresponding to the correct answer and then click the Continue button. The web page is redisplayed with a new question and an updated score. If you select the wrong answer, you are notified with an alert message, and the question is redisplayed. When you have successfully answered all of the questions in the quiz, you will be congratulated with the web page shown in Figure 9.10.

FIGURE 9.9:

The Quiz Program opening display lists a quiz question and a group of possible answers. (Listing 9.7)

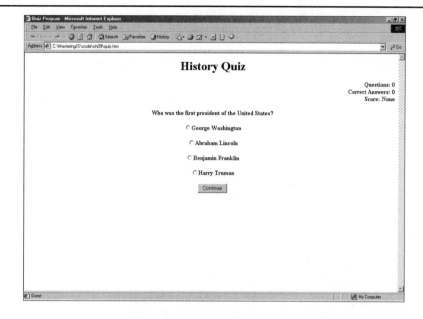

FIGURE 9.10:

The Quiz Program final display tells users how well they scored. (Listing 9.7)

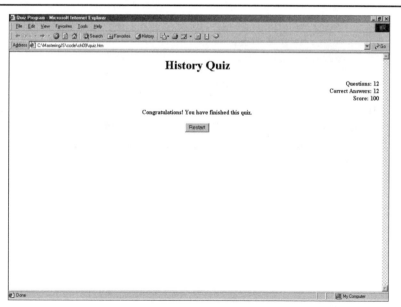

The quiz.htm file is shown in Listing 9.7. It consists almost entirely of JavaScript code. This code is organized into three scripts. Two of the scripts are in the document's head; the other, a short script, is located in the document's body. The second script of the document's head loads the JavaScript code contained in the history.js file (Listing 9.8), which contains the questions that are used in the quiz. The quiz questions are contained in a separate file so that the quiz can be easily tailored to different sets of questions.

TIP   You can improve the quiz by adding graphics and links to related topics.

Listing 9.7:   Quiz Program (quiz.htm)

```
<HTML>
<HEAD>
<TITLE>Quiz Program</TITLE>
<SCRIPT LANGUAGE="JavaScript"><!--
//Question object
function Question() {
 this.question=Question.arguments[0]
 var n=Question.arguments.length
 this.answers = new Array(n-2)
 for(var i=1; i<n-1; ++i)
  this.answers[i-1]=Question.arguments[i]
 this.correctAnswer=Question.arguments[n-1]
}
function readCookie() {
 currentQuestion=0
 numberOfQuestions=0
 correctAnswers=0
 score="None"
 cookie=document.cookie
 currentQuestion=getNumberValue(cookie,"currentQuestion")
 numberOfQuestions=getNumberValue(cookie,"numberOfQuestions")
 correctAnswers=getNumberValue(cookie,"correctAnswers")
 if(numberOfQuestions>0)
  score=Math.round(correctAnswers*100/numberOfQuestions)
}
function getNumberValue(s,n) {
 s=removeBlanks(s)
 var pairs=s.split(";")
 for(var i=0;i<pairs.length;++i) {
  var pairSplit=pairs[i].split("=")
  if(pairSplit[0]==n) {
   if(pairSplit.length>1) return parseInt(pairSplit[1])
   else return 0
  }
 }
 return 0
}
function removeBlanks(s) {
 var temp=""
```

```
  for(var i=0;i<s.length;++i) {
   var c=s.charAt(i)
   if(c!=" ") temp += c
  }
  return temp
 }
 function askNextQuestion() {
  document.writeln("<H4 ALIGN='CENTER'>"
   +qa[currentQuestion].question+"</H4>")
  displayAnswers()
 }
 function displayAnswers() {
  document.writeln('<FORM NAME="answerForm">')
  for(var ii=0;ii<qa[currentQuestion].answers.length;++ii) {
   document.writeln('<H4 ALIGN="CENTER">')
   document.writeln('<INPUT TYPE="RADIO" NAME="answer"> ')
   document.writeln(qa[currentQuestion].answers[ii])
   if(ii+1==qa[currentQuestion].answers.length) {
    document.writeln('<BR><BR><INPUT TYPE="BUTTON"')
    document.writeln('NAME="continue" VALUE="Continue" ')
    document.writeln(' onClick="checkAnswers()">')
   }
   document.writeln('</H4>')
  }
  document.writeln('</FORM>')
 }
 function checkAnswers() {
  var numAnswers=qa[currentQuestion].answers.length
  var correctAnswer=qa[currentQuestion].correctAnswer
  for(var jj=0;jj<numAnswers;++jj) {
   if(document.answerForm.elements[jj].checked) {
    if(jj==correctAnswer){
     correct()
      break
    }else{
      incorrect()
      break
    }
   }
   if(jj==numAnswers){
    incorrect()
    break
   }
  }
 }
 function correct() {
  ++currentQuestion
  ++numberOfQuestions
  ++correctAnswers
  updateCookie()
  location.reload(true)
```

```
}
function incorrect() {
 ++numberOfQuestions
 updateCookie()
 alert("Incorrect!")
 location.reload(true)
}
function updateCookie() {
 document.cookie="currentQuestion="+currentQuestion
 document.cookie="numberOfQuestions="+numberOfQuestions
 document.cookie="correctAnswers="+correctAnswers
}
function endQuiz() {
 document.cookie="currentQuestion=0"
 document.cookie="numberOfQuestions=0"
 document.cookie="correctAnswers=0"
 document.writeln('<FORM NAME="finishedForm">')
 document.write("<H4 ALIGN='CENTER'>")
 document.write("Congratulations! You have finished this quiz.")
 document.write('<BR><BR><INPUT TYPE="BUTTON" ')
 document.writeln('NAME="restart" VALUE="Restart" ')
 document.writeln(' onClick="restartQuiz()">')
 document.writeln("</H4>")
 document.writeln('</FORM>')
}
function restartQuiz() {
 location.reload(true)
}
// --></SCRIPT>
<SCRIPT LANGUAGE="JavaScript" SRC="history.js"><!--
// --></SCRIPT>
</HEAD>
<BODY>
<SCRIPT LANGUAGE="JavaScript"><!--
readCookie()
document.writeln("<H1 ALIGN='CENTER'>"+pageHeading+"</H1>")
document.writeln("<P ALIGN='RIGHT'><B>Questions: "
 +numberOfQuestions+"<BR>")
document.writeln("Correct Answers: "+correctAnswers+"<BR>")
document.writeln("Score: "+score+"</B></P>")
if(currentQuestion >= qa.length) endQuiz()
else askNextQuestion()
// --></SCRIPT>
</BODY>
</HTML>
```

We'll examine the code contained in the body of quiz.htm and then study the code in the document's head. After that, we'll cover history.js.

The Code in the Document Body

The code in the body of `quiz.htm` is very short. The `readCookie()` function is invoked to read the cookies associated with the document and use the cookie's `name=value` pairs to initialize the script's variables to the current state of the quiz. The cookies contain the number of the current question, the number of questions asked so far, and the number of correct answers. Next, the script creates a document heading based on the value of the `pageHeading` variable. (The `pageHeading` variable is initialized in `history.js`.)

The number of questions asked, number of correct answers, and quiz score are then displayed. The script checks to see if the value of `currentQuestion` is equal to or greater than the length of the qa array. (The qa array is also defined in `history.js`.) It is used to store all of the quiz's questions and answers. If the `currentQuestion` variable is greater than or equal to the length of the qa array, all questions have been asked, and the `endQuiz()` function is invoked to end the quiz. Otherwise, the `askNextQuestion()` function is invoked to present the user with another question.

The Code in the Document Head

The first script in the head of `quiz.htm` defines 12 functions. These functions are used as described in the following subsections.

The *Question()* Function

This function is used in `history.js` to create `Question` objects. It uses the `arguments` property of the `function` object to determine how many arguments were passed in the `Question()` invocation. The first argument is the text of the question. The last argument is an integer that identifies the correct answer. All arguments between the first and the last are used to define the answers to a question.

The *readCookie()* Function

This function reads the cookies of the current document; and sets the `currentQuestion`, `numberOfQuestions`, and `correctAnswers` variables. It then uses these values to calculate the value of the `score` variable.

The *getNumberValue()* Function

This function is used by `readCookie()` to parse the cookie string s and return the value associated with a particular name n. It does this by removing all blanks from s and then splitting s by means of the field separator ";". Having separated the string into `name=value` fields, it then separates these fields by "=". It checks to see if the name component of the split field matches n, and returns the value associated with the name as an integer. If the name does not have a value, it returns 0.

The *removeBlanks()* Functions

This function removes all blanks contained in a string, and returns this value as a result.

The *askNextQuestion()* Function

This function displays the current question in a centered Heading 4. It then invokes `displayAnswers()` to display the possible answers associated with this question.

The *displayAnswers()* Function

This function displays the possible answers of the current question as a form. A radio button is displayed with each answer. A Continue button follows the answers. The Continue button's onClick event handler is set to the `checkAnswers()` function.

The *checkAnswers()* Function

This function is invoked when a user answers a question and clicks the Continue button. It determines how many answers are associated with a question and then checks the radio button of each answer to see if it is checked. When it finds a checked button, it determines whether the checked button is the correct answer. If the answer is correct, it invokes the `correct()` function; otherwise, it invokes the `incorrect()` function. If no radio buttons have been clicked, the `incorrect()` function is invoked.

The *correct()* Function

This function increments the `currentQuestion`, `numberOfQuestions`, and `correctAnswers` variables, and invokes `updateCookie()` to write the values of these variables to the document's cookie jar. It then reloads the `quiz.htm` file to process the next question.

The *incorrect()* Function

This function increments the `numberOfQuestions` variable, and invokes `updateCookie()` to write the value of this variable to the document's cookie jar. It then reloads the `quiz.htm` file to reprocess the same question.

The *updateCookie()* Function

This function uses the document's cookie jar to temporarily store the program's state while the `quiz.htm` file is reloaded. It stores the values of the `currentQuestion`, `numberOf-Questions`, and `correctAnswers` variables.

The *endQuiz()* Function

This function ends the quiz by setting the document's cookies back to their initial state. It then displays a form that congratulates the user for finishing the quiz, and displays a Restart button so that the user can restart the quiz if they wish. The onClick event handler for the Restart button is `restartQuiz()`.

The *restartQuiz()* Function

This function handles the clicking of the Restart button by reloading the `quiz.htm` file so that the quiz may be restarted.

The Source File

Having gone through the description of `quiz.htm`, the `history.js` file (Listing 9.8) is easy to understand. It defines the `pageHeading` variable that is used to display the heading on each quiz page. It then creates the `qa` array. Each element of `qa` is a `Question` object, and 12 questions are defined. Feel free to add your own questions or delete the ones that I've created—you can change the entire content of the quiz by modifying `history.js`. You can also substitute your own question file for `history.js` by modifying the SRC attribute value of the second script of `quiz.htm`.

Listing 9.8:   Quiz Questions (history.js)

```
//Heading displayed on the quiz page
pageHeading="History Quiz"
//Questions
qa = new Array()
qa[0] = new Question("Who was the first president of the United States?",
  "George Washington",
  "Abraham Lincoln",
  "Benjamin Franklin",
  "Harry Truman",
  0)
qa[1] = new Question("When did Columbus discover America?",
  "1249",
  "1942",
  "1492",
  "1294",
  2)
qa[2] = new Question("Who commanded the Macedonian army?",
  "Napoleon",
  "Alexander the Great",
  "Cleopatra",
  "George Patton",
  1)
qa[3] = new Question("Where did Davy Crockett lose his life?",
  "The Spanish Inquisition",
  "The Alamo",
  "Miami, Florida",
  "On the Oregon Trail",
  1)
qa[4] = new Question("Who was the first man to walk on the moon?",
  "Louis Armstrong",
  "Buzz Armstrong",
  "Jack Armstrong",
  "Neil Armstrong",
  3)
qa[5] = new Question("Who wrote the <I>Scarlet Letter</I>?",
  "Michael Crichton",
  "Ernest Hemingway",
```

```
  "Nathaniel Hawthorne",
  "Charles Dickens",
  2)
qa[6] = new Question("Eli Whitney invented:",
  "Mad Cow's Disease",
  "the Cotton Gin",
  "whisky",
  "the automobile",
  1)
qa[7] = new Question("Who was known as the King of the Fauves?",
  "Salvatore Dali",
  "Henri Matisse",
  "Pablo Picasso",
  "Vincent Van Gogh",
  1)
qa[8] = new Question("Who discovered the force of gravity?",
  "Isaac Newton",
  "Galileo",
  "Copernicus",
  "Albert Einstein"
  ,0)
qa[9] = new Question("Who created HTML?",
  "Tim Berners-Lee",
  "Marc Andreessen",
  "Bill Gates",
  "Jim Barksdale",
  0)
qa[10] = new Question("Leonardo da Vinci was born in Greece.",
  "True",
  "False",
  1)
qa[11] = new Question("Louisiana was purchased from France.",
  "True",
  "False",
  0)
```

This example showed how JavaScript can use cookies to create a complex web application without the use of a CGI program. All the cookie processing was performed locally on the browser.

Comparison—Cookies versus Hidden Form Fields

Now that you've learned how both hidden fields and cookies can be used to maintain state information, you might be wondering which one you should use and when. In general, cookies are the preferred option because they allow persistent storage of state information, and hidden fields do not. However, cookies may not be the right choice for all applications. Table 9.1 summarizes the trade-offs between cookies and hidden fields.

TABLE 9.1: Cookies versus Hidden Fields

Trade-Off	Cookies	Hidden Fields
Ease of use	Requires cookie string parsing	Requires form setup and access
Browser support	Navigator, Internet Explorer, other browsers	Almost all browsers
Server support	May not be supported by some servers	Supported by all servers
Performance	Slower—requires disk I/O	Faster—implemented in RAM
Persistent storage	Supported	Not supported
Availability	Maximum cookie storage may be reached	No practical storage limitation

Both cookies and hidden fields are easy to use; however, both also have some coding overhead associated with them. Cookie strings need to be parsed when they are read. Hidden fields require invisible forms to be set up. As far as ease of use is concerned, I prefer cookies because all of the setup processing is performed in JavaScript.

Although cookies are supported by Navigator, Internet Explorer, and other browsers, they are not supported by all browsers. On the other hand, hidden fields are supported by all HTML 2-compatible browsers.

Not all web servers support cookies, though they do support hidden form fields. Cookies are not as performance-efficient as hidden fields because cookie operations require disk I/O to the local cookie file. However, in most applications, this performance difference is not noticeable.

Cookies provide persistent storage. That is their biggest advantage and why they were developed in the first place. If you require persistent storage, you have to use cookies.

Cookies may not always be available to your scripts. The cookie specification states that a browser cannot claim that it is cookie-capable unless it provides a minimum cookie storage capacity of 300 (currently, this limit is not a problem for most browsers). However, with the increase in cookie popularity, it could be an issue in the future. In addition, most browsers limit the number of cookies that can be stored for a given domain. Netscape Navigator 4 has a 20-cookie-per-domain limit, and Internet Explorer 3 has a single-cookie-per-domain limit. Hidden fields do not have any practical limits.

Summary

In this chapter, you learned how to use hidden fields and cookies to maintain browser state information. You learned how JavaScript enhances the capabilities that both hidden fields and cookies provide by maximizing local processing and reducing the need for CGI programming. In the next chapter, you'll learn how to work with the link-related objects that are available in JavaScript. You'll learn how to attach scripts to link events and how to use the `location` object to dynamically load web pages under script control.

CHAPTER **10**

Working with Links

- Standard URL protocols

- The *javascript:* and *about:* protocols

- The *location* object

- The *link* object

- The *link()* method

- The *anchor* object

- The *history* object

The ability to quickly move from one web page to another in search of information (and entertainment) is at the heart of the Web's popularity. With a click of the mouse, we can travel from a web page about native cultures to recipes of exotic foods. The single-click simplicity with which we traverse the Web is provided by *links*.

Most links are *static*. Static links always take you to the same destination. This type of link can be written entirely in HTML. Other links are *dynamic*, such as those used to link forms to CGI programs. When you submit a form, especially a search form, the web page to which you link is often a page that is generated according to data submitted with the form. Until JavaScript, most dynamic links were created using CGI programs. Now, with JavaScript, you can develop browser-side dynamic links, which can eliminate the need for CGI programming and reduce the load on your web server.

In this chapter, you'll learn how to use JavaScript objects that provide control over the way that links are implemented. You'll learn how to use the `location` object to load documents at various URLs, how to attach JavaScript code to a document's links, and how to use the `history` object to keep track of the URLs that have been visited within a window. When you finish this chapter, you'll be able to use link-related objects to implement dynamically programmable links within your own web pages.

Uniform Resource Locators (URLs)

A Uniform Resource Locator, or URL, is the standard type of Internet address used on the Web. It is used to locate resources and services associated with a variety of protocols. The syntax of a URL varies with the particular protocol used to access a resource or service. For example, most URLs do not contain spaces, but URLs that use the *javascript:* protocol may include spaces, as you'll learn later in this section.

The most common format of a URL is as follows:

```
protocol//hostname[:port] path search hash
```

The `protocol` element of the previous URL syntax identifies the protocol to be used to access a resource or service. Examples of protocols include *http:*, *ftp:*, *mailto:*, and *file:*. More-specialized JavaScript protocols are presented later in this section.

The `hostname` element of the URL identifies the fully qualified domain name of the host where the resource is located. Examples are `home.netscape.com`, `www.w3.org`, `www.microsoft.com`, and `java.sun.com`.

The `port` element of the URL identifies the TCP port number to use with the protocol. The port is optional. If it is omitted, the colon preceding the port is also omitted, and the protocol's "well-known" port is assumed. *Well-known ports* are the ports that servers "listen to" when implementing a protocol. For example, the well-known port of HTTP is 80.

The path element of the URL is the directory/file path to the resource. It is written in the Unix forward-slash format. An example path is `/javascript/index.htm`. The path is usually relative to a directory used by the server. For example, my web server uses the following directory as the base directory from which it services HTTP requests:

```
/usr/local/etc/httpd/htdocs
```

Thus, the following URL:

```
www.jaworski.com/javascript/index.htm
```

addresses the following file:

```
/usr/local/etc/httpd/htdocs/javascript/index.htm.Verify the above base
address.
```

The search element of the URL identifies a query string passed in a URL. *Query strings* are data that is passed to CGI programs via the `QUERY_STRING` environment variable. The query string begins with a question mark (?) followed by the query data. Spaces are encoded using plus (+) signs. For example, the query string *?tall+dark+handsome* passes the words *tall, dark,* and *handsome* to a CGI program.

The hash element of the URL identifies a named file offset. It consists of a hash character (#) (some of you may know this as a pound sign), followed by the name of the anchor associated with the file offset. For example, if you want to create a link to the part of the file associated with the anchor `section3`, you would append the hash `#section3` to the link's URL.

The *javascript:* and *about:* Protocols

In addition to the standard protocols used with URLs, Netscape Navigator supports the *javascript:* and *about:* protocols. Internet Explorer supports the *javascript:* protocol, but not the *about:* protocol.

The *javascript:* Protocol

This protocol is used to evaluate a JavaScript expression and load a web page that contains the value of the expression. If the expression does not evaluate to a defined value, no web page is loaded.

NOTE   Spaces may be included in URLs that use the *javascript:* protocol.

In order to see how the *javascript:* protocol works, open your browser and load the following URL:

```
javascript:new Date()
```

As shown in Figure 10.1, this URL (which, incidentally, contains a space) opens a document that displays the value of the current date.

FIGURE 10.1:

Using the *javascript:* protocol to display the current date

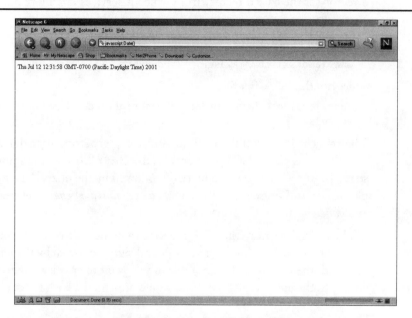

Try opening the following URL with Netscape Navigator:

```
javascript:"<H1>"+"What's up?"+"</H1>"
```

This one results in the document shown in Figure 10.2 being displayed. Note that the H1 tags were used to display *What's up?* as a Heading 1. Figure 10.3 shows what happens when you use Internet Explorer to display the same URL.

FIGURE 10.2:

Using Netscape Navigator and the *javascript:* protocol to display HTML tags

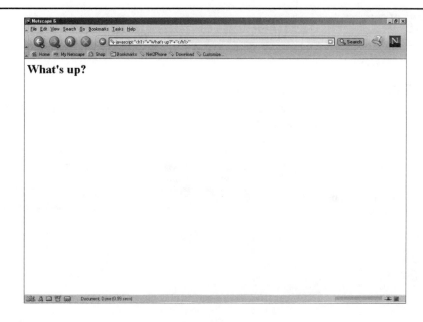

FIGURE 10.3:

Using Internet Explorer and the *javascript:* protocol to display HTML tags

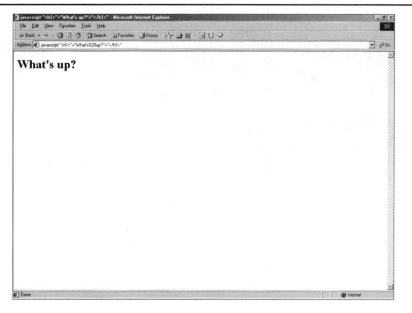

TIP   The URL, `javascript:void(0)`, can be used to create a link that does nothing when the user clicks on it. The `void()` operator is used to evaluate an expression without returning a value.

NEW! Netscape Navigator 4.06 and later versions support a JavaScript console window that you can use to debug your scripts. To open this window, simply open the URL *javascript:*, as shown in Figure 10.4. Internet Explorer does not support this feature.

FIGURE 10.4:

Using the *javascript:* protocol to open the JavaScript console window

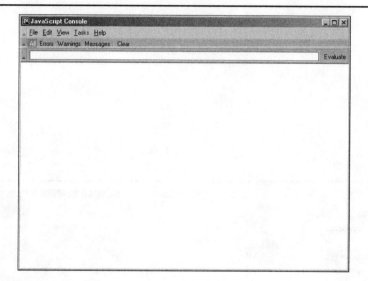

The *about:* Protocol

This protocol provides access to built-in Navigator information. The URL *about:* loads a web page that identifies the current Navigator version and other related information as shown in Figure 10.5. Loading *about:* has the same result as selecting About Netscape from the Navigator Help pull-down menu.

FIGURE 10.5:

Loading *about:* displays
the same information as
selecting About Netscape
from Navigator's Help
menu.

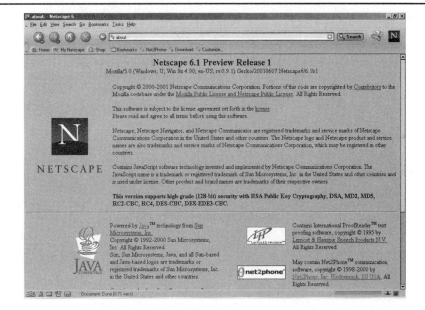

If the *about:cache* URL is loaded, then Navigator displays statistics on the current state of its cache, as shown in Figure 10.6.

FIGURE 10.6:

Loading *about:cache*
displays information about
the current state of the disk
cache.

If the *about:plugins* URL is loaded, Navigator displays information about the plug-ins that are currently configured, as shown in Figure 10.7. The resulting display is the same as that obtained by selecting About Plugins from the Help menu.

FIGURE 10.7:

Loading *about:plugins* displays information about the plug-ins your browser has installed.

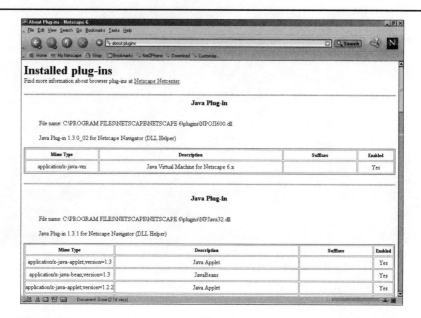

The *location* Object

JavaScript uses the location object to access the URL of the current document that is loaded in a window. The location object contains properties that describe the various parts of the URL. These properties are summarized in Table 10.1.

TABLE 10.1: Properties of the *location* Object

Property	Description
hash	The anchor part of the URL (if any)
host	The hostname:port part of the URL
hostname	The hostname part of the URL
href	The entire URL
pathname	The pathname part of the URL
port	The port part of the URL
protocol	The protocol part of the URL, which includes the colon following the protocol name
search	The query string part of the URL

The `location` object is a property of the `window` object. If the `location` object of a window is modified, the browser attempts to load the document specified by the modified URL into the window. For this reason, you should use the `href` property to modify the entire URL at a single time, rather than sequentially modifying each of the parts of the URL.

NOTE The `document` object also contains a `location` property. This property is read-only and cannot be modified to load a new document. You should not plan on using this property because it will be deleted in future versions of JavaScript. Instead, use the `href` property of the `location` property of the `window` object.

The `location` object has two methods—`reload()` and `replace()`. The `reload()` method causes the current document of a window to be reloaded according to the policy used by the browser's Reload button. This policy allows a document to be reloaded from the server in one of the following three ways:

Every time The document is reloaded from the server every time.

Once per session The document is reloaded from the server once per session if the document's date on the server indicates that it is newer than the document stored in cache. If the document is not in the cache, it is loaded from the server.

Never The document is reloaded from cache, if possible. Otherwise, it is loaded from the server.

If `true` is passed as an argument to the `reload()` method, the document is unconditionally loaded from the server.

The `replace()` method takes a URL as a parameter, and loads the document at the specified URL over the current document in the current document history list. This prevents the user from returning to the previous document by clicking the browser's Back button.

The `location` object does not have any events.

Example Application Using the *location* Object

The `location` object is a simple object with which to work. It is usually used to load a new document or to access individual parts of a document's URL. Listing 10.1 provides an example of the `location` object's use.

Listing 10.1:   Using the location Object (load-url.htm)

```
<HTML>
<HEAD>
<TITLE>Load URL</TITLE>
</HEAD>
```

```
<FRAMESET ROWS="200,*" BORDER=10>
<FRAME SRC="url-form.htm">
<FRAME SRC="blank.htm">
</FRAMESET>
</HTML>
```

Open the file `load-url.htm` with your browser, and it will display the form shown in Figure 10.8. This form lets you enter simple URLs that use the *file:*, *http:*, and *ftp:* protocols. You can enter a hostname and path to further specify the URLs. When you click the Load URL button, the document at the specified URL is displayed in the bottom frame of the window, as shown in Figure 10.9.

FIGURE 10.8:

The Load URL form lets you enter a URL part by part. (Listing 10.1)

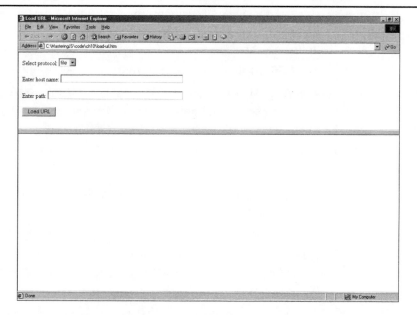

The `load-url.htm` file is shown in Listing 10.1. It sets up a two-row frame set. The file `url-form.htm` is loaded in the top row, and `blank.htm` is loaded in the bottom row. The `url-form.htm` file is shown in Listing 10.2, and the `blank.htm` file is shown in Chapter 7, "Creating Frames and Windows."

FIGURE 10.9:

The Load URL form lets you load Netscape's home page. (Listing 10.2)

Listing 10.2:   **A Form for Entering a URL (url-form.htm)**

```
<HTML>
<HEAD>
<TITLE>Load URL</TITLE>
<SCRIPT LANGUAGE="JavaScript"><!--
function loadFrames() {
 ix = document.URLform.protocol.options.selectedIndex
 urlString = document.URLform.protocol.options[ix].value+"//"
 urlString += document.URLform.hostname.value
 path =      document.URLform.path.value
 if(path.length > 0) {
   if(path.charAt(0)!="/") path = "/"+path
 }
 urlString += path
 parent.frames[1].location.href=urlString
}
// --></SCRIPT>
</HEAD>
<BODY>
<FORM ACTION="" NAME="URLform">
<P>Select protocol:
<SELECT NAME="protocol" SIZE="1">
<OPTION VALUE="file:" SELECTED="SELECTED">file</OPTION>
<OPTION VALUE="http:">http</OPTION>
<OPTION VALUE="ftp:">ftp</OPTION></SELECT></P>
```

```
<P>Enter host name:
<INPUT TYPE="TEXT" NAME="hostname" SIZE="45"></P>
<P>Enter path:
<INPUT TYPE="TEXT" NAME="path" SIZE="50"></P>
<P></P>
<INPUT TYPE="BUTTON" NAME="load" VALUE="Load URL"
 ONCLICK="loadFrames()">
</FORM>
</BODY>
</HTML>
```

There is a single script in the head of url-form.htm. This script defines the loadFrames() function, which is invoked to handle the onClick event of the Load URL button. It determines which of the protocol options were selected, and uses that option to build urlString. It appends the string "//" and the value of the hostname field to urlString followed by the value of the path variable. The path variable is set based on the value of the path field. If the first character of the path field is not "/", it prepends a slash to the path variable before appending its value to urlString. Finally, it loads the document specified by urlString in the second frame by setting the frame's location.href property to urlString.

The *link* Object

The link object encapsulates a text or image link contained in a document. It is a property of the document object. The links array is an array of all links contained in a document, and is also a property of the document object. A link object is similar to a location object in that it contains a URL. Because of this, link objects have many of the same properties as location objects; these properties are shown in Table 10.2. The only additional property that the link object has in comparison with the location object is the target property. This property is the HTML target attribute of the link that identifies the window where the document referenced by the link's URL is to be loaded.

TABLE 10.2: Properties of the *link* Object

Property	Description
hash	The anchor part of the URL (if any)
host	The hostname:port part of the URL
hostname	The hostname part of the URL
href	The entire URL
pathname	The pathname part of the URL
port	The port part of the URL

Continued on next page

TABLE 10.2 CONTINUED: Properties of the *link* Object

Property	Description
protocol	The protocol part of the URL, which includes the colon following the protocol name
search	The query string part of the URL
target	The link's HTML `target` attribute

 The `link` object does not have any methods that are supported by both Navigator and Internet Explorer. It has nine events—onClick, onDblClick, onKeyDown, onKeyPress, onKeyUp, onMouseDown, onMouseUp, onMouseOver, and onMouseOut—as described in Chapter 4, "Handling Events."

NOTE   Internet Explorer combines the `link` object with the `anchor` object. You'll learn about the `anchor` object later in this chapter. Internet Explorer's combined implementation has additional properties, methods, and events besides those described in this section.

The following section presents an example of using the `link` object. After this example, the `JavaScript link()` method is introduced.

Example Application Using *link*: A Pair-Matching Game

To see how the `link` object may be used in a web application, we'll develop a JavaScript version of a familiar pattern-matching game. In this game, you are faced with an array of 16 cards. These 16 cards represent eight pairs of matching images, randomly arranged. Initially, you see only the backs of the cards; the images are hidden face-down. Your goal is to turn over one card and then another to see if the images on the cards match. If they do, the pair remains face up, and you take another turn—that is, you try to find another pair by choosing two of the remaining cards. Whenever the second card of one of your attempts doesn't match the first card, both of those two cards flip over again, and you must take another turn. You continue taking turns until you have uncovered all the matching pairs.

To get a better feel for how the game is played, open the file click1.htm with your browser. You will see a display similar to the one shown in Figure 10.10. In order to play the game, click any one of the cards, as shown in Figure 10.11. Now, click on any other card, as shown in Figure 10.12. Your objective is to click a card whose image matches the first. Your odds at getting it right are 1 out of 15. However, with repeated tries, you can improve those odds. If the card you clicked is a match, the matching images will remain face-up until the end of the game. If you missed, click the Continue button to try again. The mismatched pair you clicked is then hidden (that is, turned face-down) again. Continue taking turns until you have finally turned over all of the pairs, two cards at a time. By the time you have won a game, you will be ready to go on to see how the game is implemented.

NOTE   In Chapter 11, "Using Images," you will learn how to enhance the pair-match program with JavaScript's dynamic image display capabilities.

FIGURE 10.10:

The pair-match opening screen shows all cards turned over. (Listings 10.3 through 10.6)

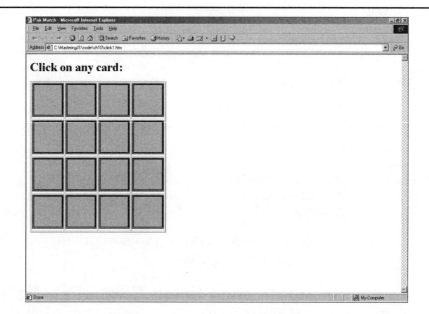

FIGURE 10.11:

A single image has been clicked—try to find a match! (Listings 10.3 through 10.6)

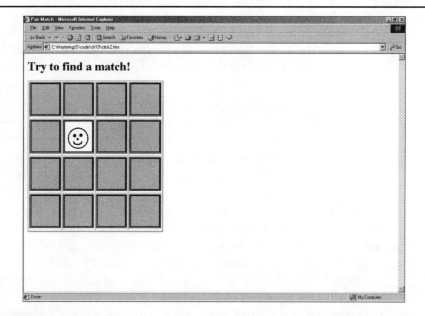

FIGURE 10.12:

Two images have been clicked. They don't match, so you must click the Continue button to take your next turn. (The images will automatically flip face-down again.) (Listings 10.3 through 10.6)

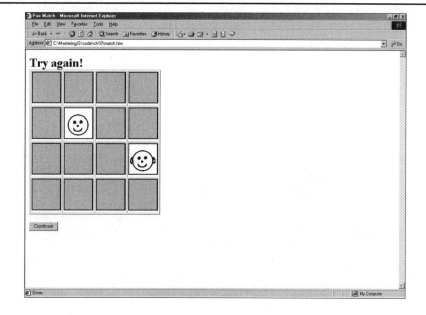

FIGURE 10.13:

The game has been won— all images have been matched. (Listings 10.3 through 10.6)

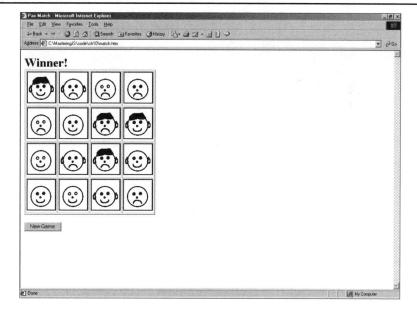

Listing 10.3 contains the code of the `click1.htm` file. This file is rather short, considering the complexity of the pair-matching application, and consists mostly of JavaScript code. The code is organized into three scripts—two in the header and one in the body.

Listing 10.3:   The Startup File for the Pair-Matching Game (click1.htm)

```
<HTML>
<HEAD>
<TITLE>Pair Match</TITLE>
<SCRIPT LANGUAGE="JavaScript" SRC="pairs.js"><!--
// --></SCRIPT>
<SCRIPT LANGUAGE="JavaScript"><!--
function readCookie() {
 var cookie=document.cookie
 if(nameDefined(cookie,"displayedImages")){
  displayedImages=getCookieValue(cookie,"displayedImages")
 }else{
  displayedImages="0000000000000000"
 }
 imageSequence = ""
 if(nameDefined(cookie,"imageSequence")){
  imageSequence=getCookieValue(cookie,"imageSequence")
 }
 if(imageSequence == "") {
  imageSequence=permuteString("0123456701234567")
 }
 initializeImageArray()
 initializeDisplayedArray()
}
function displayCell(n) {
 var f="none.gif"
 if(displayed[n]) f=images[n]
 document.write('<A HREF="click2.htm" ')
 document.write('onClick="userClick('+n+')">')
 document.write('<IMG SRC="'+f+'" WIDTH="80" HEIGHT="83">')
 document.write('')
}
function userClick(n) {
 document.cookie="displayedImages="+displayedImages
 document.cookie="imageSequence="+imageSequence
 document.cookie="click1="+n
}
// --></SCRIPT>
</HEAD>
<BODY BGCOLOR="#FFFFFF">
<H1>Click on any card:</H1>
<SCRIPT LANGUAGE="JavaScript"><!--
readCookie()
displayTable()
// --></SCRIPT>
</BODY>
</HTML>
```

The script in the document's body invokes the `readCookie()` function to read the cookies used by `click1.htm`. (Cookies were covered in Chapter 9, "Using Hidden Fields and Cookies." If you skipped Chapter 9, you should go back and read it before going on.) The `displayTable()` function is used to display the table of images shown in Figure 10.10.

The first header script imports JavaScript code from the `pairs.js` file (Listing 10.4). The code in `pairs.js` is common to `click2.htm` (Listing 10.5) and `match.htm` (Listing 10.6), which are also used in the pair-matching program.

The second header script contains the functions `readCookie()`, `displayCell()`, and `useClick()`. These functions are unique to `click1.htm`. However, modified versions of these functions are used in `click2.htm` and `match.htm`. Their use in `click1.htm` is described in the following subsections.

NOTE   To fully understand `readCookie()`, `displayCell()`, and `userClick()`, you need to read the description of `pairs.js` (see Listing 10.4 later in this section).

The *readCookie()* Function

This function reads the cookies that are available to `click1.htm`, and looks for cookies that have the names `displayedImages` and `imageSequence`. The `displayedImages` cookie contains 16 characters that are either 0 or 1. The value 1 at position n indicates that the user has successfully matched the nth image. The value 0 indicates that they have not. The `imageSequence` is a permuted string that identifies which of the 16 image positions are occupied by image pairs 0 through 7. The `initializeImageArray()` function is invoked to initialize the `images` array with the filenames of the images that are at each image position. The `initializeDisplayedArray()` is invoked to initialize the `displayed` array with Boolean values based upon the `displayedImages` cookie.

The *displayCell()* Function

This function creates the image link of each cell of the four-row by four-column image table shown in Figure 10.10. Each cell links to the `click2.htm` file. The image associated with the link is either `none.gif` (corresponding to a hidden image) or one of the images contained in the `images` array. The onClick event of the link is handled by the `userClick()` function, which is passed the index (n) of the table cell being displayed. When `userClick()` returns, the `click2.htm` file is loaded because it is the HREF attribute of the image link.

The *userClick()* Function

This function handles the onClick event associated with each of the table's image link cells. It updates the document's `displayedImages` and `imageSequence` cookies; and creates a third cookie, `click1`, which stores the index of the cell that was clicked.

The pairs.js file shown in Listing 10.4 contains the common code used by click1.htm, click2.htm, and match.htm. It defines the images and displayed arrays, and seven functions: nameDefined(), removeBlanks(), getCookieValue(), permuteString(), initializeImage-Array(), initializeDisplayedArray(), and displayTable(). These arrays and functions are discussed in the following subsections.

Listing 10.4:   Common Code for the Pair-Matching Game (pairs.js)

```
images = new Array(16)
displayed = new Array(16)
function nameDefined(c,n) {
 var s=removeBlanks(c)
 var pairs=s.split(";")
 for(var i=0;i<pairs.length;++i) {
  var pairSplit=pairs[i].split("=")
  if(pairSplit[0]==n) return true
 }
 return false
}
function removeBlanks(s) {
 var temp=""
 for(var i=0;i<s.length;++i) {
  var c=s.charAt(i)
  if(c!=" ") temp += c
 }
 return temp
}
function getCookieValue(c,n) {
 var s=removeBlanks(c)
 var pairs=s.split(";")
 for(var i=0;i<pairs.length;++i) {
  var pairSplit=pairs[i].split("=")
  if(pairSplit[0]==n) return pairSplit[1]
 }
 return ""
}
function permuteString(s) {
 var len=s.length
 var sArray = new Array(len)
 for(var i=0;i<len;++i) sArray[i]=s.charAt(i)
 for(var i=0;i<len;++i) {
  var currentValue=sArray[i]
  ix=Math.round(Math.random()*(len-1))
  sArray[i]=sArray[ix]
  sArray[ix]=currentValue
 }
 t=""
 for(var i=0;i<len;++i) t+=sArray[i]
 return t
```

```
}
function initializeImageArray() {
 for(var i=0;i<16;++i) {
  var ch=imageSequence.charAt(i)
  var n=parseInt(ch)
  if(n>3) images[i]="frown"+(n-3)+".gif"
  else images[i]="smile"+(n+1)+".gif"
 }
}
function initializeDisplayedArray() {
 for(var i=0;i<16;++i) {
  var ch=displayedImages.charAt(i)
  if(ch=="1") displayed[i]=true
  else displayed[i]=false
 }
}
function displayTable(){
 document.writeln('<TABLE BORDER="2">')
 for(var i=0;i<4;++i) {
  document.writeln('<TR>')
  for(var j=0;j<4;++j) {
   document.writeln('<TD>')
   document.writeln('<SCRIPT LANGUAGE="JavaScript">')
   document.writeln('displayCell('+(i*4+j)+')')
   document.writeln('</SCRIPT>')
   document.writeln('</TD>')
  }
  document.writeln('</TR>')
 }
 document.writeln('</TABLE>')
}
```

The *images* Array

This array contains the names of the image files that are displayed in each cell of the table.

The *displayed* Array

This array consists of 16 Boolean values, indicating which images have been matched by the user.

The *nameDefined()* Function

This function checks the cookie passed via the c argument to see if it contains a name=value pair with the name passed by the n argument. It returns true if a matching name is found and false otherwise.

The *removeBlanks()* Function

This function returns a string that has all blank spaces removed.

The *getCookieValue()* Function

This function returns the value of the name=value pair of the cookie passed via the c argument and the name passed via the n argument.

The *permuteString()* Function

This function is passed a string s, and returns a string t where t is a random permutation of s. It is used to randomly distribute the images contained in the image table.

The *initializeImageArray()* Function

This function is invoked by readCookie() to initialize the images array based upon the imageSequence cookie value. The files smile1.gif through smile4.gif correspond to imageSequence values 0 through 3. The files frown1.gif through frown4.gif correspond to imageSequence values 4 through 7.

The *initializeDisplayedArray()* Function

This function initializes the Boolean displayed array based on the displayedImages cookie.

The *displayTable()* Function

This function displays the image link table. It generates the HTML code for the table as a whole, as well as for each of its rows and for all of its cells. It writes a script that invokes the displayCell() function as the contents of each table cell. The displayCell() function is invoked when the table is being formatted. It generates each cell's image link.

When a user clicks any image link displayed by click1.htm, the userClick() function is invoked to handle the event. Each image displayed by click1.htm is used as the anchor of a link. The destination of this link is click2.htm; this file processes the second click of a pair of clicks. Its code is shown in Listing 10.5.

The only differences between click2.htm and click1.htm are in click2's implementation of the readCookie(), displayCell(), and userClick() functions. These differences are explained in the following subsections.

The *readCookie()* Function

In click2.htm, readCookie() reads three cookies: displayedImages, imageSequence, and click1. The additional click1 cookie contains the index of the image that the user selected with his or her first click.

The *displayCell()* Function

In click2.htm, the displayCell() function displays an image if it has already been matched by the user (that is, if displayed[n] is true), or if it was selected on the user's first click. Also, all links created by click2.htm now point to match.htm. When a user clicks on a link, userClick() is invoked to handle the onClick event; then match.htm is loaded.

The *userClick()* Function

In click2.htm, the userClick() function creates an additional cookie, click2, which records the user's second image selection.

Listing 10.5:   The Document Used to Process the Second Click (click2.htm)

```
<HTML>
<HEAD>
<TITLE>Pair Match</TITLE>
<SCRIPT LANGUAGE="JavaScript" SRC="pairs.js"><!--
// --></SCRIPT>
<SCRIPT LANGUAGE="JavaScript"><!--
function readCookie() {
 var cookie=document.cookie
 displayedImages=getCookieValue(cookie,"displayedImages")
 imageSequence=getCookieValue(cookie,"imageSequence")
 click1=parseInt(getCookieValue(cookie,"click1"))
 initializeImageArray()
 initializeDisplayedArray()
}
function displayCell(n) {
 var f="none.gif"
 if(displayed[n] || click1==n) f=images[n]
 document.write('<A HREF="match.htm" ')
 document.write('onClick="userClick('+n+')">')
 document.write('<IMG SRC="'+f+'" WIDTH="80" HEIGHT="83">')
 document.write('</A>')
}
function userClick(n) {
 document.cookie="displayedImages="+displayedImages
 document.cookie="imageSequence="+imageSequence
 document.cookie="click1="+click1
 document.cookie="click2="+n
}
// --></SCRIPT>
</HEAD>
<BODY BGCOLOR="#FFFFFF">
<H1>Try to find a match!</H1>
<SCRIPT LANGUAGE="JavaScript"><!--
readCookie()
displayTable()
// --></SCRIPT>
</BODY>
</HTML>
```

The match.htm file is loaded each time the user has clicked two cards. It checks to see if the images match and whether the game has been won. It is similar to click1.htm and click2.htm, but it provides the capability to check for and display a match and to determine when the game is over.

The Script in the Document's Body

The script in the document's body invokes the displayMatchStatus() function before going on to display the image table. The displayMatchStatus() determines whether the user has matched a pair of images, and it displays an appropriate heading. After the image table is displayed, a form with a single button is generated. The button's label is *New Game* if the user has just matched all image pairs, and *Continue* otherwise. Clicking the button results in click1.htm being reloaded.

The *readCookie()* Function

The readCookie() function reads four cookies: displayedImages, imageSequence, click1, and click2.

The *displayCell()* Function

The displayCell() function displays an image if its index is click1 or click2, or if that image has already been matched. It does not generate image links for the table's cells. Simple images are used instead. By the time a user gets to match.htm, they will not be clicking an image. Instead, they will click the New Game or Continue button.

The *displayMatchStatus()* Function

This function checks to see if a user has matched two images. In this case, click1 must be different from click2 (the user can't click on the same image twice) and the value of the images array for both clicks must be the same (the image files must match). If the user has successfully matched two images, the value of the displayed array is updated to reflect the fact that the images match. The displayedImages cookie value is then updated, based upon the revised displayed array. The winner() function is invoked to determine whether all images have been matched, and an appropriate heading is displayed.

The *winner()* Function

This function checks to see if all images have been matched. If they have, then it returns true. Otherwise, it returns false.

Listing 10.6:   The Document Used to Check for Matching Clicks (match.htm)

```
<HTML>
<HEAD>
<TITLE>Pair Match</TITLE>
<SCRIPT LANGUAGE="JavaScript" SRC="pairs.js"><!--
// --></SCRIPT>
<SCRIPT LANGUAGE="JavaScript"><!--
function readCookie() {
 var cookie=document.cookie
 displayedImages=getCookieValue(cookie,"displayedImages")
 imageSequence=getCookieValue(cookie,"imageSequence")
 click1=parseInt(getCookieValue(cookie,"click1"))
 click2=parseInt(getCookieValue(cookie,"click2"))
 initializeImageArray()
 initializeDisplayedArray()
}
function displayCell(n) {
 var f="none.gif"
 if(displayed[n] || click1==n || click2==n) f=images[n]
 document.write('<IMG SRC="'+f+'" WIDTH="80" HEIGHT="83">')
}
function displayMatchStatus() {
 if(click1!=click2 && images[click1]==images[click2]){
  displayed[click1]=true
  displayed[click2]=true
  displayedImages=""
  for(var i=0;i<16;++i) {
   if(displayed[i]) displayedImages+="1"
   else displayedImages+="0"
  }
  if(winner()){
   document.writeln("<H1>Winner!")
   displayedImages="0000000000000000"
   imageSequence=permuteString("0123456701234567")
   state="winner"
  }else{
   document.writeln("<H1>They matched!")
   state="matched"
  }
 }else{
  document.writeln("<H1>Try again!")
  state="notMatched"
 }
 document.cookie="displayedImages="+displayedImages
 document.cookie="imageSequence="+imageSequence
}
function winner() {
 for(var i=0;i<16;++i)
  if(displayed[i]!=true) return false
```

```
  return true
}
// --></SCRIPT>
</HEAD>
<BODY BGCOLOR="#FFFFFF">
<SCRIPT LANGUAGE="JavaScript"><!--
readCookie()
displayMatchStatus()
displayTable()
document.write('<FORM><INPUT TYPE="BUTTON" NAME="goToClick1"')
if(state=="winner") document.writeln(' VALUE="New Game" ')
else document.writeln(' VALUE="Continue" ')
document.write('onClick="window.location.href=')
document.write("'click1.htm'")
document.writeln('"></FORM>')
// --></SCRIPT>
</BODY>
</HTML>
```

The *link()* Method

The link object is not the only way of creating a link. A link may be created using the link() method of the String object. This method takes the hypertext reference (HREF) attribute of the link as a parameter, and creates a link to the specified HREF. For example, the following statements create a link to the *Mastering JavaScript* home page.

```
mjLink="Mastering
JavaScript".link("http://www.jaworski.com/javascriptdocument.writeln(mjLink)
```

The previous statements result in the following HTML being generated for the current document:

```
<A HREF="http://www.jaworski.com/javascript/">Mastering JavaScript</A>
```

As another example, consider Listing 10.7. It contains the code of the linkx.htm file, and generates the web page shown in Figure 10.14.

Listing 10.7:   Using the *link()* Method (linkx.htm)

```
<HTML>
<HEAD>
<TITLE>Using the link() Method</TITLE>
</HEAD>
<BODY>
<H1>Using the link() Method</H1>
<SCRIPT LANGUAGE="JavaScript"><!--
text=new Array(5)
text[0]="Mastering JavaScript Home Page"
```

```
text[1]="Sybex Home Page"
text[2]="Netscape Home Page"
text[3]="Microsoft Home Page"
text[4]="JavaSoft Home Page"
linkx=new Array(5)
linkx[0]=text[0].link("http://www.jaworski.com/javascript/")linkx[1]=text[1].l
ink("http://www.sybex.com")
linkx[2]=text[2].link("http://home.netscape.com")
linkx[3]=text[3].link("http://www.microsoft.com")
linkx[4]=text[4].link("http://www.javasoft.com")
for(var i=0;i<linkx.length;++i)
 document.writeln("<P>"+linkx[i]+"</P>")
// --></SCRIPT>
</BODY>
</HTML>
```

FIGURE 10.14:

The *link()* method makes it easy to insert URLs in a Web page. (Listing 10.7)

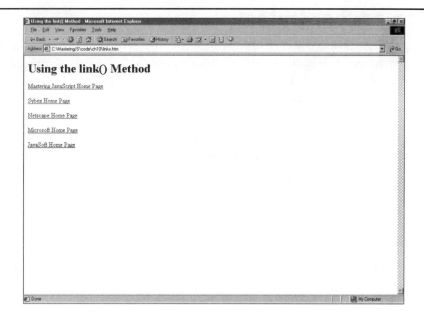

The linkx.htm file creates an array of strings, called text, with the following anchor text:

Mastering JavaScript Home Page

Sybex Home Page

Netscape Home Page

Microsoft Home Page

JavaSoft Home Page

It then creates an array of links, called linkx, using the link() method of the String object. These links are to the following URLs:

- www.jaworski.com/javascript/
- www.sybex.com
- home.netscape.com
- www.microsoft.com
- www.javasoft.com

Finally, it writes these links to the current document using the writeln() method of the document object.

The *anchor* Object

The anchor object represents an anchor that is used as a named offset within an HTML document. It is a property of the document object. The anchors array contains all of the anchors of a document. The anchor object has no properties, methods, or events. It is used to keep track of the named offsets that are defined relative to an HTML document. For example, anchors.length can be used to step through all of a document's anchors.

An anchor object is also a link object if it contains an HREF attribute. In this case, it will have an entry in both the anchors and links arrays.

The anchor() method is a method of the String object that can be used to generate the hypertext used to create an anchor object. It is similar to the link() method. For example, the following code can be used to create an anchor in the current document:

```
anchorString="Section 5".anchor("sect5")
document.write(anchorString)
```

The anchor created by the above code is equivalent to the following HTML:

```
<A NAME="sect5">Section 5</A>
```

Internet Explorer's Links and Anchors

Internet Explorer combines the link object with the anchor object. In the Internet Explorer object model, the document.links[] array refers to a collection of anchor and area objects. (You'll learn about area objects in the next chapter.) A *link* is differentiated from an *anchor* in that the anchor object's href property is set if the anchor represents a link, and its name property is set if it represents a named anchor. It is possible for an anchor object to be used as both a link and an anchor. In this case, both properties will be set. The important thing to remember is that either href or name must be set.

The *history* Object

The `history` object is used by Navigator to keep track of the URLs that have been displayed within a window during the current browser session. It displays this information in the history list that is accessed via Navigator's Go menu. The `history` object is a property of the `window` object. The `history` object has no events, but it has the four following properties:

current   The URL of the current document displayed in the window

length   The length of the history list

next   The next URL in the history list

previous   The previous URL in the history list

The `history` object has three methods—`back()`, `forward()`, and `go()`—which can be used to travel to documents contained in the history list:

back()   Loads the previous document in the history list. It produces the same effect as clicking your browser's Back button.

forward()   Loads the next document in the history list. It produces the same effect as clicking your browser's Forward button.

go()   Goes to a specific document in the history list. It can take either an integer parameter (positive or negative, indicating whether to go forward or back in the history list) or a string parameter (a keyword—see the next two items).

go(n)   When $n>0$, this method loads the document that is n entries ahead (forward) in the history list. When $n=0$, it reloads the current document. When $n<0$, go loads the document that is n entries behind (back) in the history list.

go(string)   When used in this manner, `go()` loads the closest document in the history list whose URL contains this string as a substring. For example, `history.go("chargers")` loads the closest history entry that contains the string `"chargers"` in its URL.

The JavaScript history object may be used to help users navigate your website. For example, it can be used to create simple direction buttons that allow users to revisit previously traversed web pages. More elaborate navigation aids may be developed using a standard site navigation form.

JavaScript security places restrictions on the use of the history object. In particular, a script that executes as part of a document in one frame can access the history object of a different frame only if the history object refers to documents that are loaded from the same web server as the script's document. This restriction is implemented by both Navigator and Internet Explorer. Chapter 34, "Securing Your Scripts," covers this and other aspects of JavaScript security in more detail. It also shows how signed scripts can be used to avoid some security restrictions.

Summary

In this chapter, you learned how to use link-related objects to exercise greater control over your document's links. You learned how to load documents via the location object, how to attach JavaScript code to a document's links, and how to use the history object to keep track of the URLs that have been visited within a window. In the next chapter, you'll learn how to use JavaScript's image and area objects to perform animation and to implement advanced client-side image map programs.

CHAPTER 11

Using Images

- The *image* object and its properties

- Dynamic image display

- Images and animation

- Image maps and the area object

- Working with image maps

The old adage that a picture is worth a thousand words has never been more appropriate than it is to the Web. Images transform web pages from fancy formatted text to professional graphical presentations. They allow drawings, photographs, and other graphics to be used to present the information that words alone cannot describe. Images can also be used as the source anchor for links or as clickable image maps. When images are used with links, they provide a highly intuitive approach to navigating the Web.

Until JavaScript, however, images could not be displayed dynamically because HTML's image-display capabilities have one significant limitation—once you've displayed an image, you cannot change it without loading a new web page. JavaScript overcomes the static image-display limitations of HTML by allowing you to dynamically update images without having to load a new web page. This single JavaScript feature can greatly enhance the attractiveness of your web pages. It allows you to provide timely graphical feedback in response to user actions, and can be used to include sophisticated animation sequences in your web pages.

In this chapter, you'll learn how to use the excellent image-handling features that JavaScript provides. I'll cover the image object and show you how to control the way images are displayed with respect to surrounding text. You'll learn how to dynamically display images in your web pages and how to use dynamic images to create animation effects. You'll also learn how to develop sophisticated client-side image maps using the area object. When you finish this chapter, you'll be able to use images to create web applications that are highly informative, user-friendly, and entertaining.

The *image* Object

The image object provides access to the images that are loaded with a document. It is a property of the document object. The images array contains an entry for each <img> tag that is specified within a document. The images array is also a property of the document object.

The properties of the image object that are supported by both Navigator and Internet Explorer are shown in Table 11.1. These properties reflect the attributes of the <img> tag. Internet Explorer supports many more properties than those shown in Table 11.1.

TABLE 11.1: *image* Properties

Property	Description
border	The value of the <img> tag's BORDER attribute
complete	Identifies whether an image has been completely loaded

Continued on next page

TABLE 11.1 CONTINUED: *image* Properties

Property	Description
height	The value of the <img> tag's HEIGHT attribute
hspace	The value of the <img> tag's HSPACE attribute
lowsrc	The value of the <img> tag's LOWSRC attribute
name	The value of the <img> tag's NAME attribute
prototype	Used to add user-specified properties to an image object
src	The value of the <img> tag's SRC attribute
vspace	The value of the <img> tag's VSPACE attribute
width	The value of the <img> tag's WIDTH attribute

The image object has no methods that are common to Internet Explorer and Navigator. Navigator defines the handleEvent() method, which is used to directly invoke an image's event handler. Internet Explorer defines 10 methods that support event handling and DHTML. Appendix C, "JavaScript and JScript Object Reference," covers the differences between Internet Explorer's and Navigator's implementation of the image object. Both Internet Explorer and Navigator support the six events listed in Table 4.1. The image object type allows new image objects to be explicitly created with the new keyword and a *constructor*. (Constructors were introduced in Chapter 5, "Working with Objects.") The Image() constructor is used to create and preload images that aren't initially displayed as part of a web page. These image objects are stored in the browser's cache and are used to replace images that have already been displayed.

An example of creating a cached image via the Image() constructor follows:

```
cachedImage = new Image()
cachedImage.src = "myImage.gif"
```

The first statement creates a new image object, and assigns it to the cachedImage variable. The second statement sets the image object's src property to the image file myImage.gif. This causes myImage.gif to be loaded into the browser cache. The loaded image can then be referenced using the cachedImage variable.

The image constructor takes optional width and height parameters. For example, myImage = new Image(40,50) creates an image object that is 40 pixels wide and 50 pixels high.

NOTE   Images that are created using the Image() constructor are not accessible via the images array.

Image Display Properties

Before I get into dynamic image display, I'll cover the image properties that affect the way an image is displayed with respect to surrounding text. These properties reflect the attributes of the `<img>` tag used to place an image in a document.

The `border` property identifies the thickness of an image's border in pixels. Images that are created using the `Image()` constructor have their border set to 0. The `border` property is read-only.

The `height` and `width` properties of an image specify the height and width of the window area in which the image is to be displayed. If the image is larger than the specified area, the browser will scale the image to fit in the allocated space. The `height` and `width` properties can be specified in pixels or as a percentage of the window's dimensions; a percent sign (%) is used to specify a percentage value. Images that are created using the `Image()` constructor have their `height` and `width` properties set to their actual dimensions. The `height` and `width` properties are read-only.

The `hspace` and `vspace` properties are used to specify a margin between an image and surrounding text. The `hspace` attribute specifies the size of an image's left and right margins in pixels. The `vspace` attribute specifies an image's top and bottom margins in pixels. Images that are created using the `Image()` constructor have their `hspace` and `vspace` properties set to 0. These properties are read-only.

Other Image Properties

The `image` object has other properties that can be used to monitor and control image loading and display:

- The `name` property is a read-only property that specifies the image's `name` attribute.

- The `lowsrc` property can be modified to quickly load and display a low-resolution image while a slower-loading, high-resolution image is being loaded.

- The `src` property is used to load a new image in the place of a currently displayed image. (You'll learn more about this property in the next section on dynamic image display.)

- The `complete` property is a read-only property that indicates whether an image has been completely loaded.

- The `prototype` property allows other user-defined properties to be created for all objects of the `image` object type. (This property is covered in Chapter 5.)

Dynamic Image Display

JavaScript's dynamic image display capabilities are easy to use. Just follow these three steps:

1. Use the Image() constructor to create image objects for storing the images that you'll display dynamically.

2. Load the image files associated with the newly created images by setting the image's src attribute to the image file's name.

3. Display the images by setting the src attribute of an image in the document's images array to the src attribute of a cached image.

For example, suppose you have a document that contains two <img> tags. When the document is loaded by your browser, the image files that are specified in the <img> tags' src attributes are displayed. You can load and display two new images using the following JavaScript code:

```
//Step 1: Create image objects
newImage1 = new Image()
newImage2 = new Image()
//Step 2: Load the image files
newImage1.src = "new1.gif"
newImage2.src = "new2.gif"
//Step 3: Display the images
document.images[0].src = newImage1.src
document.images[1].src = newImage2.src
```

In Chapter 10, "Working with Links," you developed an image pair-matching program. This program was designed to illustrate link-event handling and to develop your skills in using cookies. The program did not take advantage of JavaScript's dynamic image display capabilities, and as a result, it required a new web page to be loaded whenever a new image was displayed. Now that you know how to display images dynamically, let's revise the pair-matching program to take advantage of these capabilities.

A revised pair-matching program is contained in Listing 11.1. This single file (pairs.htm) takes the place of the click1.htm, click2.htm, match.htm, and pairs.js files used in Chapter 10. It also implements the image map program in a much smoother fashion, because it does not load an entire web page to display a single image. Figure 11.1 shows the program's opening display. Figure 11.2 provides a sample snapshot of a game in mid-progress. You can play the new game by opening the pairs.htm file with your browser. You should immediately notice the improvement in the way the program displays images.

Listing 11.1:   Pair Matching Revisited (pairs.htm)

```
<HTML>
<HEAD>
<TITLE>Pair Match</TITLE>
<SCRIPT LANGUAGE="JavaScript"><!--
function initialize() {
 imageSource=new Array(9)
 for(var i=0;i<9;++i) imageSource[i]=new Image()
 imageSource[0].src="smile1.gif"
 imageSource[1].src="smile2.gif"
 imageSource[2].src="smile3.gif"
 imageSource[3].src="smile4.gif"
 imageSource[4].src="frown1.gif"
 imageSource[5].src="frown2.gif"
 imageSource[6].src="frown3.gif"
 imageSource[7].src="frown4.gif"
 imageSource[8].src="none.gif"
 imageSequence=new Array(16)
 for(var i=0;i<16;++i) imageSequence[i]=i%8
 for(var i=0;i<16;++i) {
  var currentValue=imageSequence[i]
  var ix=Math.round(Math.random()*(15))
  imageSequence[i]=imageSequence[ix]
  imageSequence[ix]=currentValue
 }
 click0=0
 click1=0
 click2=0
}
function displayTable(){
 document.writeln('<TABLE BORDER="2">')
 for(var i=0;i<4;++i) {
  document.writeln('<TR>')
  for(var j=0;j<4;++j) {
   document.writeln('<TD>')
   document.write('<A HREF="javascript:void(0)" ')
   document.write('onClick="userClick('+(i*4+j)+')">')
   document.write('<IMG SRC="none.gif" WIDTH="80" HEIGHT="83">')
   document.write('</A>')
   document.writeln('</TD>')
  }
  document.writeln('</TR>')
 }
 document.writeln('</TABLE>')
}
function userClick(n) {
 if(click0==0){
  click0=1
  click1=n
  document.images[n].src=imageSource[imageSequence[n]].src
 }else if(click0==1){
```

```
  click0=0
  click2=n
  document.images[n].src=imageSource[imageSequence[n]].src
  if(click1==click2 ||
   imageSequence[click1]!=imageSequence[click2])
    setTimeout("resetImages()",1500)
 }
}
function resetImages() {
 document.images[click1].src=imageSource[8].src
 document.images[click2].src=imageSource[8].src
}
// --></SCRIPT>
</HEAD>
<BODY BGCOLOR="#FFFFFF">
<H1>Try to find a matching pair!</H1>
<SCRIPT LANGUAGE="JavaScript"><!--
initialize()
displayTable()
// --></SCRIPT>
<FORM>
<P ALIGN="CENTER">
<INPUT TYPE="BUTTON" NAME="replay" VALUE="Play again!"
 ONCLICK="window.location='pairs.htm'">
</P>
</FORM>
</BODY>
</HTML>
```

FIGURE 11.1:

The revised pair-matching program takes advantage of dynamic image display. (pairs.htm)

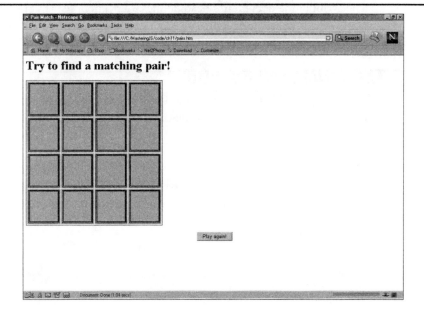

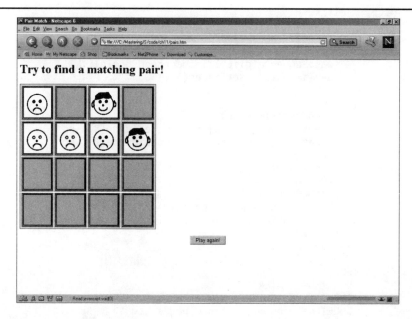

The pairs.htm file contains a large script in the document's head and a small script in the document's body. The script in the document's body invokes the initialize() function to initialize the arrays and variables used in the program. It invokes the displayTable() function to display the table of image links.

The script in the document's head defines four functions: initialize(), displayTable(), userClick(), and resetImages(). The use of these functions is described in the following subsections.

The *initialize()* Function

This function initializes the arrays and variables used throughout the script. The image-Source array is used to load and cache the images to be displayed throughout the script's execution. The imageSequence array is used to identify in which table cells the images are to be stored. It randomizes the location of pairs of the digits 0 through 7. These digits correspond to the first eight images stored in imageSource. The click0 variable is used to keep track of whether the user has clicked on the first or second image of the two-image sequence. The click1 and click2 variables identify the index of the image that the user clicked.

The *displayTable()* Function

This function displays the initial image link table. It is similar to the `displayTable()` function used in Chapter 10. However, it displays the table only once—when the document is loaded. Thus, it displays the `none.gif` image in each table cell. The table images are updated dynamically by the `userClick()` function.

The *userClick()* Function

This function handles the `onClick` event that is generated when a user clicks on an image link. If the user has clicked on the first image of the two-click sequence, the `click` variable is set to 1, `click1` is set to the index of the clicked cell, and the image associated with the cell is displayed. If the user has clicked on the second image of the two-click sequence, the `click` variable is reset to 0, `click2` is set to the index of the clicked cell, and the image associated with the cell is displayed. If the images do not match, the `resetImages()` function is invoked to reset the image display after a 1.5-second timeout period.

The *resetImages()* Function

This function resets the table cells pointed to by the `click1` and `click2` variables; it resets them to the `none.gif` image.

Images and Animation

JavaScript's dynamic image display capabilities can be used to create animation effects. *Animation* basically involves displaying one image after another in sequence. The quality of the animation depends on the quality of the images displayed, the delay between successive image displays, and the ability of your browser to reduce any deviations in this delay.

The quality of the images displayed depends on your taste in choosing images or your artistic skills in creating them; we can't provide you with much help in those areas. The delay between images is usually a fraction of a second (assuming that all images are downloaded prior to performing the animation). Higher-performance computers may be able to minimize this delay and reduce deviations in the average delay. These deviations are caused by the performance load on your system that results from other concurrently executing tasks.

Even if you already know the basics of how to perform animation, there are a few tips that will improve your results. These are as follows:

- Make sure that all images are loaded before you start your animation sequence. This will eliminate any additional delays associated with image loading.

- Schedule successive image displays using the onLoad event handler of the <img> tag to which the images are to be written. This will ensure that an image has been loaded and displayed before the next image is processed.

- Use the setTimeout() method of the window object to implement delays between images. This method will help to reduce any deviations in your average delay.

- Experiment with the delay value to see what delay is best for your animation. Although a lower delay value provides a smoother animation, a delay that is too small can result in images being displayed at a comically quick pace.

The file animate.htm provides a simple example of JavaScript animation (see Figure 11.3). It displays a five-frame animation of me working out. The first and last frames are the same; so are the second and fourth frames. Admittedly, this is not a very exciting animation, but it illustrates the principles of animation without getting wrapped up in the images being displayed. You can apply these principles to your own animation needs. If you haven't already done so, open animate.htm with your browser. Experiment with the faster and slower buttons to change the delay between successive images. Notice how this delay affects the quality of the animation.

FIGURE 11.3:

A snapshot of the animation sequence displays one of the images.
(animate.htm)

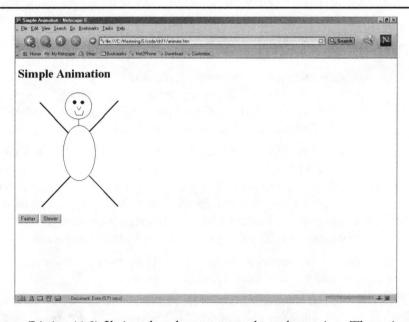

The animate.htm (Listing 11.2) file is rather short compared to other scripts. The script in the document's body simply invokes the initialize() function to create and load the animation images, set the value of the delay variable, and initialize other variables. Note that the onLoad event handler of the <img> tag invokes the setStart() function to start the animation. The setStart() function sets the start variable to *true*. The animate() function waits until start is true before beginning the animation.

Listing 11.2:   JavaScript Animation (animate.htm)

```
<HTML>
<HEAD>
<TITLE>Simple Animation</TITLE>
<SCRIPT LANGUAGE="JavaScript"><!--
function initialize() {
 start=false
 imageSource=new Array(5)
 for(var i=0;i<5;++i){
  imageSource[i]=new Image()
  imageSource[i].src="image"+i+".gif"
 }
 delay=500
 delta=100
 nextImage=1
 startAnimation()
}
function startAnimation() {
 interval=setInterval('animate()',delay)
}
function setStart() {
 start = true
}
function animate() {
 if(start==true){
  i=nextImage
  ++nextImage
  nextImage%=5
  if(imageSource[i].complete)
    document.display.src=imageSource[i].src
 }
}
function goFaster() {
 clearInterval(interval)
 delay-=delta
 if(delay<100) delay=100
 startAnimation()
}
function goSlower() {
 clearInterval(interval)
 delay+=delta
 startAnimation()
}
// --></SCRIPT>
</HEAD>
```

```
<BODY BGCOLOR="#FFFFFF">
<SCRIPT LANGUAGE="JavaScript"><!--
initialize()
// --></SCRIPT>
<H1>Simple Animation</H1>
<IMG NAME="display" SRC="image0.gif" onLoad="setStart()">
<BR>
<FORM>
<INPUT TYPE="BUTTON" NAME="faster" VALUE="Faster" ONCLICK="goFaster()">
<INPUT TYPE="BUTTON" NAME="slower" VALUE="Slower" ONCLICK="goSlower()">
</FORM>
</BODY>
</HTML>
```

The script in the document's head defines four functions: `initialize()`, `startAnimation()`, `setStart()`, `animate()`, `goFaster()`, and `goSlower()`. The use of these functions is described in the following subsections.

The *initialize()* Function

This function creates and loads the images used in the animation, and sets the `delay` variable to 500. Because the delay is specified in milliseconds, this initial delay is a one-half second. The `delta` variable is set to 100. This variably is used to increment or decrement the delay when the user clicks on the Slower or Faster buttons. The `nextImage` variable identifies the next image to be displayed.

The *startAnimation()* Function

This function invokes the `animate()` function at an interval of `delay` milliseconds.

The *setStart()* Function

Sets the value of `start` to `true` to begin the animation.

The *animate()* Function

This function performs the actual animation. It displays the next image, and updates `nextImage` to point to a new image.

The *goFaster()* Function

This function handles the `onClick` event associated with the Faster button by decreasing the `delay` value by the amount indicated by the `delta` variable.

The *goSlower()* Function

This function handles the onClick event associated with the Slower button by increasing the delay value by the amount indicated by the delta variable.

Image Maps and the *area* Object

Clickable image maps provide a graphical, intuitive, and easy-to-use way to navigate the Web. An *image map* is an image that is divided into different areas, each of which is associated with its own URL. When a user clicks on a particular area of the image map, the document at the URL associated with the area is loaded. Chapter 4, "Handling Events," introduces image maps and shows how to handle image map events.

JavaScript supports client-side image maps, and provides the area object as a way of handling user actions related to specific image areas. These areas are defined by the <area> tag.

The properties of the area object that are common to Navigator and Internet Explorer are shown in Table 11.2. These properties reflect the HREF and TARGET attributes of the <area> tag, and are equivalent to those of the location and link objects that you studied in Chapter 10. The area object does not have any methods that are common to Navigator and Internet Explorer. It has three common events: onDblClick, onMouseOut, and onMouseOver, as described in Chapter 4.

TABLE 11.2: *area* Properties

Property	Description
hash	The file offset part of an **area** object's HREF attribute
host	The hostname part of an **area** object's HREF attribute
hostname	The host:port part of an **area** object's HREF attribute
href	An **area** object's complete HREF attribute
pathname	The pathname part of an **area** object's HREF attribute
port	The port part of an **area** object's HREF attribute
protocol	The protocol part of an **area** object's HREF attribute
search	The query string part of an **area** object's HREF attribute
target	An **area** object's TARGET attribute

Working with Image Maps

The HTML `<map>` and `<area>` tags can be used to implement effective client-side image maps. However, as is usually the case, JavaScript provides some additional features that further enhance the capabilities of HTML. With respect to image maps, these features are the onMouseOver and onMouseOut events associated with the area object. The onMouseOver event is generated when a user moves the mouse pointer over an image area. The onMouseOut event is generated when a user moves the mouse pointer away from an image area. Of the two events, the onMouseOver event is generally more useful. To illustrate its use, I'll create an image map for lazy people. With this image map, users will not have to *click* the image for an action to be performed—they only have to move the mouse over an image area.

The `imap.htm` file is shown in Listing 11.3. It creates a simple two-frame document with `map.htm` (Listing 11.4) loaded in the first frame. Open `imap.htm` with your web browser; the two-frame document shown in Figure 11.4 is displayed.

Listing 11.3:   A Client-side Image Map (imap.htm)

```
<HTML>
<HEAD>
<TITLE>Client-Side Image Maps</TITLE>
</HEAD>
<FRAMESET COLS="415,*" BORDER="1">
<FRAME SRC="map.htm">
<FRAME SRC="blank.htm">
</FRAMESET>
</HTML>
```

Listing 11.4:   Creating the Image Map (map.htm)

```
<HTML>
<HEAD>
<TITLE>Client-Side Image Maps</TITLE>
<SCRIPT LANGUAGE="JavaScript"><!--
function goWhatsNew() {
 parent.frames[1].location.href="whatsnew.htm"
}
function goProducts() {
 parent.frames[1].location.href="products.htm"
}
function goCompany() {
 parent.frames[1].location.href="company.htm"
}
function goField() {
 parent.frames[1].location.href="field.htm"
```

```
        }
        // --></SCRIPT>
        </HEAD>
        <BODY BGCOLOR="#FFFFFF">
        <MAP NAME="bizmap">
          <AREA NAME="whatsNew" COORDS="219,250,50" shape="circle"
           HREF="javascript:void(0)" onMouseOver="goWhatsNew();
              return true">
          <AREA NAME="products" COORDS="205,226,100" shape="circle"
           HREF="javascript:void(0)" onMouseOver="goProducts();
              return true">
          <AREA NAME="company" COORDS="192,202,155" shape="circle"
           HREF="javascript:void(0)" onMouseOver="goCompany()">
          <AREA NAME="field" COORDS="183,189,188" shape="circle"
           HREF="javascript:void(0)" onMouseOver="goField()">
        </MAP>
        <IMG SRC="map.gif" BORDER="0" USEMAP="#bizmap">
        </HTML>
```

FIGURE 11.4:

The image map opening display provides an interesting company home page. (Listing 11.3)

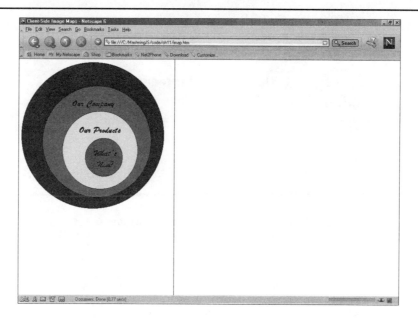

The map.htm file creates a client-side image map and defines four <area> tags. These <area> tags correspond to each of the four circles of the map.gif file. The HREF attribute of each <area> tag is set to the URL *javascript:void(0)*. This URL causes user clicks to be ignored. The onMouseOver events of the four <area> tags are handled by invoking the goWhatsNew(), goProducts(), goCompany(), and goField() functions, as appropriate. These functions display the files shown in Listings 11.5 through 11.8. (In a real company home page, the files shown in Listings 11.5 through 11.8 would contain real links, as opposed to the fake ones shown in the example.)

Listing 11.5:   What's New! (whatsnew.htm)

```
<HTML>
<HEAD>
<TITLE>What's New!</TITLE>
</HEAD>
<BODY BGCOLOR="#FFFFFF">
<H1 ALIGN="CENTER">What's New!</H1>
<DL>
<DT><I>October 10, 2002</I></DT>
<DD>Our lastest virtual widget has been released...</DD>
<DT><I>February 29, 2002</I></DT>
<DD>We've developed a special millenium leap year widget...</DD>
<DT><I>January 1, 2002</I></DT>
<DD>Our X Widget has led the way into the 21st century...</DD>
</DL>
</BODY>
</HTML>
```

Listing 11.6:   Our Products! (products.htm)

```
<HTML>
<HEAD>
<TITLE>Our Products!</TITLE>
</HEAD>
<BODY BGCOLOR="#FFFFFF">
<H1 ALIGN="CENTER">Our Products!</H1>
<P>Our product line includes the following
 state-of-the-art widgets:</P>
<DL>
<DT><A HREF="javascript:void(0)">X Widget</A></DT>
<DD>The most advanced widget available today.</DD>
<DT><A HREF="javascript:void(0)">Y Widget</A></DT>
<DD>A low power version of the X Widget.</DD>
<DT><A HREF="javascript:void(0)">Z Widget</A></DT>
<DD>Our lowest cost X-compatible widget. </DD>
</DL>
</BODY>
</HTML>
```

Listing 11.7:   Our Company! (company.htm)

```
<HTML>
<HEAD>
<TITLE>Our Company!</TITLE>
</HEAD>
<BODY BGCOLOR="#FFFFFF">
<H1 ALIGN="CENTER">Our Company!</H1>
<P>XYZ Corporation has remained at the forefront of advanced
  widget research. We have pioneered the development of the
  new X widget, the low power Y widget, and the low cost Z
  widget....</P>
</BODY>
</HTML>
```

Listing 11.8:   Our Field! (field.htm)

```
<HTML>
<HEAD>
<TITLE>Our Field!</TITLE>
</HEAD>
<BODY BGCOLOR="#FFFFFF">
<H1 ALIGN="CENTER">Our Field!</H1>
<P>Our field has witnessed a number of breakthroughs in the
  last year. Advanced widget research at the university level
  has led to whole new ways of designing widgets. New widget
  designs have revolutionized the end products built from these
  widgets....</P>
</BODY>
</HTML>
```

When you move your mouse over the What's New? circle, the second frame displays the relevant page, as shown in Figure 11.5. When you move your mouse over the Our Products circle, the second frame shows the document shown in Figure 11.6. Move your mouse over the Our Company and Our Field circles, and the frame shows the documents shown in Figures 11.7 and 11.8. Isn't this much more efficient than having to move *and* click individual image areas?

FIGURE 11.5:

The What's New? document display provides up-to-date news about a company. (Listing 11.5)

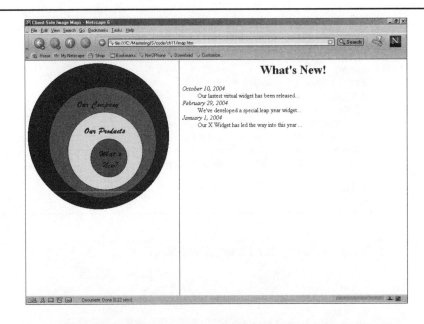

FIGURE 11.6:

The Our Products document display provides access to information about a company's products. (Listing 11.6)

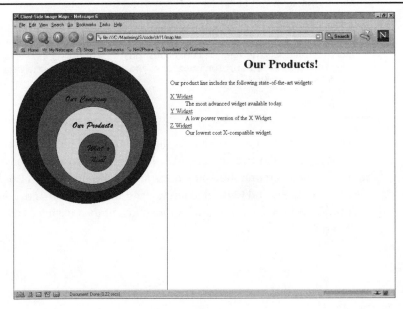

FIGURE 11.7:

The Our Company document display provides high-level information about a company. (Listing 11.7)

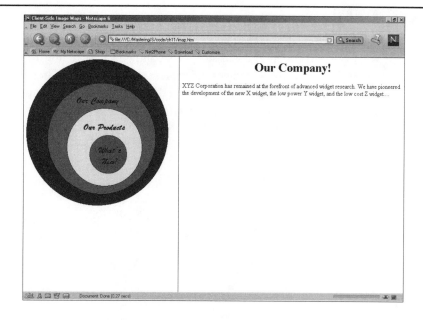

FIGURE 11.8:

The Our Field document display provides new information about the technical fields in which the company is engaged. (Listing 11.8)

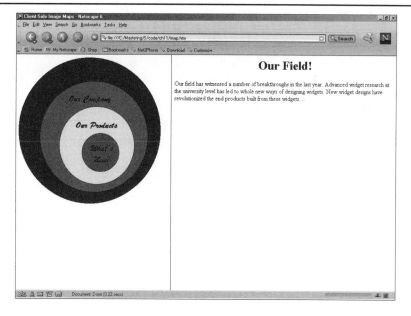

Summary

In this chapter, you learned how to use the image-handling features provided by JavaScript. You were introduced to the `image` object, and you learned how to control the way images are formatted with respect to surrounding text. You also learned how to dynamically display images in your web pages. You covered the basics of animation and learned how to use dynamic images to create animation effects. You also learned how to use the `area` object to enhance the attractiveness of client-side image maps. In the following chapter, you'll learn about JavaScript's support for Dynamic HTML (DHTML).

CHAPTER 12

Working with Styles and DHTML

- What are style sheets?

- Cascading style sheets versus JavaScript style sheets

- Defining style sheets

- Using the *<LINK>* tag to include styles

- Using multiple style sheets

- Using the DHTML capabilities of Navigator 6 and Internet Explorer

One of the most exciting capabilities provided with Cascading Style Sheets, or CSS, is the capability to specify the style in which different HTML elements are formatted and displayed. Before the advent of style sheets, web page authors were confined to using the standard formatting provided by individual HTML elements. Headings, paragraphs, lists, and other text elements provided little variety or flexibility in the way that they were presented. Style sheets changed all that—now, web authors can control the color, font, margins, and many other aspects of individual HTML elements. This powerful capability results in web pages that are livelier, more colorful, and more closely tailored to their target audience. This means that you can create more stirring pages for those who want to be moved; on the other hand, you can create more tightly organized pages for those who admire standardization.

In this chapter, you'll be introduced to style sheets. You'll learn the differences between *Cascading Style Sheets (CSS)* that were developed by the World Wide Web Consortium and the now-defunct JavaScript style sheets that were a part of Netscape Navigator 4. You'll cover the tags and attributes used with CSS, and learn how to work with both internally and externally defined styles. You'll also learn how styles can be dynamically updated using DHTML. When you finish this chapter, you'll be able to take advantage of CSS style sheets and DHTML to add both flair and consistency to your web applications.

What Are Style Sheets?

Style sheets provide the capability to control the way in which HTML elements (such as headings, paragraphs, and lists) are laid out and displayed. They enable web page designers to use standard HTML elements in a limitless variety of new ways. For example, before style sheets were developed, web authors had six heading levels to work with. These headings could be right-justified, left-justified, or centered. They could be made to use a different size font or display style, but not much more. Style sheets let you specify the display of different level headings with various colors, font styles, font sizes, and more. You can also specify the way that headings are laid out—the spacing before and after the heading and the margins used with the heading. You can collect styles for certain types of projects and save them in style sheets. Style sheets give you complete flexibility and control in the way that the pages of your web applications are presented.

You may wonder what possible uses you can make of all this flexibility. Well, if you develop web pages for a number of different audiences, style sheets are an absolute must. You can create a standard company style sheet to lay out the pages that you develop at work, a style sheet to lay out documents that are unique to your department at school, a style sheet to create your own casual-looking personal web pages, and a style sheet of really outrageous styles for the web pages that you develop for your friends, kids, or hobbies.

Within an organization, different styles can be used for different departments (engineering versus marketing), different types of documents (product descriptions versus design specifications), or different types of information (company-sensitive versus material that can be distributed freely).

Cascading Style Sheets versus JavaScript Style Sheets

Much of the underlying technology of the Web—including HTML, web browsers, and web servers—was developed at the CERN physics laboratory in Geneva, Switzerland. For a bunch of scientists, they sure turn out some amazing internetworking technologies. Style sheets are another development of CERN. In 1994, work on HTML style sheets was initiated, and a specification called *Cascading Style Sheets* was proposed in December 1996. The style sheets are referred to as *cascading* because the specification allows for multiple levels of styles to be applied to a single document in which the output of some styles are the input of others.

The Cascading Style Sheets, referred to by their acronym *CSS1*, are a natural outgrowth of CERN's involvement in the development of HTML. HTML 4 and CSS1 are implemented by most modern browsers from Netscape Navigator 4 and Internet Explorer 4 onward. In addition to supporting CSS1, Netscape Navigator 4 also supports a JavaScript-based approach to style sheets, referred to as *JavaScript Style Sheets*, or *JSS* for short. JavaScript style sheets support the styles provided by CSS1, and have the advantage of making these styles available as JavaScript properties. However, JSS were a non-standard solution and were limited to Navigator 4. Throughout the rest of this chapter, I'll refer exclusively to CSS style sheets.

NOTE   Several different versions of CSS have been defined by the W3C. Most browsers support CSS1. However, CSS2 and CSS3 will eventually be supported.

NOTE   For a complete treatment of CSS1, refer to the W3C CSS1 recommendation. It is available at the URL www.w3.org/TR/REC-CSS1.

An Introductory Example

To give you a better feel for how style sheets work, we'll start off with a simple example. Listing 12.1 contains a document that displays a few headings and paragraphs in different colors using CSS. Figure 12.1 provides a black-and-white representation of the web page that is displayed by Navigator 6.

Listing 12.1:   An Introductory Style Sheet Example (style1.htm)

```
<HTML>
<HEAD>
<TITLE>Using CSS Styles</TITLE>
<STYLE TYPE="text/css">
body {
 background-color: cyan;
}
h1 {
 color: red;
}
h2 {
 color: blue;
}
p {
 color: green;
}
</STYLE>
</HEAD>
<BODY>
<H1>This is a first level heading</H1>
<P>This is the first paragraph.</P>
<H2>This is a second level heading.</H2>
<P>This is the second paragraph.</P>
<H1>Here is another first level heading</H1>
</BODY>
</HTML>
```

FIGURE 12.1:

A simple introduction to
style sheets

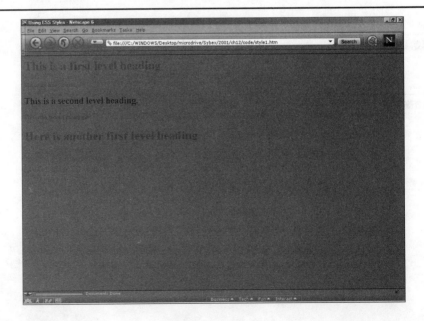

Open `style1.htm` with your browser to see how the document is displayed. You'll probably be aghast at the awful color scheme that I've chosen—style sheets make it as easy to convey a poor sense of style as easily as a well-developed sense of style. But please bear with me. Your document background color should be set to cyan. The first and last headings in the document are level-1 headings that are displayed in red. In the middle of the document is a level-2 heading that is displayed in blue. The document contains two one-line paragraphs that are displayed in green.

If you look at Listing 12.1, you'll see that except for the `<STYLE>` element in the document head, the rest of the document appears to be just regular HTML. That's the power of style sheets—you can change the formatting and display of an entire document by just changing the style of the document. In the case of `style1.htm`, all you had to do was add the `<STYLE>` element to change a very normal-looking HTML document into a very unusual-looking one.

The `<STYLE>` tags shown in Listing 12.1 are surrounding tags. They surround four style descriptions that assign color values to the `body`, `h1`, `h2`, and `p` tags. The syntax used for style rules in Listing 12.1 is as follows:

```
selector {
  propertyName: propertyValue;
}
```

The *selector* specifies the document elements to which the style applies. In the case of Listing 12.1, tag names were used as selectors. Multiple style properties may be defined in a style rule. Common CSS property names and values will be introduced in this chapter. Consult Appendix F, "Cascading Style Sheets," for a more detailed reference of these properties and values.

The `<STYLE>` tag uses the `TYPE` attribute to determine what type of style sheet is in effect. The `text/css` value is used to identify a CSS style sheet (as opposed to a JavaScript style sheet). The `text/javascript` value would be used to identify a JavaScript style sheet.

NOTE   Appendix F provides a CSS1 reference.

Defining Styles

As you saw in the previous example, using styles is easy. You write your HTML documents using traditional HTML tags and then define style rules to specify the style changes to be used with selected HTML elements. This is the preferred way to use styles, although a number of usage options are provided.

Styles may be defined in any of the following ways:

- The `<STYLE>` tag may be used to define styles in the document head.

- The <LINK> tag may be used to refer to a style sheet that is in a separate, external document.

- The <SPAN> tag may be used to surround text to which a particular style is to be applied.

The following sections show how to use each of the preceding mechanisms to define and use styles within your documents.

The *<STYLE>* Tag

You already learned to use the <STYLE> tag in the first example of this chapter, as follows:

- You put <STYLE> and </STYLE> tags in a document's header.

- You set the TYPE attribute to text/css.

- You defined styles between the <STYLE> tags.

The <STYLE> tag is very easy to use. The hard part is figuring out what kind of styles you want to define.

The styles used in Listing 12.1 showed how the styles associated with individual HTML elements can be defined. Basically, you redefined all level-1 and level-2 headings and paragraphs to use certain colors. The statements that are included between the <STYLE> tags may be used to provide much more power and flexibility in the way that styles are defined. For example, you can do the following:

- Specify the style and size of fonts to be used with specific HTML elements.

- Specify the way that text is to be aligned (vertically and horizontally), indented, capitalized, and decorated (underline, overline, blink, and strikethrough).

- Specify foreground and background colors, and the use of background images.

- Identify the margins, borders, padding, and alignment to be used to lay out block-formatted HTML elements.

- Define classes of styles and specify which HTML elements belong to each class.

- Define exceptions to a style or class of styles.

- Insert comments that document your style definitions.

Although the preceding list may seem daunting, don't worry. We will cover each of these capabilities, one at a time, in the following sections.

NOTE   If your machine doesn't have a font that the style needs, your browser will try to find a font with the closest fit to the one it requires.

Inserting Comments

Multiline JavaScript comments /* */ can be used to document your style sheets.

The *ID* Attribute

Listing 12.1 shows how you can define style rules for individual HTML tags. You simply identify the tag name to which the style will be applied. This approach is quick and easy. However, for better or worse, it affects all tags with the specified style name.

Sometimes, you'll want to identify exceptions to a style rule. That's where the HTML ID attribute comes in handy. You can identify a particular ID attribute for specific tags, and associate them with a style rule. For example, you can create an ID to specify that a particular HTML element is to be displayed in red, as shown in Listing 12.2. A hash mark (#) is placed in front of a selector to indicate that it represents the value of an element's ID attribute.

In Listing 12.2, tag selectors are used to define styles for the <BODY> and <P> tags. An ID selector, named WARNING, is used in the second paragraph and the last heading. This causes the second paragraph and last heading shown in Figure 12.2 to be displayed in red.

Listing 12.2:   Using the ID Attribute (ids.htm)

```
<HTML>
<HEAD>
<TITLE>Using the CSS ID attribute</TITLE>
<STYLE TYPE="text/css">
BODY {background-color: white;}
P {color: blue;}
#WARNING {color: red;}
</STYLE>
</HEAD>
<BODY>
<P>This is the first paragraph.
It uses the redefined paragraph style.</P>
<P ID="WARNING">This is the second paragraph.
It has its ID attribute set to WARNING.</P>
<P>This is the third paragraph.
It uses the redefined paragraph style.</P>
<H1>This is a normal H1 heading.</H1>
<H1 ID="WARNING">This H1 heading uses the WARNING ID.</H1>
</BODY>
</HTML>
```

FIGURE 12.2:

How the *ID* attribute and *Warning* style are used

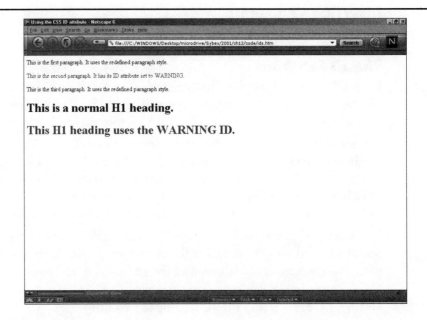

Setting Font Properties

The font-style, font-variant, and font-size style properties of an HTML element may be specified as part of the element's style definition. For example:

```
<STYLE TYPE="text/css">
h1 {
 font-size: smaller;
 font-style: italic;
}
</STYLE>
```

The font-style property may be assigned the following values:

- normal

- italic

- oblique

The font-variant style property may be normal or small-caps.

The italic and oblique values may be combined with the small-caps font-variant style property. Use of the oblique style causes text to be slanted to the left; this is different from an italic font, which is explicitly designed to look slanted. Use of small-caps causes text to appear in uppercase, but with a much smaller font.

The font-size property may be used to change the size of the font in which text is displayed. Fonts may be specified using a numeric size, such as 12pt; a descriptive size, such as large; or a relative size, such as smaller. Consult Appendix F for a list of possible values.

Displayed font sizes depend upon the table of font sizes that your browser uses. Your browser may not have the exact font size that you specify; if this is the case, it will try to find the one closest to it in the table. Listing 12.3 shows how the font sizes and styles of the first four heading levels may be redefined. Figure 12.3 shows how a browser displays the new headings.

Listing 12.3:   Using Font Sizes and Font Styles (fonstyle.htm)

```
<HTML>
<HEAD>
<TITLE>Using CSS Font Sizes</TITLE>
<STYLE TYPE="text/css">
body {
  background-color: white;
}
h1 {
  font-size: small;
}
h2 {
  font-size: medium;
  font-style: italic;
}
h3 {
  font-size: large;
}
h4 {
  font-size: x-large;
  font-style: italic;
}
</STYLE>
</HEAD>
<BODY>
<H1>A level 1 heading</H1>
<H2>A level 2 heading</H2>
<H3>A level 3 heading</H3>
<H4>A level 4 heading</H4>
</BODY>
</HTML>
```

FIGURE 12.3:

Redefining the first four
heading levels using font
sizes and font styles

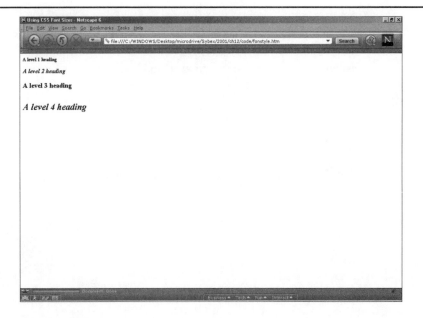

Setting Text Properties

You can define a number of properties that govern the display of text within an HTML element:

- line-height controls the spacing between lines of text.
- text-align specifies the horizontal alignment of text within an HTML element.
- vertical-align specifies the vertical alignment of text within an HTML element.
- text-transform specifies the case to be used for text within an HTML element.
- text-decoration specifies how text is to be adorned using underline, overline, blink, and strikethrough.

The line-height property is set to a number, a length, or a percentage—such as 150% for space and a half, 200% for double-spacing, 300% for triple-spacing, and so on—that identifies the line spacing to be used between adjacent lines of text.

The text-align property can be set to left, right, center, or justify to alter the way that text is aligned with respect to an HTML element.

The vertical-align property may be set to the values baseline, sub, super, top, text-top, middle, bottom, and text-bottom. The sub and super values are used to create subscripts and superscripts. The other values are similar to the HTML attribute values used to align images. The vertical-align property can also be set to a percentage.

The `text-transform` property may be set to the following values: uppercase, lowercase, capitalize, or none. The none value turns off capitalization.

The `text-decoration` property may be set to the following values: none, underline, overline, line-through, or blink. The none value turns off any previously assigned decorations.

Listing 12.4 provides an example of using text properties. Figure 12.4 shows how these properties are reflected in a browser's display.

Listing 12.4:   Using Text Properties (textyle.htm)

```
<HTML>
<HEAD>
<TITLE>Using CSS Text Properties</TITLE>
<STYLE TYPE="text/css">
BODY {background-color: white;}
#HALF {line-height: 50%;
 text-align: right;}
#ONEPT5 {line-height: 150%;
  text-align: center;
  text-transform: uppercase;
  text-decoration: blink;}
#DOUBLE {line-height: 200%;
  text-align: justify;
  text-transform: lowercase;
  text-decoration: underline;}
#TRIPLE {line-height: 300%;
  text-transform: capitalize;
  text-decoration: line-through;}
</STYLE>
</HEAD>
<BODY>
<P>This is a normal paragraph without any text styling.
Check out its line height, alignment, text case, and
decoration. Use this as a standard to judge subsequent
paragraphs.</P>
<P ID="HALF">This paragraph has a line height of 50%
and right alignment. It does not have any special text
decoration. Check out what happens when this line wraps.
The lines overlap because of the line height.</P>
<P ID="ONEPT5">This paragraph has a line height of 150%
and center alignment. It also uses the uppercase text
transform and the blink text decoration. Internet Explorer
does not currently support blink but Navigator does.</P>
<P ID="DOUBLE">This paragraph has a line height of 200%
and justify alignment. It also uses the lowercase text
transform and the underline decoration. Both Navigator
and Internet Explorer support the underline decoration.</P>
<P ID="TRIPLE">This paragraph has a line height of 300%.
It does not specify an alignment style. It also uses the
```

```
capitalize text transform and the line-through decoration.
Both Navigator and Internet Explorer support the line-through
decoration.</P>
</BODY>
</HTML>
```

FIGURE 12.4:

Changing paragraph
formats using text styles

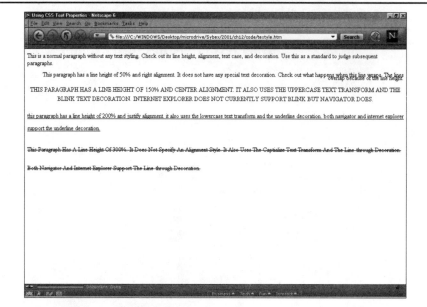

Using Colors and Background Images

You are already familiar with using the color and background-color properties from previous examples in this chapter. The color property is used to set the text foreground color and the background-color property is used to set the color of the background occupied by an HTML element. The RGB values of custom colors may be specified using the rgb() function. For example, a color with a 50 red value, 100 green value, and 150 blue value may be specified using rgb(50,100,150). Listing 12.5 shows how background and foreground colors can be specified using the background-color and color properties. Figure 12.5 shows a black-and-white version of the web page displayed by Listing 12.5. If it were in color, it would show a cyan document background, a level-1 heading with red foreground and yellow background colors, and a paragraph with white foreground and blue background colors.

Listing 12.5:   Using Backgrounds and Foregrounds (colors.htm)

```
<HTML>
<HEAD>
<TITLE>Using CSS Colors</TITLE>
<STYLE TYPE="text/css">
BODY {background-color: cyan;}
H1 {background-color: yellow;
 color: red;}
P {background-color: blue;
 color: white;}
</STYLE>
</HEAD>
<BODY>
<H1>This is a level 1 heading.</H1>
<P>This is a paragraph.</P>
</BODY>
</HTML>
```

FIGURE 12.5:

Background and foreground colors may be set using color styles.

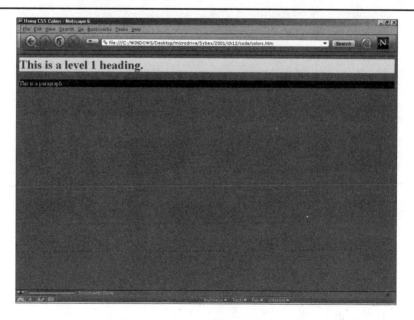

The background-image property may be used to identify a background image to be used with an HTML element. The property takes a URL as its value. Background images are typically used with the document as a whole by assigning an image to the <BODY> tag. However,

CSS allows background images to be assigned to block-formatted elements. Block-formatted elements are covered next.

Laying Out Block-Formatted Elements

Block-formatted elements are HTML elements that begin on a new line. Examples are headings, paragraphs, and lists. The margins, border, padding, and other aspects of block-formatted elements can be defined by styles.

Margins are defined using the `margins-right`, `margins-left`, `margins-top`, and `margins-bottom` properties. The `margin` property sets all four margins at the same time.

The width of the border around a block element is set using the `border-left-width`, `border-right-width`, `border-top-width`, and `border-bottom-width` properties. The `border-width` property can be used in the same manner as the `margin` property to set the width of all four borders at once. The `border-style` property sets the style of the border to `dotted`, `dashed`, `solid`, `double`, `groove`, `ridge`, `inset`, `outset`, or `none`.

The padding between a block element and its border is set using the `padding-right`, `padding-left`, `padding-top`, and `padding-bottom` properties. The `padding` property sets all four padding values.

The `width` and `height` properties specify the dimensions to be used in laying out block elements. If the `width` and `height` properties are set to `auto`, any replacement for the block element, such as a loaded image, will cause the block to be automatically resized. If the properties are not set to `auto`, the replacement will be resized to fit the block.

Listing 12.6 provides an example of block formatting. Figure 12.6 shows how the block formatting attributes affect the margins, border, and padding of paragraphs.

Listing 12.6:   Using Block Formatting Properties (blocks.htm)

```
<HTML>
<HEAD>
<TITLE>Formatting CSS Block Properties</TITLE>
<STYLE TYPE="text/css">
BODY {background-color: white;}
P {margin-left: 10;
  border-left-width: 1;
  border-style: solid;
  background-color: cyan;}
#para2 {margin-left: 50;
  padding-left: 10;
  padding-top: 15;
  padding-bottom: 0;}
</STYLE>
</HEAD>
```

```
<BODY>
<P>This is a paragraph.</P>
<P ID="para2">This is another paragraph.</P>
</BODY>
</HTML>
```

FIGURE 12.6:

Block-formatting styles can be used to change the margins, border, and padding of block elements.

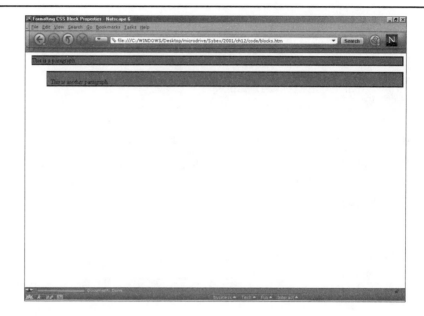

Using Measurement Units

CSS measurement units are used to specify font sizes, margins, and other element properties. They are organized into three categories:

- **Absolute units**. These units specify the actual magnitude of a property. For example, 14pt may be used to identify a 14-point font.

- **Relative units**. These units specify the magnitude of a property relative to the element being defined. For example, 5em may be used to identify a 5-em margin. (An *em* is a real unit of measure: It's defined as the width of the capital letter M. Obviously, this unit changes from one font to another.)

- **Proportional units.** These units specify the size of a property in proportion to the element being defined. For example, 50% may be used to reduce the font size of a heading by half.

Listing 12.7 shows how absolute, relative, and proportional units may be used in CSS. Figure 12.7 shows how the document of Listing 12.7 is displayed.

Listing 12.7: **Using Measurement Units (units.htm)**

```
<HTML>
<HEAD>
<TITLE>CSS Measurement Units</TITLE>
<STYLE TYPE="text/css">
BODY {background-color: white;}
H1 {font-size: 75%;}
P {margin-left: 5em;}
#para2 {font-size: 36pt;}
</STYLE>
</HEAD>
<BODY>
<H1>This level 1 heading is reduced 75%.</H1>
<P>This is a normal paragraph with a 5 em margin.</P>
<P ID="para2">This paragraph uses a 36 point font and
has a 5 em margin.</P>
</BODY>
</HTML>
```

FIGURE 12.7:

CSS measurement units

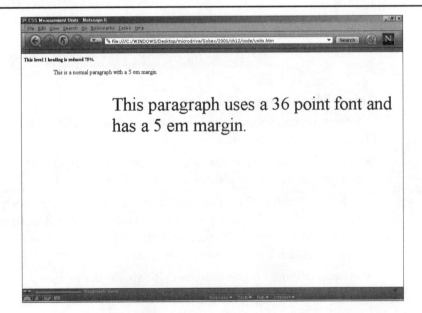

Using Classes

With CSS, you can define classes of styles that can be applied to different parts of a document. For example, you can define a class for marking company-sensitive data within a document, highlighting important text, or inserting revisions into a document. Classes are identified using the HTML CLASS attribute. For example, the following identifies a heading as being in the important class:

```
<H1 CLASS="important">This is an important heading.</H1>
```

The selector of a class is preceded with a period (.). Class selectors are defined in <STYLE> tags using the following syntax:

```
.className {
 propertyName: propertyValue;
}
```

For example, the following rule defines the style of the important class:

```
.important {
 font-style: italic;
 text-decoration: underline;
 color: red;
 background-color: yellow;
}
```

A class may be tailored for use with a particular tag by preceding the period with the tag name. For example, the following specifies that the important class shall use a 36-point font with the H1 tag:

```
H1.important {font-size: 36pt;}
```

Listing 12.8 provides an example of using classes to define important text. Figure 12.8 shows how the document described by Listing 12.8 is displayed.

Listing 12.8:   Using Classes to Define Important Text (classes.htm)

```
<HTML>
<HEAD>
<TITLE>Using CSS Classes</TITLE>
<STYLE TYPE="text/css">
BODY {background-color: white;}
.important {
 font-style: italic;
 text-decoration: underline;
 color: red;
 background-color: yellow;}
H1.important {font-size: 36pt;}
P.important {font-size: 18pt;}
UL.important {font-size: 12pt;}
</STYLE>
```

```
</HEAD>
<BODY>
<H1>This is a normal heading.</H1>
<P>This is a normal paragraph.</P>
<H1 CLASS="important">This is an important heading.</H1>
<P CLASS="important">This paragraph contains some important information.</P>
<P>This is a normal paragraph, but an important list follows.</P>
<UL CLASS="important">
<LI>item 1
<LI>item 2
<LI>item 3
</UL>
</BODY>
</HTML>
```

FIGURE 12.8:

Classes add power and flexibility to style sheets.

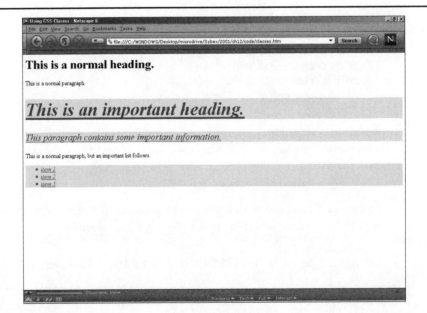

The <*SPAN*> Tag

What happens if you want to change the style of a selected portion of text, and do not want to redefine other logical and physical formatting tags? For example, suppose that you want to develop a style called highlight, which merely changes the color of the selected text to magenta so that it will stand out. You could redefine the <EM> tag, but you still want to be able to emphasize text that is highlighted. The <SPAN> tag provides the solution you need.

The <SPAN> tag is used to apply styles to selected text. Use the <SPAN> and </SPAN> tags to surround the text to which the style is to be applied. You can then use the CLASS and ID attributes to apply a style to the text.

For example, consider Listing 12.9. It defines a highlight style that changes the text foreground color to magenta. Highlighted text is selected by the <SPAN> tags, and the ID attribute of the <SPAN> tag is set to highlight. Use of the <SPAN> tags does not conflict with the <EM> tag. Figure 12.9 shows how the document of Listing 12.9 is displayed.

Listing 12.9:   Using the <SPAN> Tag to Change the Style of Selected Text (span.htm)

```
<HTML>
<HEAD>
<TITLE>Using the SPAN tag with CSS</TITLE>
<STYLE TYPE="text/css">
BODY {background-color: white;}
P {font-size: 36pt;
 margin-left: 5em;
 margin-right: 5em;
 margin-top: 1em;}
.highlight {color: magenta;}
</STYLE>
</HEAD>
<BODY>
<P>This paragraph contains some
<SPAN CLASS="highlight">highlighted</SPAN> text.</P>
<P>This paragraph contains some
<SPAN CLASS="highlight">highlighted and <EM>emphasized</EM></SPAN>
text.</P>
</BODY>
</HTML>
```

FIGURE 12.9:

The *<SPAN>* tag allows styles to be applied to selected text.

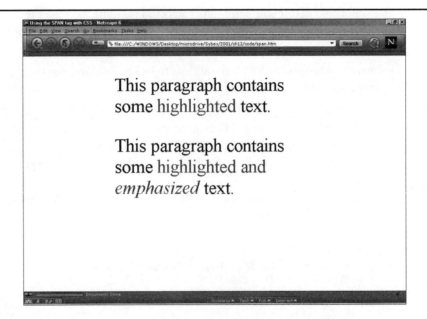

Using the *<LINK>* Tag to Include Styles

Now that you are familiar with styles, you're probably wondering whether you have to re-enter your favorite style definitions in all the documents that use those styles. The answer is no—you can use the <LINK> tag to use styles that are defined in external files. This means that you can define your styles once and then reuse them over and over again. It also means that you can update the styles used for multiple documents by changing a single file.

The external style files define styles using the syntax that we covered in previous sections. Style rules are specified without the surrounding <STYLE> tags. For example, Listing 12.10 contains style definitions for the document body and paragraph tags.

Listing 12.10:   External Style Definitions (favstyle)

```
BODY {background-color: blue;}
P {font-size: 24pt;
 font-style: italic;
 color: white;
 margin-left: 5em;
 margin-right: 5em;
 margin-top: 5em;}
```

The style definitions of Listing 12.10 can be included using the following <LINK> tag:

```
<LINK REL=STYLESHEET TYPE="text/css" HREF="favstyle">
```

The <LINK> tag is defined in the HTML specification (www.w3.org/TR/html401/struct/links.html#edef-LINK). The REL attribute identifies the relationship with the linked document. It should always be set to STYLESHEET. The TYPE attribute identifies the MIME type of the linked file. It should always be set to text/css. The HREF attribute identifies the URL of the external file containing the style definitions. Listing 12.11 shows how the <LINK> tag can be used to include externally defined styles. Figure 12.10 shows how this document is displayed.

Listing 12.11:   Using the *<LINK>* Tag (usestyle.htm)

```
<HTML>
<HEAD>
<TITLE>Using the LINK tag</TITLE>
<LINK REL=STYLESHEET TYPE="text/css" HREF="favstyle">
</HEAD>
<BODY>
<P>This paragraph uses the style sheet that is contained in
the favstyle file. You can modify favstyle to update the styles
used for all of your favorite documents.</P>
</BODY>
</HTML>
```

FIGURE 12.10:

The *<LINK>* tag allows externally defined styles to be included in a document.

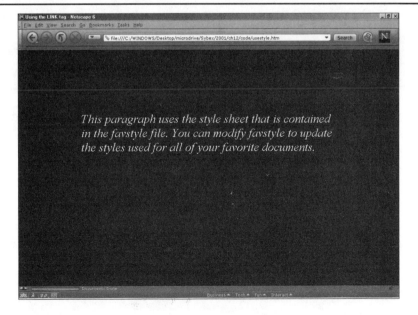

Using Multiple Style Sheets

Multiple JavaScript style sheets can be used in a single document. Externally defined style sheets can also be combined with internally defined style sheets. The internally defined styles take precedence over the externally defined styles. Later referenced external styles take precedence over earlier referenced external styles.

Using the DHTML Capabilities of Navigator 6 and Internet Explorer

About the time that Netscape was developing its proprietary JavaScript style sheets in Navigator 4, Microsoft was providing extensive support for CSS in Internet Explorer 4. In addition, Internet Explorer also provided the capability to dynamically change styles using JavaScript. This capability was commonly referred to as Internet Explorer *Dynamic HTML*, or *DHTML*. Later versions of Internet Explorer extended this capability with extensive support for DOM 1.

Meanwhile, Netscape built its own DHTML using another proprietary, dead-end technology known as *layers*. However, Netscape eventually gave up on both JSS and layers and built Navigator 6 (via the Mozilla project) into a standards-based browser with support for CSS scripting and DOM 1. Because Navigator 4's support for DHTML is extinct, we won't cover it in this chapter. Instead, we'll look at DHTML from the perspective of CSS scripting and DOM 1. We'll also show how to provide backward compatibility for Internet Explorer 4.

NOTE   A detailed introduction to DOM 1 is provided in Chapter 13, "Using the W3C DOM Level 1."

Accessing HTML Elements as Objects

In order to use JavaScript to dynamically change the styles associated with HTML elements, it is necessary to access those elements as JavaScript objects. In most cases, you'll want to access specific HTML elements. The easiest way to do this is to identify the objects to be accessed by their ID attributes.

The DOM 1 (supported by Internet Explorer 5 and later and Navigator 6 and later) provides a standard way to access elements by their ID attribute using the getElementById() method of the document object. For example, suppose you have an HTML DIV element with an ID of "div123". You can obtain a reference to this object using the following:

```
divRef = document.getElementById("d123")
```

Starting with version 4, Internet Explorer provided a mechanism for accessing all of the HTML elements of a document via the `all` property of the document object. The IE4 equivalent of the above statement follows:

```
divRef = document.all["d123"]
```

Starting with version 5 of Internet Explorer, you can use either `document.getElementById()` or `document.all`. However, because `document.getElementById()` is standardized by DOM 1, it is preferred over `document.all`.

The Style Property

Starting with Internet Explorer 4 and Navigator 6, each HTML object has a `style` property that can be used to access the CSS styles of the corresponding HTML element. This `style` property is an object itself, referred to as the `style` object, and has properties that correspond to the CSS style properties. Table 12.1 lists some of these properties. Appendix F contains a complete description.

TABLE 12.1: Properties of the *style* Object

Properties	Description
background backgroundAttachment backgroundColor backgroundImage backgroundPosition backgroundPositionX backgroundPositionY backgroundRepeat	The CSS background properties
border borderBottom borderBottomColor borderBottomStyle borderBottomWidth borderColor borderLeft borderLeftColor borderLeftStyle borderLeftWidth borderRight borderRightColor borderRightStyle borderRightWidth borderStyle borderTop borderTopColor	The CSS border properties

Continued on next page

TABLE 12.1 CONTINUED: Properties of the *style* Object

Properties	Description
borderTopStyle borderTopWidth borderWidth	The CSS border properties
clear	The CSS clear property
clip	The CSS clip property
color	The CSS color property
display	The CSS display property
filter	The CSS filter property
font fontFamily fontSize fontStyle fontVariant fontWeight	The CSS font properties
height	The CSS height property
left	The CSS left property
letterSpacing	The CSS letter-spacing property
lineHeight	The CSS line-height property
listStyle listStyleImage listStylePosition listStyleType	The CSS list properties
margin marginBottom marginLeft marginRight marginTop	The CSS margin properties
overflow	The CSS overflow property
paddingBottom paddingLeft paddingRight paddingTop	The CSS padding properties
pageBreakAfter pageBreakBefore	The CSS page-break property
pixelHeight pixelLeft pixelTop pixelWidth	The dimensions and position of the element in pixels
position	The CSS position property

Continued on next page

TABLE 12.1 CONTINUED: Properties of the *style* Object

Properties	Description
posHeight	The dimensions and position of the element in units specified by the CSS height, left, top, and width properties
posLeft posTop posWidth	
styleFloat	The CSS float property
textAlign textDecoration textDecorationBlink textDecorationLineThrough textDecorationNone textDecorationOverline textDecorationUnderline textIndent textTransform	The CSS text properties
top	The CSS top property
verticalAlign	The CSS vertical-align property
visibility	The CSS visibility property
width	The CSS width property
zIndex	The CSS z-index property

The important point about the `style` object is that you can dynamically change the CSS style of an HTML object by setting the properties of its `style` object. You'll see an extended example of dynamically updated styles in the next section.

A Style Sampler

To appreciate the power of being able to change styles dynamically, you need to see them in action. I'll give you a short tour and then explain how the scripts work. Open `dhtml.htm` (Listing 12.13) with Internet Explorer 4 or later, or Navigator 6 or later. It displays the screen shown in Figure 12.11. Click the Apply DHTML Style button; the characteristics of the displayed text are updated, as shown in Figure 12.12. Click the button again; the text colors change, as shown in Figure 12.13. Click one more time; the text layout is altered, as shown in Figure 12.14.

FIGURE 12.11:

Displaying simple text

FIGURE 12.12:

Changing the text's font characteristics

FIGURE 12.13:

Changing text colors

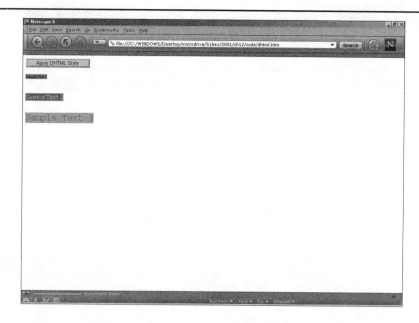

FIGURE 12.14:

Changing the text's position

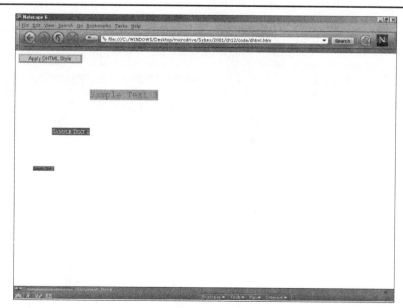

If you think that what you have seen so far is impressive, hang in there because it gets better. Click the Apply DHTML Style button again; the text is animated, as shown in Figure 12.15.

Click the button again; the animation stops with the text aligned, as shown in Figure 12.16. Click three more times; the area occupied by each text segment is enlarged, as shown in Figure 12.17.

FIGURE 12.15:

Animating the text

FIGURE 12.16:

Lining up the text

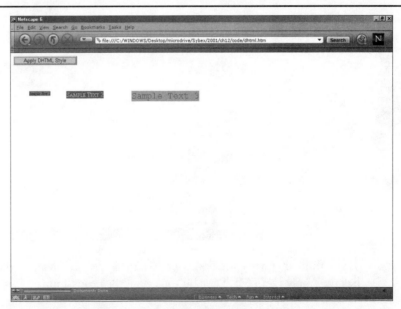

FIGURE 12.17:

Resizing the area occupied
by the text

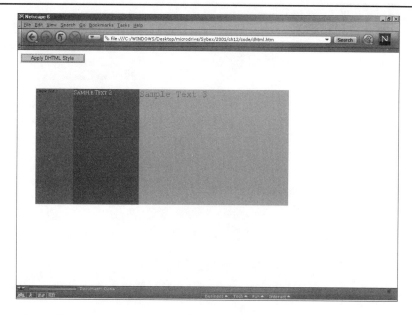

You're almost at the end of the style sampler. Click the Apply DHTML Style again; the
text regions move and overlap, as shown in Figure 12.18. Click one last time; the content,
location, and font characteristics of the text are dynamically updated in an animation effect,
as shown in Figure 12.19.

FIGURE 12.18:

Overlapping text regions

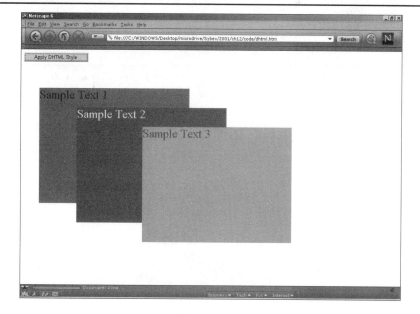

FIGURE 12.19:

More text animation

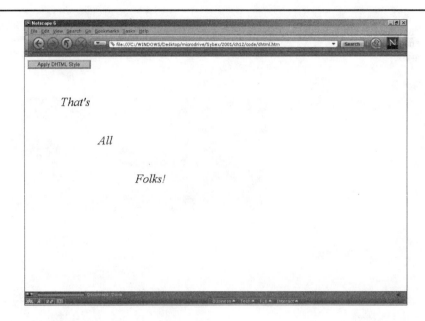

How the Style Sampler Works

The scripting behind the style sampler script is actually fairly simple. The `applyDHTML()` function is invoked to handle the button's `onClick` event. This function creates an array of `div` objects via the `document.all` (IE4) collection and the `document.getElementById()` method (DOM1-capable browsers).

It uses the `state` variable to keep track of which display state it is in, and updates the `style` object of each `div` object in a long case statement. Each case is described in the following paragraphs.

case 0:

The `fontSize`, `fontStyle`, `fontVariant`, and `fontFamily` properties of the paragraphs' `style` objects are updated to change the text styles.

case 1:

The `backgroundColor` and `color` properties are updated to change the text background and foreground colors.

case 2:

The position of each paragraph is updated using the moveDivTo() method. This method takes the division's number (0, 1, or 2) and the xy-coordinates of where the division should be moved as arguments. In the case of Internet Explorer 4, it sets the style object's posLeft and posTop properties to move the div object. For DOM 1-capable browsers, it sets the style object's left and top properties.

case 3:

The moveParagraphs() function is used to animate the paragraphs by moving them around the document window.

case 4:

The animation is stopped via the clearInterval() method, and the paragraphs are lined up at 100 pixels from the top of the page.

cases 5 through 7:

The stacking order (zIndex) of each paragraph is updated to place it above the others, and its height and width dimensions are enlarged.

case 8:

The paragraphs are converted to an xx-large Times font and repositioned.

case 9:

The paragraphs are converted to black and white, hidden, and repositioned to the left of the document window. The text of each paragraph is then changed via the div object's innerHTML property. The slideText() function is invoked to animate each paragraph so the paragraph moves from left to right. The italicize() method is then invoked to change each paragraph's text to italics.

Listing 12.13:   Dynamically Updating Styles Using DHTML (dhtml.htm)

```
<HTML>
<HEAD>
<TITLE></TITLE>
<SCRIPT LANGUAGE="JavaScript"><!--
function initialize() {
  state = 0
  if(document.all && !document.getElementById) {
    div0 = document.all["d0"]
    div1 = document.all["d1"]
    div2 = document.all["d2"]
```

```
  browser = "ie4"
 }else if(document.getElementById){
  div0 = document.getElementById("d0")
  div1 = document.getElementById("d1")
  div2 = document.getElementById("d2")
  browser = "dom1"
 }else{
  browser = "unknown"
  return
 }
 divs = new Array(div0, div1, div2)
 divStyles = new Array(div0.style, div1.style, div2.style)
}
function moveParagraphs() {
 for(var i=0; i<divStyles.length; ++i) {
  var x = Math.random()*400
  var y = Math.random()*400
  moveDivTo(i, x, y)
 }
}
function moveDivTo(i, x, y) {
 if(browser == "ie4") {
  divStyles[i].posLeft = x
  divStyles[i].posTop = y
 }else if(browser == "dom1") {
  divStyles[i].left = x
  divStyles[i].top = y
 }
}
function slideText(n) {
 divStyles[n].visibility = "visible"
 var max = (n+1)*100
 for(var i=0;i<max;++i) {
  setTimeout("moveDivTo("+n+","+i+","+max+")",500)
 }
}
function italicize() {
 divStyles[0].fontStyle = "italic"
 divStyles[1].fontStyle = "italic"
 divStyles[2].fontStyle = "italic"
}
function applyDHTML() {
 if(browser == "unknown") {
  alert("Sorry. Your browser does not provide sufficient DHTML support to run
this example.")
  return
 }
 switch(state) {
  case 0:
   divStyles[0].fontSize = "x-small"
   divStyles[0].fontStyle = "italic"
   divStyles[1].fontSize = "medium"
   divStyles[1].fontVariant = "small-caps"
```

```
 divStyles[2].fontSize = "x-large"
 divStyles[2].fontFamily = "Courier"
 break
case 1:
 divStyles[0].backgroundColor = "cyan"
 divStyles[0].color = "blue"
 divStyles[1].backgroundColor = "green"
 divStyles[1].color = "yellow"
 divStyles[2].backgroundColor = "orange"
 divStyles[2].color = "red"
 break
case 2:
 moveDivTo(0, 50, 300)
 moveDivTo(1, 100, 200)
 moveDivTo(2, 200, 100)
 break
case 3:
 interval = setInterval("moveParagraphs()",750)
 break
case 4:
 clearInterval(interval)
 moveDivTo(0, 50, 100)
 moveDivTo(1, 150, 100)
 moveDivTo(2, 325, 100)
 break
case 5:
 divStyles[0].zIndex = 100
 divStyles[0].width = 400
 divStyles[0].height = 300
 break
case 6:
 divStyles[0].zIndex = 0
 divStyles[1].zIndex = 100
 divStyles[1].width = 400
 divStyles[1].height = 300
 break
case 7:
 divStyles[1].zIndex = 1
 divStyles[2].zIndex = 100
 divStyles[2].width = 400
 divStyles[2].height = 300
 break
case 8:
 for(var i=0;i<divStyles.length;++i) {
  divStyles[i].fontFamily = "Times"
  divStyles[i].fontSize = "xx-large"
  divStyles[i].fontStyle = "normal"
  divStyles[i].fontVariant = "normal"
 }
 moveDivTo(1, 150, 150)
 moveDivTo(2, 325, 200)
 break
```

```
      case 9:
        for(var i=0;i<divStyles.length;++i) {
          divStyles[i].color = "black"
          divStyles[i].backgroundColor = "white"
          divStyles[i].visibility = "hidden"
          moveDivTo(i, 0, (i+1)*100)
        }
        divs[0].innerHTML = "That's"
        divs[1].innerHTML = "All"
        divs[2].innerHTML = "Folks!"
        setTimeout("slideText(0)",500)
        setTimeout("slideText(1)",1500)
        setTimeout("slideText(2)",2500)
        setTimeout("italicize()",5000)
        break
      case 10:
        window.location.reload()
        break
    }
   ++state
  }
//--></SCRIPT>
</HEAD>
<BODY onload="initialize()">
<FORM>
<INPUT TYPE="BUTTON" VALUE="Apply DHTML Style"
 onClick="applyDHTML()">
</FORM>
<DIV ID="d0" STYLE="position:absolute; top:50px">Sample Text 1</DIV>
<DIV ID="d1" STYLE="position:absolute; top:100px">Sample Text 2</DIV>
<DIV ID="d2" STYLE="position:absolute; top:150px">Sample Text 3</DIV>
</BODY>
</HTML>
```

Summary

In this chapter, you were introduced to style sheets, and saw several examples of their application. You learned about the differences between the Cascading Style Sheets developed by the World Wide Web Consortium and the now-defunct Netscape JavaScript style sheets. You covered the tags, properties, and attributes used with styles; and learned how to work with both internally and externally defined styles. Finally, you looked at the DOM 1 and Internet Explorer 4 support for style sheets and DHTML. You also learned how to use DHTML to dynamically script styles and create interesting effects for your web pages.

In the next chapter, you'll delve into the DOM 1 and learn to use it to create web applications that use standardized, cross-browser DHTML capabilities.

CHAPTER 13

Using the W3C DOM Level 1

- Evolution of the DOM

- DOM Level 0

- DOM Level 1 Core

- DOM Level 1 HTML

- CSS and DOM

- DOM Levels 2 and 3

The *Document Object Model Level 1 (DOM 1)* provides a common standard API for accessing the objects contained in HTML or XML documents. It was developed by the W3C as the result of collaboration between major browser developers (such as Microsoft and Netscape) and web software developers (such as Sun, IBM, and SoftQuad).

The DOM 1 addresses object model incompatibilities introduced with version 4 of the Navigator and Internet Explorer browsers. It provides a standard object model for the development of scripts for Navigator 6 and Internet Explorer 5 or later browsers. Levels 2 and 3 of the DOM provide additional standardization that cover areas such as event handling and style sheets.

In this chapter, you'll be introduced to the DOM 1, learn how it is organized, and work with scripts that illustrate its features. You'll cover the DOM 1 Core and HTML APIs, and use these APIs with the latest versions of Navigator and Internet Explorer. When you have finished this chapter, you will be familiar with the DOM 1 and will be able to use the DOM 1 API for scripting Navigator and Internet Explorer.

Life Before the DOM

The JavaScript object model that you've been learning about in previous chapters has evolved considerably since it was first introduced by Netscape. The evolution of the object model closely parallels the evolution of the web browser as a whole. Netscape took the early lead in browser development with Navigator 2 and Navigator 3, but was eventually overtaken by Microsoft at the time both companies released version 4 browsers.

Navigator 3 was a significant milestone in the development of the object model because it filled in several gaps in the model presented by Navigator 2. Many of the capabilities that we've been using in previous chapters were available in the Navigator 3 object model. Internet Explorer 3 copied most (but not all) of the Navigator 3 object model. The objects, properties, and methods supported by both Navigator 3 and Internet Explorer 3 are referred to as the DOM level 0. Appendix D, "DOM 0 Object Reference," describes these objects, properties, and methods.

Although Navigator 4 and Internet Explorer 4 did introduce some common objects, properties, and methods, the object models of these browsers diverged far more than they converged. I refer to the intersection of the object models as the DOM level 0+. Appendix D also describes these DOM 0+ objects, properties, and methods.

In the previous chapter, you saw how the divergence between the Internet Explorer and Navigator object models led to incompatibility in DHTML scripting. This incompatibility started with Netscape's (now defunct) JavaScript style sheets, and widened as Internet Explorer 4 began to surpass Navigator 4 in terms of scripting capabilities.

The Document Object Model Level 1 was a response to the divergence in the object models of the version 4 browsers. Now that Internet Explorer 5, Navigator 6, and later browsers support DOM 1, as scripters we can move forward and develop more advanced cross-browser scripts.

DOM 1 Overview

The DOM 1 is an object model for HTML and XML documents. The DOM 1 focuses on document objects and does not address browser-specific objects that are not part of a document. The DOM 1 provides complete access to the elements of a document. It allows new document elements to be created and allows existing document elements to be modified or deleted.

NOTE The latest version of the DOM 1 recommendation is available at www.w3.org/TR/REC-DOM-Level-1.

NOTE If you are not familiar with XML, you may want to browse Chapter 21, "Learning XML," to get a top-level understanding of what XML is all about.

The DOM 1 models documents using a tree-based structural model. The elements of a document are represented as nodes that form the branches and leaves of the tree. Trees are represented upside-down. The root of the tree is on top, and its branches grow downward. In this model, for HTML documents, the <HTML> element is the root of the tree. The <HEAD> and <BODY> elements, which are enclosed by the <HTML> element, are branches from the root. Consider the HTML document shown in Listing 13.1. Figure 13.1 provides a graphical depiction of the DOM 1 tree representation of this document.

As you can see from Figure 13.1, outer (enclosing) HTML elements, such as the <BODY> element are the parent nodes of inner (enclosed) nodes, such as the <H1> and <P> nodes.

Listing 13.1:   An Example HTML Document (html-example.htm)

```
<html>
<head><title>Example HTML Document</title></head>
<body>
<h1>Example HTML Document</h1>
<p>This is an example of an HTML document.</p>
</body>
</html>
```

FIGURE 13.1:

Representing *html-example.htm* as a tree

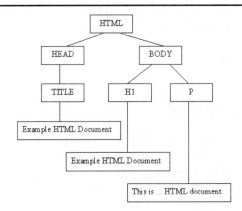

Listing 13.2 shows a simple XML document, and Figure 13.2 provides a tree representation of the document shown in Listing 13.2. The tree-based modeling of XML documents is analogous to the way HTML documents are modeled. Enclosing elements are modeled as the parents of the elements that they enclose.

Listing 13.2:   An Example XML Document (xml-example.htm)

```
<?xml version="1.0" encoding="iso-8859-1"?>
<!DOCTYPE dom1 SYSTEM "dom1.dtd">
<dom1>
<interface>
<name>Document</name>
<extends>Node</extends>
<description>
Document is the root node of the DOM document tree.
It provides properties and methods by which the other document
objects are accessed. It also provides methods for creating
these objects.
</description>
</interface>
</dom1>
```

FIGURE 13.2:

Representing *xml-example.htm* as a tree

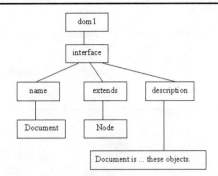

Now that you've seen a few examples of how documents can be represented as trees, you may be wondering why the DOM 1 has adopted this model. There are actually a few reasons:

- A tree model is analogous to the way HTML and XML documents are structured. A tree representation of these documents is both natural and intuitive.

- Documents are represented in a consistent (but not equivalent) manner by all browsers. A given browser represents the same HTML or XML document using the same tree structure.

- All elements of a document can be accessed by starting at the root element and then following parent-child relationships until the element is reached. This is analogous to climbing the branches of a tree until you reach the leaf you want.

Because the DOM 1 supports both XML and HTML documents, it is natural that it would be organized according to its support for these types of documents. We'll cover the Core XML part of the DOM 1 first, followed by its more specific support for HTML.

DOM 1 Core

The DOM 1 Core consists of a set of interfaces that provides access to the parts of XML and HTML documents. The DOM 1 is identified in terms of *interfaces* instead of object types. You can think of an interface as a specification for an object type. The interfaces that are defined by the DOM 1 specify the properties and methods of the object types that comprise the DOM. However, these interfaces do not provide an implementation of the object types, properties, and methods. You can look at the DOM 1 as a design document. It specifies the design for a DOM 1-compliant browser. However, it leaves it up to the browser to provide the implementation of these interfaces.

The interfaces provided by the DOM 1 Core provide the foundation for the DOM HTML interfaces. The DOM 1 Core interfaces must be implemented by XML-compliant browsers. However, they need not be implemented by browsers that support only HTML.

TABLE 13.1: DOM 1 Core Interfaces

Core Interface	Description
Attr	Represents an XML/HTML attribute name/value pair.
CDATASection	Represents a CDATA section. CDATA sections are used to escape blocks of text containing characters that would otherwise be regarded as markup.
CharacterData	The CharacterData interface extends Node with a set of attributes and methods for accessing character data in the DOM. This interface, like Node, is an abstract interface. No DOM objects correspond directly to CharacterData. It is extended by Text and other interfaces. It supports UTF-16 text characters.

Continued on next page

TABLE 13.1 CONTINUED: DOM 1 Core Interfaces

Core Interface	Description
Comment	Represents the content of an XML or HTML comment.
Document	**Document** is the root node of the DOM document tree. It provides properties and methods by which the other document objects are accessed. It also provides methods for creating these objects.
DocumentFragment	**DocumentFragment** is described as a "lightweight" or "minimal" **Document** object. It is used to create or access a fragment of a document. **DocumentFragment** extends **Node,** but does not define any additional properties or methods.
DocumentType	Each **Document** has a **doctype** attribute whose value is either **null** or a **Document-Type** object. The **DocumentType** interface in the DOM Level 1 Core provides an interface to the list of entities that are defined for the document.
DOMException	**DOMException** is used to signal the fact that a particular operation cannot be performed because of an abnormal condition.
DOMImplementation	Provides access to information about the underlying DOM implementation support.
Element	Represents an element of an XML or HTML document.
Entity	Represents an entity, either parsed or unparsed, in an XML document. Note that this models the entity itself not the entity declaration.
EntityReference	Represents an entity reference in an XML or HTML document. Note that character references and references to predefined entities are considered to be expanded by the HTML or XML processor so that characters are represented by their Unicode equivalent rather than by an entity reference. Moreover, the XML processor may completely expand references to entities while building the structure model, instead of providing **EntityReference** objects.
NamedNodeMap	Represents a collection of nodes that can be accessed by name.
Node	**Node** interface is the primary interface type of the DOM. All document objects, including **Document**, extend **Node**. Therefore, the properties and methods of **Node** are available to all of these document objects.
NodeList	Defines an ordered collection of **Node** objects.
Notation	Represents a notation declared in the DTD. (See Chapter 21 for more information on DTDs.) A notation either declares, by name, the format of an unparsed entity, or it is used for formal declaration of processing instruction targets. The **nodeName** attribute (inherited from **Node**) is set to the declared name of the notation.
ProcessingInstruction	The **ProcessingInstruction** interface represents a "processing instruction," which is used in XML as a way to keep processor-specific information in the text of the document.
Text	Represents the textual content of an **Element** or **Attr**.

In the following sections, we'll investigate some of the primary DOM 1 Core interfaces and provide examples of their use. We'll come back to these interfaces in Chapter 22, "Displaying XML with Internet Explorer and Navigator."

DOMImplementation

The `DOMImplementation` interface provides access to the features supported by a particular DOM implementation. It has a single method `hasFeature(feature, version)`, which returns a `boolean` value indicating whether or not the implementation of the DOM supports a feature. The allowed values for feature are `XML` and `HTML`. The version is an optional parameter that allows a version of the DOM (such as "1.0") to be specified.

Listing 13.3 provides an example of using the `DOMImplementation` interface. A reference to a `DOMImplementation` object is obtained through the `implementation` property of the document object. Currently, Navigator 6 supports this property, but Internet Explorer 6 does not. Figure 13.3 shows the result of executing this script in Navigator 6.

Listing 13.3:   Using DOMImplementation to See What DOM Features Are Supported by Your Browser (domfeatures.htm)

```
<html>
<head><title>DOM Feature Test</title></head>
<body>
<script language="JavaScript">
try {
 var impl = document.implementation
 var xml = impl.hasFeature("XML", "1.0")
 var html = impl.hasFeature("HTML", "1.0")
 if(xml)
   document.write("<p><strong>Your browser supports the DOM XML Core Version
1.0</strong></p>")
 if(html)
   document.write("<p><strong>Your browser supports DOM HTML Version
1.0</strong></p>")
}catch(e) {
 document.write("<p>Your browser does not support the
<code>document.implementation</code> property.</p>")
}
</script>
</body>
</html>
```

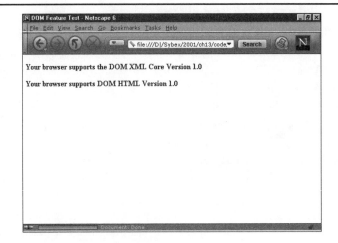

Node

The Node interface is a fundamental interface type of the DOM 1 Core. All document
objects, including Document, extend Node and inherit the properties and methods of Node.
There is no generic Node object contained in an XML or HTML document, but nearly all
objects are a specific type of Node.

Figure 13.4 shows the Node interface and the hierarchy of DOM 1 Core interfaces that
extend Node. These interfaces represent the types of objects that may appear in an XML document. Note that the CharacterData interface provides common properties and methods for
interfaces (such as Comment, Text, and CDATASection) that contain text.

The properties and methods provided by the Node interface are inherited by the interfaces
shown in Figure 13.4. Tables 13.2 and 13.3 summarize the Node properties. Table 13.4 summarizes the Node methods.

FIGURE 13.4:

The *Node* interface
hierarchy

Node

- Document
- DocumentFragment
- Element
- Attr
- CharacterData
  - o Text
    - ▪ CDATASection
  - o Comment
- DocumentType
- Notation
- ProcessingInstruction
- Entity
- EntityReference

TABLE 13.2: Properties of the *Node* Object

Property	Type	Description
nodeName	String	The name of the node. (See Table 13.3.)
nodeValue	String	The value of the node. (See Table 13.3.)
nodeType	short	An integer constant that identifies the type of the node. (See Table 13.3.)
parentNode	Node	The parent of this node, or **null** if this node doesn't have a parent.
childNodes	NodeList	A **NodeList** that contains all children of this node.
firstChild	Node	The first child of this node (if there is one), or **null** otherwise.
lastChild	Node	The last child of this node (if there is one), or **null** otherwise.
previousSibling	Node	The node immediately before this node (if there is one), or **null** otherwise.
nextSibling	Node	The node immediately after this node (if there is one), or **null** otherwise.
attributes	NamedNodeMap	Provides a **NamedNodeMap** containing the attributes of this node (if it is an **Element**), or **null** otherwise.
ownerDocument	Document	The **Document** object associated in which this node is contained. If this node is a **Document**, **ownerDocument** is **null**.

TABLE 13.3: Values of the *nodeName*, *nodeValue*, and *nodeType* Properties

Node Type	Node Name	Node Value	Node Type Constant
Attr	name of attribute	value of the attribute	2
CDATASection	#cdata-section	contents of the CDATA section	4
Comment	#comment	content of the comment	8
Document	#document	null	9
DocumentFragment	#document-fragment	null	11
DocumentType	document type name	null	10
Element	tag name	null	1
Entity	entity name	null	6
EntityReference	name of entity referenced	null	5
Notation	notation name	null	12
ProcessingInstruction	target	entire content excluding the target	7
Text	#text	content of the text node	3

TABLE 13.4: Methods of the *Node* Object

Method	Description
insertBefore(**newChild, refChild**)	Inserts the node **newChild** before the existing child node **refChild**.
replaceChild(**newChild, oldChild**)	Replaces the child node **oldChild** with newChild in the list of children, and returns the **oldChild** node.
removeChild(**oldChild**)	Removes the child node indicated by **oldChild** from the list of children, and returns it.
appendChild(**newChild**)	Adds the node **newChild** to the end of the list of children of this node. If the **newChild** is already in the tree, it is first removed.
hasChildNodes()	Returns a **boolean** value indicating whether or not a node has any children.
cloneNode(**deep**)	Returns a duplicate copy of this node (including attributes). If **deep** is set to **true**, all contained nodes are copied. If **deep** is set to **false**, only this node is copied.

Document

The DOM 1 Core Document interface corresponds to the JavaScript document object that you've been using in previous chapters. It extends the Node interface, and provides properties and methods that are the primary hooks for accessing the DOM 1 objects that are contained in a document. Table 13.5 describes the properties of the Document interface. Table 13.6 summarizes its methods.

TABLE 13.5: Properties of the *Document* Interface

Name	Type	Description
doctype	DocumentType	Identifies the Document Type Declaration (DTD) associated with the document. Its value is **null** if the document does not have a DTD.
documentElement	Element	Provides direct access to the **child** node that is the root element of the document. For HTML documents, this is the element with the tag named **HTML**.
implementation	DOMImplementation	Provides access to the **DOMImplementation** object associated with the document.

TABLE 13.6: Methods of the *Document* Interface

Method	Description
createElement(tagName)	Creates a new **document** element of the type specified by **tagName**.
createDocumentFragment()	Creates a new **DocumentFragment** object.
createTextNode(data)	Creates a text node with the specified **data**.
createComment(data)	Creates a comment whose value is set by **data**.
createCDATASection(data)	Creates a **CDATA** section whose value is set by **data**.
createProcessingInstruction(target, data)	Creates a processing instruction with the specified **target** and **data**.
createAttribute(name)	Creates an attribute with the specified **name**. The attribute's value is set to a blank string.
createEntityReference(name)	Creates an entity reference with the specified **name**.
getElementsByTagName(tagname)	Returns a **NodeList** object of all the elements with the specified **tagName**. A **tagName** of * is used as a wildcard character and matches all tag names.

NodeList

The NodeList interface specifies an ordered collection of nodes. It has a single property, length, which identifies the number of elements in the NodeList. It also has a single method, item(index), which returns the node of the NodeList specified by **index**.

NamedNodeMap

The NamedNodeMap interface specifies an ordered collection of nodes. It has the length property and item(index) method, as described for NodeList. It also has the following three methods:

- getNamedItem(name). Returns the named node of the NamedNodeMap.
- setNamedItem(arg). Adds a node to the NamedNodeMap based on its nodeName property. If a node with that name is already present in this map, it is replaced by the new one.
- removeNamedItem(name). Removes the specified node and returns the node.

NamedNodeMap is typically used to contain the attributes of an element.

A DOM Core Document Analyzer

Now that you have been exposed to the DOM Core, let's look at how we can put these interfaces into action. Listing 13.4 provides a script that displays the tree structure of a document, using the objects prescribed by the DOM Core interfaces. (The DOM Core applies to HTML as well as XML documents.) When the document loads, it invokes the `analyzeDocument()` function to open a new window and display the structure.

This script works with the DOM 1-capable versions of Internet Explorer and Navigator. Figure 13.5 shows the results that it displays for Internet Explorer, and Figure 13.6 shows the results that it displays for Navigator. You can see that Navigator displays a lot more #text nodes than Internet Explorer because it assumes the existence of a #text node between adjacent tags. This is just one of the browser-specific idiosyncrasies that you'll have to deal with when writing DOM 1-oriented scripts.

NOTE   Even if Internet Explorer and Navigator both support the DOM 1, each browser differs in the completeness and manner in which it provides this support.

The `analyzeDocument()` function opens a new browser window, writes the document's header, and then invokes `getDocumentStructure()` to fill in the document's body. It then closes the document's body and the document. It passes the `documentElement` property of the document object as an argument to `getDocumentStructure`. The `documentElement` property refers to the top-level document element. In the case of HTML documents, it is the <HTML> tag.

The `getDocumentStructure()` function displays a document node and all of its children. It does this by writing the node's `nodeName` property and then using its `childNodes` property to obtain a list of child nodes. It then displays the children as an unordered list by calling `get-DocumentStructure()` for each child.

Listing 13.4:   The *coreanalyzer.htm* Script

```
<html>
<head><title>DOM Core Analyzer</title>
<script language="JavaScript">
function analyzeDocument() {
 var win = open("","results")
 var doc = win.document
 doc.open()
 doc.writeln("<html><head><title>Results</title></head><body>")
 getDocumentStructure(document.documentElement, doc)
 doc.writeln("</body></html>")
 doc.close()
}
function getDocumentStructure(node, doc) {
 doc.write(node.nodeName)
 var children = node.childNodes
```

```
    if(children != null && children.length > 0) {
     doc.writeln("<ul>")
     for(var i=0; i<children.length; ++i) {
      var child = children.item(i)
      doc.write("<li>")
      getDocumentStructure(child, doc)
     }
     doc.writeln("</ul>")
    }
}
</script>
</head>
<body onload="analyzeDocument()">
<h1 align="center">DOM Core Analyzer</h1>
<p>The <code>analyzeDocument()</code> function is used to display a map of the
document tree.</p>
<p>It displays the document tree in a separate window.</p>
</body>
</html>
```

FIGURE 13.5:

How Internet Explorer 5.5 displays the document structure

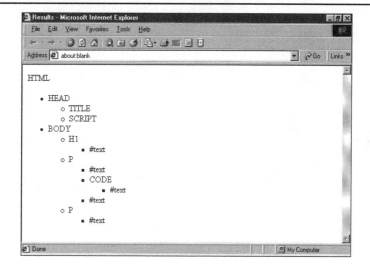

FIGURE 13.6:

How Navigator 6 displays
the document structure

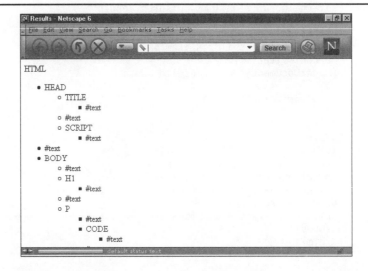

DOM HTML

In the previous sections, you were introduced to the DOM 1 Core interfaces. (You'll cover these interfaces in greater detail in Chapter 22.) However, for the most part, your DOM 1 scripting will focus on the DOM HTML interfaces. As you might surmise, these interfaces are oriented toward scripting HTML documents.

Table 13.7 summarizes the DOM 1 HTML interfaces. As you can see, these interfaces are closely aligned to the various types of HTML elements that may appear in a document. Appendix E, "DOM 1 Object Reference," provides a complete description of these interfaces, their properties, and their methods. We'll cover some of the more important ones in the following subsections.

TABLE 13.7: DOM 1 HTML Interfaces

Core Interface	Description
HTMLAnchorElement	Represents an HTML A element.
HTMLAppletElement	Represents an HTML APPLET element.
HTMLAreaElement	Represents an HTML AREA element.
HTMLBaseElement	Represents an HTML BASE element.
HTMLBaseFontElement	Represents an HTML BASEFONT element.

Continued on next page

TABLE 13.7 CONTINUED: DOM 1 HTML Interfaces

Core Interface	Description
HTMLBodyElement	Represents an HTML BODY element.
HTMLBRElement	Represents an HTML BR element.
HTMLButtonElement	Represents an HTML BUTTON element.
HTMLCollection	An HTMLCollection is a list of nodes. An individual node may be accessed by the ordinal index or the node's name or id attributes.
HTMLDirectoryElement	Represents an HTML DIR element.
HTMLDivElement	Represents an HTML DIV element.
HTMLDListElement	Represents an HTML DL element.
HTMLDocument	The root of the HTML hierarchy that holds the entire content of the document. Besides providing access to the hierarchy, it also provides some convenient methods for accessing certain sets of information from the document.
HTMLElement	Base interface for defining all other HTML elements. The other HTML elements extend and inherit from this interface.
HTMLFieldSetElement	Represents an HTML LEGEND element.
HTMLFontElement	Represents an HTML FONT element.
HTMLFormElement	Represents an HTML FORM element.
HTMLFrameElement	Represents an HTML FRAME element.
HTMLFrameSetElement	Represents an HTML FRAMESET element.
HTMLHeadElement	The HEAD element of an HTML document.
HTMLHeadingElement	Represents an HTML heading (H1 through H6) element.
HTMLHRElement	Represents an HTML HR element.
HTMLHtmlElement	The root of an HTML document. Corresponds to the HTML tag.
HTMLIFrameElement	Represents an HTML IFRAME element.
HTMLImageElement	Represents an HTML IMG element.
HTMLInputElement	Represents an HTML INPUT element.
HTMLIsIndexElement	Represents an HTML ISINDEX element.
HTMLLabelElement	Represents an HTML LABEL element.
HTMLLegendElement	Represents an HTML FIELDSET element.
HTMLLIElement	Represents an HTML LI element.
HTMLLinkElement	Represents an HTML LINK element.
HTMLMapElement	Represents an HTML MAP element.
HTMLMenuElement	Represents an HTML MENU element.
HTMLMetaElement	Represents an HTML META element.
HTMLModElement	Represents the HTML INS and DEL elements.
HTMLObjectElement	Represents an HTML OBJECT element.
HTMLOListElement	Represents an HTML OL element.

Continued on next page

TABLE 13.7 CONTINUED: DOM 1 HTML Interfaces

Core Interface	Description
HTMLOptGroupElement	Represents an HTML **OPTGROUP** element.
HTMLOptionElement	Represents an HTML **OPTION** element.
HTMLParagraphElement	Represents an HTML **P** element.
HTMLParamElement	Represents an HTML **PARAM** element.
HTMLPreElement	Represents an HTML **PRE** element.
HTMLQuoteElement	Represents the HTML **BLOCKQUOTE** and **Q** elements.
HTMLScriptElement	Represents an HTML **SCRIPT** element.
HTMLSelectElement	Represents an HTML **SELECT** element.
HTMLStyleElement	Represents an HTML **STYLE** element.
HTMLTableCaptionElement	Represents an HTML **CAPTION** element.
HTMLTableCellElement	Represents an HTML **TD** element.
HTMLTableColElement	Represents an HTML **COL** element.
HTMLTableElement	Represents an HTML **TABLE** element.
HTMLTableRowElement	Represents an HTML **TR** element.
HTMLTableSectionElement	Represents the HTML **THEAD**, **TFOOT**, and **TBODY** elements.
HTMLTextAreaElement	Represents an HTML **TEXTAREA** element.
HTMLTitleElement	Represents an HTML **TITLE** element.
HTMLUListElement	Represents an HTML **UL** element.

HTMLElement

The HTMLElement interface is a basic interface that is extended by most of the other DOM HTML interfaces. The HTMLElement interface extends the Element interface of the DOM Core. This means that most of the DOM HTML interfaces inherit properties and methods from Node, Element, and HTMLElement. The HTMLElement interface defines the five properties that are described in Table 13.8. It does not define any methods.

TABLE 13.8: Properties of the *HTMLElement* Interface

Name	Type	Description
id	String	The element's identifier.
title	String	The element's advisory title.
lang	String	Language code defined in RFC 1766.

Continued on next page

TABLE 13.8 CONTINUED: Properties of the *HTMLElement* Interface

Name	Type	Description
dir	String	Specifies the base direction of directionally neutral text and the directionality of tables. Although most languages, such as English, read from left to right, some languages, such as Hebrew, read from right to left.
className	String	The class attribute of the element.

The id and className properties can be used to gain access to an element's ID and CLASS attributes. The title, lang, and dir attributes provide access to the less commonly used TITLE, LANG, and DIR attributes.

HTMLCollection

The HTMLCollection interface is similar to the NodeList and NamedNodeMap interfaces of the DOM 1 Core. It is simply a collection of HTMLElement objects. The length property identifies the number of objects in the collection. The item(index) method returns the specified item from the collection. The namedItem(name) returns an item from the collection based on its ID or NAME attribute.

HTMLDocument

The HTMLDocument interface extends the Document interface of the DOM 1 Core. The HTML-Document interface is the root element of an HTML document, and it contains the entire content of the document. It provides properties and methods for accessing this content. Table 13.9 describes the HTMLDocument properties. Table 13.10 summarizes its methods. Note the similarity between these properties and methods and the DOM 0 document object.

TABLE 13.9: Properties of the *HTMLDocument* Interface

Name	Type	Description
title	String	The title of a document as specified by the TITLE element in the head of the document.
referrer	String	Returns the URL of the page that linked to this page. The value is an empty string if the user navigated to the page directly.
domain	String	The domain name of the server that served the document, or null if the server cannot be identified by a domain name.
URL	String	The complete URL of the document.

Continued on next page

TABLE 13.9: Properties of the *HTMLDocument* Interface

Name	Type	Description
body	HTMLElement	The element that contains the content for the document. In documents with BODY contents, this returns the BODY element. In frameset documents, this returns the outermost FRAMESET element.
images	HTMLCollection	A collection of all the IMG elements in a document. The behavior is limited to IMG elements for backward compatibility.
applets	HTMLCollection	A collection of all the OBJECT elements that include applets and APPLET elements in a document.
links	HTMLCollection	A collection of all AREA elements and anchor (A) elements in a document with a value for the **href** attribute.
forms	HTMLCollection	A collection of all the forms of a document.
anchors	HTMLCollection	A collection of all the anchor (A) elements in a document with a value for the **name** attribute. For reasons of backward compatibility, the returned set of anchors contains only those anchors created with the **name** attribute, not those created with the **id** attribute.
cookie	String	The cookies associated with this document. If there are none, the value is an empty string. Otherwise, the value is a string: a semicolon-delimited list of name=value pairs for all the cookies associated with the page.

TABLE 13.10: Methods of the *HTMLDocument* Interface

Method	Description
open()	Opens a document stream for writing. If a document exists in the target, this method clears it.
close()	Closes a document stream opened by **open()** and forces rendering.
write(text)	Writes a string of text to a document stream opened by **open()**. The text is parsed into the document's structure model.
writeln(text)	Writes a string of text followed by a newline character to a document stream opened by **open()**. The text is parsed into the document's structure model.
getElementById(elementId)	Returns the Element whose id is given by elementId. If no such element exists, returns null. Behavior is not defined if more than one element has this id.
getElementsByName(elementName)	Returns the (possibly empty) collection of elements whose name value is given by elementName.

Dynamically Generating HTML Documents

One of the more powerful capabilities provided with the DOM 1 is the capability to insert and delete HTML elements on the fly. This capability makes dynamic HTML even more dynamic. Listing 13.5 (dyngen.htm) displays the page shown in Figure 13.7. Select a tag type from the drop-down list, and enter some text in the text area. Then click the Insert element button. A new HTML element is created and inserted between the horizontal rules. Refer to Figure 13.8. The element has the specified tag type and text. Add a few more elements, as shown in Figure 13.9. Now, click the Delete element button. The last element that you inserted is deleted, as shown in Figure 13.10. Delete a few more elements if you like. This script performs in the same way on both Navigator and Internet Explorer.

The script consists of three functions: initializeDiv(), insertElement(), and delete-Element(). The initializeDiv() function uses the getElementById() method of the HTML-Document interface to obtain a reference to the division with the ID of testdiv.

The insertElement() function determines which tag the user selected, and creates a new Element object using the createElement() method of the Document interface. It then creates a new TextElement with the text entered by the user, and adds this element as a child of the newly created tag. Finally, it uses the appendChild() method of Node to add the new tag as a child of the division element referenced by the div variable.

The deleteElement() function uses the hasChildNodes() method of Node to determine whether the division element has any children. If it does, it uses the childNodes property of Node to obtain a NodeList of the children. It then obtains the last element of the NodeList via the item() method and removes it from the division element using the removeChild() method of Node.

Listing 13.5: Generating HTML On the Fly (dyngen.htm)

```
<html>
<head><title>Dynamically Generated HTML</title>
<script language="JavaScript">
function initializeDiv() {
 div = document.getElementById("testdiv")
}
function insertElement() {
 var tagIX = document.forms["genform"].elements["elementType"].selectedIndex
 var tagName = "p"
 if(tagIX == 1) tagName = "h1"
 else if(tagIX == 2) tagName = "blockquote"
 else if(tagIX == 3) tagName = "pre"
 var text = document.forms["genform"].elements["ta"].value
 var newElement = document.createElement(tagName)
 var newText = document.createTextNode(text)
 newElement.appendChild(newText)
 div.appendChild(newElement)
}
function deleteElement() {
 if(div.hasChildNodes()) {
```

```
      var children = div.childNodes
      var n = children.length - 1
      var lastChild = children.item(n)
      div.removeChild(lastChild)
    }
  }
</script>
</head>
<body onload="initializeDiv()">
<h1 align="center">Dynamically Generated HTML</h1>
<hr align="center">
<div id="testdiv">
</div>
<hr align="center">
<form name="genform">
<p><b>Tag: </b><select name="elementType" size="1">
<option selected="true">P
<option>H1
<option>BLOCKQUOTE
<option>PRE
</select>
<input type="button" value="Insert element" onclick="insertElement()">
<input type="button" value="Delete element" onclick="deleteElement()"></p>
<textarea name="ta" rows="5" cols="40">
Text of element goes here.
</textarea>
</form>
</body>
</html>
```

FIGURE 13.7:

The *dyngen.htm* Display

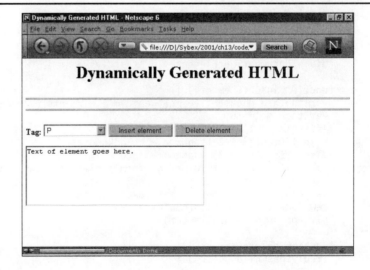

FIGURE 13.8:

Inserting an Element

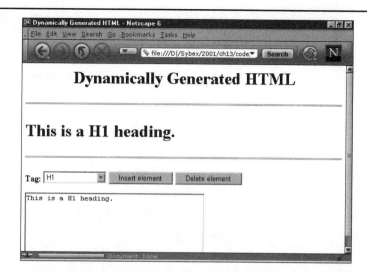

FIGURE 13.8:

Inserting an Element

FIGURE 13.9:

Inserting Multiple Elements

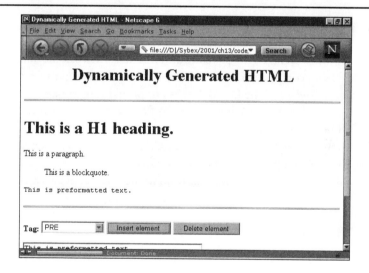

FIGURE 13.9:

Inserting Multiple Elements

FIGURE 13.10:

Deleting an Element

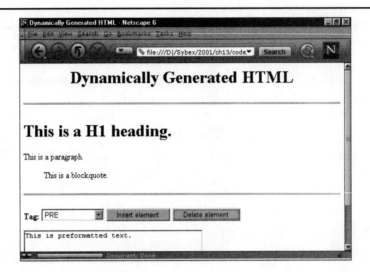

DOM 1, DOM 2, and DOM 3

Although the DOM 1 provides a standard framework for developing DHTML scripts, it is far from complete. The DOM 1 does not provide support for styles (other than the HTML-StyleElement). The DOM 1 does not provide any support for defining events and event handlers, either. Both of these are put off to future extensions to the DOM. Fortunately, the DOM Level 2 picks up where the DOM 1 leaves off. The DOM 2 provides support for both events and styles. Unfortunately, current browsers are even less DOM 2-compliant than DOM 1-compliant. In addition, work on the DOM 3 is nearing completion. The DOM 3 will provide further standardization in the areas of events and XML support.

Summary

In this chapter, you were introduced to the DOM 1. You covered the DOM Core and the DOM HTML, and learned to use the DOM interfaces to access the elements of HTML documents. This concludes Part II. In the next part, you'll focus on using JavaScript to create components for use in your web pages.

PART III

Developing Components and Applications

CHAPTER 14

Creating Basic JavaScript Components

- Including advertisements in your web pages

- Usage counters for tabulating "hits"

- Page format preferences

It seems like the most popular web pages always have the best adornments—scrolling marquees, animated icons, or dynamically updated advertisements. To some extent, these novelties help to contribute to the popularity of these pages. The Web, after all, is the showcase for everything that is new and cool.

In this chapter, we'll explore using JavaScript to create a variety of interesting components for your web pages. *Components* are common pieces of code that can be used over and over. They have been developed to fill a common need and can be easily tailored for use in a variety of situations. These components can be used to simplify the development of your pages and to add features that your users will find helpful and interesting.

In this chapter, you'll learn how to develop and use a variety of components with your web pages. I'll present a variety of ways in which JavaScript can be used to facilitate the way you display advertisements, and I'll show you how to develop and display the number of "hits" your websites and web pages are enjoying (and usage counters for measuring hits, can be reused with little or no tailoring). Finally, I'll present examples of features that allow users to control how your web pages are displayed. When you finish this chapter you'll be able to enhance your web pages with all of these new features.

Including Advertisements in Your Web Pages

The Web has become a mecca for advertisement. It is hard to find a popular web page that does not have some sort of colorful ad strategically positioned across the top or along the side of the page. And why not? It's a great way to generate interest in your products or services, and thus possibly some extra income to pay for Internet access. I can think of harder ways to make money!

In this section, you'll learn how JavaScript can be used to simplify the placement and management of ads in your web pages. You'll learn how to display fixed ads, for specific time intervals, and how to randomly sequence your ads in a continuous display. You'll also learn how to tailor your ad display based on user preferences.

Working with Fixed Ads

Fixed ads are ads that stay in place for a given period of time—a day, a week, a month, and so on. After the ad's time interval expires, a new ad is displayed. JavaScript can be used to simplify the management of fixed ads by automatically displaying the next ad at the proper time.

Listing 14.1 provides an example of a script that displays a different ad for each day of the week. To see how it works, open the file fixedad.htm with your browser. Your browser will display a web page similar to the one shown in Figure 14.1 except that the ad displayed by your browser will vary according to which day of the week it is.

FIGURE 14.1:

This component displays the ad of the day. (Listing 14.1)

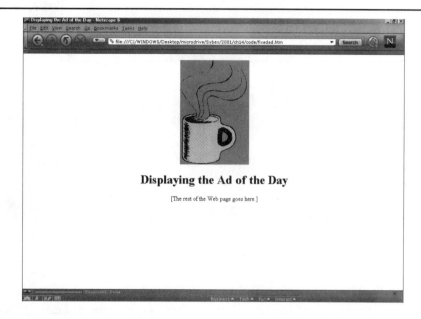

◠ **Listing 14.1:   Displaying a New Ad Every Day (fixedad.htm)**

```
<HTML>
<HEAD>
<TITLE>Displaying the Ad of the Day</TITLE>
<SCRIPT LANGUAGE="JavaScript"><!--
urls = new Array("components.htm",
"webmstr.htm",
"coffee.htm",
"sports.htm",
"news.htm",
"stocks.htm",
"travel.htm")
function insertAd() {
 var today = new Date()
 adIX = today.getDay()
 document.write('<P ALIGN="CENTER"><A HREF="'+urls[adIX]+'">')
 document.write('<IMG SRC="i'+adIX+'.gif" BORDER="0">')
 document.writeln('</A></P>')
}
```

```
// --></SCRIPT>
</HEAD>
<BODY BGCOLOR="#FFFFFF">
<SCRIPT LANGUAGE="JavaScript"><!--
insertAd()
// --></SCRIPT>
</P><H1 ALIGN="CENTER">Displaying the Ad of the Day</H1>
<P ALIGN="CENTER">[The rest of the Web page goes here.]</P>
</BODY>
</HTML>
```

The fixed ad display is easy to implement. You create an array of URLs corresponding to each day of the week. You also create the ad images associated with each URL and give them indexed names (for example, i0.gif, i1.gif, i2.gif, etc).

When your web page is being loaded, you use the Date object to determine what ad to display for the current month, date, day, hour, and so on. The ad is displayed as an image link using the appropriate image and URL.

Placing Random Ads

Random ads are ads that are randomly selected and displayed, usually each time a web page is loaded. Random ads change often and are usually used by websites with lots of advertisers. JavaScript can be used to simplify the processing of these ads by randomly selecting and displaying a new ad each time a web page is loaded.

Listing 14.2 shows how random ads can be implemented using JavaScript. Open randad.htm with your browser. It will display a web page similar to the one shown in Figure 14.2 except that the ad displayed by your browser will probably differ, since the ad is randomly selected from a set of seven.

Click on your browser's Reload button and another randomly selected ad is displayed, as shown in Figure 14.3.

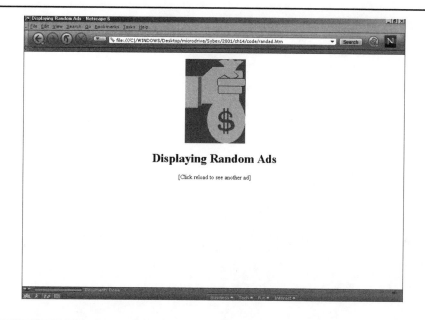

Listing 14.2: **A Random Ad Display Page (randad.htm)**

```
<HTML>
<HEAD>
<TITLE>Displaying Random Ads</TITLE>
<SCRIPT LANGUAGE="JavaScript"><!--
urls = new Array("components.htm",
"webmstr.htm",
"coffee.htm",
"sports.htm",
"news.htm",
"stocks.htm",
"travel.htm")
function insertAd() {
 adIX = Math.round(Math.random()*(urls.length-1))
 document.write('<P ALIGN="CENTER"><A HREF="'+urls[adIX]+'">')
 document.write('<IMG SRC="i'+adIX+'.gif" BORDER="0">')
 document.writeln('</A></P>')
}
// --></SCRIPT>
</HEAD>
<BODY BGCOLOR="#FFFFFF">
<SCRIPT LANGUAGE="JavaScript"><!--
insertAd()
// --></SCRIPT>
<H1 ALIGN="CENTER">Displaying Random Ads</H1>
<P ALIGN="CENTER">[Click reload to see another ad]</P>
</BODY>
</HTML>
```

The file randad.htm is very similar to fixedad.htm. It differs only in the way it selects the ad to be displayed. Instead of selecting an ad based on the Date object, it generates a random number, which is used to select an ad.

Enabling User-Selected Ads

For an ad to be successful, a user must respond to it. Ideally, they will respond by buying the product or service you're advertising, but the first step to getting them to do that is usually getting them to click on the ad. There are a number of strategies that can be used to get users to click on an ad. For example, you can use offbeat messages, colorful image links, or animated icons in the hope of catching the user's attention. You can also display only ads that the user is likely to be interested in. For example, a web page that is devoted to sports is a better place to advertise sports equipment than handmade blankets.

In fact, it's a good idea to let the user decide what kind of ads he or she is interested in seeing. The web page generated by Listing 14.3 does just that. It allows the user to set his or her ad preferences and it permanently stores the user's preference via a cookie.

Listing 14.3: Code to Display an Ad Based on User Preferences (prefad.htm)

```
<HTML>
<HEAD>
<TITLE>Displaying Ads Based on User Preferences</TITLE>
<SCRIPT LANGUAGE="JavaScript"><!--
function nameDefined(c,n) {
 var s=removeBlanks(c)
 var pairs=s.split(";")
 for(var i=0;i<pairs.length;++i) {
  var pairSplit=pairs[i].split("=")
  if(pairSplit[0]==n) return true
 }
 return false
}
function removeBlanks(s) {
 var temp=""
 for(var i=0;i<s.length;++i) {
  var c=s.charAt(i)
  if(c!=" ") temp += c
 }
 return temp
}
function getCookieValue(c,n) {
 var s=removeBlanks(c)
 var pairs=s.split(";")
 for(var i=0;i<pairs.length;++i) {
  var pairSplit=pairs[i].split("=")
  if(pairSplit[0]==n) return pairSplit[1]
 }
 return ""
}
preferences = new Array("Random","Home","Business","Computers",
 "Travel","Entertainment")
urls = new Array("decorate.htm",
"coffee.htm",
"repair.htm",
"news.htm",
"stocks.htm",
"components.htm",
"software.htm",
"hardware.htm",
"webmstr.htm",
"travel.htm",
"travel2.htm",
"sports.htm",
```

```
"tv.htm")
prefIX=new Array(0,0,3,6,9,11)
function insertAd() {
 readCookie()
 setUserPreferences()
 displayAd()
}
function displayAd() {
 if(userPref==0){
   adIX = Math.round(Math.random()*(urls.length-1))
 }else{
  var startIX=prefIX[userPref]
  var numPrefs=urls.length-startIX
  if(userPref!=prefIX.length-1)
   numPrefs=prefIX[userPref+1] - startIX
  adIX = Math.round(Math.random()*(numPrefs-1))
  adIX += startIX
 }
 document.write('<P ALIGN="CENTER">')
 document.write('<A HREF="'+urls[adIX]+'">')
 document.write('<IMG SRC="ir'+adIX+'.gif" BORDER="0">')
 document.writeln('</A></P>')
 document.write('<FORM NAME="setPref">')
 document.write('<P><B> Current ad preference: ')
 document.write(preferences[userPref]+' ')
 document.write('</B></P>')
 displaySelectionList()
 document.write(' <INPUT TYPE="BUTTON" NAME="update"' )
 document.write('VALUE="Update" onClick="updatePrefs()">')
 document.writeln('</FORM>')
}
function displaySelectionList() {
 document.write('<SELECT NAME="prefsList">')
 for(var i=0;i<preferences.length;++i) {
  if(i==userPref)
   document.write('<OPTION DEFAULT>'+preferences[i])
  else document.write('<OPTION>'+preferences[i])
  }
 document.write('</SELECT>')
}
function updatePrefs() {
 var list = window.document.setPref.prefsList
 var selectedOption=list.options[list.selectedIndex].text
 var newCookie="adPref="+selectedOption
 newCookie += "; expires=Wednesday, 10-Nov-10 23:12:40 GMT"
 window.document.cookie=newCookie
 window.location="prefad.htm"
}
function setUserPreferences() {
 userPref=0
 for(var i=0;i<preferences.length;++i) {
```

```
   if(adPref==preferences[i]){
    userPref=i
    break
   }
  }
 }
 function readCookie() {
  var cookie=document.cookie
  adPref="random"
  if(nameDefined(cookie,"adPref"))
   adPref=getCookieValue(cookie,"adPref")
 }
// --></SCRIPT>
</HEAD>
<BODY BGCOLOR="#FFFFFF">
<SCRIPT LANGUAGE="JavaScript"><!--
insertAd()
// --></SCRIPT>
<H1 ALIGN="CENTER">Displaying Ads Based on User Preferences</H1>
<P ALIGN="CENTER">[The rest of the Web page goes here.]</P>
</BODY>
</HTML>
```

To see how it works, open prefad.htm with your browser. It will display a web page similar to that shown in Figure 14.4. Note that a small form is provided for you to select what type of ads you are interested in seeing. Select Travel from the selection list and click on the Update button. All the ads that you see in the future will be travel-related ads, as shown in Figure 14.5.

FIGURE 14.4:

Select ad preferences to determine what types of ads will be displayed. (Listing 14.3)

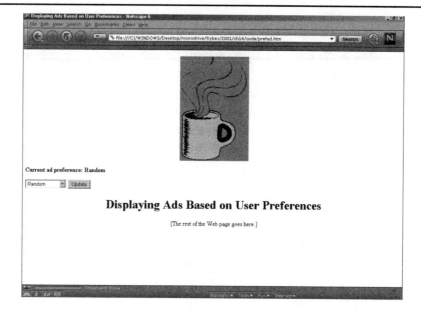

Even though `prefad.htm` is noticeably longer than `fixedad.htm` and `randad.htm`, it is only slightly more complex. It consists of some familiar code. You're already familiar with `nameDefined()`, `removeBlanks()`, and `getCookieValue()`; these functions are used to parse cookies. The rest of the script's arrays and functions are as follows.

The *preferences* array This array identifies the ad categories that a user is allowed to select.

The *urls* array This array lists the URLs to be used in the ads.

The *prefIX* array This array identifies the index into the `urls` array of the first ad in each ad category specified by the `preferences` array.

The *insertAd()* function This function is used to insert an ad and the preferences form into a document. It invokes `readCookie()` to load any preferences that were previously selected by the user, `setPreferences()` to set those preferences, and `displayAd()` to display the ad.

The *displayAd()* function This function displays an ad based on user preferences. It sets `adIX` to the index of the ad (with respect to `urls`) to be displayed. It calculates this index (for non-random preferences) by selecting a random index within the portion of the `urls` array occupied by URLs of the user-preferred category. After computing `adIX`, `displayAd()` displays the ad and is followed by the preference selection form.

The *displaySelectionList()* **function** This function displays the selection list containing the ad categories identified in the `preferences` array.

The *updatePrefs()* **function** This function updates the `adPref` cookie with the value of the preference selected in the `prefsList` selection list. It then reloads the current document with the selected preference in effect.

The *setUserPreferences()* **function** This function sets the `userPref` variable to the index within the `preferences` array of the current user preferences, as identified by the `adPref` cookie.

The *readCookie()* **function** This function reads the `adPref` cookie value and stores it in the `adPref` variable.

NOTE You may wonder why `displayAd()` generated the entire preferences selection form. Why not just put it in the HTML code? The reason for generating the HTML from JavaScript was to combine the ad and the preference selection form into a single component, which could be inserted into a document using the simple `insertAd()` function invocation.

Tabulating Hits with Usage Counters

Many websites display usage counters of the form "This website has been visited 102,987 times." These counters help keep track of how many times a site has been visited and display this number to users (and would-be advertisers). In Internet lingo, the visits are called *hits*.

In this section, we'll look at how you can use JavaScript to create usage counters that are tailored to the individual user rather than the mass of humanity that visits your website.

Web Page Access Counters

Most usage counters keep track of how many times web surfers as a whole access a website. Wouldn't it be nice to have a counter that reported to each user how many times each individual user had accessed your site?

Let's start with tabulating individual user accesses to a web page before we move on to tracking accesses to your website as a whole. The script shown in Listing 14.4 tallies web page accesses. Run this script by opening `pagecnt.htm` with your browser. You will see the display shown in Figure 14.6. It tells you that you've loaded the web page for the first time. Click your browser's Reload button and you will see the display shown in Figure 14.7. It tells you that you've accessed the web page for the second time.

FIGURE 14.6:

Opening a page for the first time results in this display. (Listing 14.4)

FIGURE 14.7:

Opening a page for the second time shows the counter in operation. (Listing 14.4)

Listing 14.4:   A Personal Web Page Access Counter (pagecnt.htm)

```
<HTML>
<HEAD>
<TITLE>Keeping track of Web page access</TITLE>
<SCRIPT LANGUAGE="JavaScript"><!--
function nameDefined(c,n) {
 var s=removeBlanks(c)
 var pairs=s.split(";")
 for(var i=0;i<pairs.length;++i) {
  var pairSplit=pairs[i].split("=")
  if(pairSplit[0]==n) return true
 }
 return false
}
function removeBlanks(s) {
 var temp=""
 for(var i=0;i<s.length;++i) {
  var c=s.charAt(i)
  if(c!=" ") temp += c
 }
 return temp
}
function getCookieValue(c,n) {
 var s=removeBlanks(c)
 var pairs=s.split(";")
 for(var i=0;i<pairs.length;++i) {
  var pairSplit=pairs[i].split("=")
  if(pairSplit[0]==n) return pairSplit[1]
 }
 return ""
}
function insertCounter() {
 readCookie()
 displayCounter()
}
function displayCounter() {
 document.write('<H3 ALIGN="CENTER">')
 document.write("Welcome! You've accessed this page ")
 if(counter==1) document.write("for the first time.")
 else document.write(counter+" times!")
 document.writeln('</H3>')
}
function readCookie() {
 var cookie=document.cookie
 counter=0
 if(nameDefined(cookie,"pageCount"))
  counter=parseInt(getCookieValue(cookie,"pageCount"))
 ++counter
 var newCookie="pageCount="+counter
```

```
    newCookie += "; expires=Wednesday, 10-Nov-10 23:12:40 GMT"
    window.document.cookie=newCookie
    }
    // --></SCRIPT>
    </HEAD>
    <BODY BGCOLOR="#FFFFFF">
    <SCRIPT LANGUAGE="JavaScript"><!--
    insertCounter()
    // --></SCRIPT>
    <H1 ALIGN="CENTER">Keeping track of Web page access</H1>
    <P ALIGN="CENTER">[The rest of the Web page goes here.]</P>
    </BODY>
    </HTML>
```

The script in the document body invokes the insertCounter() function to generate and insert the counter in the web page. The script in the document head defines three new functions—insertCounter(), readCookie(), and displayCounter(). These functions are used as follows:

The *insertCounter()* function   Invokes readCookie() to load the current access counter and displayCounter() to display the counter.

The *readCookie()* function   Reads the pageCount cookie, increments it by 1, and then stores it as an updated cookie.

The *displayCounter()* function   Displays the counter message.

Website Access Counters

The script shown in Listing 14.4 can be easily extended to report how many times a single user has accessed your website as a whole. This is accomplished by storing the usage counter in a cookie that has the path set to / (simply a forward slash). This causes the cookie to apply to all web pages located on a particular host.

To see how the counter works, follow these steps:

1.   Open sitecnt.htm (Listing 14.5) with your browser. It will display the web page shown in Figure 14.8.

2.   Close your browser and copy sitecnt.htm and counter.js to another directory. This will demonstrate the effect of having two web pages at your site.

3.   Open the copied file. It will be displayed as shown in Figure 14.9. Note that the counter was updated even though the second file you opened was in another directory (representing a separate web page at the same site).

NOTE   In order for this counter to keep an accurate count of accesses to your website, you must use the files `sitecnt.htm` and `counter.js` with all the web pages at your site.

FIGURE 14.8:

Opening `sitecnt.htm` (Listing 14.5) for the first time shows that you're visiting this site for the first time.

FIGURE 14.9:

The counter (Listing 14.5) tallies your additional accesses to the site, even though your accesses may be to different pages at the site.

Listing 14.5:   A Website Access Counter (sitecnt.htm)

```
<HTML>
<HEAD>
<TITLE>Keeping track of Web site access</TITLE>
<SCRIPT LANGUAGE="JavaScript" SRC="counter.js"><!--
// --></SCRIPT>
</HEAD>
<BODY BGCOLOR="#FFFFFF">
<SCRIPT LANGUAGE="JavaScript"><!--
insertSiteCounter()
// --></SCRIPT>
<H1 ALIGN="CENTER">Keeping track of Web site access</H1>
<P ALIGN="CENTER">[The rest of the Web page goes here.]</P>
</BODY>
</HTML>
```

To show how easy it is to include a counter in your web pages, I've separated the code that implements the counter from the code that displays it. The sitecnt.htm file shown in Listing 14.5 includes the counter.js file shown in Listing 14.6. In Listing 14.5, only a single JavaScript line is needed to insert the site counter into the web page.

Listing 14.6:   The Code That Implements the Counter (counter.js)

```
function nameDefined(c,n) {
 var s=removeBlanks(c)
 var pairs=s.split(";")
 for(var i=0;i<pairs.length;++i) {
  var pairSplit=pairs[i].split("=")
  if(pairSplit[0]==n) return true
 }
 return false
}
function removeBlanks(s) {
 var temp=""
 for(var i=0;i<s.length;++i) {
  var c=s.charAt(i)
  if(c!=" ") temp += c
 }
 return temp
}
function getCookieValue(c,n) {
 var s=removeBlanks(c)
 var pairs=s.split(";")
 for(var i=0;i<pairs.length;++i) {
  var pairSplit=pairs[i].split("=")
  if(pairSplit[0]==n) return pairSplit[1]
 }
```

```
   return ""
}
function insertSiteCounter() {
 readCookie()
 displayCounter()
}
function displayCounter() {
 document.write('<H3 ALIGN="CENTER">')
 document.write("Welcome! You've accessed this site ")
 if(counter==1) document.write("for the first time.")
 else document.write(counter+" times!")
 document.writeln('</H3>')
}
function readCookie() {
 var cookie=document.cookie
 counter=0
 if(nameDefined(cookie,"siteCount"))
  counter=parseInt(getCookieValue(cookie,"siteCount"))
 ++counter
 var newCookie="siteCount="+counter
 newCookie += "; expires=Wednesday, 10-Nov-10 23:12:40 GMT"
 newCookie += "; path=/"
 window.document.cookie=newCookie
}
```

You probably noticed that counter.js is very similar to pagecnt.htm. The only significant difference between the two files is that counter.js stores the cookie with the path set to /. This enables the cookie to work with any file in any directory on your system. However, the cookie cannot be shared among pages from different domains.

Time Usage Counters

In some cases, you may be more interested in telling users how many hours or minutes they have spent at your website, rather than how many times they have accessed it. This is especially true if your website provides some sort of interactive content, like a game or tutorial. In this case, you may want to display a message of the form "You've accessed this website for over 120 hours—Get a life!" This type of usage counter can be easily implemented with JavaScript, as shown in Listing 14.7. Note that this file uses timecnt.js (Listing 14.8).

NOTE Don't rely on this technique being secure—mischievous users could manipulate their cookie files to change the time value recorded.

Listing 14.7:   Keeping Track of User Access Time (timecnt.htm)

```
<HTML>
<HEAD>
<TITLE>Keeping track of Web site access time</TITLE>
<SCRIPT LANGUAGE="JavaScript" SRC="timecnt.js"><!--
// --></SCRIPT>
</HEAD>
<BODY BGCOLOR="#FFFFFF">
<SCRIPT LANGUAGE="JavaScript"><!--
insertTimeCounter()
// --></SCRIPT>
<H1 ALIGN="CENTER">Keeping track of Web site access time</H1>
<P ALIGN="CENTER">[The rest of the Web page goes here.]</P>
</BODY>
</HTML>
```

Listing 14.8:   Implementing the Time Counter (timecnt.js)

```
function nameDefined(c,n) {
 var s=removeBlanks(c)
 var pairs=s.split(";")
 for(var i=0;i<pairs.length;++i) {
  var pairSplit=pairs[i].split("=")
  if(pairSplit[0]==n) return true
 }
 return false
}
function removeBlanks(s) {
 var temp=""
 for(var i=0;i<s.length;++i) {
  var c=s.charAt(i)
  if(c!=" ") temp += c
 }
 return temp
}
function getCookieValue(c,n) {
 var s=removeBlanks(c)
 var pairs=s.split(";")
 for(var i=0;i<pairs.length;++i) {
  var pairSplit=pairs[i].split("=")
  if(pairSplit[0]==n) return pairSplit[1]
 }
 return ""
}
function insertTimeCounter() {
```

```
    today = new Date()
    startTime = today.getTime()
    readCookie()
    displayCounter()
    setInterval("setCookie()",1000)
    }
function displayCounter() {
  document.write('<H3 ALIGN="CENTER">')
  document.write("Welcome! You've accessed this site ")
  if(prevTime==0) document.write("for the first time.")
  else document.write("over "+displayTime())
  document.writeln('</H3>')
  }
function displayTime() {
  var seconds=Math.round(prevTime/1000)
  var minutes=Math.round(seconds/60)
  var hours=Math.round(minutes/60)
  if(seconds<60) return ""+seconds+ " seconds."
  else if(minutes<60) return ""+minutes+ " minutes."
  else return ""+hours+" hours "
  }
function readCookie() {
  var cookie=document.cookie
  prevTime=0
  if(nameDefined(cookie,"timeCount"))
    prevTime=parseInt(getCookieValue(cookie,"timeCount"))
  }
function setCookie() {
  now = new Date()
  endTime = now.getTime()
  duration = endTime-startTime
  var newCookie="timeCount="+(prevTime+duration)
  newCookie += "; expires=Wednesday, 10-Nov-10 23:12:40 GMT"
  newCookie += "; path=/"
  window.document.cookie=newCookie
  }
```

Open timecnt.htm with your browser. Your display should look like Figure 14.10. Wait a few seconds and then click your browser's reload button. It should display the web page shown in Figure 14.11. Notice how it tracked the time in which the page was loaded.

The time counter display shows that you're accessing this site for the first time (Listing 14.7).

The time counter can also be used to track the amount of time the user has spent at your site (Listing 14.7).

The `timecnt.js` file uses five new functions—insertTimeCounter(), displayCounter(), displayTime(), readCookie(), and setCookie(). These functions are used as follows.

The *insertTimeCounter()* function   Sets the starting time in which a page is loaded, invokes `readCookie()` to load the previous elapsed time, and then invokes `displayCounter()` to display the current elapsed time.

The *displayCounter()* function   Displays the total time that a page was accessed up to the time that it was loaded.

The *displayTime()* function   Converts elapsed time from milliseconds to seconds, minutes, and hours.

The *readCookie()* function   Reads the `timeCount` cookie and stores its value in the `prevTime` variable.

The *setCookie()* Function   Updates the `timeCount` cookie with by adding the time in which a web page is loaded to the previous value of the cookie.

Implementing Nag Counters

As a final example of usage counters, consider a situation in which you want to inform your users that they need to do something like register or pay their usage bills. In this case, you may want to display a message along the lines of "You've used this web page 75 times, and you still haven't registered!" These types of nag messages can be easily added to a usage counter. Listing 14.9 shows how. It uses the `counter.js` file that you studied in the "Website Access Counters" section earlier in this discussion, and it displays an alert message after the user has accessed your website 10 or more times. Figure 14.12 shows how this message is displayed. As a practical matter, you would also want to tie the alert message to the value of a cookie that tracked user registration.

Listing 14.9:   Implementing a Nag Counter (nag.htm)

```
<HTML>
<HEAD>
<TITLE>Nagging the user to register</TITLE>
<SCRIPT LANGUAGE="JavaScript" SRC="counter.js"><!--
// --></SCRIPT>
</HEAD>
<BODY BGCOLOR="#FFFFFF">
<SCRIPT LANGUAGE="JavaScript"><!--
insertSiteCounter()
if(counter>=10) alert("Don't you think its time you registered?")
// --></SCRIPT>
<H1 ALIGN="CENTER">Nagging the user to register</H1>
<P ALIGN="CENTER">[The rest of the Web page goes here.]</P>
</BODY>
</HTML>
```

FIGURE 14.12:

Nagging the user is easy using counters and alert dialog boxes. (Listing 14.9)

Selecting Page Format Preferences

As a final type of web page component, you'll create a simple form that can be used to control the way that your web pages are displayed. There are a number of page formatting and display options that you may wish to allow users to control:

- Whether to use frames

- Whether to display images

- What colors to use for the document background, text, and links

- Whether to display navigation buttons, a usage clock, or other components

By giving users control over these options, you can get them more involved with your web pages and heighten their awareness and interest in what you publish.

Listing 14.10 shows how simple page format controls can be added to a web page to permit the user to change the text and background colors. Figure 14.13 shows the browser display that it produces. Experiment with the document's background and text colors by changing them to different color combinations. Doesn't this simple component make you feel like you have greater control over what's displayed and that you are interacting with and improving upon it?

Listing 14.10:   Implementing User Preferences (prefs.htm)

```
<HTML>
<HEAD>
<TITLE>Setting color preferences</TITLE>
<SCRIPT LANGUAGE="JavaScript"><!--
function nameDefined(c,n) {
 var s=removeBlanks(c)
 var pairs=s.split(";")
 for(var i=0;i<pairs.length;++i) {
  var pairSplit=pairs[i].split("=")
  if(pairSplit[0]==n) return true
 }
 return false
```

```
}
function removeBlanks(s) {
 var temp=""
 for(var i=0;i<s.length;++i) {
  var c=s.charAt(i)
  if(c!=" ") temp += c
 }
 return temp
}
function getCookieValue(c,n) {
 var s=removeBlanks(c)
 var pairs=s.split(";")
 for(var i=0;i<pairs.length;++i) {
  var pairSplit=pairs[i].split("=")
  if(pairSplit[0]==n) return pairSplit[1]
 }
 return ""
}
function readCookie() {
 var cookie=document.cookie
 background="white"
 text="black"
 if(nameDefined(cookie,"background"))
  background=getCookieValue(cookie,"background")
 if(nameDefined(cookie,"text"))
  text=getCookieValue(cookie,"text")
}
function setCookie() {
 var newCookie="background="+background
 newCookie += "; expires=Wednesday, 10-Nov-10 23:12:40 GMT"
 window.document.cookie=newCookie
 var newCookie="text="+text
 newCookie += "; expires=Wednesday, 10-Nov-10 23:12:40 GMT"
 window.document.cookie=newCookie
 window.location="prefs.htm"
}
function prefsForm() {
 document.writeln('<FORM name="prefs">')
 document.writeln('Background color: ')
 document.writeln('<SELECT name="bg" size="1">')
 document.writeln('<OPTION>black')
 document.writeln('<OPTION SELECTED>white')
 document.writeln('<OPTION>red')
 document.writeln('<OPTION>orange')
 document.writeln('<OPTION>yellow')
 document.writeln('<OPTION>green')
 document.writeln('<OPTION>blue')
 document.writeln('<OPTION>brown')
 document.writeln('</SELECT>')
 document.writeln(' Text color: ')
 document.writeln('<SELECT name="fg" size="1">')
```

```
document.writeln('<OPTION SELECTED>black')
document.writeln('<OPTION>white')
document.writeln('<OPTION>red')
document.writeln('<OPTION>orange')
document.writeln('<OPTION>yellow')
document.writeln('<OPTION>green')
document.writeln('<OPTION>blue')
document.writeln('<OPTION>brown')
document.writeln('</SELECT>')
document.writeln('<INPUT type="button" value="Set Colors"
↳onClick="setPrefs()"')
document.writeln('</FORM>')
}
function setPrefs() {
 bgField = window.document.prefs.bg
 bgIndex = bgField.selectedIndex
 background = bgField.options[bgIndex].text
 fgField = window.document.prefs.fg
 fgIndex = fgField.selectedIndex
 text = fgField.options[fgIndex].text
 setCookie()
}
// --></SCRIPT>
</HEAD>
<BODY>
<SCRIPT LANGUAGE="JavaScript"><!--
readCookie()
document.bgColor=background
document.fgColor=text
prefsForm()
// --></SCRIPT>
<H1 ALIGN="CENTER">Setting color preferences</H1>
<P ALIGN="CENTER">[The rest of the Web page goes here.]</P>
</BODY>
</HTML>
```

To insert the color preferences form into a web page, you invoke the prefsForm() function. You do so after executing the following three lines of code:

```
readCookie()
document.bgColor=background
document.fgColor=text
```

These statements read the current cookie value (if any) and update the document's background and foreground colors.

NOTE   The SRC attribute of the script tag may be used to include the JavaScript code shown in the document head.

FIGURE 14.13:

JavaScript makes it easy to change document colors. (Listing 14.13)

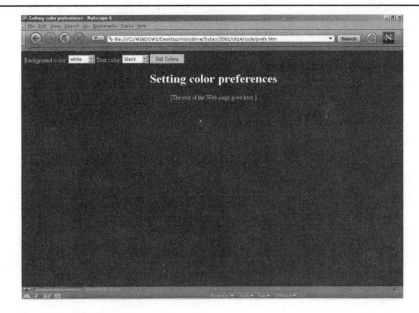

The new functions defined in the document's head are used as follows:

The *readCookie()* function   Reads the cookies containing the background and text colors.

The *setCookie()* function   Sets the background and text color cookies to the values selected by the user. It then reloads the web page to bring the new values into effect.

The *prefsForm()* function   Displays the color preferences selection form.

The *setPrefs()* function   Handles the onClick event associated with the Set Colors button by reading the color values selected by the user and invoking setCookie() to store the cookie values.

Summary

In this chapter, you learned how to create a variety of interesting components for use in your web pages. You learned how to develop and display ads and usage counters. You also learned how to create scrolling text and images and animated icons. Finally, you learned how to include format controls in your web pages. In the next chapter you'll learn more about JavaScript animation and you'll develop a JavaScript slide show component.

CHAPTER 15

Developing Animations and Slide Shows

- Animating text and images

- Creating slide shows

- Setting up autobrowsing

It's no secret that people want to be entertained—even more so on the Web. Browsing plain old text web pages can be as dull as reading the phone book. A little style and animation can do a lot to add increase interest in a website. In this chapter, you'll learn how you can use JavaScript to animate text and images. You'll learn how to use JavaScript to organize your content into slide shows and even provide an autobrowsing capability for your laziest users. When you finish this chapter, you'll be able to create a number of JavaScript effects that will make your pages livelier and more attractive.

Using Animation Effects

Animation effects can add a lot of visual appeal to your web pages. While they may appear complicated, they're actually easy to implement in JavaScript. You simply set an interval timer and make periodic changes to the way your pages are displayed. We'll cover text animations first, followed by image-based animations.

Animating Text

Text animations are very easy to implement in JavaScript—you just periodically change some aspect of the way the text is displayed. For example, you can change the position of text, its style, or even its content.

The Blink and Marquee Tags

There are two HTML tags, blink and marquee, that can be used to implement simple animation effects. The blink tag was developed by Netscape and only works with Navigator. It causes marked-up text to blink on and off. The marquee tag was developed by Microsoft and only works with Internet Explorer. So, unless you are coding for a single brand of browser, these tags are fairly useless. Listing 15.1 provides an example of their use. If you open it using Navigator, the first paragraph will blink and the second will do nothing. If you open it with Internet Explorer, the second paragraph will scroll and the first will do nothing.

Listing 15.1:   The blink and marquee Tags (blink.htm)

```
<html>
<head>
<title>Blinking and Scrolling Text</title>
</head>
<body>
<p><blink>Watch this text blink!</blink></p>
<p><marquee>Watch this text scroll!!!</marquee></p>
</body>
</html>
```

Scrolling Text

One of the simplest JavaScript animations is to scroll text in the browser's status window. Listing 15.2 provides an example. It scrolls the message "Watch this text scroll!!!" as shown in Figure 15.1.

Upon loading of the document, the scrollText() function sets an interval timer to invoke the displayText() function every 300 milliseconds. The displayText() function progressively prepends between 0 and 100 space characters to the message to create the scrolling effect.

FIGURE 15.1:

A message is scrolled in the status window.

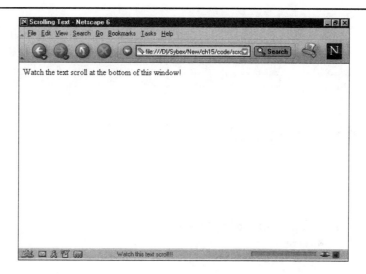

Listing 15.2:   Scrolling Text in the Status Window (scrolltext.htm)

```
<html>
<head>
<title>Scrolling Text</title>
<script language="JavaScript">
var scrollPos = 0
var maxScroll = 100
var blanks = ""
function scrollText(text, milliseconds) {
 window.setInterval("displayText('"+text+"')", milliseconds)
}
function displayText(text) {
 window.defaultStatus = blanks + text
 ++scrollPos
 blanks += " "
 if(scrollPos > maxScroll) {
```

```
  scrollPos = 0
  blanks = ""
 }
}
</script>
</head>
<body onload="scrollText('Watch this text scroll!!!', 300)">
<p>Watch the text scroll at the bottom of this window!</p>
</body>
</html>
```

Replacing Text

A more interesting and useful effect is to periodically change the text that is displayed in an HTML element as shown in Listing 15.3. It displays the text shown in Figure 15.2. After two seconds the text is changed to that shown in Figure 15.3. A total of three new messages are displayed.

Listing 15.3: **Periodically Updating the Text Displayed by an HTML Element (changetext.htm)**

```
<html>
<head>
<title>Replacing Text</title>
<script language="JavaScript">
var msgIX = 0
var msgs = new Array(
 "Notice anything different?",
 "The text you are looking at has changed.",
 "This is a handy way of sending messages to your users."
)

function scrollMessages(milliseconds) {
 window.setInterval("displayMessage()", milliseconds)
}
function displayMessage() {
 if(document.getElementById != null) {
  var heading = document.getElementById("scrollme")
  heading.firstChild.nodeValue = msgs[msgIX]
 }else{
  if(navigator.appName == "Microsoft Internet Explorer") {
   var heading = document.all.item("scrollme")
   heading.innerText = msgs[msgIX]
  }
 }
 ++msgIX
 msgIX %= msgs.length
}
```

```
    </script>
    </head>
    <body onload="scrollMessages(2000)">
    <h1 align="center" id="scrollme">Watch this text very carefully!</h1>
    </body>
    </html>
```

FIGURE 15.2:

The initial text displayed by
`changetext.htm`

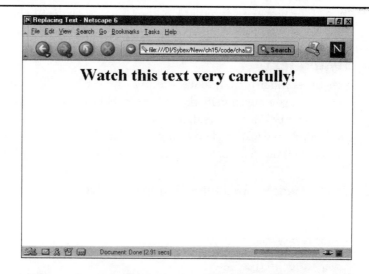

FIGURE 15.3:

The initial text is replaced.

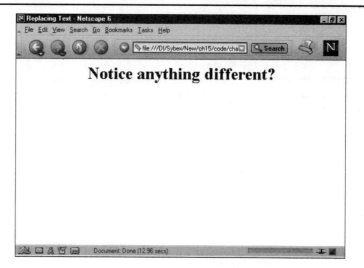

The scrollMessages() function is invoked when the page is initially loaded. It sets a two-second interval timer for invoking the displayMessage() function.

The displayMessage() function supports DOM1-capable browsers and Internet Explorer 4, but does not support Navigator 4. If the browser is DOM1-capable (i.e., document.get-ElementById() is defined), it obtains access to the H1 element with the id attribute of scrollme and changes the value of the marked-up text using the next message of the msgs array. If the browser is Internet Explorer 4, access to the H1 element is obtained through the document.all property and its text is updated via the innerText property.

Styling Text

Sometimes you may want to just create a simple effect, like that of the Netscape blink tag. In these cases, you can animate the style of an HTML element as shown in Listing 15.4. When styletext.htm is first opened, it displays the bland text shown in Figure 15.4. However, after two seconds, the text's style is changed to that shown in Figure 15.5. The two styles (bland and colorful) then alternate every two seconds to create a blinking effect.

Listing 15.4:   Animating Text Styles (styletext.htm)

```
<html>
<head>
<title>Styling Text</title>
<script language="JavaScript">
var color = true
var heading = null
function styleText(milliseconds) {
 window.setInterval("changeColors()", milliseconds)
}
function changeColors() {
 if(document.getElementById != null)
  var heading = document.getElementById("styleme")
 else if(navigator.appName == "Microsoft Internet Explorer")
  var heading = document.all.item("styleme")
 if(color && heading != null) {
  heading.style.backgroundColor = "rgb(255,0,0)"
  heading.style.color = "rgb(0,0,255)"
 }else if(heading != null) {
  heading.style.backgroundColor = "rgb(255,255,255)"
  heading.style.color = "rgb(0,0,0)"
 }
 color = ! color
}
</script>
</head>
<body onload="styleText(2000)" bgcolor="white">
```

```
<h1 align="center" id="styleme" style="background-color: rgb(255,255,255)">Watch
this text very carefully!</h1>
</body>
</html>
```

FIGURE 15.4:

The bland text

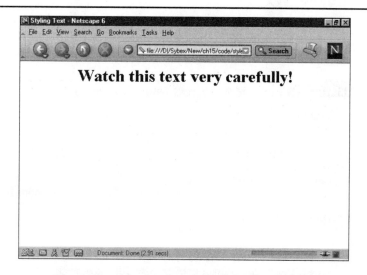

FIGURE 15.5:

The styled text

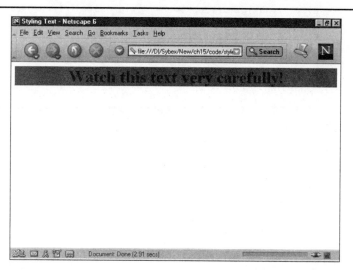

The styleText() function is invoked when the page is loaded. It sets a two-second interval timer for invoking the changeColors() function.

The changeColors() function supports DOM1-capable browsers and Internet Explorer 4. It obtains access to the heading identified by the id attribute of styleme and then sets its foreground and background colors based on the value of the color variable.

Moving Text

The last text animation shows how to move text around a page. You've encountered this technique in Chapter 12, "Working with Styles and DHTML." The example shown in Listing 15.5 supports Navigator 4, Internet Explorer 4, and DOM1-capable browsers.

Listing 15.5: **Moving Text (movetext.htm)**

```
<html>
<head>
<title>Moving Text</title>
<script language="JavaScript">
var heading = null
function moveText(milliseconds) {
 window.setInterval("changePosition()", milliseconds)
}
function changePosition() {
 var x = Math.random()*400
 var y = Math.random()*400
 if(document.getElementById)
  heading = document.getElementById("moveme")
 else if(navigator.appName == "Microsoft Internet Explorer")
  heading = document.all.item("moveme")
 else if(document.layers)
  heading = document.layers["moveme"]
 if(heading != null) {
  if(heading.style == null) { // Navigator 4
   heading.left = x
   heading.top = y
  }else if(heading.style.left != null) { // DOM-capable
   heading.style.left = x
   heading.style.top = y
  }else{ // IE 4
   heading.style.posLeft = x
   heading.style.posTop = y
  }
 }
}
</script>
</head>
<body onload="moveText(2000)">
<div id="moveme" style="position:absolute;font-size:xx-large;">This text
moves!</div>
</body>
</html>
```

The heading text shown in Figure 15.6 moves around the page randomly every 2 seconds.

FIGURE 15.6:

Randomly moving text

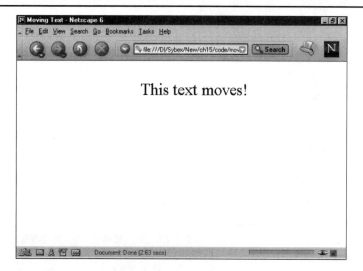

The moveText() function is invoked when the document is loaded to kick off the animation. It sets an interval timer to invoke the changePosition() function every two seconds.

The changePosition() function calculates random x and y coordinates (between 0 and 400) and then updates the position of the division identified with the id of moveme according to capabilities of the browser's object model.

Animating Images

Animating text is a great way to learn animation effects, but animated images are far more eye-catching. The good news is that the same techniques that you learned from text animation apply to image animation.

Replacing Images

One of the easiest ways to achieve an interesting animation effect is to display a series of images in a fixed location over time. The images blend together to give the impression that the image is moving. Listing 15.6 provides an example. It displays a sequence of six images to create the impression of an animated face (refer to Figure 15.7).

Listing 15.6:   Simple Image Replacement (changeimages.htm)

```
<html>
<head>
<title>Replacing Images</title>
```

```
<script language="JavaScript">
var ix = 0
function changeImages(milliseconds) {
 window.setInterval("changeImage()", milliseconds)
}
function changeImage() {
 ++ix
 ix %= 6
 var imageRef = document.images[0]
 imageRef.src = "face"+ix+".gif"
}
</script>
</head>
<body onload="changeImages(500)">
<p align="center"><img id="changeme" src="face0.gif"></p>
</body>
</html>
```

FIGURE 15.7:

An animated face

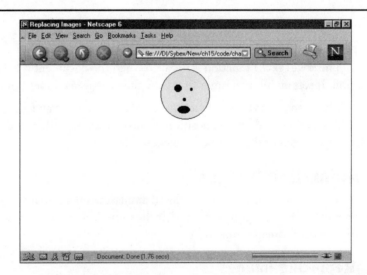

The changeImages() function sets an interval timer of 500 milliseconds for invoking the changeImage() function. The changeImage() function changes the src property of the document's image to the next image in the series.

Blowing Up Images

Image blowups are a handy technique for including images in your web pages. Instead of wasting all of your document's space displaying an image, you display a reduced-size version of the image (Figure 15.8). When the user moves his or her mouse over the image, a full-size version of the image is displayed. When the user moves the mouse away from the image, the full-size image goes away and the reduced-size image is shown (see Figure 15.9).

FIGURE 15.8:

A reduced-sized image is displayed.

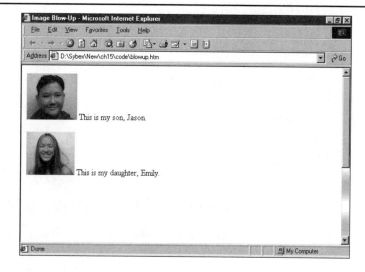

FIGURE 15.9:

A full-sized image is displayed when the user moves the mouse over the reduced-size image.

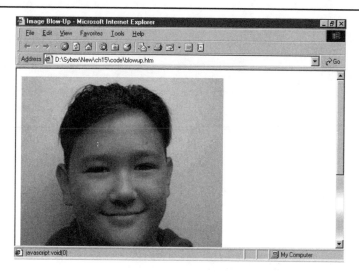

Listing 15.7 shows how to implement image blowups. It uses the `blowup.js` script shown in Listing 15.8.

Listing 15.7: **Image Blowups (blowup.htm)**

```
<html>
<head>
<title>Image Blow-Up</title>
<script language="JavaScript" src="blowup.js">
</script>
</head>
<body>
<p><a href="javascript:void(0)"
 onmouseover="showBlowup('jason','eg1')"
 onclick="showBlowupInNewWindow('jason-large.jpg',525,425)">
<img name="eg1" src="jason-small.jpg" border=0></a>
This is my son, Jason.</p>
<p><a href="javascript:void(0)"
 onmouseover="showBlowup('emily','eg2')"
 onclick="showBlowupInNewWindow('emily-large.jpg',525,425)">
<img name="eg2" src="emily-small.jpg" border=0></a>
This is my daughter, Emily.</p>
<div id="jason" style="position:absolute;height:300;visibility:hidden;margin:-
2px;">
<a href="javascript:void(0)" onmouseout="hideBlowup('jason')"
onclick="hideBlowup('jason')"><img src="jason-large.jpg" border=0></a>
</div>
<div id="emily" style="position:absolute;height:300;visibility:hidden;margin:-
2px;">
<a href="javascript:void(0)" onmouseout="hideBlowup('emily')"
onclick="hideBlowup('emily')"><img src="emily-large.jpg" border=0></a>
</div>
</body>
</html>
```

Listing 15.8: **The Blowup Script (blowup.js)**

```
// blowup.js

function showBlowup(divID, imageID) {
 if(document.layers) {
  // Navigator 4 model
  var divObject = document.layers[divID]
  var imageObject = document.images[imageID]
  divObject.pageX = imageObject.x
  divObject.pageY = imageObject.y
  divObject.visibility = "visible"
 } else if(document.all) {
  // Internet Explorer model
  var divStyle = document.all.item(divID).style
  var imageObject = document.images[imageID]
```

```
      divStyle.posLeft = (window.event.clientX - window.event.offsetX)
      divStyle.posTop = (window.event.clientY - window.event.offsetY +
  document.body.scrollTop)
      if (navigator.appVersion.indexOf("Mac") >= 0) { // work around Mac IE bug
        divStyle.posTop -= document.body.scrollTop
        }
      divStyle.visibility = "visible"
    }
  }

  function showBlowupInNewWindow(imageFileURL,width,height) {
    // Workaround for Navigator 6
    windowOptions =
  "directories=0,menubar=0,personalbar=0,status=0,resizable=1,width="
    windowOptions += width + ",height=" + height
    window.open(imageFileURL,"nav6workaround",windowOptions)
  }

  function hideBlowup(divID) {
    if(document.layers) {
      var divObject = document.layers[divID]
      divObject.visibility = "hidden"
    } else if (document.all) {
    // Use IE DHTML
      var divStyle = document.all.item(divID).style
      divStyle.visibility = "hidden"
    }
  }
```

Anchor tags surround the reduced-size images. The onmouseover and onclick event handlers of the anchor tags are set to invoke the showBlowup() and showBlowupInNewWindow() functions. (The showBlowupInNewWindow() function is a Navigator 6 workaround).

Two hidden divisions contain the full-size images. These images are also wrapped in anchor tags. The onmouseout and onclick event handlers of the anchor tags are set to the hideBlowup() function.

The showBlowup(), showBlowupInNewWindow(), and hideBlowup() functions are defined in blowup.js. The showBlowup() and hideBlowup() functions don't support Navigator 6 because Navigator 6 doesn't implement the x and y properties of image objects.

The showBlowup() function moves the hidden division containing the full-size version of an image to the same location as the reduced-size image and then makes the division visible. In the case of Navigator 4, this amounts to getting the reduced-size image's coordinates and using them as the location for the division. In the case of Internet Explorer, this involves calculating the position of where the mouse event occurred with respect to the current window's scroll position.

The `hideBlowup()` function simply sets the visibility of the division containing the full-size image to `hidden`.

The `showBlowupInNewWindow()` opens a new browser window to display the full-size image.

Moving Images

Moving images can be used to direct the user's attention to your web pages. Listing 15.9 moves a hand across the top of a web page to focus your attention on a link. Refer to Figure 15.10. Listing 15.10 moves a plane across the page to give it a fun effect, as shown in Figure 15.11.

Listing 15.9:   Moving a Hand Across the Top of a Web Page (movehand.htm)

```
<html>
<head>
<title>Scrolling an image across the page</title>
<script language="JavaScript">
function loadImages() {
 hand = new Image()
 blank = new Image()
 hand.src = "hand.gif"
 blank.src = "blnkhand.gif"
 max = 5
 current = 4
}
function scrollImages() {
 window.document.images[current].src = blank.src
 current = (current + 1) % max
 window.document.images[current].src = hand.src
}
</script>
</head>
<body bgcolor="#FFFFFF"
 onLoad="setInterval('scrollImages()',500)">
<script language="JavaScript">
loadImages()
</script>
<p align="center">
<img src="blnkhand.gif" border="0">
<img src="blnkhand.gif" border="0">
<img src="blnkhand.gif" border="0">
<img src="blnkhand.gif" border="0">
<IMG SRC="blnkhand.gif" BORDER="0">
<a href="javascript: void(0)">Click here!</a>
</P>
<h1 align="center">Scrolling an image across the screen</h1>
</body>
</html>
```

FIGURE 15.10:

A moving hand

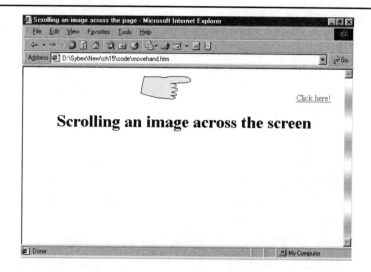

Listing 15.10:   Moving an Airplane Across a Web Page (fly.htm)

```html
<html>
<head>
<title>Animation with Divisions</title>
</head>
<script language="JavaScript">
function fly() {
 if(document.getElementById) {
  var planeStyle = document.getElementById("plane").style
  window.defaultStatus = "("+planeStyle.left+","+planeStyle.top+")"
  if(parseInt(planeStyle.top) < 10) {
   planeStyle.left = 0
   planeStyle.top = 400
  }else{
   planeStyle.left = parseInt(planeStyle.left) + 8
   planeStyle.top = parseInt(planeStyle.top) - 5
  }
 }else if(document.all) {
  var planeStyle=window.document.all.plane.style
  window.defaultStatus = "("+planeStyle.posLeft+","+planeStyle.posTop+")"
  if(planeStyle.posTop < 10) {
   planeStyle.posLeft = 0
   planeStyle.posTop = 400
  }else{
   planeStyle.posLeft += 8
   planeStyle.posTop -= 5
  }
 }
```

```
}
</script>
<body bgcolor="blue" onload="setInterval('fly()',100)">
<div name="heading" style="position:absolute;left:100;top:100;z-index:3">
<h1 style="color: rgb(255,255,0);">Welcome to the Aviation Home Page!</h1>
</div>
<div id="plane" style="position:absolute;left:0;top:400;z-index:2">
<img src="plane.png">
</div>
<div id="cloud1" style="position:absolute;left:150;top:300;z-index:3">
<img src="cloud.gif">
</div>
<div id="cloud2" style="position:absolute;left:250;top:200;z-index:3">
<img src="cloud.gif">
</div>
<div id="cloud3" style="position:absolute;left:350;top:150;z-index:1">
<img src="cloud.gif">
</div>
<div id="cloud4" style="position:absolute;left:350;top:250;z-index:1">
<img src="cloud.gif">
</div>
</BODY>
</HTML>
```

FIGURE 15.11:

A moving plane

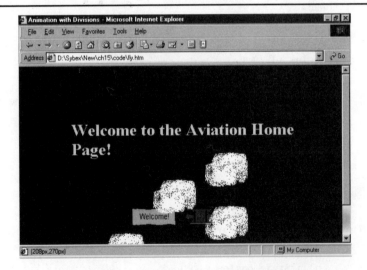

These examples illustrate two different approaches to moving images. In Listing 15.9, a series of five blank images is displayed across the top of the page. The image of the hand replaces each of the blank images in succession. In Listing 15.10, the image of the plane is put in a division tag. The division is moved across the page by changing its left and top style attributes. Note that the first approach works with Navigator 4 while the second approach does not. To implement the second type of animation with Navigator 4, you'll have to use the now-defunct `layer` object.

Creating Slide Shows

Slide shows are a great way to organize pages that should be viewed in sequence. They are web incarnations of the classic PowerPoint presentation. Programs like PowerPoint and Freelance Graphics provide capabilities for translating traditional presentations into web pages. The problem is that the translated presentations are noticeably stiff and not web oriented.

Organizing Pages into a Show

When it comes to slide shows, a little JavaScript goes a long way. Listing 15.11 presents a two-frame set. The top frame (Listing 15.12) contains the controls for a slide show, and the bottom frame contains its contents (page0.htm through page4.htm). Listing 15.13 contains a style sheet for the controls and presentation slides.

Listing 15.11:   The Slide Show Frame Set (pageshow.htm)

```
<html>
<head><title>Page Show</title></head>
<frameset rows="120,*" border="0">
<frame src="controls.htm" name="controls">
<frame src="page0.htm" name="bottom">
</frameset>
</html>
```

Listing 15.12:   The Slide Show Controls (controls.htm)

```
<html>
<head>
<link rel="stylesheet" type="text/css" href="pageshow.css">
<script language="JavaScript" src="pageshow.js">
</script>
</head>
<body>
<script language="JavaScript">
var pages = new Array("page0.htm", "page1.htm", "page2.htm", "page3.htm",
 "page4.htm")
var pageShow = new PageShow("pageShow", "bottom", pages)
pageShow.displayControls()
</script>
</body>
</html>
```

Listing 15.13:   The Slide Show's Style Sheet (pageshow.css)

```
p.pageshow
{text-align: right}

h1
{background-color: #c5c5e2;
border: 5px red groove;
color: #004080;
font-family: Verdana, Helvetica, Arial, sans-serif;
font-style: italic;
text-align: center}

a.pageshow
{background-color: #0000a0;
color: #ffffff;
font-weight: bold;
padding: 2px;
text-decoration: none}
```

When you open pageshow.htm in your browser, you see the first page of the slide show with four navigation controls in the upper-right corner. Refer to Figure 15.12. You can use these controls to move between the pages of the presentation.

FIGURE 15.12:

The slide show display

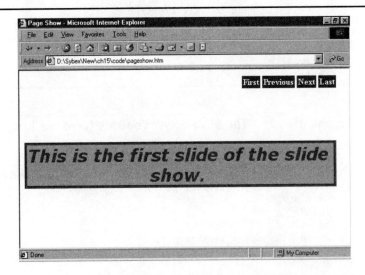

The top frame (controls.htm) uses the pageshow.js (Listing 15.14) script to display and implement the slide show's navigation controls. It builds an array of page URLs and then constructs a PageShow object. It then uses the displayControls() method to display the navigation controls.

Listing 15.14: The Slide Show Script (pageshow.js)

```
// pageshow.js

function PageShow(varName, winName, pages) {
 this.varName = varName
 this.winName = winName
 this.pages = pages
 this.current = 0
 this.displayControls = PageShow_displayControls
 this.goFirst = PageShow_goFirst
 this.goNext = PageShow_goNext
 this.goPrevious = PageShow_goPrevious
 this.goLast = PageShow_goLast
}

function PageShow_displayControls() {
 document.write("<p class='pageshow'>")
 document.write("<a class='pageshow'
href='javascript:"+this.varName+".goFirst()'>First</a> ")
 document.write("<a class='pageshow'
href='javascript:"+this.varName+".goPrevious()'>Previous</a> ")
 document.write("<a class='pageshow'
href='javascript:"+this.varName+".goNext()'>Next</a> ")
 document.write("<a class='pageshow'
href='javascript:"+this.varName+".goLast()'>Last</a>")
 document.write("</p>")
}

function PageShow_goFirst() {
 this.current = 0
 var win = window.parent.frames[this.winName]
 win.location.href = this.pages[this.current]
}

function PageShow_goNext() {
 if(this.current == this.pages.length - 1) return
 this.current++
 var win = window.parent.frames[this.winName]
 win.location.href = this.pages[this.current]
}

function PageShow_goPrevious() {
 if(this.current == 0) return
 this.current-
 var win = window.parent.frames[this.winName]
 win.location.href = this.pages[this.current]
```

```
     }
     function PageShow_goLast() {
      this.current = this.pages.length - 1
      var win = window.parent.frames[this.winName]
      win.location.href = this.pages[this.current]
     }
```

The PageShow constructor takes the name of the variable that references the PageShow object (for event-handling call-backs), the name of the window (or frame) where the slide show pages are to be displayed, and the URL array as arguments. It uses the current property to keep track of the current page being displayed.

The PageShow object has the following five methods:

displayControls()   Displays the navigation buttons.

goFirst()   Loads the first page of the show.

goNext()   Loads the next page of the show.

goPrevious()   Loads the previous page of the show.

goLast()   Loads the last page of the show.

The pages array can be initialized with simple file names or complete URLs. The URLs may point to different Internet hosts.

Organizing Markup into a Show

The slide show presented in the previous section displayed the pages of a slide show in the bottom half of a two-page frame set. This approach is fine for many presentations, but there are times when you may want to include the presentation inline to a single web page. The slide show presented in Listing 15.14 does just that. When you open it, you'll see a boxed division that displays an image and HTML markup (see Figure 15.13). The page also has a set of navigation controls for displaying different slides within the boxed division.

Listing 15.14:   **An Inline Slide Show (slideshow.htm)**

```
<html>
<head>
<title>Slide Show</title>
<link rel="stylesheet" type="text/css" href="slideshow.css">
<script language="JavaScript">
var numSlides
var currentSlide = 0
function initializeSlideShow(n) {
 numSlides = n
```

```
  showSlide(currentSlide, true)
 }
 function displaySlide(n) {
  showSlide(currentSlide, false)
  currentSlide = n
  showSlide(currentSlide, true)
 }
 function showSlide(n, display) {
  if(document.getElementById) {
   var slide = document.getElementById("slide"+n).style
   if(display) slide.display = "block"
   else slide.display = "none"
  }else if(document.all){
   var slide=window.document.all.item("slide"+n).style
   if(display) slide.display = "block"
   else slide.display = "none"
  }
 }
 function goFirst() {
  displaySlide(0)
 }
 function goLast() {
  displaySlide(numSlides - 1)
 }
 function goNext() {
  if(currentSlide < numSlides - 1)
   displaySlide(currentSlide+1)
 }
 function goPrevious() {
  if(currentSlide > 0)
   displaySlide(currentSlide-1)
 }
</script>
</head>
<body onload="initializeSlideShow(6)">
<div id="slide0" class="slide">
<img src="image0.jpg" border="0"><br>
<b>The Great Buddha at Kamakura</b>
</div>
<div id="slide1" class="slide">
<img src="image1.jpg" border="0"><br>
<b>A Small House at the Corner of the Imperial Palace</b>
</div>
<div id="slide2" class="slide">
<img src="image2.jpg" border="0"><br>
<b>Entrance to the Meiji Shrine</b>
</div>
<div id="slide3" class="slide">
<img src="image3.jpg" border="0"><br>
<b>A Piece of the Tokyo Skyline</b>
</div>
```

```
<div id="slide4" class="slide">
<img src="image4.jpg" border="0"><br>
<b>Crowded Streets of Shibuya</b>
</div>
<div id="slide5" class="slide">
<img src="image5.jpg" border="0"><br>
<b>A Street Corner Off Shinjuku-dori Avenue</b>
</div>
<div style="position:absolute;left:40;top:250">
<form class="slide">
<input type="button" value="First" onclick="goFirst()">
<input type="button" value="Previous" onclick="goPrevious()">
<input type="button" value="Next" onclick="goNext()">
<input type="button" value="Last" onclick="goLast()">
</form>
</div>
</body>
</html>
```

FIGURE 15.13:

An inline slide show

The slides of the slide show are implemented as a sequence of HTML divisions. The form buttons invoke the goFirst(), goPrevious(), goNext(), and goLast() functions to move between the slides of the slide show. These functions calculate the index of the next slide and use the displaySlide() function to display the slide.

The displaySlide() function uses the showSlide() function to hide the display of the current slide division and to display the new slide. The showSlide() method takes the index of the slide and a Boolean display value as arguments. The display value determines whether a slide is displayed or hidden. It supports DOM1-capable browsers and Internet Explorer 4 but does not support Navigator 4. Listing 15.15 provides a style sheet for the slide show.

Listing 15.15:   A Style Sheet for the Slide Show (slideshow.css)

```
div.slide
{background-color: #ffffd2;
border: 1px solid;
display: none;
height: 200px;
left: 20px;
padding: 10px;
position: absolute;
text-align: center;
top: 20px;
width: 400px}
```

Autobrowsing

The slide shows presented in the previous sections provided controls for navigating between slides. Sometimes you may want to automate the navigation of your slide show by having the browser automatically load a new slide every few seconds. Listing 15.16 provides an example of an *autobrowsing* slide show. It displays a new page every five seconds but can be configured to display pages more quickly or slowly. Figure 15.14 shows how the first slide of the show is displayed. Unlike previous slide shows, there is no master controlling page. Each page of the show implements the slide show logic.

Listing 15.16:   The First Page of the Slide Show (p0.htm)

```
<html>
<head>
<title>The Great Buddha at Kamakura</title>
<script language="JavaScript" src="pagesequence.js">
</script>
<script language="JavaScript" src="autobrowsing.js">
</script>
</head>
<body>
<p align="center"><img src="image0.jpg" border="0"><br>
<b>The Great Buddha at Kamakura</b></p>
</body>
</html>
```

FIGURE 15.14:

The first page of the
slide show

This logic consists of the pagesequence.js file (Listing 15.17) and the autobrowsing.js file (Listing 15.18). The pagesequence.js file defines the array of pages that are to be a part of the slide show. You'll need to modify this for your slide shows.

The autobrowsing.js file is a configuration file that you can modify to change the way the slide show is displayed. You can change the time between slides or use the insertAuto-BrowserControl() function to display controls that enable the user to modify the way in which autobrowsing is performed.

Listing 15.17:   The Page Sequence (pagesequence.js)

```
var pageSequence = new Array ("p0.htm", "p1.htm", "p2.htm",
  "p3.htm", "p4.htm", "p5.htm")
```

Listing 15.18:   The Autobrowsing Configuration Parameters (autobrowsing.js)

```
// Declare timeout variable
var pageTimeout

// Number of milliseconds to display each page
// This can be overridden by the user
var displayTime = 5000

// Is autobrowsing on by default?
var autoBrowsingOn = true

// Index within pageSequence of next page to load
```

```
var nextIndex = 0

window.onload = setupAutoBrowse

// Get any stored settings and set page timeout
function setupAutoBrowse() {
 // Load current settings from cookie
 autoBrowseCookie = getCookie("autobrowse")
 if(autoBrowseCookie == "true") autoBrowsingOn = true
 else if(autoBrowseCookie == "false") autoBrowsingOn = false
 timeoutCookie = getCookie("timeout")
 if(timeoutCookie != null) displayTime = parseInt(timeoutCookie)
 // Determine which page is the current page
 var currentURL = window.location.href
 var currentIndex = -1
 for(var i=0; i<pageSequence.length; ++i) {
  if(currentURL.indexOf(pageSequence[i]) != -1) {
   currentIndex = i
   break
  }
 }
 // Determine which page is the next page
 nextIndex = (currentIndex + 1) % pageSequence.length
 // Set a timeout to load the next page
 if(autoBrowsingOn) setPageTimeout()
}

// Function to load the next page
function loadNextPage() {
 window.location.href = pageSequence[nextIndex]
}

// Set the page timeout
function setPageTimeout() {
 pageTimeout = window.setTimeout("loadNextPage()", displayTime)
}

// Allow the user to cancel the timeout
function cancelPageTimeout() {
 window.clearTimeout(pageTimeout)
}

function getCookie(name) {
 var cookie = removeBlanks(document.cookie)
 var nameValuePairs = cookie.split(";")
 for(var i=0; i<nameValuePairs.length; ++i) {
  var pairSplit = nameValuePairs[i].split("=")
  if(pairSplit[0] == name && pairSplit.length > 1) return pairSplit[1]
 }
 return null
}
```

```
function setCookie(name, value, expirationDate) {
 document.cookie = name+"="+value
}

function removeBlanks(s) {
 var temp = ""
 for(var i=0; i<s.length; ++i) {
  var c = s.charAt(i)
  if(c != " ") temp += c
 }
 return temp
}

function insertAutoBrowserControl() {
 document.writeln('<FORM name="autobrowseform">')
 document.writeln('<B>AutoBrowsing: </B>')
 document.writeln('<SELECT name="autobrowseselect" size="1"
onChange="updateAutoBrowsing()">')
 document.writeln('<option value="-1"></option>')
 document.writeln('<option value="5">Display a new page every 5
seconds</option>')
 document.writeln('<option value="10">Display a new page every 10
seconds</option>')
 document.writeln('<option value="30">Display a new page every 30
seconds</option>')
 document.writeln('<option value="60">Display a new page every minute</option>')
 document.writeln('<option value="120">Display a new page every 2
minutes</option>')
 document.writeln('<option value="300">Display a new page every 5
minutes</option>')
 document.writeln('<option value="0">Turn off autobrowsing</option>')
 document.writeln('</SELECT>')
 document.writeln('</FORM>')
}

function updateAutoBrowsing() {
 var selections =
window.document.forms["autobrowseform"].elements["autobrowseselect"].options
 for(var i=0; i<selections.length; ++i) {
  if(selections[i].selected) {
   var v = selections[i].value
   if(v == -1) break
   cancelPageTimeout()
   if(v == 0) {
    autoBrowsingOn = false
   }else {
    autoBrowsingOn = true
    displayTime = v * 1000
    setPageTimeout()
   }
   setCookie("autobrowse", autoBrowsingOn)
```

```
    setCookie("timeout", displayTime)
    break
  }
 }
}
```

Summary

In this chapter, you learned how to use JavaScript to animate text and images. You also learn how to create slide shows and implement autobrowsing features. In the next chapter, you'll learn how to create pull-down menus, tabbed panels, and tree components.

CHAPTER 16

Building Tabbed Panels, Trees, and Menu Bars

- Exploring JavaScript components

- Creating tabbed panels

- Building collapsible trees

- Implementing menu bars

HTML forms provide a number of GUI components (such as text fields, buttons, and selection lists) that you can use to build your web applications. However, these basic HTML components are quite simple and may not be sufficient for all of your needs. Fortunately, you can build a wide variety of custom components using JavaScript.

In this chapter, we'll create three custom JavaScript components: a tabbed panel, a collapsible tree, and a menu bar with pull-down menus. These components will work with Internet Explorer 4 and later and Navigator 4 and later. When you finish this chapter, you'll be able to integrate these components into your own web applications.

Building Tabbed Panels

Tabbed panels provide a great way to maximize the amount of information that you can deliver in a fixed area of a web page. Figure 16.1 shows an example of a tabbed panel that is displayed by Listing 16.1. When you click on a tab, the panel associated with that tab is displayed, as shown in Figure 16.2. The tabbed panel allows you to organize information about a number of topics in a compact space. Moreover, the tabbed panel makes this information easily accessible to your users.

FIGURE 16.1:

Tabbed panel display

FIGURE 16.2:

The panels change when you click on the tabs.

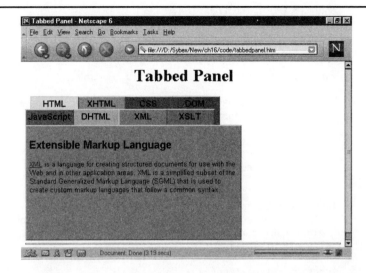

The tabbed panel shown in Listing 16.1 works with versions 4 and later of Internet Explorer and Navigator. Listing 16.2 shows the style sheet that is used with the tabs and panels. Listing 16.3 shows the special workaround that is used to accommodate Navigator 4.

Getting back to Listing 16.1, you'll see that an ilayer tag is used to insert the Navigator 4 workaround (nav4.html) into tabbedpanel.htm. The ilayer tag is a defunct tag that only works with Navigator 4. The nolayer tag includes the HTML div tags that are used with Internet Explorer 4 and later and Navigator 6 and later. I'll cover the nav4.html file first and then get back to these div tags.

Listing 16.1:   The Tabbed Panel HTML and Script (tabbedpanel.htm)

```
<html>
<head><title>Tabbed Panel</title>
<link rel="stylesheet" type="text/css" href="tabbedpanel.css">
<script language="JavaScript">
var panelID = "p1"
var numDiv = 8
var numRows = 2
var tabsPerRow = 4
var numLocations = numRows * tabsPerRow
var tabWidth = 90
var tabHeight = 30
var vOffset = 6
var hOffset = 10

var divLocation = new Array(numLocations)
var newLocation = new Array(numLocations)
```

```
    for(var i=0; i<numLocations; ++i) {
     divLocation[i] = i
     newLocation[i] = i
    }

    function getDiv(s,i) {
     var div
     if(navigator.appName == "Microsoft Internet Explorer"
       && navigator.appVersion.charAt(0) < 5)
      div = document.all.item(panelID+s+i)
     else if(navigator.appName == "Netscape" && navigator.appVersion.charAt(0) < 5)
      div = document.layers[panelID].layers[panelID+s+i]
     else div = document.getElementById(panelID+s+i)
     return div
    }
    function setZIndex(div, zIndex) {
     if(navigator.appName == "Netscape" && navigator.appVersion.charAt(0) < 5)
      div.zIndex = zIndex
     else div.style.zIndex = zIndex
    }
    function getLocation(i) {
     return divLocation[i]
    }
    function setLocation(i, j) {
     divLocation[i] = j
    }
    function getNewLocation(i) {
     return newLocation[i]
    }
    function setNewLocation(i, j) {
     newLocation[i] = j
    }
    function updatePosition(div, newPos) {
     if(navigator.appName == "Netscape" && navigator.appVersion.charAt(0) < 5) {
      div.top = (numRows-(Math.floor(newPos/tabsPerRow) + 1)) * (tabHeight-vOffset)
      div.left = (newPos % tabsPerRow) * tabWidth +
       (hOffset * (Math.floor(newPos / tabsPerRow)))
     }else {
      div.style.top = (numRows-(Math.floor(newPos/tabsPerRow) + 1))
    ↳  * (tabHeight-vOffset)
      div.style.left = (newPos % tabsPerRow) * tabWidth +
       (hOffset * (Math.floor(newPos / tabsPerRow)))
     }
    }

    function selectTab(n) {
     // n is the ID of the division that was clicked
     // firstTab is the location of the first tab in the selected row
     var firstTab = Math.floor(getLocation(n) / tabsPerRow) * tabsPerRow
     // newLoc is its new location
     for(var i=0; i<numDiv; ++i) {
```

```
     // loc is the current location of the tab
     var loc = getLocation(i)
     // If in the selected row
     if(loc >= firstTab && loc < (firstTab + tabsPerRow))
         setNewLocation(i, loc - firstTab)
     else if(loc < tabsPerRow) setNewLocation(i,firstTab+(loc % tabsPerRow))
     else setNewLocation(i, loc)
   }
   // Set tab positions & zIndex
   // Update location
   for(var i=0; i<numDiv; ++i) {
    var div = getDiv("tab",i)
    var loc = getNewLocation(i)
    updatePosition(div, loc)
    if(i == n) setZIndex(div, numLocations +1)
    else setZIndex(div,numLocations - loc)
    div = getDiv("panel",i)
    if(i == n) setZIndex(div, numLocations +1)
    else setZIndex(div, numLocations - loc)
    setLocation(i, loc)
   }
}
</script>
</head>
<body>
<h1>Tabbed Panel</h1>
<ilayer  id="p1" width="400" height="200" src="nav4.html">
</ilayer>
<nolayer>
<div style="background-color: transparent; position: relative;
  width: 400px; height: 200px">
<div class="tab" style="background-color: yellow;
 height: 78px;
 left: 0px;
 top: 24px;
 z-index: 8"
 id="p1tab0" onclick="selectTab(0)">HTML
</div>
<div class="tab" style="background-color: orange;
 height: 78px;
 left: 90px;
 top: 24px;
 z-index: 7"
 id="p1tab1" onclick="selectTab(1)">XHTML
</div>
<div class="tab" style="background-color: red;
 height: 78px;
 left: 180px;
 top: 24px;
 z-index: 6"
 id="p1tab2" onclick="selectTab(2)">CSS
```

```
</div>
<div class="tab" style="background-color: green;
 height: 78px;
 left: 270px;
 top: 24px;
 z-index: 5"
 id="p1tab3" onclick="selectTab(3)">DOM
</div>
<div class="tab" style="background-color: cyan;
 height: 78px;
 left: 10px;
 top: 0px;
 z-index: 4"
 id="p1tab4" onclick="selectTab(4)">JavaScript
</div>
<div class="tab" style="background-color: silver;
 height: 78px;
 left: 100px;
 top: 0px;
 z-index: 3"
 id="p1tab5" onclick="selectTab(5)">DHTML
</div>
<div class="tab" style="background-color: violet;
 height: 78px;
 left: 190px;
 top: 0px;
 z-index: 2"
 id="p1tab6" onclick="selectTab(6)">XML
</div>
<div class="tab" style="background-color: gray;
 height: 78px;
 left: 280px;
 top: 0px;
 z-index: 1"
 id="p1tab7" onclick="selectTab(7)">XSLT
</div>
<div class="panel" style="background-color: yellow;
 z-index: 8"
 id="p1panel0">
<h2>Hypertext Markup Language</h2>
<p><a href="http://www.w3.org/MarkUp/" target="external">HTML</a> is
 the language in which Web pages are written. HTML uses tags to
 identify how text is to be structured and formatted within a
 document. </p>
</div>
<div class="panel" style="background-color: orange;
 z-index: 7"
 id="p1panel1">
<h2>Extensible HyperText Markup Language</h2>
<p><a href="http://www.w3.org/TR/xhtml1/"
 target="external">XHTML</a>
```

```
 is a redevelopment and extension of HTML that makes HTML compatible
 with XML. XHTML specifies a family of markup languages that are
 based on HTML but take advantage of the simplicity, extensibility,
 and powerful toolset of XML. </p>
</div>
<div class="panel" style="background-color: red;
 z-index: 6"
 id="p1panel2">
<h2>Cascading Style Sheets</h2>
<p>CSS is a style sheet language that enables Web page writers to
 specify presentation, sizing, and positioning properties of HTML
 and XML documents. CSS is used to describe the appearance of a
 document in a manner that is independent of its content. There
 are currently two versions of CSS (referred to as
<a href="http://www.w3.org/TR/REC-CSS1" target="external">CSS1</a>
 and <a href="http://www.w3.org/TR/REC-CSS2"
 target="external">CSS2</a>). CSS2 extends CSS1.</p>
</div>
<div class="panel" style="background-color: green;
 z-index: 5"
 id="p1panel3">
<h2>Document Object Model</h2>
<p>The <a href="http://www.w3.org/DOM/" target="external">DOM</a>
 is a model that describes the objects that are available within
 HTML and XML documents. It describes these objects in a programming
 language-independent manner as a system of interfaces. It defines
 the properties of these objects and methods for accessing these
 objects. The objects can be accessed via programming languages,
 such as JavaScript and Java.</p>
</div>
<div class="panel" style="background-color: cyan;
 z-index: 4"
 id="p1panel4">
<h2>JavaScript</h2>
<p><a href="http://developer.netscape.com/javascript/"
 target="external">JavaScript</a> is a programming language for
 scripting Web pages that was developed by Netscape. It has been
 standardized by the ECMA and is referred to as ECMAScript.
 JavaScript has evolved into a general-purpose scripting language
 -- it is no longer limited to Web pages. Microsoft has also
 developed a version of JavaScript that is named JScript.</p>
</div>
<div class="panel" style="background-color: silver;
 z-index: 3"
 id="p1panel5">
<h2>Dynamic HTML</h2>
<p><a href="http://developer.netscape.com/dhtml/"
 target="external">DHTML</a> is a combination of HTML, CSS, and
 JavaScript that enables Web page content to exhibit dynamic
 behavior. This is accomplished by dynamically changing the
 properties of document objects in response to user actions and
```

```
  other events.</p>
</div>
<div class="panel" style="background-color: violet;
 z-index: 2"
 id="p1panel6">
<h2>Extensible Markup Language</h2>
<a href="http://www.w3.org/XML/" target="external">XML</a> is a
 language for creating structured documents for use with the Web and
 in other application areas. XML is a simplified subset of the
 Standard Generalized Markup Language (SGML) that is used to create
 custom markup languages that follow a common syntax.
</div>
<div class="panel" style="background-color: gray;
 z-index: 1"
 id="p1panel7">
<h2>XSL Transformations</h2>
<a href="http://www.w3.org/TR/xslt" target="external">XSLT</a> is a
 part of the Extensible Stylesheet Language (XSL) that is used to
 transform XML documents from one format into another format. XSLT
 style sheets are written in XML. These style sheets specify how XML
 documents are to be translated. They are provided as input to a
 translation program, which performs the actual translation.
</div>
</div>
<!-- The following tag is a spacer that is used to make sure that
markup that follows the tabbed panel is not covered by the panel.
Adjust the height attribute as desired. -->
<img border="0" height="50"><p>
</nolayer>
<hr>
</body>
</html>
```

Listing 16.2:   The Tabbed Panel Style Sheet (tabbedpanel.css)

```
.tab {font-family: sans-serif; line-height:150%;
   font-weight: bold; position:absolute;
   text-align: center; border: 2px; border-color:#999999;
   border-style: outset; border-bottom-style: none;
   width: 90px; margin:0px}

.panel {font-family: sans-serif; font-size: smaller;
   position:absolute; border: 2px; border-color:#999999;
   border-style:outset; width: 400px; height: 200px;
   left:0px; top:54px; margin:0px; padding:6px}

h1 {text-align: center}
```

The nav4.html file (Listing 16.3) contains a number of layer tags. The layer tags are defunct and only work with Navigator 4. Some of these layer tags define the tabs of the tabbed panel. Others define the panels. The onfocus event handlers of the tabs are set to the selectTab() function. This function switches the tabbed panel from one tab and panel to another.

Listing 16.3:   The Navigator 4 WorkAround (nav4.html)

```
<layer bgcolor="yellow"
 style="font-weight: bold; text-align: center"
 width="90"
 height="78"
 left="0"
 top="24"
 z-index="8" id="p1tab0"
 onfocus="selectTab(0)">HTML
</layer>

<layer bgcolor="orange"
 style="font-weight: bold; text-align: center"
 width="90"
 height="78"
 left="90"
 top="24"
 z-index="7" id="p1tab1"
 onfocus="selectTab(1)">XHTML
</layer>

<layer bgcolor="red"
 style="font-weight: bold; text-align: center"
 width="90"
 height="78"
 left="180"
 top="24"
 z-index="6" id="p1tab2"
 onfocus="selectTab(2)">CSS
</layer>

<layer bgcolor="green"
 style="font-weight: bold; text-align: center"
 width="90"
 height="78"
 left="270"
 top="24"
 z-index="5" id="p1tab3"
 onfocus="selectTab(3)">DOM
</layer>

<layer bgcolor="cyan"
```

```
 style="font-weight: bold; text-align: center"
 width="90"
 height="78"
 left="10"
 top="0"
 z-index="4" id="p1tab4"
 onfocus="selectTab(4)">JavaScript
</layer>

<layer bgcolor="silver"
 style="font-weight: bold; text-align: center"
 width="90"
 height="78"
 left="100"
 top="0"
 z-index="3" id="p1tab5"
 onfocus="selectTab(5)">DHTML
</layer>

<layer bgcolor="violet"
 style="font-weight: bold; text-align: center"
 width="90"
 height="78"
 left="190"
 top="0"
 z-index="2" id="p1tab6"
 onfocus="selectTab(6)">XML
</layer>

<layer bgcolor="gray"
 style="font-weight: bold; text-align: center"
 width="90"
 height="78"
 left="280"
 top="0"
 z-index="1" id="p1tab7"
 onfocus="selectTab(7)">XSLT
</layer>


<layer bgcolor="yellow"
 width="400"
 height="200"
 left="0"
 top="54"
 z-index="8"
 id="p1panel0">
<h2>Hypertext Markup Language</h2>
<p><a href="http://www.w3.org/MarkUp/" target="external">HTML</a> is
 the language in which Web pages are written. HTML uses tags to
 identify how text is to be structured and formatted within a
```

```
  document. </p>
</layer>

<layer bgcolor="orange"
 width="400"
 height="200"
 left="0"
 top="54"
 z-index="7"
 id="p1panel1">
<h2>Extensible HyperText Markup Language</h2>
<p><a href="http://www.w3.org/TR/xhtml1/"
 target="external">XHTML</a> is a redevelopment and extension of
 HTML that makes HTML compatible with XML. XHTML specifies a family
 of markup languages that are based on HTML but take advantage of
 the simplicity, extensibility, and powerful toolset of XML. </p>

</layer>

<layer bgcolor="red"
 width="400"
 height="200"
 left="0"
 top="54"
 z-index="6"
 id="p1panel2">
<h2>Cascading Style Sheets</h2>
<p>CSS is a style sheet language that enables Web page writers to
 specify presentation, sizing, and positioning properties of HTML
 and XML documents. CSS is used to describe the appearance of a
 document in a manner that is independent of its content. There are
 currently two versions of CSS (referred to as
<a href="http://www.w3.org/TR/REC-CSS1" target="external">CSS1</a>
 and <a href="http://www.w3.org/TR/REC-CSS2"
 target="external">CSS2</a>). CSS2 extends CSS1.</p>
</layer>

<layer bgcolor="green"
 width="400"
 height="200"
 left="0"
 top="54"
 z-index="5"
 id="p1panel3">
<h2>Document Object Model</h2>
<p>The <a href="http://www.w3.org/DOM/" target="external">DOM</a> is
 a model that describes the objects that are available within HTML
 and XML documents. It describes these objects in a programming
 language-independent manner as a system of interfaces. It defines
 the properties of these objects and methods for accessing these
 objects. The objects can be accessed via programming languages,
```

```
such as JavaScript and Java.</p>
</layer>

<layer bgcolor="cyan"
 width="400"
 height="200"
 left="0"
 top="54"
 z-index="4"
 id="p1panel4">
<h2>JavaScript</h2>
<p><a href="http://developer.netscape.com/javascript/"
 target="external">JavaScript</a> is a programming language for
 scripting Web pages that was developed by Netscape. It has been
 standardized by the ECMA and is referred to as ECMAScript.
 JavaScript has evolved into a general-purpose scripting language
 -- it is no longer limited to Web pages. Microsoft has also
 developed a version of JavaScript that is named JScript.</p>
</layer>

<layer bgcolor="silver"
 width="400"
 height="200"
 left="0"
 top="54"
 z-index="3"
 id="p1panel5">
<h2>Dynamic HTML</h2>
<p><a href="http://developer.netscape.com/dhtml/"
 target="external">DHTML</a> is a combination of HTML, CSS, and
 JavaScript that enables Web page content to exhibit dynamic
 behavior. This is accomplished by dynamically changing the
 properties of document objects in response to user actions and
 other events.</p>
</layer>

<layer bgcolor="violet"
 width="400"
 height="200"
 left="0"
 top="54"
 z-index="2"
 id="p1panel6">
<h2>Extensible Markup Language</h2>
<a href="http://www.w3.org/XML/" target="external">XML</a> is a
 language for creating structured documents for use with the Web and
 in other application areas. XML is a simplified subset of the
 Standard Generalized Markup Language (SGML) that is used to create
 custom markup languages that follow a common syntax.

</layer>
```

```
<layer bgcolor="gray"
  width="400"
  height="200"
  left="0"
  top="54"
  z-index="1"
  id="p1panel7">
<h2>XSL Transformations</h2>
<a href="http://www.w3.org/TR/xslt" target="external">XSLT</a> is a
  part of the Extensible Stylesheet Language (XSL) that is used to
  transform XML documents from one format into another format. XSLT
  style sheets are written in XML. These style sheets specify how XML
  documents are to be translated. They are provided as input to a
  translation program, which performs the actual translation.
</layer>
```

The `div` tags that are defined in `tabbedpanel.htm` (Listing 16.1) define tabs and panels that are analogous to the layers of Listing 16.3. The `onclick` event handlers of the `div` tags are set to the `selectTab()` function.

A number of variables are defined in the head of Listing 16.1. These variables are used by the script to access and manipulate the tabbed panels:

panelID   Gives the first part of each panel's `id` attribute. It is used to differentiate between multiple panels on the same page.

numDiv   Specifies the number of tab divisions.

numRows   Identifies the number of rows in the tabbed panel.

tabsPerRow   Specifies the number of tabs per row.

numLocations   Equals `numRows * tabsPerRow`.

tabWidth   Identifies the width of each tab.

tabHeight   Identifies the height of each tab.

vOffset   Specifies the vertical offset between tabs in adjacent rows.

hOffset   Specifies the horizontal offset between tabs in adjacent rows.

divLocation   Identifies the current location of each division. The location is the order that it appears in the tabbed panel.

newLocation   Specifies the new location of each division after tabs are changed.

The script in the document's head also defines the following functions:

getDiv(s, i)   Returns the *i*th tab or panel depending upon whether s is set to `tab` or `panel`.

setZIndex(div, zIndex)   Sets the zIndex property of the specified division. The zIndex determines the stacking order of a division. Higher zIndex divisions appear on top of lower zIndex divisions.

getLocation(i)   Returns the location of the *i*th tab. The location is the order that it appears in the tabbed panel.

setLocation(i, j)   Sets the location of the *i*th division to *j*.

getNewLocation(i)   Returns the new location of the *i*th division.

setNewLocation(i, j)   Sets the new location of the *i*th division.

updatePosition(div, newPos)   Updates the position of the specified division to newPos. Sets the division's style parameters (e.g., left and top) to reposition the division within the tabbed panel.

selectTab(n)   Handles the clicking of a tab. Moves the tabs and panels of the tabbed panel to display the selected tab and panel.

Creating a tabbed panel by hand can be a tedious process since it involves determining the absolute position of each tab and panel. In Chapter 24, "Working with XSLT," I'll show you how to specify the tabs and content of the panel using XML and then automatically generate the required JavaScript and XML via XSLT.

Building Collapsible Trees

Trees are one of my favorite GUI components. I like to collapse selected branches of a tree to focus on the top-level view of the information contained within the tree and then expand the branches of the tree to access important details. Listing 16.4 (tree.htm) provides an example tree that is implemented in JavaScript. Listing 16.5 (tree.css) provides a style sheet for the tree.

Listing 16.4:   The Tree HTML and Script (tree.htm)

```
<html>
<head>
<title>Tree Test</title>
<link rel="stylesheet" type="text/css" href="tree.css">
<script language="JavaScript">
var tree
if(isNav4() && navigator.tree8487 != undefined)
  // Use a unique value to differentiate with other concurrent tree objects
  tree = navigator.tree8487
else tree = createTree()
```

```
function isDOM1Capable() {
 if(document.getElementById) return true
 return false
}

function isIE4() {
 if(!isDOM1Capable() && document.all) return true
 return false
}

function isNav4() {
 if(navigator.appName == "Netscape" &&
   parseInt(navigator.appVersion) >= 4 &&
   parseInt(navigator.appVersion) < 5) return true
 return false
}

function createTree() {
 var nodes = new Array(
   "Tree Component",
   "Tackles problems of persistence and redisplay",
   "How can a complex object persist between page loadings?",
   "How can I redisplay a portion of a page?",
   "Exploits browser-unique features",
   "Navigator 4",
   "Uses <code>navigator</code> property for persistence.",
   "Internet Explorer 4 and DOM1-capable browsers",
   "Uses <code>innerHTML</code> property for redisplay",
   "Just a touch of DHTML",
   "Style sheets are used to shrink margins and hide links",
   "Easily tailored")
 var branches = new Array(new Array(0,1), new Array(0,4),
  new Array(0,10), new Array(0,11), new Array(1,2), new Array(1,3),
  new Array(4,5), new Array(4,7), new Array(5,6), new Array(7,8),
  new Array(7,9)
 )
 branchID = 0
 var subtrees = new Array()
 for(var i=0; i<nodes.length; ++i)
  subtrees[i] = new Tree(nodes[i])
 for(var i=0; i<branches.length; ++i)
  subtrees[branches[i][0]].addBranch(subtrees[branches[i][1]])
 return subtrees[0]
}

function Tree(root) {
 this.text = root
 this.id = branchID
 ++branchID
 this.expanded = true
 this.branches = new Array()
```

```
   this.addBranch = Tree_addBranch
   this.changeState = Tree_changeState
   this.handleClick = Tree_handleClick
   this.processClick = Tree_processClick
   this.display = Tree_display
   this.getTreeString = Tree_getTreeString
}
function Tree_addBranch(tree) {
   this.branches[this.branches.length] = tree
}
function Tree_changeState() {
   this.expanded = !this.expanded
}
function Tree_handleClick(branch) {
   this.processClick(branch)
   if(isNav4()) {
    navigator.tree8487 = tree
    window.location.reload()
   }else if(isDOM1Capable()) {
    var d = document.getElementById("tree")
    if(d != null) d.innerHTML = this.getTreeString()
   }else if(isIE4()) {
    var d = document.all("tree")
    if(d != null) d.innerHTML = this.getTreeString()
   }
}
function Tree_processClick(branch) {
   if(this.id == branch) this.changeState()
   else {
    for(var i=0; i<this.branches.length; ++i)
     this.branches[i].processClick(branch)
   }
}
function Tree_getTreeString() {
   var s = "<blockquote>"
   s += '<table border="0">'
   s += "<tr>"
   s += "<td>"
   if(this.branches.length > 0)
    s += '<a href="javascript:tree.handleClick('+this.id+')">+</a>'
   else s += "-"
   s += "</td>"
   s += "<td>"
   s += this.text
   s += "</td>"
   s += "</tr>"
   s += "</table>"
   if((this.branches.length > 0) && (this.expanded == true)) {
    for(var i=0; i<this.branches.length; ++i)
     s += this.branches[i].getTreeString()
   }
```

```
  s += "</blockquote>"
  return s
}
function Tree_display() {
  document.writeln(this.getTreeString())
}
</script>
</head>
<body>
<hr>
<div id="tree">
<script language="JavaScript">
tree.display()
</script>
</div>
<hr>
</body>
</html>
```

Listing 16.5: **The Tree Style Sheet (tree.css)**

```
BLOCKQUOTE {
margin-top: -5;
margin-bottom: -5;
}
TABLE {
margin-top: 0;
margin-bottom: 0;
}
A:link, A:visited {
  color: black;
  text-decoration: none;
}
```

When you open tree.htm, it displays the tree shown in Figure 16.3. You can collapse a branch of the tree by clicking on the plus sign (+) that appears in front of the branch (see Figure 16.4). If you click the plus sign a second time the branch is reopened, as shown in Figure 16.5.

FIGURE 16.3:

The initial tree display

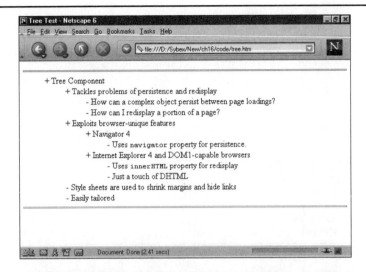

FIGURE 16.4:

You can collapse an outline level.

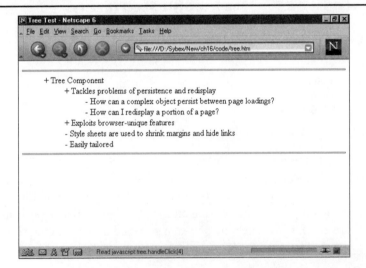

The tree is implemented as a JavaScript Tree object. As usual, a special workaround is provided to accommodate Navigator 4. The tree is displayed by constructing a Tree object and then invoking its display() method.

The Tree object shown in Listing 16.4 is created using the createTree() method. This method is invoked when the page is first loaded. In the case of Navigator 4, the tree is reloaded each time it is displayed/redisplayed. The tree8487 property of the navigator object is used to hold the state of the tree between reloads. The navigator object is unique to

Navigator and can be used to retain complex objects between documents. This capability is not needed with Internet Explorer 4 or later or Navigator 6 or later because these browsers are able to dynamically update a document without reloading it. The choice of `tree8487` for the name of the property is to emphasize that this property is dynamically defined (i.e., you pick the name) and that you should use a unique name that won't collide with other properties referencing other trees.

The `isDOM1Capable()`, `isIE4()`, and `isNav4()` methods are convenient methods for identifying the current browser.

Getting back to `createTree()`, you should note that the nodes (branches and leaves) of the tree are defined as a flat array. The structure of the tree is defined in the `branches` array. Each branch is a two-element array that identifies the index (within `nodes`) of the parent node and a child node. The `subtrees` array consists of an array of `Tree` objects, one for each node of the tree. The subtrees are pieced together to create the overall tree, which is returned by the `createTree()` method.

The `Tree` object defines the following properties:

text   The text associated with the tree node.

id   A unique ID for the tree node.

expanded   Whether the branch is expanded or collapsed.

branches   The subtrees that are branches of this tree.

The following methods are defined for the `Tree` object:

addBranch(tree)   Adds a `tree` as a branch of this tree.

changeState()   Changes the state of the expanded property.

handleClick(branch)   Handles the clicking of the branch's plus sign.

processClick(branch)   Supports by changing the expanded state of the appropriate branch of the tree.

display()   Displays the tree using the HTML returned by `getTreeString()`.

getTreeString()   Returns the HTML associated with the tree's display.

The `Tree` object reflects a compromise between the DOM1 and the capabilities of Navigator 4. A pure DOM1 `Tree` object could be defined to simply use HTML divisions and CSS.

FIGURE 16.5:

The outline is expanded again.

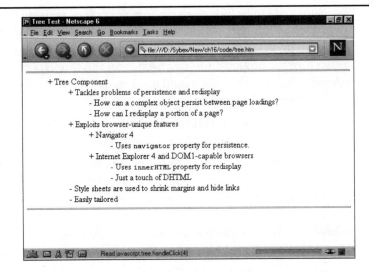

Creating Menu Bars

Menu bars are carried over from windows-based operating systems, like the MacOS, the X-Window system, and Microsoft Windows. They provide a handy way to organize a series of commands and to make these commands available without taking up too much display space. Listing 16.6 provides an example menu bar. When you open it in your browser, it displays the menu bar shown in Figure 16.6. If you click on a menu name, a list of menu items drops down, as shown in Figure 16.7. If you click on a menu item a command is executed. In the case of Listing 16.6, the commands are to display messages via alert dialog boxes. However, you can change these to load URLs or do other things.

Listing 16.6:   **A Menu Bar Example (menu.htm)**

```
<html>
<head>
<title>Menus</title>
<script language="JavaScript" src="menu.js">
</script>
<script language="JavaScript">
var menuBar1 = new MenuBar("menuBar1",70)
var companyMenu = new Menu("Company","#6666ff","black")
companyMenu.addMenuItem("General Info","alert('You selected: General Info')")
companyMenu.addMenuItem("History","alert('You selected: History')")
companyMenu.addMenuItem("Contact Us","alert('You selected: Contact Us')")
var servicesMenu = new Menu("Services","#ff6666","black")
```

```
servicesMenu.addMenuItem("Software Design","alert('You selected: Software
Design')")
servicesMenu.addMenuItem("Programming","alert('You selected: Programming')")
servicesMenu.addMenuItem("Training","alert('You selected: Training')")
var productsMenu = new Menu("Products","#66ff66","black")
productsMenu.addMenuItem("JavaScript Components","alert('You selected:
JavaScript Components')")
productsMenu.addMenuItem("Java Applets","alert('You selected: Java Applets')")
var supportMenu = new Menu("Support","#cccccc","black")
supportMenu.addMenuItem("FAQ","alert('You selected: FAQ')")
supportMenu.addMenuItem("Email Support","alert('You selected: Email Support')")
supportMenu.addMenuItem("Downloads","alert('You selected: Downloads')")
menuBar1.addMenu(companyMenu)
menuBar1.addMenu(servicesMenu)
menuBar1.addMenu(productsMenu)
menuBar1.addMenu(supportMenu)
</script>
</head>
<body>
<p> <br> </p>
<script language="JavaScript">
menuBar1.display(20,20)
</script>
<h1>A DHTML Menu Bar</h1>
<p>This menu works with DOM1-capable browsers,
Internet Explorer 4, and Navigator 4.</p>
<p>Click on a menu and a set of menu items appear. Then
click on the menu item to invoke the action associated
with the menu item.</p>
</body>
</html>
```

FIGURE 16.6:

The initial menu bar display

FIGURE 16.7:

A pull-down menu is displayed.

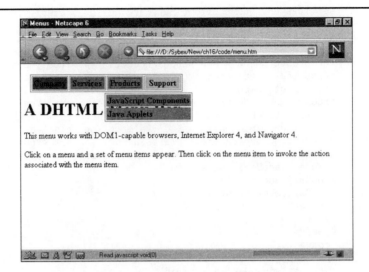

The menu bar is implemented using the MenuBar, Menu, and MenuItem objects defined in Listing 16.7. A menu bar consists of one or menus, each of which consists of one or more menu items.

The script shown in the head of the document of Listing 16.6 creates a MenuBar object and four Menu objects. It adds MenuItem objects to each of the Menu objects and the Menu objects to the MenuBar object. The display() method of the MenuBar object is used to display the menu bar.

Listing 16.7:   The Menu Script (menu.js)

```
// menu.js

// The MenuBar object

function MenuBar(reference, menuwidth) {
 this.reference = reference
 this.menuwidth = menuwidth
 this.menus = null
 this.menuClicked = -1
 this.browser = "unknown"
 if(navigator.appName == "Microsoft Internet Explorer" &&
   parseInt(navigator.appVersion) >= 4) this.browser = "ie4"
 else if(navigator.appName == "Netscape" &&
  parseInt(navigator.appVersion) >= 4 &&
   parseInt(navigator.appVersion) < 5) this.browser = "nav4"
 else if(navigator.appName == "Netscape" &&
   parseInt(navigator.appVersion) >= 5) this.browser = "nav6"
```

```
   this.addMenu = MenuBar_addMenu
   this.handleClick = MenuBar_handleClick
   this.hideMenu = MenuBar_hideMenu
   this.display = MenuBar_display
   this.displayIE4 = MenuBar_displayIE4
   this.displayNav4 = MenuBar_displayNav4
   this.displayNav6 = MenuBar_displayNav6
   this.showMenu = MenuBar_showMenu
   this.showMenuIE4 = MenuBar_showMenuIE4
   this.showMenuNav4 = MenuBar_showMenuNav4
   this.showMenuNav6 = MenuBar_showMenuNav6
}

function MenuBar_addMenu(menu) {
 if(this.menus == null) {
  this.menus = new Array(1)
  this.menus[0] = menu
 }else{
  var n = this.menus.length
  this.menus[n] = menu
 }
}

function MenuBar_handleClick(n) {
 if(this.menuClicked >= 0) {
  if(n == this.menuClicked) {
   this.hideMenu(n)
   this.menuClicked = -1
  }else{
   this.hideMenu(this.menuClicked)
   this.showMenu(n)
   this.menuClicked = n
  }
 }else{
  this.showMenu(n)
  this.menuClicked = n
 }
}

function MenuBar_hideMenu(n) {
 var menuItemDiv
 if(this.browser == "ie4") {
  menuItemDiv = document.all(this.reference+"."+n+".mi",0)
  menuItemDiv.style.visibility = "hidden"
 }else if(this.browser == "nav4") {
  menuItemDiv = document.layers[this.reference+"."+n+".mi"]
  menuItemDiv.visibility = "hidden"
 }else if(this.browser == "nav6") {
  menuItemDiv = document.getElementById(this.reference+"."+n+".mi")
  menuItemDiv.style.zIndex = -100
  menuItemDiv.style.visibility = "hidden"
```

```
 }
}

function MenuBar_showMenu(n) {
 if(this.browser == "ie4") this.showMenuIE4(n)
 else if(this.browser == "nav4") this.showMenuNav4(n)
 else if(this.browser == "nav6") this.showMenuNav6(n)
}

function MenuBar_showMenuIE4(n) {
 var menuBarDiv = document.all(this.reference,0)
 var menuDiv = document.all(this.reference+"."+n,0)
 var menuItemDiv = document.all(this.reference+"."+n+".mi",0)
 var menuBarX = menuBarDiv.offsetLeft
 var menuBarY = menuBarDiv.offsetTop
 var menuBarWidth = menuBarDiv.offsetWidth
 var menuBarHeight = menuBarDiv.offsetHeight
 var delta = 0
 for(var i=0; i<n; ++i) {
  var tempDiv = document.all(this.reference+"."+i,0)
   delta += tempDiv.offsetWidth + 6
 }
 menuItemDiv.style.left = menuBarX + delta
 menuItemDiv.style.top = menuBarY + menuBarHeight
 menuItemDiv.style.visibility = "visible"
}

function MenuBar_showMenuNav4(n) {
 var menuBarDiv = document.layers[this.reference]
 var menuItemDiv = document.layers[this.reference+"."+n+".mi"]
 var menuBarX = menuBarDiv.pageX
 var menuBarY = menuBarDiv.pageY
 var menuWidth = menuBarDiv.clip.width
 var menuHeight = menuBarDiv.clip.height
 var avgWidth = (n*(menuWidth/this.menus.length))
 menuItemDiv.pageX = menuBarX+avgWidth
 menuItemDiv.pageY = menuBarY+menuHeight
 menuItemDiv.visibility = "visible"
}

function MenuBar_showMenuNav6(n) {
 var menuBarDiv = document.getElementById(this.reference)
 var menuDiv = document.getElementById(this.reference+"."+n)
 var menuItemDiv = document.getElementById(this.reference+"."+n+".mi")
 var menuBarX = parseInt(menuBarDiv.style.left)
 var menuBarY = parseInt(menuBarDiv.style.top)
 var menuBarWidth = parseInt(menuBarDiv.style.marginTop)
 var menuBarHeight = parseInt(menuBarDiv.style.marginRight)
 var delta = this.menuwidth + 2
 if(delta == 2) delta = 75
 delta *= n
```

```
 menuItemDiv.style.left = menuBarX + delta + "px"
 menuItemDiv.style.top = menuBarY + 35 + "px"
 menuItemDiv.style.zIndex = 100
 menuItemDiv.style.visibility = "visible"
}

function MenuBar_display(x, y) {
 if(this.browser == "ie4") this.displayIE4(x,y)
 else if(this.browser == "nav4") this.displayNav4(x,y)
 else if(this.browser == "nav6") this.displayNav6(x,y)
}

function MenuBar_displayIE4(x,y) {
 var styleString = 'position: absolute; left: '+x+'; top: '+y
 document.writeln('<div id="'+this.reference+'" style="'+styleString+'">')
 document.write('<table border="1"><colgroup span="'+this.menus.length)
 document.writeln('" width="'+this.menuwidth+'"><tr>')
 for(var i=0; i<this.menus.length; ++i)
  this.menus[i].displayIE4(this.reference,i)
 document.writeln('</tr></table>')
 document.writeln('</div>')
 for(var i=0; i<this.menus.length; ++i)
  this.menus[i].displayMenuItemsIE4(this.reference,i)
}

function MenuBar_displayNav4(x,y) {
 var styleString = 'position: absolute; left: '+x+'; top: '+y
 document.writeln('<layer id="'+this.reference+'" pagex="'+x+'" pagey="'+y+'">')
 document.writeln('<table border="1"><tr>')
 for(var i=0; i<this.menus.length; ++i)
  this.menus[i].displayNav4(this.reference,i)
 document.writeln('</tr></table>')
 document.writeln('</layer>')
 for(var i=0; i<this.menus.length; ++i)
  this.menus[i].displayMenuItemsNav4(this.reference,i)
}

function MenuBar_displayNav6(x,y) {
 for(var i=0; i<this.menus.length; ++i)
  this.menus[i].displayMenuItemsNav6(this.reference,i)
 var styleString = 'position: absolute; left: '+x+'; top: '+y
 document.writeln('<div id="'+this.reference+'" style="'+styleString+'">')
 document.write('<table border="1"><colgroup span="'+this.menus.length)
 document.writeln('" width="'+this.menuwidth+'"><tr>')
 for(var i=0; i<this.menus.length; ++i)
  this.menus[i].displayNav6(this.reference,i)
 document.writeln('</tr></table>')
 document.writeln('</div>')
}

// The Menu object
```

```
function Menu(name, backgroundColor, textColor) {
 if(arguments.length < 3) textColor = "black"
 if(arguments.length < 2) backgroundColor = "white"
 this.name = name
 this.backgroundColor = backgroundColor
 this.textColor = textColor
 this.menuItems = null

 this.addMenuItem = Menu_addMenuItem
 this.displayIE4 = Menu_displayIE4
 this.displayNav4 = Menu_displayNav4
 this.displayNav6 = Menu_displayNav6
 this.displayMenuItemsIE4 = Menu_displayMenuItemsIE4
 this.displayMenuItemsNav4 = Menu_displayMenuItemsNav4
 this.displayMenuItemsNav6 = Menu_displayMenuItemsNav6
}

function Menu_addMenuItem(name, action) {
 var menuItem = new MenuItem(name, action)
 if(this.menuItems == null) {
  this.menuItems = new Array(1)
  this.menuItems[0] = menuItem
 }else{
  var n = this.menuItems.length
  this.menuItems[n] = menuItem
 }
}

function Menu_displayIE4(reference, menuNumber) {
 document.writeln('<th>')
 var id = ""+reference + "." + menuNumber
 document.write('<div id="'+id+'"'
↦ onclick="'+reference+'.handleClick('+menuNumber+')"')
 document.write(' style="padding: 2; background-color: '
↦ '+this.backgroundColor+'; color: ')
 document.writeln(this.textColor+'">')
 var styleString = "text-decoration: none; color: "+this.textColor
 document.writeln('<a href="javascript:void(0)"'
↦ style="'+styleString+'">'+this.name+'</a>')
 document.writeln('</div></th>')
}

function Menu_displayMenuItemsIE4(reference, menuNumber) {
 var id = ""+reference + "." + menuNumber + ".mi"
 var style="position: absolute; left: 10; top:10; visibility: hidden"
 document.write('<div id="'+id+'" style="'+style+'">')
 document.write('<table border="1">')
 for(var i=0; i<this.menuItems.length; ++i) {
  document.write('<tr><td bgcolor="'+this.backgroundColor+'">')
↦ color: "+this.textColor
```

```
    document.write('<a
href="javascript:'+reference+'.handleClick('+menuNumber+');')
    document.writeln(this.menuItems[i].action+'" style="'+styleString+'">')
    document.writeln(this.menuItems[i].name+'</a>')
    document.write('</td></tr>')
  }
  document.writeln('</table></div>')
}

function Menu_displayNav4(reference, menuNumber) {
  document.writeln('<th bgcolor="'+this.backgroundColor+'">')
  var anchorStart = '<a href="javascript:void(0)" '
  anchorStart += 'onclick="window.'+reference+'.handleClick('+menuNumber+')">'
  anchorStart += '<font color="'+this.textColor+'">'
  document.writeln(anchorStart+this.name+'</a>')
  document.writeln('</font></th>')
}

function Menu_displayMenuItemsNav4(reference, menuNumber) {
  var id = ""+reference + "." + menuNumber + ".mi"
  document.write('<layer id="'+id+'" pagex="10 pagey="10"')
  document.write(' visibility="hidden"><table border="1">')
  for(var i=0; i<this.menuItems.length; ++i) {
    document.write('<tr><td bgcolor="'+this.backgroundColor+'">')
    document.write('<a href="javascript:'+reference+'.handleClick('
↳
+menuNumber+');')
    document.writeln(this.menuItems[i].action+'"><font color="'+
↳
this.textColor+'"><b>')
    document.writeln(this.menuItems[i].name+'</b></font></a>')
    document.write('</td></tr>')
  }
  document.writeln('</table></layer>')
}

function Menu_displayNav6(reference, menuNumber) {
  document.writeln('<th>')
  var id = ""+reference + "." + menuNumber
  document.write('<div id="'+id+'"'
↳ onclick="'+reference+'.handleClick('+menuNumber+')"')
  document.write(' style="padding: 2; background-color:
↳ '+this.backgroundColor+'; color: ')
  document.writeln(this.textColor+'">')
  var styleString = "text-decoration: none; color: "+this.textColor
  document.writeln('<a href="javascript:void(0)"
↳ style="'+styleString+'">'+this.name+'</a>')
  document.writeln('</div></th>')
}

function Menu_displayMenuItemsNav6(reference, menuNumber) {
```

```
var id = ""+reference + "." + menuNumber + ".mi"
var style="position: absolute; left: 10; top:10; visibility: hidden"
document.write('<div id="'+id+'" style="'+style+'">')
document.write('<table border="1">')
for(var i=0; i<this.menuItems.length; ++i) {
  document.write('<tr><td bgcolor="'+this.backgroundColor+'">')
  var styleString = "font-weight: bold; text-decoration: none;
↳ color: "+this.textColor
  document.write('<a
href="javascript:'+reference+'.handleClick('+menuNumber+');')
  document.writeln(this.menuItems[i].action+'" style="'+styleString+'">')
  document.writeln(this.menuItems[i].name+'</a>')
  document.write('</td></tr>')
  }
  document.writeln('</table></div>')
}

// The MenuItem object

function MenuItem(name, action) {
  this.name = name
  this.action = action
  }
```

The *MenuBar* object

The MenuBar object defines the following properties:

reference   The name of a variable that references this MenuBar object.

menuwidth   The width of the menu bar.

menus   An array of menus contained in the menu bar.

menuClicked   The number of the menu bar that was clicked.

browser   The type of browser displaying the menu bar.

The following methods are defined for the MenuBar object:

addMenu(menu)   Adds a menu to the menu bar.

handleClick(n)   Handles the clicking of a menu.

hideMenu(n)   Hides the specified menu.

display(x, y)   Creates the HTML for the menu bar.

displayIE4(x, y)   Creates the HTML for the menu bar using the capabilities of Internet
Explorer 4 and later.

displayNav4(x, y) Creates the HTML for the menu bar using the capabilities of Navigator 4.

displayNav6(x, y) Creates the HTML for the menu bar using the capabilities of Navigator 6.

showMenu(n) Displays the specified menu.

showMenuIE4(n) Displays the specified menu using the capabilities of Internet Explorer 4 and later.

showMenuNav4(n) Displays the specified menu using the capabilities of Navigator 4.

showMenuNav6(n) Displays the specified menu using the capabilities of Navigator 6.

The *Menu* object

The Menu object defines the following properties:

textColor The color of the text of the menu.

backgroundColor The background color of the menu.

name The text of the menu.

menuItems An array of MenuItem objects.

The following methods are defined for the Menu object:

addMenuItem(name, action) Creates a MenuItem object and adds it to the menu.

displayIE4(reference, menuNumber) Displays a menu using the capabilities of Internet Explorer 4 or later.

displayNav4(reference, menuNumber) Displays a menu using the capabilities of Navigator 4.

displayNav6(reference, menuNumber) Displays a menu using the capabilities of Navigator 6.

displayMenuItemsIE4(reference, menuNumber) Displays the menu items of the specified menu using the capabilities of Internet Explorer 4 or later.

displayMenuItemsNav4(reference, menuNumber) Displays the menu items of the specified menu using the capabilities of Navigator 4.

displayMenuItemsNav6(reference, menuNumber) Displays the menu items of the specified menu using the capabilities of Navigator 6.

The *MenuItem* Object

The MenuItem object is pretty simple. It has two properties (name and action) and no methods. The name property specifies the text of the menu item. The action property is the action that is performed (i.e., JavaScript code that is executed) when the menu item is clicked.

Summary

In this chapter, you created three custom JavaScript components: a tabbed panel, a collapsible tree, and a menu bar with pull-down menus. These components work with Internet Explorer 4 and later and Navigator 4 and later. In the following chapter, you'll learn how to create additional components that provide accessories, such as a calendar and calculator, for use in your web pages.

CHAPTER 17

Developing Web Page Accessories

- The calendar accessory

- The calculator accessory

- To-do list

- World clock

- Assembling the desktop

One of the reasons for the success of windows-based operating systems is their ability to take the objects of your physical desktop—the clock, calendar, notepad, calculator, files, and so on—and make them available in electronic form. Software such as MacOS and Microsoft Windows were developed around this desktop metaphor. The World Wide Web, on the other hand, was designed using the metaphor of a library—we access electronic documents and view electronic pages. Now the Web and the desktop are beginning to converge. The browser has been integrated into windows-based operating systems and desktop programs are being executed on the Web.

In previous chapters, you developed several components that enhance the effectiveness of your web pages. These components are generic and can be tailored to a variety of needs. In this chapter, you'll learn how to develop JavaScript components that are not only eye-catching, but also useful. As you have probably guessed by now, you'll be developing desktop accessories—a calendar, a calculator, a to-do list, and a clock—that you'll be able to use with your own web pages. By themselves, these simple accessories won't likely make you a more productive person, but I will show you how you can incorporate such accessories into your web applications, which may be very useful for your business or personal needs.

Developing a Calendar Accessory

The first accessory that you'll develop is a calendar. Calendars are required by anyone who works or lives by a schedule. I constantly consult a calendar to schedule meetings, conferences, travel, and parties. In most cases, a simple monthly view is all I need to make these scheduling decisions. Why would you want to put a calendar on a web page? Well, if you were the leader of a rock band, you might want to tell your fans when and where to go for your next month's gigs. If you were an astronomer, you could let people know when to look for interesting celestial events. If you were a soccer coach, you could inform your players when practices and games would be held. Get the idea? In short, when there's a need to publicize a schedule, making it available electronically is a good way to do it.

The calendar that you'll develop in this section is only a calendar—it won't let you publish your schedule, it will just show you the days of the month. However, it can easily be added as an accessory to any schedule publishing application.

NOTE   When you run the calendar scripts of this chapter, they will display a calendar for the current month. The screen captures shown in this chapter were current for the month in which this chapter was written. Thus, your display and the chapter's screens will differ.

Listing 17.1 defines a `Calendar` object that displays the monthly calendar shown in Figure 17.1. The `calendar.js` serves as a building block for a general calendar application. It defines six functions: the `Calendar()` constructor, `displayCalendar()`, `displayCalendar-Header()`, `displayDates()`, `numberOfDays()`, and `writeDate()`. These functions are used as explained in the following subsections.

Listing 17.1:   The Calendar Object (calendar.js)

```
function Calendar() {
 var len = Calendar.arguments.length
 if(len == 2){
  this.month = Calendar.arguments[0]
  this.year = Calendar.arguments[1]
 }else{
  today = new Date()
  this.month = today.getMonth()
  this.year = today.getFullYear()
 }
 this.display = displayCalendar
}

function displayCalendar() {
 document.writeln("<TABLE BORDER='0' BGCOLOR='white'>")
 displayCalendarHeader(this.month,this.year)
 if(displayCalendar.arguments.length>0){
  var day = displayCalendar.arguments[0]-1
  displayDates(day,this.month,this.year,true)
 }else displayDates(0,this.month,this.year,false)
 document.writeln("</TABLE>")
}

function displayCalendarHeader(month,year) {
 var days = new Array("Sun","Mon","Tue","Wed","Thu",
  "Fri","Sat")
 var months = new Array("January","February","March","April",
  "May","June","July","August","September","October",
  "November","December")
 document.writeln("<TR><TH COLSPAN='7'><H2 ALIGN='CENTER'>")
 document.writeln(months[month])
 document.writeln(year+"</H2></TH></TR>")
 document.writeln("<TR>")
 for(var i=0;i<days.length;++i)
  document.writeln("<TH> "+days[i]+" </TH>")
 document.writeln("</TR>")
}

function displayDates(day,month,year,shade) {
 d = new Date(year,month,1)
 var startDay = d.getDay()
```

```
     var numDays = numberOfDays(month,year)
     var numRows = Math.floor((numDays+startDay)/7)
     if((numDays+startDay)%7 > 1) ++numRows
     var currentDate=0
     for(var i=0;i<numRows;++i) {
      document.writeln("<TR>")
      for(var j=0;j<7;++j) {
       if(shade && day==currentDate)
        document.write("<TD BGCOLOR='red'>")
       else document.write("<TD>")
       if(currentDate>=numDays) document.write(" ")
       else if(currentDate>0){
        ++currentDate
        writeDate(currentDate)
       }else if(i*7+j>=startDay){
        ++currentDate
        writeDate(currentDate)
       }else document.write(" ")
       document.writeln("</TD>")
      }
      document.writeln("</TR>")
     }
    }

    function numberOfDays(month,year) {
     var numDays=new Array(31,28,31,30,31,30,31,31,30,31,30,31)
     n = numDays[month]
     if(month == 1 && year % 4 == 0) ++n
     return n
    }

    function writeDate(n) {
     document.write("<H3 ALIGN='CENTER'>"+n+"</H3>")
    }
```

The *Calendar()* Constructor

This is the constructor for the Calendar object. It checks the number of arguments passed to it and creates a calendar using the current date or a specified month and year. It also defines the display() method using the displayCalendar() function.

The *displayCalendar()* Function

This function displays a monthly calendar as an HTML table. It invokes displayCalendar-Header() to display the table header and displayDates() to display the actual calendar dates. If a day of the month is passed as an argument to this function, then that day is highlighted in red when the calendar is displayed.

FIGURE 17.1:

Displaying the calendar
(Listing 17.1)

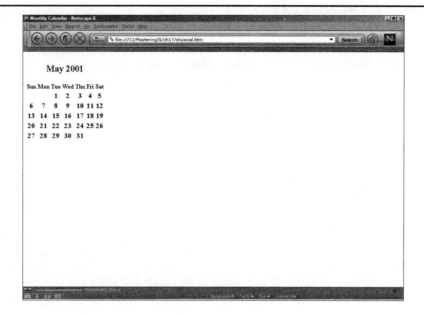

The *displayCalendarHeader()* Function

This function displays the calendar header—month, year, and days of the week.

The *displayDates()* Function

This function displays the days of the month. It figures out what day the month should begin on by creating a Date object for the first day of the month and by accessing its getDay() method. It invokes the numberOfDays() function to get the number of days in a particular month. It calculates the number of rows in the calendar table and then fills in those rows with the appropriate dates. If the shade argument is set to true, then the specified day is highlighted in red. Calendar days outside of the current month are ignored (a non-breaking space, , is used to fill the calendar entry of these days).

The *numberOfDays()* Function

This function calculates the number of days in a month. It takes leap years into account.

The *writeDate()* Function

This function writes the cells of the calendar table as centered Heading 3's.

To see how the Calendar object and functions of the calendar.js file work, open show-cal.htm (Listing 17.2) with your browser. It generates the display shown in Figure 17.1. The file showcal.htm is a simple HTML file with two scripts—one to read calendar.js and one to create and display a calendar. You can use calendar.js in your scripts in a similar fashion.

Listing 17.2:   Displaying the Calendar (showcal.htm)

```
<HTML>
<HEAD>
<TITLE>Monthly Calendar</TITLE>
<SCRIPT LANGUAGE="JavaScript" SRC="calendar.js"><!--
// --></SCRIPT>
</HEAD>
<BODY>
<SCRIPT LANGUAGE="JavaScript"><!--
cal=new Calendar()
cal.display()
// --></SCRIPT>
</BODY>
</HTML>
```

Because calendar.js is fairly modular, its functions can be used to build larger calendar applications. Let's do so now as a prelude to using calendar.js in your own web applications.

Open cal.htm with your browser, and it displays the web page shown in Figure 17.2. At the top of your screen are three buttons for displaying different monthly views. If you click the left arrow, the previous month is displayed, as shown in Figure 17.3. If you click the right arrow, the next month is displayed. Of course, if you click the Current Month button, the current month's calendar is displayed.

FIGURE 17.2:

The Calendar program opening display (Listing 17.3)

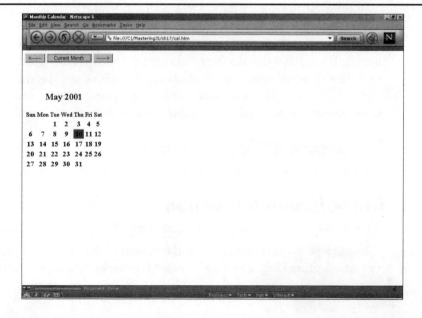

FIGURE 17.3:

FIGURE 17.3:

Displaying the previous month (Listing 17.3)

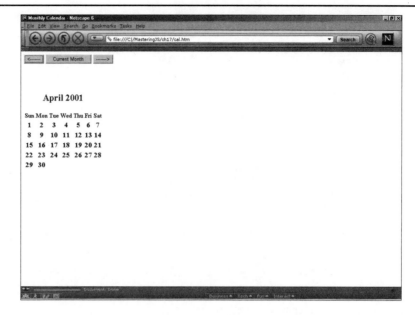

The button controls at the top of the calendar were added by creating a two-frame set. The buttons are placed in the top frame set and the calendar is displayed in the bottom frame set. Listing 17.3 shows how the frame sets were set up.

Listing 17.3:   Setting Up a Two-Frame Calendar (cal.htm)

```
<HTML>
<HEAD>
<TITLE>Monthly Calendar</TITLE>
<FRAMESET ROWS="77,*" BORDER="0">
<FRAME SRC="control.htm">
<FRAME SRC="calendar.htm">
</FRAMESET>
</HTML>
```

The control.htm file (Listing 17.4) is used to display the buttons in the top frame. Note that two hidden fields are used to hold the values of the current month and year of the calendar being displayed. These values are initially set to 99 and 0. The calendar.htm file recognizes these values as invalid and sets them to the values of the current month to mark them as invalid entries. (You can't have a month 99 and year 0 has long since passed. The calendar doesn't work for all historical dates.)

Listing 17.4:   The Calendar Controls (control.htm)

```
<HTML>
<HEAD>
<TITLE>Monthly Calendar</TITLE>
<SCRIPT LANGUAGE="JavaScript"><!--
function updateCalendar(month,year) {
 document.forms[0].monthValue.value=month
 document.forms[0].yearValue.value=year
 parent.frames[1].location="calendar.htm"
}
function previousMonth() {
 month=document.forms[0].monthValue.value
 year=document.forms[0].yearValue.value
 --month
 if(month<0) {
  if(year==0) month=0
  else{
   --year
   month=11
  }
 }
 updateCalendar(month,year)
}
function currentMonth() {
 var today=new Date()
 updateCalendar(today.getMonth(),today.getFullYear())
}
function nextMonth() {
 month=document.forms[0].monthValue.value
 year=document.forms[0].yearValue.value
 ++month
 if(month>11) {
  if(year==99) month=11
  else{
   ++year
   month=0
  }
 }
 updateCalendar(month,year)
}
// --></SCRIPT>
</HEAD>
<BODY>
<FORM NAME="changeMonth">
<INPUT TYPE="HIDDEN" NAME="monthValue" VALUE="99">
<INPUT TYPE="HIDDEN" NAME="yearValue" VALUE="0">
<INPUT TYPE="BUTTON" NAME="previous" VALUE="<-------"
 onClick="previousMonth()">
<INPUT TYPE="BUTTON" NAME="current" VALUE="Current Month"
```

```
 onClick="currentMonth()">
<INPUT TYPE="BUTTON" NAME="next" VALUE="------->"
 onClick="nextMonth()">
</FORM>
</BODY>
</HTML>
```

The previousMonth(), currentMonth(), and nextMonth() functions are used to handle the events associated with the clicking of the three buttons. They update the month and year as appropriate, and invoke updateCalendar() to store the new month and year values in the monthValue and yearValue hidden fields. The updateCalendar() function then reloads the bottom frame so that the calendar displayed reflects the new month and year values.

The calendar.htm file (Listing 17.5) displays the calendar in the bottom frame. It uses the calendar.js file to accomplish this purpose. It contains a small script that reads the month-Value and yearValue fields of the control.htm file and creates a calendar for the specified month and year. If the month is 99, then the script sets the month and year to the current date and updates the monthValue and yearValue fields with these values. If the month and year are current, then the current date is highlighted in red on the calendar.

Listing 17.5:   The Calendar Update Frame (calendar.htm)

```
<HTML>
<HEAD>
<TITLE>Monthly Calendar</TITLE>
<SCRIPT LANGUAGE="JavaScript" SRC="calendar.js"><!--
// --></SCRIPT>
</HEAD>
<BODY>
<SCRIPT LANGUAGE="JavaScript"><!--
formRef = parent.frames[0].document.forms[0]
month = parseInt(formRef.monthValue.value)
year = parseInt(formRef.yearValue.value)
today = new Date()
if(month==99) {
 month = today.getMonth()
 year = today.getFullYear()
 formRef.monthValue.value=""+month
 formRef.yearValue.value=""+year
}
cal=new Calendar(month,year)
if(month==today.getMonth() && year==today.getFullYear())
 cal.display(today.getDate())
else cal.display()
// --></SCRIPT>
</BODY>
</HTML>
```

Building a Calculator

Whenever I buy something online I always like to check the math on the final purchase price. I use a desktop calculator to do this. When I'm doing price comparisons between websites, I usually like to compare price, tax, and shipping to see where I can get the best deal. The calculator accessory introduced in this section can be added to a web page as a convenience to your users. It performs all the basic math needed to make price calculations.

To see the components in action, open `calc.htm` (see Listing 17.6) in your browser. It will display the calculator shown in Figure 17.6. Try using it to make some sample calculations. In Appendix A, "Doing Math," we'll build a more powerful scientific version of this calculator. The calculator is implemented as an HTML form. The calculator buttons are form buttons and the calculated value is stored in a text field. The `addDigit()`, `addDecimalPoint()`, `performOp()`, `calc()`, `changeSign()`, and `clearDisplay()` functions are used to handle the clicking of the calculator's buttons.

The calculator uses the `r` array to keep track of the operands entered by the user. The `ix` variable is an index into the `r` array. The `operand` variable identifies the operand (+, -, *, /, etc.) of the mathematical operation. The `state` variable identifies the current state of the calculator's processing. Valid states are `start`, `gettingInteger`, `gettingFloat`, `haveOperand`, and `getOperand2`. The `setStateState()` function initializes each of these variables.

The `addDigit()` function handles the clicking of the numbered buttons. It adds the digit to the appropriate operand and displays it. The `appendDigit()` function appends the last digit to the current digits of the current operand.

The `display()` function displays a string in the calculator's display field. The `clearDisplay()` function reinitializes the calculator and its display field.

The `addDecimalPoint()` function adds a decimal point to the current operand. The `changeSign()` function changes the sign of the current operand.

The `performOp()` function handles the clicking of a button that is associated with a mathematical operation. The `calc()` function handles the clicking of the equals button. The `calculateOperation()` function calculates the result of the operation.

FIGURE 17.4:

The simplified calculator
(Listing 17.6)

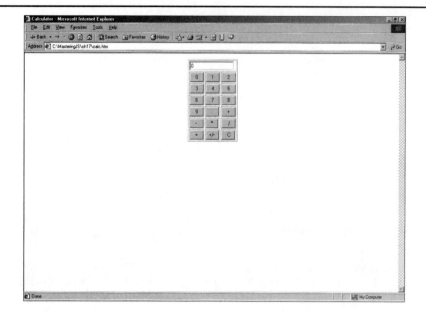

Listing 17.6:   The Calculator Program (calc.htm)

```
<HTML>
<HEAD>
<TITLE>Calculator</TITLE>
<SCRIPT LANGUAGE="JavaScript"><!--
r = new Array(2)
function setStartState(){
 state="start"
 r[0] = "0"
 r[1] = "0"
 operand=""
 ix=0
}
function addDigit(n){
 if(state=="gettingInteger" || state=="gettingFloat")
  r[ix]=appendDigit(r[ix],n)
 else{
  r[ix]=""+n
  state="gettingInteger"
 }
 display(r[ix])
}
function appendDigit(n1,n2){
 if(n1=="0") return ""+n2
 var s=""
```

```
  s+=n1
  s+=n2
  return s
}
function display(s){
 document.calculator.total.value=s
}
function addDecimalPoint(){
 if(state!="gettingFloat"){
  decimal=true
  r[ix]+="."
  if(state=="haveOperand" || state=="getOperand2") r[ix]="0."
  state="gettingFloat"
  display(r[ix])
 }
}
function clearDisplay(){
 setStartState()
 display(r[0])
}
function changeSign(){
 if(r[ix].charAt(0)=="-") r[ix]=r[ix].substring(1,r[ix].length)
 else if(parseFloat(r[ix])!=0) r[ix]="-"+r[ix]
 display(r[ix])
}
function calc(){
 if(state=="gettingInteger" || state=="gettingFloat" ||
  state=="haveOperand"){
  if(ix==1){
   r[0]=calculateOperation(operand,r[0],r[1])
   ix=0
  }
 }else if(state=="getOperand2"){
  r[0]=calculateOperation(operand,r[0],r[0])
  ix=0
 }
 state="haveOperand"
 decimal=false
 display(r[ix])
}
function calculateOperation(op,x,y){
 var result=""
 if(op=="+"){
  result=""+(parseFloat(x)+parseFloat(y))
 }else if(op=="-"){
  result=""+(parseFloat(x)-parseFloat(y))
 }else if(op=="*"){
  result=""+(parseFloat(x)*parseFloat(y))
 }else if(op=="/"){
  if(parseFloat(y)==0){
   alert("Division by 0 not allowed.")
```

```
    result=0
   }else result=""+(parseFloat(x)/parseFloat(y))
  }
  return result
}
function performOp(op){
 if(state=="start"){
  ++ix
  operand=op
 }else if(state=="gettingInteger" || state=="gettingFloat" ||
  state=="haveOperand"){
  if(ix==0){
   ++ix
   operand=op
  }else{
   r[0]=calculateOperation(operand,r[0],r[1])
   display(r[0])
   operator=op
  }
 }
 state="getOperand2"
 decimal=false
}
// --></SCRIPT>
</HEAD>
<BODY>
<SCRIPT LANGUAGE="JavaScript"><!--
setStartState()
// --></SCRIPT>
<FORM NAME="calculator">
<TABLE BORDER="BORDER" ALIGN="CENTER">
<TR>
<TD COLSPAN="3"><INPUT TYPE="TEXT" NAME="total" VALUE="0"
 SIZE="15"></TD></TR>
<TR>
<TD><INPUT TYPE="BUTTON" NAME="n0" VALUE="   0   "
 ONCLICK="addDigit(0)"></TD>
<TD><INPUT TYPE="BUTTON" NAME="n1" VALUE="   1   "
 ONCLICK="addDigit(1)"></TD>
<TD><INPUT TYPE="BUTTON" NAME="n2" VALUE="   2   "
 ONCLICK="addDigit(2)"></TD>
</TR>
<TR>
<TD><INPUT TYPE="BUTTON" NAME="n3" VALUE="   3   "
 ONCLICK="addDigit(3)"></TD>
<TD><INPUT TYPE="BUTTON" NAME="n4" VALUE="   4   "
 ONCLICK="addDigit(4)"></TD>
<TD><INPUT TYPE="BUTTON" NAME="n5" VALUE="   5   "
 ONCLICK="addDigit(5)"></TD>
</TR>
<TR>
```

```
<TD><INPUT TYPE="BUTTON" NAME="n6" VALUE="    6    "
  ONCLICK="addDigit(6)"></TD>
<TD><INPUT TYPE="BUTTON" NAME="n7" VALUE="    7    "
  ONCLICK="addDigit(7)"></TD>
<TD><INPUT TYPE="BUTTON" NAME="n8" VALUE="    8    "
  ONCLICK="addDigit(8)"></TD>
</TR>
<TR>
<TD><INPUT TYPE="BUTTON" NAME="n9" VALUE="    9    "
  ONCLICK="addDigit(9)"></TD>
<TD><INPUT TYPE="BUTTON" NAME="decimal" VALUE="    .    "
  ONCLICK="addDecimalPoint()"></TD>
<TD><INPUT TYPE="BUTTON" NAME="plus" VALUE="    +    "
  ONCLICK="performOp('+')"></TD>
</TR>
<TR>
<TD><INPUT TYPE="BUTTON" NAME="minus" VALUE="    -    "
  ONCLICK="performOp('-')"></TD>
<TD><INPUT TYPE="BUTTON" NAME="multiply" VALUE="    *    "
  ONCLICK="performOp('*')"></TD>
<TD><INPUT TYPE="BUTTON" NAME="divide" VALUE="    /    "
  ONCLICK="performOp('/')"></TD>
</TR>
<TR>
<TD><INPUT TYPE="BUTTON" NAME="equals" VALUE="    =    "
  ONCLICK="calc()"></TD>
<TD COLSPAN="1" ROWSPAN="1"><INPUT TYPE="BUTTON"
  NAME="sign" VALUE=" +/-  " ONCLICK="changeSign()"></TD>
<TD><INPUT TYPE="BUTTON" NAME="clearField" VALUE="    C    "
  ONCLICK="clearDisplay()"></TD>
</TR>
</TABLE>
</FORM>
</BODY>
</HTML>
```

Creating a To-Do List

When you're browsing the Web, would you like to take notes on a particular web page and have those notes available to you whenever you revisit the page? I know I would. You could take notes to summarize the important points of a web-based document, to identify other relevant URLs, or just to keep track of when or why you last visited the page.

This section presents an approach to maintaining private notes on public websites. In keeping with the desktop metaphor, it implements this approach in terms of a to-do list—a very handy tool for people who have a lot to do! It can easily be tailored to a general-purpose notepad by just changing its heading.

Open `notes.htm` with your browser. It generates the display shown in Figure 17.5. Now type a list of things that you have to do—your to-do list—as shown in Figure 17.6. Exit your browser, wait a few seconds, and then reopen `notes.htm`. Your notes are still there, on that web page! The best thing about it is that nobody else can read them. This may not seem all that exciting, but it is an important capability. You can add the same type of note area to your web pages. People can jot down notes to themselves about your web pages and when they return to your web page, their notes will still be there—but only for their own use.

FIGURE 17.5:

The to-do list opening display (Listing 17.7)

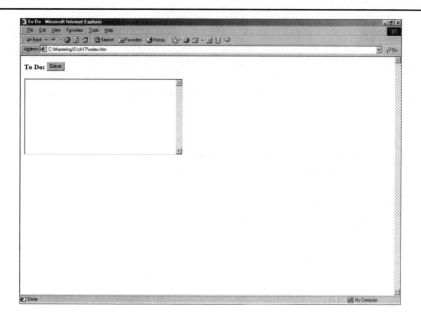

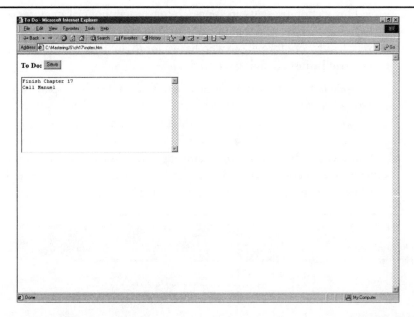

How does notes.htm (Listing 17.7) work? You probably guessed it—cookies. Cookies are used to store the notes entered by the user. These notes are stored on the user's system, so you don't have to worry about making disk space available for them. When the user revisits your web page, they are automatically reloaded by his or her browser.

Listing 17.7:   The To-Do List Script (notes.htm)

```
<HTML>
<HEAD>
<TITLE>To Do</TITLE>
<SCRIPT LANGUAGE="JavaScript" SRC="cookie.js"><!--
// --></SCRIPT>
<SCRIPT LANGUAGE="JavaScript"><!--
function loadNotes() {
 var cookie=document.cookie
 if(nameDefined(cookie,"toDo")) {
  todo=getCookieValue(cookie,"toDo")
  todo=decode(todo)
 }else todo=""
 document.forms[0].notes.value=todo
}
function saveNotes() {
 todo=window.document.forms[0].notes.value
 todo=encode(todo)
 var newCookie = "toDo="+todo+"; expires="
```

```
  newCookie += "Tuesday, 09-Nov-10 23:12:40 GMT"
  document.cookie=newCookie
}
function encode(s) {
 t=""
 for(var i=0;i<s.length;++i) {
  ch=s.charAt(i)
  if(ch=="/") t += "//"
  else if(ch==" ") t += "/b"
  else if(ch==",") t += "/."
  else if(ch==";") t += "/:"
  else if(ch=="\n") t += "/n"
  else if(ch=="\r") t += "/r"
  else if(ch=="\t") t += "/t"
  else if(ch=="\b") t += "/b"
  else t += ch
 }
 return t
}
function decode(s) {
 // Decode the encoded cookie value
 t=""
 if(s==null) return t
 for(var i=0;i<s.length;++i) {
  var ch=s.charAt(i)
  if(ch=="/") {
   ++i
   if(i<s.length){
   ch=s.charAt(i)
   if(ch=="/") t += ch
   else if(ch==".") t += ","
   else if(ch==":") t += ";"
   else if(ch=="n") t += "\n"
   else if(ch=="r") t += "\r"
   else if(ch=="t") t += "\t"
   else if(ch=="b") t += " "
   }
  }else t += ch
 }
 return t
}
// --></SCRIPT>
</HEAD>
<BODY>
<FORM>
<H3>To Do:
<INPUT NAME="save" TYPE="BUTTON" VALUE="Save"
 onClick="saveNotes()"></H3>
<TEXTAREA NAME="notes" ROWS="12" COLS="50"
 VALUE=""></TEXTAREA>
</FORM>
```

```
<SCRIPT LANGUAGE="JavaScript"><!--
  loadNotes()
// --></SCRIPT>
</BODY>
</HTML>
```

The notes.htm file uses the cookie-reading functions of cookie.js (Listing 17.8). You've already used these functions in Chapter 10, "Working with Links," and Chapter 11, "Using Images." They are nameDefined(), removeBlanks(), and getCookieValue().

Listing 17.8:   Common Cookie Functions (cookie.js)

```
function nameDefined(c,n) {
 var s=removeBlanks(c)
 var pairs=s.split(";")
 for(var i=0;i<pairs.length;++i) {
  var pairSplit=pairs[i].split("=")
  if(pairSplit[0]==n) return true
 }
 return false
}
function removeBlanks(s) {
 var temp=""
 for(var i=0;i<s.length;++i) {
  var c=s.charAt(i)
  if(c!=" ") temp += c
 }
 return temp
}
function getCookieValue(c,n) {
 var s=removeBlanks(c)
 var pairs=s.split(";")
 for(var i=0;i<pairs.length;++i) {
  var pairSplit=pairs[i].split("=")
  if(pairSplit[0]==n) return pairSplit[1]
 }
 return ""
}
```

The file notes.htm defines four other functions—loadNotes(), saveNotes(), encode(), and decode()—to process the text that is entered into its text area field. These functions are used as explained in the following subsections.

The *loadNotes()* Function

This function uses nameDefined() and getCookieValue() to read the value of the toDo cookie. It invokes decode() to decode the cookie value.

The *saveNotes()* Function

This function reads the notes entered into the text area field and invokes encode() to encode them in a form that is suitable for storage in a cookie. It then creates a new toDo cookie with a 2010 expiration date. (I picked 2010 arbitrarily. There is no reason you can't go beyond the year 2010.)

The *encode()* Function

White-space characters, semicolons, and commas cannot be stored as part of a cookie's name=value pair. This function encodes such strings into a form that is suitable for cookie storage. The conversions carried out by the encode() function are listed in Table 17.1.

TABLE 17.1: String to Cookie Encoding Performed by encode() and decode()

String character	Cookie character
/	//
space	/b
,	/.
;	/:
\n (new line)	/n
\r (carriage return)	/r
\t (tab)	/t
\b (backspace)	/b

The *decode()* Function

This function decodes a stored cookie string in accordance with Table 17.1.

Using the World Clock Accessory

The Web never sleeps. Someone could be browsing your web page at any time of the day. They could be viewing it from Europe, Asia, Africa, Australia, or North or South America. In some cases, you may want to display the current date and time along with your web page. But when people view your web page, they are more concerned about the time of day where they are rather than the time of day where your web page is located.

If you add the time to your web pages via a CGI program, you will have a hard time converting your time to the local time of your web users. Fortunately, JavaScript can be easily used to display the user's local time and identify the user's time-zone offset from Greenwich Mean Time (GMT).

Open clock.htm with your browser and your browser will display the day of the week, the date, your local time, and your time-zone offset from GMT, as shown in Figure 17.7. Take a closer look at your browser display. Notice the seconds tick by. Your browser updates the time in one-second intervals. This allows you to update the time as your web page sits on your user's browser. You can even tell your user how long he or she has been at your web page—an important capability if you decide to charge someone based on access time.

FIGURE 17.7:

The world-clock display
(Listing 17.9)

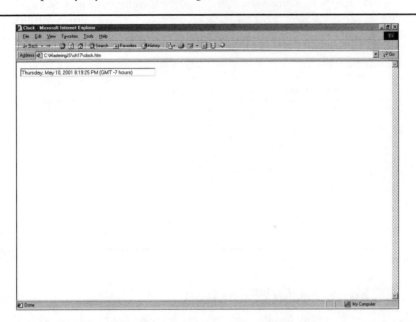

The script used in clock.htm (Listing 17.9) is fairly short, but it illustrates some important points. The clock text field takes its value directly from the dateTime() function. The tick() function is then invoked to start the clock running. This function updates the value of the clock field and then sets a one-second timeout so it can reinvoke itself. The dateTime() function returns a string containing the day, date, time, and time-zone offset.

Listing 17.9:   A Clock Script (clock.htm)

```
<HTML>
<HEAD>
<TITLE>Clock</TITLE>
<SCRIPT LANGUAGE="JavaScript"><!--
function dateTime() {
```

```
    var now = new Date()
    var result = now.toLocaleString()
    var tzOffset=-now.getTimezoneOffset()/60
    if(tzOffset<0) result += " (GMT "+tzOffset+" hours)"
    else result += " (GMT +"+tzOffset+" hours)"
    return result
}
function tick() {
  document.forms[0].clock.value=dateTime()
  setTimeout("tick()",1000)
}
// --></SCRIPT>
</HEAD>
<BODY>
<FORM>
<INPUT NAME="clock" TYPE="TEXT" SIZE="50"
  VALUE="&{dateTime()};">
</FORM>
<SCRIPT LANGUAGE="JavaScript"><!--
tick()
// --></SCRIPT>
</BODY>
</HTML>
```

Assembling the Desktop

Now that you've developed the clock, calendar, calculator, and to-do list, wouldn't you like to put them all together in one web page? You'll learn how to do that, so you can see them working together and envision how to integrate them with your own web pages. The hard part has been completed—the accessories have been developed. All you need to do now is to assemble them into a common desktop.

Open desktop.htm and you'll see the web page shown in Figure 17.8. You can watch the clock tick, flip through the calendar, make some notes, or calculate how much your next raise should be.

FIGURE 17.8:

The desktop display integrates each of the desktop accessories. (Listing 17.10)

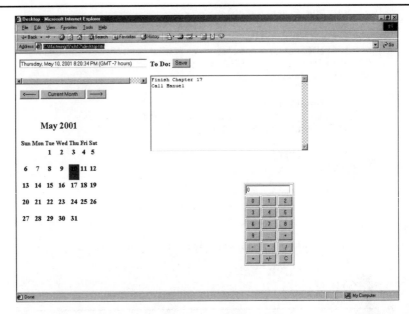

The desktop.htm file (Listing 17.10) is the first of two levels of frame sets. It defines two columns that contain the files cal-clock.htm (Listing 17.11) and notes-calc.htm (Listing 17.12). The cal-clock.htm file creates a frame set for displaying the clock and the calendar. The notes-calc.htm file creates a frame set for displaying the to-do list and the calculator. Notice how simple it is to integrate all four accessories into a single web application.

Listing 17.10:   Defining the Top-Level Frame Set (desktop.htm)

```
<HTML>
<HEAD>
<TITLE>Desktop</TITLE>
<FRAMESET COLS="350,*" BORDER="0">
<FRAME SRC="cal-clock.htm">
<FRAME SRC="notes-calc.htm">
</FRAMESET>
</HTML>
```

Listing 17.11:   Defining the Left Frame Set (cal-clock.htm)

```
<HTML>
<HEAD>
<TITLE>Desktop</TITLE>
<FRAMESET ROWS="80,*" BORDER="0">
<FRAME SRC="clock.htm">
```

```
<FRAME SRC="cal.htm">
</FRAMESET>
</HTML>
```

Listing 17.12:   Defining the Right Time Set (notes-calc.htm)

```
<HTML>
<HEAD>
<TITLE>Desktop</TITLE>
<FRAMESET ROWS="325,*" BORDER="0">
<FRAME SRC="notes.htm">
<FRAME SRC="calc.htm">
</FRAMESET>
</HTML>
```

Summary

In this chapter, you learned how to develop four common desktop accessories—a calendar, a calculator, a clock, and a to-do list—and integrate them into a web page–based application: a web desktop. You are finally learning how to develop scripts that are both useful and reusable. In the next chapter, you'll learn how to use JavaScript to help your users navigate your website.

CHAPTER 18

Developing Search Tools

- Using search forms

- Including search engines

- Connecting search forms to search engines

- Creating local search engines

Some of the most frequently visited websites are those that help you to find other web pages. Google, Yahoo!, Go, and Lycos are some of the many popular search sites. In addition, many large sites (such as Microsoft's and CNN's) provide site-specific search capabilities.

JavaScript makes implementing search capabilities in your web pages easy. You can use JavaScript to develop a full-featured search interface to connect to existing search engines or to implement your own browser-based search scripts.

In this chapter, you'll learn to integrate search capabilities in your web pages. You'll learn to use JavaScript to write interfaces to search engines and to implement local search capabilities. When you finish this chapter, you'll be able to incorporate advanced search features in your web pages.

Search Forms

Search forms are used to gather search information from a user and forward it to one or more search engines. The search engines then perform the search and forward the search results back to the user. Because the search form is what the user sees when he or she performs the search, it is important to provide an interface that is flexible, efficient, and easy to use.

JavaScript-based search forms have a major advantage over those that are implemented in HTML alone—they allow form-related events to be handled locally. This lets you develop forms that can dynamically adapt to entries the user may have made previously. These dynamic forms help users to specify search criteria more easily and efficiently. Dynamic search forms can also be used to present a more flexible and intuitive interface to the user. They can also be used to validate form data and provide users with suggestions on how to enter data correctly.

NOTE   In this chapter, I've provided three different search engines for different purposes. For each example in the chapter, I'll instruct you to rename `engines1.htm`, `engines2.htm`, or `engines3.htm` to simply `engines.htm` to run the appropriate search engine in the particular example being discussed. Go ahead and rename `engines1.htm` to `engines.htm` before running the first example. These files need to be copied from the CD to a working directory in order to be renamed and work correctly.

To get a better feel for how JavaScript can be used to enhance a search interface, consider the search form shown in Figure 18.1. This form allows you to select a particular web technology area of interest and then a specific topic within that area. Open the file search.htm (Listing 18.1) with your browser to see how this form works.

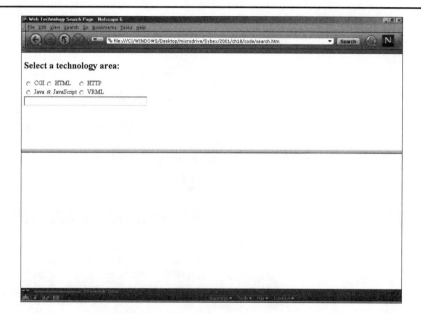

When you click on a Select a Technology Area radio button, the list of topic links to the right changes to reflect the area you selected. For this example, click the HTTP technology area and the list of topics is updated with links that are specific to HTTP—Specification, Security, and Versions—as shown in Figure 18.2. Click the Security link; a web search engine form is displayed, as shown in Figure 18.3. Note that the area and topic the user selected, in this case HTTP and security, are automatically inserted into the search text field. Forms such as the ones shown in this example make it much easier for the user to formulate a search query. In "Connecting Search Forms to Search Engines" section later in this chapter, you'll learn how to connect this form to a search engine.

FIGURE 18.2:

Selecting a technology area
(Listings 18.1 through 18.3)

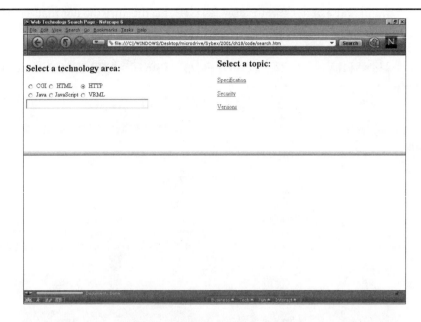

FIGURE 18.3:

Selecting a search engine
(Listing 18.4)

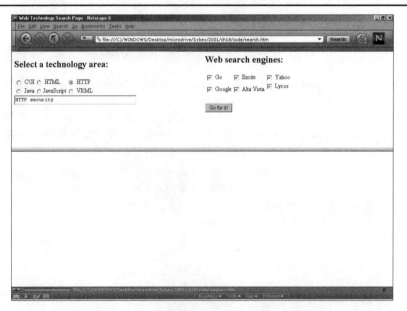

Listing 18.1 contains the search.htm file. This file sets up a two-frame set with sform.htm (Listing 18.2) loaded into the top frame. Listing 18.2 shows that sform.htm breaks the top

frame into two columns, with topic.htm loaded into the left frame. The topic.htm file is shown in Listing 5.3.

Listing 18.1:   The Search Form's Top-Level Frame Set (search.htm)

```
<HTML>
<HEAD>
<TITLE>Web Technology Search Page</TITLE>
</HEAD>
<FRAMESET ROWS="250,*" BORDER="10">
<FRAME SRC="sform.htm">
<FRAME SRC="blank.htm">
</FRAMESET>
</HTML
```

Listing 18.2:   The Search Form's Second-Level Frame Set (sform.htm)

```
<HTML>
<HEAD>
<TITLE>Web Technology Search Page</TITLE>
</HEAD>
<FRAMESET COLS="*,*" BORDER="0">
<FRAME SRC="topic.htm">
<FRAME SRC="blank.htm">
</FRAMESET>
</HTML>
```

The topic.htm file implements the search form. It creates the radio button form shown in the upper-left frame of Figure 18.1 and implements the following functions and arrays.

The *Topic()* Function

This function is the constructor of the search's Topic object. A Topic consists of a topic title and a string of keywords to search for that are related to this topic.

The *topics* Array

The topics array is an array of the arrays of all topics supported for each technology area. For example, topics[0] identifies the topics related to the CGI area, topics[1] identifies the topics related to HTML, and so on.

The *displayTopics()* Function

The displayTopics() function creates the document shown in the upper-right frame of the window. It creates a link for each topic in the topics array related to the technology area.

The engines.htm file is the destination of each link. The setSearch() function is the onClick event handler for each link. The setSearch() function displays the link's search string in the text field of the frame located in the upper left of the window.

Listing 18.3: Implementing the Search Form (topic.htm)

```
<HTML>
<HEAD>
<TITLE>Web Technologies Search Form</TITLE>
<SCRIPT LANGUAGE="JavaScript"><!--
function Topic(desc,search) {
 this.desc=desc
 this.search=search
}

topics = new Array()
topics[0] = new Array(
 new Topic("Tutorials","CGI tutorial"),
 new Topic("Documentation","CGI documentation"),
 new Topic("Examples","CGI example"),
 new Topic("Using cookies","CGI cookies")
)
topics[1] = new Array(
 new Topic("HTML 2.0","HTML 2.0"),
 new Topic("HTML 3.0","HTML 3.0"),
 new Topic("HTML 3.2","HTML 3.2"),
 new Topic("Extensions","HTML extensions"),
 new Topic("Tutorials","HTML tutorial")
)
topics[2] = new Array(
 new Topic("Specification","HTTP specification"),
 new Topic("Security","HTTP security"),
 new Topic("Versions","HTTP version")
)
topics[3] = new Array(
 new Topic("Documentation","Java documentation"),
 new Topic("Tutorials","Java tutorial"),
 new Topic("Examples","Java example"),
 new Topic("Shareware","Java shareware")
)
topics[4] = new Array(
 new Topic("Documentation","JavaScript documentation"),
 new Topic("Tutorials","JavaScript tutorial"),
 new Topic("Examples","JavaScript example")
)
topics[5] = new Array(
 new Topic("Documentation","VRML documentation"),
 new Topic("Tutorials","VRML tutorial"),
 new Topic("Examples","VRML example"),
 new Topic("Web sites","VRML sites")
```

```
)

function displayTopics(n) {
 var doc=parent.frames[1].document
 doc.open()
 doc.writeln('<HTML>')
 doc.writeln('<HEAD>')
 doc.writeln('<SCRIPT LANGUAGE="JavaScript">')
 doc.writeln('function setSearch(s) {')
 doc.writeln('text=parent.frames[0].document.forms[0].srch')
 doc.writeln('text.value=s')
 doc.writeln('}')
 doc.writeln('</SCRIPT>')
 doc.writeln('</HEAD>')
 doc.writeln('<BODY BGCOLOR="white">')
 doc.writeln('<H2>Select a topic:</H2>')
 for(var i=0;i<topics[n].length;++i) {
  doc.writeln('<P><A HREF="engines.htm" ')
  doc.writeln('onClick="setSearch(\''+topics[n][i].search+'\')">')
  doc.writeln(topics[n][i].desc+'</A></P>')
 }
 doc.writeln('</BODY>')
 doc.writeln('</HTML>')
 doc.close()
}
// --></SCRIPT>
</HEAD>
<BODY BGCOLOR="white">
<FORM>
<H2>Select a technology area:</H2>
<TABLE>
<TR><TD><P>
<INPUT TYPE="RADIO" NAME="area" VALUE="cgi"
 onClick="displayTopics(0)"> CGI</P></TD>
<TD><P>
<INPUT TYPE="RADIO" NAME="area" VALUE="html"
 onClick="displayTopics(1)"> HTML</P></TD>
<TD><P>
<INPUT TYPE="RADIO" NAME="area" VALUE="http"
 onClick="displayTopics(2)"> HTTP</P></TD>
</TR>
<TR><TD><P>
<INPUT TYPE="RADIO" NAME="area" VALUE="java"
 onClick="displayTopics(3)"> Java</P></TD>
<TD><P>
<INPUT TYPE="RADIO" NAME="area" VALUE="javascript"
 CHECKED="CHECKED" onClick="displayTopics(4)">JavaScript</P>
<TD><P>
<INPUT TYPE="RADIO" NAME="area" VALUE="vrml"
 onClick="displayTopics(5)"> VRML</P></TD>
</TR>
```

```
</TABLE>
<INPUT TYPE="text" NAME="srch" SIZE="40">
</FORM>
<SCRIPT LANGUAGE="JavaScript"><!--
displayTopics(4)
// --></SCRIPT>
</BODY>
</HTML>
```

Search Engines

Search engines are programs (usually CGI scripts) that perform a search and generate search results. They commonly use one or more databases to keep track of a large collection of URLs for web pages and the keywords that the pages contain. JavaScript scripts can make use of and enhance the capabilities provided by these CGI-based search engines. The following sections show how to design a JavaScript-based search page and how to connect your scripts to available search engines.

The First Search Engine

The engines1.htm file (see Listing 18.4) is the first of three search "engines" that you'll be creating in the examples in this chapter. You must rename this file to engines.htm for it to be used with the current version of our search form. This file is not in itself a search engine—in fact, this version doesn't actually perform any searching at all. Instead, it displays a handful of popular and freely available web search engines, shown in the upper-right frame of Figure 18.3. It also handles the onClick event of the Go for It! button using the goSearch() function (which is a function stub that will implemented in engines2.htm and engines3.htm, search engines that are introduced in later sections of this chapter).

NOTE
The file engines1.htm we're using in this example will be the basis of the other two engines we develop later in the chapter. The file engines2.htm will make use of the six web search engines listed in this example to perform actual searching, and the file engines3.htm will be adapted for use as a local search engine.

Listing 18.4: Selecting a Search Engine (engines1.htm)

```
<HTML>
<HEAD>
<TITLE>Web Search Engines</TITLE>
<SCRIPT LANGUAGE="JavaScript"><!--
function goSearch() {
```

```
doc = top.frames[1].document
doc.write("<H2>This function is implemented in ")
doc.write("<CODE>engines2.htm</CODE> and ")
doc.writeln("<CODE>engines3.htm</CODE>.</H2>")
}
// --></SCRIPT>
</HEAD>
<BODY BGCOLOR="white">
<H2>Web search engines:</H2>
<FORM>
<TABLE>
<TR>
<TD><INPUT TYPE="CHECKBOX" CHECKED NAME="go"> Go
</TD>
<TD><INPUT TYPE="CHECKBOX" CHECKED NAME="excite"> Excite
</TD>
<TD><INPUT TYPE="CHECKBOX" CHECKED NAME="yahoo"> Yahoo
</TD>
</TR>
<TR>
<TD><INPUT TYPE="CHECKBOX" CHECKED NAME="google"> Google
</TD>
<TD><INPUT TYPE="CHECKBOX" CHECKED NAME="altaVista"> Alta Vista
</TD>
<TD><INPUT TYPE="CHECKBOX" CHECKED NAME="lycos"> Lycos</P>
</TD>
</TR>
</TABLE>
<P><INPUT TYPE="BUTTON" VALUE="Go for it!"
 onClick="goSearch()"></P>
</FORM>
</BODY>
</HTML>
```

Connecting Search Forms to Search Engines

To perform a search, you must pass the search criteria gathered from the user (via the search form) to the CGI program implementing the search engine. This search criteria is generally passed in the form of a query string.

A query string passes data to a CGI program via the URL used to access the CGI program. It consists of a question mark (?) followed by the data to be passed. For example, the following URL passes the string This is a test to the echo-query.cgi CGI program:

```
http://www.jaworski.com/cgi-bin/echo-query.cgi?This+is+a+test
```

You may have noticed in this URL that spaces are encoded with plus signs (+) when they are passed via query strings. Other codings are used to pass special characters and binary data as described in RFC 1738, "Uniform Resource Locators (URL)." This RFC is available at http://nic.mil/ftp/rfc/rfc1738.txt. The coding of form data is covered in the HTML 4 specification (www.w3.org/TR/REC-html40/html140.txt).

Listing 18.5 shows how search data can be passed to more than one search engine at the same time. It builds upon the first example shown in this chapter by adding the JavaScript necessary to implement the goSearch() function. First, you must rename engines2.htm as engines.htm (in order to install that file as the new search engine for the search form introduced in the previous section). Then open search.htm with your browser. Finally, make sure that you are connected to the Internet, because the engines2.htm file contains links to connect your search form to popular online search engines.

Listing 18.5:   **Connecting to Other Search Engines (engines2.htm)**

```
<HTML>
<HEAD>
<TITLE>Web Search Engines</TITLE>
<SCRIPT LANGUAGE="JavaScript"><!--
function goSearch() {
 searchString=parent.frames[0].document.forms[0].srch.value
 searchString=convertToQueryString(searchString)
 var n=numberOfSearchSites()
 createFrames(n)
 setTimeout("loadFrames("+n+")",2000)
}
function convertToQueryString(s) {
 var result=""
 for(var i=0;i<s.length;++i)
  if(s.charAt(i)==' ') result+="+"
  else result+=s.charAt(i)
 return result
}
function numberOfSearchSites() {
 var result=0
 var elements=window.document.forms[0].elements
 for(var i=0;i<elements.length-1;++i)
  if(elements[i].checked) ++result
 return result
}
function createFrames(n) {
 if(n>1)
   parent.parent.frames[1].location.href="frames"+n+".htm"
}
function loadFrames(n) {
 var mainFrame=parent.parent.frames[1]
 var newStart
 if(n==1) loadNextFrame(mainFrame,0)
 else if(n==2) {
```

```
  newStart=loadNextFrame(mainFrame.frames[0],0)
  loadNextFrame(mainFrame.frames[1],newStart)
}else if(n==3) {
  newStart=loadNextFrame(mainFrame.frames[0],0)
  newStart=loadNextFrame(mainFrame.frames[1],newStart)
  loadNextFrame(mainFrame.frames[2],newStart)
}else if(n==4) {
  newStart=loadNextFrame(mainFrame.frames[0].frames[0],0)
  newStart=loadNextFrame(mainFrame.frames[0].frames[1],newStart)
  newStart=loadNextFrame(mainFrame.frames[1].frames[0],newStart)
  loadNextFrame(mainFrame.frames[1].frames[1],newStart)
}else if(n==5) {
  newStart=loadNextFrame(mainFrame.frames[0].frames[0],0)
  newStart=loadNextFrame(mainFrame.frames[0].frames[1],newStart)
  newStart=loadNextFrame(mainFrame.frames[1].frames[0],newStart)
  newStart=loadNextFrame(mainFrame.frames[1].frames[1],newStart)
  loadNextFrame(mainFrame.frames[2],newStart)
}else if(n==6) {
  newStart=loadNextFrame(mainFrame.frames[0].frames[0],0)
  newStart=loadNextFrame(mainFrame.frames[0].frames[1],newStart)
  newStart=loadNextFrame(mainFrame.frames[1].frames[0],newStart)
  newStart=loadNextFrame(mainFrame.frames[1].frames[1],newStart)
  newStart=loadNextFrame(mainFrame.frames[2].frames[0],newStart)
  loadNextFrame(mainFrame.frames[2].frames[1],newStart)
 }
}
function loadNextFrame(frameObj,start) {
 var elements=window.document.forms[0].elements
 for(var i=start;i<elements.length-1;++i) {
  if(elements[i].checked){
   var searchURL="http://"
   if(elements[i].name=="go")
    searchURL+=" www.goto.com/d/search/p/go/?Partner=go_home&Keywords="
   else if(elements[i].name=="excite")
    searchURL+="www.excite.com/search.gw?search="
   else if(elements[i].name=="yahoo")
    searchURL+="search.yahoo.com/bin/search?p="
   else if(elements[i].name=="google")
    searchURL+="www.google.com/search?q="
   else if(elements[i].name=="altaVista"){
    searchURL+="www.altavista.digital.com"
    searchURL+="/cgi-bin/query?pg=q&what=web&fmt=.&q="
   }else if(elements[i].name=="lycos")
    searchURL+="www.lycos.com/cgi-bin/pursuit?query="
   searchURL+=searchString
   frameObj.location.href=searchURL
   return (i+1)
  }
 }
 return start
```

```
        }
        // --></SCRIPT>
        </HEAD>
        <BODY BGCOLOR="white">
        <H2>Web search engines:</H2>
        <FORM>
        <TABLE>
        <TR>
        <TD><INPUT TYPE="CHECKBOX" CHECKED NAME="go"> Go
        </TD>
        <TD><INPUT TYPE="CHECKBOX" CHECKED NAME="excite"> Excite
        </TD>
        <TD><INPUT TYPE="CHECKBOX" CHECKED NAME="yahoo"> Yahoo
        </TD>
        </TR>
        <TR>
        <TD><INPUT TYPE="CHECKBOX" CHECKED NAME="google"> Google
        </TD>
        <TD><INPUT TYPE="CHECKBOX" CHECKED NAME="altaVista"> Alta Vista
        </TD>
        <TD><INPUT TYPE="CHECKBOX" CHECKED NAME="lycos"> Lycos</P>
        </TD>
        </TR>
        </TABLE>
        <P><INPUT TYPE="BUTTON" VALUE="Go for it!"
         onClick="goSearch()"></P>
        </FORM>
        </BODY>
        </HTML>
```

For this example, click on the VRML radio button and then on the Examples link. The Web Search Engines form appears in the upper-right frame. Click on the Go for It! button to perform a search for the string "VRML example" using all of the six major search engines. The search results produced by these engines are provided in six separate frames at the bottom of the window (refer to Figure 18.4). You can click on the links in each of these frames to find more information on VRML examples. Wouldn't it be impressive to provide the same search capabilities in your web pages?

FIGURE 18.4:

Using all six search engines at once (Listing 18.5)

Figure 18.5 shows the results of a search that uses only four search engines. Figure 18.6 shows the results of a single engine search.

FIGURE 18.5:

Using four search engines (Listing 18.5)

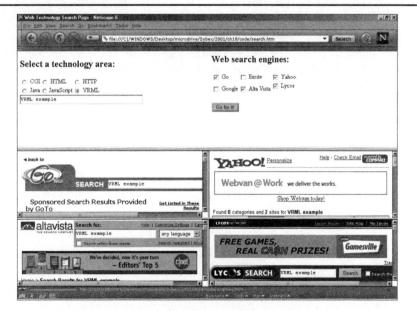

FIGURE 18.6:

Using a single search
engine (Listing 18.5)

The Second Search Engine

The engines2.htm search engine is more of a transmission than an engine. It takes the search string produced by the search form introduced in the previous section and converts it into a form that can be used with popular web search engines. It then prompts these engines to perform a search of the search string and displays the results they return in separate frames. The following functions are implemented by engines2.htm:

The *goSearch()* function   This function handles the onClick event of the Go for It! button and initiates the search. It retrieves the search string contained in the text field of the frame in the upper-left corner of the window and converts it to a URL query string using the convertToQueryString() function. It determines how many search sites the user selected in the Web Search Engines form, creates that many frames to store the query results, and waits two seconds before invoking loadFrames() to load the search results into these frames. The two-second delay is used to make sure that the new frames are created before the search is initiated. If you have a low-powered computer, then you may wish to increase the delay. You can also use an onLoad event handler to check for form loading.

The *convertToQueryString()* function   This function converts spaces in the search string to plus signs (+) so that the search string can be passed via a query string.

The *numberOfSearchSites()* function   This function determines how many web search sites were chosen by the user in the Web Search Engines form.

The *createFrames()* function   This function creates the required number of frames to display the search results by loading the appropriate document (from the set of documents named `frames2.htm` through `frames6.htm`) into the lower frame of the window. These files are shown in Listings 18.6 through 18.11.

The *loadFrames()* function   This function uses the `loadNextFrame()` function to perform the search and loads the results into the frames created by the `createFrames()` function. The `loadNextFrame()` function is passed the frame that the search results should be loaded into; it is also passed the index of the next search site to be considered as a candidate for searching.

The *loadNextFrame()* function   This function uses a search site to perform a search and stores the results in a designated frame. The `frameObj` parameter identifies the frame in which the search results should be loaded. The `start` parameter identifies the index of the next search site to be considered as a candidate for searching. If the check box at the specified index is not selected, then subsequent check boxes are examined for the next search site to be used. This function prepares the URLs necessary to using the Go, Excite, Yahoo!, Google, AltaVista, and Lycos search engines and appends the value of the `search-String` variable to these URLs. The search is initiated by setting the destination frame's location property to the search URL.

NOTE   The URLs of the search engines used in `loadNextFrame()` were determined by trial and error, playing with the search engines at each search site. The conventions used in these URLs are specific to each site.

The following `frames*.htm` files (Listings 18.6–18.10) are used by the `engines2.htm` file to create frames to display the results of the web search engines. The `double.htm` file (Listing 18.11) splits a frame into a two-column frame set.

Listing 18.6:   Displaying the Results of Two Search Engines (frames2.htm)

```
<HTML>
<FRAMESET ROWS="*,*" BORDER="5">
<FRAME SRC="blank.htm">
<FRAME SRC="blank.htm">
</FRAMESET>
</HTML>
```

Listing 18.7:   Displaying the Results of Three Search Engines (frames3.htm)

```
<HTML>
<FRAMESET ROWS="*,*,*" BORDER="5">
<FRAME SRC="blank.htm">
<FRAME SRC="blank.htm">
<FRAME SRC="blank.htm">
</FRAMESET>
</HTML>
```

Listing 18.8:   Displaying the Results of Four Search Engines (frames4.htm)

```
<HTML>
<FRAMESET ROWS="*,*" BORDER="5">
<FRAME SRC="double.htm">
<FRAME SRC="double.htm">
</FRAMESET>
</HTML>
```

Listing 18.9:   Displaying the Results of Five Search Engines (frames5.htm)

```
<HTML>
<FRAMESET ROWS="*,*,*" BORDER="5">
<FRAME SRC="double.htm">
<FRAME SRC="double.htm">
<FRAME SRC="blank.htm">
</FRAMESET>
</HTML>
```

Listing 18.10:   Displaying the Results of Six Search Engines (frames6.htm)

```
<HTML>
<FRAMESET ROWS="*,*,*" BORDER="5">
<FRAME SRC="double.htm">
<FRAME SRC="double.htm">
<FRAME SRC="double.htm">
</FRAMESET>
</HTML>
```

> **Listing 18.11:   Creating Two Columns (double.htm)**

```
<HTML>
<FRAMESET COLS="*,*" BORDER="5">
<FRAME SRC="blank.htm">
<FRAME SRC="blank.htm">
</FRAMESET>
</HTML>
```

Local Search Engines

A local search engine is one that implements search algorithms on the browser instead of using a server-based CGI program. The main advantage of local search engines is that they take the processing load off of your server and put it on the browser. Their main disadvantage is that they are downloaded to the browser and are therefore limited in the amount of search data that they can contain. Local search engines may be impractical for searching large websites (such as those of Microsoft, IBM, and Sun), but they may be the perfect solution for searching the websites of small- to medium-size companies. Local search engines may also be combined with server-based search engines to take some of the processing load off the server-based search engines.

Keyword Search Scripts

For small to medium-size websites, simple *keyword search scripts* may be used as local search engines. These scripts present a selection list of terms (keywords) that categorize or describe web pages that you think may be of interest to the user. The keywords you provide should be categories that you think the page's topics might fall into or words and phrases that you think users might use to describe the page's content. For example, for a document about server-side web programming, you might list the keywords *CGI*, *LiveWire*, *Perl* as categories, and/or *programming*, *client/server*, and so on as descriptions.

The advantages of keyword scripts are that they are small, user-friendly, and easy to develop. Their main disadvantage is that they become unwieldy when the number of keywords used becomes large.

Keyword search scripts can be created in such a way that when the user clicks on a keyword, the URLs for relevant web pages are displayed. Of course, you can also create a script that first offers topic or category keywords (as you first saw in search.htm at the beginning of the chapter), which would link to more-detailed lists of keywords that are linked to specific URLs. This latter approach is the one we've been building up to throughout the chapter and is the approach I'll be illustrating with the following listing.

Listing 18.12 provides an example of a local search engine that provides lists of keywords to choose from in various categories and at various levels of focus (for documents of interest to the entire company, to a company division, or to a single department). To run this example, rename engines3.htm to engines.htm to use it with the search form developed in the first section of this chapter. After renaming it, open search.htm and, for this example, try the following keyword searches:

1. Click on the Java radio button in the Select a Technology Area frame, then click the Documentation link in the Select a Topic frame.

2. Scroll to the right (if necessary) in the upper panel to see the choices offered by the Search Depth form.

3. Choose the Department button to perform a department-level search, then click on the Go for It! button. The search results are shown in Figure 18.7.

Listing 18.12:   A Local Search Engine (engines3.htm)

```
<HTML>
<HEAD>
<TITLE>Local Search Engine</TITLE>
<SCRIPT LANGUAGE="JavaScript" SRC="db.js"><!--
// --></SCRIPT>
<SCRIPT LANGUAGE="JavaScript"><!--
scope=0
function goSearch() {
 searchString=parent.frames[0].document.forms[0].srch.value
 searchString=convertToQueryString(searchString)
 performSearch()
 listURLs()
}
function convertToQueryString(s) {
 var result=""
 for(var i=0;i<s.length;++i)
  if(s.charAt(i)==' ') result+="+"
  else result+=s.charAt(i)
 return result
}
function performSearch() {
 strings=searchString.split("+")
 buildHitList()
 for(var i=0;i<strings.length;++i)
  updateSearch(strings[i])
}
function buildHitList() {
 if(scope==0) hitList = new Array(deptURLs.length)
 else if(scope==1) hitList = new Array(divURLs.length)
 else if(scope==2) hitList = new Array(sectURLs.length)
```

```
   for(var i=0;i<hitList.length;++i) hitList[i]=true
  }
 function updateSearch(s) {
  var mask = new Array(hitList.length)
  for(var i=0;i<mask.length;++i) mask[i]=false
  for(var i=0;i<dictionary.length;++i) {
   if(dictionary[i]==s) {
    for(var j=0;j<db[i][scope].length;++j) {
     mask[db[i][scope][j]]=true
    }
   }
  }
  for(var i=0;i<hitList.length;++i)
   hitList[i]=hitList[i] && mask[i]
 }
 function listURLs() {
  doc=parent.parent.frames[1].document
  doc.open()
  var hitCount=0
  var urlSet = deptURLs
  if(scope==1) urlSet=divURLs
  else if(scope==2) urlSet=sectURLs
  doc.writeln("<HTML><BODY BGCOLOR='white'>")
  for(var i=0;i<hitList.length;++i) {
   if(hitList[i]) {
    ++hitCount
    doc.writeln("<P>"+urlSet[i].link(urlSet[i])+" ")
    doc.writeln("<B>"+urlDescs[scope][i]+"</B></P>")
   }
  }
  doc.writeln("<H2>"+hitCount+" matches.</H2>")
  doc.writeln("</BODY></HTML>")
  doc.close()
 }
// --></SCRIPT>
</HEAD>
<BODY BGCOLOR="white">
<H2>Search depth:</H2>
<FORM>
<P><INPUT TYPE="RADIO" CHECKED NAME="depth" VALUE="dept"
 onClick="scope=0">Department
</P><P><INPUT TYPE="RADIO" NAME="depth" VALUE="div"
 onClick="scope=1"> Division
</P><P><INPUT TYPE="RADIO" NAME="depth" VALUE="sect"
 onClick="scope=2"> Sector
</P>
<P><INPUT TYPE="BUTTON" VALUE="Go for it!"
 onClick="goSearch()"></P>
</FORM>
</BODY>
</HTML>
```

FIGURE 18.7:

Searching for documents
related to Java at the
department level
(Listing 18.12)

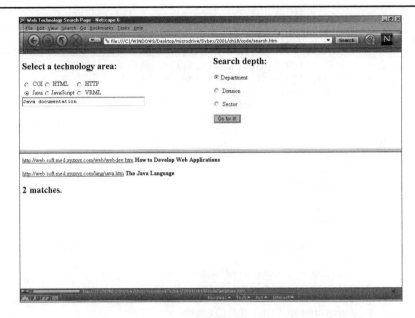

The Search depth form in this example provides local search capabilities at different levels, in this case at department, division, and sector levels. I chose these levels to reflect the differences in scope you might want to address within a company's organization. In this example, the company is considered to be comprised of sectors, which are made up of divisions, which consist of departments. Documents that are intended for readership at the sector level are for the use of all divisions and departments within the sector. Other documents may be intended for both the division and sector levels, and still others may be of interest only within a department.

When you perform a similar search for JavaScript documentation at the division level, you see the results shown in Figure 18.8. Searching for VRML tutorials at the sector level produces the result shown in Figure 18.9.

FIGURE 18.8:

Searching for documents relating to JavaScript at the division level (Listing 18.12)

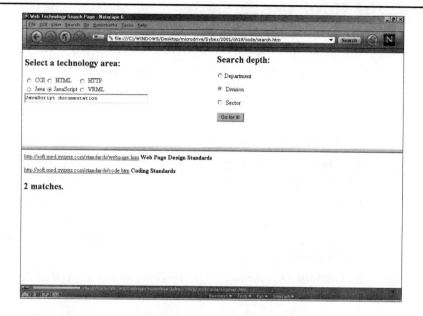

FIGURE 18.9:

Searching for documents relating to VRML at the sector level (Listing 18.12)

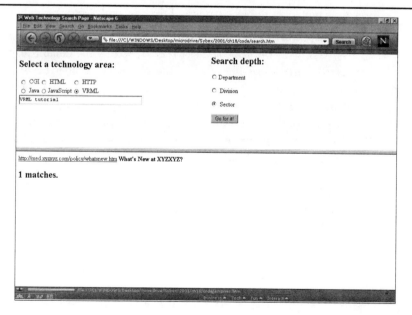

The Third Search Engine

The engines3.htm file implements the local search engine using the following functions. Note that the JavaScript code it includes is contained in db.js.

The *goSearch()* function   This function handles the onClick event of the Go for It! button and initiates the search. It retrieves the search string contained in the text field of the frame in the upper-left corner of the window and converts it to a URL query string using the convertToQueryString() function. It then invokes performSearch() to perform the search and listURLs() to display the search results.

The *convertToQueryString()* function   This function converts spaces in the search string to plus signs (+) so that it can be passed via a query string.

The *performSearch()* function   This function searches the search database for each word in the search string. The buildHitList() function builds a list of candidate URLs, referred to as a *hit list*. The updateSearch() function updates the hitList array based on the search for each word.

The *buildHitList()* function   This function creates a list of all URLs that are candidates for the search. This hitList is implemented as indices into the deptURLs, divURLs, or sectURLs arrays defined in db.js. The scope variable is set to 0, 1, or 2 by the onClick event handlers of the Department, Division, and Sector radio buttons.

The *updateSearch()* function   This function performs the central search processing. It creates a mask array the same size as hitList, setting the default search value to false. It then finds the search word identified by the s variable in the dictionary array (defined in db.js). It sets the values of the mask array to true depending on whether the value of s is contained in a document in the list of URLs specified by the scope variable. Refer to the description of the db array (defined in db.js) for more information on how this is accomplished. The values of the elements of the mask array are then logically *AND*ed with the values of the elements of the hitList array to identify which URLs are still search candidates.

The *listURLs()* function   This function uses the hitList array to display the URLs and their descriptions in the lower frame of the window. The urlSet variable is assigned the deptURLs, divURLs, or sectURLs array depending upon the value of scope. It then uses urlSet and the urlDescs array to display and describe the URLs that have met the search criteria. The urlSet and the urlDescs array are defined in db.js (Listing 18.13).

Listing 18.13:   The Search Database (db.js)

```
dictionary = new Array(
  "CGI",
  "tutorial",
```

```
  "documentation",
  "example",
  "cookies",
  "HTML",
  "2.0",
  "3.0",
  "3.2",
  "extensions",
  "HTTP",
  "specification",
  "security",
  "version",
  "Java",
  "shareware",
  "JavaScript",
  "VRML",
  "sites"
)
deptURLs = new Array(
 "http://web.soft.med.xyzxyz.com/web/webdev.htm",
 "http://web.soft.med.xyzxyz.com/web/webtut.htm",
 "http://web.soft.med.xyzxyz.com/web/examples.htm",
 "http://web.soft.med.xyzxyz.com/spec/http.htm",
 "http://web.soft.med.xyzxyz.com/spec/vrml.htm",
 "http://web.soft.med.xyzxyz.com/lang/java.htm",
 "http://web.soft.med.xyzxyz.com/lang/javascript.htm",
 "http://web.soft.med.xyzxyz.com/lang/vrml.htm",
 "http://web.soft.med.xyzxyz.com/lang/html.htm"
)
divURLs = new Array(
 "http://soft.med.xyzxyz.com/standards/webpage.htm",
 "http://soft.med.xyzxyz.com/standards/code.htm",
 "http://soft.med.xyzxyz.com/standards/http.htm",
 "http://soft.med.xyzxyz.com/tutorials/html.htm",
 "http://soft.med.xyzxyz.com/tutorials/cgi.htm",
 "http://soft.med.xyzxyz.com/tutorials/java.htm",
 "http://soft.med.xyzxyz.com/tutorials/javascript.htm",
 "http://soft.med.xyzxyz.com/tutorials/vrml.htm"
)
sectURLs = new Array(
 "http://med.xyzxyz.com/policy/web.htm",
 "http://med.xyzxyz.com/policy/whatsnew.htm"
)
urlDescs = new Array(
 new Array(
  "How to Develop Web Applications",
  "A Web Tutorial",
  "Examples of Web Application Development",
  "The HTTP Specification",
  "The VRML Specification",
  "The Java Language",
```

```
  "The JavaScript Language",
  "The VRML Language",
  "The HTML Language"
 ),
 new Array(
  "Web Page Design Standards",
  "Coding Standards",
  "The HTTP Specification",
  "An HTML Tutorial",
  "A CGI Tutorial",
  "A Java Tutorial",
  "A JavaScript Tutorial",
  "A VRML Tutorial"
 ),
 new Array(
  "The XYZXYZ Company Web Policy",
  "What's New at XYZXYZ?"
 )
)
db = new Array(dictionary.length)
db[0]=new Array(
 new Array("0","1","2"),
 new Array("0","1","4"),
 new Array()
)
db[1]=new Array(
 new Array("1"),
 new Array("3","4","5","6","7"),
 new Array("1")
)
db[2]=new Array(
 new Array("0","3","4","5","6","7","8"),
 new Array("0","1","2"),
 new Array("1")
)
db[3]=new Array(
 new Array("2"),
 new Array("3","4","5","6","7"),
 new Array()
)
db[4]=new Array(
 new Array("0","3"),
 new Array("1","2","4"),
 new Array()
)
db[5]=new Array(
 new Array("0","1","2","5","6","8"),
 new Array("0","1","3","4","5","6"),
 new Array("0","1")
)
db[6]=new Array(
```

```
  new Array("0","1","2","8"),
  new Array("0","1","3"),
  new Array("0")
)
db[7]=new Array(
  new Array("8"),
  new Array("0"),
  new Array("0")
)
db[8]=new Array(
  new Array("0","8"),
  new Array("0","3"),
  new Array("0","1")
)
db[9]=new Array(
  new Array("0","1","8"),
  new Array("0","3"),
  new Array("0","1")
)
db[10]=new Array(
  new Array("3"),
  new Array("2"),
  new Array()
)
db[11]=new Array(
  new Array("0","3","4"),
  new Array("0","1","2"),
  new Array()
)
db[12]=new Array(
  new Array(),
  new Array("0","1","2","4"),
  new Array("0","1")
)
db[13]=new Array(
  new Array("3","4"),
  new Array("0","1","2"),
  new Array("0","1")
)
db[14]=new Array(
  new Array("0","1","2","5"),
  new Array("0","1","5"),
  new Array("0","1")
)
db[15]=new Array(
  new Array("2"),
  new Array("4","5"),
  new Array()
)
db[16]=new Array(
  new Array("0","1","2","6"),
```

```
 new Array("0","1","6"),
 new Array("0","1")
 )
db[17]=new Array(
 new Array("4","7"),
 new Array("7"),
 new Array("1")
 )
db[18]=new Array(
 new Array("7"),
 new Array("7"),
 new Array("1")
 )
```

The db.js file contains the search database used by engines3.htm. It consists of the following arrays:

The *dictionary* array   This array contains all of the keywords that are supported by the search engine. The list presented here is small. Most search engines would have a list containing between 100 and 1,000 words.

The *deptURLs* array   This array identifies the department-level URLs that are covered by the search engine. The script here lists only a few, for example purposes. A list of hundreds of URLs would be more normal for a real application, and would still be manageable by most local search engines.

The *divURLs* array   This array identifies the division-level URLs that are covered by the search engine.

The *sectURLs* array   This array identifies the sector-level URLs that are covered by the search engine.

The *urlDescs* array   This array provides a description of the department, division, and sector URLs. It is an array of arrays of descriptions that can be indexed by the scope variable (see Listing 18.12, engines3.htm) to provide department, division, or sector URL descriptions.

The *db* Array   This array is the heart of the search database. Each element of db contains information on a specific word in the dictionary array. For example, db[0] contains info pertaining to the keyword *CGI*, db[1] contains info pertaining to the keyword *Tutorial*, and db[18] contains info pertaining to the keyword *Sites*. In addition, every db[n] is itself a three-element array, for it contains the aforementioned information at the department, division, and sector levels respectively. These arrays are created using the new operator and Array() constructor. For example, in theListing 18.13, db[5][0] is an array containing the indices for the HTML keyword for department-level URLs. These URLs are deptURLs[0], deptURLs[1], deptURLs[2], deptURLs[5], deptURLs[6], and deptURLs[8].

Similarly, db[5][1] is an array containing the indices for the HTML keyword for division-level URLs. These URLs are divURLs[0], divURLs[1], divURLs[3], divURLs[4], divURLs[5] and divURLs[6].

> **NOTE** The elements of the **db** arrays are initialized as strings to avoid ambiguities in the array definitions. For example, `new Array(5)` results in a new array of five elements, and `new Array("5")` results in a new array of one element whose value is `"5"`.

Summary

In this chapter you learned how to develop and integrate JavaScript-based search capabilities in your web pages. You learned how to connect your scripts to existing web search engines and how to implement local search engines using JavaScript. In the next chapter you'll have a little fun. You'll learn how to develop an interesting e-commerce application using JavaScript.

CHAPTER 19

Developing E-commerce Applications

- Running the example application

- Developing an online catalog

- Adding a client-side shopping cart

Most web developers want to get paid for their efforts. This means that someone, some-where on the Web, has to sell something. That's where e-commerce comes in.

E-commerce, in a simple sense, involves four things:

- Providing customers with information about your products and services
- Enabling customers to order your products and services
- Fulfilling customer orders
- Maintaining an on-going relationship with your customers

In this chapter, we're going to address the first two items. You'll learn how to use JavaScript to build an online product catalog for a hypothetical home-furnishing company. You'll also build a JavaScript shopping cart that will allow customers to order multiple products and manage the products they are ordering. This chapter's example will gather billing and shipping information and take your customer's up to the check out page. All you'll need is some server-side code to do credit card processing and a warehouse full of products to start an online business of your own.

Running the Example Application

The best way to understand the application that we're building is to run it on your own. Open `catalog.htm` (Listing 19.1) in your browser, the window shown in Figure 19.1 is displayed. The product catalog enables you to search for home furnishings by furniture category or by room. Select the default settings of Furniture and Living room, and click the List products button. The list of products shown in Figure 19.2 is displayed. Click on the product number to display detailed information on a specific product. For now, click on F-120 to display more information on the arm chair (Figure 19.3).

Listing 19.1:   The Opening Page of the Product Catalog (catalog.htm)

```
<html>
<head>
<script language="JavaScript" src="catalog.js">
</script>
<script language="JavaScript" src="productdesc.js">
</script>
<script language="JavaScript" src="database.js">
</script>
<script language="JavaScript" src="cookie.js">
</script>
```

```
<script language="JavaScript" src="cart.js">
</script>
<script language="JavaScript" src="accesscart.js">
</script>
<script language="JavaScript">
document.write("<title>"+catalog.title+"</title>")
</script>
<link rel="stylesheet" type="text/css"
 href="catstyle.css">
</head>
<body>
<script language="JavaScript">
displayViewCheckoutButtons()
catalog.displayCatalogForm()
</script>
</body>
</html>
```

FIGURE 19.1:

The catalog search page
(catalog.htm)

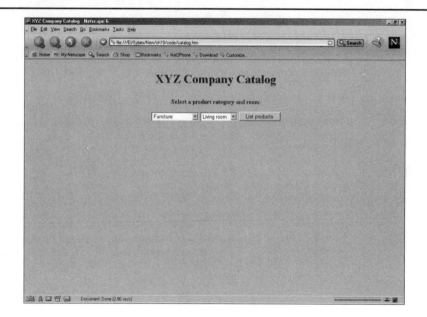

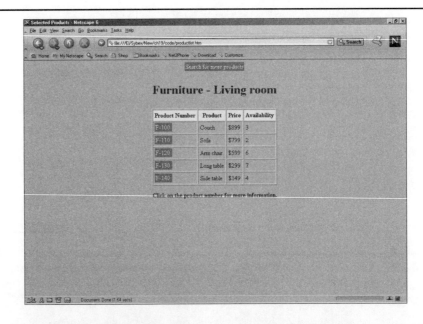

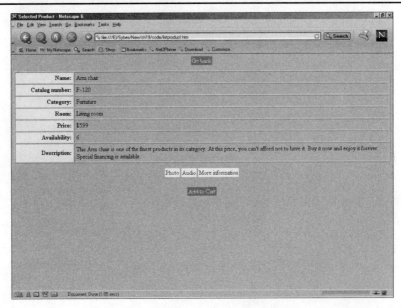

The page shown in Figure 19.3 provides information on a specific product. The Photo, Audio, and More Information links provide access to a photo (Figure 19.4), an audio description, and a product-specific web page (Figure 19.5). If you click these links, a new window will be opened to display the additional information.

FIGURE 19.4:

A photo of the armchair product (i2.jpg)

FIGURE 19.5:

The product page (d2.htm)

Click the Add to Cart button to add the armchair to your shopping cart. The alert dialog shown in Figure 19.6 provides confirmation that the product has been added to your cart. The View Shopping Cart and Check Out links are added to the product information page as shown in Figure 19.7.

FIGURE 19.6:

The armchair was added to the shopping cart.

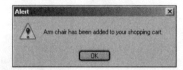

FIGURE 19.7:

The View Shopping Cart and Check Out links are added to the product information page (`listproduct.htm`).

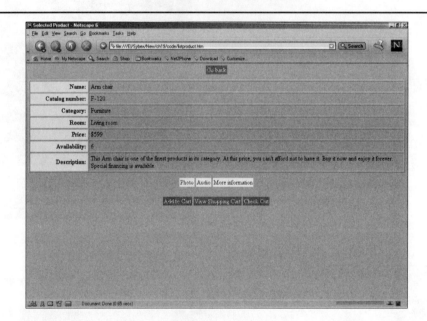

Click the View Shopping Cart link to take a look at what's in your cart (Figure 19.8). If you click the Change quantity link, the dialog box shown in Figure 19.9 is displayed. Change the quantity to 2 and click OK. The change is reflected in the shopping cart as shown in Figure 19.10.

FIGURE 19.8:

The shopping cart lets customers manage their order.
(viewcart.htm)

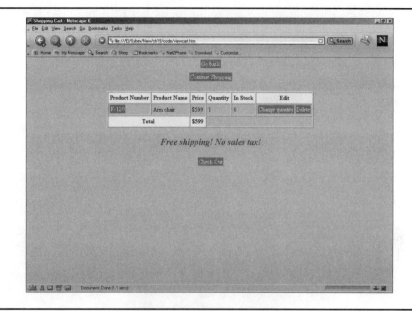

FIGURE 19.9:

Changing the number of products that are ordered

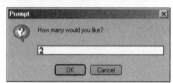

FIGURE 19.10:

The number of armchairs is updated
(viewcart.htm).

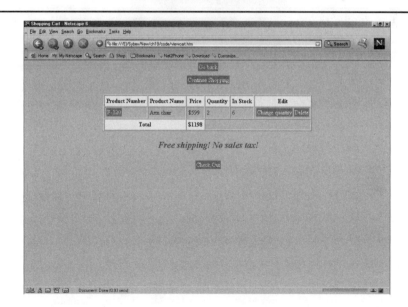

Let's add another product to the cart. Click the Continue Shopping link to go back to the main catalog page. Select Carpeting and Bed Room to obtain a list of bedroom carpeting products as shown in Figure 19.11. Click on C-300 to get more information on the lamb skin carpet as shown in Figure 19.12.

FIGURE 19.11:

Looking for bedroom carpeting
(productlist.htm)

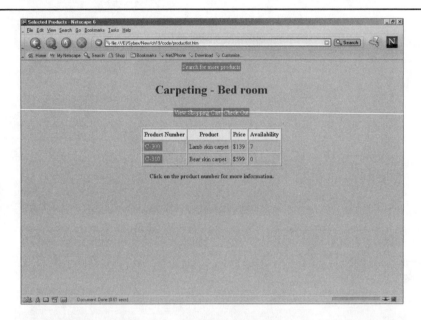

FIGURE 19.12:

The details of the lamb skin carpet
(listproduct.htm)

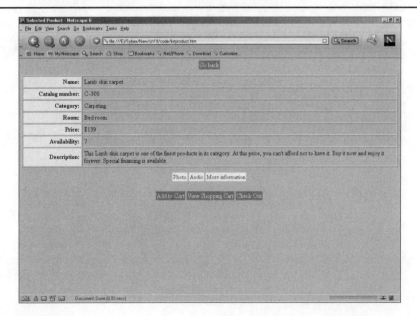

Go ahead and add the lamb skin carpet to your cart and then click the Check Out button. The check out form shown in Figure 19.13 is displayed. Don't bother filling in the details of the form. There is no server-side code to perform the credit card processing. If you click on the Check Out button at the bottom of the form, the alert box shown in Figure 19.14 is displayed.

FIGURE 19.13:

The check out form
(checkout.htm)

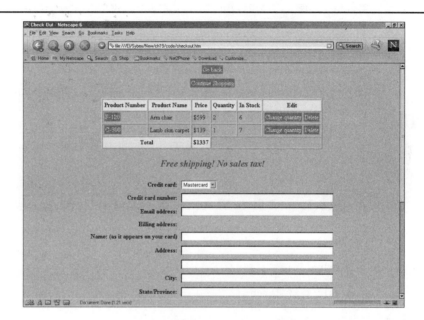

FIGURE 19.14:

This is where you put your
credit card processing code.

Developing an Online Catalog

The opening page of the catalog is shown in listing 19.1. As you can see, most of the processing is performed in JavaScript. The following six JavaScript source files are included:

catalog.js   Defines the Catalog object that implements the product catalog.

productdesc.js   Defines the ProductDesc object that provides information about a specific product.

database.js   Contains the product database of the XYZ Company. Provides an instance of the `Catalog` object type (referenced via the `catalog` variable).

cookie.js   Provides functions for streamlining access to cookies.

cart.js   Defines the `Cart` object that provides an implementation of a shopping cart.

accesscart.js   Provides functions that simplify access to the shopping cart.

These JavaScript files are covered throughout the rest of this chapter. The `displayView-CheckoutButtons()` function is implemented in `accesscart.js` and the `displayCatalog-Form()` function is implemented in `catalog.js`.

Listing 19.2 shows the style sheet that's used with the catalog and shopping cart.

WARNING   If you use this example to build a real-world, e-commerce application, be sure to use Secure Sockets Layer (SSL) encryption to protect communication between your customers and your website.

Listing 19.2:   A Style Sheet for the Catalog (catstyle.css)

```
body
{background-color: #ddddff}

p.catalogtitle
{color: #0000a0;
font-size: xx-large;
font-weight: bold;
text-align: center}

p.catalog
{color: #0000a0;
font-weight: bold;
text-align: center}

form.catalog
{text-align: center}

a.info
{background-color: #ffffcc;
color: #0000a0}

p.back
{text-align: center}

td
{padding: 4px}
```

```
th.productdesc
{text-align: right;
width: 150px}

th
{background-color: #ffff80;
padding: 4px}

p.cart
{margin-bottom: 30px;
margin-top: 30px;
text-align: center}

p.search
{margin-bottom: 30px;
text-align: center}

p.slogan
{color: #df0000;
font-size: x-large;
font-style: italic;
font-weight: bold;
text-align: center}

td.form
{font-weight: bold;
text-align: right}

a
{background-color: #8080c0;
color: #ffffff;
padding: 2px;
text-decoration: none}

p.info
{text-align: center}
```

The *Catalog* Object

The Catalog object (Listing 19.3) implements the product catalog. It has the following four properties:

title   The title of the catalog page.

categories   An array of product category names.

rooms   An array of room names.

products   An array of ProductDesc objects (covered in the next section).

The Catalog object provides three methods that help to display the catalog and its products:

displayCatalogForm()   Creates the catalog search form shown in Listing 19.1.

listProducts()   Handles the clicking of the List Products button of the catalog search form. Sets the category and room cookies with the values of the user's selection and loads the productlist.htm page (Listing 19.7).

hasProducts(category, room)   Returns a Boolean value indicating whether or not products are associated with a particular category and room combination.

A separate listProducts() function is used to connect event handlers to the listProducts() method. It is used with the displayCatalogForm() method.

Listing 19.3:   **The *Catalog* Object (catalog.js)**

```
// catalog.js

function Catalog(title, categories, rooms, products) {
  this.title = title
  this.categories = categories
  this.rooms = rooms
  this.products = products
  this.displayCatalogForm = Catalog_displayCatalogForm
  this.listProducts = Catalog_listProducts
  this.hasProducts = Catalog_hasProducts
}

function Catalog_displayCatalogForm() {
  document.writeln("<p class='catalogtitle'>"+this.title+"</p>")
  document.writeln("<form name='catalog' class='catalog'>")
  document.writeln("<p class='catalog'>Select a product category and room:</p>")
  document.writeln("<select name='categories' class='categories'>")
  for(var i=0; i<this.categories.length; ++i)
    document.writeln("<option>"+this.categories[i]+"</option>")
  document.writeln("</select>")
  document.writeln("<select name='rooms' class='rooms'>")
  for(var i=0; i<this.rooms.length; ++i)
    document.writeln("<option>"+this.rooms[i]+"</option>")
  document.writeln("</select>")
  document.writeln("<input type='button' ")
  document.write("onclick='listProducts()' ")
  document.write("value='List products' class='catalog'>")
  document.writeln("</form>")
}

function listProducts() {
  catalog.listProducts()
}
```

```
function Catalog_listProducts() {
 var catalogForm = document.forms["catalog"]
 var category = catalogForm.elements["categories"].selectedIndex
 var room = catalogForm.elements["rooms"].selectedIndex
 setCookie("category", category)
 setCookie("room", room)
 window.location.href = "productlist.htm"
}

function Catalog_hasProducts(category, room) {
 for(var i=0; i<this.products.length; ++i) {
  if(category == "All" ||
    this.products[i].category == category) {
   if(room == "All" || this.products[i].room == room)
    return true
  }
 }
 return false
}
```

The *ProductDesc* Object

The ProductDesc object provides information about a specific product. It has the following 10 properties:

name   The product's name.

category   The product category to which the product belongs.

room   The room in which the product is used.

price   The product's price.

availability   The number of products of this kind in stock.

product_number   A product identifier.

image_url   The URL of the product's photo.

audio_url   The URL of the product's audio description.

data_url   The product's home page.

description   A short description of the product.

The ProductDesc object defines the following four methods to simplify the display of product-related information:

displayProductInfo()   Displays the product information table shown in Figure 19.3.

displayProductImage(win)   Displays a photo of the product (see Figure 19.4).

displayProductAudio(win)   Plays an audio description of the product.

displayProductData(win)   Loads the product's home page (see Figure 19.5).

In addition, the listProduct() information is defined to handle the selection of a product from the displayed product list. It sets the listproduct cookie with the user's selection and loads the listproduct.htm file (Listing 19.4).

Listing 19.4:   The *ProductDesc* Object (productdesc.js)

```
// productdesc.js

function ProductDesc(name, category, room, price, availability,
  product_number, image_url, audio_url, data_url, description) {
  this.name = name
  this.category = category
  this.room = room
  this.price = price
  this.availability = availability
  this.product_number = product_number
  this.image_url = image_url
  this.audio_url = audio_url
  this.data_url = data_url
  this.description = description
  this.displayProductInfo = ProductDesc_displayProductInfo
  this.displayProductImage = ProductDesc_displayProductImage
  this.displayProductAudio = ProductDesc_displayProductAudio
  this.displayProductData = ProductDesc_displayProductData
}

function ProductDesc_displayProductInfo() {
  document.writeln("<table border='1' align='center' valign='top'>")
  document.writeln("<tr><th
class='productdesc'>Name:</th><td>"+this.name+"</td></tr>")
  document.writeln("<tr><th class='productdesc'>Catalog
number:</th><td>"+this.product_number+"</td></tr>")
  document.writeln("<tr><th
class='productdesc'>Category:</th><td>"+this.category+"</td></tr>")
  document.writeln("<tr><th
class='productdesc'>Room:</th><td>"+this.room+"</td></tr>")
  document.writeln("<tr><th
class='productdesc'>Price:</th><td>$"+this.price+"</td></tr>")
  document.writeln("<tr><th
class='productdesc'>Availability:</th><td>"+this.availability+"</td></tr>")
  document.writeln("<tr><th
class='productdesc'>Description:</th><td>"+this.description+"</td></tr>")
  document.writeln("</table>")
  document.writeln("<p class='info'><a href='products/"+this.image_url+"'
class='info' target='info'>Photo</a>")
```

```
 document.writeln("<a href='products/"+this.audio_url+"'
class='info'>Audio</a>")
 document.writeln("<a href='products/"+this.data_url+"' class='info'
target='info'>More information</a></p>")
}

function ProductDesc_displayProductImage(win) {
 win.location = this.image_url
}

function ProductDesc_displayProductAudio(win) {
 win.location = this.audio_url
}

function ProductDesc_displayProductData(win) {
 win.location = this.data_url
}

function listProduct(n) {
 setCookie("listproduct",n)
 window.location.href = "listproduct.htm"
}
```

The Product Database

Listing 19.5 contains the database used to implement the product catalog. While this may seem like a large file, it is actually much smaller (24 kilobytes) than most image files and should not slow down the user's browser (unless the user has a very slow computer and Internet connection).

The file creates an instance of the ProductDesc object for each product in the catalog and then assembles these instances into the products array. It defines the catalog's categories, rooms, and title and then uses these objects to create an instance of the catalog that is referenced by the catalog variable.

Listing 19.5:   The XYZ Company Product Database (database.js)

```
var p0 = new ProductDesc("Couch", "Furniture", "Living room",
 899.00, 3, "F-100", "i0.jpg", "a0.wav", "d0.htm",
 "This Couch is one of the finest " +
"products in its category. At this price, you can't afford " +
"not to have it. Buy it now and enjoy it forever. Special " +
"financing is available.")

var p1 = new ProductDesc("Sofa", "Furniture", "Living room",
 799.00, 2, "F-110", "i1.jpg", "a1.wav", "d1.htm",
 "This Sofa is one of the finest " +
"products in its category. At this price, you can't afford " +
```

```
    "not to have it. Buy it now and enjoy it forever. Special " +
    "financing is available.")

    var p2 = new ProductDesc("Arm chair", "Furniture", "Living room",
      599.00, 6, "F-120", "i2.jpg", "a2.wav", "d2.htm",
      "This Arm chair is one of the finest " +
    "products in its category. At this price, you can't afford " +
    "not to have it. Buy it now and enjoy it forever. Special " +
    "financing is available.")

    var p3 = new ProductDesc("Long table", "Furniture", "Living room",
      299.00, 7, "F-130", "i3.jpg", "a3.wav", "d3.htm",
      "This Long table is one of the finest " +
    "products in its category. At this price, you can't afford " +
    "not to have it. Buy it now and enjoy it forever. Special " +
    "financing is available.")

    var p4 = new ProductDesc("Side table", "Furniture", "Living room",
      149.00, 4, "F-140", "i4.jpg", "a4.wav", "d4.htm",
      "This Side table is one of the finest " +
    "products in its category. At this price, you can't afford " +
    "not to have it. Buy it now and enjoy it forever. Special " +
    "financing is available.")

    var p5 = new ProductDesc("Persian rug", "Carpeting", "Living room",
      1249.00, 2, "C-100", "i5.jpg", "a5.wav", "d5.htm",
      "This Persian rug is one of the finest " +
    "products in its category. At this price, you can't afford " +
    "not to have it. Buy it now and enjoy it forever. Special " +
    "financing is available.")

    var p6 = new ProductDesc("Cheap rug", "Carpeting", "Living room",
      79.00, 13, "C-110", "i6.jpg", "a6.wav", "d6.htm",
      "This Cheap rug is one of the finest " +
    "products in its category. At this price, you can't afford " +
    "not to have it. Buy it now and enjoy it forever. Special " +
    "financing is available.")

    var p7 = new ProductDesc("Recessed ceiling light", "Lighting", "Living room",
      359.00, 9, "L-100", "i7.jpg", "a7.wav", "d7.htm",
      "This Recessed ceiling light is one of the finest " +
    "products in its category. At this price, you can't afford " +
    "not to have it. Buy it now and enjoy it forever. Special " +
    "financing is available.")

    var p8 = new ProductDesc("Floor light", "Lighting", "Living room",
      139.00, 0, "L-110", "i8.jpg", "a8.wav", "d8.htm",
      "This Floor light is one of the finest " +
    "products in its category. At this price, you can't afford " +
    "not to have it. Buy it now and enjoy it forever. Special " +
    "financing is available.")
```

```
var p9 = new ProductDesc("Table light", "Lighting", "Living room",
  49.00, 0, "L-120", "i9.jpg", "a9.wav", "d9.htm",
  "This Table light is one of the finest " +
"products in its category. At this price, you can't afford " +
"not to have it. Buy it now and enjoy it forever. Special " +
"financing is available.")

var p10 = new ProductDesc("Big TV", "Electronics", "Living room",
  1499.00, 2, "E-100", "i10.jpg", "a10.wav", "d10.htm",
  "This Big TV is one of the finest " +
"products in its category. At this price, you can't afford " +
"not to have it. Buy it now and enjoy it forever. Special " +
"financing is available.")

var p11 = new ProductDesc("Small TV", "Electronics", "Living room",
  299.00, 3, "E-110", "i11.jpg", "a11.wav", "d11.htm",
  "This Small TV is one of the finest " +
"products in its category. At this price, you can't afford " +
"not to have it. Buy it now and enjoy it forever. Special " +
"financing is available.")

var p12 = new ProductDesc("Entertainment center", "Electronics", "Living room",
  649.00, 2, "E-120", "i12.jpg", "a12.wav", "d12.htm",
  "This Entertainment center is one of the finest " +
"products in its category. At this price, you can't afford " +
"not to have it. Buy it now and enjoy it forever. Special " +
"financing is available.")

var p13 = new ProductDesc("Stereo", "Electronics", "Living room",
  1499.00, 3, "E-130", "i13.jpg", "a13.wav", "d13.htm",
  "This Stereo is one of the finest " +
"products in its category. At this price, you can't afford " +
"not to have it. Buy it now and enjoy it forever. Special " +
"financing is available.")

var p14 = new ProductDesc("Large painting", "Accessories", "Living room",
  769.00, 11, "A-100", "i14.jpg", "a14.wav", "d14.htm",
  "This Large painting is one of the finest " +
"products in its category. At this price, you can't afford " +
"not to have it. Buy it now and enjoy it forever. Special " +
"financing is available.")

var p15 = new ProductDesc("Small painting", "Accessories", "Living room",
  139.00, 14, "A-110", "i15.jpg", "a15.wav", "d15.htm",
  "This Small painting is one of the finest " +
"products in its category. At this price, you can't afford " +
"not to have it. Buy it now and enjoy it forever. Special " +
"financing is available.")

var p16 = new ProductDesc("Large fake plant", "Accessories", "Living room",
  89.00, 16, "A-120", "i16.jpg", "a16.wav", "d16.htm",
  "This Large fake plant is one of the finest " +
```

```
"products in its category. At this price, you can't afford " +
"not to have it. Buy it now and enjoy it forever. Special " +
"financing is available.")

var p17 = new ProductDesc("Small fake plant", "Accessories", "Living room",
  39.00, 20, "A-130", "i17.jpg", "a17.wav", "d17.htm",
  "This Small fake plant is one of the finest " +
"products in its category. At this price, you can't afford " +
"not to have it. Buy it now and enjoy it forever. Special " +
"financing is available.")

var p18 = new ProductDesc("Expensive knick knack", "Accessories", "Living room",
  179.00, 12, "A-140", "i18.jpg", "a18.wav", "d18.htm",
  "This Expensive knick knack is one of the finest " +
"products in its category. At this price, you can't afford " +
"not to have it. Buy it now and enjoy it forever. Special " +
"financing is available.")

var p19 = new ProductDesc("Cheap knick knack", "Accessories", "Living room",
  19.00, 34, "A-150", "i19.jpg", "a19.wav", "d19.htm",
  "This Cheap knick knack is one of the finest " +
"products in its category. At this price, you can't afford " +
"not to have it. Buy it now and enjoy it forever. Special " +
"financing is available.")

var p20 = new ProductDesc("Expensive dining set", "Furniture", "Dining room",
  2499.00, 3, "F-200", "i20.jpg", "a20.wav", "d20.htm",
  "This Expensive dining set is one of the finest " +
"products in its category. At this price, you can't afford " +
"not to have it. Buy it now and enjoy it forever. Special " +
"financing is available.")

var p21 = new ProductDesc("Cheap dining set", "Furniture", "Dining room",
  799.00, 6, "F-210", "i21.jpg", "a21.wav", "d21.htm",
  "This Cheap dining set is one of the finest " +
"products in its category. At this price, you can't afford " +
"not to have it. Buy it now and enjoy it forever. Special " +
"financing is available.")

var p22 = new ProductDesc("China cabinet", "Furniture", "Dining room",
  1199.00, 8, "F-220", "i22.jpg", "a22.wav", "d22.htm",
  "This China cabinet is one of the finest " +
"products in its category. At this price, you can't afford " +
"not to have it. Buy it now and enjoy it forever. Special " +
"financing is available.")

var p23 = new ProductDesc("Serving table", "Furniture", "Dining room",
  249.00, 0, "F-230", "i23.jpg", "a23.wav", "d23.htm",
  "This Serving table is one of the finest " +
"products in its category. At this price, you can't afford " +
"not to have it. Buy it now and enjoy it forever. Special " +
"financing is available.")
```

```
var p24 = new ProductDesc("Stain-proof rug", "Carpeting", "Dining room",
  1239.00, 5, "C-200", "i24.jpg", "a24.wav", "d24.htm",
  "This Stain-proof rug is one of the finest " +
"products in its category. At this price, you can't afford " +
"not to have it. Buy it now and enjoy it forever. Special " +
"financing is available.")

var p25 = new ProductDesc("Plastic floor covering", "Carpeting", "Dining room",
  49.00, 7, "C-210", "i25.jpg", "a25.wav", "d25.htm",
  "This Plastic floor covering is one of the finest " +
"products in its category. At this price, you can't afford " +
"not to have it. Buy it now and enjoy it forever. Special " +
"financing is available.")

var p26 = new ProductDesc("Chandalier", "Lighting", "Dining room",
  3499.00, 1, "L-200", "i26.jpg", "a26.wav", "d26.htm",
  "This Chandalier is one of the finest " +
"products in its category. At this price, you can't afford " +
"not to have it. Buy it now and enjoy it forever. Special " +
"financing is available.")

var p27 = new ProductDesc("Ceiling lamp/fan", "Lighting", "Dining room",
  279.00, 2, "L-210", "i27.jpg", "a27.wav", "d27.htm",
  "This Ceiling lamp/fan is one of the finest " +
"products in its category. At this price, you can't afford " +
"not to have it. Buy it now and enjoy it forever. Special " +
"financing is available.")

var p28 = new ProductDesc("China set", "Accessories", "Dining room",
  399.00, 1, "A-200", "i28.jpg", "a28.wav", "d28.htm",
  "This China set is one of the finest " +
"products in its category. At this price, you can't afford " +
"not to have it. Buy it now and enjoy it forever. Special " +
"financing is available.")

var p29 = new ProductDesc("Silver set", "Accessories", "Dining room",
  599.00, 3, "A-210", "i29.jpg", "a29.wav", "d29.htm",
  "This Silver set is one of the finest " +
"products in its category. At this price, you can't afford " +
"not to have it. Buy it now and enjoy it forever. Special " +
"financing is available.")

var p30 = new ProductDesc("King bed", "Furniture", "Bed room",
  999.00, 6, "F-300", "i30.jpg", "a30.wav", "d30.htm",
  "This King bed is one of the finest " +
"products in its category. At this price, you can't afford " +
"not to have it. Buy it now and enjoy it forever. Special " +
"financing is available.")

var p31 = new ProductDesc("Queen bed", "Furniture", "Bed room",
  799.00, 8, "F-310", "i31.jpg", "a31.wav", "d31.htm",
  "This Queen bed is one of the finest " +
```

```
   "products in its category. At this price, you can't afford " +
   "not to have it. Buy it now and enjoy it forever. Special " +
   "financing is available.")

   var p32 = new ProductDesc("Single bed", "Furniture", "Bed room",
      399.00, 12, "F-320", "i32.jpg", "a32.wav", "d32.htm",
      "This Single bed is one of the finest " +
   "products in its category. At this price, you can't afford " +
   "not to have it. Buy it now and enjoy it forever. Special " +
   "financing is available.")

   var p33 = new ProductDesc("End table", "Furniture", "Bed room",
      199.00, 5, "F-330", "i33.jpg", "a33.wav", "d33.htm",
      "This End table is one of the finest " +
   "products in its category. At this price, you can't afford " +
   "not to have it. Buy it now and enjoy it forever. Special " +
   "financing is available.")

   var p34 = new ProductDesc("Dresser", "Furniture", "Bed room",
      499.00, 7, "F-340", "i34.jpg", "a34.wav", "d34.htm",
      "This Dresser is one of the finest " +
   "products in its category. At this price, you can't afford " +
   "not to have it. Buy it now and enjoy it forever. Special " +
   "financing is available.")

   var p35 = new ProductDesc("Lamb skin carpet", "Carpeting", "Bed room",
      139.00, 7, "C-300", "i35.jpg", "a35.wav", "d35.htm",
      "This Lamb skin carpet is one of the finest " +
   "products in its category. At this price, you can't afford " +
   "not to have it. Buy it now and enjoy it forever. Special " +
   "financing is available.")

   var p36 = new ProductDesc("Bear skin carpet", "Carpeting", "Bed room",
      599.00, 0, "C-310", "i36.jpg", "a36.wav", "d36.htm",
      "This Bear skin carpet is one of the finest " +
   "products in its category. At this price, you can't afford " +
   "not to have it. Buy it now and enjoy it forever. Special " +
   "financing is available.")

   var p37 = new ProductDesc("Ceiling lamp", "Lighting", "Bed room",
      239.00, 4, "L-300", "i37.jpg", "a37.wav", "d37.htm",
      "This Ceiling lamp is one of the finest " +
   "products in its category. At this price, you can't afford " +
   "not to have it. Buy it now and enjoy it forever. Special " +
   "financing is available.")

   var p38 = new ProductDesc("Table lamp", "Lighting", "Bed room",
      59.00, 9, "L-310", "i38.jpg", "a38.wav", "d38.htm",
      "This Table lamp is one of the finest " +
   "products in its category. At this price, you can't afford " +
   "not to have it. Buy it now and enjoy it forever. Special " +
   "financing is available.")
```

```
var p39 = new ProductDesc("Clock radio", "Electronics", "Bed room",
  129.00, 15, "E-300", "i39.jpg", "a39.wav", "d39.htm",
  "This Clock radio is one of the finest " +
"products in its category. At this price, you can't afford " +
"not to have it. Buy it now and enjoy it forever. Special " +
"financing is available.")

var p40 = new ProductDesc("Electronic head board", "Electronics", "Bed room",
  499.00, 5, "E-310", "i40.jpg", "a40.wav", "d40.htm",
  "This Electronic head board is one of the finest " +
"products in its category. At this price, you can't afford " +
"not to have it. Buy it now and enjoy it forever. Special " +
"financing is available.")

var p41 = new ProductDesc("Pillow set", "Accessories", "Bed room",
  69.00, 6, "A-300", "i41.jpg", "a41.wav", "d41.htm",
  "This Pillow set is one of the finest " +
"products in its category. At this price, you can't afford " +
"not to have it. Buy it now and enjoy it forever. Special " +
"financing is available.")

var p42 = new ProductDesc("Linen set", "Accessories", "Bed room",
  329.00, 8, "A-310", "i42.jpg", "a42.wav", "d42.htm",
  "This Linen set is one of the finest " +
"products in its category. At this price, you can't afford " +
"not to have it. Buy it now and enjoy it forever. Special " +
"financing is available.")

var p43 = new ProductDesc("Bed spread", "Accessories", "Bed room",
  59.00, 7, "A-320", "i43.jpg", "a43.wav", "d43.htm",
  "This Bed spread is one of the finest " +
"products in its category. At this price, you can't afford " +
"not to have it. Buy it now and enjoy it forever. Special " +
"financing is available.")

var p44 = new ProductDesc("Refrigerator", "Appliances", "Kitchen",
  899.00, 5, "P-400", "i44.jpg", "a44.wav", "d44.htm",
  "This Refrigerator is one of the finest " +
"products in its category. At this price, you can't afford " +
"not to have it. Buy it now and enjoy it forever. Special " +
"financing is available.")

var p45 = new ProductDesc("Stove - oven", "Appliances", "Kitchen",
  799.00, 11, "P-410", "i45.jpg", "a45.wav", "d45.htm",
  "This Stove - oven is one of the finest " +
"products in its category. At this price, you can't afford " +
"not to have it. Buy it now and enjoy it forever. Special " +
"financing is available.")

var p46 = new ProductDesc("Microwave oven", "Appliances", "Kitchen",
  79.00, 6, "P-420", "i46.jpg", "a46.wav", "d46.htm",
```

```
    "This Microwave oven is one of the finest " +
    "products in its category. At this price, you can't afford " +
    "not to have it. Buy it now and enjoy it forever. Special " +
    "financing is available.")

var p47 = new ProductDesc("Toaster", "Appliances", "Kitchen",
    39.00, 4, "P-430", "i47.jpg", "a47.wav", "d47.htm",
    "This Toaster is one of the finest " +
    "products in its category. At this price, you can't afford " +
    "not to have it. Buy it now and enjoy it forever. Special " +
    "financing is available.")

var p48 = new ProductDesc("Coffee maker", "Appliances", "Kitchen",
    69.00, 8, "P-440", "i48.jpg", "a48.wav", "d48.htm",
    "This Coffee maker is one of the finest " +
    "products in its category. At this price, you can't afford " +
    "not to have it. Buy it now and enjoy it forever. Special " +
    "financing is available.")

var p49 = new ProductDesc("Dish washer", "Appliances", "Kitchen",
    399.00, 9, "P-450", "i49.jpg", "a49.wav", "d49.htm",
    "This Dish washer is one of the finest " +
    "products in its category. At this price, you can't afford " +
    "not to have it. Buy it now and enjoy it forever. Special " +
    "financing is available.")

var p50 = new ProductDesc("Delux cabinets", "Cabinets", "Kitchen",
    659.00, 5, "B-400", "i50.jpg", "a50.wav", "d50.htm",
    "This Delux cabinets is one of the finest " +
    "products in its category. At this price, you can't afford " +
    "not to have it. Buy it now and enjoy it forever. Special " +
    "financing is available.")

var p51 = new ProductDesc("Standard cabinets", "Cabinets", "Kitchen",
    399.00, 8, "B-410", "i51.jpg", "a51.wav", "d51.htm",
    "This Standard cabinets is one of the finest " +
    "products in its category. At this price, you can't afford " +
    "not to have it. Buy it now and enjoy it forever. Special " +
    "financing is available.")

var p52 = new ProductDesc("Delux counter", "Cabinets", "Kitchen",
    499.00, 4, "B-420", "i52.jpg", "a52.wav", "d52.htm",
    "This Delux counter is one of the finest " +
    "products in its category. At this price, you can't afford " +
    "not to have it. Buy it now and enjoy it forever. Special " +
    "financing is available.")

var p53 = new ProductDesc("Standard counter", "Cabinets", "Kitchen",
    399.00, 4, "B-430", "i53.jpg", "a53.wav", "d53.htm",
    "This Standard counter is one of the finest " +
    "products in its category. At this price, you can't afford " +
    "not to have it. Buy it now and enjoy it forever. Special " +
    "financing is available.")
```

```
var p54 = new ProductDesc("Kitchen ceiling light", "Lighting", "Kitchen",
  89.00, 7, "L-400", "i54.jpg", "a54.wav", "d54.htm",
  "This Kitchen ceiling light is one of the finest " +
"products in its category. At this price, you can't afford " +
"not to have it. Buy it now and enjoy it forever. Special " +
"financing is available.")

var p55 = new ProductDesc("Counter light", "Lighting", "Kitchen",
  29.00, 9, "L-410", "i55.jpg", "a55.wav", "d55.htm",
  "This Counter light is one of the finest " +
"products in its category. At this price, you can't afford " +
"not to have it. Buy it now and enjoy it forever. Special " +
"financing is available.")

var p56 = new ProductDesc("Cookware", "Accessories", "Kitchen",
  229.00, 13, "A-400", "i56.jpg", "a56.wav", "d56.htm",
  "This Cookware is one of the finest " +
"products in its category. At this price, you can't afford " +
"not to have it. Buy it now and enjoy it forever. Special " +
"financing is available.")

var p57 = new ProductDesc("Storage containers", "Accessories", "Kitchen",
  39.00, 12, "A-410", "i57.jpg", "a57.wav", "d57.htm",
  "This Storage containers is one of the finest " +
"products in its category. At this price, you can't afford " +
"not to have it. Buy it now and enjoy it forever. Special " +
"financing is available.")

var p58 = new ProductDesc("Wall clock", "Accessories", "Kitchen",
  49.00, 5, "A-420", "i58.jpg", "a58.wav", "d58.htm",
  "This Wall clock is one of the finest " +
"products in its category. At this price, you can't afford " +
"not to have it. Buy it now and enjoy it forever. Special " +
"financing is available.")

var p59 = new ProductDesc("Delux sink", "Sinks", "Bath room",
  399.00, 7, "N-500", "i59.jpg", "a59.wav", "d59.htm",
  "This Delux sink is one of the finest " +
"products in its category. At this price, you can't afford " +
"not to have it. Buy it now and enjoy it forever. Special " +
"financing is available.")

var p60 = new ProductDesc("Standard sink", "Sinks", "Bath room",
  199.00, 8, "N-510", "i60.jpg", "a60.wav", "d60.htm",
  "This Standard sink is one of the finest " +
"products in its category. At this price, you can't afford " +
"not to have it. Buy it now and enjoy it forever. Special " +
"financing is available.")

var p61 = new ProductDesc("Delux toilet", "Toilets", "Bath room",
  449.00, 11, "T-500", "i61.jpg", "a61.wav", "d61.htm",
```

```
    "This Delux toilet is one of the finest " +
"products in its category. At this price, you can't afford " +
"not to have it. Buy it now and enjoy it forever. Special " +
"financing is available.")

var p62 = new ProductDesc("Standard toilet", "Toilets", "Bath room",
    209.00, 24, "T-510", "i62.jpg", "a62.wav", "d62.htm",
    "This Standard toilet is one of the finest " +
"products in its category. At this price, you can't afford " +
"not to have it. Buy it now and enjoy it forever. Special " +
"financing is available.")

var p63 = new ProductDesc("Ceiling light", "Lighting", "Bath room",
    119.00, 0, "T-520", "i63.jpg", "a63.wav", "d63.htm",
    "This Ceiling light is one of the finest " +
"products in its category. At this price, you can't afford " +
"not to have it. Buy it now and enjoy it forever. Special " +
"financing is available.")

var p64 = new ProductDesc("Wall light", "Lighting", "Bath room",
    89.00, 6, "L-500", "i64.jpg", "a64.wav", "d64.htm",
    "This Wall light is one of the finest " +
"products in its category. At this price, you can't afford " +
"not to have it. Buy it now and enjoy it forever. Special " +
"financing is available.")

var p65 = new ProductDesc("Delux bath tub", "Bath and shower", "Bath room",
    359.00, 3, "S-500", "i65.jpg", "a65.wav", "d65.htm",
    "This Delux bath tub is one of the finest " +
"products in its category. At this price, you can't afford " +
"not to have it. Buy it now and enjoy it forever. Special " +
"financing is available.")

var p66 = new ProductDesc("Standard bath tub", "Bath and shower", "Bath room",
    249.00, 4, "S-510", "i66.jpg", "a66.wav", "d66.htm",
    "This Standard bath tub is one of the finest " +
"products in its category. At this price, you can't afford " +
"not to have it. Buy it now and enjoy it forever. Special " +
"financing is available.")

var p67 = new ProductDesc("Shower stall", "Bath and shower", "Bath room",
    349.00, 2, "S-520", "i67.jpg", "a67.wav", "d67.htm",
    "This Shower stall is one of the finest " +
"products in its category. At this price, you can't afford " +
"not to have it. Buy it now and enjoy it forever. Special " +
"financing is available.")

var p68 = new ProductDesc("Wall cabinet", "Bath and shower", "Bath room",
    139.00, 1, "S-530", "i68.jpg", "a68.wav", "d68.htm",
    "This Wall cabinet is one of the finest " +
"products in its category. At this price, you can't afford " +
```

```
"not to have it. Buy it now and enjoy it forever. Special " +
"financing is available.")

var p69 = new ProductDesc("Towel rack", "Accessories", "Bath room",
 12.00, 8, "A-500", "i69.jpg", "a69.wav", "d69.htm",
 "This Towel rack is one of the finest " +
"products in its category. At this price, you can't afford " +
"not to have it. Buy it now and enjoy it forever. Special " +
"financing is available.")

var p70 = new ProductDesc("Towels", "Accessories", "Bath room",
 35.00, 3, "A-510", "i70.jpg", "a70.wav", "d70.htm",
 "This Towels is one of the finest " +
"products in its category. At this price, you can't afford " +
"not to have it. Buy it now and enjoy it forever. Special " +
"financing is available.")

var products = new Array(p0, p1, p2, p3, p4, p5, p6, p7, p8,
 p9, p10, p11, p12, p13, p14, p15, p16, p17, p18, p19, p20,
 p21, p22, p23, p24, p25, p26, p27, p28, p29, p30, p31, p32,
 p33, p34, p35, p36, p37, p38, p39, p40, p41, p42, p43, p44,
 p45, p46, p47, p48, p49, p50, p51, p52, p53, p54, p55, p56,
 p57, p58, p59, p60, p61, p62, p63, p64, p65, p66, p67, p68,
 p69, p70)

var categories = new Array(
 "Furniture",
 "Electronics",
 "Accessories",
 "Bath and shower",
 "Carpeting",
 "Lighting",
 "Appliances",
 "Cabinets",
 "Sinks",
 "Toilets"
)

var rooms = new Array(
 "Living room",
 "Dining room",
 "Bed room",
 "Kitchen",
 "Bath room"
)

var title = "XYZ Company Catalog"

var catalog = new Catalog(title, categories, rooms, products)
```

Cookie Code

The cookie.js file (Listing 19.6) provides the now-familiar functions for getting and setting cookie values:

nameDefined(name)   Returns a Boolean value indicating whether a cookie with the specified name has been defined.

removeBlanks(s)   Removes any space characters in a string.

getCookie(name)   Retrieves the value of the named cookie. Returns an empty string if the cookie doesn't exist.

setCookie(name, value)   Creates a cookie with the specified name and value.

These functions were defined and used in earlier chapters.

Listing 19.6:   Functions for Accessing Cookies (cookie.js)

```
// cookie.js

function nameDefined(name) {
 var cookie=document.cookie
 var s=removeBlanks(cookie)
 var pairs=s.split(";")
 for(var i=0;i<pairs.length;++i) {
  var pairSplit=pairs[i].split("=")
  if(pairSplit[0]==name) return true
 }
 return false
}

function removeBlanks(s) {
 var temp=""
 for(var i=0;i<s.length;++i) {
  var c=s.charAt(i)
  if(c!=" ") temp += c
 }
 return temp
}

function getCookie(name) {
 var cookie=document.cookie
 var s=removeBlanks(cookie)
 var pairs=s.split(";")
 for(var i=0;i<pairs.length;++i) {
  var pairSplit=pairs[i].split("=")
  if(pairSplit[0]==name) return pairSplit[1]
 }
 return ""
}
```

```
function setCookie(name, value) {
  var newCookie = name + "=" +value
  window.document.cookie=newCookie
}
```

Listing Products

The productlist.htm page (Listing 19.7) is used to display a list of products within a specified category and from a particular room. These values are passed via the category and room cookies. The products are displayed in tabular form (refer to Figure 19.2).

Listing 19.7: Listing Selected Products (productlist.htm)

```
<html>
<head>
<script language="JavaScript" src="catalog.js">
</script>
<script language="JavaScript" src="productdesc.js">
</script>
<script language="JavaScript" src="database.js">
</script>
<script language="JavaScript" src="cookie.js">
</script>
<script language="JavaScript" src="cart.js">
</script>
<script language="JavaScript" src="accesscart.js">
</script>
<title>Selected Products</title>
<link rel="stylesheet" type="text/css"
 href="catstyle.css">
<body>
<p class="search"><a href="catalog.htm" class="search">Search for more
products</a></p>
<script language="JavaScript">
var category = getCookie("category")
var room = getCookie("room")
var categoryName = "All"
var roomName = "All"
if(category != "" && category != -1)
 categoryName = catalog.categories[category]
if(room != "" && room != -1)
 roomName = catalog.rooms[room]
document.writeln("<p class='catalogtitle'>"+categoryName + " - " + roomName +
"</p>")
if(catalog.hasProducts(categoryName, roomName)) {
 displayViewCheckoutButtons()
 document.writeln("<table border='1' align='center'>")
```

```
  document.writeln("<tr><th>Product
Number</th><th>Product</th><th>Price</th><th>Availability</th>")
  for(var i=0; i<catalog.products.length; ++i) {
   if(categoryName == "All" ||
     catalog.products[i].category == categoryName) {
    if(roomName == "All" || catalog.products[i].room == roomName) {
     document.write("<tr><td><a href='javascript:listProduct("+i+")'>")
     document.write(catalog.products[i].product_number)
     document.write("<a></td>")
     document.write("<td>" + catalog.products[i].name + "</td>")
     document.write("<td>$" + catalog.products[i].price + "</td>")
     document.writeln("<td>" + catalog.products[i].availability + "</td></tr>")
    }
   }
  }
  document.writeln("</table>")
  document.writeln("<p class='catalog'>Click on the product number for more
information.</p>")
 }else document.writeln("<p>No products were found!</p>")
</script>
</body>
</html>
```

Providing Product Details

The productlist.htm page (Listing 19.8) is used to display information about a specific product, as identified by the listproduct cookie. The displayProductInfo() method of the ProductDesc object creates the product description table (refer to Figure 19.3).

Listing 19.8:   Providing Detailed Information about a Specific Product (listproduct.htm)

```
<html>
<head>
<script language="JavaScript" src="catalog.js">
</script>
<script language="JavaScript" src="productdesc.js">
</script>
<script language="JavaScript" src="database.js">
</script>
<script language="JavaScript" src="cookie.js">
</script>
<script language="JavaScript" src="cart.js">
</script>
<script language="JavaScript" src="accesscart.js">
</script>
<title>Selected Product</title>
<link rel="stylesheet" type="text/css"
```

```
  href="catstyle.css">
<body>
<p class="back"><a href="javascript:window.history.back()">Go back</a></p>
<script language="JavaScript">
 var n = getCookie("listproduct")
 catalog.products[n].displayProductInfo()
 displayAddViewCheckoutButtons(n)
</script>
</body>
</html>
```

Adding a Client-Side Shopping Cart

Implementing a shopping cart is easy using JavaScript and cookies. The cart.js file (Listing 19.9) makes use of the cookie functions defined in cookie.js. The Cart object is constructed using the values defined in the cart cookie. The Cart object defines the product and quantity properties. These properties are arrays that keep track of the number of products of each type that the user has added to his or her shopping cart.

Listing 19.9:   The *Cart* Object (cart.js)

```
// cart.js

function Cart() {
 var cart = getCookie("cart")
 this.product = new Array()
 this.quantity = new Array()
 if(cart != "") {
  var pairs=cart.split("|")
  for(var i=0;i<pairs.length;++i) {
   var pairSplit=pairs[i].split("-")
   this.product[i] = pairSplit[0]
   this.quantity[i] = pairSplit[1]
  }
 }
 this.save = Cart_save
 this.addProduct = Cart_addProduct
 this.deleteProduct = Cart_deleteProduct
 this.changeQuantity = Cart_changeQuantity
}

function Cart_save() {
 var cart = ""
 for(var i=0; i<this.product.length; ++i) {
  cart += "" + this.product[i] + "-" + this.quantity[i]
  if(i != this.product.length - 1) cart += "|"
```

```
    }
    setCookie("cart", cart)
}

function Cart_addProduct(n) {
  for(var i=0; i<this.product.length; ++i) {
   if(this.product[i] == n) {
    this.quantity[i]++
    return
   }
  }
  var last = this.product.length
  this.product[last] = n
  this.quantity[last] = 1
}

function Cart_deleteProduct(n) {
  for(var i=0; i<this.product.length; ++i) {
   if(this.product[i] == n) {
    this.product.splice(i, 1)
    this.quantity.splice(i, 1)
    break
   }
  }
}

function Cart_changeQuantity(n, q) {
  if(q < 0) return
  if(q == 0) {
   this.deleteProduct(n)
   return
  }
  for(var i=0; i<this.product.length; ++i) {
   if(this.product[i] == n) {
    this.quantity[i] = q
    break
   }
  }
}
```

The product numbers are indices into the `products` property of the `Catalog` object. The product/quantity values are stored in the single `cart` cookie. The cookie has the following string format:

$$p_0\text{-}q_0|p_1\text{-}q_1| \cdots |p_n\text{-}q_n$$

The p_0 , p_1 , ... p_n are the numbers of the products in the cart and q_0 , q_1 , ... q_n are their associated quantities.

The Cart object defines the following four methods:

save()   Saves the object as the cart cookie.

addProduct(n)   Adds a product to the cart. If the product already exists in the cart, its quantity is incremented.

deleteProduct(n)   Removes a product from the cart.

changeQuantity(n, q)   Changes the quantity of a product. If the value of q is 0, then the product is removed from the cart.

These methods are used by the functions of accesscart.js (Listing 19.10). The following functions defined by accesscart.js simplify access to the shopping cart:

addToCart(n)   Creates a new Cart object from the cart cookie, adds the specified product to the cart, and then saves the Cart object as a cookie. Displays a message to the user that the product was added to the cart. Reloads the current page.

deleteProduct(n)   Creates a new Cart object from the cart cookie, adds the specified product to the cart, and then saves the Cart object as a cookie. Reloads the current page.

changeQuantity(n, q)   Creates a new Cart object from the cart cookie, changes the quantity of the specified product in the cart, and then saves the Cart object as a cookie. Reloads the current page.

displayViewCheckoutButtons()   Displays the View Shopping Cart and Check Out links if the user has something in his or her cart.

displayCheckoutButton()   Displays the Check Out link if the user has something in his or her cart. If the user's cart is empty, a message is displayed to the user.

displayAddViewCheckoutButtons(n)   Displays the Add to Cart link, and if the user's cart is not empty, displays the View Shopping Cart and Check Out links.

cartIsEmpty()   Returns a Boolean value indicating whether or not the user's cart is empty (i.e., contains no products).

Listing 19.10:   Simplifying Access to the Shopping Cart (accesscart.js)

```
// accesscart.js

function addToCart(n) {
 var cart = new Cart()
 cart.addProduct(n)
 cart.save()
 var msg = catalog.products[n].name
 msg += " has been added to your shopping cart."
 alert(msg)
```

```
 window.location.reload()
 }

function deleteProduct(n) {
 var cart = new Cart()
 cart.deleteProduct(n)
 cart.save()
 window.location.reload()
 }

function changeQuantity(n, q) {
 var newQ = window.prompt("How many would you like?", q)
 if(newQ >= 0) {
  var cart = new Cart()
  cart.changeQuantity(n, newQ)
  cart.save()
  window.location.reload()
 }else alert("The quantity must be zero or greater.")
 }

function displayViewCheckoutButtons() {
 if(cartIsEmpty()) return
 document.write("<p class='cart'>")
 document.write("<a href='viewcart.htm' class='cartbutton'>")
 document.write("View Shopping Cart</a> ")
 document.write("<a href='checkout.htm' class='cartbutton'>")
 document.writeln("Check Out</a></p>")
 }

function displayCheckoutButton() {
 if(cartIsEmpty()) {
  alert("Your cart is empty.")
  return
 }
 document.write("<p class='cart'>")
 document.write("<a href='checkout.htm' class='cartbutton'>")
 document.writeln("Check Out</a></p>")
 }

function displayAddViewCheckoutButtons(n) {
 document.write("<p class='cart'>")
 document.write("<a href='javascript:addToCart("+n+")' class='cartbutton'>")
 document.write("Add to Cart</a> ")
 if(!cartIsEmpty()) {
  document.write("<a href='viewcart.htm' class='cartbutton'>")
  document.write("View Shopping Cart</a> ")
  document.write("<a href='checkout.htm' class='cartbutton'>")
  document.writeln("Check Out</a>")
 }
 document.writeln("</p>")
 }
```

```
function cartIsEmpty() {
 if(getCookie("cart") == "") return true
 return false
 }
```

Viewing the Cart

The viewcart.htm file (Listing 19.11) displays the contents of the shopping cart (refer to Figure 19.8). It uses the Cart object (see cart.js) stored in the cart cookie and displays the contents of the cart as a table.

Listing 19.11: Viewing the Contents of the Shopping Cart (viewcart.htm)

```
<html>
<head>
<title>Shopping Cart</title>
<script language="JavaScript" src="catalog.js">
</script>
<script language="JavaScript" src="productdesc.js">
</script>
<script language="JavaScript" src="database.js">
</script>
<script language="JavaScript" src="cookie.js">
</script>
<script language="JavaScript" src="cart.js">
</script>
<script language="JavaScript" src="accesscart.js">
</script>
</head>
<link rel="stylesheet" type="text/css"
 href="catstyle.css">
<body>
<p class="back"><a href="javascript:window.history.back()">Go back</a></p>
<p class="search"><a href="catalog.htm">Continue Shopping</a></p>
<script language="JavaScript">
var cart = new Cart()
if(cart.product.length == 0) {
 document.write("<p class='empty'>Your shopping cart is empty.</p>")
}else{
 document.writeln("<table border='1' align='center'>")
 document.writeln("<tr><th>Product Number</th><th>Product
 Name</th><th>Price</th><th>Quantity</th><th>In
 Stock</th><th>Edit</th></tr>")
 var cost = 0
 for(var i=0; i<cart.product.length; ++i) {
 var n = cart.product[i]
 var q = cart.quantity[i]
 cost += catalog.products[n].price * q
 document.write("<tr>")
```

```
  document.write("<td><a href='javascript:listProduct("+n+")'>" +
↳ catalog.products[n].product_number + "</a></td>")
  document.write("<td>" + catalog.products[n].name + "</td>")
  document.write("<td>$" + catalog.products[n].price + "</td>")
  document.write("<td>" + q + "</td>")
  var available = catalog.products[n].availability
  document.write("<td>" + available + "</td>")
  var commands = "<a href='javascript:changeQuantity("+n+","+q+")'
↳ class='command'>Change quantity</a> "
  commands = commands + "<a href='javascript:deleteProduct("+n+")'
↳ class='command'>Delete</a>"
  document.write("<td>" + commands + "</td>")
  document.writeln("</tr>")
  }
  document.writeln("<tr><th colspan='2'>Total</th><th
↳$"+cost+"</th><td colspan='3'> </td></tr>")
  document.writeln("</table>")
  document.writeln("<p class='slogan'>Free shipping! No sales tax!</p>")
  displayCheckoutButton()
}
</script>
</body>
</html>
```

The Check Out Form

The checkout.htm file (Listing 19.12) displays a fairly standard web checkout form. It duplicates the code of viewcart.htm (Listing 19.11) to display the products contained in the user's cart.

Listing 19.12: Obtaining Billing and Shipping Information (checkout.htm)

```
<html>
<head>
<script language="JavaScript" src="catalog.js">
</script>
<script language="JavaScript" src="productdesc.js">
</script>
<script language="JavaScript" src="database.js">
</script>
<script language="JavaScript" src="cookie.js">
</script>
<script language="JavaScript" src="cart.js">
</script>
<script language="JavaScript" src="accesscart.js">
</script>
<title>Check Out</title>
<link rel="stylesheet" type="text/css"
 href="catstyle.css">
```

```
</head>
<body>
<p class="back"><a href="javascript:window.history.back()">Go back</a></p>
<p class="search"><a href="catalog.htm">Continue Shopping</a></p>
<script language="JavaScript">
var cart = new Cart()
if(cart.product.length == 0) {
 document.write("<p class='empty'>Your shopping cart is empty.</p>")
}else{
 document.writeln("<table border='1' align='center'>")
 document.writeln("<tr><th>Product Number</th>
⤷<th>Product Name</th><th>Price</th>
⤷<th>Quantity</th><th>In Stock</th>
⤷<th>Edit</th></tr>")
 var cost = 0
 for(var i=0; i<cart.product.length; ++i) {
  var n = cart.product[i]
  var q = cart.quantity[i]
  cost += catalog.products[n].price * q
  document.write("<tr>")
  document.write("<td><a href='javascript:listProduct("+n+")'>"
⤷ + catalog.products[n].product_number + "</a></td>")
  document.write("<td>" + catalog.products[n].name + "</td>")
  document.write("<td>$" + catalog.products[n].price + "</td>")
  document.write("<td>" + q + "</td>")
  var available = catalog.products[n].availability
  document.write("<td>" + available + "</td>")
  var commands = "<a href='javascript:changeQuantity("+n+","+q+")'
⤷ class='command'>Change quantity</a> "
  commands = commands + "<a href='javascript:deleteProduct("+n+")'
⤷ class='command'>Delete</a>"
  document.write("<td>" + commands + "</td>")
  document.writeln("</tr>")
 }
 document.writeln("<tr><th colspan='2'>Total</th>
⤷<th>$"+cost+"</th><td colspan='3'> </td></tr>")
 document.writeln("</table>")
 document.writeln("<p class='slogan'>Free shipping! No sales tax!</p>")
}
</script>
<form name="checkout" action="javascript:alert('You need
⤷server-side code to process the submission of this form!')">
<table border="0" align="center">
<tr><td class="form">Credit card:<td>
<select name="card"><option>Mastercard</option>
<option>Visa</option></select></td></tr>
<tr><td class="form">Credit card number:</td>
<td><input type="text" size="50" name="cardnumber"></td></tr>
<tr><td class="form">Email address:</td>
<td><input type="text" size="50" name="email"></td></tr>
<tr><td class="form">Billing address:</td><td> </td></tr>
```

```
<tr><td class="form">Name: (as it appears on your
card)</td><td><input type="text" size="50"
name="billname"></td></tr>
<tr><td class="form">Address:</td>
<td><input type="text" size="50" name="billaddr1"></td></tr>
<tr><td class="form"> </td>
<td><input type="text" size="50" name="billaddr2"></td></tr>
<tr><td class="form">City:</td>
<td><input type="text" size="50" name="billcity"></td></tr>
<tr><td class="form">State/Province:</td>
<td><input type="text" size="50" name="billstate"></td></tr>
<tr><td class="form">Postal Code:</td>
<td><input type="text" size="15" name="billzip"></td></tr>
<tr><td class="form">Country:</td>
<td><input type="text" size="50" name="billcountry"></td></tr>
<tr><td class="form">Shipping address:</td>
<td>(if different than the billing address)</td></tr>
<tr><td class="form">Name:</td>
<td><input type="text" size="50" name="shipname"></td></tr>
<tr><td class="form">Address:</td>
<td><input type="text" size="50" name="shipaddr1"></td></tr>
<tr><td class="form"> </td>
<td><input type="text" size="50" name="shipaddr2"></td></tr>
<tr><td class="form">City:</td>
<td><input type="text" size="50" name="shipcity"></td></tr>
<tr><td class="form">State/Province:</td>
<td><input type="text" size="50" name="shipstate"></td></tr>
<tr><td class="form">Postal Code:</td>
<td><input type="text" size="15" name="shipzip"></td></tr>
<tr><td class="form">Country:</td>
<td><input type="text" size="50" name="shipcountry"></td></tr>
<tr><td class="form"> </td>
<td><input type="submit" size="50" value="Check Out"></td>
</tr>
</form>
</body>
</html>
```

Summary

In this chapter, you learned how to use JavaScript to build an online product catalog for the hypothetical XYZ home-furnishing company. You also built a JavaScript shopping cart that enabled customers to order multiple products and manage the products they order. In the next chapter, you'll have a little fun learning how to use JavaScript to create games.

Game Programming

- Developing a poker machine

- Creating a board game

You've worked hard over the last 19 chapters to learn the JavaScript language and many of its applications. In this chapter, you'll have some fun as you learn more JavaScript game programming. First, you'll develop a poker machine that will let you play poker against your browser. Then you'll develop a board game that I call Web Walk, which will test your knowledge of the Web. Of course, the chapter isn't only fun and games—by programming these entertaining projects, you'll learn some very useful skills, including how to use JavaScript to build appealing user interfaces, to work with images, and to respond to a variety of user interface events. When you finish this chapter, you'll be able to develop your own games in JavaScript.

Developing a Poker Machine

The first game that you'll develop is a JavaScript version of a Vegas-style poker machine. In this game, you place an initial bet of $1.00 and are dealt five cards that you use to try to form a poker hand. Refer to Table 20.1 for a description and ranking of possible poker hands.

TABLE 20.1: Ranking of Poker Hands

Rank	Hand	Description
1	Royal flush	10 through ace of the same suit
2	Straight flush	Five consecutive cards of the same suit
3	Four of a kind	Four cards of the same rank
4	Full house	Three cards of one rank and two cards of another
5	Flush	Five cards of the same suit
6	Straight	Five consecutive cards
7	Three of a kind	Three cards of the same rank
8	Two pair	Two cards of the same rank and two cards of another rank
9	One pair	Two cards of the same rank
10	Everything else	

After receiving your five cards, you are allowed to discard any unwanted cards and receive an equal number of replacement cards in return. (You discard a card by clicking on it.) Once you have been dealt your replacement cards, you will receive a payoff based on the value of your hand. Table 20.2 summarizes the payoff algorithm.

TABLE 20.2: The Payoff Algorithm

Hand	Payoff
Royal flush	$1,000.00
Straight flush	$ 500.00
Four of a kind	$ 250.00
Full house	$ 100.00
Flush	$ 50.00
Straight	$ 25.00
Three of a kind	$ 10.00
Two pair	$ 5.00
One pair of jacks or higher	$ 1.00

To play this game, open `poker.htm` (Listing 20.1). The program will deal you a five-card hand, as shown in Figure 20.1. You are also given $100.00 dollars to start with—the You have $ text box displays your current stake for the game. The amount is updated after each hand. (Each hand costs $1.00 to play.)

FIGURE 20.1:

Poker machine initial deal
(Listing 20.1)

If you're happy with the hand you were dealt, click the Continue button to play the next hand. Otherwise, click on any cards that you want to discard—they will be turned over, as shown in Figure 20.2—and then click the Continue button. You can discard only once per each hand. The cards you indicated as discards will be replaced, and you will be told of your winnings in your browser's status bar, as shown in Figure 20.3. Click the Continue button to play another hand.

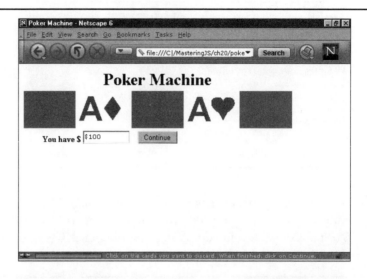

Listing 20.1 shows the source code of poker.htm. It is mostly JavaScript except for the HTML in the document body that creates the table used to display the card images. Temporary green images (turned-over cards) are initially loaded and displayed until all 52 cards have been loaded. The script in the document body invokes startGame() to begin play.

Listing 20.1:   A Poker Machine (poker.htm)

```
<HTML>
<HEAD>
<TITLE>Poker Machine</TITLE>
<SCRIPT LANGUAGE="JavaScript"><!--

cardImages=new Array(52)
deck=new Array(52)
cards = new Array(5)
replacements = new Array(5)
rank = new Array(5)
suit = new Array(5)

function startGame() {
 state="load"
 budget=100
 loadImages()
 setTimeout("checkImageLoading()",1000)
}
function checkImageLoading() {
 var allLoaded=false
 for(var i=0;i<52;++i){
  if(!cardImages[i].complete){
   setTimeout("checkImageLoading()",1000)
   break
  }else if(i==51) play()
 }
}
function loadImages() {
 blankCard = new Image()
 blankCard.src="blank.gif"
 for(var i=0;i<52;++i) {
  cardImages[i]=new Image()
  cardImages[i].src="card"+i+".gif"
 }
}
function play() {
 state="deal"
 shuffleDeck()
 dealCards()
}
function shuffleDeck() {
 for(var i=0;i<52;++i) deck[i]=i
 for(var i=0;i<52;++i) {
  var temp=deck[i]
  var rand=Math.round(Math.random()*51)
  deck[i]=deck[rand]
  deck[rand]=temp
 }
```

```
}
function dealCards() {
 for(var i=0;i<5;++i){
  cards[i]=deck[i]
  replacements[i]=deck[5+i]
 }
 displayCards()
 window.document.forms[0].status.value="$"+budget
 var msg="Click on the cards you want to discard. "
 msg+="When finished, click on Continue."
 window.defaultStatus=msg
 state="draw"
}
function displayCards() {
 for(var i=0;i<5;++i)
  window.document.images[i].src=cardImages[cards[i]].src
}
function processCard(n) {
 if(state=="draw") {
  var img=window.document.images[n]
  if(img.src!=cardImages[cards[n]].src)
   img.src=cardImages[cards[n]].src
  else img.src="blank.gif"
 }
}
function statusChange() {
 alert("Are you cheating?")
 window.document.forms[0].status.value="$"+budget
}
function continueClicked() {
 if(state=="draw") {
  state="payoff"
  for(var i=0;i<5;++i) {
   var img=window.document.images[i]
   if(img.src!=cardImages[cards[i]].src) {
    cards[i]=replacements[i]
    img.src=cardImages[cards[i]].src
   }
  }
  showPayoff()
 }else if(state=="payoff") play()
}
function showPayoff() {
 var payoff=-1
 evaluateHand()
 if(isRoyalFlush()) payoff=1000
 else if(isStraightFlush()) payoff=500
 else if(isFourOfAKind()) payoff=250
 else if(isFullHouse()) payoff=100
 else if(isFlush()) payoff=50
 else if(isStraight()) payoff=25
```

```
    else if(isThreeOfAKind()) payoff=10
    else if(isTwoPair()) payoff=5
    else if(isJacksOrBetter()) payoff=1
    else msg="You lose $1."
    window.defaultStatus=msg+" Click on Continue to play again."
    budget+=payoff
    window.document.forms[0].status.value="$"+budget
  }
function compare(a,b) {
  return a-b
}
function evaluateHand() {
  for(var i=0;i<5;++i) {
   rank[i]=cards[i]%13+1
   suit[i]=Math.floor(cards[i]/13)
  }
  rank=rank.sort(compare)
}
function isRoyalFlush()    {
  if(sameSuit() && straight()) {
   if(rank[0]==1 && rank[1]==10) {
    msg="A ROYAL FLUSH! You win $1000."
    return true
   }
  }
  return false
}
function sameSuit() {
  if(suit[0]==suit[1] && suit[0]==suit[2]
   && suit[0]==suit[3] && suit[0]==suit[4]) return true
  return false
}
function straight() {
  var aceHi = new Array(5)
  for(var i=0;i<5;++i) {
   aceHi[i]=rank[i]
   if(aceHi[i]==1) aceHi[i]=14
  }
  if(straightCheck(rank)) return true
  if(straightCheck(aceHi.sort(compare))) return true
  return false
}
function straightCheck(a) {
  for(var i=0;i<4;++i)
   if(a[i]+1!=a[i+1]) return false
  return true
}
function isStraightFlush()     {
  if(sameSuit() && straight()) {
   msg="A STRAIGHT FLUSH! You win $500."
   return true
```

```
 }
 return false
}
function isFlush()   {
 if(sameSuit()) {
  msg="A FLUSH! You win $50."
  return true
 }
 return false
}
function isStraight()   {
 if(straight()) {
  msg="A STRAIGHT! You win $25."
  return true
 }
 return false
}
function isFourOfAKind() {
 for(var i=0;i<2;++i) {
  if(matches(rank[i])==4) {
   msg="FOUR OF A KIND! You win $250."
   return true
  }
 }
 return false
}
function matches(n) {
 var count=0
 for(var i=0;i<5;++i)
  if(rank[i]==n) ++count
 return count
}
function isThreeOfAKind() {
 for(var i=0;i<3;++i) {
  if(matches(rank[i])==3) {
   msg="THREE OF A KIND! You win $10."
   return true
  }
 }
 return false
}
function isFullHouse() {
 var matched3 = false
 var matched2 = false
 for(var i=0;i<4;++i) {
  if(matches(rank[i])==3) matched3=true
  else if(matches(rank[i])==2) matched2=true
 }
 if(matched3 && matched2) {
   msg="A FULL HOUSE! You win $100."
   return true
```

```
  }
  return false
 }
 function isTwoPair() {
  var count = 0
  for(var i=0;i<5;++i)
   if(matches(rank[i])==2) ++count
  if(count==4) {
    msg="TWO PAIR! You win $5."
    return true
  }
  return false
 }
 function isJacksOrBetter() {
  for(var i=0;i<5;++i) {
   if(matches(rank[i])==2){
    if(rank[i]==1 || rank[i]>10){
     msg="A PAIR OF "
     msg+=jacksOrBetterPairName(rank[i])
     msg+="! You win $1."
     return true
    }
   }
  }
  return false
 }
 function jacksOrBetterPairName(n) {
  if(n==1) return "ACES"
  if(n==11) return "JACKS"
  if(n==12) return "QUEENS"
  if(n==13) return "KINGS"
  return ""
 }
// --></SCRIPT>
</HEAD>
<BODY BGCOLOR="white">
<TABLE>
<TR>
<TD COLSPAN="5">
<H1 ALIGN="CENTER">Poker Machine</H1></TD>
</TR>
<TR>
<TD><A HREF="javascript:void(0)" onClick="processCard(0)">
<IMG SRC="blank.gif" BORDER="0"></A></TD>
<TD><A HREF="javascript:void(0)" onClick="processCard(1)">
<IMG SRC="blank.gif" BORDER="0"></A></TD>
<TD><A HREF="javascript:void(0)" onClick="processCard(2)">
<IMG SRC="blank.gif" BORDER="0"></A></TD>
<TD><A HREF="javascript:void(0)" onClick="processCard(3)">
<IMG SRC="blank.gif" BORDER="0"></A></TD>
<TD><A HREF="javascript:void(0)" onClick="processCard(4)">
```

```
<IMG SRC="blank.gif" BORDER="0"></A></TD>
</TR>
<TR>
<TD ALIGN="RIGHT" COLSPAN="2">
<FORM>
<B>You have $</B>
<INPUT TYPE="TEXT" NAME="status" VALUE="" SIZE="10"
onChange="statusChange()">
</FORM>
</TD>
<TD ALIGN="CENTER">
<FORM>
<INPUT TYPE="BUTTON" NAME="continue" VALUE="Continue"
onClick="continueClicked()">
</FORM>
</TD>
<TD>
</TD>
<TD>
</TD>
</TR>
</TABLE>
<SCRIPT LANGUAGE="JavaScript"><!--
startGame()
// --></SCRIPT>
</BODY>
</HTML>
```

The following are the arrays and functions defined in the document head:

The *cardImages* array   Contains the images to be displayed for each card. They are loaded from the files card0.gif through card51.gif.

The *deck* array   Is used to simulate a deck of cards. They are identified numerically as shown in Table 20.3.

TABLE 20.3: Numerical Coding of Card Values

Value range	Description
0 through 12	Ace through king of spades
13 through 25	Ace through king of clubs
26 through 38	Ace through king of hearts
39 through 51	Ace through king of diamonds

The *cards* array   Contains the cards that are initially dealt to the user.

The *replacements* array   Contains replacement cards for those cards that the user discards.

The *rank* array   Identifies the numerical ranking of each card in the cards array. Values range from 1 (ace) through 13 (king).

The *suit* array   Identifies the suit of each card in cards. Suits are 0 (spades), 1 (clubs), 2 (hearts), and 3 (diamonds).

The *startGame()* function   Is invoked to begin play of the game. It sets the program state to load, gives the user a budget of $100.00, loads the card images, and sets a timeout to check for the completion of image loading.

The *checkImageLoading()* function   Because there are so many GIF images used in this program, it would probably take a significant amount of time for them to be loaded over a low-speed modem line. This function repeatedly checks (through timeouts) to determine if all card images have been loaded. The play() method is invoked when all images have been loaded.

TIP

Whenever you require images to be loaded before the main part of a script begins, use timeouts to check for the completion of image loading.

The *loadImages()* function   Performs the loading of the card images.

The *play()* function   Is invoked when all images have been loaded. It sets the program state to *deal*, shuffles the deck, and deals a hand to the user.

The *shuffleDeck()* function   Shuffles the deck array by switching the 52 cards to random positions within the deck.

The *dealCards()* function   Assigns five cards from the deck to the cards array and five to the replacements array. It then displays the cards to the user, identifies how much money the user has available, and displays a help message in the window's status bar. It then sets the program state to *draw*.

The *displayCards()* function   Is used by dealCards() to display the value of the cards array to the user.

The *processCard()* function   Handles the event that occurs when the user clicks on a card. It checks to make sure the program is in the *draw* state, and if so, flips the designated card over (flips it face-down or face-up depending on its current display status).

The *statusChange()* function   Handles the onChange event associated with the status text field by preventing the user from modifying the field's value.

The *continueClicked()* function   Handles the clicking of the Continue button. If the state is *draw*, then the state is changed to *payoff*; replacement cards are displayed to the user; and the showPayoff() function is invoked to compute a new total based on how much the user won or lost. Because users bet $1.00 per hand, they cannot lose more than a dollar at a time. If the state is *payoff*, then a new round of play is initiated.

The *showPayoff()* function   Checks to see how much the user won or lost by invoking functions that evaluate the hand. The user's budget is updated by this amount.

The *compare()* function   Is used for numerical comparison by the sort() method of the array object.

The *evaluateHand()* function   Generates the rank and suit arrays from the cards array and then sorts the rank array.

The *isRoyalFlush()* function   Checks a hand to see if it is a royal flush. A royal flush is ace, king, queen, jack, and ten of the same suit.

The *sameSuit()* function   Checks a hand to see if all the cards are the same suit.

The *straight()* function   Checks a hand to see if it is a straight (five cards in a row). It checks for both ace low and ace high.

The *straightCheck()* function   Is used by straight() to check a hand to see if it is a straight.

The *isStraightFlush()* function   Checks a hand to see if it is a straight flush (five cards in a row of the same suit).

The *isFlush()* function   Checks a hand to see if it is a flush (five cards of the same suit).

The *isStraight()* function   Checks a hand to see if it is a straight.

The *isFourOfAKind()* function   Checks a hand to see if it contains four of a kind.

The *matches()* function   Returns the number of cards in a hand that are of the same rank.

The *isThreeOfAKind()* function   Checks a hand to see if it contains three of a kind.

The *isFullHouse()* function   Checks a hand to see if it is a full house.

The *isTwoPair()* function   Checks a hand to see if it contains two pairs.

The *isJacksOrBetter()* function   Checks a hand to see if it contains a pair of jacks or higher.

The *jacksOrBetterPairName()* function   If the hand contains a pair of aces, kings, queens, or jacks, this function returns the name of the highest pair contained in the hand.

Developing a Board Game—Web Walk

Board games, such as Parker Brothers' Monopoly, Milton Bradley's Life, and the traditional backgammon, have been popular for a long time. They are easy to learn, present a variety of interesting situations, and include an element of risk. In this section, you'll learn how to create a simple JavaScript board game that is based on a simple "advance around the board" concept, with multiple-choice questions about the World Wide Web. I call the game Web Walk, and though it will probably never be as popular as backgammon, it should be entertaining.

Web Walk is played like Life. To see how it's played, open webwalk.htm. (Listing 20.2). (The webwalk.htm file uses the ww.htm file of Listing 20.3.) You start off at a fixed starting point and move across a path to a fixed destination. The path consists of marked squares.

Listing 20.2:   The Web Walk Top-Level Frame Set (webwalk.htm)

```
<HTML>
<HEAD>
<TITLE>Web Walk</TITLE>
<FRAMESET COLS="500,*" BORDER="0">
<FRAME SRC="ww.htm">
<FRAME SRC="blank.htm">
</FRAMESET>
</HTML>
```

Listing 20.3:   The Web Walk Implementation (ww.htm)

```
<HTML>
<HEAD>
<TITLE>Web Walk</TITLE>
<SCRIPT LANGUAGE="JavaScript"><!--
state="load"

boardLayout = new Array(
 new Array("s","6","3","1","q","q","-2","q"),
 new Array("","6","","","","","","-3"),
 new Array("","1","","","","q","q","-5"),
 new Array("3","q","","","","q","",""),
 new Array("q","","-1","q","q","q","q","q"),
 new Array("q","","q","","-1","","","q"),
 new Array("q","","-6","","1","q","q","-10"),
 new Array("q","q","q","","","","","e"))

function Move(p1,p2) {
 this.from=p1
 this.to=p2
}
```

```
validMoves=new Array(
 new Move(0,1), new Move(1,2), new Move(1,9),
 new Move(2,3), new Move(3,4), new Move(4,5),
 new Move(5,6), new Move(6,7), new Move(7,15),
 new Move(9,17), new Move(15,23), new Move(17,25),
 new Move(21,29), new Move(22,21), new Move(23,22),
 new Move(24,32), new Move(25,24), new Move(29,37),
 new Move(32,40), new Move(34,35), new Move(35,36),
 new Move(36,37), new Move(36,44), new Move(37,38),
 new Move(38,39), new Move(39,47), new Move(40,48),
 new Move(42,34), new Move(44,52), new Move(47,55),
 new Move(48,56), new Move(50,42), new Move(52,53),
 new Move(53,54), new Move(54,55), new Move(55,63),
 new Move(56,57), new Move(57,58), new Move(58,50)
)

function loadImages() {
 questionGIF=new Image(); questionGIF.src="question.gif"
 feetGIF=new Image(); feetGIF.src="feet.gif"
 plus1GIF=new Image(); plus1GIF.src="plus1.gif"
 plus3GIF=new Image(); plus3GIF.src="plus3.gif"
 plus6GIF=new Image(); plus6GIF.src="plus6.gif"
 minus1GIF=new Image(); minus1GIF.src="minus1.gif"
 minus2GIF=new Image(); minus2GIF.src="minus2.gif"
 minus3GIF=new Image(); minus3GIF.src="minus3.gif"
 minus5GIF=new Image(); minus5GIF.src="minus5.gif"
 minus6GIF=new Image(); minus6GIF.src="minus6.gif"
 minus10GIF=new Image(); minus10GIF.src="minus10.gif"
}
function startGame() {
 state="start"
 position=0
 direction="F"
 stepsToMove=0
 msg("Click on Start to begin.")
}
function msg(s) {
 var doc=parent.frames[1].document
 doc.open()
 doc.writeln('<BODY BGCOLOR="white">')
 doc.writeln(s)
 doc.writeln('</BODY>')
 doc.close()
}
function square(n) {
 nextPos=parseInt(n)
 if(board(nextPos)=="s"){
  if(state=="start") {
   state="move"
   stepsToMove=steps()
   msg(move())
```

```
    }else alert("Game is already started.")
   }else if(state=="move"){
    if(canMove(nextPos)){
     if(board(nextPos)=="e") {
      state="end"
      restoreCurrentPosition()
     showMovement(nextPos)
      winner()
     }else{
      state="wait"
      restoreCurrentPosition()
     showMovement(nextPos)
     processMovement(nextPos)
     }
    }else msg("Can't move there!")
  }
}
function board(n) {
 return boardLayout[Math.floor(n/8)][n%8]
}
function steps() {
 return Math.floor((Math.random()*3)+1)
}
function move() {
 var squares=" squares."
 if(stepsToMove==1) squares=" square."
 var dir=" forward "
 if(direction=="B") dir=" backward "
 return "Move"+dir+stepsToMove+squares
}
function canMove(n) {
 for(var i=0;i<validMoves.length;++i){
  if(direction=="F" && validMoves[i].from==position &&
   validMoves[i].to==n) return true
  if(direction=="B" && validMoves[i].from==n &&
   validMoves[i].to==position) return true
 }
 return false
}
function restoreCurrentPosition() {
 var sq=board(position)
 var imgPos=imagePosition(position)
 var oldImage=questionGIF
 if(sq=="s") return
 else if(sq=="1") oldImage=plus1GIF
 else if(sq=="3") oldImage=plus3GIF
 else if(sq=="6") oldImage=plus6GIF
 else if(sq=="-1") oldImage=minus1GIF
 else if(sq=="-2") oldImage=minus2GIF
 else if(sq=="-3") oldImage=minus3GIF
 else if(sq=="-5") oldImage=minus5GIF
```

```
  else if(sq=="-6") oldImage=minus6GIF
  else if(sq=="-10") oldImage=minus10GIF
  window.document.images[imgPos].src=oldImage.src
}
function imagePosition(n) {
 imageCount=0
 for(var i=0;i<n;++i)
  if(board(i)!="") ++imageCount
 var len=window.document.images.length
 // Fixes bug in Navigator 3.0
 if(len>38) imageCount+=Math.floor(len/2)
 return imageCount
}
function showMovement(n) {
 var imgPos=imagePosition(n)
 window.document.images[imgPos].src=feetGIF.src
}
function processMovement(n) {
 position=n
 --stepsToMove
 if(stepsToMove==0){
  var sq=board(position)
  var num=0
  if(sq=="q") askQuestion()
  else{
   num=parseInt(sq)
   if(num<0) direction="B"
   else direction="F"
   stepsToMove=Math.abs(num)
   state="move"
   msg(move())
  }
 }else{
  state="move"
  msg(move())
 }
}
function winner() {
 var doc=parent.frames[1].document
 doc.open()
 doc.writeln('<BODY BGCOLOR="white">')
 doc.writeln('<H3>Congratulations -- You Won!!!</H3>')
 doc.writeln('Click Reload to play again.')
 doc.writeln('</BODY>')
 doc.close()
}
function Question() {
 this.question=Question.arguments[0]
 var n=Question.arguments.length
 this.answers = new Array(n-2)
 for(var i=1; i<n-1; ++i) this.answers[i-1]=Question.arguments[i]
```

```
   this.correctAnswer=Question.arguments[n-1]
}
function askQuestion() {
 rnd=Math.round(Math.random()*(qa.length-1))
 var doc=parent.frames[1].document
 doc.open()
 doc.writeln('<HTML>')
 doc.writeln('<BODY BGCOLOR="white">')
 doc.writeln("<H4 ALIGN='CENTER'>"+qa[rnd].question+"</H4>")
 doc.writeln('<FORM NAME="answerForm">')
 for(var ii=0;ii<qa[rnd].answers.length;++ii) {
  doc.writeln('<H4 ALIGN="CENTER">')
  doc.write('<INPUT TYPE="RADIO" NAME="answer">')
  doc.writeln(qa[rnd].answers[ii])
  if(ii+1==qa[rnd].answers.length) {
   doc.write('<BR><BR><INPUT TYPE="BUTTON"')
   doc.writeln('NAME="continue" VALUE="Continue" ')
   doc.writeln(' onClick="parent.frames[0].focus()">')
  }
  doc.writeln('</H4>')
 }
 doc.writeln('</FORM>')
 doc.writeln('</BODY></HTML>')
 doc.close()
}
function checkAnswers() {
 if(state!="wait") return
 var numAnswers=qa[rnd].answers.length
 var correctAnswer=qa[rnd].correctAnswer
 var doc=parent.frames[1].document
 for(var jj=0;jj<numAnswers;++jj) {
  if(doc.answerForm.elements[jj].checked) {
   if(jj==correctAnswer){
    correct()
    break
   }else{
    incorrect()
    break
   }
  }
  if(jj==numAnswers){
   incorrect()
   break
  }
 }
}
function correct() {
 var num=steps()
 direction="F"
 stepsToMove=num
 state="move"
```

```
  msg("<H4>Correct!</H4>"+move())
}
function incorrect() {
 var num=steps()
 direction="B"
 stepsToMove=num
 state="move"
 msg("<H4>Incorrect.</H4>"+move())
}

//Questions
qa = new Array()

qa[0] = new Question("Who created the Web?",
 "Marc Andreessen",
 "James Gosling",
 "Tim Berners-Lee",
 "Bill Gates",
 2)

qa[1] = new Question("Who invented HTML?",
 "Marc Andreessen",
 "James Gosling",
 "Tim Berners-Lee",
 "Bill Gates",
 2)

qa[2] = new Question("Who is the creator of Mosaic?",
 "Marc Andreessen",
 "James Gosling",
 "Tim Berners-Lee",
 "Bill Gates",
 0)

qa[3] = new Question("Who is the creator of JavaScript?",
 "Tim Berners-Lee",
 "Spike Lee",
 "Brendan Eich",
 "Marc Andreessen",
 2)

qa[4] = new Question("What is Lynx?",
 "A mark-up language",
 "A Web browser",
 "A Web server",
 "A protocol",
 1)

qa[5] = new Question("What company created Java?",
 "Microsoft",
 "Sun Microsystems",
```

```
  "Netscape",
  "IBM",
  1)

qa[6] = new Question("What company created JavaScript ?",
  "Microsoft",
  "Sun Microsystems",
  "Netscape",
  "IBM",
  2)

qa[7] = new Question("Where was the Web created?",
  "CERN",
  "NCSA",
  "MIT",
  "USC",
  0)

qa[8] = new Question("Where was Mosaic created?",
  "CERN",
  "NCSA",
  "MIT",
  "USC",
  1)

qa[9] = new Question("What is HTTP?",
  "A mark-up language",
  "A protocol",
  "A Web server",
  "A Web browser",
  1)

qa[10] = new Question("Which of the following speak HTTP?",
  "Web browsers",
  "Web servers",
  "Both Web browsers and servers",
  "None of the above",
  2)

qa[11] = new Question("Where do CGI programs run?",
  "On browsers",
  "On Web servers",
  "On both Web browsers and servers",
  "None of the above",
  1)

qa[12] = new Question("What is a MIME type?",
  "A CGI program",
  "A file type identifier",
  "A plug-in",
  "A protocol",
```

```
  1)

qa[13] = new Question("What is a plug-in?",
 "A CGI program",
 "A helper program that executes in the context of a browser",
 "An external helper program",
 "A protocol",
 1)

qa[14] = new Question("What is LiveScript?",
 "The precursor to JavaScript",
 "An ActiveX scripting language",
 "A Visual Basic scripting language",
 "A C++ scripting language",
 0)

qa[15] = new Question("What is an event?",
 "An object that represents the occurrence of an action",
 "A function that responds to an action",
 "An HTML tag",
 "A protocol data unit",
 0)

qa[16] = new Question("What is an event handler?",
 "An object that represents the occurrence of an action",
 "A function that responds to an action",
 "An HTML tag",
 "A protocol data unit",
 1)

qa[17] = new Question("What is an object type?",
 "A MIME type",
 "An HTML tag",
 "An HTML attribute",
 "A template for defining and creating objects",
 3)

qa[18] = new Question("What is an object?",
 "A function that does not return a value",
 "An HTML tag",
 "A VRML document",
 "An instance of an object type",
 3)

qa[19] = new Question("What is a property?",
 "A function that is associated with an object",
 "A data item that is associated with an object",
 "A JavaScript syntax rule",
 "An object type",
 1)

qa[20] = new Question("What is a method?",
 "A function that is associated with an object",
```

```
 "A data item that is associated with an object",
 "A JavaScript syntax rule",
 "An object type",
 0)

qa[21] = new Question("What is an applet?",
 "A Macintosh program",
 "A small script",
 "An ActiveX script",
 "A Java program that executes in the context of a browser",
 3)
// --></SCRIPT>
</HEAD>
<BODY BGCOLOR="white" onLoad="startGame()" onFocus="checkAnswers()">
<TABLE BGCOLOR="black">
<TR>
<TD><A HREF="javascript:void(0)" onClick="square(0)">
<IMG SRC="start.gif" BORDER="0"></A></TD>
<TD><A HREF="javascript:void(0)" onClick="square(1)">
<IMG SRC="plus6.gif" BORDER="0"></A></TD>
<TD><A HREF="javascript:void(0)" onClick="square(2)">
<IMG SRC="plus3.gif" BORDER="0"></A></TD>
<TD><A HREF="javascript:void(0)" onClick="square(3)">
<IMG SRC="plus1.gif" BORDER="0"></A></TD>
<TD><A HREF="javascript:void(0)" onClick="square(4)">
<IMG SRC="question.gif" BORDER="0"></A></TD>
<TD><A HREF="javascript:void(0)" onClick="square(5)">
<IMG SRC="question.gif" BORDER="0"></A></TD>
<TD><A HREF="javascript:void(0)" onClick="square(6)">
<IMG SRC="minus2.gif" BORDER="0"></A></TD>
<TD><A HREF="javascript:void(0)" onClick="square(7)">
<IMG SRC="question.gif" BORDER="0"></A></TD>
</TR>
<TR>
<TD> </TD>
<TD><A HREF="javascript:void(0)" onClick="square(9)">
<IMG SRC="plus6.gif" BORDER="0"></A></TD>
<TD> </TD><TD> </TD><TD> </TD><TD> </TD><TD> </TD>
<TD><A HREF="javascript:void(0)" onClick="square(15)">
<IMG SRC="minus3.gif" BORDER="0"></A></TD>
</TR>
<TR>
<TD> </TD>
<TD><A HREF="javascript:void(0)" onClick="square(17)">
<IMG SRC="plus1.gif" BORDER="0"></A></TD>
<TD> </TD><TD> </TD><TD> </TD>
<TD><A HREF="javascript:void(0)" onClick="square(21)">
<IMG SRC="question.gif" BORDER="0"></A></TD>
<TD><A HREF="javascript:void(0)" onClick="square(22)">
<IMG SRC="question.gif" BORDER="0"></A></TD>
<TD><A HREF="javascript:void(0)" onClick="square(23)">
<IMG SRC="minus5.gif" BORDER="0"></A></TD>
</TR>
```

```
<TR>
<TD><A HREF="javascript:void(0)" onClick="square(24)">
<IMG SRC="plus3.gif" BORDER="0"></A></TD>
<TD><A HREF="javascript:void(0)" onClick="square(25)">
<IMG SRC="question.gif" BORDER="0"></A></TD>
<TD> </TD><TD> </TD><TD> </TD>
<TD><A HREF="javascript:void(0)" onClick="square(29)">
<IMG SRC="question.gif" BORDER="0"></A></TD>
<TD> </TD><TD> </TD>
</TR>
<TR>
<TD><A HREF="javascript:void(0)" onClick="square(32)">
<IMG SRC="question.gif" BORDER="0"></A></TD>
<TD> </TD>
<TD><A HREF="javascript:void(0)" onClick="square(34)">
<IMG SRC="minus1.gif" BORDER="0"></A></TD>
<TD><A HREF="javascript:void(0)" onClick="square(35)">
<IMG SRC="question.gif" BORDER="0"></A></TD>
<TD><A HREF="javascript:void(0)" onClick="square(36)">
<IMG SRC="question.gif" BORDER="0"></A></TD>
<TD><A HREF="javascript:void(0)" onClick="square(37)">
<IMG SRC="question.gif" BORDER="0"></A></TD>
<TD><A HREF="javascript:void(0)" onClick="square(38)">
<IMG SRC="question.gif" BORDER="0"></A></TD>
<TD><A HREF="javascript:void(0)" onClick="square(39)">
<IMG SRC="question.gif" BORDER="0"></A></TD>
</TR>
<TR>
<TD><A HREF="javascript:void(0)" onClick="square(40)">
<IMG SRC="question.gif" BORDER="0"></A></TD>
<TD> </TD>
<TD><A HREF="javascript:void(0)" onClick="square(42)">
<IMG SRC="question.gif" BORDER="0"></A></TD>
<TD> </TD>
<TD><A HREF="javascript:void(0)" onClick="square(44)">
<IMG SRC="minus1.gif" BORDER="0"></A></TD>
<TD> </TD><TD> </TD>
<TD><A HREF="javascript:void(0)" onClick="square(47)">
<IMG SRC="question.gif" BORDER="0"></A></TD>
</TR>
<TR>
<TD><A HREF="javascript:void(0)" onClick="square(48)">
<IMG SRC="question.gif" BORDER="0"></A></TD>
<TD> </TD>
<TD><A HREF="javascript:void(0)" onClick="square(50)">
<IMG SRC="minus6.gif" BORDER="0"></A></TD>
<TD> </TD>
<TD><A HREF="javascript:void(0)" onClick="square(52)">
<IMG SRC="plus1.gif" BORDER="0"></A></TD>
<TD><A HREF="javascript:void(0)" onClick="square(53)">
<IMG SRC="question.gif" BORDER="0"></A></TD>
```

```
<TD><A HREF="javascript:void(0)" onClick="square(54)">
<IMG SRC="question.gif" BORDER="0"></A></TD>
<TD><A HREF="javascript:void(0)" onClick="square(55)">
<IMG SRC="minus10.gif" BORDER="0"></A></TD>
</TR>
<TR>
<TD><A HREF="javascript:void(0)" onClick="square(56)">
<IMG SRC="question.gif" BORDER="0"></A></TD>
<TD><A HREF="javascript:void(0)" onClick="square(57)">
<IMG SRC="question.gif" BORDER="0"></A></TD>
<TD><A HREF="javascript:void(0)" onClick="square(58)">
<IMG SRC="question.gif" BORDER="0"></A></TD>
<TD> </TD><TD> </TD><TD> </TD><TD> </TD>
<TD><A HREF="javascript:void(0)" onClick="square(63)">
<IMG SRC="end.gif" BORDER="0"></A></TD>
</TR>
</TABLE>
<SCRIPT LANGUAGE="JavaScript"><!--
loadImages()
// --></SCRIPT>
</BODY>
</HTML>
```

You begin the game by clicking the Start square shown in the upper-left corner of Figure 20.4. This generates a random number, between 1 and 3, telling you how many squares you must move, as shown in Figure 20.5. You then move by clicking on the squares in your chosen path (refer to Figure 20.6). Footprints mark your move.

FIGURE 20.4:

The opening screen of Web Walk (Listing 20.2)

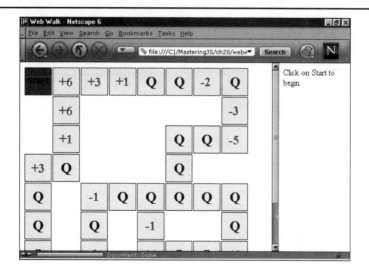

FIGURE 20.5:

The message in the right frame tells you how many squares to move.
(Listing 20.3)

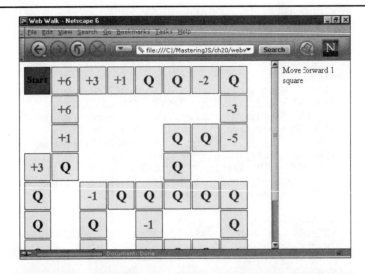

FIGURE 20.6:

Footprints mark your move.
(Listing 20.3)

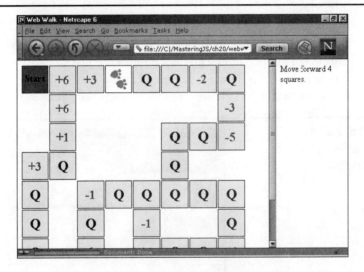

When you click on the last square of your move, you will either be told to move again (Figure 20.7) or a question will appear in the right side of the window (Figure 20.8). This is determined by the type of square you have landed on. If the square is labeled with an integer, then you will be told to move the indicated number of squares forward or backward. If you land on a square that is labeled with a Q, then you will be asked a question. If you answer the question correctly (Figure 20.9), you will be told to move forward 1, 2, or 3 squares. If you answer the question incorrectly, you will be told to move backward 1, 2, or 3 squares.

FIGURE 20.7:

A new message appears when you finish your move on a numbered square. (Listing 20.3)

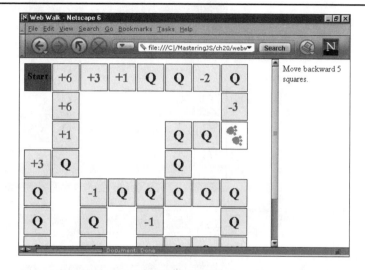

FIGURE 20.8:

A question appears when you land on a square labeled Q. (Listing 20.3)

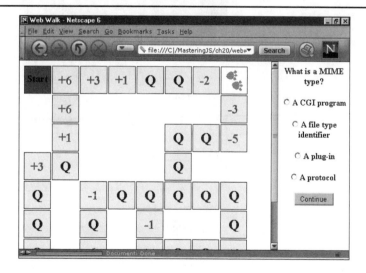

FIGURE 20.9:

Answer the question correctly to move forward.
(Listing 20.3)

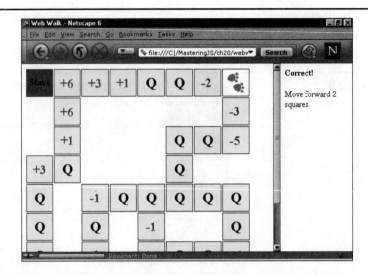

The object of the game is to get to the End square, as shown in Figure 20.10. To get there, you must correctly answer the questions along the way.

FIGURE 20.10:

Work your way to the End square to win.
(Listing 20.3)

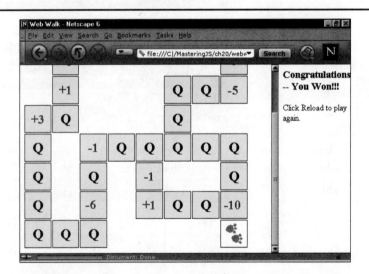

The number of ways to tailor Web Walk is infinite—feel free to substitute your own questions and adapt the game to your needs.

The webwalk.htm file sets up a two-frame set: the left frame runs the JavaScript code in ww.htm and the right frame is used to display messages and questions.

The ww.htm file is very long. It contains the code to implement the game plus all of the questions and answers displayed in the right frame set. To understand how ww.htm works, start with the document body. The generateBoard() function is invoked to display the game board, and the loadImages() function is used to load copies of the images to be displayed in the game into the cache. When these documents have completed their processing, the startGame() function is invoked to handle the document's onLoad event. The checkAnswers() function is invoked to handle the onFocus event. This occurs when the user has answered a question that is displayed in the right frame of the window. The following are the data and functions defined in the document head:

The *state* variable   Is used to identify the current state of the program's loading and interaction with the user.

The *boardLayout* array   Identifies the design of the board's layout. It consists of eight array elements that are used to describe the elements of each row of the board table. Table 20.4 describes the values used to identify board elements.

TABLE 20.4: Board Layout Description

Value	Board Element
(Blank)	None (blank area of board)
s	Starting square
e	Ending square
q	Question square
An integer	Square that specifies a forward (positive integer) or backward (negative integer) movement

The *Move()* function   Is the constructor for the Move object type. A Move object identifies whether a user may move from one square to another.

The *validMoves* array   Identifies all permitted square-to-square moves.

The *generateBoard()* function   Generates the board in terms of a table based on the values of the boardLayout array.

The *loadImages()* function   Loads all images that are required to be cached so that they may be displayed during the course of the play of the game.

The *startGame()* function   Handles the event associated with the document loading, initializes the main program variables, and sends a start message to the user. The position variable identifies the square (0 to 63) that the user is currently occupying. The direction variable identifies whether the user is moving forward (F) or backward (B). The stepsToMove variable identifies how many more squares the user must move until that move is completed.

The *msg()* function   Displays a message in the right frame of the window.

The *square()* function   Handles the event that occurs when the user clicks on a square. It stores the index of the clicked square using the nextPos variable. It checks to see if the user clicked on the Start square. If the state is *start*, then the state is set to *move* and the user is given a random number (from 1 through 3) of squares to move. If the state is already *move* when this function is invoked, then canMove() is invoked to determine whether it is permitted to move to the square that was clicked. If it is permitted, then the destination square is checked to see if it is the End square (and if so, the user is moved to that square, congratulated, and the game is ended). If the destination square is not the End square, the user is moved to the square and the state is set to *wait*, which prevents the user from clicking on other squares while the move is being processed. The restoreCurrentPosition() function is invoked to clear previous footprints. The showMovement() function is invoked to display new footprints. The processMovement() function is invoked to determine how the new position will affect what the user must do.

The *board()* function   Returns the value of the boardLayout array for a single-value (0 to 63) index.

The *steps()* function   Returns a random integer value of 1, 2, or 3.

The *move()* function   Creates a text string that identifies how many more steps the user must move.

The *canMove()* function   Returns true if a user is permitted to move to a specified square and false if they are not permitted to do so.

The *restoreCurrentPosition()* function   Displays the image of the square that was present before the user moved onto that square.

The *imagePosition()* function   Determines the index in the images array of the image displayed at a square.

NOTE   I've included a fix in the imagePosition() function to address a Navigator bug that sometimes causes the length of the images array to be doubled.

The *showMovement()* function   Moves the footprint's image onto a square.

The *processMovement()* function   Determines what processing should be performed as the result of a movement onto a square. If there are no more squares to move in the current move, then the two possibilities are as follows:

- The user has landed on a number square; the method automatically moves the user that many squares forward or backward.
- The user has landed on a Q square; askQuestion() is invoked to ask the user a question.

The *winner()* function   Notifies the user that the game has been successfully completed.

The *Question()* function   Is the constructor of the Question object (which was introduced in Chapter 9, "Using Hidden Fields and Cookies").

The *askQuestion()* function   Displays a question to the user in the right frame of the window. Note that the onClick event of the question's Continue button causes the left window to come into focus. This allows the event to be handled in the left frame of the window.

The *checkAnswers()* function   Is invoked to handle the onFocus event of the left frame of the window. This event is generated as the result of the user clicking the Continue button that appears when a question is displayed in the right frame. This little trick allows events to be propagated from one frame to another. The checkAnswers() function checks to see if the user answered the question correctly and invokes correct() or incorrect() depending on the result.

The *correct()* function   Causes the user to move 1, 2, or 3 steps forward as the result of answering a question correctly.

The *incorrect()* function   Causes the user to move 1, 2, or 3 steps backward as the result of answering a question incorrectly.

The *qa* array   Is used to store the Question objects used in the game. (Refer to Chapter 9.)

Summary

In this chapter you learned to program JavaScript games. You created a poker game that lets you play against your browser—good luck collecting your winnings! You also developed the Web Walk board game, which can be easily tailored to a variety of subjects.

This chapter was the last chapter in Part III, "Developing Components and Applications." In Part IV, "Working with XML-Capable Browsers," you'll learn to use JavaScript to script XML.

PART IV

Working with XML-Capable Browsers

Learning XML

- Simple XML examples

- XML syntax

- Document Type Definitions

- Using DTDs

Many of the advanced features introduced with Internet Explorer 5 and Navigator 6 center around browser support for XML. This support enables browsers to go beyond the limitations of HTML to parse and render documents that take advantage of the flexibility and customization provided by XML. This chapter introduces XML, discusses the similarities and differences between XML and HTML, and explains the advantages of using XML. When you finish this chapter, you will be introduced to the basics of XML, and you'll be able to create your own XML documents.

NOTE   This chapter is a quick introduction to XML for those who have never used XML. If you are already familiar with XML, you may want to skim this chapter because it reviews XML basic concepts and introduces XML examples that will be used in later chapters.

Introduction to XML

XML, like HTML, JavaScript, and Java, is a fundamental technology for building both web and non-web applications. It is also a relatively new technology whose impact has yet to be felt. However, many experts are claiming that the use of XML will become pervasive in all aspects of information technology. In the six chapters of Part IV, we'll gradually build up your XML skills. By the time you finish Chapter 24, "Creating XML-Based Web Applications," you'll have a clear understanding of what XML has to offer, and you'll be able to use it to build your own web applications.

XML, like HTML, is a markup language. This means that it uses tags to structure data. It also supports attributes for markup tags in the same way as HTML. Because of its similarity to HTML, you'll find XML to be immediately familiar and easy to use.

XML differs from HTML in that it does not define a standard set of tags and attributes. Instead, it allows you to define your own tags and attributes. This means that you have the power to use whatever tags you need to structure your information—no matter what kind of information you work with. XML has been used to specify chemical compounds, write music, and encode medical records. Its applications are endless.

For example, a pet shop owner could use tags such as <dog> and <cat> and attributes such as weight and sex to describe her pets. If you were a librarian, you could use tags such as <book> and <catalog> to describe your collection of books. A farmer could use tags such as <crop> and <livestock> to describe and manage his farm.

You are probably wondering, "If farmers, librarians, and pet shop owners are free to define their own tags, what exactly does XML provide?" The answer is that XML defines a syntax and a set of rules so that once you define your tags and attributes, they can be easily read and used by others. In other words, if one farmer creates an XML-compliant document, it can be parsed and read by other farmers (and non-farmers). Likewise, if a pet shop owner provides you with an XML-compliant document describing her pet collection, you'll be able to parse and read the information that is contained in the document.

Simple XML Examples

The nice thing about XML is that it is simple and easy to learn, especially if you have a background in HTML. And the easiest way to learn is by looking at a few examples.

NOTE   If you are looking for a difficult way to learn XML, try reading the W3C XML recommendation. It is available at `http://www.w3.org/TR/2000/REC-xml-20001006`. The W3C XML recommendation is a formal definition of XML.

Listing 21.1 provides an example of a simple XML document. The document contains a fictitious list of contacts. I'll walk you through the document and explain what it contains.

The first line of the document is the XML declaration:

```
<?xml version="1.0" encoding="iso-8859-1" standalone="yes"?>
```

The declaration identifies the document as an XML document. You should always have a declaration at the top of your document. The XML `version` attribute is mandatory and should always be specified. The current version of XML is 1.0, so your document should always appear as shown previously.

The `encoding` and `standalone` attributes are optional. However, it's a good idea to always specify a character encoding. The iso-8859-1 is a fairly standard Western encoding. However, you can use other encodings, such as UTF-16. I'll use iso-8859-1 throughout this book.

You should use `standalone="yes"` if you are developing an XML document that does not have a Document Type Definition (DTD) and does not depend on any other documents. A DTD is a document that defines the tags and attributes that may appear in an XML document. We'll cover DTDs later in this chapter. Suppose that we created a file named contacts.dtd (see Listing 21.3) that defines the tags and attributes for our contact lists. We would use this XML declaration:

```
<?xml version="1.0" encoding="iso-8859-1"?>
```

followed by a DOCTYPE declaration that identifies the DTD:

```
<!DOCTYPE contacts SYSTEM "contacts.dtd">
```

The previous DOCTYPE declaration identifies the DTD as contacts.dtd with contacts as the document element. The document element is the first and outermost tag in the document. For example, the document element of HTML documents is html.

NOTE   The term *element* is synonymous with *tag* when referring to the parts of an XML document.

You'll notice that the <contacts> and </contacts> tags enclose the rest of the tags of the document. All XML documents have a document element, such as contacts, that surrounds all other elements.

NOTE   White space is ignored when it appears between tags. Use it liberally to make your documents more readable.

Between the <contacts> and </contacts> tags is the rest of the document. This markup is organized into six sections enclosed with the <contact> and </contact> tags. These tags represent individual contacts.

Between the contact tags are the following types of tags:

- name—the name of the contact
- address—the contact's address
- phone—the contact's phone number
- email—the contact's e-mail address
- note—a note about the contact

Each contact has a name element and at least one phone element. But some contacts do not have address, email, or note elements. Multiple address, phone, email, and note elements may be used with a particular contact.

The address, phone, email, and note elements may contain an optional description element that describes the element. For example, it can be used to specify a *home* address or a *work* phone number.

The address tag is composed of street_address, city, state, postal_code, and country tags that further specify the address. The phone tag contains a phone_number tag that identifies the actual phone number. The email tag contains an email_address tag that contains the actual e-mail address. The note tag contains a text tag that contains the body of the note.

Are there other ways that I could have specified a contact list? Sure. This is just the way that works best for me. You can define your own contact list tags that work better for you. For example, you may use first_name and last_name tags, or maybe an organization tag.

Listing 21.1:   An XML Contact List (contacts1.xml)

```xml
<?xml version="1.0" encoding="iso-8859-1" standalone="yes"?>

<contacts>

<contact><name>Dad</name>
 <address>
  <description>Home</description>
  <street_address>1234 Main Street</street_address>
  <city>Chula Vista</city>
  <state>CA</state>
  <postal_code>92154</postal_code>
 </address>
 <address>
  <description>Work</description>
  <street_address>567 Toolery Avenue</street_address>
  <city>Chula Vista</city>
  <state>CA</state>
  <postal_code>91910</postal_code>
 </address>
 <phone>
  <description>Home</description>
  <phone_number>619-555-1234</phone_number>
 </phone>
 <phone>
  <description>Work</description>
  <phone_number>619-555-5678</phone_number>
 </phone>
 <phone>
  <description>Mobile</description>
  <phone_number>619-555-9012</phone_number>
 </phone>
 <email>
  <description>Work</description>
  <email_address>dad@toolery.com</email_address>
 </email>
 <email>
  <description>Yahoo</description>
  <email_address>dad@yahoo.com</email_address>
 </email>
 <note>
  <description>Birthday</description>
  <text>June 27</text>
 </note>
</contact>

<contact><name>Grandma</name>
 <address>
  <description>Home</description>
```

```xml
  <street_address>6 Rue de Gears</street_address>
  <city>Puymoyen</city>
  <postal_code>16400</postal_code>
  <country>France</country>
 </address>
 <phone>
  <description>Home</description>
  <phone_number>33-5-45-97-1234</phone_number>
 </phone>
 <email>
  <email_address>grandma@france.org</email_address>
 </email>
 <note>
  <description>Birthday</description>
  <text>October 10</text>
 </note>
</contact>

<contact><name>Work</name>
 <address>
  <street_address>789 West H Street</street_address>
  <city>Chula Vista</city>
  <state>CA</state>
  <postal_code>91912</postal_code>
 </address>
 <phone>
  <description>Voice</description>
  <phone_number>619-555-9876</phone_number>
 </phone>
 <phone>
  <description>Fax</description>
  <phone_number>619-555-9877</phone_number>
 </phone>
</contact>

<contact><name>Pizza</name>
 <phone>
  <phone_number>619-555-8765</phone_number>
 </phone>
</contact>

<contact><name>Betty</name>
 <phone>
  <description>Home</description>
  <phone_number>619-555-4321</phone_number>
 </phone>
 <phone>
  <description>Work</description>
  <phone_number>619-555-5432</phone_number>
 </phone>
 <phone>
```

```
<description>Mobile</description>
<phone_number>619-555-6543</phone_number>
</phone>
<phone>
<description>Sister's House</description>
<phone_number>619-555-7654</phone_number>
</phone>
<email>
<email_address>betty@hotmail.com</email_address>
</email>
<note>
<description>Likes</description>
<text>Shopping</text>
</note>
<note>
<description>Dislikes</description>
<text>Sports</text>
</note>
</contact>

<contact><name>Bob</name>
<phone>
<description>Mobile</description>
<phone_number>619-555-2468</phone_number>
</phone>
<email>
<email_address>bob@yahoo.com</email_address>
</email>
</contact>

</contacts>
```

Listing 21.2 provides another example of an XML document. You'll notice that this document contains a DOCTYPE declaration and specifies attributes for some XML tags. The document element is album. This element has a title element and four event elements. Each event element consists of a caption and one or more photo or video elements. Each photo and video element contains a caption element.

The photo element contains two attributes, src and orientation. The src attribute identifies the location of the image file. The orientation attribute identifies the picture as landscape or portrait.

The video element only specifies the src attribute.

Listing 21.2:   An XML Photo Album (album.xml)

```
<?xml version="1.0" encoding="iso-8859-1"?>
<!DOCTYPE album SYSTEM "album.dtd">
```

```xml
<album>
<title>June 2001 Cancun Trip</title>
 <event><caption>Chichen Itza</caption>
  <photo src="disk1/dscf0054.jpg" orientation="landscape">
   <caption>The observatory</caption>
  </photo>
  <photo src="disk1/dscf0055.jpg" orientation="landscape">
   <caption>Nun's house</caption>
  </photo>
  <photo src="disk1/dscf0056.jpg" orientation="landscape">
   <caption>Pyramid of Kulkulcan #1</caption>
  </photo>
  <photo src="disk1/dscf0057.jpg" orientation="landscape">
   <caption>Pyramid of Kulkulcan #2</caption>
  </photo>
  <photo src="disk1/dscf0058.jpg" orientation="landscape">
   <caption>Temple of the Warriors</caption>
  </photo>
  <photo src="disk1/dscf0060.jpg" orientation="landscape">
   <caption>View of the Temple of the Warriors from the Pyramid of
   Kulkulcan</caption>
  </photo>
  <photo src="disk1/dscf0062.jpg" orientation="landscape">
   <caption>View of the Pelota Court from the Pyramid of Kulkulcan</caption>
  </photo>
  <photo src="disk1/dscf0067.jpg" orientation="landscape">
   <caption>Pyramid of Kulkulcan #4</caption>
  </photo>
  <photo src="disk1/dscf0068.jpg" orientation="landscape">
   <caption>Pyramid of Kulkulcan #5</caption>
  </photo>
  <video src="disk1/dscf0069.avi">
   <caption>Cenote #1</caption>
  </video>
  <video src="disk2/dscf0001.avi">
   <caption>Cenote #2</caption>
  </video>
  <photo src="disk2/dscf0009.jpg" orientation="landscape">
   <caption>Pelota court</caption>
  </photo>
  <photo src="disk2/dscf0010.jpg" orientation="landscape">
   <caption>Who moved the hoop?</caption>
  </photo>
  <photo src="disk2/dscf0011.jpg" orientation="portrait">
   <caption>The winners!</caption>
  </photo>
  <photo src="disk2/dscf0012.jpg" orientation="landscape">
   <caption>Ouch!</caption>
  </photo>
  <photo src="disk2/dscf0013.jpg" orientation="landscape">
   <caption>Pyramid of Kulkulcan #6</caption>
```

```
  </photo>
 </event>
<event><caption>Tulum</caption>
 <photo src="disk4/dscf0010.jpg" orientation="portrait">
  <caption>Read this!</caption>
 </photo>
 <video src="disk4/dscf0009.avi">
  <caption>Panorama</caption>
 </video>
 <video src="disk4/dscf0018.avi">
  <caption>The Mayans</caption>
 </video>
 <photo src="disk4/dscf0011.jpg" orientation="landscape">
  <caption>Zaira and her uncles #1</caption>
 </photo>
 <photo src="disk4/dscf0012.jpg" orientation="landscape">
  <caption>Zaira and her uncles #2</caption>
 </photo>
 <photo src="disk4/dscf0013.jpg" orientation="landscape">
  <caption>Iguana #1</caption>
 </photo>
 <photo src="disk4/dscf0014.jpg" orientation="landscape">
  <caption>Iguana #2</caption>
 </photo>
 <photo src="disk4/dscf0015.jpg" orientation="landscape">
  <caption>Lisa and Yvonne</caption>
 </photo>
</event>
<event><caption>Aktun Chen</caption>
 <photo src="disk4/dscf0054.jpg" orientation="landscape">
  <caption>Oscar and friends</caption>
 </photo>
 <photo src="disk4/dscf0057.jpg" orientation="landscape">
  <caption>Let me in!</caption>
 </photo>
 <photo src="disk4/dscf0058.jpg" orientation="landscape">
  <caption>Who is feeding who?</caption>
 </photo>
 <video src="disk5/dscf0002.avi">
  <caption>Monkey movie #1</caption>
 </video>
 <video src="disk5/dscf0003.avi">
  <caption>Monkey movie #2</caption>
 </video>
 <video src="disk5/dscf0006.avi">
  <caption>Cave movie #1</caption>
 </video>
 <video src="disk5/dscf0030.avi">
  <caption>Cave movie #2</caption>
 </video>
 <photo src="disk5/dscf0004.jpg" orientation="landscape">
```

```
  <caption>Lisa #1</caption>
 </photo>
 <photo src="disk5/dscf0005.jpg" orientation="landscape">
  <caption>The way in</caption>
 </photo>
 <photo src="disk5/dscf0017.jpg" orientation="landscape">
  <caption>Who is that alien girl?</caption>
 </photo>
 <photo src="disk5/dscf0025.jpg" orientation="landscape">
  <caption>Waterfall</caption>
 </photo>
</event>
<event><caption>Chichen Itza (with Lisa)</caption>
 <photo src="disk6/dscf0001.jpg" orientation="landscape">
  <caption>The Pyramid #1</caption>
 </photo>
 <photo src="disk6/dscf0002.jpg" orientation="landscape">
  <caption>The Pyramid #2</caption>
 </photo>
 <photo src="disk6/dscf0003.jpg" orientation="landscape">
  <caption>The Pyramid #3</caption>
 </photo>
 <photo src="disk6/dscf0004.jpg" orientation="landscape">
  <caption>The Pyramid #4</caption>
 </photo>
 <photo src="disk6/dscf0007.jpg" orientation="landscape">
  <caption>Pelota hoop</caption>
 </photo>
 <photo src="disk6/dscf0008.jpg" orientation="landscape">
  <caption>Carvings in the Pelota court</caption>
 </photo>
 <photo src="disk6/dscf0012.jpg" orientation="landscape">
  <caption>Kissing kulkulcan</caption>
 </photo>
 <video src="disk6/dscf0016.avi">
  <caption>Sacrificial altar</caption>
 </video>
 <video src="disk6/dscf0024.avi">
  <caption>Video of the observatory</caption>
 </video>
 <photo src="disk6/dscf0034.jpg" orientation="landscape">
  <caption>The Nun House and the Church #1</caption>
 </photo>
 <photo src="disk6/dscf0035.jpg" orientation="landscape">
  <caption>The Nun House and the Church #2</caption>
 </photo>
 <photo src="disk6/dscf0044.jpg" orientation="landscape">
  <caption>Lisa on top of pyramid #1</caption>
 </photo>
 <photo src="disk6/dscf0045.jpg" orientation="landscape">
  <caption>Lisa on top of pyramid #2</caption>
```

```
      </photo>
      <photo src="disk7/dscf0001.jpg" orientation="landscape">
       <caption>Cenote #1</caption>
      </photo>
      <photo src="disk7/dscf0002.jpg" orientation="landscape">
       <caption>Cenote #2</caption>
      </photo>
     </event>
   </album>
```

XML Syntax

From the last two examples, you should have a pretty good idea of how XML documents are structured. In this section, I'll give you the detailed rules of XML syntax. These rules are somewhat simplified. For a formal definition of XML, refer to the W3C XML recommendation at http://www.w3.org/TR/2000/REC-xml-20001006.

XML Declaration

Every document should begin with an XML declaration. The following is a minimal declaration:

```
<?xml version="1.0"?>
```

However, it's a good idea to specify a character encoding:

```
<?xml version="1.0" encoding="iso-8859-1"?>
```

If your document is a stand-alone XML document without a DTD and with no other dependencies, you should include the standalone attribute:

```
<?xml version="1.0" encoding="iso-8859-1" standalone="yes"?>
```

DOCTYPE Declaration

If you have defined a DTD for your document and you want to have your document validated against the DTD, you should include a DOCTYPE declaration after the XML declaration. The following is a typical DOCTYPE declaration:

```
<!DOCTYPE document_element SYSTEM "URLofDTD">
```

The document_element should identify your document's document element. The document element is the first and most enclosing tag in the document. The URL of the DTD is enclosed in double quotes after the SYSTEM keyword.

If your document references a publicly available DTD, you can use a DOCTYPE declaration of the following form:

```
<!DOCTYPE document_element PUBLIC "URLofDTD">
```

The PUBLIC keyword is substituted for the SYSTEM keyword.

Tags

The tags of an XML document come in three forms:

- Opening tags—tags of the form `<tagname>`
- Closing tags—tags of the form `</tagname>`
- Separating tags—tags of the form `<tagname/>`

Opening and closing tags of the same tag name are paired. For example, `<mytag>` and `</mytag>`. Separating tags (which are similar to the HTML `<br>` and `<hr>` tags) may appear in isolation (for example, `<mytag/>`.)

Opening and closing tags are nested. This means that if `<tag1>` appears before `<tag2>`, the matching `</tag2>` must appear before the matching `</tag1>`. Neither the opening nor the closing tag may be omitted.

Tag names must begin with a letter or underscore (_). Subsequent letters may consist of letters, digits, periods (.), hyphens (-), and underscores (_). Tags cannot begin with the letters "xml" regardless of case. Tags cannot contain spaces. Tags are case-sensitive!

It's a good idea to choose human-readable names for your tags.

NOTE   Special types of tag names refer to XML name spaces. These are covered in Chapter 22, "Using XML Support in Communicator and Internet Explorer."

Attributes

XML attributes are written in the following form:

```
name = "value"
```

or

```
name = 'value'
```

The attribute name must follow the same rules as a tag name. Attribute names are case-sensitive. The attribute value is a string of characters that is enclosed by double or single quotes. Attribute values may not be omitted, and must be quoted (unlike HTML).

Comments

XML comments are written as follows:

```
<!-- This is a comment -->
```

Comments may not appear within the name of a tag, an attribute name, an attribute value, nor marked-up text. Double dashes (--) may not appear within the body of the comment.

Marked-Up Text

The text that is marked up by tags may not contain the less than (<), greater than (>), or ampersand (&) characters unless the text is escaped in a CDATA section. However, the ampersand (&) character may appear as the first character of a character or entity reference.

The following character references may be used to represent the less than (<), greater than (>), or ampersand (&) characters.

- &lt—less than

- &gt—greater than

- &amp—ampersand

You should note that the preceding XML character references are equivalent to those used in HTML. For more character references, consult the W3C XML recommendation.

CDATA Sections

CDATA sections may be used to escape text containing the less than (<), greater than (>), or ampersand (&) characters:

```
<![CDATA[ This text contains >, <, and &. ]]>
```

CDATA sections begin with `<![CDATA[` and end with `]]>`. CDATA sections cannot be nested. The following is an example of using a CDATA section:

```
<outertag>
<innertag><![CDATA[ Escaped text: >, <, and &. ]]></innertag>
</outertag>
```

Entities and Entity References

XML supports character entities in much the same way as HTML. It also supports other types of entities, referred to as *parsed entities*. Parsed entities are a mechanism for naming text and then referring to the text by its name. Parsed entities are defined as follows:

```
<!ENTITY entityname "replacement text">
```

Entity definitions typically appear in DTDs. Entities are referenced by placing an ampersand (&) before the entity name and following the entity name with a semicolon (;). For example, `myEntity` can be referenced using `&myEntity;`. An entity's text replaces the entity referenced when the XML document is parsed. XML entities are similar to HTML character entities, such as `&copy;`. You won't need to know how to define or use entities for the examples in this book.

XML also supports *parameter entities*, which are used exclusively in DTDs, and *unparsed entities*, which can be used to reference data that is not parsed text. Consult the W3C XML recommendation for more information on these types of entities.

Processing Instructions

Processing instructions are special instructions that you can embed in your XML documents. They are specific to the program that processes your XML documents. Processing instructions have the following syntax:

```
<?application instructions?>
```

The `application` is the name of the application that will process the instruction. The `instructions` are the specific instructions to be processed. An example of a processing instruction follows:

```
<?sqlprocessor select * from db?>
```

The use of processing instructions is rare.

Notations

Notations are declarations that provide further information about an external object. They are typically used to associate a URL with an image name. For example, the following notation associates `"myImage.gif"` with me:

```
<!NOTATION me SYSTEM "myImage.gif">
```

Notations are declared using the following syntax:

```
<!NOTATION name SYSTEM "url">
```

or

```
<!NOTATION name PUBLIC "url">
```

For more information on notations, consult the W3C XML recommendation.

Document Type Definitions

The previous sections provided an introduction to the syntax of XML. We mentioned that the power of XML lies in the fact that it lets us decide what tags and attributes we want to use in our documents. That flexibility is great, but it comes at the expense of standardization.

Document Type Definitions (DTDs) let us enjoy the flexibility of XML while being able to define standard types of XML documents. Suppose you and your friends liked the tags that I used in my contacts list (refer to Listing 21.1) and decided to develop a web standard for managing contacts. You would want everyone to use the same tags in their applications so that contacts could be freely exchanged. In order to come up with a standard type of XML document for contacts, you could define a contacts DTD. Listing 21.3 provides an example.

You'll notice that the first line of the DTD is an XML declaration, and the second line is a comment. The rest of the document consists of tags of the following form:

```
<!ELEMENT tagname (content model)>
```

Each element declaration defines a single markup tag. Element declarations of the following form identify elements (that is, tags) that mark up text:

```
<!ELEMENT tagname (#PCDATA)>
```

The #PCDATA stands for parsed character data, and identifies the fact that text appears between the tags.

Other element declarations identify the tags that occur within a particular tag. For example, the following declaration specifies that a contacts tag contains one or more contact tags:

```
<!ELEMENT contacts (contact+)>
```

The + stands for one or more, and * stands for zero or more.

The contact tag is defined as containing a name tag, followed by zero or more address tags, followed by one or more phone tags, followed by zero or more email tags, followed by zero or more note tags.

```
<!ELEMENT contact (name, address*, phone+, email*, note*)> [based on previous
text that implied at least one phone – stoney – Thanks – jamie]
```

Suppose that we wanted to allow the address, phone, email, and note tags to appear in any order with zero or more of each being possible. We could have defined the contact element as follows:

```
<!ELEMENT contact (name, (address | phone | email | note)*)>
```

The | stands for "or."

The address element is defined as containing zero or one `description` tags, followed by zero or more `street_address` tags, followed by zero or one `city`, `state`, `postal_code`, or country tags. The ? stands for zero or one.

```
<!ELEMENT address (description?, street_address*, city?, state?,
        postal_code?, country?)>
```

Tags may also be declared as belonging to a particular category. This syntax is as follows:

```
<!ELEMENT tagname category>
```

For example, the following defines myTag as containing any XML:

```
<!ELEMENT myTag ANY>
```

The EMPTY category is used to define a tag that does not contain markup (that is, a separating tag):

```
<!ELEMENT mySeparatingTag EMPTY>
```

NOTE   The + character stands for one or more, the * character stands for zero or more, and the ? character stands for zero or one.

NOTE   Writing DTDs can be (but doesn't have to be) more involved than the examples presented in this section. Consult the W3C XML recommendation for more information about DTDs.

Listing 21.3:   A Contacts DTD (contacts.dtd)

```
]
<?xml version='1.0' encoding='ISO-8859-1'?>
<!-- DTD for representing contact lists -->

<!ELEMENT contacts (contact+)>
<!ELEMENT contact (name, address*, phone+, email*, note*)>
<!ELEMENT name (#PCDATA)>
<!ELEMENT address (description?, street_address*, city?, state?,
        postal_code?, country?)>
<!ELEMENT description (#PCDATA)>
<!ELEMENT street_address (#PCDATA)>
<!ELEMENT city (#PCDATA)>
<!ELEMENT state (#PCDATA)>
<!ELEMENT postal_code (#PCDATA)>
<!ELEMENT country (#PCDATA)>
<!ELEMENT phone (description?, phone_number)>
<!ELEMENT phone_number (#PCDATA)>
<!ELEMENT email (description?, email_address)>
<!ELEMENT email_address (#PCDATA)>
<!ELEMENT note (description?, text?)>
<!ELEMENT text (#PCDATA)>
```

Declaring Attributes

In addition to defining entities, DTDs are used to identify the attributes that may be contained in an XML document. This is accomplished through the ATTLIST declaration. Listing 21.4 presents the DTD for the photo album of Listing 21.2. It defines attributes for the photo and video elements.

The following defines the photo element as having two attributes, src and orientation. The src tag is a required tag, and contains arbitrary character data. The orientation tag may take the values landscape or portrait with the default value being landscape.

```
<!ATTLIST photo
    src CDATA #REQUIRED
    orientation (landscape | portrait) "landscape"
>
```

The general syntax for an ATTLIST declaration is as follows:

```
<!ATTLIST tagname attributename type valuedescription>
```

Multiple attributes may be defined for a single tag within a single ATTLIST declaration, as shown in the previous example. The types that may appear in an ATTLIST declaration are as follows:

- CDATA—Character data. This is the typical type of attribute that you'll define.
- (value1 | value2 | ... | valuen)—A list of the possible values
- ID—Identifies the attribute as being unique for each element. Analogous to the HTML ID attribute
- IDREF—A reference to the ID attribute of an element
- IDREFS—A reference to a space-delimited list of ID values
- NMTOKEN—CDATA that is restricted to valid XML names
- NMTOKENS—A list of NMTOKEN values separated by spaces
- ENTITY—The name of a predefined entity
- ENTITIES—A space-separated list of entities
- NOTATION—An XML notation name

The value description may be any of the following:

- A default value—The value is simply listed
- #REQUIRED—Specifies that the attribute is not optional
- #IMPLIED—Identifies the value as optional in that no default value is provided
- #FIXED value—Identifies the value and requires that it not change

Listing 21.4:   An Album DTD (album.dtd)

```
<?xml version='1.0' encoding='ISO-8859-1'?>
<!- DTD for representing photo albums ->

<!ELEMENT album (title, event*)>
<!ELEMENT event (caption, description?, (photo | video)*)>
<!ELEMENT photo (caption, description?)>
<!ELEMENT video (caption, description?)>
<!ELEMENT title (#PCDATA)>
<!ELEMENT caption (#PCDATA)>
<!ELEMENT description (#PCDATA)>

<!ATTLIST photo
    src CDATA #REQUIRED
    orientation (landscape | portrait) "landscape"
>

<!ATTLIST video src CDATA #REQUIRED>
```

Using DTDs

You may be wondering how DTDs are used by XML documents. Recall that the DOCTYPE declaration specifies a document's DTD. If a DOCTYPE declaration is included in an XML document, a validating XML parser will check the document against the DTD to make sure that the document complies with the DTD. If the document doesn't comply, an error message is displayed. That way, you can check your XML documents for any errors before publishing or distributing them.

Summary

In this chapter, you were introduced to XML. You learned how to design custom documents using XML and how to create DTDs that defined the documents you created. You covered a lot of material that will be used in the other chapters of this part. In the following chapter, you'll learn how to display XML documents using Internet Explorer and Navigator.

Displaying XML with Internet Explorer and Navigator

- Displaying XML with Internet Explorer and Navigator

- Using CSS with XML

- Using XML namespaces

In the previous chapter, you learned the basics of XML, but you didn't open a single browser window. In this chapter, you'll learn how to display XML using Internet Explorer and Navigator. If you haven't read Chapter 12, "Working with Styles and DHTML," now would be a good time to do so. That's because the predominant means for displaying XML is to use CSS style sheets.

This chapter will show you how to style XML documents for browser display. There's not much to it other than making the connection between XML and CSS. But it covers basics that you'll need to know before you can go on to learning how to script XML with JavaScript in Chapter 23, "Scripting XML in Communicator and Internet Explorer."

NOTE   If your CSS is rusty, you may want to check Appendix F, "Cascading Style Sheets," to brush up on your knowledge of CSS.

Displaying XML with Internet Explorer

Internet Explorer 5 and later has a great feature. You can display arbitrary XML documents in an intuitive and easy-to-use manner. To see this, open the `contacts1.xml` file from Chapter 22, "Using XML Support in Communicator and Internet Explorer." Internet Explorer displays the window shown in Figure 22.1. It's easy to access the document's structure using this view.

Click the hyphen before the first `<contact>` tag. The contents of the contact collapse, and the dash turns into a plus sign (see Figure 22.2). Click the plus sign, and the contact is expanded. I love that feature.

FIGURE 22.1:

Internet Explorer displays
contacts1.xml.

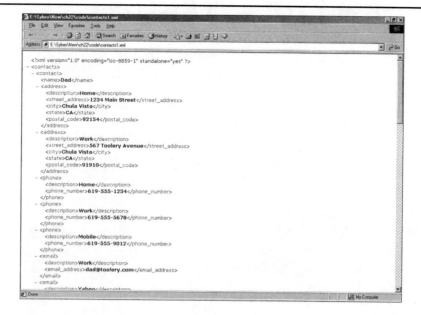

FIGURE 22.2:

Tags can be collapsed and
expanded.

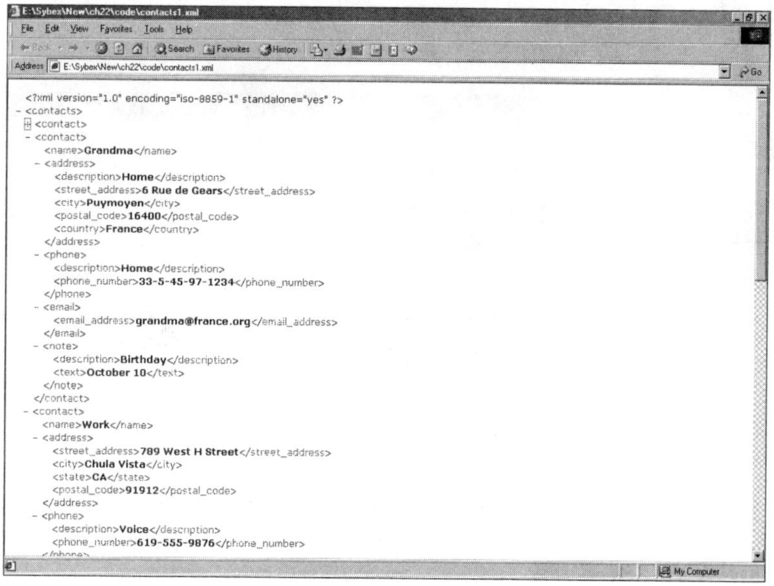

Displaying XML with Navigator

Navigator 6 isn't nearly as pretty. It just strings together the marked-up text, as shown in Figure 22.3. Don't uninstall Navigator just yet, however. Even if Navigator doesn't display raw XML files well, it excels at displaying styled XML.

FIGURE 22.3:

Navigator displays *contacts1.xml.*

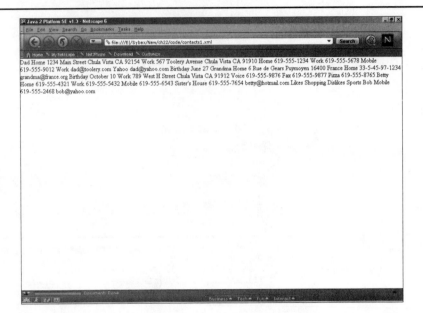

Using CSS with XML

The solution to making XML files presentable in current browsers is to attach a CSS style sheet to the XML document. Even if XML has its own style language—known as eXtensible Stylesheet Language, or XSL—current browsers don't provide full XSL support. So the best solution is to use good old CSS.

You can associate a CSS style sheet with an XML document by putting a processing instruction in the XML document:

```
<?xml-stylesheet href="mystyle.css" type="text/css"?>
```

The previous instruction tells the browser to display the document using the styles contained in `mystyle.css`.

Displaying a Contact List

Now that you know the secret of styling XML, let's try it out on contacts1.xml. I inserted the following processing instruction to the top of contacts1.xml and saved it as contacts2.xml. Listing 22.1 shows the contents of the contactstyle.css file.

```
<?xml version="1.0" encoding="iso-8859-1" standalone="yes"?>
<?xml-stylesheet href="contactstyle.css" type="text/css"?>
```

Figure 22.4 shows how Navigator 6 renders the styled XML. Looks pretty good, considering my poor taste in styles. However, Internet Explorer 5.5 displays it using the blotchy background colors shown in Figure 22.5.

FIGURE 22.4:

Navigator displays the styled contacts.

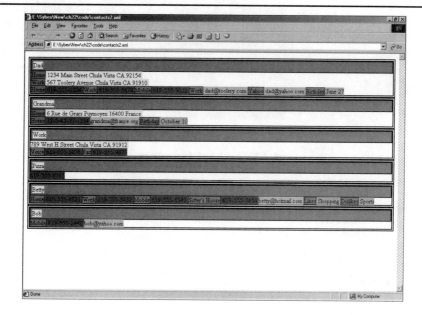

FIGURE 22.5:

Internet Explorer displays the styled contacts.

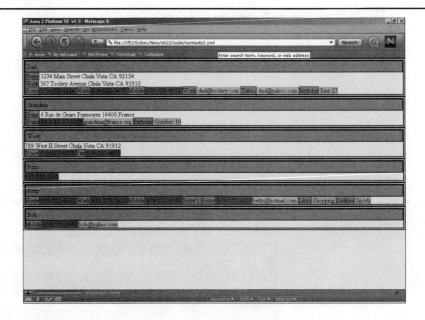

Listing 22.1:   A Style Sheet for contacts2.xml (contactstyle.css)

```
contacts
{background-color: #ffff80}

contact
{border: 6px double;
display: block}

name
{background-color: #ff8000;
border: 2px solid;
display: block;
padding: 4px}

address
{display: block}

description
{background-color: #ff8080;
border: 1px solid}

phone
{background-color: #8080ff}

email
```

```
{background-color: #c0c0c0}

note
{background-color: #abd6d6}
```

Displaying an Outline

Because XML files are hierarchical and tree-structured, they are often displayed using outlines and indented text. Listing 22.2 (outline.xml) contains a simple outline written in XML. Listing 22.3 (outline.dtd) provides the DTD for the outline. Listing 22.4 provides a style sheet for the outline file. Both Navigator 6 and Internet Explorer 6 display the outline in a similar manner, as shown in Figures 22.6 and 22.7. However, if we change the name tag's display style from block to list-item, Navigator displays it correctly, as shown in Figure 22.8. Internet Explorer messes it up, however, as shown in Figure 22.9. The lesson learned is that you have to find the common ground of style support between the two browsers if you want similar displays. This requires a little experimentation when creating your display styles.

FIGURE 22.6:

Navigator displays the styled outline.

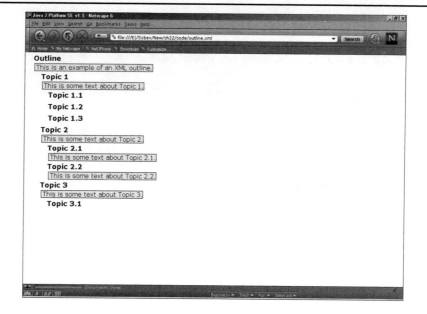

FIGURE 22.7:

Internet Explorer displays the outline.

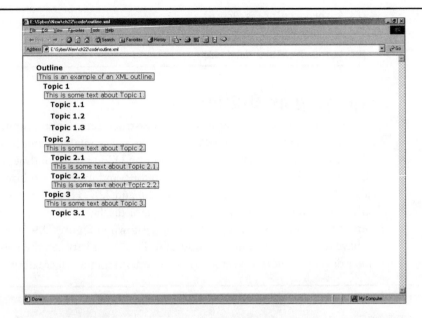

FIGURE 22.8:

Navigator correctly handles the list items.

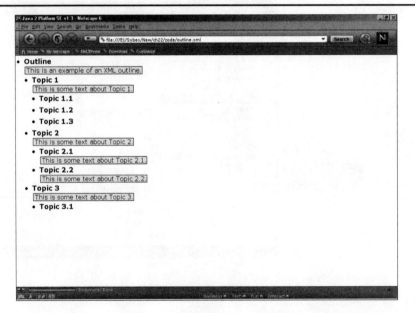

FIGURE 22.9:

Internet Explorer messes up
the list items.

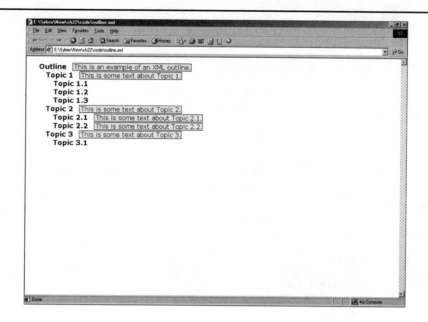

Listing 22.2:   An XML Outline (outline.xml)

```
<?xml version="1.0" encoding="iso-8859-1"?>
<!DOCTYPE topic SYSTEM "outline.dtd">
<?xml-stylesheet href="outline1.css" type="text/css"?>

<topic><name>Outline</name>
 <text>This is an example of an XML outline.</text>
 <topic><name>Topic 1</name>
  <text>This is some text about Topic 1.</text>
  <topic><name>Topic 1.1</name></topic>
  <topic><name>Topic 1.2</name></topic>
  <topic><name>Topic 1.3</name></topic>
 </topic>
 <topic><name>Topic 2</name>
  <text>This is some text about Topic 2.</text>
  <topic><name>Topic 2.1</name>
   <text>This is some text about Topic 2.1.</text>
  </topic>
  <topic><name>Topic 2.2</name>
   <text>This is some text about Topic 2.2.</text>
  </topic>
 </topic>
 <topic><name>Topic 3</name>
  <text>This is some text about Topic 3.</text>
  <topic><name>Topic 3.1</name></topic>
 </topic>
</topic>
```

Listing 22.3: **The Outline DTD (outline.dtd)**

```
<?xml version='1.0' encoding='ISO-8859-1'?>
<!-- DTD for representing outlines -->

<!ELEMENT topic (name, text?, topic*)>
<!ELEMENT name (#PCDATA)>
<!ELEMENT text (#PCDATA)>
```

Listing 22.4: **An Outline Style Sheet (outline1.css)**

```
topic
{display: block;
font-family: Verdana, Helvetica, Arial, sans-serif;
margin-left: +2%}

name
{display: block;
font-size: larger;
font-weight: bold;
padding: 4px}

text
{background-color: #ffff80;
border: 1px solid;
margin-left: 6px;
padding-left: 4px}
```

Listing 22.5: **An Outline Style Sheet that Uses List Elements (outline2.css)**

```
topic
{display: block;
font-family: Verdana, Helvetica, Arial, sans-serif;
margin-left: +2%}

name
{display: list-item;
font-size: larger;
font-weight: bold;
list-style-position: outside;
list-style-type: disc;
padding: 4px}

text
{background-color: #ffff80;
border: 1px solid;
margin-left: 6px;
padding-left: 4px}
```

Displaying a Catalog

XML documents often contain information, such as price or parts listings, that is more easily accessed when rendered as tables. Tabular displays can be rigged using CSS1 styles, but they are most easily displayed using the CSS2 `display` styles. Unfortunately, CSS2 support is marginal in both Navigator and Internet Explorer.

Listing 22.6 (`catalog.xml`) presents a furniture and electronics catalog of the XYZ Corporation. This catalog lists the company's products, identifies its product category, and identifies what room they are used in. Listing 22.7 provides a DTD for the catalog, and Listing 22.8 provides a CSS1 style sheet that displays the catalog as a table. Figure 22.10 shows how the catalog is displayed by Internet Explorer, which does a fairly good job. Figure 22.11 shows how the catalog is displayed by Navigator 6, which fails to correctly set the widths of each row entry.

FIGURE 22.10:

Internet Explorer displays the product catalog well.

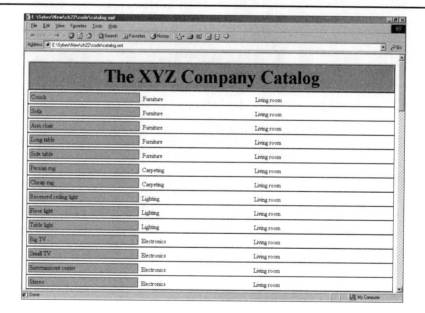

FIGURE 22.11:

Navigator fails to display
the row elements with the
proper width.

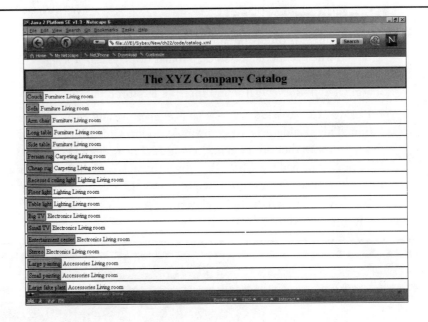

Listing 22.6:   An XML Catalog (catalog.xml).

```
<?xml version="1.0" encoding="iso-8859-1"?>
<!DOCTYPE catalog SYSTEM "catalog.dtd">
<?xml-stylesheet href="catalog.css" type="text/css"?>

<catalog>
<description>The XYZ Company Catalog</description>
<!-- Living room products -->
<product><name>Couch</name>
 <descriptor>
  <name>category</name>
  <value>Furniture</value>
 </descriptor>
 <descriptor>
  <name>room</name>
  <value>Living room</value>
 </descriptor>
</product>
<product><name>Sofa</name>
 <descriptor>
  <name>category</name>
  <value>Furniture</value>
 </descriptor>
 <descriptor>
  <name>room</name>
```

```
    <value>Living room</value>
  </descriptor>
</product>
<product><name>Arm chair</name>
 <descriptor>
  <name>category</name>
  <value>Furniture</value>
 </descriptor>
 <descriptor>
  <name>room</name>
  <value>Living room</value>
 </descriptor>
</product>
<product><name>Long table</name>
 <descriptor>
  <name>category</name>
  <value>Furniture</value>
 </descriptor>
 <descriptor>
  <name>room</name>
  <value>Living room</value>
 </descriptor>
</product>
<product><name>Side table</name>
 <descriptor>
  <name>category</name>
  <value>Furniture</value>
 </descriptor>
 <descriptor>
  <name>room</name>
  <value>Living room</value>
 </descriptor>
</product>
<product><name>Persian rug</name>
 <descriptor>
  <name>category</name>
  <value>Carpeting</value>
 </descriptor>
 <descriptor>
  <name>room</name>
  <value>Living room</value>
 </descriptor>
</product>
<product><name>Cheap rug</name>
 <descriptor>
  <name>category</name>
  <value>Carpeting</value>
 </descriptor>
 <descriptor>
  <name>room</name>
  <value>Living room</value>
```

```
  </descriptor>
 </product>
 <product><name>Recessed ceiling light</name>
  <descriptor>
   <name>category</name>
   <value>Lighting</value>
  </descriptor>
  <descriptor>
   <name>room</name>
   <value>Living room</value>
  </descriptor>
 </product>
 <product><name>Floor light</name>
  <descriptor>
   <name>category</name>
   <value>Lighting</value>
  </descriptor>
  <descriptor>
   <name>room</name>
   <value>Living room</value>
  </descriptor>
 </product>
 <product><name>Table light</name>
  <descriptor>
   <name>category</name>
   <value>Lighting</value>
  </descriptor>
  <descriptor>
   <name>room</name>
   <value>Living room</value>
  </descriptor>
 </product>
 <product><name>Big TV</name>
  <descriptor>
   <name>category</name>
   <value>Electronics</value>
  </descriptor>
  <descriptor>
   <name>room</name>
   <value>Living room</value>
  </descriptor>
 </product>
 <product><name>Small TV</name>
  <descriptor>
   <name>category</name>
   <value>Electronics</value>
  </descriptor>
  <descriptor>
   <name>room</name>
   <value>Living room</value>
  </descriptor>
```

```
</product>
<product><name>Entertainment center</name>
 <descriptor>
  <name>category</name>
  <value>Electronics</value>
 </descriptor>
 <descriptor>
  <name>room</name>
  <value>Living room</value>
 </descriptor>
</product>
<product><name>Stereo</name>
 <descriptor>
  <name>category</name>
  <value>Electronics</value>
 </descriptor>
 <descriptor>
  <name>room</name>
  <value>Living room</value>
 </descriptor>
</product>
<product><name>Large painting</name>
 <descriptor>
  <name>category</name>
  <value>Accessories</value>
 </descriptor>
 <descriptor>
  <name>room</name>
  <value>Living room</value>
 </descriptor>
</product>
<product><name>Small painting</name>
 <descriptor>
  <name>category</name>
  <value>Accessories</value>
 </descriptor>
 <descriptor>
  <name>room</name>
  <value>Living room</value>
 </descriptor>
</product>
<product><name>Large fake plant</name>
 <descriptor>
  <name>category</name>
  <value>Accessories</value>
 </descriptor>
 <descriptor>
  <name>room</name>
  <value>Living room</value>
 </descriptor>
</product>
```

```
<product><name>Small fake plant</name>
 <descriptor>
  <name>category</name>
  <value>Accessories</value>
 </descriptor>
 <descriptor>
  <name>room</name>
  <value>Living room</value>
 </descriptor>
</product>
<product><name>Expensive knick knack</name>
 <descriptor>
  <name>category</name>
  <value>Accessories</value>
 </descriptor>
 <descriptor>
  <name>room</name>
  <value>Living room</value>
 </descriptor>
</product>
<product><name>Cheap knick knack</name>
 <descriptor>
  <name>category</name>
  <value>Accessories</value>
 </descriptor>
 <descriptor>
  <name>room</name>
  <value>Living room</value>
 </descriptor>
</product>
<!-- Dining room products -->
<product><name>Expensive dining set</name>
 <descriptor>
  <name>category</name>
  <value>Furniture</value>
 </descriptor>
 <descriptor>
  <name>room</name>
  <value>Dining room</value>
 </descriptor>
</product>
<product><name>Cheap dining set</name>
 <descriptor>
  <name>category</name>
  <value>Furniture</value>
 </descriptor>
 <descriptor>
  <name>room</name>
  <value>Dining room</value>
 </descriptor>
</product>
```

```
<product><name>China cabinet</name>
 <descriptor>
  <name>category</name>
  <value>Furniture</value>
 </descriptor>
 <descriptor>
  <name>room</name>
  <value>Dining room</value>
 </descriptor>
</product>
<product><name>Serving table</name>
 <descriptor>
  <name>category</name>
  <value>Furniture</value>
 </descriptor>
 <descriptor>
  <name>room</name>
  <value>Dining room</value>
 </descriptor>
</product>
<product><name>Stain-proof rug</name>
 <descriptor>
  <name>category</name>
  <value>Carpeting</value>
 </descriptor>
 <descriptor>
  <name>room</name>
  <value>Dining room</value>
 </descriptor>
</product>
<product><name>Plastic floor covering</name>
 <descriptor>
  <name>category</name>
  <value>Carpeting</value>
 </descriptor>
 <descriptor>
  <name>room</name>
  <value>Dining room</value>
 </descriptor>
</product>
<product><name>Chandalier</name>
 <descriptor>
  <name>category</name>
  <value>Lighting</value>
 </descriptor>
 <descriptor>
  <name>room</name>
  <value>Dining room</value>
 </descriptor>
</product>
<product><name>Ceiling lamp/fan</name>
```

```
<descriptor>
 <name>category</name>
 <value>Lighting</value>
</descriptor>
<descriptor>
 <name>room</name>
 <value>Dining room</value>
</descriptor>
</product>
<product><name>China set</name>
 <descriptor>
  <name>category</name>
  <value>Accessories</value>
 </descriptor>
 <descriptor>
  <name>room</name>
  <value>Dining room</value>
 </descriptor>
</product>
<product><name>Silver set</name>
 <descriptor>
  <name>category</name>
  <value>Accessories</value>
 </descriptor>
 <descriptor>
  <name>room</name>
  <value>Dining room</value>
 </descriptor>
</product>
<!-- Bed room products -->
<product><name>King bed</name>
 <descriptor>
  <name>category</name>
  <value>Furniture</value>
 </descriptor>
 <descriptor>
  <name>room</name>
  <value>Bed room</value>
 </descriptor>
</product>
<product><name>Queen bed</name>
 <descriptor>
  <name>category</name>
  <value>Furniture</value>
 </descriptor>
 <descriptor>
  <name>room</name>
  <value>Bed room</value>
 </descriptor>
</product>
<product><name>Single bed</name>
```

```
  <descriptor>
   <name>category</name>
   <value>Furniture</value>
  </descriptor>
  <descriptor>
   <name>room</name>
   <value>Bed room</value>
  </descriptor>
 </product>
 <product><name>End table</name>
  <descriptor>
   <name>category</name>
   <value>Furniture</value>
  </descriptor>
  <descriptor>
   <name>room</name>
   <value>Bed room</value>
  </descriptor>
 </product>
 <product><name>Dresser</name>
  <descriptor>
   <name>category</name>
   <value>Furniture</value>
  </descriptor>
  <descriptor>
   <name>room</name>
   <value>Bed room</value>
  </descriptor>
 </product>
 <product><name>Lamb skin carpet</name>
  <descriptor>
   <name>category</name>
   <value>Carpeting</value>
  </descriptor>
  <descriptor>
   <name>room</name>
   <value>Bed room</value>
  </descriptor>
 </product>
 <product><name>Bear skin carpet</name>
  <descriptor>
   <name>category</name>
   <value>Carpeting</value>
  </descriptor>
  <descriptor>
   <name>room</name>
   <value>Bed room</value>
  </descriptor>
 </product>
 <product><name>Ceiling lamp</name>
  <descriptor>
```

```
   <name>category</name>
   <value>Lighting</value>
  </descriptor>
  <descriptor>
   <name>room</name>
   <value>Bed room</value>
  </descriptor>
 </product>
 <product><name>Table lamp</name>
  <descriptor>
   <name>category</name>
   <value>Lighting</value>
  </descriptor>
  <descriptor>
   <name>room</name>
   <value>Bed room</value>
  </descriptor>
 </product>
 <product><name>Clock radio</name>
  <descriptor>
   <name>category</name>
   <value>Electronics</value>
  </descriptor>
  <descriptor>
   <name>room</name>
   <value>Bed room</value>
  </descriptor>
 </product>
 <product><name>Electronic head board</name>
  <descriptor>
   <name>category</name>
   <value>Electronics</value>
  </descriptor>
  <descriptor>
   <name>room</name>
   <value>Bed room</value>
  </descriptor>
 </product>
 <product><name>Pillow set</name>
  <descriptor>
   <name>category</name>
   <value>Accessories</value>
  </descriptor>
  <descriptor>
   <name>room</name>
   <value>Bed room</value>
  </descriptor>
 </product>
 <product><name>Linen set</name>
  <descriptor>
   <name>category</name>
```

```xml
    <value>Accessories</value>
   </descriptor>
   <descriptor>
    <name>room</name>
    <value>Bed room</value>
   </descriptor>
  </product>
  <product><name>Bed spread</name>
   <descriptor>
    <name>category</name>
    <value>Accessories</value>
   </descriptor>
   <descriptor>
    <name>room</name>
    <value>Bed room</value>
   </descriptor>
  </product>
  <!-- Kitchen products -->
  <product><name>Refrigerator</name>
   <descriptor>
    <name>category</name>
    <value>Appliances</value>
   </descriptor>
   <descriptor>
    <name>room</name>
    <value>Kitchen</value>
   </descriptor>
  </product>
  <product><name>Stove - oven</name>
   <descriptor>
    <name>category</name>
    <value>Appliances</value>
   </descriptor>
   <descriptor>
    <name>room</name>
    <value>Kitchen</value>
   </descriptor>
  </product>
  <product><name>Microwave oven</name>
   <descriptor>
    <name>category</name>
    <value>Appliances</value>
   </descriptor>
   <descriptor>
    <name>room</name>
    <value>Kitchen</value>
   </descriptor>
  </product>
  <product><name>Toaster</name>
   <descriptor>
    <name>category</name>
```

```
  <value>Appliances</value>
 </descriptor>
 <descriptor>
  <name>room</name>
  <value>Kitchen</value>
 </descriptor>
</product>
<product><name>Coffee maker</name>
 <descriptor>
  <name>category</name>
  <value>Appliances</value>
 </descriptor>
 <descriptor>
  <name>room</name>
  <value>Kitchen</value>
 </descriptor>
</product>
<product><name>Dish washer</name>
 <descriptor>
  <name>category</name>
  <value>Appliances</value>
 </descriptor>
 <descriptor>
  <name>room</name>
  <value>Kitchen</value>
 </descriptor>
</product>
<product><name>Delux cabinets</name>
 <descriptor>
  <name>category</name>
  <value>Cabinets</value>
 </descriptor>
 <descriptor>
  <name>room</name>
  <value>Kitchen</value>
 </descriptor>
</product>
<product><name>Standard cabinets</name>
 <descriptor>
  <name>category</name>
  <value>Cabinets</value>
 </descriptor>
 <descriptor>
  <name>room</name>
  <value>Kitchen</value>
 </descriptor>
</product>
<product><name>Delux counter</name>
 <descriptor>
  <name>category</name>
  <value>Cabinets</value>
```

```
 </descriptor>
 <descriptor>
  <name>room</name>
  <value>Kitchen</value>
 </descriptor>
</product>
<product><name>Standard counter</name>
 <descriptor>
  <name>category</name>
  <value>Cabinets</value>
 </descriptor>
 <descriptor>
  <name>room</name>
  <value>Kitchen</value>
 </descriptor>
</product>
<product><name>Kitchen ceiling light</name>
 <descriptor>
  <name>category</name>
  <value>Lighting</value>
 </descriptor>
 <descriptor>
  <name>room</name>
  <value>Kitchen</value>
 </descriptor>
</product>
<product><name>Counter light</name>
 <descriptor>
  <name>category</name>
  <value>Lighting</value>
 </descriptor>
 <descriptor>
  <name>room</name>
  <value>Kitchen</value>
 </descriptor>
</product>
<product><name>Cookware</name>
 <descriptor>
  <name>category</name>
  <value>Accessories</value>
 </descriptor>
 <descriptor>
  <name>room</name>
  <value>Kitchen</value>
 </descriptor>
</product>
<product><name>Storage containers</name>
 <descriptor>
  <name>category</name>
  <value>Accessories</value>
 </descriptor>
```

```xml
  <descriptor>
   <name>room</name>
   <value>Kitchen</value>
  </descriptor>
</product>
<product><name>Wall clock</name>
 <descriptor>
  <name>category</name>
  <value>Accessories</value>
 </descriptor>
 <descriptor>
  <name>room</name>
  <value>Kitchen</value>
 </descriptor>
</product>
<!-- Bath room products -->
<product><name>Delux sink</name>
 <descriptor>
  <name>category</name>
  <value>Sinks</value>
 </descriptor>
 <descriptor>
  <name>room</name>
  <value>Bath room</value>
 </descriptor>
</product>
<product><name>Standard sink</name>
 <descriptor>
  <name>category</name>
  <value>Sinks</value>
 </descriptor>
 <descriptor>
  <name>room</name>
  <value>Bath room</value>
 </descriptor>
</product>
<product><name>Delux toilet</name>
 <descriptor>
  <name>category</name>
  <value>Toilets</value>
 </descriptor>
 <descriptor>
  <name>room</name>
  <value>Bath room</value>
 </descriptor>
</product>
<product><name>Standard toilet</name>
 <descriptor>
  <name>category</name>
```

```
 <value>Toilets</value>
 </descriptor>
 <descriptor>
  <name>room</name>
  <value>Bath room</value>
 </descriptor>
</product>
<product><name>Ceiling light</name>
 <descriptor>
  <name>category</name>
  <value>Lighting</value>
 </descriptor>
 <descriptor>
  <name>room</name>
  <value>Bath room</value>
 </descriptor>
</product>
<product><name>Wall light</name>
 <descriptor>
  <name>category</name>
  <value>Lighting</value>
 </descriptor>
 <descriptor>
  <name>room</name>
  <value>Bath room</value>
 </descriptor>
</product>
<product><name>Delux bath tub</name>
 <descriptor>
  <name>category</name>
  <value>Bath and shower</value>
 </descriptor>
 <descriptor>
  <name>room</name>
  <value>Bath room</value>
 </descriptor>
</product>
<product><name>Standard bath tub</name>
 <descriptor>
  <name>category</name>
  <value>Bath and shower</value>
 </descriptor>
 <descriptor>
  <name>room</name>
  <value>Bath room</value>
 </descriptor>
</product>
<product><name>Shower stall</name>
 <descriptor>
```

```
   <name>category</name>
   <value>Bath and shower</value>
  </descriptor>
  <descriptor>
   <name>room</name>
   <value>Bath room</value>
  </descriptor>
 </product>
 <product><name>Wall cabinet</name>
  <descriptor>
   <name>category</name>
   <value>Bath and shower</value>
  </descriptor>
  <descriptor>
   <name>room</name>
   <value>Bath room</value>
  </descriptor>
 </product>
 <product><name>Towel rack</name>
  <descriptor>
   <name>category</name>
   <value>Accessories</value>
  </descriptor>
  <descriptor>
   <name>room</name>
   <value>Bath room</value>
  </descriptor>
 </product>
 <product><name>Towels</name>
  <descriptor>
   <name>category</name>
   <value>Accessories</value>
  </descriptor>
  <descriptor>
   <name>room</name>
   <value>Bath room</value>
  </descriptor>
 </product>
 </catalog>
```

Listing 22.7: The Catalog's DTD (catalog.dtd)

```
<?xml version='1.0' encoding='ISO-8859-1'?>
<!-- DTD for representing catalogs -->

<!ELEMENT catalog (description?, product*)>
<!ELEMENT description (#PCDATA)>
<!ELEMENT product (name, descriptor*)>
<!ELEMENT descriptor (name, value)>
<!ELEMENT name (#PCDATA)>
<!ELEMENT value (#PCDATA)>
```

⤵ Listing 22.8:   A Catalog Style Sheet (catalog.css)

```
catalog
{display: block;
text-align: left}

description
{background-color: #bbbbff;
border: 5px ridge;
display: block;
font-size: xx-large;
font-weight: bold;
margin-top: 25px;
padding: 5px;
text-align: center}

product
{border: 1px solid;
display: block;
padding: 5px}

descriptor
{background-color: #ffffff}

product name
{background-color: #d5d5ff;
border: 1px solid;
padding: 2px;
width: 30%}

descriptor name
{background-color: #8080ff;
display: none}

value
{width: 30%}
```

XML Namespaces

You should have a feel for how XML markup can be styled with CSS. With a little experimentation, you'll quickly become an XML style master. However, there are two more tricks that you'll want to learn: how to insert HTML into XML documents, and how to display the inserted HTML.

Consider Listing 22.9 (`rapsheet1.xml`). It provides a rap sheet about an individual, complete with photos. I can style the markup so that it looks nice, but how do I display the photos? If there were only one photo, I could display it as a background image. But I may have to display several photos.

XML doesn't provide any easy-to-use facilities for displaying image files. A convenient solution is to use XML to structure the overall document, and use HTML to display images and other elements that are difficult to display using XML. This approach involves the use of XML namespaces.

XML namespaces are a mechanism for using elements from multiple document types in a single document. Tag names use prefixes that identify the document type to which a tag belongs. The easiest way to see how this works is through an example. Listing 22.10 (rap-sheet2.xml) presents an updated rap sheet. There are two significant changes:

- The document element contains two namespace definitions.
- The src tags were replaced by HTML img tags.

The document element defines two namespaces: the default namespace, which is associated with the URL www.toolery.com/rapsheet, and the html namespace, which is associated with www.w3.org/1999/xhtml.

```
<rapsheet xmlns="http://www.toolery.com/rapsheet"
  xmlns:html="http://www.w3.org/1999/xhtml">
```

The default namespace is used by all document elements that don't have prefixes in their tag names. The html namespace is associated with all document elements whose tag names begin with the prefix html:. These are the three elements of the following form:

```
<html:img src="url"/>
```

The html namespace definition and the use of the html: prefixes allows us to embed HTML elements in our XML document. You may be wondering what's at the URLs specified in the namespace definitions. The answer is nothing. The URLs are just used to uniquely define the namespaces. I chose www.toolery.com/rapsheet because I own the toolery.com domain. The URL associated with HTML and XHTML is standard. It's just something that you learn.

Listing 22.11 (rapsheet.css) presents a style sheet for rapsheet2.xml. Figures 22.12 and 22.13 show how it is rendered by Internet Explorer and Navigator 6.

FIGURE 22.12:

Internet Explorer displays the rap sheet.

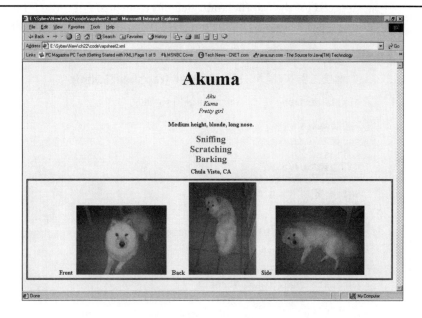

FIGURE 22.13:

Navigator displays the rap sheet.

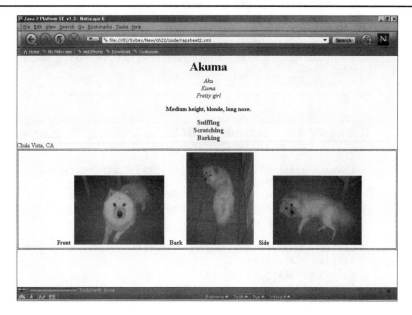

You can also use namespaces to incorporate XML elements from other document types into your XML documents. Just associate a namespace with the other XML document, and use a prefix for the external (non-default) elements. For more information on XML namespaces, check out the W3C namespaces recommendation at www.w3.org/TR/1999/REC-xml-names-19990114/.

Listing 22.9:   An XML Dossier (rapsheet1.xml)

```
<?xml version="1.0" encoding="iso-8859-1"?>

<rapsheet>
<name>Akuma</name>
<aliases>
<alias>Aku</alias>
<alias>Kuma</alias>
<alias>Pretty girl</alias>
</aliases>
<description>
Medium height, blonde, long nose.
</description>
<arrests>
<arrest>Sniffing</arrest>
<arrest>Scratching</arrest>
<arrest>Barking</arrest>
</arrests>
<last_seen>Chula Vista, CA</last_seen>
<photos>
<photo><caption>Front</caption><src>front.jpg</src></photo>
<photo><caption>Back</caption><src>back.jpg</src></photo>
<photo><caption>Side</caption><src>side.jpg</src></photo>
</photos>
</rapsheet>
```

Listing 22.10:   Embedding HTML in XML (rapsheet2.xml)

```
<?xml version="1.0" encoding="iso-8859-1"?>
<?xml-stylesheet href="rapsheet.css" type="text/css"?>

<rapsheet xmlns="http://www.toolery.com/rapsheet"
 xmlns:html="http://www.w3.org/1999/xhtml">
<name>Akuma</name>
<aliases>
<alias>Aku</alias>
<alias>Kuma</alias>
<alias>Pretty girl</alias>
</aliases>
<description>
Medium height, blonde, long nose.
</description>
<arrests>
```

```
<arrest>Sniffing</arrest>
<arrest>Scratching</arrest>
<arrest>Barking</arrest>
</arrests>
<last_seen>Chula Vista, CA</last_seen>
<photos>
<photo><caption>Front</caption><html:img src="front.jpg"/></photo>
<photo><caption>Back</caption><html:img src="back.jpg"/></photo>
<photo><caption>Side</caption><html:img src="side.jpg"/></photo>
</photos>
</rapsheet>
```

Listing 22.11: A Style Sheet for the Rap Sheet (rapsheet.css)

```
dossier
{background-color: #ffffff}

name
{display: block;
font-size: xx-large;
font-weight: bolder;
margin: 10px;
text-align: center}

aliases
{display: block;
text-align: center}

alias
{display: block;
font-style: italic}

description
{display: block;
font-weight: bold;
margin: 1em;
text-align: center}

last_seen
{display: block;
font-weight: bolder;
margin-bottom: 10px;
margin-top: 10px;
text-align: center}

arrests
{display: block;
text-align: center}

arrest
```

```
{color: #ff0000;
display: block;
font-size: large;
font-weight: bold}

photos
{border: 4px double;
display: block;
padding: 5px;
text-align: center}

caption
{font-weight: bold;
padding: 10px}
```

Summary

In this chapter, you learned how to style XML for display with Internet Explorer and Navigator. You learned how to associate CSS style sheets with XML documents, and you experimented with a few different style sheets. You also learned about differences in the style sheet support provided by Navigator and Internet Explorer. You learned about XML namespaces, how to embed HTML in XML documents, and how to use HTML to display images in XML documents.

In the next chapter, you'll learn how to insert JavaScript into XML documents; how to set XML event handlers; and how to access the objects, properties, and methods of XML objects.

Scripting XML

- Adding scripts to XML files

- Understanding DOM 2 events

- Handling HTML events in XML documents

In the previous chapters of this section, you learned how to create XML documents, style them with CSS, and display them using Internet Explorer and Navigator. In this chapter, you'll learn how to script XML files with JavaScript. If you haven't read Chapter 13, "Using the W3C DOM Level 1," now would be a good time to do so. That's because the predominant means for scripting XML is to use the DOM 1 Core objects.

This chapter will show you how to write scripts for XML documents that work with both Internet Explorer 5.5, Navigator 6, and later. The later versions of these browsers provide better support for DOM 1 Core objects and CSS. By the time you finish this chapter, you'll know how to script XML documents, and you'll have a good idea of the XML-scripting capabilities provided by Internet Explorer and Navigator.

NOTE   Appendix E, "DOM 1 Object Reference," provides a summary of the DOM 1 interfaces.

Adding Scripts to XML Files

In the previous chapter, you learned how to insert HTML in XML files using XML namespaces. You'll use the same technique to insert JavaScript scripts in XML files. Listing 23.1 (`script1.xml`) provides a simple example. The following script is inserted at the bottom of the document:

```
<html:script language="JavaScript">
window.alert("I can script XML!")
</html:script>
```

It works in XML documents just as it does in HTML documents. An alert dialog box is displayed when the document is loaded, as shown in Figure 23.1. The script works the same way in both Navigator and Internet Explorer. Listing 23.2 provides the `script1.css` style sheet that is referenced by `script1.xml`.

FIGURE 23.1:

An alert dialog box is generated by the script.

Listing 23.3 (`script2.xml`) shows how to include a JavaScript `.js` file in an XML file:

```
<html:script language="JavaScript" src="update.js"/>
```

You don't need to use enclosing tags—a single separating tag will do. Remember to end the tag with a />.

Listing 23.4 shows the script that's contained in `update.js`. The following code is executed when the tag is encountered. It sets the `text` variable to the first and only `text` element, initializes the `msgs` array to a list of messages to be displayed, initializes `index` to 0, and sets an interval timer to execute the `update()` function every five seconds.

```
var nl = document.getElementsByTagName("text")
var text = nl.item(0).firstChild
var msgs = new Array(
 "Hello XML!",
 "It's great to be able to update text dynamically!",
 "This script works in both Navigator 6 and Internet Explorer 5.5.",
 "You can use it to display news items to your users."
)
var index = 0
window.setInterval("update()",5000)
```

The `update()` function sets the `nodeValue` property of the `text` node to an element of the `msgs` array.

```
function update() {
 text.nodeValue = msgs[index]
 index = (index + 1) % msgs.length
}
```

Listing 23.1:   A Simple XML Script (script1.xml)

```
<?xml version="1.0" encoding="iso-8859-1"?>
<?xml-stylesheet href="script1.css" type="text/css"?>

<document  xmlns="http://www.toolery.com/script"
 xmlns:html="http://www.w3.org/1999/xhtml">
<text>This XML document is scripted using JavaScript!</text>
<html:script language="JavaScript">
window.alert("I can script XML!")
</html:script>
</document>
```

Listing 23.2:   The Style Sheet for script1.xml (script1.css)

```
text
{display: block;
font-family: Verdana, Helvetica, Arial, sans-serif;
font-size: larger;
font-weight: bold;
text-align: center;
```

```
border: 1px solid;
padding: 4px;
margin-top: +2%;
margin-left: +2%}
```

Listing 23.3:   An XML File that Includes a .js file (script2.xml)

```
<?xml version="1.0" encoding="iso-8859-1"?>
<?xml-stylesheet href="script2.css" type="text/css"?>

<document  xmlns="http://www.toolery.com/script"
 xmlns:html="http://www.w3.org/1999/xhtml">
<text>This XML document is scripted using update.js.
It uses a timer to change the content of this element.</text>
<html:script language="JavaScript" src="update.js"/>
</document>
```

Listing 23.4:   The update.js File

```
// update.js

function update() {
 text.nodeValue = msgs[index]
 index = (index + 1) % msgs.length
}

var nl = document.getElementsByTagName("text")
var text = nl.item(0).firstChild
var msgs = new Array(
 "Hello XML!",
 "It's great to be able to update text dynamically!",
 "This script works in both Navigator 6 and Internet Explorer 5.5.",
 "You can use it to display news items to your users."
)
var index = 0
window.setInterval("update()",5000)
```

Listing 23.5:   The script2.css File

```
text
{display: block;
background-color: white;
font-family: Verdana, Helvetica, Arial, sans-serif;
font-size: larger;
font-weight: bold;
text-align: center;
```

```
border: 1px solid;
padding: 4px;
margin-top: +2%;
margin-left: +2%}

document
{background-color: #ffffff}
```

DOM 2 Events and Styles

At this point, you might be thinking that scripting XML is easy. Unfortunately, as you go beyond simple examples, incompatibilities between Navigator and Internet Explorer make things complicated. Two areas in which this is a major problem are event handling and dynamic styles. Navigator does things by the book using DOM 2 events and styles. Internet Explorer doesn't support DOM 2 events and styles, but it provides great support for using HTML events and styles with XML. I'll cover DOM 2 events and styles first, and then I'll address using HTML events and styles later in this chapter.

DOM 2 Events and XML Elements

When it comes to event handling in XML, you have two choices: using DOM 2 events with XML elements, or handling HTML events. Currently, only Netscape Navigator 6 and later allow you to define DOM 2 events for XML elements.

The W3C DOM Level 2 Events recommendation (www.w3.org/TR/2000/REC-DOM-Level-2-Events-20001113/) defines a generic event system that extends HTML events to the XML documents and the DOM as a whole. I'm not going to cover all of the DOM 2 events because they are only supported by Navigator. However, I'll give you some examples of DOM 2 event handling and explain how they work. For more information, read the W3C recommendation.

Listing 23.6 (clickme.xml) provides a simple XML document that is scripted to use DOM 2 events with XML elements. The clickme.js script is shown in Listing 23.7, and the clickme .css style sheet is shown in Listing 23.8.

The script gets the text element, assigns it to the text variable, and then adds an event handler using the DOM 2 addEventListener() method:

```
nl.item(0).addEventListener("click", changeText, false)
```

The method takes the name of the event, the name of the event handling function, and a Boolean value as arguments. The event names are defined in the DOM 2 Events recommendation. For the most part, the event names are analogous to those used in HTML. For example, the previous statement is equivalent to setting an HTML element's `onclick` attribute to `changeText()`:

```
onclick="changeText()"
```

The Boolean value indicates whether or not events should be captured by the event handler. Event capturing allows an event listener to intercept events before they are signaled to their target. Event capturing is the opposite of event bubbling, in that its direction of flow is reversed so that it acts in a top-down manner. (Refer to Chapter 4, "Handling Events.")

When you open `clickme.xml` in Navigator, the window shown in Figure 23.2 is displayed. Click the text box, and a new text message is displayed, as shown in Figure 23.3.

FIGURE 23.2:

The opening display of *clickme.xml*

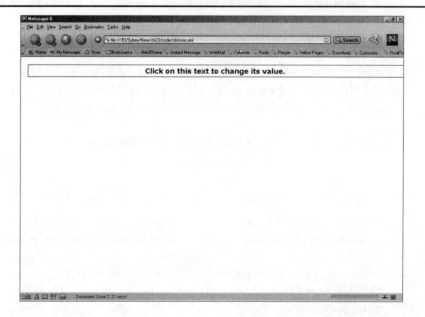

FIGURE 23.3:

The click event is handled by displaying a new message.

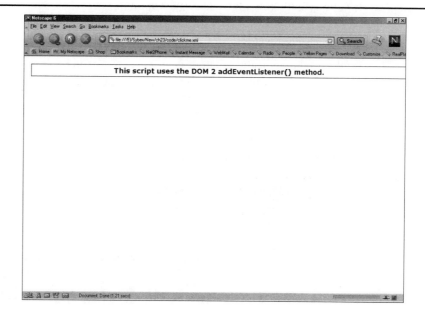

Listing 23.6:   The clickme.xml File

```
<?xml version="1.0" encoding="iso-8859-1"?>
<?xml-stylesheet href="clickme.css" type="text/css"?>

<document  xmlns="http://www.toolery.com/script"
 xmlns:html="http://www.w3.org/1999/xhtml">
<text>Click on this text to change its value.</text>
<html:script language="JavaScript" src="clickme.js"/>
</document>
```

Listing 23.7:   A Script that Uses DOM 2 Events with XML Elements

```
// clickme.js

function changeText(e) {
 text.nodeValue = msgs[index]
 index = (index + 1) % msgs.length
}

var nl = document.getElementsByTagName("text")
var text = nl.item(0).firstChild
nl.item(0).addEventListener("click", changeText, false)
var msgs = new Array(
 "This script uses the DOM 2 addEventListener() method.",
```

```
"You can define events for your XML tags.",
"Navigator 6 supports DOM 2 events, but Internet Explorer 5.5 does not."
)
var index = 0
```

Listing 23.8: **The clickme.css Style Sheet**

```
text
{display: block;
background-color: white;
font-family: Verdana, Helvetica, Arial, sans-serif;
font-size: larger;
font-weight: bold;
text-align: center;
border: 1px solid;
padding: 4px;
margin-top: +2%;
margin-left: +2%}
```

Dynamically Updating XML Styles Using DOM 2 Styles

In Dynamic HTML, we change the style of HTML elements based upon timers and events generated by users. So it's reasonable to expect a similar capability with XML. The DOM 2 Style recommendation (www.w3.org/TR/2000/REC-DOM-Level-2-Style-20001113/) provides an API for dynamically updating styles in XML and HTML documents. This API is supported by Navigator, but not Internet Explorer.

Listing 22.9 (style.xml) shows a document that has two style sheets (style1.css and style2.css). It is scripted by the style.js file (Listing 22.10). Listings 22.11 and 22.12 show the style1.css and style2.css files.

When style.xml is loaded in Navigator, it displays the window shown in Figure 23.4. When you click the text box, the document's appearance changes, as shown in Figure 23.5. This amounts to toggling between style1.css and style2.css.

The script in style.js sets the onclick event handler of the text element to the toggleStyles() function.

```
nl.item(0).addEventListener("click", toggleStyles, false)
```

The toggleStyles() function uses the DOM 2 stylesheets property to toggle between the two style sheets. Normally, the second style sheet takes precedence over the first. When the second style sheet is disabled, the first style sheet goes into effect.

```
document.styleSheets[1].disabled = !document.styleSheets[1].disabled
```

In the following section, I'll show you how to update the style of individual elements using the DOM 2 API.

FIGURE 23.4:

The *style.xml* initial display

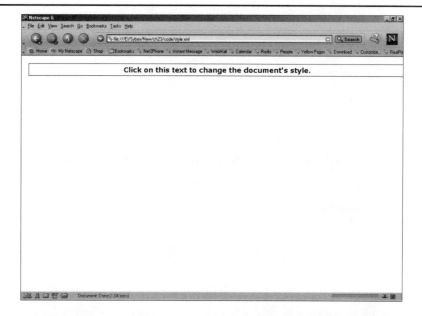

FIGURE 23.5:

The document style is updated when the text box is clicked.

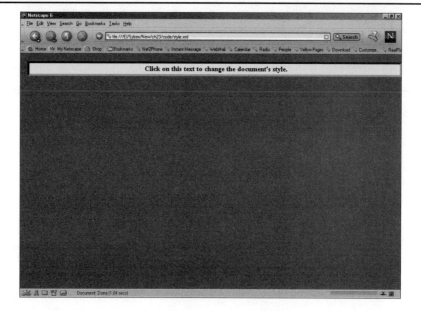

Listing 22.9:   The style.xml Example

```
<?xml version="1.0" encoding="iso-8859-1"?>
<?xml-stylesheet href="style1.css" type="text/css"?>
<?xml-stylesheet href="style2.css" type="text/css"?>

<document  xmlns="http://www.toolery.com/style"
 xmlns:html="http://www.w3.org/1999/xhtml">
<text>Click on this text to change the document's style.</text>
<html:script language="JavaScript" src="style.js"/>
</document>
```

Listing 22.10:   Scripting Styles with DOM 2 (style.js)

```
// style.js

function toggleStyles() {
 document.styleSheets[1].disabled = !document.styleSheets[1].disabled
}

var nl = document.getElementsByTagName("text")
var text = nl.item(0).firstChild
nl.item(0).addEventListener("click", toggleStyles, false)
```

Listing 22.11:   The First Style Sheet for style.xml (style1.css)

```
text
{background-color: #ffff80;
border: 5px inset;
display: block;
font-family: Times, "Times New Roman", serif;
font-size: larger;
font-weight: bold;
margin-left: +2%;
margin-top: +2%;
padding: 4px;
text-align: center}

document
{background-color: #8080ff}
```

Listing 22.12:   The Second Style Sheet for style.xml (style2.css)

```
text
{display: block;
```

```
background-color: white;
font-family: Verdana, Helvetica, Arial, sans-serif;
font-size: larger;
font-weight: bold;
text-align: center;
border: 1px solid;
padding: 4px;
margin-top: +2%;
margin-left: +2%}

document
{background-color: #ffffff}
```

Using DOM 2 Events and Styles with *outline.xml*

In Chapter 22, "Displaying XML with Internet Explorer and Navigator," you created an XML outline (outline.xml), and displayed it with CSS styles (outline1.css and outline2 .css). Listing 23.13 updates outline.xml to use the script outline.js (Listing 23.14). Besides using XML namespaces and including outline.js, outline.xml also sets id attributes for each topic. These id attributes are used to uniquely identify each topic.

When you open outline.xml in Navigator, it displays the window shown in Figure 23.6. If you click a topic, the topic is collapsed, and all subtopics and text are hidden, as shown in Figure 23.7. If you click again, the topic is expanded back to its original display state.

FIGURE 23.6:

The *outline.xml* opening window

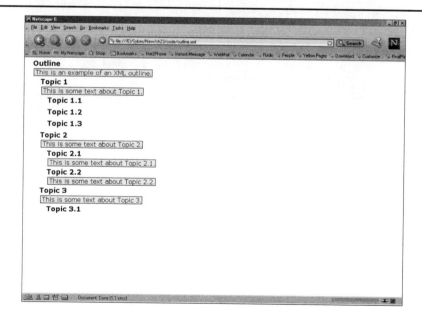

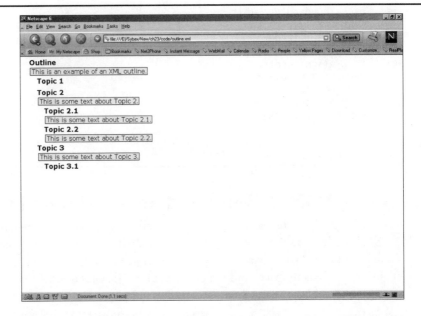

The outline.js script selects all the name elements, and sets their onclick event handler to
the updateOutline() function. It also sets their state attribute to open. I often use the attributes of XML elements to store state information in a persistent manner. The stylesheet
variable is set to the document's one and only style sheet. The rules variable is set to the
cssRules property of the style sheet. This property is a collection of all rules that are contained in the style sheet.

```
var nl = document.getElementsByTagName("name")
for(var i=0; i<nl.length; ++i) {
 var nameTag = nl.item(i)
 nameTag.addEventListener("click", updateOutline, false)
 nameTag.setAttribute("state", "open")
}
var stylesheet = document.styleSheets[0]
var rules = stylesheet.cssRules
```

The updateOutline() function is a fairly long function. It is automatically passed an Event
object (the e parameter) when it is invoked. The Event object provides information about the
event that caused the handler to be invoked. In particular, its target property identifies the
element that was clicked.

```
var target = e.target
```

The `target` can be either marked-up text or the element that holds the marked-up text (a `name` element). If it is marked-up text, we set the `target` variable to its parent, which is a `name` element.

```
// If the target is text then get its parent
if(target.nodeType == 3 || target.nodeType == 4)
  target = e.target.parentNode
```

Next, we get the value of the element's `state` variable (`open` or `closed`), and retrieve the style rules that are associated with that element (and stored as attributes of the element). The first time the `rule1` and `rule2` attributes are accessed, they are blank strings. They are updated when the element's style is changed. The `deleteRule()` function is invoked to delete any existing style rules for the element.

```
// Get the name's state, rule1, and rule2 attributes
var state = target.getAttribute("state")
var oldRule1 = target.getAttribute("rule1")
var oldRule2 = target.getAttribute("rule2")
deleteRule(oldRule1)
deleteRule(oldRule2)
```

The `state` attribute is then updated to its new state.

```
if(state == "closed") target.setAttribute("state", "open")
else  target.setAttribute("state", "closed")
```

The parent of the `name` element is a `topic` element. This element has an `id` attribute that uniquely identifies that element. This element is used to build the new style rules for the element. For example, if a `topic` element with an `id` of t2 is expanded, the following CSS2 style rules will be added to the style sheet:

```
topic[id=t2] > text { display: inline; }
topic[id=t2] > topic { display: block; }
```

These rules cause all child `text` and `topic` elements to be displayed normally. (Refer to the CSS2 recommendation at www.w3.org/TR/1998/REC-CSS2-19980512/ for more information on style rules.)

If topic t2 is collapsed, the following style rules will be inserted into the style sheet:

```
topic[id=t2] > text { display: none; }
topic[id=t2] > topic { display: none; }
```

These rules cause all child `text` and `topic` elements to be hidden. The code that implements this functionality follows.

```
// Get the name tag's parent
var topic = target.parentNode
// Get the parent's id attribute
var attr = topic.getAttribute("id")
```

```
var rule1 = "topic[id=" + attr + "] > text { display: inline; }"
var rule2 = "topic[id=" + attr + "] > topic { display: block; }"
if(state == "open") {
 var rule1 = "topic[id=" + attr + "] > text { display: none; }"
 var rule2 = "topic[id=" + attr + "] > topic { display: none; }"
 }
```

The rules are inserted into the style sheet using the `insertRule()` method of the
`CSSStyleSheet` object referenced by `stylesheet`. The `insertRule()` method takes two arguments: the rules to be inserted and the location within the style sheet where they are to be inserted. In this case, they are added to the end of the style sheet.

```
var ix = rules.length
stylesheet.insertRule(rule1, ix)
target.setAttribute("rule1", rules.item(ix).cssText)
++ix
stylesheet.insertRule(rule2, ix)
target.setAttribute("rule2", rules.item(ix).cssText)
```

The `deleteRule()` function uses the `cssText` property of the `CSSRule` interface to convert an existing rule back into a text string, and uses the `deleteRule()` method of the `CSSStyleSheet` interface to delete the `i`th rule of the style sheet.

```
if(rule.length > 0) {
  for(var i=0; i<rules.length; ++i) {
   var r = rules.item(i).cssText
   if(r == rule) {
    stylesheet.deleteRule(i)
    break
   }
  }
 }
```

If you think that this is a really complicated way to update the styles of XML elements, you're right. Netscape does it by the book, but Internet Explorer does it much more simply, as you'll learn in the following sections.

Listing 23.13:   Revised outline.xml

```
<?xml version="1.0" encoding="iso-8859-1"?>
<?xml-stylesheet href="outline1.css" type="text/css"?>

<topic id="t0" xmlns="http://www.toolery.com/outline"
 xmlns:html="http://www.w3.org/1999/xhtml">
 <name>Outline</name>
 <text>This is an example of an XML outline.</text>
 <topic id="t1"><name>Topic 1</name>
  <text>This is some text about Topic 1.</text>
```

```
    <topic id="t1_1"><name>Topic 1.1</name></topic>
    <topic id="t1_2"><name>Topic 1.2</name></topic>
    <topic id="t1_3"><name>Topic 1.3</name></topic>
   </topic>
   <topic id="t2"><name>Topic 2</name>
    <text>This is some text about Topic 2.</text>
    <topic id="t2_1"><name>Topic 2.1</name>
     <text>This is some text about Topic 2.1.</text>
    </topic>
    <topic id="t2_2"><name>Topic 2.2</name>
     <text>This is some text about Topic 2.2.</text>
    </topic>
   </topic>
   <topic id="t3"><name>Topic 3</name>
    <text>This is some text about Topic 3.</text>
    <topic id="t3_1"><name>Topic 3.1</name></topic>
   </topic>
   <html:script language="JavaScript" src="outline.js"/>
  </topic>
```

Listing 23.14:   Adding DOM2 Events to outline.xml (outline.js)

```
// outline.js

function updateOutline(e) {
 var target = e.target
 // If the target is text then get its parent
 if(target.nodeType == 3 || target.nodeType == 4)
  target = e.target.parentNode
 // Get the name's state, rule1, and rule2 attributes
 var state = target.getAttribute("state")
 var oldRule1 = target.getAttribute("rule1")
 var oldRule2 = target.getAttribute("rule2")
 deleteRule(oldRule1)
 deleteRule(oldRule2)
 if(state == "closed") target.setAttribute("state", "open")
 else  target.setAttribute("state", "closed")
 // Get the name tag's parent
 var topic = target.parentNode
 // Get the parent's id attribute
 var attr = topic.getAttribute("id")
 var rule1 = "topic[id=" + attr + "] > text { display: inline; }"
 var rule2 = "topic[id=" + attr + "] > topic { display: block; }"
 if(state == "open") {
  var rule1 = "topic[id=" + attr + "] > text { display: none; }"
  var rule2 = "topic[id=" + attr + "] > topic { display: none; }"
 }
 var ix = rules.length
 stylesheet.insertRule(rule1, ix)
 target.setAttribute("rule1", rules.item(ix).cssText)
```

```
  ++ix
  stylesheet.insertRule(rule2, ix)
  target.setAttribute("rule2", rules.item(ix).cssText)
 }

 function deleteRule(rule) {
  if(rule.length > 0) {
   for(var i=0; i<rules.length; ++i) {
    var r = rules.item(i).cssText
    if(r == rule) {
     stylesheet.deleteRule(i)
     break
    }
   }
  }
 }

 var nl = document.getElementsByTagName("name")
 for(var i=0; i<nl.length; ++i) {
  var nameTag = nl.item(i)
  nameTag.addEventListener("click", updateOutline, false)
  nameTag.setAttribute("state", "open")
 }
 var stylesheet = document.styleSheets[0]
 var rules = stylesheet.cssRules
```

Handling HTML Events in XML Documents

If the DOM 2 events and styles seem to be a lot more involved than what you've been doing with HTML, don't worry. You can use HTML events with both Navigator and Internet Explorer, and you can use the simple style property with Internet Explorer. This greatly simplifies your XML scripting and allows for cross-browser compatibility.

Listing 23.15 (contactlist.xml) updates the contacts1.xml and contacts2.xml files of Chapter 22 to support event handling and dynamic styles. It is scripted using contactlist.js (Listing 23.16) and styled using contactstyle.css (Listing 23.17). It works with both Navigator and Internet Explorer.

When you open contactlist.xml in Internet Explorer, it displays the simple search form shown in Figure 23.8. Enter some text (for example, birthday) in the search form, and click the Search button. The script looks through the XML contact records, and selects those that contain the search text. It then displays these contact records, as shown in Figure 23.9. Play around with it a little to get a feel for how it works.

FIGURE 23.8:

The *contactlist.xml* search form

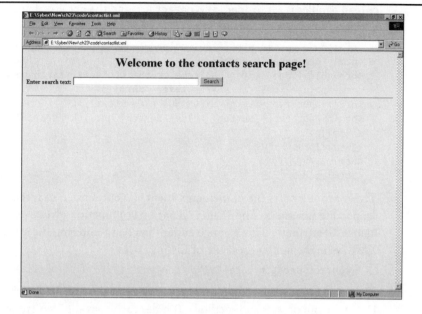

FIGURE 23.9:

Searching the contacts for "birthday."

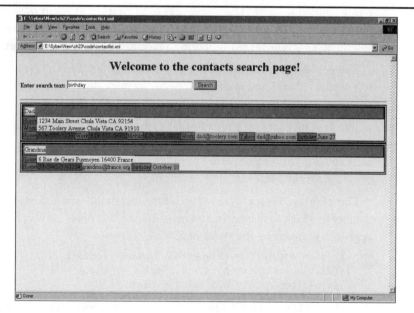

The contactlist.xml file uses XML namespaces to include some HTML markup. This markup implements the search form shown in Figure 23.8. Note that the document's onload handler is set to identifyContacts(), and the onclick handler of the form's Search button is set to searchContacts().

```
<html:body bgcolor="#ffff80" onload="identifyContacts()">
<html:form name="searchForm">
<html:h1 align="center">Welcome to the contacts search page!</html:h1>
<html:p><html:b>Enter search text: </html:b>
<html:input type="text" size="50" name="text"/>
<html:input type="button" value="Search" onclick="searchContacts()"/>
</html:p>
</html:form>
<html:hr/>
</html:body>
```

The contactlist.js file implements identifyContacts(), searchContacts(), and four other supporting functions. The identifyContacts() function gives each contact element a unique id attribute. This is much easier than hand-entering the attributes in the source XML, as in the outline.xml file of Listing 23.13.

```
contact.setAttribute("id", "contact"+i)
```

The searchContacts() function gets the value of the text field of the HTML form using DOM 1 Core objects and methods. It hides each contact element in case the contact is currently being displayed. Then, it checks each contact element to see whether it contains the text entered in the search form. It uses the getText() function to retrieve the contained text and the displayContact() function to hide or display the contact element.

The getText() function checks to see whether a node is a text node. If it is, it returns the text associated with the node. Otherwise, it checks its children (recursively) to see if they contain text, and returns the concatenated text of its children.

The displayContact() function takes the index of a contact and a Boolean value as its arguments. If the value is true, it displays the contact. Otherwise, it hides the contact. It accomplishes this in a browser-specific manner using the displayContactInExplorer() and displayContactInNavigator() functions.

The displayContactInExplorer() function simply sets the style.display property of the contact to block to display it, and none to hide it. This is a convenient and easy-to-use approach to updating the styles of XML elements.

```
var nl = document.getElementsByTagName("contact")
if(display) nl.item(n).style.display = "block"
else nl.item(n).style.display = "none"
```

The displayContactInNavigator() function updates the document's style sheet to change the style of a single contact. It uses the same approach that you learned in the previous section with outline.js.

Listing 23.15:   The contactlist.xml File

```
<?xml version="1.0" encoding="iso-8859-1" standalone="yes"?>
<?xml-stylesheet href="contactstyle.css" type="text/css"?>

<contacts xmlns="http://www.toolery.com/contactlist"
 xmlns:html="http://www.w3.org/1999/xhtml">
<html:script language="JavaScript" src="contactlist.js"/>
<html:body bgcolor="#ffff80" onload="identifyContacts()">
<html:form name="searchForm">
<html:h1 align="center">Welcome to the contacts search page!</html:h1>
<html:p><html:b>Enter search text: </html:b>
<html:input type="text" size="50" name="text"/>
<html:input type="button" value="Search" onclick="searchContacts()"/>
</html:p>
</html:form>
<html:hr/>
</html:body>
<contact>
 <name>Dad</name>
 <address>
  <description>Home</description>
  <street_address>1234 Main Street</street_address>
  <city>Chula Vista</city>
  <state>CA</state>
  <postal_code>92154</postal_code>
 </address>
 <address>
  <description>Work</description>
  <street_address>567 Toolery Avenue</street_address>
  <city>Chula Vista</city>
  <state>CA</state>
  <postal_code>91910</postal_code>
 </address>
 <phone>
  <description>Home</description>
  <phone_number>619-555-1234</phone_number>
 </phone>
 <phone>
  <description>Work</description>
  <phone_number>619-555-5678</phone_number>
 </phone>
 <phone>
  <description>Mobile</description>
  <phone_number>619-555-9012</phone_number>
 </phone>
 <email>
  <description>Work</description>
  <email_address>dad@toolery.com</email_address>
 </email>
```

```
<email>
 <description>Yahoo</description>
 <email_address>dad@yahoo.com</email_address>
</email>
<note>
 <description>Birthday</description>
 <text>June 27</text>
</note>
</contact>

<contact><name>Grandma</name>
 <address>
  <description>Home</description>
  <street_address>6 Rue de Gears</street_address>
  <city>Puymoyen</city>
  <postal_code>16400</postal_code>
  <country>France</country>
 </address>
 <phone>
  <description>Home</description>
  <phone_number>33-5-45-97-1234</phone_number>
 </phone>
 <email>
  <email_address>grandma@france.org</email_address>
 </email>
 <note>
  <description>Birthday</description>
  <text>October 10</text>
 </note>
</contact>

<contact><name>Work</name>
 <address>
  <street_address>789 West H Street</street_address>
  <city>Chula Vista</city>
  <state>CA</state>
  <postal_code>91912</postal_code>
 </address>
 <phone>
  <description>Voice</description>
  <phone_number>619-555-9876</phone_number>
 </phone>
 <phone>
  <description>Fax</description>
  <phone_number>619-555-9877</phone_number>
 </phone>
</contact>

<contact><name>Pizza</name>
 <phone>
   <phone_number>619-555-8765</phone_number>
```

```
  </phone>
</contact>

<contact><name>Betty</name>
 <phone>
  <description>Home</description>
  <phone_number>619-555-4321</phone_number>
 </phone>
 <phone>
  <description>Work</description>
  <phone_number>619-555-5432</phone_number>
 </phone>
 <phone>
  <description>Mobile</description>
  <phone_number>619-555-6543</phone_number>
 </phone>
 <phone>
  <description>Sister's House</description>
  <phone_number>619-555-7654</phone_number>
 </phone>
 <email>
  <email_address>betty@hotmail.com</email_address>
 </email>
 <note>
  <description>Likes</description>
  <text>Shopping</text>
 </note>
 <note>
  <description>Dislikes</description>
  <text>Sports</text>
 </note>
</contact>

<contact><name>Bob</name>
 <phone>
  <description>Mobile</description>
  <phone_number>619-555-2468</phone_number>
 </phone>
 <email>
  <email_address>bob@yahoo.com</email_address>
 </email>
</contact>

</contacts>
```

Listing 23.16:   The contactlist.js File Used with contactlist.xml

```
// contactlist.js

function searchContacts() {
```

```
// Get search text
var nl = document.getElementsByTagName("input")
var textField = nl.item(0)
var searchText = textField.value
// Get all contacts
nl = document.getElementsByTagName("contact")
// Hide them
for(var i=0; i<nl.length; ++i) displayContact(i, false)
// Check each contact for search text
for(var i=0; i<nl.length; ++i) {
 var contact = nl.item(i)
 var text = getText(contact).toLowerCase()
 if(text.indexOf(searchText.toLowerCase()) != -1)
   displayContact(i, true)
 }
}

function identifyContacts() {
 // Get all contacts
 var nl = document.getElementsByTagName("contact")
 // Assign them an id attribute
 for(var i=0; i<nl.length; ++i) {
  var contact = nl.item(i)
  contact.setAttribute("id", "contact"+i)
 }
}

function displayContact(n, display) {
 if(navigator.appName == "Netscape") displayContactInNavigator(n, display)
 else if(navigator.appName == "Microsoft Internet Explorer")
displayContactInExplorer(n, display)
}

function displayContactInExplorer(n, display) {
 var nl = document.getElementsByTagName("contact")
 if(display) nl.item(n).style.display = "block"
 else nl.item(n).style.display = "none"
}

function displayContactInNavigator(n, display) {
 var stylesheet = document.styleSheets[0]
 var rules = stylesheet.cssRules
 var nl = document.getElementsByTagName("contact")
 var contact = nl.item(n)
 // Delete old CSS rule
 var oldRule = contact.getAttribute("rule")
 if(oldRule.length > 0) {
  for(var i=0; i<rules.length; ++i) {
   var r = rules.item(i).cssText
   if(r == oldRule) {
    stylesheet.deleteRule(i)
```

```
    break
   }
  }
 }
 // Insert new CSS rule
 var show = "none"
 if(display) show = "block"
 var newRule = "contact[id=contact" + n + "] { display: " + show +"; }"
 var ix = rules.length
 stylesheet.insertRule(newRule, ix)
 contact.setAttribute("rule", rules.item(ix).cssText)
}

function getText(node) {
 if(node.nodeName == "#text") {
  return node.nodeValue
 }else{
  var nl = node.childNodes
  var s = ""
  for(var i=0; i<nl.length; ++i) {
   s += getText(nl.item(i))
  }
  return s
 }
}
```

Listing 23.17:   The Style Sheet for contactlist.xml (contactstyle.css)

```
contacts
{background-color: #ffff80}

contact
{border: 6px double;
display: none}

name
{background-color: #ff8000;
border: 2px solid;
display: block;
padding: 4px}

address
{display: block}

description
{background-color: #ff8080;
border: 1px solid}

phone
{background-color: #8080ff}
```

```
email
{background-color: #c0c0c0}

note
{background-color: #abd6d6}
```

Scripting *catalog.xml*

You can use the same scripting techniques that you learned in the previous section to provide an HTML interface to the catalog.xml file of Chapter 22. Listing 23.18 presents an updated version of catalog.xml, and Listings 23.19 and 23.20 present the script (catalog.js) and style sheet (catalog.css) files. The files work with both Navigator and Internet Explorer.

When you open catalog.xml in Internet Explorer, it displays the form shown in Figure 23.10. Select a product type and a room from the drop-down lists, and click the List products button. A list of products that meet the criteria is displayed, as shown in Figure 23.11.

FIGURE 23.10:

The opening display of *catalog.xml*

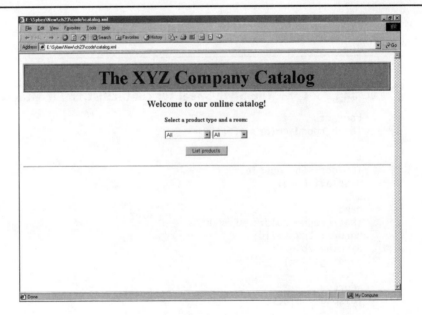

FIGURE 23.11:

The script searches the XML elements, and displays those that meet the search criteria.

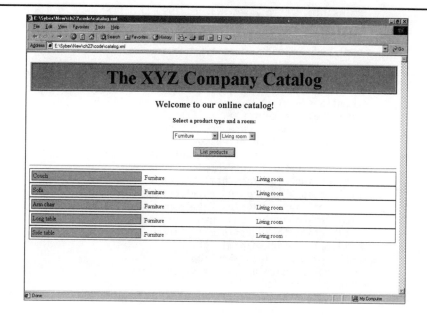

NOTE   The script takes much longer to run in Navigator because of the way styles are updated in Navigator.

The HTML form that is inserted in catalog.xml uses the searchCatalog() function to handle the clicking of the List products button. Note that the identifyProducts() function handles the document's onload event.

The identifyProducts() function is equivalent to the identifyContacts() function of Listing 23.16. It gives each product a unique id attribute.

The searchCatalog() function gets the values of the form's select fields, and matches them against the value elements of each product's descriptors. If a match occurs, the product is displayed. Otherwise, it is hidden. The displayProduct(), displayProductInExplorer(), and displayProductInNavigator() functions display or hide a product using the same approach as the displayContact(), displayContactInExplorer(), and displayContactIn-Navigator() functions of Listing 23.16.

Listing 23.18:   The Updated catalog.xml

```
<?xml version="1.0" encoding="iso-8859-1"?>
<?xml-stylesheet href="catalog.css" type="text/css"?>

<catalog xmlns="http://www.toolery.com/catalog"
```

```
 xmlns:html="http://www.w3.org/1999/xhtml">
<description>The XYZ Company Catalog</description>
<html:script language="JavaScript" src="catalog.js"/>
<html:body onload="identifyProducts()">
<html:form name="searchForm">
<html:h2 align="center">Welcome to our online catalog!</html:h2>
<html:p align="center"><html:b>Select a product type and a room:
</html:b></html:p>
<html:p align="center">
<html:select name="category">
<html:option>All</html:option>
<html:option>Furniture</html:option>
<html:option>Carpeting</html:option>
<html:option>Lighting</html:option>
<html:option>Electronics</html:option>
<html:option>Accessories</html:option>
<html:option>Appliances</html:option>
<html:option>Cabinets</html:option>
<html:option>Sinks</html:option>
<html:option>Toilets</html:option>
<html:option>Bath and shower</html:option>
</html:select>
<html:select name="room">
<html:option>All</html:option>
<html:option>Living room</html:option>
<html:option>Dining room</html:option>
<html:option>Bed room</html:option>
<html:option>Kitchen</html:option>
<html:option>Bath room</html:option>
</html:select>
</html:p>
<html:p align="center">
<html:input type="button" value="List products" onclick="searchCatalog()"/>
</html:p>
</html:form>
<html:hr/>
</html:body>
<!-- Living room products -->
<product><name>Couch</name>
 <descriptor>
  <name>category</name>
  <value>Furniture</value>
 </descriptor>
 <descriptor>
  <name>room</name>
  <value>Living room</value>
 </descriptor>
</product>
<product><name>Sofa</name>
 <descriptor>
  <name>category</name>
```

```
     <value>Furniture</value>
    </descriptor>
    <descriptor>
     <name>room</name>
     <value>Living room</value>
    </descriptor>
   </product>
   <product><name>Arm chair</name>
    <descriptor>
     <name>category</name>
     <value>Furniture</value>
    </descriptor>
    <descriptor>
     <name>room</name>
     <value>Living room</value>
    </descriptor>
   </product>
   <product><name>Long table</name>
    <descriptor>
     <name>category</name>
     <value>Furniture</value>
    </descriptor>
    <descriptor>
     <name>room</name>
     <value>Living room</value>
    </descriptor>
   </product>
   <product><name>Side table</name>
    <descriptor>
     <name>category</name>
     <value>Furniture</value>
    </descriptor>
    <descriptor>
     <name>room</name>
     <value>Living room</value>
    </descriptor>
   </product>
   <product><name>Persian rug</name>
    <descriptor>
     <name>category</name>
     <value>Carpeting</value>
    </descriptor>
    <descriptor>
     <name>room</name>
     <value>Living room</value>
    </descriptor>
   </product>
   <product><name>Cheap rug</name>
    <descriptor>
     <name>category</name>
     <value>Carpeting</value>
```

```
  </descriptor>
  <descriptor>
   <name>room</name>
   <value>Living room</value>
  </descriptor>
 </product>
 <product><name>Recessed ceiling light</name>
  <descriptor>
   <name>category</name>
   <value>Lighting</value>
  </descriptor>
  <descriptor>
   <name>room</name>
   <value>Living room</value>
  </descriptor>
 </product>
 <product><name>Floor light</name>
  <descriptor>
   <name>category</name>
   <value>Lighting</value>
  </descriptor>
  <descriptor>
   <name>room</name>
   <value>Living room</value>
  </descriptor>
 </product>
 <product><name>Table light</name>
  <descriptor>
   <name>category</name>
   <value>Lighting</value>
  </descriptor>
  <descriptor>
   <name>room</name>
   <value>Living room</value>
  </descriptor>
 </product>
 <product><name>Big TV</name>
  <descriptor>
   <name>category</name>
   <value>Electronics</value>
  </descriptor>
  <descriptor>
   <name>room</name>
   <value>Living room</value>
  </descriptor>
 </product>
 <product><name>Small TV</name>
  <descriptor>
   <name>category</name>
   <value>Electronics</value>
  </descriptor>
```

```
<descriptor>
 <name>room</name>
 <value>Living room</value>
</descriptor>
</product>
<product><name>Entertainment center</name>
 <descriptor>
 <name>category</name>
 <value>Electronics</value>
</descriptor>
 <descriptor>
 <name>room</name>
 <value>Living room</value>
</descriptor>
</product>
<product><name>Stereo</name>
 <descriptor>
 <name>category</name>
 <value>Electronics</value>
</descriptor>
 <descriptor>
 <name>room</name>
 <value>Living room</value>
</descriptor>
</product>
<product><name>Large painting</name>
 <descriptor>
 <name>category</name>
 <value>Accessories</value>
</descriptor>
 <descriptor>
 <name>room</name>
 <value>Living room</value>
</descriptor>
</product>
<product><name>Small painting</name>
 <descriptor>
 <name>category</name>
 <value>Accessories</value>
</descriptor>
 <descriptor>
 <name>room</name>
 <value>Living room</value>
</descriptor>
</product>
<product><name>Large fake plant</name>
 <descriptor>
 <name>category</name>
 <value>Accessories</value>
</descriptor>
 <descriptor>
```

```
  <name>room</name>
  <value>Living room</value>
 </descriptor>
</product>
<product><name>Small fake plant</name>
 <descriptor>
  <name>category</name>
  <value>Accessories</value>
 </descriptor>
 <descriptor>
  <name>room</name>
  <value>Living room</value>
 </descriptor>
</product>
<product><name>Expensive knick knack</name>
 <descriptor>
  <name>category</name>
  <value>Accessories</value>
 </descriptor>
 <descriptor>
  <name>room</name>
  <value>Living room</value>
 </descriptor>
</product>
<product><name>Cheap knick knack</name>
 <descriptor>
  <name>category</name>
  <value>Accessories</value>
 </descriptor>
 <descriptor>
  <name>room</name>
  <value>Living room</value>
 </descriptor>
</product>
<!-- Dining room products -->
<product><name>Expensive dining set</name>
 <descriptor>
  <name>category</name>
  <value>Furniture</value>
 </descriptor>
 <descriptor>
  <name>room</name>
  <value>Dining room</value>
 </descriptor>
</product>
<product><name>Cheap dining set</name>
 <descriptor>
  <name>category</name>
  <value>Furniture</value>
 </descriptor>
 <descriptor>
```

```
   <name>room</name>
   <value>Dining room</value>
  </descriptor>
 </product>
 <product><name>China cabinet</name>
  <descriptor>
   <name>category</name>
   <value>Furniture</value>
  </descriptor>
  <descriptor>
   <name>room</name>
   <value>Dining room</value>
  </descriptor>
 </product>
 <product><name>Serving table</name>
  <descriptor>
   <name>category</name>
   <value>Furniture</value>
  </descriptor>
  <descriptor>
   <name>room</name>
   <value>Dining room</value>
  </descriptor>
 </product>
 <product><name>Stain-proof rug</name>
  <descriptor>
   <name>category</name>
   <value>Carpeting</value>
  </descriptor>
  <descriptor>
   <name>room</name>
   <value>Dining room</value>
  </descriptor>
 </product>
 <product><name>Plastic floor covering</name>
  <descriptor>
   <name>category</name>
   <value>Carpeting</value>
  </descriptor>
  <descriptor>
   <name>room</name>
   <value>Dining room</value>
  </descriptor>
 </product>
 <product><name>Chandalier</name>
  <descriptor>
   <name>category</name>
   <value>Lighting</value>
  </descriptor>
  <descriptor>
   <name>room</name>
```

```xml
   <value>Dining room</value>
  </descriptor>
 </product>
 <product><name>Ceiling lamp/fan</name>
  <descriptor>
   <name>category</name>
   <value>Lighting</value>
  </descriptor>
  <descriptor>
   <name>room</name>
   <value>Dining room</value>
  </descriptor>
 </product>
 <product><name>China set</name>
  <descriptor>
   <name>category</name>
   <value>Accessories</value>
  </descriptor>
  <descriptor>
   <name>room</name>
   <value>Dining room</value>
  </descriptor>
 </product>
 <product><name>Silver set</name>
  <descriptor>
   <name>category</name>
   <value>Accessories</value>
  </descriptor>
  <descriptor>
   <name>room</name>
   <value>Dining room</value>
  </descriptor>
 </product>
 <!-- Bed room products -->
 <product><name>King bed</name>
  <descriptor>
   <name>category</name>
   <value>Furniture</value>
  </descriptor>
  <descriptor>
   <name>room</name>
   <value>Bed room</value>
  </descriptor>
 </product>
 <product><name>Queen bed</name>
  <descriptor>
   <name>category</name>
   <value>Furniture</value>
  </descriptor>
  <descriptor>
   <name>room</name>
```

```
      <value>Bed room</value>
     </descriptor>
    </product>
    <product><name>Single bed</name>
     <descriptor>
      <name>category</name>
      <value>Furniture</value>
     </descriptor>
     <descriptor>
      <name>room</name>
      <value>Bed room</value>
     </descriptor>
    </product>
    <product><name>End table</name>
     <descriptor>
      <name>category</name>
      <value>Furniture</value>
     </descriptor>
     <descriptor>
      <name>room</name>
      <value>Bed room</value>
     </descriptor>
    </product>
    <product><name>Dresser</name>
     <descriptor>
      <name>category</name>
      <value>Furniture</value>
     </descriptor>
     <descriptor>
      <name>room</name>
      <value>Bed room</value>
     </descriptor>
    </product>
    <product><name>Lamb skin carpet</name>
     <descriptor>
      <name>category</name>
      <value>Carpeting</value>
     </descriptor>
     <descriptor>
      <name>room</name>
      <value>Bed room</value>
     </descriptor>
    </product>
    <product><name>Bear skin carpet</name>
     <descriptor>
      <name>category</name>
      <value>Carpeting</value>
     </descriptor>
     <descriptor>
      <name>room</name>
      <value>Bed room</value>
```

```xml
  </descriptor>
 </product>
 <product><name>Ceiling lamp</name>
  <descriptor>
   <name>category</name>
   <value>Lighting</value>
  </descriptor>
  <descriptor>
   <name>room</name>
   <value>Bed room</value>
  </descriptor>
 </product>
 <product><name>Table lamp</name>
  <descriptor>
   <name>category</name>
   <value>Lighting</value>
  </descriptor>
  <descriptor>
   <name>room</name>
   <value>Bed room</value>
  </descriptor>
 </product>
 <product><name>Clock radio</name>
  <descriptor>
   <name>category</name>
   <value>Electronics</value>
  </descriptor>
  <descriptor>
   <name>room</name>
   <value>Bed room</value>
  </descriptor>
 </product>
 <product><name>Electronic head board</name>
  <descriptor>
   <name>category</name>
   <value>Electronics</value>
  </descriptor>
  <descriptor>
   <name>room</name>
   <value>Bed room</value>
  </descriptor>
 </product>
 <product><name>Pillow set</name>
  <descriptor>
   <name>category</name>
   <value>Accessories</value>
  </descriptor>
  <descriptor>
   <name>room</name>
   <value>Bed room</value>
  </descriptor>
```

```
  </product>
  <product><name>Linen set</name>
   <descriptor>
    <name>category</name>
    <value>Accessories</value>
   </descriptor>
   <descriptor>
    <name>room</name>
    <value>Bed room</value>
   </descriptor>
  </product>
  <product><name>Bed spread</name>
   <descriptor>
    <name>category</name>
    <value>Accessories</value>
   </descriptor>
   <descriptor>
    <name>room</name>
    <value>Bed room</value>
   </descriptor>
  </product>
  <!-- Kitchen products -->
  <product><name>Refrigerator</name>
   <descriptor>
    <name>category</name>
    <value>Appliances</value>
   </descriptor>
   <descriptor>
    <name>room</name>
    <value>Kitchen</value>
   </descriptor>
  </product>
  <product><name>Stove - oven</name>
   <descriptor>
    <name>category</name>
    <value>Appliances</value>
   </descriptor>
   <descriptor>
    <name>room</name>
    <value>Kitchen</value>
   </descriptor>
  </product>
  <product><name>Microwave oven</name>
   <descriptor>
    <name>category</name>
    <value>Appliances</value>
   </descriptor>
   <descriptor>
    <name>room</name>
    <value>Kitchen</value>
   </descriptor>
```

```xml
   </product>
   <product><name>Toaster</name>
    <descriptor>
     <name>category</name>
     <value>Appliances</value>
    </descriptor>
    <descriptor>
     <name>room</name>
     <value>Kitchen</value>
    </descriptor>
   </product>
   <product><name>Coffee maker</name>
    <descriptor>
     <name>category</name>
     <value>Appliances</value>
    </descriptor>
    <descriptor>
     <name>room</name>
     <value>Kitchen</value>
    </descriptor>
   </product>
   <product><name>Dish washer</name>
    <descriptor>
     <name>category</name>
     <value>Appliances</value>
    </descriptor>
    <descriptor>
     <name>room</name>
     <value>Kitchen</value>
    </descriptor>
   </product>
   <product><name>Delux cabinets</name>
    <descriptor>
     <name>category</name>
     <value>Cabinets</value>
    </descriptor>
    <descriptor>
     <name>room</name>
     <value>Kitchen</value>
    </descriptor>
   </product>
   <product><name>Standard cabinets</name>
    <descriptor>
     <name>category</name>
     <value>Cabinets</value>
    </descriptor>
    <descriptor>
     <name>room</name>
     <value>Kitchen</value>
    </descriptor>
   </product>
```

```
<product><name>Delux counter</name>
 <descriptor>
  <name>category</name>
  <value>Cabinets</value>
 </descriptor>
 <descriptor>
  <name>room</name>
  <value>Kitchen</value>
 </descriptor>
</product>
<product><name>Standard counter</name>
 <descriptor>
  <name>category</name>
  <value>Cabinets</value>
 </descriptor>
 <descriptor>
  <name>room</name>
  <value>Kitchen</value>
 </descriptor>
</product>
<product><name>Kitchen ceiling light</name>
 <descriptor>
  <name>category</name>
  <value>Lighting</value>
 </descriptor>
 <descriptor>
  <name>room</name>
  <value>Kitchen</value>
 </descriptor>
</product>
<product><name>Counter light</name>
 <descriptor>
  <name>category</name>
  <value>Lighting</value>
 </descriptor>
 <descriptor>
  <name>room</name>
  <value>Kitchen</value>
 </descriptor>
</product>
<product><name>Cookware</name>
 <descriptor>
  <name>category</name>
  <value>Accessories</value>
 </descriptor>
 <descriptor>
  <name>room</name>
  <value>Kitchen</value>
 </descriptor>
</product>
<product><name>Storage containers</name>
```

```xml
   <descriptor>
    <name>category</name>
    <value>Accessories</value>
   </descriptor>
   <descriptor>
    <name>room</name>
    <value>Kitchen</value>
   </descriptor>
  </product>
  <product><name>Wall clock</name>
   <descriptor>
    <name>category</name>
    <value>Accessories</value>
   </descriptor>
   <descriptor>
    <name>room</name>
    <value>Kitchen</value>
   </descriptor>
  </product>
  <!-- Bath room products -->
  <product><name>Delux sink</name>
   <descriptor>
    <name>category</name>
    <value>Sinks</value>
   </descriptor>
   <descriptor>
    <name>room</name>
    <value>Bath room</value>
   </descriptor>
  </product>
  <product><name>Standard sink</name>
   <descriptor>
    <name>category</name>
    <value>Sinks</value>
   </descriptor>
   <descriptor>
    <name>room</name>
    <value>Bath room</value>
   </descriptor>
  </product>
  <product><name>Delux toilet</name>
   <descriptor>
    <name>category</name>
    <value>Toilets</value>
   </descriptor>
   <descriptor>
    <name>room</name>
    <value>Bath room</value>
   </descriptor>
  </product>
  <product><name>Standard toilet</name>
```

```
 <descriptor>
  <name>category</name>
  <value>Toilets</value>
 </descriptor>
 <descriptor>
  <name>room</name>
  <value>Bath room</value>
 </descriptor>
</product>
<product><name>Ceiling light</name>
 <descriptor>
  <name>category</name>
  <value>Lighting</value>
 </descriptor>
 <descriptor>
  <name>room</name>
  <value>Bath room</value>
 </descriptor>
</product>
<product><name>Wall light</name>
 <descriptor>
  <name>category</name>
  <value>Lighting</value>
 </descriptor>
 <descriptor>
  <name>room</name>
  <value>Bath room</value>
 </descriptor>
</product>
<product><name>Delux bath tub</name>
 <descriptor>
  <name>category</name>
  <value>Bath and shower</value>
 </descriptor>
 <descriptor>
  <name>room</name>
  <value>Bath room</value>
 </descriptor>
</product>
<product><name>Standard bath tub</name>
 <descriptor>
  <name>category</name>
  <value>Bath and shower</value>
 </descriptor>
 <descriptor>
  <name>room</name>
  <value>Bath room</value>
 </descriptor>
</product>
<product><name>Shower stall</name>
 <descriptor>
```

```
      <name>category</name>
      <value>Bath and shower</value>
     </descriptor>
     <descriptor>
      <name>room</name>
      <value>Bath room</value>
     </descriptor>
    </product>
    <product><name>Wall cabinet</name>
     <descriptor>
      <name>category</name>
      <value>Bath and shower</value>
     </descriptor>
     <descriptor>
      <name>room</name>
      <value>Bath room</value>
     </descriptor>
    </product>
    <product><name>Towel rack</name>
     <descriptor>
      <name>category</name>
      <value>Accessories</value>
     </descriptor>
     <descriptor>
      <name>room</name>
      <value>Bath room</value>
     </descriptor>
    </product>
    <product><name>Towels</name>
     <descriptor>
      <name>category</name>
      <value>Accessories</value>
     </descriptor>
     <descriptor>
      <name>room</name>
      <value>Bath room</value>
     </descriptor>
    </product>
    </catalog>
```

Listing 23.19: The catalog.js Script

```
// catalog.js

function searchCatalog() {
 // Get search text
 var nl = document.getElementsByTagName("select")
 var select0 = nl.item(0)
 var select1 = nl.item(1)
 var room = ""
 var category = ""
```

```
  if(select0.selectedIndex > 0)
   room = select0.options.item(select0.selectedIndex).text
  if(select1.selectedIndex > 0)
   category = select1.options.item(select1.selectedIndex).text
  // Get all products
  nl = document.getElementsByTagName("product")
  // Match each product to room and category
  for(var i=0; i<nl.length; ++i) {
   var product = nl.item(i)
   var display = true
   var descriptors = product.getElementsByTagName("value")
   if(room != "") {
    display = false
    for(var j=0; j<descriptors.length; ++j) {
     var descriptor = descriptors.item(j)
     var text = getText(descriptor)
     if(text == room) {
      display = true
      break
     }
    }
   }
   if(display && category != "") {
    display = false
    for(var j=0; j<descriptors.length; ++j) {
     var descriptor = descriptors.item(j)
     var text = getText(descriptor)
     if(text == category) {
      display = true
      break
     }
    }
   }
   displayProduct(i, display)
  }
}

function identifyProducts() {
 // Get all products
 var nl = document.getElementsByTagName("product")
 // Assign them an id attribute
 for(var i=0; i<nl.length; ++i) {
  var product = nl.item(i)
  product.setAttribute("id", "product"+i)
 }
}

function displayProduct(n, display) {
 if(navigator.appName == "Netscape") displayProductInNavigator(n, display)
 else if(navigator.appName == "Microsoft Internet Explorer")
displayProductInExplorer(n, display)
```

```
}

function displayProductInExplorer(n, display) {
 var nl = document.getElementsByTagName("product")
 if(display) nl.item(n).style.display = "block"
 else nl.item(n).style.display = "none"
}

function displayProductInNavigator(n, display) {
 var stylesheet = document.styleSheets[0]
 var rules = stylesheet.cssRules
 var nl = document.getElementsByTagName("product")
 var product = nl.item(n)
 // Delete old CSS rule
 var oldRule = product.getAttribute("rule")
 if(oldRule.length > 0) {
  for(var i=0; i<rules.length; ++i) {
   var r = rules.item(i).cssText
   if(r == oldRule) {
    stylesheet.deleteRule(i)
    break
   }
  }
 }
 // Insert new CSS rule
 var show = "none"
 if(display) show = "block"
 var newRule = "product[id=product" + n + "] { display: " + show +"; }"
 var ix = rules.length
 stylesheet.insertRule(newRule, ix)
 product.setAttribute("rule", rules.item(ix).cssText)
}

function getText(node) {
 if(node.nodeName == "#text") {
  return node.nodeValue
 }else{
  var nl = node.childNodes
  var s = ""
  for(var i=0; i<nl.length; ++i) {
   s += getText(nl.item(i))
  }
  return s
 }
}
```

Listing 23.20:   A Style Sheet for catalog.xml (catalog.css)

```
catalog
{display: block;
text-align: left}
```

```
description
{background-color: #bbbbff;
border: 5px ridge;
display: block;
font-size: xx-large;
font-weight: bold;
margin-top: 25px;
padding: 5px;
text-align: center}

product
{border: 1px solid;
display: none;
padding: 5px}

descriptor
{background-color: #ffffff}

product name
{background-color: #d5d5ff;
border: 1px solid;
padding: 2px;
width: 30%}

descriptor name
{background-color: #8080ff;
display: none}

value
{width: 30%}
```

Summary

In this chapter, you learned how to script XML using JavaScript. We covered DOM 2 events and styles, and you learned how to work with HTML events in XML scripting. You should now be capable of writing XML scripts of your own. But before you go off to develop an XML application for your web site, be sure to read the next chapter, which will introduce you to XSL transforms. XSL transforms enable you to translate XML documents from one form into another. They also enable you to translate XML documents into HTML for easy browser display.

Working with XSLT

- Understanding XSL and XSLT

- Learning XSLT and XPath

- Working with XSLT translators

- Using XSLT syntax

In the previous three chapters, you learned how to create XML documents, style them with CSS, and script them using JavaScript. However, XML has much more to offer than you've learned so far. In this chapter, you'll learn about a very powerful XML tool called the XML Stylesheet Language for Transformations, or XSLT. XSLT provides you with the capability to transform XML documents into other forms, into HTML, and even into plain text. You'll learn how to use XSLT to transform your XML documents into formats that look great when they're viewed by browsers. You'll also learn how XML and XSLT can simplify the creation of JavaScript components. When you finish this chapter, you'll be able to create custom components in XML and transform them into HTML and JavaScript using XSLT.

XSL and XSLT

The purpose of XML is to add structure to information. It enables us to define custom tags that help us organize information into structured documents and make it universally accessible. We use style sheets to display our documents in a format that is easy to read and highlights different aspects of the information contained in the documents.

As you learned in Chapter 22, "Displaying XML with Internet Explorer and Navigator," Cascading Style Sheets (CSS) are the primary means of styling XML documents for display with Navigator and Internet Explorer. CSS were originally designed to support HTML, but they also work well with XML. In addition to CSS, the Extensible Stylesheet Language (XSL) was developed to support the styling of XML documents. XSL consists of three components:

1. XSL Transformations (XSLT). An XML-based language for specifying how XML documents can be transformed into other formats (www.w3.org/TR/xslt.html).

2. XML Path Language (XPath). An expression syntax for referring to parts of XML documents (www.w3.org/TR/xpath.html).

3. XSL Formatting Objects. A language for specifying the formatting of XML documents (www.w3.org/TR/xsl/).

Of these three, the first two (XSLT and XPath) are mature and have been implemented by Navigator and Internet Explorer. Because XSL formatting objects aren't currently supported, we won't waste any time covering them.

XSLT and XPath

XSLT is a language for translating XML documents from one XML document type into another. It also can be used to translate XML documents into HTML and plain text. XSLT makes use of XPath to refer to parts of XML documents. *XSLT transforms* are documents that are written in XSLT that act as programs for specifying the details of a specific transformation.

At this point, you're probably wondering why you would want to translate a document from one type into another. The main reason is to support information exchange. For example, suppose that I have a product catalog written in XML, and you want to become a reseller of my products as well as products of other vendors. You can use an XSLT transform to transform my catalog as well as those of other vendors into a format that can be inserted into your catalog.

XSLT's capability to translate XML into HTML and text is also very useful. It enables you to design your web site in XML and then translate it into HTML for use by older, non-XML capable browsers. You can also translate your XML documents into plain text, PostScript, or even Adobe's Portable Document Format (PDF).

XSLT Translators

Because XML is all about transformations, the first thing that you'll want to get is an XSLT translator. There are a number of freely available translators that you can download—just search for "XSLT translator."

There are two translators that I recommend: Instant Saxon and Xalan. If you are a Windows user, Instant Saxon is an easy-to-install and easy-to-use solution. You can download it from `http://saxon.sourceforge.net/`. I'll use Instant Saxon for the examples in this chapter.

If you're up to speed with Java, Xalan is a good choice. Xalan was developed as part of the XML-Apache project. It is available at `http://xml.apache.org/`.

TIP   Please take the time to install an XSLT translator before going on to the next section.

Learning XSLT

XSLT is a programming language that is expressed in XML. By this, I mean that the statements of the language are written in an XML notation. For most of us, this seems cumbersome, and it takes some time and practice before we become comfortable with it. However, once you do get up to speed with XSLT, you'll be able to do a lot more with XML, as you'll see in this chapter and the next.

The best way to get up to speed with XSLT is to study a few examples and then try some on your own. Listing 24.1 (`prices.xml`) provides a simple XML file that contains a list of products, product numbers, and prices. Listing 24.2 (`pricelist.dtd`) provides a DTD for Listing 24.1.

Suppose that you maintain your company's price list as an XML file, and you want to convert it to HTML so that you can display it on the company's web site. The transform shown in Listing 24.3 (`prices2html.xsl`) will do just that. Copy all three files into the same directory and then open a console (that is, MS-DOS) window in that directory. Then run the following command (make sure that you have Instant Saxon installed!):

```
saxon -o prices.htm prices.xml prices2html.xsl
```

The preceding command tells Saxon to translate `prices.xml` into `prices.htm` using the transform contained in `prices2html.xsl`. The output of the transformation (`prices.htm`) is shown in Listing 24.4. As you can see, it is a simple HTML file containing a table. If you open it in your browser, you'll see the output shown in Figure 24.1.

FIGURE 24.1:

The price list generated by *prices2html.xsl*

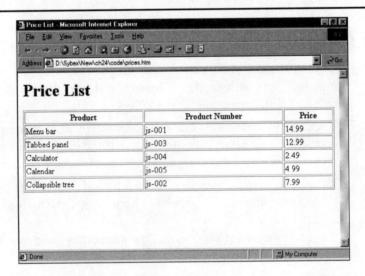

Now the big question is, "What's in `prices2html.xsl`, and how does it work?" You'll notice that the first line identifies the file as an XML document:

```
<?xml version="1.0" encoding="iso-8859-1"?>
```

The next element identifies it as an XSLT stylesheet that uses the `xsl:` prefix to refer to elements out of the XSLT namespace. You should begin all of your XSLT documents using the XML document identifier (preceding) and the stylesheet tag (following).

```
<xsl:stylesheet
    xmlns:xsl="http://www.w3.org/1999/XSL/Transform"
    version="1.0"
>
```

The stylesheet ends with a matching `</xsl:stylesheet>` tag.

XSLT can be used to transform XML into XML, HTML, or other types of formatted text. However, you must tell the translator what the output format should be, or it will assume that it is XML. That's what the following tag does:

```
<xsl:output
    method="html"
    indent="yes"
    encoding="iso-8859-1"/>
```

The `method` attribute identifies the format. The `indent` attribute turns output indenting on or off. The `encoding` attribute selects a character encoding.

The rest of the document is organized into two `<xsl:template>` elements. XSLT documents are organized into a series of *templates*. The templates identify patterns to match in the input XML document, and text and markup to be placed in the output document. The first template of Listing 24.3 matches the `pricelist` tag of the input document. The second template matches the `product` tag.

When the `prices.xml` file is processed by Saxon (or other XSLT processors), it looks for a tag that matches the templates of the XSLT transform. When it finds a match, it processes that template. The first template is matched immediately because the `pricelist` tag is the document tag of `prices.xml`.

What happens inside the `pricelist` template? Well, you probably noticed the following chunk of HTML:

```
<html>
<head><title>Price List</title></head>
<body>
<h1>Price List</h1>
<table border="1" width="100%">
<tr><th>Product</th><th>Product
    Number</th><th>Price</th></tr>
```

It is simply written to the output document (`prices.htm`). Then comes the `<xsl:apply-templates>` tag:

```
<xsl:apply-templates select="product"/>
```

The preceding tag tells Saxon to select all the `product` elements in the input document (`prices.xml`), and apply any matching templates to these elements.

After the `product` elements are processed, the following HTML is written to the output document:

```
</table>
</body>
</html>
```

The preceding HTML closes the table and the output document.

TIP   When using XSLT to generate HTML, make sure that your HTML consists of matching enclosing tags (for example, `<p>` and `</p>`), or that you write your separating tags using XHTML notation (for example, `<br>` becomes `<br/>`).

The second template processes individual product elements. It begins by writing the HTML table row tag (`<tr>`), followed by the following three sets of elements:

```
<td><xsl:value-of select="./name"/></td>
<td><xsl:value-of select="./product_number"/></td>
<td><xsl:value-of select="./price"/></td>
```

As you can probably guess, the preceding statements generate the HTML for the cells of the row. The `<xsl:value-of>` tag tells the processor to write the value of the expression given by the `select` attribute to the output document. The `select` attribute (as well as the `select` attribute of the `<xsl:apply-templates>` element) makes use of expressions that are defined by XPath. The expressions that we'll be using are simple and intuitive (besides, I'll explain what they mean). However, it's a good idea to download and read the XPath recommendation so that you'll know the full capabilities of the language.

In the case of the previous elements, the values of the `select` attributes are `./name`, `./product_number`, and `./price`. The `.` refers to the current element being matched (that is, the `product` tag). The `/` refers to an element that is contained in the element and the `name`, `product_number`, and `price` parts name the next-level element.

So the `./name` expression results in the markup contained in the `name` element of the product element being generated as output. The `./product_number` and `./price` expressions result in the markup contained in the `product_number` and `price` elements being generated as output.

Finally, the `product` template generates the closing `</tr>` tag and then completes its processing.

Listing 24.1:   An XML Price List (prices.xml)

```xml
<?xml version="1.0" encoding="iso-8859-1"?>
<!DOCTYPE pricelist SYSTEM "pricelist.dtd">

<pricelist>
<product>
<name>Menu bar</name>
<product_number>js-001</product_number>
<price>14.99</price>
</product>
<product>
<name>Tabbed panel</name>
<product_number>js-003</product_number>
<price>12.99</price>
</product>
<product>
<name>Calculator</name>
<product_number>js-004</product_number>
<price>2.49</price>
</product>
<product>
<name>Calendar</name>
<product_number>js-005</product_number>
<price>4.99</price>
</product>
<product>
<name>Collapsible tree</name>
<product_number>js-002</product_number>
<price>7.99</price>
</product>
</pricelist>
```

Listing 24.2:   A DTD for the Price List (pricelist.dtd).

```xml
<?xml version='1.0' encoding='ISO-8859-1'?>
<!- DTD for representing price lists ->

<!ELEMENT pricelist (product+)>
<!ELEMENT product (name, product_number, price)>
<!ELEMENT name (#PCDATA)>
<!ELEMENT product_number (#PCDATA)>
<!ELEMENT price (#PCDATA)>
```

Listing 24.3:   An XSLT Transform (prices2html.xsl).

```
<?xml version="1.0" encoding="iso-8859-1"?>
<xsl:stylesheet
    xmlns:xsl="http://www.w3.org/1999/XSL/Transform"
    version="1.0"
>
<xsl:output
    method="html"
    indent="yes"
    encoding="iso-8859-1"/>

<xsl:template match="pricelist">
<html>
<head><title>Price List</title></head>
<body>
<h1>Price List</h1>
<table border="1" width="100%">
<tr><th>Product</th><th>Product
    Number</th><th>Price</th></tr>
<xsl:apply-templates select="product"/>
</table>
</body>
</html>
</xsl:template>

<xsl:template match="product">
<tr>
<td><xsl:value-of select="./name"/></td>
<td><xsl:value-of select="./product_number"/></td>
<td><xsl:value-of select="./price"/></td>
</tr>
</xsl:template>

</xsl:stylesheet>
```

Listing 24.4:   The Generated HTML Price List (prices.htm).

```
<html>
   <head>
      <meta http-equiv="Content-Type" content="text/html; charset=iso-8859-1">

      <title>Price List</title>
   </head>
   <body>
      <h1>Price List</h1>
      <table border="1" width="100%">
         <tr>
            <th>Product</th>
```

```
            <th>Product Number</th>
            <th>Price</th>
        </tr>
        <tr>
            <td>Menu bar</td>
            <td>js-001</td>
            <td>14.99</td>
        </tr>
        <tr>
            <td>Tabbed panel</td>
            <td>js-003</td>
            <td>12.99</td>
        </tr>
        <tr>
            <td>Calculator</td>
            <td>js-004</td>
            <td>2.49</td>
        </tr>
        <tr>
            <td>Calendar</td>
            <td>js-005</td>
            <td>4.99</td>
        </tr>
        <tr>
            <td>Collapsible tree</td>
            <td>js-002</td>
            <td>7.99</td>
        </tr>
    </table>
  </body>
</html>
```

Sorting and Reorganizing the Output

Looking at Figure 24.1, you may wonder how hard it is to make the product number column the first column and sort by product number. Listing 24.5 does just that. You can run it using the following Saxon command:

```
saxon -o sortedprices.htm prices.xml sortbynumber.xsl
```

It will generate the HTML file shown in Listing 24.6. Figure 24.2 shows how it is displayed in your browser.

FIGURE 24.2:

A sorted price list

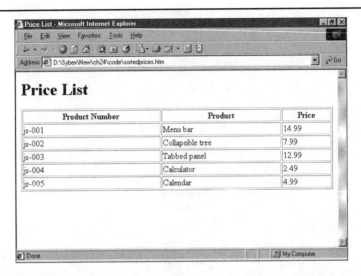

The changes required to rearrange the columns and sort by product number were minimal. In the `pricelist` template, the column headings were rearranged, and the `<xsl:sort>` element was added to the `<xsl:apply-templates>` element:

```
<tr><th>Product
    Number</th><th>Product</th><th>Price</th></tr>
<xsl:apply-templates select="product">
<xsl:sort select="product_number"/>
</xsl:apply-templates>
```

Note that the `<xsl:apply-templates>` element changed from a separating element to an enclosing element in order to accommodate the `<xsl:sort>` element. The `<xsl:sort>` element sorts the elements selected by the `<xsl:apply-templates>` tag. The value of the `select` attribute is an XPath expression that identifies the sort key.

The other change was to the `product` template. The second table cell was moved ahead of the first table cell:

```
<td><xsl:value-of select="./product_number"/></td>
<td><xsl:value-of select="./name"/></td>
```

What you should take away from this second example is that XSLT provides a lot of power and flexibility in transforming XML into HTML.

Listing 24.5:   A Transform that Sorts its Output (sortbynumber.xsl).

```
<?xml version="1.0" encoding="iso-8859-1"?>
<xsl:stylesheet
    xmlns:xsl="http://www.w3.org/1999/XSL/Transform"
    version="1.0"
```

```
>
<xsl:output
    method="html"
    indent="yes"
    encoding="iso-8859-1"/>

<xsl:template match="pricelist">
<html>
<head><title>Price List</title></head>
<body>
<h1>Price List</h1>
<table border="1" width="100%">
<tr><th>Product
   Number</th><th>Product</th><th>Price</th></tr>
<xsl:apply-templates select="product">
<xsl:sort select="./product_number"/>
</xsl:apply-templates>
</table>
</body>
</html>
</xsl:template>

<xsl:template match="product">
<tr>
<td><xsl:value-of select="./product_number"/></td>
<td><xsl:value-of select="./name"/></td>
<td><xsl:value-of select="./price"/></td>
</tr>
</xsl:template>

</xsl:stylesheet>
```

Listing 24.6:   The Sorted Price List (sortedprices.htm).

```
<html>
   <head>
      <meta http-equiv="Content-Type" content="text/html;
   charset=iso-8859-1">

      <title>Price List</title>
   </head>
   <body>
      <h1>Price List</h1>
      <table border="1" width="100%">
         <tr>
            <th>Product Number</th>
            <th>Product</th>
            <th>Price</th>
         </tr>
         <tr>
            <td>js-001</td>
            <td>Menu bar</td>
```

```
                    <td>14.99</td>
                </tr>
                <tr>
                    <td>js-002</td>
                    <td>Collapsible tree</td>
                    <td>7.99</td>
                </tr>
                <tr>
                    <td>js-003</td>
                    <td>Tabbed panel</td>
                    <td>12.99</td>
                </tr>
                <tr>
                    <td>js-004</td>
                    <td>Calculator</td>
                    <td>2.49</td>
                </tr>
                <tr>
                    <td>js-005</td>
                    <td>Calendar</td>
                    <td>4.99</td>
                </tr>
            </table>
        </body>
    </html>
```

Creating JavaScript Components

At this point, you may be wondering what, if anything, XSLT has to do with JavaScript. The answer is that not only is XSLT useful for transforming XML into HTML, it is also great for creating JavaScript components from XML.

Do you remember the tabbed panel from Chapter 16, "Using Tabbed Panel, Tree, and Menu Components?" If you tried to figure out the parameters of the tabbed panel's divisions by hand, you probably found it rather tedious. However, with XML and XSLT, creating a tabbed panel is easy.

Listing 24.7 provides an XML representation of the tabbed panel shown in Chapter 16. Listing 24.8 provides its DTD. Listing 24.9 contains an XSLT transform that transforms XML representations of a tabbed panel to their JavaScript and HTML implementation. To see how it works, run the following Saxon command:

```
saxon -o tabbedpanel.htm tabbedpanel.xml tabbedpanel.xsl
```

It will generate the HTML file shown in Listing 24.10 (tabbedpanel.htm). To run it, you will need the JavaScript source file shown in Listing 24.11 and the style sheet provided in Listing 24.12. Figure 24.3 shows the output it displays.

Creating the tabbed panel in XML is much easier than figuring out the positions of each of its HTML div tags. The XML is also much easier to update and maintain. You begin by creating a dimensions element to specify the size of the tabs and panels (as well as horizontal and vertical offsets). The offsets specify the offsets between tabs in different rows of the tabbed panel.

The dimensions element is followed by a panels element. The panels element contains a unique panel element for each tab-panel combination. The panel tag contains the color, tab_markup, and panel_markup elements. The color element specifies the background color of the tab and panel. The tab_markup tag identifies the HTML markup that goes into the tab, and the panel_markup tag identifies the HTML markup that goes into the panel. Make sure that you surround the markup using the XML escape tags <![CDATA[and]]>.

You'll notice that the style sheet in Listing 24.12 has some hard-coded size information. Don't worry about editing that either—Listing 24.13 provides an XML transform for generating the style sheet. You can use it as follows:

```
saxon -o tabbedpanel.css tabbedpanel.xml tabstyle.xsl
```

After you learn to program with XSLT, you'll be able to automate a lot of your web development.

The transform in Listing 24.9 may look a lot different than the ones in Listing 24.3 and 24.5. That's because I want to expose you to some new XSLT coding techniques.

You'll notice that Listing 24.9 begins with 13 `<xsl:variable>` tags. These tags are used to compute positioning-related information and store them in variables for later use in the transform. These variables are as follows:

- `id`–Used to uniquely identify the divisions of the tabbed panel. You should note that the XPath expression `/tabbed_panel/@id` is used as the value of the `select` attribute. This refers to the `id` attribute of the `tabbed_panel` tag.

- `numPanels`–Identifies the number of panels in the tabbed panel. It is calculated using the expression `count(/tabbed_panel/panels/panel)`. This expression determines the number of `panel` tags that are contained in a `panels` tag that is contained in a `tabbed_panel` tag. The `<xsl:value-of>` tag returns the value of the expression given by the `select` attribute.

- `height`–The height of the tabbed panel in pixels. It is determined by the XPath expression `/tabbed_panel/dimensions/panel_size/height`.

- `width`–The width of the tabbed panel in pixels.

- `panelWidth`–The same value as width. I used separate variables for `panelWidth` and `panelHeight` in case I want to change the way the panels are laid out.

- `panelHeight`–The same value as height.

- `tabWidth`–The width of a tab.

- `tabHeight`–The height of a tab.

- `tabsPerRow`–The number of tabs in each row.

- `numRows`–The number of rows in the tabbed panel. It is calculated from the expression `ceiling($numPanels div $tabsPerRow)`, which divides the value of the `numPanels` variable by the value of the `tabsPerRow` variable and then rounds the result up to the next higher integer value. The dollar sign ($) is used to indicate the value of the variable following the dollar sign.

- `vOffset`–The vertical overlap of tabs in adjacent rows.

- `hOffset`–The number of pixels in which the horizontal position of a tab in one row differs from the corresponding tab in an adjacent row.

- `panelY`–The vertical position (in pixels) of the panels of the tabbed panel.

The definition of the `tabsPerRow` variable makes use of an `<xsl:choose>` element. This element selects one value from a set of alternatives. The alternatives are tested in order. One or more `<xsl:when>` elements are used to test the value of an expression (given by the `test` attribute). If the expression is true, the value of the markup surrounded by the `<xsl:when>` and `</xsl:when>` tags is returned.

The expression ($panelWidth div $tabWidth) < 1 tests to see if the value of the panelWidth variable divided by the tabWidth variable is less than one. Note that the character code (<) is used for the less than (<) character.

If no test attribute of an <xsl:when> tag evaluates to true, the value of the markup of the <xsl:otherwise> element is returned. In this case, the expression floor($panelWidth div $tabWidth) is the value returned by the <xsl:otherwise> element. This expression divides the panelWidth by the tabWidth, and rounds down to the next lowest integer.

You'll notice that only one template is defined for the transform and that its match attribute is set to "/". This value indicates the root of the document. It is always matched first—even before the document element tabbed_panel. The template begins by generating the following HTML:

```
<html>
<head><title>Tabbed Panel</title>
<link rel="stylesheet" type="text/css"
    href="tabbedpanel.css"/>
<script language="JavaScript">
```

It then sets the values for a number of JavaScript variables:

```
var panelID = "<xsl:value-of select="$id"/>"
var numDiv = <xsl:value-of select="$numPanels"/>
var numRows = <xsl:value-of select="$numRows"/>
var tabsPerRow = <xsl:value-of select="$tabsPerRow"/>
var numLocations = numRows * tabsPerRow
var tabWidth = <xsl:value-of select="$tabWidth"/>
var tabHeight = <xsl:value-of select="$tabHeight"/>
var vOffset = <xsl:value-of select="$vOffset"/>
var hOffset = <xsl:value-of select="$hOffset"/>
```

The values of these variables are set from the corresponding XSLT variables.

After that, some more HTML is generated, followed by the first div tag:

```
<div style="background-color: transparent; position: relative; width:
    {$width}px; height: {$height}px">
```

The expressions {$width} and {$height} return the values of the XSLT width and height variables.

Next, an <xsl:for-each> element is used to implement a for loop.

```
<xsl:for-each select="/tabbed_panel/panels/panel">
  .
  .
  .
</xsl:for-each>
```

The loop iterates over each panel. The variable i is set to the position of each panel minus 1. The position() function returns the value of 1 for the first element in a set of elements.

```
<xsl:variable name="i">
<xsl:value-of select="position() - 1"/>
</xsl:variable>
```

The div tag of each tag is generated using the following HTML and XSLT:

```
<div class="tab" style="font-weight: bold; background-color: {./color}; left:
    {($i mod $tabsPerRow) * $tabWidth + ($hOffset * (floor($i div
    $tabsPerRow)))}px; top: {($numRows - (floor($i div $tabsPerRow) + 1)) *
    ($tabHeight - $vOffset)}px; z-index: {$numPanels - $i}" id="{$id}tab{$i}"
    onclick="selectTab({$i})">
```

The value of the i variable, combined with the previously defined variables, is used to compute the div tag's attributes and styles. The markup contained in the div tag is generated using the following:

```
<xsl:value-of select="./tab_markup" disable-output-escaping="yes"/>
```

The disable-output-escaping attribute is set to yes to prevent Saxon from escaping any contained HTML tags using < and >.

A second <xsl:for-each> element is used to generate the div tags of the panels:

```
<xsl:for-each select="/tabbed_panel/panels/panel">
    .
    .
    .
</xsl:for-each>
```

The loop index i is set as in the previous loop. The panel's div tag is then generated using the following:

```
<div class="panel" style="background-color: {./color};  z-index: {$numPanels -
$i}" id="{$id}panel{$i}">
```

The disable-output-escaping attribute is set to yes in order to prevent the HTML of the panel from being escaped using < and >:

```
<xsl:value-of select="./panel_markup" disable-output-escaping="yes"/>
```

That's all for tabbedpanel.xsl. Now let's go to the transform shown in Listing 24.13. This one is much shorter and simpler. You'll notice many of the variable definitions that were defined in tabbedpanel.xsl. In addition, you should note that the method attribute of the <xsl:output> tag is set to text. That's because the style sheet consists of plain text and not HTML nor XML.

```
<xsl:output
    method="text"
    indent="no"
```

```
                     encoding="iso-8859-1"/>
```

A single root template is used to generate the styles. The tab's style is generated using the following. The <xsl:value-of> element is used to insert values into the text.

```
.tab {font-family: sans-serif; line-height:150%;
    font-weight: bold; position:absolute;
    text-align: center; border: 2px; border-color:#999999;
    border-style: outset; border-bottom-style: none;
    height: <xsl:value-of select="$numRows * $tabHeight -
    ($numRows - 1) * $vOffset"/>px; width: <xsl:value-of select="$tabWidth"/>px;
    margin:0px}
```

The panel's styles are generated in a similar manner.

NOTE   I left Navigator 4 support out of the tabbed panel. Refer to Chapter 16 for information on how it can be implemented using Netscape layers.

Listing 24.7:   An XML Representation of a Tabbed Panel (tabbedpanel.xml)

```
<?xml version='1.0'?>
<!DOCTYPE tabbed_panel SYSTEM 'tabbedPanel.dtd'>
<tabbed_panel id="p1">
<dimensions>
<tab_size>
<width>90</width>
<height>30</height>
</tab_size>
<panel_size>
<width>400</width>
<height>200</height>
</panel_size>
<horizontal_offset>10</horizontal_offset>
<vertical_offset>6</vertical_offset>
</dimensions>
<panels>
<panel>
<color>yellow</color>
<tab_markup>HTML</tab_markup>
<panel_markup><![CDATA[
<h2>Hypertext Markup Language</h2>
<p><a href="http://www.w3.org/MarkUp/"
    target="external">HTML</a> is the language in which Web pages are written.
    HTML uses tags like &lt;p&gt; and &lt;/p&gt; to identify how text is to be
    structured and formatted within a document. </p>
]]></panel_markup>
</panel>
<panel>
<color>orange</color>
<tab_markup>XHTML</tab_markup>
```

```
<panel_markup><![CDATA[
<h2>Extensible HyperText Markup Language</h2>
<p><a href="http://www.w3.org/TR/xhtml1/"
    target="external">XHTML</a> is a redevelopment and extension of HTML that
    makes HTML compatible with XML. XHTML specifies a family of markup languages
    that are based on HTML but take advantage of the simplicity, extensibility,
    and powerful toolset of XML. </p>
]]></panel_markup>
</panel>
<panel>
<color>red</color>
<tab_markup>CSS</tab_markup>
<panel_markup><![CDATA[
<h2>Cascading Style Sheets</h2>
<p>CSS is a style sheet language that enables Web page writers to specify
    presentation, sizing, and positioning properties of HTML and XML documents.
    CSS is used to describe the appearance of a document in a manner that is
    independent of its content. There are currently two versions of CSS (referred
    to as <a href="http://www.w3.org/TR/REC-CSS1" target="external">CSS1</a> and
    <a href="http://www.w3.org/TR/REC-CSS2" target="external">CSS2</a>). CSS2
    extends CSS1.</p>]]></panel_markup>
</panel>
<panel>
<color>cyan</color>
<tab_markup>DOM</tab_markup>
<panel_markup><![CDATA[
<h2>Document Object Model</h2>
<p>The <a href="http://www.w3.org/DOM/"
    target="external">DOM</a> is a model that describes the objects that are
    available within HTML and XML documents. It describes these objects in a
    programming language-independent manner as a system of interfaces. It defines
    the properties of these objects and methods for accessing these objects. The
    objects can be accessed via programming languages, such as JavaScript and
    Java.</p>
]]></panel_markup>
</panel>
<panel>
<color>rgb(170,170,255)</color>
<tab_markup>JavaScript</tab_markup>
<panel_markup><![CDATA[
<h2>JavaScript</h2>
<p><a href="http://developer.netscape.com/javascript/"
    target="external">JavaScript</a> is a programming language for scripting Web
    pages that was developed by Netscape. It has been standardized by the ECMA
    and is referred to as ECMAScript. JavaScript has evolved into a general-
    purpose scripting language – it is no longer limited to Web pages. Microsoft
    has also developed a version of JavaScript that is named JScript.</p>
]]></panel_markup>
</panel>
<panel>
<color>fuchsia</color>
```

```
<tab_markup>DHTML</tab_markup>
<panel_markup><![CDATA[
<h2>Dynamic HTML</h2>
<p><a href="http://developer.netscape.com/dhtml/" target="external">DHTML</a> is
    a combination of HTML, CSS, and JavaScript that enables Web page content to
    exhibit dynamic behavior. This is accomplished by dynamically changing the
    properties of document objects in response to user actions and other
    events.</p>
]]></panel_markup>
</panel>
<panel>
<color>lime</color>
<tab_markup>XML</tab_markup>
<panel_markup><![CDATA[
<h2>Extensible Markup Language</h2>
<a href="http://www.w3.org/XML/" target="external">XML</a> is a language for
    creating structured documents for use with the Web and in other application
    areas. XML is a simplified subset of the Standard Generalized Markup Language
    (SGML) that is used to create custom markup languages that follow a common
    syntax.
]]></panel_markup>
</panel>
<panel>
<color>silver</color>
<tab_markup>XSLT</tab_markup>
<panel_markup><![CDATA[
<h2>XSL Transformations</h2>
<a href="http://www.w3.org/TR/xslt" target="external">XSLT</a> is a part of the
    Extensible Stylesheet Language (XSL) that is used to transform XML documents
    from one format into another format. XSLT style sheets are written in XML.
    These style sheets specify how XML documents are to be translated. They are
    provided as input to a translation program, which performs the actual
translation.
]]></panel_markup>
</panel>
</panels>
</tabbed_panel>
```

Listing 24.8:   A Tabbed Panel DTD (tabbedpanel.dtd)

```
<?xml version='1.0' encoding='ISO-8859-1'?>
<!- DTD for a tabbed panel object ->
<!ELEMENT tabbed_panel (dimensions, panels)>
<!ELEMENT dimensions (tab_size, panel_size, horizontal_offset, vertical_offset)>
<!ELEMENT tab_size (width, height)>
<!ELEMENT horizontal_offset (#PCDATA)>
<!ELEMENT vertical_offset (#PCDATA)>
<!ELEMENT panel_size (width, height)>
<!ELEMENT width (#PCDATA)>
<!ELEMENT height (#PCDATA)>
<!ELEMENT panels (panel+)>
```

```
<!ELEMENT panel (color, tab_markup, panel_markup)>
<!ELEMENT color (#PCDATA)>
<!ELEMENT tab_markup (#PCDATA)>
<!ELEMENT panel_markup (#PCDATA)>
<!ATTLIST tabbed_panel id ID #REQUIRED>
```

Listing 24.9:   A Tabbed Panel Transform (tabbedpanel.xsl)

```xml
<?xml version='1.0'?>
<xsl:stylesheet xmlns:xsl="http://www.w3.org/1999/XSL/Transform" version="1.0">
<xsl:output
    method="html"
    indent="no"
    encoding="iso-8859-1"/>

<xsl:variable name="id"><xsl:value-of select="/tabbed_panel/@id"/>
</xsl:variable>

<xsl:variable name="numPanels"><xsl:value-of
    select="count(/tabbed_panel/panels/panel)"/>
</xsl:variable>

<xsl:variable name="height"><xsl:value-of
    select="/tabbed_panel/dimensions/panel_size/height"/>
</xsl:variable>

<xsl:variable name="width"><xsl:value-of
    select="/tabbed_panel/dimensions/panel_size/width"/>
</xsl:variable>

<xsl:variable name="panelWidth"><xsl:value-of
    select="/tabbed_panel/dimensions/panel_size/width"/>
</xsl:variable>

<xsl:variable name="panelHeight"><xsl:value-of
    select="/tabbed_panel/dimensions/panel_size/height"/>
</xsl:variable>

<xsl:variable name="tabWidth"><xsl:value-of
    select="/tabbed_panel/dimensions/tab_size/width"/>
</xsl:variable>

<xsl:variable name="tabHeight"><xsl:value-of
    select="/tabbed_panel/dimensions/tab_size/height"/>
</xsl:variable>

<xsl:variable name="tabsPerRow">
<xsl:choose>
<xsl:when test="($panelWidth div $tabWidth) &lt; 1">1</xsl:when>
<xsl:otherwise><xsl:value-of select="floor($panelWidth div
    $tabWidth)"/></xsl:otherwise>
```

```
</xsl:choose>
</xsl:variable>

<xsl:variable name="numRows">
<xsl:value-of select="ceiling($numPanels div $tabsPerRow)"/>
</xsl:variable>

<xsl:variable name="vOffset"><xsl:value-of
   select="/tabbed_panel/dimensions/vertical_offset"/></xsl:variable>

<xsl:variable name="hOffset"><xsl:value-of
   select="/tabbed_panel/dimensions/horizontal_offset"/></xsl:variable>

<xsl:variable name="panelY"><xsl:value-of select="$numRows * ($tabHeight -
   $vOffset) + $vOffset"/></xsl:variable>

<xsl:template match="/">
<html>
<head><title>Tabbed Panel</title>
<link rel="stylesheet" type="text/css" href="tabbedpanel.css"/>
<script language="JavaScript">
var panelID = "<xsl:value-of select="$id"/>"
var numDiv = <xsl:value-of select="$numPanels"/>
var numRows = <xsl:value-of select="$numRows"/>
var tabsPerRow = <xsl:value-of select="$tabsPerRow"/>
var numLocations = numRows * tabsPerRow
var tabWidth = <xsl:value-of select="$tabWidth"/>
var tabHeight = <xsl:value-of select="$tabHeight"/>
var vOffset = <xsl:value-of select="$vOffset"/>
var hOffset = <xsl:value-of select="$hOffset"/>
</script>
<script language="JavaScript" src="tabbedpanel.js">
</script>
</head>
<body>
<h1>Tabbed Panel</h1>
<div style="background-color: transparent; position: relative; width:
   {$width}px; height: {$height}px">
<xsl:for-each select="/tabbed_panel/panels/panel">
<xsl:variable name="i"><xsl:value-of select="position() - 1"/></xsl:variable>
<!- Layout the tabs ->
<div class="tab" style="font-weight: bold; background-color: {./color}; left:
   {($i mod $tabsPerRow) * $tabWidth + ($hOffset * (floor($i div
   $tabsPerRow)))}px; top: {($numRows - (floor($i div $tabsPerRow) + 1)) *
   ($tabHeight - $vOffset)}px; z-index: {$numPanels - $i}" id="{$id}tab{$i}"
   onclick="selectTab({$i})">
<xsl:value-of select="./tab_markup" disable-output-escaping="yes"/>
</div>
</xsl:for-each>
<xsl:for-each select="/tabbed_panel/panels/panel">
<xsl:variable name="i"><xsl:value-of select="position() - 1"/></xsl:variable>
```

```
<!- Layout the panels ->
<div class="panel" style="background-color: {./color};  z-index: {$numPanels -
    $i}" id="{$id}panel{$i}">
<xsl:value-of select="./panel_markup" disable-output-escaping="yes"/>
</div>
</xsl:for-each>
</div>
<!- The following tag is a spacer that is used to make sure that markup that
    follows the tabbed panel is not covered by the panel. Adjust the height
    attribute as desired. ->
<img border="0" height="50"/><p></p>
</body>
</html>
</xsl:template>

</xsl:stylesheet>
```

Listing 24.10: The Tabbed Panel that Was Generated by the Transform (tabbedpanel.htm)

```
<html><head>
    <meta http-equiv="Content-Type" content="text/html; charset=iso-8859-1">
    <title>Tabbed Panel</title><link rel="stylesheet" type="text/css"
    href="tabbedpanel.css"><script language="JavaScript">
var panelID = "p1"
var numDiv = 8
var numRows = 2
var tabsPerRow = 4
var numLocations = numRows * tabsPerRow
var tabWidth = 90
var tabHeight = 30
var vOffset = 6
var hOffset = 10</script><script language="JavaScript"
    src="tabbedpanel.js"></script></head><body><h1>Tabbed Panel</h1><div
    style="background-color: transparent; position: relative; width: 400px;
    height: 200px"><div class="tab" style="font-weight: bold; background-color:
    yellow; left: 0px; top: 24px; z-index: 8" id="p1tab0"
    onclick="selectTab(0)">HTML</div><div class="tab" style="font-weight: bold;
    background-color: orange; left: 90px; top: 24px; z-index: 7" id="p1tab1"
    onclick="selectTab(1)">XHTML</div><div class="tab" style="font-weight: bold;
    background-color: red; left: 180px; top: 24px; z-index: 6" id="p1tab2"
    onclick="selectTab(2)">CSS</div><div class="tab" style="font-weight: bold;
    background-color: cyan; left: 270px; top: 24px; z-index: 5" id="p1tab3"
    onclick="selectTab(3)">DOM</div><div class="tab" style="font-weight: bold;
    background-color: rgb(170,170,255); left: 10px; top: 0px; z-index: 4"
    id="p1tab4" onclick="selectTab(4)">JavaScript</div><div class="tab"
    style="font-weight: bold; background-color: fuchsia; left: 100px; top: 0px;
    z-index: 3" id="p1tab5" onclick="selectTab(5)">DHTML</div><div class="tab"
    style="font-weight: bold; background-color: lime; left: 190px; top: 0px; z-
```

```
     index: 2" id="p1tab6" onclick="selectTab(6)">XML</div><div class="tab"
     style="font-weight: bold; background-color: silver; left: 280px; top: 0px; z-
     index: 1" id="p1tab7" onclick="selectTab(7)">XSLT</div><div class="panel"
     style="background-color: yellow;  z-index: 8" id="p1panel0">
<h2>Hypertext Markup Language</h2>
<p><a href="http://www.w3.org/MarkUp/" target="external">HTML</a> is the
     language in which Web pages are written. HTML uses tags like &lt;p&gt; and
     &lt;/p&gt; to identify how text is to be structured and formatted within a
     document. </p>
</div><div class="panel" style="background-color: orange;  z-index: 7"
     id="p1panel1">
<h2>Extensible HyperText Markup Language</h2>
<p><a href="http://www.w3.org/TR/xhtml1/" target="external">XHTML</a> is a
     redevelopment and extension of HTML that makes HTML compatible with XML.
     XHTML specifies a family of markup languages that are based on HTML but take
     advantage of the simplicity, extensibility, and powerful toolset of XML. </p>
</div><div class="panel" style="background-color: red;  z-index: 6"
     id="p1panel2">
<h2>Cascading Style Sheets</h2>
<p>CSS is a style sheet language that enables Web page writers to specify
     presentation, sizing, and positioning properties of HTML and XML documents.
     CSS is used to describe the appearance of a document in a manner that is
     independent of its content. There are currently two versions of CSS (referred
     to as <a href="http://www.w3.org/TR/REC-CSS1" target="external">CSS1</a> and
     <a href="http://www.w3.org/TR/REC-CSS2" target="external">CSS2</a>). CSS2
     extends CSS1.</p></div><div class="panel" style="background-color: cyan;
     z-index: 5" id="p1panel3">
<h2>Document Object Model</h2>
<p>The <a href="http://www.w3.org/DOM/" target="external">DOM</a> is a model
     that describes the objects that are available within HTML and XML documents.
     It describes these objects in a programming language-independent manner as a
     system of interfaces. It defines the properties of these objects and methods
     for accessing these objects. The objects can be accessed via programming
     languages, such as JavaScript and Java.</p>
</div><div class="panel" style="background-color: rgb(170,170,255);  z-index: 4"
     id="p1panel4">
<h2>JavaScript</h2>
<p><a href="http://developer.netscape.com/javascript/"
     target="external">JavaScript</a> is a programming language for scripting Web
     pages that was developed by Netscape. It has been standardized by the ECMA
     and is referred to as ECMAScript. JavaScript has evolved into a general-
     purpose scripting language – it is no longer limited to Web pages. Microsoft
     has also developed a version of JavaScript that is named JScript.</p>
</div><div class="panel" style="background-color: fuchsia;  z-index: 3"
     id="p1panel5">
<h2>Dynamic HTML</h2>
<p><a href="http://developer.netscape.com/dhtml/" target="external">DHTML</a> is
     a combination of HTML, CSS, and JavaScript that enables Web page content to
     exhibit dynamic behavior. This is accomplished by dynamically changing the
     properties of document objects in response to user actions and other
     events.</p>
```

```
</div><div class="panel" style="background-color: lime;  z-index: 2"
    id="p1panel6">
<h2>Extensible Markup Language</h2>
<a href="http://www.w3.org/XML/" target="external">XML</a> is a language for
    creating structured documents for use with the Web and in other application
    areas. XML is a simplified subset of the Standard Generalized Markup Language
    (SGML) that is used to create custom markup languages that follow a common
    syntax.
</div><div class="panel" style="background-color: silver;  z-index: 1"
    id="p1panel7">
<h2>XSL Transformations</h2>
<a href="http://www.w3.org/TR/xslt" target="external">XSLT</a> is a part of the
    Extensible Stylesheet Language (XSL) that is used to transform XML documents
    from one format into another format. XSLT style sheets are written in XML.
    These style sheets specify how XML documents are to be translated. They are
    provided as input to a translation program, which performs the actual
    translation.
</div></div><img border="0" height="50"><p></p></body></html>
```

Listing 24.11:   The Supporting JavaScript File (tabbedpanel.js)

```javascript
// tabbedpanel.js

var divLocation = new Array(numLocations)
var newLocation = new Array(numLocations)

for(var i=0; i<numLocations; ++i) {
 divLocation[i] = i
 newLocation[i] = i
}

function getDiv(s,i) {
 var div
 if(navigator.appName == "Microsoft Internet Explorer"
   && navigator.appVersion.charAt(0) < 5)
  div = document.all.item(panelID+s+i)
 else div = document.getElementById(panelID+s+i)
 return div
}
function setZIndex(div, zIndex) {
 div.style.zIndex = zIndex
}
function getLocation(i) {
 return divLocation[i]
}
function setLocation(i, j) {
 divLocation[i] = j
}
function getNewLocation(i) {
 return newLocation[i]
```

```
}
function setNewLocation(i, j) {
 newLocation[i] = j
}
function updatePosition(div, newPos) {
 div.style.top = (numRows-(Math.floor(newPos/tabsPerRow) + 1)) * (tabHeight-
   vOffset)
 div.style.left = (newPos % tabsPerRow) * tabWidth +
  (hOffset * (Math.floor(newPos / tabsPerRow)))
}

function selectTab(n) {
 // n is the ID of the division that was clicked
 // firstTab is the location of the first tab in the selected row
 var firstTab = Math.floor(getLocation(n) / tabsPerRow) * tabsPerRow
 // newLoc is its new location
 for(var i=0; i<numDiv; ++i) {
   // loc is the current location of the tab
   var loc = getLocation(i)
   // If in the selected row
   if(loc >= firstTab && loc < (firstTab + tabsPerRow)) setNewLocation(i, loc -
   firstTab)
   else if(loc < tabsPerRow) setNewLocation(i,firstTab+(loc % tabsPerRow))
   else setNewLocation(i, loc)
 }
 // Set tab positions & zIndex
 // Update location
 for(var i=0; i<numDiv; ++i) {
  var div = getDiv("tab",i)
  var loc = getNewLocation(i)
  updatePosition(div, loc)
  if(i == n) setZIndex(div, numLocations +1)
  else setZIndex(div,numLocations - loc)
  div = getDiv("panel",i)
  if(i == n) setZIndex(div, numLocations +1)
  else setZIndex(div, numLocations - loc)
  setLocation(i, loc)
 }
}
```

Listing 24.12: A Tabbed Panel Style Sheet (tabbedpanel.css)

```
.tab {font-family: sans-serif; line-height:150%;
   font-weight: bold; position:absolute;
   text-align: center; border: 2px; border-color:#999999;
   border-style: outset; border-bottom-style: none;
   height: 54px; width: 90px; margin:0px}
```

```
.panel {font-family: sans-serif; font-size: smaller;
   position:absolute; border: 2px; border-color:#999999;
   border-style:outset; width: 400px; height: 200px;
   left:0px; top:54px; margin:0px; padding:6px}

h1 {text-align: center}
```

Listing 24.13:   A Transform to Generate the Style Sheet (tabstyle.xsl)

```xml
<?xml version='1.0'?>
<xsl:stylesheet xmlns:xsl="http://www.w3.org/1999/XSL/Transform" version="1.0">
<xsl:output
    method="text"
    indent="no"
    encoding="iso-8859-1"/>

<xsl:variable name="numPanels"><xsl:value-of
    select="count(/tabbed_panel/panels/panel)"/>
</xsl:variable>

<xsl:variable name="height"><xsl:value-of
    select="/tabbed_panel/dimensions/panel_size/height"/>
</xsl:variable>

<xsl:variable name="width"><xsl:value-of
    select="/tabbed_panel/dimensions/panel_size/width"/>
</xsl:variable>

<xsl:variable name="panelWidth"><xsl:value-of
    select="/tabbed_panel/dimensions/panel_size/width"/>
</xsl:variable>

<xsl:variable name="panelHeight"><xsl:value-of
    select="/tabbed_panel/dimensions/panel_size/height"/>
</xsl:variable>

<xsl:variable name="tabWidth"><xsl:value-of
    select="/tabbed_panel/dimensions/tab_size/width"/>
</xsl:variable>

<xsl:variable name="tabHeight"><xsl:value-of
    select="/tabbed_panel/dimensions/tab_size/height"/>
</xsl:variable>

<xsl:variable name="tabsPerRow">
<xsl:choose>
<xsl:when test="($panelWidth div $tabWidth) &lt; 1">1</xsl:when>
<xsl:otherwise><xsl:value-of select="floor($panelWidth div
    $tabWidth)"/></xsl:otherwise>
</xsl:choose>
```

```
    </xsl:variable>

    <xsl:variable name="numRows">
    <xsl:value-of select="ceiling($numPanels div $tabsPerRow)"/>
    </xsl:variable>

    <xsl:variable name="vOffset"><xsl:value-of
        select="/tabbed_panel/dimensions/vertical_offset"/></xsl:variable>

    <xsl:variable name="hOffset"><xsl:value-of
        select="/tabbed_panel/dimensions/horizontal_offset"/></xsl:variable>

    <xsl:variable name="panelY"><xsl:value-of select="$numRows * ($tabHeight -
        $vOffset) + $vOffset"/></xsl:variable>

    <xsl:template match="/">
    .tab {font-family: sans-serif; line-height:150%;
        font-weight: bold; position:absolute;
        text-align: center; border: 2px; border-color:#999999;
        border-style: outset; border-bottom-style: none;
        height: <xsl:value-of select="$numRows * $tabHeight - ($numRows - 1) *
        $vOffset"/>px; width: <xsl:value-of select="$tabWidth"/>px; margin:0px}

    .panel {font-family: sans-serif; font-size: smaller;
        position:absolute; border: 2px; border-color:#999999;
        border-style:outset; width: <xsl:value-of select="$panelWidth"/>px; height:
        <xsl:value-of select="$panelHeight"/>px;
        left:0px; top:<xsl:value-of select="$numRows * $tabHeight - ($numRows - 1) *
        $vOffset"/>px; margin:0px; padding:6px}

    h1 {text-align: center}
    </xsl:template>

    </xsl:stylesheet>
```

Updating the Tabbed Panel

One of the benefits of using XML and XSLT to generate a JavaScript component is that you can easily update or modify the component. If you want to add another tab to the tabbed panel, you'd have to recalculate the positions of all the tabs and panels, which is a pretty time-consuming and boring thing to do. With XML and XSLT, it's no problem.

Listing 24.14 (tabbedpanel2.xml) updates tabbedpanel.xml to add a new Java tab. You can generate a new tabbed panel by running the following command:

```
saxon -o tabbedpanel2.htm tabbedpanel2.xml tabbedpanel.xsl
```

You can then generate a new style sheet just as easily:

```
saxon -o tabbedpanel2.css tabbedpanel2.xml tabstyle.xsl
```

Figure 24.4 shows how the new tabbed panel is displayed.

FIGURE 24.4:

The new tabbed panel, as
displayed by Internet
Explorer

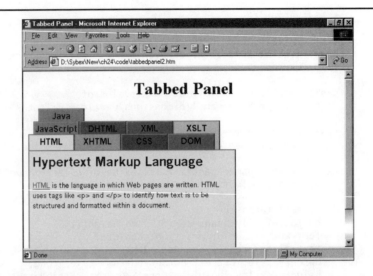

Listing 24.14:   Adding a Tab to the Tabbed Panel (tabbedpanel2.xml)

```xml
<?xml version='1.0'?>
<!DOCTYPE tabbed_panel SYSTEM 'tabbedPanel.dtd'>
<tabbed_panel id="p1">
<dimensions>
<tab_size>
<width>90</width>
<height>30</height>
</tab_size>
<panel_size>
<width>400</width>
<height>250</height>
</panel_size>
<horizontal_offset>10</horizontal_offset>
<vertical_offset>6</vertical_offset>
</dimensions>
<panels>
<panel>
<color>yellow</color>
<tab_markup>HTML</tab_markup>
<panel_markup><![CDATA[
<h2>Hypertext Markup Language</h2>
<p><a href="http://www.w3.org/MarkUp/"
   target="external">HTML</a> is the language in which Web pages are written.
   HTML uses tags like &lt;p&gt; and &lt;/p&gt; to identify how text is to be
   structured and formatted within a document. </p>
]]></panel_markup>
</panel>
```

```
<panel>
<color>orange</color>
<tab_markup>XHTML</tab_markup>
<panel_markup><![CDATA[
<h2>Extensible HyperText Markup Language</h2>
<p><a href="http://www.w3.org/TR/xhtml1/"
    target="external">XHTML</a> is a redevelopment and extension of HTML that
    makes HTML compatible with XML. XHTML specifies a family of markup languages
    that are based on HTML but take advantage of the simplicity, extensibility,
    and powerful toolset of XML. </p>
]]></panel_markup>
</panel>
<panel>
<color>red</color>
<tab_markup>CSS</tab_markup>
<panel_markup><![CDATA[
<h2>Cascading Style Sheets</h2>
<p>CSS is a style sheet language that enables Web page writers to specify
    presentation, sizing, and positioning properties of HTML and XML documents.
    CSS is used to describe the appearance of a document in a manner that is
    independent of its content. There are currently two versions of CSS (referred
    to as <a href="http://www.w3.org/TR/REC-CSS1" target="external">CSS1</a> and
    <a href="http://www.w3.org/TR/REC-CSS2" target="external">CSS2</a>). CSS2
    extends CSS1.</p>]]></panel_markup>
</panel>
<panel>
<color>cyan</color>
<tab_markup>DOM</tab_markup>
<panel_markup><![CDATA[
<h2>Document Object Model</h2>
<p>The <a href="http://www.w3.org/DOM/"
    target="external">DOM</a> is a model that describes the objects that are
    available within HTML and XML documents. It describes these objects in a
    programming language-independent manner as a system of interfaces. It defines
    the properties of these objects and methods for accessing these objects. The
    objects can be accessed via programming languages, such as JavaScript and
    Java.</p>
]]></panel_markup>
</panel>
<panel>
<color>rgb(170,170,255)</color>
<tab_markup>JavaScript</tab_markup>
<panel_markup><![CDATA[
<h2>JavaScript</h2>
<p><a href="http://developer.netscape.com/javascript/"
    target="external">JavaScript</a> is a programming language for scripting Web
    pages that was developed by Netscape. It has been standardized by the ECMA
    and is referred to as ECMAScript. JavaScript has evolved into a general-
    purpose scripting language - it is no longer limited to Web pages. Microsoft
    has also developed a version of JavaScript that is named JScript.</p>
]]></panel_markup>
```

```
</panel>
<panel>
<color>fuchsia</color>
<tab_markup>DHTML</tab_markup>
<panel_markup><![CDATA[
<h2>Dynamic HTML</h2>
<p><a href="http://developer.netscape.com/dhtml/"
    target="external">DHTML</a> is a combination of HTML, CSS, and JavaScript
    that enables Web page content to exhibit dynamic behavior. This is
    accomplished by dynamically changing the properties of document objects in
    response to user actions and other events.</p>
]]></panel_markup>
</panel>
<panel>
<color>lime</color>
<tab_markup>XML</tab_markup>
<panel_markup><![CDATA[
<h2>Extensible Markup Language</h2>
<a href="http://www.w3.org/XML/"
    target="external">XML</a> is a language for creating structured documents for
    use with the Web and in other application areas. XML is a simplified subset
    of the Standard Generalized Markup Language (SGML) that is used to create
    custom markup languages that follow a common syntax.
]]></panel_markup>
</panel>
<panel>
<color>silver</color>
<tab_markup>XSLT</tab_markup>
<panel_markup><![CDATA[
<h2>XSL Transformations</h2>
<a href="http://www.w3.org/TR/xslt"
    target="external">XSLT</a> is a part of the Extensible Stylesheet Language
    (XSL) that is used to transform XML documents from one format into another
    format. XSLT style sheets are written in XML. These style sheets specify how
    XML documents are to be translated. They are provided as input to a
    translation program, which performs the actual translation.
]]></panel_markup>
</panel>
<panel>
<color>rgb(128,128,128)</color>
<tab_markup>Java</tab_markup>
<panel_markup><![CDATA[
<h2>Java</h2>
Java is a programming language that supports the development of Web
    applications. You can use it to develop applets, servlets, and JavaServer
    Pages.
]]></panel_markup>
</panel>
</panels>
</tabbed_panel>
```

Listing 24.15:   A New Tabbed Panel (tabbedpanel2.htm)

```
<html><head>
     <meta http-equiv="Content-Type" content="text/html; charset=iso-8859-1">
     <title>Tabbed Panel</title><link rel="stylesheet" type="text/css"
     href="tabbedpanel.css"><script language="JavaScript">
var panelID = "p1"
var numDiv = 9
var numRows = 3
var tabsPerRow = 4
var numLocations = numRows * tabsPerRow
var tabWidth = 90
var tabHeight = 30
var vOffset = 6
var hOffset = 10</script><script language="JavaScript"
src="tabbedpanel.js"></script></head><body><h1>Tabbed Panel</h1><div
     style="background-color: transparent; position: relative; width: 400px;
     height: 250px"><div class="tab" style="font-weight: bold; background-color:
     yellow; left: 0px; top: 48px; z-index: 9" id="p1tab0"
     onclick="selectTab(0)">HTML</div><div class="tab" style="font-weight: bold;
     background-color: orange; left: 90px; top: 48px; z-index: 8" id="p1tab1"
     onclick="selectTab(1)">XHTML</div><div class="tab" style="font-weight: bold;
     background-color: red; left: 180px; top: 48px; z-index: 7" id="p1tab2"
     onclick="selectTab(2)">CSS</div><div class="tab" style="font-weight: bold;
     background-color: cyan; left: 270px; top: 48px; z-index: 6" id="p1tab3"
     onclick="selectTab(3)">DOM</div><div class="tab" style="font-weight: bold;
     background-color: rgb(170,170,255); left: 10px; top: 24px; z-index: 5"
     id="p1tab4" onclick="selectTab(4)">JavaScript</div><div class="tab"
     style="font-weight: bold; background-color: fuchsia; left: 100px; top: 24px;
     z-index: 4" id="p1tab5" onclick="selectTab(5)">DHTML</div><div class="tab"
     style="font-weight: bold; background-color: lime; left: 190px; top: 24px;
     z-index: 3" id="p1tab6" onclick="selectTab(6)">XML</div><div class="tab"
     style="font-weight: bold; background-color: silver; left: 280px; top: 24px;
     z-index: 2" id="p1tab7" onclick="selectTab(7)">XSLT</div><div class="tab"
     style="font-weight: bold; background-color: rgb(128,128,128); left: 20px;
     top: 0px; z-index: 1" id="p1tab8" onclick="selectTab(8)">Java</div><div
     class="panel" style="background-color: yellow;  z-index: 9" id="p1panel0">
<h2>Hypertext Markup Language</h2>
<p><a href="http://www.w3.org/MarkUp/" target="external">HTML</a> is the
     language in which Web pages are written. HTML uses tags like &lt;p&gt; and
     &lt;/p&gt; to identify how text is to be structured and formatted within a
     document. </p>
</div><div class="panel" style="background-color: orange;  z-index: 8"
     id="p1panel1">
<h2>Extensible HyperText Markup Language</h2>
<p><a href="http://www.w3.org/TR/xhtml1/" target="external">XHTML</a> is a
     redevelopment and extension of HTML that makes HTML compatible with XML.
     XHTML specifies a family of markup languages that are based on HTML but take
     advantage of the simplicity, extensibility, and powerful toolset of XML. </p>
```

```
</div><div class="panel" style="background-color: red;  z-index: 7"
    id="p1panel2">
<h2>Cascading Style Sheets</h2>
<p>CSS is a style sheet language that enables Web page writers to specify
    presentation, sizing, and positioning properties of HTML and XML documents.
    CSS is used to describe the appearance of a document in a manner that is
    independent of its content. There are currently two versions of CSS (referred
    to as <a href="http://www.w3.org/TR/REC-CSS1" target="external">CSS1</a> and
    <a href="http://www.w3.org/TR/REC-CSS2" target="external">CSS2</a>). CSS2
    extends CSS1.</p></div><div class="panel" style="background-color: cyan;
    z-index: 6" id="p1panel3">
<h2>Document Object Model</h2>
<p>The <a href="http://www.w3.org/DOM/" target="external">DOM</a> is a model
    that describes the objects that are available within HTML and XML documents.
    It describes these objects in a programming language-independent manner as a
    system of interfaces. It defines the properties of these objects and methods
    for accessing these objects. The objects can be accessed via programming
    languages, such as JavaScript and Java.</p>
</div><div class="panel" style="background-color: rgb(170,170,255);  z-index: 5"
    id="p1panel4">
<h2>JavaScript</h2>
<p><a href="http://developer.netscape.com/javascript/"
    target="external">JavaScript</a> is a programming language for scripting Web
    pages that was developed by Netscape. It has been standardized by the ECMA
    and is referred to as ECMAScript. JavaScript has evolved into a general-
    purpose scripting language – it is no longer limited to Web pages. Microsoft
    has also developed a version of JavaScript that is named JScript.</p>
</div><div class="panel" style="background-color: fuchsia;  z-index: 4"
    id="p1panel5">
<h2>Dynamic HTML</h2>
<p><a href="http://developer.netscape.com/dhtml/" target="external">DHTML</a> is
    a combination of HTML, CSS, and JavaScript that enables Web page content to
    exhibit dynamic behavior. This is accomplished by dynamically changing the
    properties of document objects in response to user actions and other
    events.</p>
</div><div class="panel" style="background-color: lime;  z-index: 3"
    id="p1panel6">
<h2>Extensible Markup Language</h2>
<a href="http://www.w3.org/XML/" target="external">XML</a> is a language for
    creating structured documents for use with the Web and in other application
    areas. XML is a simplified subset of the Standard Generalized Markup Language
    (SGML) that is used to create custom markup languages that follow a common
    syntax.
</div><div class="panel" style="background-color: silver;  z-index: 2"
    id="p1panel7">
<h2>XSL Transformations</h2>
<a href="http://www.w3.org/TR/xslt" target="external">XSLT</a> is a part of the
    Extensible Stylesheet Language (XSL) that is used to transform XML documents
    from one format into another format. XSLT style sheets are written in XML.
    These style sheets specify how XML documents are to be translated. They are
    provided as input to a translation program, which performs the actual
    translation.
```

```
</div><div class="panel" style="background-color: rgb(128,128,128);  z-index: 1"
    id="p1panel8">
<h2>Java</h2>
Java is a programming language that supports the development of Web
    applications. You can use it to develop applets, servlets, and JavaServer
    Pages.
</div></div><img border="0" height="50"><p></p></body></html>
```

⤳ **Listing 24.16:   A New Style Sheet (tabbedpanel2.css)**

```
.tab {font-family: sans-serif; line-height:150%;
    font-weight: bold; position:absolute;
    text-align: center; border: 2px; border-color:#999999;
    border-style: outset; border-bottom-style: none;
    height: 78px; width: 90px; margin:0px}

.panel {font-family: sans-serif; font-size: smaller;
    position:absolute; border: 2px; border-color:#999999;
    border-style:outset; width: 400px; height: 250px;
    left:0px; top:78px; margin:0px; padding:6px}

h1 {text-align: center}
```

Basic XSLT Syntax

XSLT provides a rich syntax for creating transforms. A complete description of XSLT would require a book of its own. However, the following list of elements (see Table 24.1) should get you up and running with XSLT programming.

TABLE 24.1: XSLT Elements

Element	Description
apply-imports	Provides access to imported template rules.
apply-templates	Causes processing of the children of the current node.
attribute	Used to add attributes to output elements.
attribute-set	Defines a named set of attributes.
call-template	Invokes a template by its name.
choose	Selects a single result from among a number of possible alternatives.
comment	Creates a comment in the output.
copy	Creates a copy of the current node.
copy-of	Copies a node to the output document.

Continued on next page

TABLE 24.1 CONTINUED: XSLT Elements

Element	Description
decimal-format	Used to format numbers.
element	Creates an element with a specified name and namespace.
fallback	Supports fallback processing for an element.
for-each	Used to perform looping.
if	Used to perform conditional processing.
import	Enables rules to be imported from another style sheet. The rules of the importing style sheet take precedence over the imported rules.
include	Includes rules from another style sheet.
key	Used to declare keys. Keys are used to implement a cross-reference structure within a document.
message	Sends a message to the XSLT processor.
namespace-alias	Declares one namespace as an alias for another.
number	Used to insert a formatted number into the output.
otherwise	Identifies a default alternative for an **xsl:choose** element.
output	Specifies information about the format of the output.
param	Used to define a parameter for a template.
preserve-space	Used to preserve whitespace in a document.
processing-instruction	Creates a processing instruction in the output.
sort	Used to sort elements.
strip-space	Specifies that whitespace should be discarded.
stylesheet	Used to identify an XSLT style sheet.
template	Declares a template.
text	Used to control output escaping of text.
transform	A synonym for **xsl:stylesheet**.
value-of	Returns the value of an expression.
variable	Declares a variable and associates it with a value.
when	Used to identify an alternative in an **xsl:choose** element.
with-param	Used to pass parameters to a template.

In addition, XSLT defines a number of functions for use in expressions. These functions are defined in Section 12 of the XSLT recommendation.

XPath

The XPath recommendation provides the basis for many XSLT expressions. You've been exposed to the basic use of XPath. However, I recommend that you download and read the

XPath recommendation so that you will be familiar with the extent of the capabilities provided by XPath.

Functional Programming

XSLT supports a style of programming known as *functional programming* or *declarative programming*. In this style of programming, there are no assignment statements as in languages such as Java and JavaScript. XSLT allows you to create variables and give them values. However, you cannot update the values of these variables from other locations in the transform. This frees XSLT from the problem of *side effects*, in which one piece of code changes the value of a variable that has been set and is being used by another piece of code. The downside of XSLT's style of programming is that you cannot update variables as you do in *imperative programming* languages, such as JavaScript and Java. However, after you grow accustomed to programming in XSLT, this is not much of a problem. You'll get more hands-on experience in the next chapter.

Summary

In this chapter, you were introduced to XSLT. You learned how to create custom components in XML and how to translate them into HTML and JavaScript using XSLT. In the next chapter, you'll cover additional uses of XSLT. You'll learn how to create web applications using XML, XSLT and JavaScript, and how to use the XSLT capabilities of Navigator and Internet Explorer.

CHAPTER 25

Creating XML-Based Web Applications

- Building Web applications using XML

- Processing XML on the client

- Associating an XML Document with an XSLT style sheet

- Transforming XML into HTML and JavaScript

In the previous chapter, you learned how to use XSLT to transform XML documents into HTML and JavaScript. In this chapter, you'll extend your knowledge of XSLT and JavaScript, and use these languages to build XML-based web applications. You'll start by learning about the different ways that you can deploy XML-based web applications. Then, you'll learn how to use your browser as an XSLT processor. Finally, you'll look at how to build your application using XML and then deploy it as HTML and JavaScript. When you finish this chapter, you'll be able to create XML-based web applications using XSLT and JavaScript.

Building Web Applications Using XML

XML and XSLT provide a powerful framework for building web applications. They enable you to define custom tags to structure your application's objects and then transform them into a working combination of HTML and JavaScript. Although XML support in current browsers is relatively new, it is a major focus of browser development, and improvements will continue to occur.

There are a number of options open to web developers on how to deploy XML-based web applications—especially if you are using XSLT to transform your XML into HTML and JavaScript. In this chapter, you'll see that Internet Explorer 5 and later, and Navigator 6.1 and later can be used as XSLT processors. This means that you can send XML documents and XSLT style sheets to them, and they'll perform the transformations required to render them in HTML and JavaScript. This is a new and great capability. However, XSLT support at the browser level is still relatively new and buggy.

Another option is to deploy your XML documents and XSLT style sheets on your web server and use server-side programming technologies, such as Java servlets and JavaServer pages, to dynamically translate the XML and XSLT into HTML and JavaScript. We won't explore this option because we're not diving very deep into server-side programming.

The last and most reliable approach is to simply use an XSLT processor to statically transform your XML documents and XSLT style sheets into HTML and JavaScript before deploying them on your web server. This option is simple and straightforward, but not as technically interesting as the others.

Sending XML and XSLT to the Client

As I mentioned in the previous section, Internet Explorer 5 and later and Navigator 6.1 and later contain integrated XSLT processors. This capability enables you to send XML and XSLT directly to the browser without having to transform them into HTML and JavaScript. However, there are two little catches.

Internet Explorer 5 and later use an XSLT processor known as MSXML. These browsers come with a default XSLT implementation that is non-standard. This problem was corrected with MSXML 3.0. However, you must manually install MSXML 3.0 in replace mode in order to take full advantage of XSLT in Internet Explorer. Fortunately, it's easy to do. The Unofficial MSXML FAQ at `www.netcrucible.com/xslt/msxml-faq.htm` provides you with all the information you need to do this.

The other little catch is that as of Navigator 6.1 preview 1, the XSLT processor doesn't work very well with JavaScript. Hopefully, that problem will have already been corrected by the time you read this. The important point is that you should upgrade to the latest version of Navigator if you have not already done so.

Associating an XML Document with an XSLT Style Sheet

In order to have your browser act as an XSLT processor, you have to associate your XML files with XSLT style sheets. You use the same technique that you used with CSS style sheets. Just include a processing instruction in your XML file.

Listing 25.1 provides an example. It inserts the following line into the price list of Chapter 24, "Working with XSLT."

```
<?xml-stylesheet type="text/xsl" href="prices2html.xsl"?>
```

That's all you need to do to tell your browser to transform `prices.xml` using the `prices2html.xsl` style sheet. Figure 25.1 shows how it is displayed by Internet Explorer. Figure 25.2 shows how it is displayed by Navigator 6.1 preview 1. As you can see, Navigator doesn't quite get the table right. Make sure that `prices2html.xsl` is in the same directory as `prices.xml`.

FIGURE 25.1:

The price list displayed by
Internet Explorer

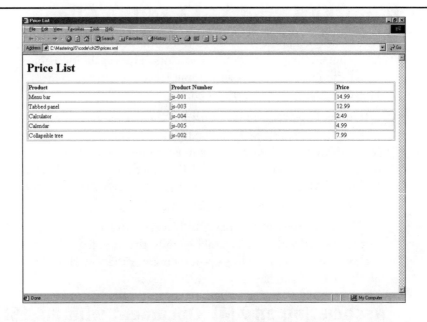

FIGURE 25.2:

The price list displayed by
Navigator

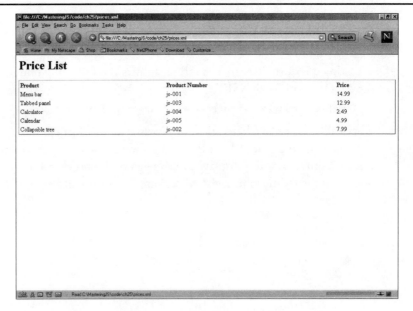

If you want to switch style sheets to sortbynumber.xsl (refer to Chapter 24), use the following processing instruction:

```
<?xml-stylesheet type="text/xsl" href="sortbynumber.xsl"?>
```

Changing transforms is as easy as changing styles. If you are using Internet Explorer and have problems displaying these files, make sure that you installed MSXML 3.0 correctly.

Listing 25.1:   Associating prices.xml with an XSLT Style Sheet (prices.xml)

```
<?xml version="1.0" encoding="iso-8859-1"?>
<!DOCTYPE pricelist SYSTEM "pricelist.dtd">
<?xml-stylesheet type="text/xsl" href="prices2html.xsl"?>

<pricelist>
<product>
<name>Menu bar</name>
<product_number>js-001</product_number>
<price>14.99</price>
</product>
<product>
<name>Tabbed panel</name>
<product_number>js-003</product_number>
<price>12.99</price>
</product>
<product>
<name>Calculator</name>
<product_number>js-004</product_number>
<price>2.49</price>
</product>
<product>
<name>Calendar</name>
<product_number>js-005</product_number>
<price>4.99</price>
</product>
<product>
<name>Collapsible tree</name>
<product_number>js-002</product_number>
<price>7.99</price>
</product>
</pricelist>
```

Using XSLT with JavaScript on the Browser

In Chapter 24, you learned how to use XML and XSLT to simplify the creation of JavaScript components. Wouldn't it be great if you could just send the XML and XSLT to the browser and have the browser sort it all out instead of having to transform it using Saxon?

Listing 25.2 (`tree.xml`) provides an XML representation of a collapsible tree. It is based on the one that you developed in Chapter 16, "Using Tabbed Panel, Tree, and Menu Components." Listing 25.3 (`tree.dtd`) shows the simple DTD used by the tree. Listing 25.4 (`tree.xsl`) provides an XSLT transform for transforming the XML version of the tree into JavaScript and HTML. To run it in your browser, you need the JavaScript file shown in Listing 25.5 (`tree.js`) and the CSS style sheet shown in Listing 25.6 (`tree.css`). Figure 25.3 shows how it is displayed by Internet Explorer. Clicking a plus sign (+) causes the associated branch of the tree to be expanded or collapsed, as shown in Figure 25.4.

FIGURE 25.3:

The initial display of the tree component

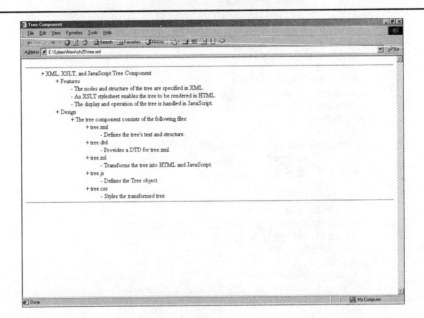

The combination of the XSLT and JavaScript seems to be too much for Navigator. It simply fails to display the tree, as shown in Figure 25.5. However, if you use Saxon to transform `tree.xml` into `tree.htm`, Navigator is able to properly display `tree.htm`, as shown in Figure 25.6.

```
saxon -o tree.htm tree.xml tree.xsl
```

FIGURE 25.4:

The branches expand or collapse when you click the plus signs.

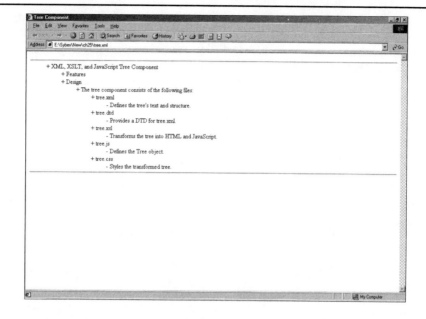

FIGURE 25.5:

Navigator can't handle the XSLT and JavaScript.

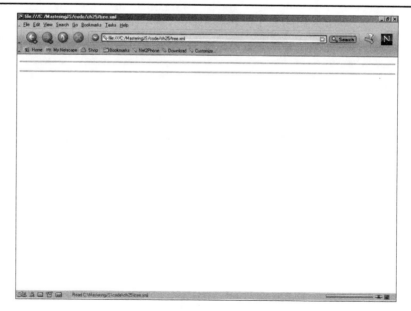

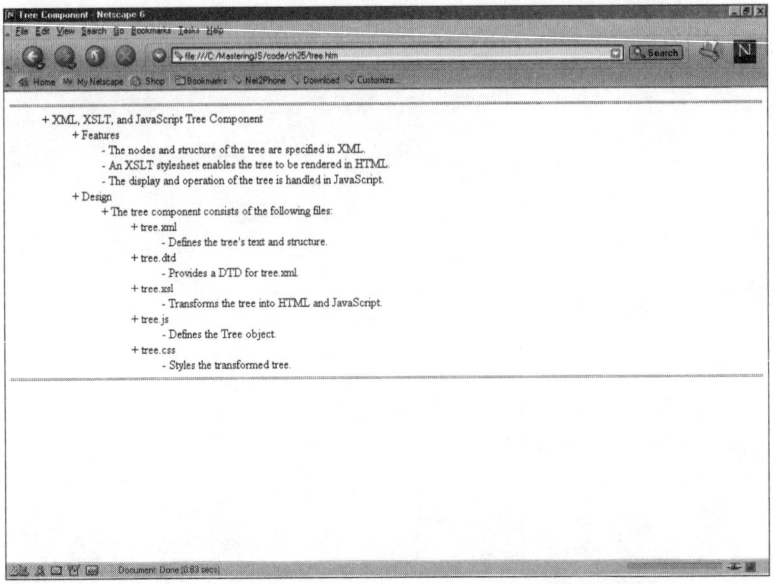

FIGURE 25.6:

If you transform the XML
into HTML first, Navigator
can display the tree.

The interesting part of the tree component lies in the fact that we use XSLT to generate
the JavaScript arrays used to build the tree. In Listing 25.4 (`tree.xsl`), the two arrays (`nodes`
and `branches`) used to create an instance of the `Tree` object are initialized.

```
var nodes = new Array(<xsl:call-template name="quoted_list">
<xsl:with-param name="names" select="//text"/></xsl:call-template>
)
var branches = new Array(
<xsl:apply-templates select="node">
</xsl:apply-templates>
new Array(-1,-1))
```

The arrays are initialized in two different ways to call attention to different coding techniques. The `nodes` array is initialized by invoking the `quoted_list` template and passing it a
parameter named `names` that has a list of the values all of the `text` tags in `tree.xml`. The
XPath notation `//nodename` results in a list of all nodes with the name *nodename* being created. The `quoted-list` template takes each node in the list, wraps double quotes around
them, and separates them by commas. It avoids adding a comma to the last string in the list:

```
<xsl:template name="quoted_list">
<xsl:param name="names"/>
<xsl:for-each select="$names"><xsl:value-of select="."/>"<xsl:if
   test="position()!=last()">, </xsl:if>
</xsl:for-each>
</xsl:template>
```

The `branches` array is initialized in a much different way. The elements of the array are generated by running `apply-templates` on the next level nodes. This creates a list of `new Array(parent, child)` elements that have a comma appended to them. A bogus `new Array(-1,-1)` element is added to the end of the array to make up for the dangling comma. This coding technique is sloppy, but it saves you the trouble of creating an array element-formatting template like `quoted-list`.

The `node` template is applied only once to the top-level element of the tree. It creates a variable named `root` that is initialized to the number associated with the node in the document. The `<xsl:number>` element provides a flexible approach to numbering elements in a document. By setting the `level` attribute to any, the numbering will apply to all node elements, no matter what level of nesting they are at within the document.

```
<xsl:template match="node">
<xsl:variable name="root"><xsl:number level="any"/></xsl:variable>
<xsl:call-template name="findbranches">
<xsl:with-param name="parent" select="$root"/>
</xsl:call-template>
</xsl:template>
```

The template invokes the `findbranches` template to find all the branches from the top-level node. It passes the number associated with the top-level node as a parameter.

The `findbranches` template uses the `parent` parameter to refer to the passed value. It uses a for loop to process each of its child nodes. The variable named `child` is created to refer to the number associated with each child. An array is created with `parent` and `child` as the elements of the array. A value of 1 is subtracted from both the `parent` and `child` because XSLT starts numbering at 1 instead of 0, and these numbers are indices into the nodes array. The array represents a branch from a parent node to that of a child node. The `findbranches` template is then invoked for each child (and the child becomes the parent).

```
<xsl:template name="findbranches">
<xsl:param name="parent"/>
<xsl:for-each select="node">
<xsl:variable name="child"><xsl:number level="any"/></xsl:variable>
new Array(<xsl:value-of select="$parent - 1"/>,<xsl:value-of select="$child -
    1"/>),
<xsl:call-template name="findbranches">
<xsl:with-param name="parent" select="$child"/>
</xsl:call-template>
</xsl:for-each>
</xsl:template>
```

The important point to take from this example is that you can use XSLT to initialize your JavaScript data structures, which is usually tedious to do by hand.

The tree.js file is very similar to the one presented in Chapter 16.

Listing 25.2:   An XML Tree Component (tree.xml)

```xml
<?xml version="1.0" encoding="iso-8859-1"?>
<!DOCTYPE tree SYSTEM "tree.dtd">
<?xml-stylesheet type="text/xsl" href="tree.xsl"?>

<tree>
<node>
<text>XML, XSLT, and JavaScript Tree Component</text>
<node>
<text>Features</text>
<node>
<text>The nodes and structure of the tree are specified in XML.</text>
</node>
<node>
<text>An XSLT stylesheet enables the tree to be rendered in HTML.</text>
</node>
<node>
<text>The display and operation of the tree is handled in JavaScript.</text>
</node>
</node>
<node>
<text>Design</text>
<node>
<text>The tree component consists of the following files:</text>
<node>
<text>tree.xml</text>
<node>
<text>Defines the tree's text and structure.</text>
</node>
</node>
<node>
<text>tree.dtd</text>
<node>
<text>Provides a DTD for tree.xml.</text>
</node>
</node>
<node>
<text>tree.xsl</text>
<node>
<text>Transforms the tree into HTML and JavaScript.</text>
</node>
</node>
<node>
<text>tree.js</text>
<node>
<text>Defines the Tree object.</text>
</node>
</node>
```

```
<node>
<text>tree.css</text>
<node>
<text>Styles the transformed tree.</text>
</node>
</node>
</node>
</node>
</node>
</tree>
```

Listing 25.3:   The Tree's DTD (tree.dtd)

```
<?xml version='1.0' encoding='ISO-8859-1'?>
<!- DTD for representing trees ->

<!ELEMENT tree (node+)>
<!ELEMENT node (text, node*)>
<!ELEMENT text (#PCDATA)>
```

Listing 25.4:   An XSLT transForm for Translating the Tree into JavaScript and HTML (tree.xsl)

```
<?xml version="1.0" encoding="iso-8859-1"?>
<xsl:stylesheet
    xmlns:xsl="http://www.w3.org/1999/XSL/Transform"
    version="1.0"
>
<xsl:output
    method="html"
    indent="no"
    encoding="iso-8859-1"/>

<xsl:template match="tree">
<html>
<head>
<title>Tree Component</title>
<link rel="stylesheet" type="text/css" href="tree.css"/>
<script language="JavaScript">
var nodes = new Array(<xsl:call-template name="quoted_list">
<xsl:with-param name="names" select="//text"/></xsl:call-template>
)
var branches = new Array(
<xsl:apply-templates select="node">
</xsl:apply-templates>
new Array(-1,-1))
</script>
<script language="JavaScript" src="tree.js">
```

```
    </script>
    </head>
    <body>
    <hr/>
    <div id="tree">
    <script language="JavaScript">
    tree.display()
    </script>
    </div>
    <hr/>
    </body>
    </html>
    </xsl:template>

    <xsl:template match="node">
    <xsl:variable name="root"><xsl:number level="any"/></xsl:variable>
    <xsl:call-template name="findbranches">
    <xsl:with-param name="parent" select="$root"/>
    </xsl:call-template>
    </xsl:template>

    <xsl:template name="quoted_list">
    <xsl:param name="names"/>
    <xsl:for-each select="$names">"<xsl:value-of select="."/>"<xsl:if
    test="position()!=last()">, </xsl:if>
    </xsl:for-each>
    </xsl:template>

    <xsl:template name="findbranches">
    <xsl:param name="parent"/>
    <xsl:for-each select="node">
    <xsl:variable name="child"><xsl:number level="any"/></xsl:variable>
    new Array(<xsl:value-of select="$parent - 1"/>,<xsl:value-of select="$child -
        1"/>),
    <xsl:call-template name="findbranches">
    <xsl:with-param name="parent" select="$child"/>
    </xsl:call-template>
    </xsl:for-each>
    </xsl:template>

    </xsl:stylesheet>
```

Listing 25.5:   An Implementation of the Tree Object (tree.js)

```
    // tree.js

    var tree = createTree()

    function createTree() {
     branchID = 0
```

```
   var subtrees = new Array()
   for(var i=0; i<nodes.length; ++i)
    subtrees[i] = new Tree(nodes[i])
   for(var i=0; i<branches.length - 1; ++i)
    subtrees[branches[i][0]].addBranch(subtrees[branches[i][1]])
   return subtrees[0]
}
function Tree(root) {
 this.text = root
 this.id = branchID
 ++branchID
 this.expanded = true
 this.branches = new Array()
 this.addBranch = Tree_addBranch
 this.changeState = Tree_changeState
 this.handleClick = Tree_handleClick
 this.processClick = Tree_processClick
 this.display = Tree_display
 this.getTreeString = Tree_getTreeString
}
function Tree_addBranch(tree) {
 this.branches[this.branches.length] = tree
}
function Tree_changeState() {
 this.expanded = !this.expanded
}
function Tree_handleClick(branch) {
 this.processClick(branch)
 var d = document.getElementById("tree")
 if(d != null) d.innerHTML = this.getTreeString()
}
function Tree_processClick(branch) {
 if(this.id == branch) this.changeState()
 else {
   for(var i=0; i<this.branches.length; ++i)
    this.branches[i].processClick(branch)
 }
}
function Tree_getTreeString() {
 var s = "<blockquote>"
 s += '<table border="0">'
 s += "<tr>"
 s += "<td>"
 if(this.branches.length > 0)
  s += '<a href="javascript:tree.handleClick('+this.id+')">+</a>'
 else s += "-"
 s += "</td>"
 s += "<td>"
 s += this.text
 s += "</td>"
 s += "</tr>"
```

```
 s += "</table>"
 if((this.branches.length > 0) && (this.expanded == true)) {
  for(var i=0; i<this.branches.length; ++i)
    s += this.branches[i].getTreeString()
 }
 s += "</blockquote>"
 return s
}
function Tree_display() {
 document.writeln(this.getTreeString())
 }
```

Listing 25.6:   A CSS Style Sheet for the Transformed Tree (tree.css)

```css
BLOCKQUOTE {
margin-top: -5;
margin-bottom: -5;
}
TABLE {
margin-top: 0;
margin-bottom: 0;
}
A:link, A:visited {
  color: black;
  text-decoration: none;
}
```

Listing 25.7:   The JavaScript and HTML that is Generated by Saxon (tree.htm)

```html
<html><head>
     <meta http-equiv="Content-Type" content="text/html; charset=iso-8859-1">
   <title>Tree Component</title>
   <link rel="stylesheet" type="text/css" href="tree.css">
   <script language="JavaScript">
var nodes = new Array("XML, XSLT, and JavaScript Tree Component",
"Features",
"The nodes and structure of the tree are specified in XML.",
"An XSLT stylesheet enables the tree to be rendered in HTML.",
"The display and operation of the tree is handled in JavaScript.",
"Design", "The tree component consists of the following files:",
"tree.xml", "Defines the tree's text and structure.",
"tree.dtd", "Provides a DTD for tree.xml.",
"tree.xsl", "Transforms the tree into HTML and JavaScript.",
"tree.js", "Defines the Tree object.",
"tree.css", "Styles the transformed tree."
)
var branches = new Array(new Array(0,1),new Array(1,2),
```

```
new Array(1,3),new Array(1,4),new Array(0,5),new Array(5,6),
new Array(6,7),new Array(7,8),new Array(6,9),new Array(9,10),
new Array(6,11),new Array(11,12),new Array(6,13),new Array(13,14),
new Array(6,15),new Array(15,16),new Array(-1,-1))
</script>
<script language="JavaScript" src="tree.js">
</script>
</head>
<body>
<hr>
<div id="tree"><script language="JavaScript">
tree.display()
</script>
</div>
<hr>
</body>
</html>
```

Transforming XML into HTML and JavaScript

As I mentioned in the beginning of this chapter, the safest and most reliable approach to building XML-based web applications is to transform your XML into HTML and JavaScript before deploying them to your web server. That way, you'll have a higher level of assurance that your application will be compatible with your user's browsers. Listing 25.8 presents an XSLT transform for the product catalog (Listing 22.6) of Chapter 22, "Displaying XML with Internet Explorer and Navigator." You can use it to easily convert the XML catalog to HTML and JavaScript. To use it, you'll also need the updated catalog.js file (Listing 25.9) and CSS style sheet (Listing 25.10).

You can run it directly using Internet Explorer by replacing the CSS style sheet with the catalog.xsl transform in the third line of Listing 22.6:

```
<?xml-stylesheet type="text/xsl" href="catalog.xsl"?>
```

Figures 25.7 and 25.8 shows how it is displayed using Internet Explorer. If you transform it into HTML using the following Saxon command, you'll be able to view it using a simple DOM-capable browser. Figures 25.9 and 25.10 show how the transformed XML is displayed by Navigator 6.1.

```
saxon -o catalog.htm catalog.xml catalog.xsl
```

FIGURE 25.7:

Displaying the catalog directly using Internet Explorer

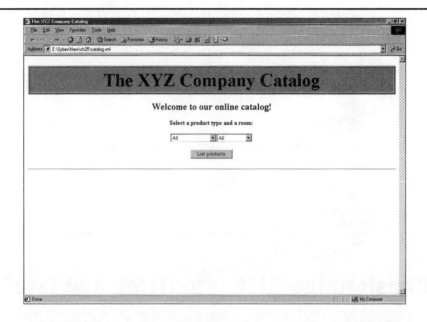

FIGURE 25.8:

Browsing the catalog using Internet Explorer

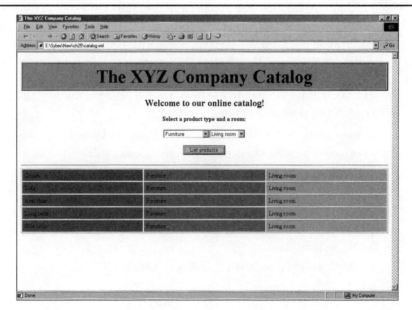

FIGURE 25.9:

Displaying the transformed catalog using Navigator

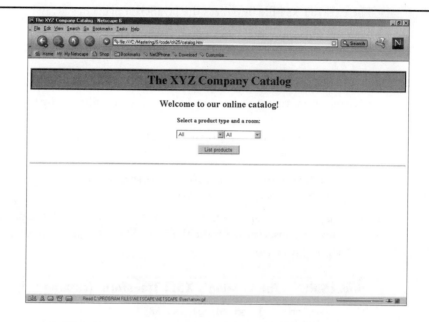

FIGURE 25.10:

Browsing the transformed catalog using Navigator

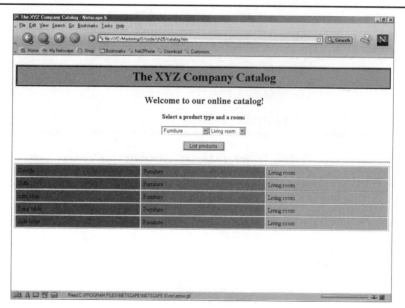

The catalog.xsl file initializes the JavaScript products array based on the content of the XML catalog:

```
var products=new Array(<xsl:apply-templates select="product"/>new Array("", "",
    ""))
```

The values of the products array are three-element arrays consisting of the product's category description, room, and name. These values are filled in by the following templates:

```
<xsl:template match="product">
new Array(<xsl:apply-templates select="descriptor"/>"<xsl:value-of
    select="./name"/>"),</xsl:template>

<xsl:template match="descriptor">"<xsl:value-of
    select="./value"/>",</xsl:template>
```

The product template applies the descriptor template to get the product's category and room values, and inserts the product's name. These simple templates are the key to going from XML to JavaScript.

Listing 25.8: The Catalog's XSLT Transform (catalog.xsl)

```
<?xml version="1.0" encoding="iso-8859-1"?>
<xsl:stylesheet
    xmlns:xsl="http://www.w3.org/1999/XSL/Transform"
    version="1.0"
>
<xsl:output
    method="html"
    indent="yes"
    encoding="iso-8859-1"/>

<xsl:template match="catalog">
<html>
<head>
<title><xsl:value-of select="./description"/></title>
<link rel="stylesheet" type="text/css" href="catalog.css"/>
<script language="JavaScript" src="catalog.js">
</script>
<script language="JavaScript">
var products=new Array(<xsl:apply-templates select="product"/>new Array("", "",
    ""))
</script>
</head>
<body>
<h1><xsl:value-of select="./description"/></h1>
<form name="searchForm">
<h2 align="center">Welcome to our online catalog!</h2>
<p align="center"><b>Select a product type and a room: </b></p>
<p align="center">
```

```
<select name="category">
<option>All</option>
<option>Furniture</option>
<option>Carpeting</option>
<option>Lighting</option>
<option>Electronics</option>
<option>Accessories</option>
<option>Appliances</option>
<option>Cabinets</option>
<option>Sinks</option>
<option>Toilets</option>
<option>Bath and shower</option>
</select>
<select name="room">
<option>All</option>
<option>Living room</option>
<option>Dining room</option>
<option>Bed room</option>
<option>Kitchen</option>
<option>Bath room</option>
</select>
</p>
<p align="center">
<input type="button" value="List products" onclick="searchCatalog()"/>
</p>
</form>
<hr/>
<div id="displayArea"> </div>
</body>
</html>
</xsl:template>

<xsl:template match="product">
new Array(<xsl:apply-templates select="descriptor"/>"<xsl:value-of
    select="./name"/>"),</xsl:template>

<xsl:template match="descriptor">"<xsl:value-of
    select="./value"/>",</xsl:template>

</xsl:stylesheet>
```

Listing 25.9: The Supporting JavaScript File (catalog.js)

```
// catalog.js

function searchCatalog() {
  // Get search text
  var select0 = document.forms["searchForm"].elements["room"]
  var select1 = document.forms["searchForm"].elements["category"]
  var room = ""
```

```
 var category = ""
 if(select0.selectedIndex >= 0)
  room = select0.options.item(select0.selectedIndex).text
 if(select1.selectedIndex >= 0)
  category = select1.options.item(select1.selectedIndex).text
 var s = "<table border='1' width='100%'>"
 // Match each product to room and category
 for(var i=0; i<products.length; ++i) {
  var pname = products[i][2]
  var proom = products[i][1]
  var pcategory = products[i][0]
  if(category == "All" || category.toLowerCase() == pcategory.toLowerCase()) {
   if(room == "All" || room.toLowerCase() == proom.toLowerCase()) {
    s += "<tr><td class='productname'>"+pname+"</td>"
    s += "<td class='category'>"+pcategory+"</td>"
    s += "<td class='room'>"+proom+"</td></tr>"
   }
  }
 }
 s += "</table>"
 var d = document.getElementById("displayArea")
 if(d != null) d.innerHTML = s
}
```

Listing 25.10:   An Updated Style Sheet (catalog.css)

```
h1
{background-color: #bbbbff;
border: 5px ridge;
display: block;
font-size: xx-large;
font-weight: bold;
margin-top: 25px;
padding: 5px;
text-align: center}

td
{padding: 5px}

.productname
{background-color: #8080ff;
width: 30%}

.category
{background-color: #a0a0ff;
width: 30%}

.room
{background-color: #d5d5ff;
width: 30%}
```

Summary

In this chapter, you learned how to use XSLT and JavaScript to build XML-based web applications. You learned about the different ways that you can deploy XML-based web applications and how to use your browser as an XSLT processor. You then looked at how to build applications using XML, transform them using XSLT, and deploy them as HTML and JavaScript. In the next chapter, you'll learn how to take advantage of browser-specific XML capabilities.

CHAPTER 26

Working with Browser-Specific XML Capabilities

- XML data islands

- The *XMLHttpRequest* object

- The *document.load()* method

So far, we've been taking the middle ground and sticking with solutions that work with both Internet Explorer and Navigator.In this chapter, however, we'll loosen up a bit and cover XML technologies that are limited to a single browser. Of course, we'll provide workarounds so similar capabilities can be implemented by the other browser.

The first technology that you'll learn about, which was developed by Microsoft, is referred to as *XML data islands*. XML data islands enable XML to be embedded in HTML documents. XML data islands are a very powerful capability, but they are limited to Internet Explorer.

Not to be outdone, the folks at Mozilla co-opted two Microsoft innovations. The first is the `XMLHttpRequest` object and the other is the `document.load()` method. Both of these innovations can be used to provide a capability that is similar to XML data islands. You'll learn how to take advantage of the features they provide.

When you finish this chapter, you'll be able to include XML in your HTML documents and to script the XML using JavaScript.

XML Data Islands: The Best of Both Worlds

XML data islands are a Microsoft technology for embedding XML in HTML documents. They are supported by Internet Explorer 5.0 and later. Their big advantage is that they provide a gradual and easy path to migrate your HTML-based web applications to XML. Their syntax is as follows:

```
<XML ID="id" SRC="url">
</XML>
```

or

```
<XML ID="id">
  .
  . XML data
  .
</XML>
```

I prefer to use the first approach because it enables you to maintain the XML separate from your HTML. It also enables you to reuse the XML with other documents and applications.

TIP Make sure that you upgrade Internet Explorer to use MSXML 3.0 or later in replace mode before viewing the examples in this chapter. Refer to **www.netcrucible.com/xslt/msxml-faq.htm** for more information on how to do this.

Listing 26.1 (`xmlisland.htm`) provides an example of an HTML document that contains embedded XML. When you open it in your browser, you'll see the display shown in Figure 26.1. After five seconds, the display is updated, as shown in Figure 26.2.

The messages that are displayed by `xmlisland.htm` are embedded as XML. They originate from `messagelist1.xml` (Listing 26.2). Listing 26.3 provides a DTD for the message list. Listing 26.4 provides a style sheet for the messages as they are displayed in HTML.

The XML data island follows the document's body tag:

```
<xml id="messages" src="messagelist1.xml"></xml>
```

The island embeds `messagelist1.xml` into the document. However, the XML is not directly displayed. Instead, it is used as data by the `displayMessages()` function.

```
function displayMessages() {
 var island = document.all("messages").XMLDocument.lastChild
 var children = island.childNodes
 var n = children.length
 for(var i=0; i<n; ++i)
  messages[i] = children.item(i).firstChild.nodeValue
 div = document.getElementById("messagedisplay")
 div.innerHTML = messages[0]
 ++messageIndex
 setInterval("displayNewMessage()", 5000)
}
```

The `displayMessages()` function gains access to the embedded document using the Internet Explorer–specific syntax `document.all("messages").XMLDocument`.

The `messagelist` element is the last child of the document's root. Its children are the individual `message` elements. The children of the message elements are the actual messages (that is, text nodes) that we want to display. The text of these nodes is copied to the `messages` array.

The HTML division identified by `messagedisplay` is then updated with the first message. A timer is used to invoke `displayNewMessage()` every five seconds to cycle through the list of messages.

The capability to embed XML within an HTML document is very powerful. It is the equivalent of storing a small database within a document. The database can be queried using the DOM to extract data to display in a web page.

FIGURE 26.1:

The XML is displayed in the bordered division.

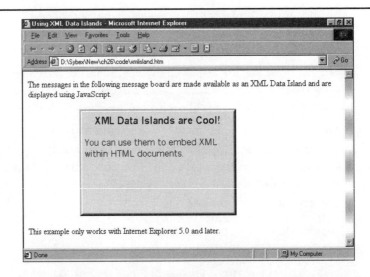

FIGURE 26.2:

The display is updated using the XML messages.

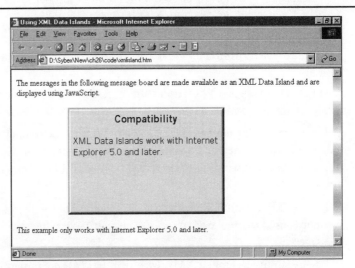

Listing 26.1:   Using XML Data Islands (xmlisland.htm).

```
<html>
<head>
<title>Using XML Data Islands</title>
<link rel="stylesheet" type="text/css" href="messagelist.css">
<script language="JavaScript">
var messages = new Array()
```

```
var messageIndex = 0
var div
function displayMessages() {
 var island = document.all("messages").XMLDocument.lastChild
 var children = island.childNodes
 var n = children.length
 for(var i=0; i<n; ++i)
  messages[i] = children.item(i).firstChild.nodeValue
 div = document.getElementById("messagedisplay")
 div.innerHTML = messages[0]
 ++messageIndex
 setInterval("displayNewMessage()", 5000)
}
function displayNewMessage() {
 div.innerHTML = messages[messageIndex]
 messageIndex = (messageIndex + 1) % messages.length
}
</script>
</head>
<body onload="displayMessages()">
<xml id="messages" src="messagelist1.xml"></xml>
<p>The messages in the following message board are
made available as an XML Data Island and are displayed
using JavaScript.</p>
<div id="messagedisplay"> </div>
<p>This example only works with Internet Explorer 5.0
and later.</p>
</body>
</html>
```

Listing 26.2:   An Embedded XML Document (messagelist1.xml).

```
<?xml version="1.0" encoding="iso-8859-1"?>
<!DOCTYPE messagelist SYSTEM "messagelist.dtd">

<messagelist>
<message>
<![CDATA[
<h3 align="center">XML Data Islands are Cool!</h3>
<p>You can use them to embed XML within HTML documents.</p>
]]>
</message>
<message>
<![CDATA[
<h3 align="center">Compatibility</h3>
<p>XML Data Islands work with Internet Explorer 5.0 and later.</p>
]]>
</message>
<message>
<![CDATA[
```

```
<h3 align="center">Usage:</h3>
<pre>
&lt;XML ID="<i>id</i>" SRC="<i>url</i>"&gt;
&lt;/XML&gt;

or

&lt;XML ID="<i>id</i>"&gt;
 .
 . <i>XML data</i>
 .
&lt;/XML&gt;
</pre>
]]>
</message>
</messagelist>
```

Listing 26.3:   **The Message List DTD (messagelist.dtd).**

```
<?xml version='1.0' encoding='ISO-8859-1'?>
<!-- DTD for representing message lists -->

<!ELEMENT messagelist (message+)>
<!ELEMENT message (#PCDATA)>
```

Listing 26.4:   **A Style Sheet for the Message List (messagelist.css).**

```
#messagedisplay {
    font-family: sans-serif; background-color: yellow;
    border: 5px; border-style:outset; width: 300px;
    height: 200px; margin-left:100px; padding:5px}
```

The *XMLHttpRequest* Object

The folks at Mozilla do not intend to support XML data islands. This greatly reduces the usefulness of this Microsoft innovation. However, Mozilla has co-opted another Microsoft development that can be used to provide a similar capability. The XMLHttpRequest object enables a browser to make an HTTP request to download an XML document. It also provides the capability to post data to a web server. These capabilities enable a JavaScript script to act as a mini-XML browser. For security reasons, a script can only make requests back to the server from which it originated.

The `XMLHttpRequest` object provides the following properties and methods:

Properties

- `channel`—The channel used to perform the request.
- `onerror`—Set this to an error-handling function.
- `onload`—Set this to a function that will respond to an asynchronous document load.
- `responseText`—The web server's response returned as text.
- `responseXML`—The web server's response returned as an XML `Document` object.
- `status`—The status code returned by the web server.
- `statusText`—The status message returned by the web server.

Methods

- `abort()`—Aborts processing of the request.
- `getAllResponseHeaders()`—Returns the HTTP response headers as a string.
- `getResponseHeader(name)`—Returns a specific HTTP response header.
- `open (method , url, asynchronous, userID, password)`—Specifies a request for a specific URL. Method is `"GET"` or `"POST"`. If the optional *aynchronous* parameter is set to *true*, the request is executed independently of the script's flow of control. The `onload` property should be set to the name of a function that handles the document's loading. The *userID* and *password* parameters are optional.
- `send(body)`—Starts the request and posts the body (for `POST` method requests).
- `setRequestHeader(name, value)`—Sets the named header to the specified value.

Listing 26.5 replaces the XML data island of Listing 26.1 with an example of using `XMLHttpRequest`. The major difference between Listing 26.5 and Listing 26.1 is as follows:

```
var xmlDocument = loadXMLDocument("messagelist2.xml")
var children = xmlDocument.lastChild.childNodes
var n = children.length
var messageCount = 0
for(var i=0; i<n; ++i) {
 var node = children.item(i)
 if(node.nodeType == 1) {
  messages[messageCount] = node.childNodes.item(1).nodeValue
  ++messageCount
 }
}
```

Instead of accessing the embedded document, the `loadXMLDocument()` function is invoked to load the method via `XMLHttpRequest`. The document is parsed slightly differently due to the differences in the way that Navigator handles white space text nodes.

The `loadXMLDocument()` function loads `messagelist2.xml` as follows:

```
function loadXMLDocument(url) {
  var obj = new XMLHttpRequest()
  obj.open("GET",url,false)
  obj.send(null)
  return obj.responseXML
}
```

A new `XMLHttpRequest` object is created. The `open()` method initializes the request as an HTTP GET request to the specified URL. Asynchronous mode is turned off, eliminating the need to handle the `onload` event. The `send()` method is used to start the request. A `null` parameter is used because we are not posting any data to the web server. When the document is loaded, the `responseXML` property of the `XMLHttpRequest` object contains a reference to the loaded document as a `Document` object.

In order to run Listing 26.5 (`xmlhttprequest.htm`), copy `xmlhttprequest.htm`, `messagelist2.xml` (refer to Listing 26.6), `messagelist.dtd`, and `messagelist.css` to an accessible directory of your web server. You can't simply run it from your file system because it requires web server support. When you open it in Navigator 6.1 or later, you'll see a document that is similar to the XML data island example (see Figure 26.3). After five seconds, another message will be displayed, as shown in Figure 26.4.

FIGURE 26.3:

The retrieved XML document is displayed.

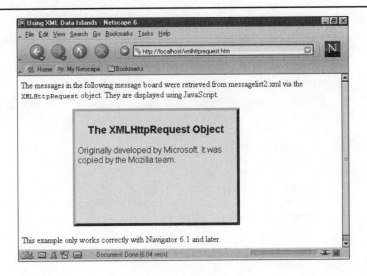

FIGURE 26.4:

The display is updated based upon other messages contained in the retrieved document.

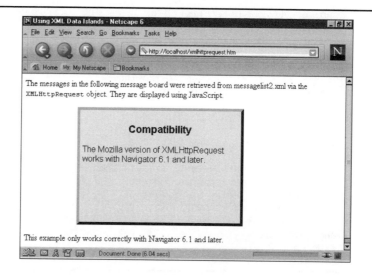

```html
<html>
<head>
<title>Using XMLHttpRequest</title>
<link rel="stylesheet" type="text/css" href="messagelist.css">
<script language="JavaScript">
var messages = new Array()
var messageIndex = 0
var div
function displayMessages() {
 var xmlDocument = loadXMLDocument("messagelist2.xml")
 var children = xmlDocument.lastChild.childNodes
 var n = children.length
 var messageCount = 0
 for(var i=0; i<n; ++i) {
  var node = children.item(i)
  if(node.nodeType == 1) {
   messages[messageCount] = node.childNodes.item(1).nodeValue
   ++messageCount
  }
 }
 div = document.getElementById("messagedisplay")
 div.innerHTML = messages[0]
 ++messageIndex
 setInterval("displayNewMessage()", 5000)
}
function loadXMLDocument(url) {
 var obj = new XMLHttpRequest()
```

```
 obj.open("GET",url,false)
 obj.send(null)
 return obj.responseXML
}
function displayNewMessage() {
 div.innerHTML = messages[messageIndex]
 messageIndex = (messageIndex + 1) % messages.length
}
</script>
</head>
<body onload="displayMessages()">
<p>The messages in the following message board were
retrieved from messagelist2.xml via the
<code>XMLHttpRequest</code> object.
They are displayed using JavaScript.</p>
<div id="messagedisplay"> </div>
<p>This example only works correctly with Navigator 6.1
and later.</p>
</body>
</html>
```

Listing 26.6:   A Second Message List (messagelist2.xml).

```
<?xml version="1.0" encoding="iso-8859-1"?>
<!DOCTYPE messagelist SYSTEM "messagelist.dtd">

<messagelist>
<message>
<![CDATA[
<h3 align="center">The XMLHttpRequest Object</h3>
<p>Originally developed by Microsoft. It was copied by
the Mozilla team.</p>
]]>
</message>
<message>
<![CDATA[
<h3 align="center">Compatibility</h3>
<p>The Mozilla version of XMLHttpRequest works with
Navigator 6.1 and later.</p>
]]>
</message>
<message>
<![CDATA[
<h3 align="center">Example</h3>
<pre>
function loadXMLDocument(url) {
 var obj = new XMLHttpRequest()
 obj.open("GET",url,false)
 obj.send(null)
 return obj.responseXML
```

```
    }
    </pre>
    ]]>
    </message>
    </messagelist>
```

The *document.load()* Method

The XMLHttpRequest object provides a powerful, low-level capability. A higher-level approach to document loading was also invented by Microsoft and borrowed by Mozilla. This approach uses the load() method of the Document object, and will most likely be standardized in the DOM Level 3 recommendation.

Listing 26.7 provides an example of using document.load() as a replacement for XML-HttpRequest. The essential difference between Listing 26.7 and Listing 26.5 follows:

```
var xmlDocument = document.implementation.createDocument("","mydoc",null)
xmlDocument.addEventListener("load", documentLoaded, false)
function displayMessages() {
 xmlDocument.load("messagelist3.xml")
}
function documentLoaded(e) {
 var children = xmlDocument.firstChild.childNodes
    .
    .
    .
}
```

The xmlDocument variable is set to a new Document object. The createDocument() method of the DOMImplementation object is defined in the DOM Core Level 2, and is implemented by Navigator 6.1. It creates a new Document object with a blank namespace and a null document type that is identified as mydoc.

The documentLoaded() function is set as an event listener for the event that is generated when the document is loaded. This makes use of the DOM Level 2 event recommendation.

The documentLoaded() event-handling function then handles the bulk of what was performed by displayMessages() in Listings 26.1 and 26.5.

Listing 26.7 does not require web server support. It can load XML documents out of the local file system. Figure 26.5 shows the output it displays for messagelist3.xml (Listing 26.8). The message is updated after five seconds, as shown in Figure 26.6.

FIGURE 26.5:

The loaded document is displayed.

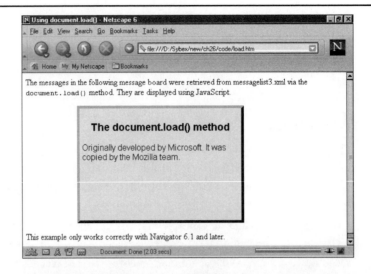

FIGURE 26.6:

The display is updated based upon other messages contained in the loaded document.

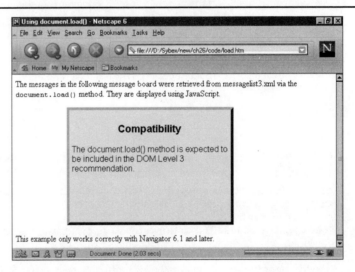

Listing 26.7:   Using *document.load* (load.htm).

```
<html>
<head>
<title>Using document.load()</title>
<link rel="stylesheet" type="text/css" href="messagelist.css">
<script language="JavaScript">
var messages = new Array()
```

```
var messageIndex = 0
var div
var xmlDocument = document.implementation.createDocument("","mydoc",null)
xmlDocument.addEventListener("load", documentLoaded, false)
function displayMessages() {
 xmlDocument.load("messagelist3.xml")
}
function documentLoaded(e) {
 var children = xmlDocument.firstChild.childNodes
 var n = children.length
 var messageCount = 0
 for(var i=0; i<n; ++i) {
  var node = children.item(i)
  if(node.nodeType == 1) {
   messages[messageCount] = node.childNodes.item(1).nodeValue
   ++messageCount
  }
 }
 div = document.getElementById("messagedisplay")
 div.innerHTML = messages[0]
 ++messageIndex
 setInterval("displayNewMessage()", 5000)
}
function loadXMLDocument(url) {
 var obj = new XMLHttpRequest()
 obj.open("GET",url,false)
 obj.send(null)
 return obj.responseXML
}
function displayNewMessage() {
 div.innerHTML = messages[messageIndex]
 messageIndex = (messageIndex + 1) % messages.length
}
</script>
</head>
<body onload="displayMessages()">
<p>The messages in the following message board were
retrieved from messagelist3.xml via the
<code>document.load()</code> method.
They are displayed using JavaScript.</p>
<div id="messagedisplay"> </div>
<p>This example only works correctly with Navigator 6.1
and later.</p>
</body>
</html>
```

Listing 26.8:   The *document.load* Message List (messagelist3.xml).

```
<?xml version="1.0" encoding="iso-8859-1"?>
<!DOCTYPE messagelist SYSTEM "messagelist.dtd">

<messagelist>
<message>
<![CDATA[
<h3 align="center">The document.load() method</h3>
<p>Originally developed by Microsoft. It was copied by
the Mozilla team.</p>
]]>
</message>
<message>
<![CDATA[
<h3 align="center">Compatibility</h3>
<p>The document.load() method is expected to be included in
the DOM Level 3 recommendation.</p>
]]>
</message>
</messagelist>
```

Summary

In this chapter, you learned about an Internet Explorer-specific XML technology, XML data islands, which enables you to embed XML in your HTML documents. You learned how to integrate this technology with JavaScript and how to create custom JavaScript components using XML. You then learned how to use the Mozilla-specific XMLHttpRequest object and the document.load() method to provide a capability similar to XML data islands. You should now feel competent and comfortable using JavaScript to script XML. In the next part of this book, you'll learn how to use JavaScript to communicate with Java, ActiveX, and plug-ins.

PART V

Communicating with Java, ActiveX, and Plug-Ins

Communicating with Java Applets

- What is Java?

- Comparing Java and JavaScript

- Working with LiveConnect

- Accessing Java methods from within JavaScript

- Accessing applets from within JavaScript

- Using JavaScript in an applet

Java is a very powerful and popular language that supports the development of browser-neutral web-based applications. It provides a number of capabilities that complement those that JavaScript provides. In this chapter, you'll learn about the similarities and differences between Java and JavaScript and how to develop simple Java programs and applets. You'll learn how to use Navigator and Internet Explorer to enable communication between JavaScript scripts and Java applets. You'll also learn how to invoke JavaScript functions from within applets. By the time you finish this chapter, you'll be able to create web applications that integrate scripts and applets.

What Is Java?

The rapid growth in the popularity of the Java language was nothing short of a phenomenon. In less than a year after Java was introduced, Java went from a relatively unknown alpha version to an incredibly successful Version 1 release. Every major computer hardware and software vendor has since endorsed Java. In this section I'll explore the features of Java that set it apart from other programming languages.

Java Is Platform Independent

Java's extraordinary success is due to the fact that it provides the capability to develop compiled software that runs, without modification, on a large variety of operating system platforms—including Microsoft Windows, Apple Macintosh, IBM OS/2, Linux, and several varieties of Unix. In addition, and perhaps more importantly, specially designed Java programs known as *applets* run in the context of Java-enabled web browsers, such as Netscape Navigator and Microsoft Internet Explorer.

> **NOTE**   Java is distributed by JavaSoft, a part of Sun Microsystems, as the Java Development Kit (JDK), a complete set of tools for developing Java applications. The latest version of the JDK can be obtained from JavaSoft via its website; browse the URL `www.java.sun.com/products/` and follow the appropriate links.

The Java Virtual Machine (JVM) is the key to Java's platform-independence. The JVM provides a machine-independent and operating system–independent platform for the execution of Java code. This program runs on your host operating system (OS) or is embedded in a browser. The JVM executes Java programs that are compiled into the JVM bytecode. This bytecode is the native machine language of the JVM and does not vary among JVM implementations.

When Java is ported to a new platform, be it an OS or a browser, the JVM itself is ported, yet its interface to compiled Java programs remains the same. The code required to port the JVM to the host OS or browser varies from system to system. In addition to the JVM, this code is required to port the Java application programming interface (API). The Java API is a common set of software packages that all Java implementations support. Much of the API is written in Java and runs on the JVM; however, some parts of the API, such as the windowing and networking software, are written in C++. The JVM, together with the additional software required to support the Java API, is referred to as the *Java Runtime Environment (JRE)*.

Java Is Object Oriented

Java is an object-oriented language and provides all of the benefits of object-oriented programming: classification, inheritance, object composition, encapsulation, and polymorphism. Java supports single inheritance but not multiple inheritance; however, it provides the interface construct that can be used to obtain the benefits of multiple inheritance without having to deal with any of its drawbacks.

NOTE   Refer to Chapter 5, "Working with Objects," for a complete discussion of object-oriented programming concepts.

Java Is Familiar

One of the most striking characteristics of Java, at least from a programmer's perspective, is its familiarity. Java is based on C++ and retains much of its syntax. This makes the language very easy to learn for C++ programmers. Because JavaScript is also based on both C++ and Java, Java's syntax will be easy for you to learn. However, because Java is a full object-*oriented* language (as opposed to an object-*based* language, like JavaScript), you will have to learn some additional programming constructs.

Java Is Simpler and Reliable

Although Java is based on C++, it is simpler and easier to use. This is because the designers of Java eliminated many of the complex and dangerous features of C++, such as pointers and address manipulation. By doing so, Java's designers also increased its overall reliability, making it an attractive language for mission-critical applications.

The Java API Supports Window and Network Programming

Another attractive feature of Java is the extensive API that comes as a standard part of the Java Developer's Kit (JDK). The API provides portable libraries for the development of window- and network-based programs. The same API is used to develop console-based programs, windowed programs, network clients and servers, applets, and fully distributed web-based applications. It also supports the development of multithreaded programs.

Java Supports Executable Web Content

The capability to develop applets for use in web applications is one of the most attractive features provided by Java. *Applets* are programs that execute in the context of a browser window; thus, they allow executable content to be embedded in a web page. This enables web pages to be more dynamic and interactive, and it greatly increases the number and types of web applications that can be supported.

NOTE   Chapter 1, "Learning the Fundamentals," presented applets within the context of a general introduction to client- and server-side web programming technologies. Chapter 5, "Working with Objects," discussed some of Java's object-oriented programming features.

Java Is Secure

The power and flexibility that applets provide requires ironclad security on the part of the Java runtime system. This high level of security is required to prevent malicious applets from disclosing or damaging the information stored on the user's computer. Java provides several levels of security protection. At the language level, Java has eliminated dangerous programming features such as pointers, memory allocation and deallocation operators, and automatic type conversion.

At the compiler level, the Java compiler performs extensive checks that prevent errors and ensure that the compiled code does not contain any inconsistencies that could allow objects to be accessed in ways other than explicitly allowed.

At the runtime level, the Java runtime system prevents applets from performing actions that could result in damage to or disclosure of information stored on your computer.

Java Is Free

Finally, if none of the above features is compelling enough to go with Java, Sun gives the JDK away for free—it is publicly available at JavaSoft's website www.java.sun.com/products/index.html.

Comparing Java and JavaScript

Although Java and JavaScript have similar names, there are a number of significant differences between the two languages. These differences do not make one language superior to the other—the features of both languages are well suited to their respective programming niches. For example, JavaScript is designed to supplement the capabilities of HTML with scripts that are capable of responding to web page events. As such, it has complete access to all aspects of the browser window. Java is designed to implement executable content that can be embedded in web pages. For this purpose, it is endowed with much more powerful programming capabilities. However, these capabilities are confined to a limited area of the browser window.

Java and JavaScript complement each other well. Java is the industrial-strength programming language for developing advanced web objects. JavaScript is the essential glue that combines HTML, Java applets, plug-ins, server-side programs, and other web components into fully integrated web applications. While Java's forte is in web component development, JavaScript excels at component integration. The following subsections identify the differences between these two languages. These discussions also show how the differences between Java and JavaScript enable each language to achieve its respective web programming goals.

Compiled versus Interpreted

The most obvious difference between Java and JavaScript is that Java is compiled and JavaScript is interpreted. As you would expect, there is a good reason for this difference.

The developers of Java intended that it be used to develop secure, high-performance web applications. The JVM executes compiled bytecodes rather than interpreting source Java statements. The bytecode instruction set is designed for quick and efficient execution, allowing Java to achieve performance comparable to native code compilers.

JavaScript, on the other hand, is intended to create scripts that can be embedded in HTML documents. These scripts control the way the documents are laid out and define functions to handle user events. JavaScript can be viewed as an extension to HTML that provides additional capabilities for browser and document control. From this perspective, it is important that JavaScript be included in HTML as source code so that the browser can inspect the code. This is the reason why it is an interpreted language instead of a compiled language, like Java.

 Although compiled JavaScript scripts would be inappropriate for web page development because of the need for cross-platform support, there is no reason why server-side scripts should not be compiled. To learn how Netscape's LiveWire tools provide a unique approach to integrating server-side scripts with web pages, see Chapter 33, "Scripting Netscape Servers," on the companion CD.

Object-Oriented versus Object-Based

Java and JavaScript differ in the degree to which they support object-oriented programming. Java is fully committed to object-oriented programming and supports all object-oriented programming features except multiple inheritance. Even so, Java's use of single inheritance combined with its interface construct provides the benefits of multiple inheritance while retaining the simple class structure that is characteristic of single inheritance. Java's commitment to object-oriented programming stems from the fact that it was originally intended to be used to develop software for consumer electronic devices. Full support of object-oriented programming is integral to the development of the simple and reliable software components that characterize these devices.

JavaScript does not share Java's commitment to object-oriented programming. JavaScript's approach is to take what's most useful from object-oriented programming and discard everything else. For example, JavaScript supports object types, instantiation, composition, reuse, and polymorphism, but it does not support classification and inheritance.

The reasons for JavaScript's pick-and-choose attitude towards object-oriented programming are based on the nature of the objects that JavaScript is compelled to support. Objects, such as windows, frames, documents, forms, and so on, are the reason for JavaScript's existence. These objects are accessed more effectively by using the document object model that was introduced in Chapter 5 than by using a pure object-oriented approach.

Strongly Typed versus Loosely Typed

JavaScript is a *loosely-typed* language and Java is a *strongly-typed* one. A *loosely-typed* language is one in which data of one type is automatically converted to another type during the runtime execution of a program or script. On the other hand, a *strongly-typed* language is one that flags inappropriate type conversions as errors instead of converting data types. Strongly-typed languages flag type-conversion errors during program compilation, loading, and execution.

Java focuses on the development of software that is secure and reliable. Strong typing is absolutely essential to achieving each of these goals. The ability to restrict operations on objects to only those that are explicitly defined is basic to Java's security approach. This control is needed to ensure that objects are not accessed in ways that circumvent the security checks imposed by the JVM.

Strong typing is also important to developing reliable software. Software reliability studies have repeatedly shown that automatic type conversion is a contributing factor in many common programming errors.

JavaScript's decision to go with loose typing can be viewed as a trade-off between expediency and reliability. This is characteristic of most scripting languages. By not enforcing strong typing, a scripting language confers more power and responsibility on the programmer. It says, "I'm going to permit you to perform this operation. It may be dangerous, but I trust your judgment."

JavaScript's support of loose typing is consistent with its role as a web scripting language. Rather than forcing you to clutter your scripts with the extra code needed to perform explicit type conversion, it automatically performs these conversions for you. This reduces the overall size of your scripts and lets you focus on the pertinent aspects of your web application.

Browser Window versus Full Browser Interaction

Perhaps the most important differences between Java and JavaScript lie in their different capabilities for interacting with the user, the browser, and the rest of the Web. These differences determine which applications each language can support.

Java applets are intended to be *embedded* in web pages, and their capabilities reflect this intent. Applets are assigned a limited area of the browser window in which they are allowed to interact with the user. Applets are not allowed to display information in other areas of the browser window or to respond to events that occur as the result of actions taken with respect to other window areas. This precludes Java from providing the controls for web page layout and event-handling support that we have seen are possible with JavaScript.

JavaScript scripts are not employed in the same manner as Java applets. JavaScript scripts are not confined to a limited area of the browser window; rather, they are allowed to control the display of an entire web page, to handle all events that occur with respect to a window, and to interact with other frames and windows. These total web-page control capabilities enable JavaScript to carry out its role of being the glue that integrates HTML, Java, plug-ins, and server-side scripts into complete web applications.

Even though JavaScript has considerably more latitude than Java in web page control, it is faced with similar security restrictions. Navigator and Internet Explorer prevent scripts that are loaded from one server from accessing the properties of documents that are loaded from other servers. This restriction prevents a script from accessing sensitive data entered in another frame or window and sending it to an arbitrary Internet host.

The Java Development Kit

In order to work the examples in this and later chapters, you will need to obtain and install a copy of the Java Development Kit (JDK) on your computer. The latest version of the JDK may be obtained by following the appropriate links from the JavaSoft home page at www.java.sun.com. Figure 27.1 shows the JavaSoft home page. It contains a number of useful links that you can follow to learn more about Java. The JDK is free to download, but make sure that you read and agree with Sun's license agreement before downloading the JDK. I use version 1.2.2 of the JDK for the examples in this chapter. This version has been renamed as Java 2.

FIGURE 27.1:

The JavaSoft home page

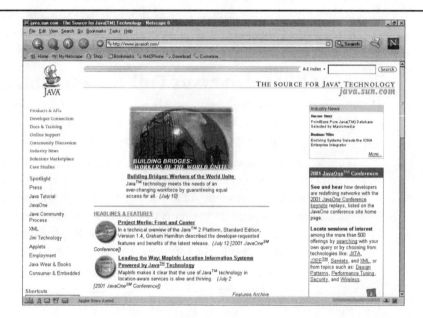

> **NOTE**   The examples in this book assume that you install the JDK in the directory `c:\jdk1.2.2` of your hard disk. I recommend that you install the JDK in this directory in order to avoid any problems in completing the examples.

Learning Java

Besides giving away the JDK for free, Sun wanted to make sure that you would be able to use it. They have included an extensive online tutorial at their website `www.java.sun.com/docs/books/tutorial/index.html`. I highly recommend that you take this tutorial if you intend to program in Java. Although Java is simple and easy to use, a complete introduction to Java is beyond the scope of this book. In this chapter, however, we will get you started by showing you how to develop a Java console program, a window program, and some applets. But first, we'll cover the Java API and differences between programs and applets.

The Java API

One of the benefits of using Java is that it comes with an extensive application programming interface (API). This API provides access to all of the objects and methods that you need to develop sophisticated window and network programs and Java applets. Sun provides excellent documentation for the Java API at its website (`www.java.sun.com/products/jdk/1.2/docs/api/index.html`). This documentation can be viewed online or downloaded to your computer.

Programs versus Applets

Java is a general-purpose programming language. You can use it to create web applets that run in the context of a web browser. But Java can also be used to develop stand-alone console and window programs that run independently of a browser and the Web. The term *console program* refers to text mode programs, such as DOS and Unix command-line programs, that do not use a windowing system, such as Microsoft Windows or the X Window System. Java *window programs* are distinguished from Microsoft Windows programs in that they can execute on Microsoft Windows, X Window System, Motif, and the Macintosh windowing system. In this section, you'll learn how to develop console and window programs and applets. In addition, later chapters will focus more on applets in particular.

Java is an easy programming language to learn—especially if you've already programmed in JavaScript. Start by browsing Sun's online Java tutorial to get a feel for the language and how it compares to JavaScript. You will find that Java's syntax is very similar to JavaScript's, but of course there are some differences between the two languages. In order to get you up and programming in Java, I'll list the most important differences here and then illustrate them in the programming examples covered in the following subsections.

Here are some of the primary differences between Java and JavaScript:

Building programs from classes   Java programs are built from *classes*. Classes are analogous to object types in JavaScript. Classes define *variables* (also called *fields*) and methods that correspond to JavaScript's properties and methods.

Organizing classes into packages   In Java, related classes are organized into *packages*. When you write a Java program, you can access previously defined classes by *importing* them into your program. JavaScript does not provide a similar capability.

The *main()* method   The main() method is the first method that is executed when you run a stand-alone Java program. JavaScript does not have a main() method.

Java Uses Variable Modifiers Java uses modifiers, like public and static, to identify additional properties of variables; JavaScript does not.

An Example Console Program

The traditional first program in any language displays the text *Hello World!*, with the objective being to create a small program that produces a visible result. In keeping with this tradition, Listing 27.1 shows the simplest possible Java program—a program that you'll soon create. Open an MS-DOS window and compile the program using the Java compiler as follows:

```
javac ConsolePrg.java
```

Then run the program using the following command line:

```
java ConsolePrg
```

It will display the text *Hello World!* to the console window.

Listing 27.1:   A Java Console Program (ConsolePrg.java)

```
import java.lang.System;
class ConsolePrg {
 public static void main (String args[]) {
  System.out.println("Hello World!");
 }
}
```

Now that you are a Java programmer, let's review the program's source code. It begins with an import statement, which imports the System class from the java.lang package into your program. By importing it, you make it available for use in your program.

Following the import statement is the declaration of the ConsolePrg class. This class declaration includes the remainder of the lines in this listing and ends with the last closing brace (}).

Within the ConsolePrg class, we define the main() method. This method is declared as public, static, and void. The public keyword identifies it as publicly accessible. The static keyword specifies that main() is used with the ConsolePrg class as a whole, rather than with an instance of the class. The void keyword identifies main() as not returning a value.

The one and only statement within main() prints the text *Hello World!* on the console window. It invokes the println() method for the out variable of the System class. The println() method is similar to the JavaScript writeln() method. The System.out variable identifies the console as the object to which the output is to be displayed. It is a standard variable provided by the System class.

In practice, `java.lang.System` (see the first line of Listing 27.1) is always imported, by default, regardless of whether it is identified in an import statement. The import statement was included in this example only so that we could cover it in the context of the first program.

An Example Windows Program

Now that you are a Java programmer and understand a little about Java programs, let's write a window-based version of the *Hello World!* program. It will quickly get you up to speed so that you can write stand-alone Java window programs.

Compile WindowsPrg.java (Listing 27.2) using the following statement,

```
javac WindowsPrg.java
```

and then run it using

```
java WindowsPrg
```

The program displays the window shown in Figure 27.2. Now we're making progress! When you've finished marveling at your creation, you can close it by clicking the X in the upper-right corner of the program's title bar.

Listing 27.2:   A Java Window Program (WindowsPrg.java)

```
import java.awt.*;
import java.awt.event.*;
public class WindowsPrg extends Frame {
 public static void main(String args[]){
  WindowsPrg program = new WindowsPrg();
 }
 public WindowsPrg() {
  super("A Java Windows Program");
  pack();
  setSize(500,250);
  addWindowListener(new WindowEventHandler());
  show();
 }
 public void paint(Graphics g) {
  g.setFont(new Font("TimesRoman",Font.BOLD+Font.ITALIC,48));
  g.setColor(Color.red);
  g.drawString("Hello World!",100,125);
 }
 class WindowEventHandler extends WindowAdapter {
  public void windowClosing(WindowEvent e){
   System.exit(0);
  }
 }
}
```

The program begins by importing java.awt.*; and java.awt.*;. This tells the Java compiler to import all classes in the java.awt and java.awt.event packages. These packages contain the classes used for window program development and event handling.

The class WindowsPrg is declared as a public class that extends the Frame class. The Frame class is a class of the java.awt package that defines the main window of an application program. Three methods and an inner class are declared in the WindowsPrg class, as discussed next.

The *main()* Method

The main() method is the first method to be executed when the WindowsPrg program is run. It creates an object of the WindowsPrg class and assigns it to the program variable. The program variable is declared as an object of the WindowsPrg class.

The *WindowsPrg()* Constructor

This is the constructor for the WindowsPrg class. Like all constructors, it does not specify a return value. It invokes the super() method to set the window's title bar to the text "A Java Windows Program". The super() method is a way of calling the constructor of WindowsPrg's parent class (Frame). The Frame() constructor takes a string as a parameter and displays it as the document's title. You may want to look up the description of the Frame class in the Java API.

WindowsPrg() then invokes the pack() method to pack the contents of the window. This is a standard method that is called when a window is constructed to place and organize any window components within the window. The window is resized to 500×250 pixels using the setSize() method. An event handler for the window-closing event is defined using the addWindowListener() method.

The window is displayed using the show() method. The pack(), setSize(), and show() methods are inherited from the Frame class by WindowsPrg.

The *paint()* Method

The paint() method is called to draw a window when it is initially displayed or needs to be redrawn. It takes a Graphics object as a parameter. The Graphics object is where the screen updates are drawn. The first statement invokes the setFont() method of the Graphics class to set the drawing font to 48-point, bold, and italic Times Roman. The Font() constructor is used to create this font. The second statement invokes the setColor() method to set the drawing color to red. The Color class provides a set of color constants. The third statement invokes the drawString() method to draw the text "Hello World!" on the screen at the offset (100,125) within the Graphics object.

The *WindowEventHandler* Class

The WindowEventHandler class is an inner class of WindowsPrg that is used to handle the event associated with the application window. It extends the WindowAdapter class, which provides default event handlers for window-related events. The windowClosing() method handles the closing of the application window by invoking the exit() method of the System class. This results in the program's termination.

An Example Applet

Now that you can develop Java window programs, you're ready to create an applet. Remember, applets execute in the context of a browser window. This means that you have to develop and compile the applet and then create an HTML document that displays the applet as part of a web page. Listing 27.3 contains the source code of an applet I've named *WebApp*. Compile it using the following statement:

```
javac WebApp.java
```

This creates the WebApp.class file, which is the compiled applet code.

NOTE   Make sure that your browser has Java enabled before trying to run the remaining examples in this chapter.

Listing 27.3:   A Java Applet (WebApp.java)

```
import java.awt.*;
import java.applet.*;
public class WebApp extends Applet {
 public void paint(Graphics g) {
  g.setFont(new Font("TimesRoman",Font.BOLD+Font.ITALIC,48));
  g.setColor(Color.red);
  g.drawString("Hello World!",50,100);
 }
}
```

The web.htm file shown in Listing 27.4 contains an HTML document that inserts the applet as part of a web page. Open web.htm with your browser. Figure 27.3 shows the web page that is displayed. The gray area of the web page is the applet's display area. I purposely set the document's background to white so that the applet would stand out.

Listing 27.4:   An HTML File That Displays a Java Applet (web.htm)

```
<HTML>
<HEAD>
<TITLE>A Java Applet</TITLE>
</HEAD>
<BODY BGCOLOR="white">
<APPLET CODE="WebApp.class" WIDTH=400 HEIGHT=200>
[WebApp applet]
</APPLET>
</BODY>
</HTML>
```

FIGURE 27.3:

A Java applet

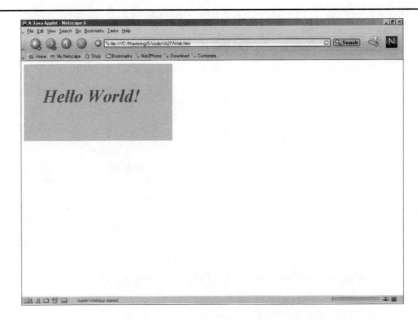

The <applet> tag shown in Listing 27.4 contains three attributes: CODE, WIDTH, and HEIGHT. The CODE attribute identifies the Java bytecode file of the applet to be loaded. The WIDTH and HEIGHT attributes identify the dimensions of the applet's display area. Any text between the <applet> and </applet> tags is displayed by browsers that are not capable of or configured to handle applets. A non–Java-capable browser would display the phrase [WebApp applet] in place of the applet.

The applet's code will be easy to follow because you've used the same methods in the earlier window programming example. In fact, applets use many of the standard java.awt window classes. The classes of the java.applet package are imported in addition to the java.awt classes. The WebApp class is declared as a class that extends the Applet class. The Applet class is the common ancestor of all applet classes in the Java class hierarchy.

The WebApp class does not define a main() method. This is because it is not a stand-alone program. It defines the paint() method to draw the Graphics object of the applet display area. The paint() method works in the same way as for window programs. The three statements contained in the paint() method are identical to those of the window program presented in the previous section except that the text is drawn at location (50,100) instead of (100,125).

LiveConnect and the Internet Explorer Object Model

Netscape Navigator 3 was the first browser to support communication between JavaScript and Java. This capability was named LiveConnect by Netscape. LiveConnect also supports communication with Navigator plug-ins. Microsoft implemented most of the features of LiveConnect in Internet Explorer 4. However, Microsoft did much more than simply re-implement LiveConnect. In its Internet Explorer Object Model, Microsoft provided the capability for scripts, applets, and ActiveX components to be seamlessly integrated within the context of a web page. Chapter 28, "Scripting ActiveX Components," shows how ActiveX components can be used with scripts and applets.

Accessing Java Methods from within JavaScript

One of the easiest ways to use Java in JavaScript is to invoke Java methods directly in your scripts. For example, consider the following Java statement, which displays the text *Hello World!* to the Java console window:

```
java.lang.System.out.println("Hello World!")
```

Using Netscape Navigator, you can execute this statement directly from within a JavaScript script, as shown in Listing 27.5 (console.htm). To see how this script works, open console.htm with Navigator 4 or later. It will display the web page shown in Figure 27.4. To view the Java console window, select Tools ➢ Java Console from the Communicator pull-down menu. The window shown in Figure 27.5 will be displayed.

NOTE   Because this approach only works with Navigator, I do not recommend using it in your web applications.

> **Listing 27.5:   Calling Java Methods (console.htm)**

```
<HTML>
<HEAD>
<TITLE>Calling Java Methods</TITLE>
</HEAD>
<BODY>
<P>This script writes the text, <EM>Hello World!</EM>
 to the Java console window.</P>
<SCRIPT LANGUAGE="JavaScript"><!--
java.lang.System.out.println("Hello World!")
// --></SCRIPT>
</BODY>
</HTML>
```

FIGURE 27.4:

The browser window
(Listing 27.5)

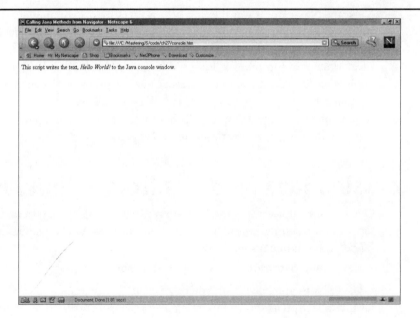

FIGURE 27.5:

The Java console window
(Listing 27.5)

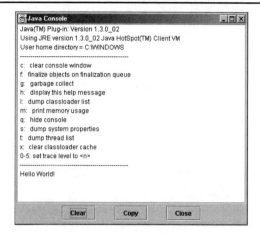

Accessing Applets from within JavaScript

As you learned in the previous section, accessing Java methods from within JavaScript is easy. When it comes to accessing the methods and variables of *applets* from within your JavaScript scripts, however, the following steps must be taken:

1. The applet methods and variables to be accessed must be declared as `public`.

2. The applet must be loaded before it can be accessed.

3. The applet must be accessed using JavaScript's `applet` object.

By simply following the above three steps, you'll be able to access the methods and properties of applets in your scripts. In addition to the above three steps, if you are using Navigator 4.*x* or later, Netscape recommends that the applet be compiled with the Netscape `java40.jar` file in your CLASSPATH. This file contains packages that provide additional security and allow Java applets to access JavaScript objects. In practice, you do not need to compile your applets with `java40.jar` unless you want to access JavaScript objects from within your applets.

NOTE   Your scripts can also use "faceless" applets, which do not display GUI output but can be used to perform internal computations.

Declaring Public Classes, Methods, and Variables

In order to access a method or variable used by an applet, the method or variable must be declared as `public` and must be declared as part of a `public` class. In practice, this is easy to accomplish—you use the `public` keyword in the class, method, or variable declaration. Listing 27.6 provides an example of an applet that displays a text string within its applet window. The `setText()` method is declared as `public`, making it accessible to JavaScript code. This method is used to change the text that is displayed by the applet. Note that the `FancyText` subclass of `applet` is also declared as `public`.

Listing 27.6:   An Applet That Displays Text (FancyText.java)

```
import java.applet.*;
import java.awt.*;
public class FancyText extends Applet {
 String text="I like Java!";
 Font font = new Font("TimesRoman",Font.BOLD+Font.ITALIC,36);
 public void paint(Graphics g) {
  g.setFont(font);
  g.drawString(text,30,30);
 }
 public void setText(String s) {
  text=s;
  repaint();
 }
}
```

Loading an Applet

An applet must be completely loaded before you can access its variables and methods. Although there is no `onLoad` event defined for the `applet` object, you can use the `window` object's `onLoad` event handler by specifying it in a document's `<body>` tag.

Consider the example shown in Listing 27.7. This example loads the applet shown in Listing 27.6. The `onLoad` event handler invokes the `accessApplet()` function after the document (and therefore the applet) has been loaded. I'll complete the discussion of Listing 27.7 after covering the `applet` object in the next section.

Listing 27.7:   Loading and Accessing an Applet (use-app1.htm)

```
<HTML>
<HEAD>
<TITLE>Accessing Applets</TITLE>
<SCRIPT LANGUAGE="JavaScript"><!--
function accessApplet() {
 setTimeout("changeText('I like JavaScript!')",2000)
 setTimeout("changeText('I like JavaScript and Java!')",4000)
```

```
   setTimeout("changeText('I like Java!')",6000)
   setTimeout("accessApplet()",8000)
  }
  function changeText(s) {
   window.document.fancyText.setText(s)
  }
  // --></SCRIPT>
  </HEAD>
  <BODY onLoad="accessApplet()">
  <APPLET CODE="FancyText.class" NAME="fancyText"
   WIDTH=450 HEIGHT=150>
  [The FancyText Applet]
  </APPLET>
  </BODY>
  </HTML>
```

Using the *applet* Object

The `applet` object is provided by JavaScript to enable JavaScript code to access Java variables and methods. This object has a single property—the `name` property—and no methods or event handlers. The `name` property is used to access the `name` attribute of the `<applet>` tag.

The `applet` object is a property of the `document` object. Individual applets can be accessed by name. For example, in the `changeText()` function of Listing 27.7, the following statement

```
window.document.fancyText.setText(s)
```

is used to invoke the `setText()` method of the applet named *fancyText*.

The `applets` array is also a property of the `document` object. This array provides access to all applets that are defined for a particular document.

My FancyText Example

Listings 27.6 and 27.7 provide a complete example of how JavaScript code is able to access a Java applet. To run this example, compile `FancyText.java` with your Java compiler. This will produce the `FancyText.class` bytecode file.

`FancyText.class` is loaded via the `<applet>` tag shown in Listing 27.7. The applet is named *fancyText*. When the `use-app1.htm` file is loaded, the `accessApplet()` function is invoked to handle the `onLoad` event. This function sets four timeouts. The first timeout invokes `changeText()` after two seconds, passing it the `I like JavaScript!` string. The second timeout invokes `changeText()` after four seconds, passing it the `I like JavaScript and Java!` string. The third timeout invokes `changeText()` after six seconds, passing it the `I like Java!` string. Finally, the fourth timeout invokes `accessApplet()` after eight seconds to cause the entire process to be repeated.

The `changeText()` function invokes the `setText()` method of the `FancyText` class defined in Listing 27.6. It uses `setText()` to change the text displayed by the applet.

To see the effect of using the JavaScript of Listing 27.7 with the Java of Listing 27.6, open
use-app1.htm with your browser. Your browser will initially display the text shown in
Figure 27.6. After two seconds, your browser will display the text shown in Figure 27.7. After
two more seconds, your browser will display the text shown in Figure 27.8.

FIGURE 27.6:

Initial text display
(Listing 27.7)

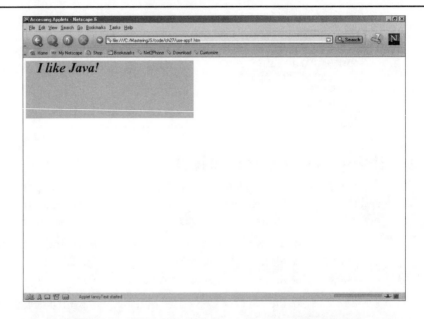

FIGURE 27.7:

The display after two
seconds (Listing 27.7)

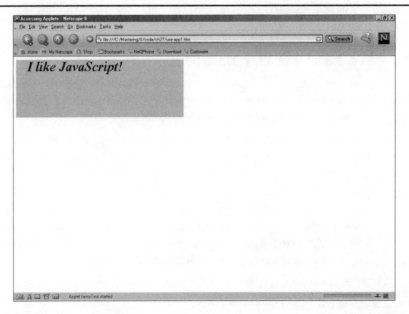

FIGURE 27.8:

The display after four seconds (Listing 27.7)

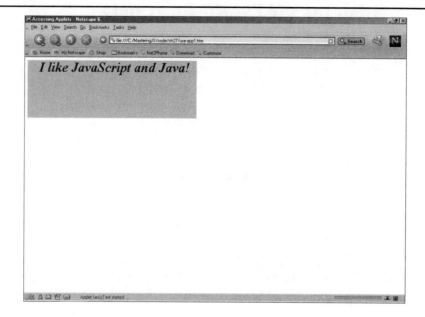

Using JavaScript in an Applet

So far, you have learned how to access and control Java applets from within JavaScript. But what if you want to do the converse, that is, access JavaScript objects and functions from within an applet? Both LiveConnect and the Internet Explorer Object Model provide an interface between Java and JavaScript that allows you to do this. However, as with JavaScript-to-Java communication, there are a few steps involved:

1. Use the MAYSCRIPT attribute of the <applet> tag to permit an applet to access a script.

2. Import the netscape.javascript package in your applet. You must do this even if the script is to run in Internet Explorer.

3. Create a handle to a JavaScript window using the JSObject class and the getWindow() method.

4. Use the getMember() method of the JSObject class to obtain access to JavaScript objects.

5. Use the eval() method of the JSObject class to invoke JavaScript methods.

These steps are covered in the following subsections.

Using the *MAYSCRIPT* Attribute

For an applet to be able to access a JavaScript object or function, the applet must be given explicit permission to do so. This prevents the applet from modifying other areas of a web page without the web page designer knowing about it. The MAYSCRIPT attribute must be placed in the `<applet>` tag to allow an applet to access JavaScript. If an applet tries to access JavaScript without the MAYSCRIPT attribute being specified, then the applet will generate an exception, display an error message, and stop running. In Listing 27.8, the ReadForm applet is loaded and given permission to access JavaScript objects and functions.

Listing 27.8:   Accessing JavaScript from an Applet (use-app2.htm)

```
<HTML>
<HEAD>
<TITLE>Accessing JavaScript from an applet</TITLE>
</HEAD>
<BODY>
<FORM NAME="textForm">
<P>Enter some text and then click Display Text:
 <INPUT TYPE="text" NAME="textField" SIZE="20"></P>
</FORM>
<APPLET CODE="ReadForm.class" WIDTH=400 HEIGHT=100
 NAME="readApp" MAYSCRIPT>
[The ReadForm Applet]
</APPLET>
</BODY>
</HTML>
```

Importing *netscape.javascript*

In order for an applet to access JavaScript objects and functions, it must import the JSObject and JSException classes of the netscape.javascript package. The import statements shown in Listing 27.9 may be used to import these classes. You only need to import JSException if you plan to handle this exception within your applet. The use of JSObject in Java-to-JavaScript communication is covered in the following sections.

NOTE   The file `java40.jar` must be in your CLASSPATH in order to access the `netscape.javascript` package.

WARNING   In some cases, importing `netscape.javascript.*;` may lead to a compilation error. To avoid this problem, import `JSObject` and `JSException` via separate import statements as shown in Listing 27.9.

> **Listing 27.9:   Reading a JavaScript Form (ReadForm.java)**

```java
import java.applet.*;
import java.awt.*;
import java.awt.event.*;
import netscape.javascript.JSObject;
import netscape.javascript.JSException;
public class ReadForm extends Applet {
 String text="Enter some text for me to display!";
 Font font = new Font("TimesRoman",Font.BOLD+Font.ITALIC,24);
 JSObject win, doc, form, textField;
 public void init() {
  win = JSObject.getWindow(this);
  doc = (JSObject) win.getMember("document");
  form = (JSObject) doc.getMember("textForm");
  textField = (JSObject) form.getMember("textField");
  setLayout(new BorderLayout());
  Panel buttons = new Panel();
  Button displayTextButton = new Button("Display Text");
  displayTextButton.addActionListener(new ButtonEventHandler());
  buttons.add(displayTextButton);
  add("South",buttons);
 }
 public void paint(Graphics g) {
  g.setFont(font);
  g.drawString(text,30,30);
 }
 class ButtonEventHandler implements ActionListener {
  public void actionPerformed(ActionEvent e){
   String s = e.getActionCommand();
   if("Display Text".equals(s)) {
    text= (String) textField.getMember("value");
    win.eval("alert(\"This alert comes from Java!\")");
    repaint();
   }
  }
 }
}
```

Creating a Handle to a JavaScript Window

When you access JavaScript methods and functions from within Java, one of the first things that you'll want to do is gain access to the JavaScript window object associated with the window in which the applet is loaded. By doing so, you'll be able to access other objects (document, form, image) that are created in the Navigator instance hierarchy.

To access the JavaScript `window` object, declare a variable of type `JSObject` and use the `getWindow()` method of the `JSObject` class to assign the `window` object to the variable. For example, in Listing 27.9 the `win` variable is declared as class `JSObject`. The first statement in the `init()` method of the `ReadForm` class assigns the `window` object to the `win` variable. The `this` parameter that is passed to the `getWindow()` method causes `getWindow()` to return the `window` object associated with the window containing the applet.

Using *getMember()*

The `getMember()` method of the `JSObject` class is used to access objects and values that are properties of a `JSObject` object. This method takes a `String` argument that identifies the object or value to be accessed. For example, in the `init()` method of Listing 27.9, the following lines of code use `getMember()` to access objects that are properties of other JavaScript objects:

```
doc = (JSObject) win.getMember("document");
form = (JSObject) doc.getMember("textForm");
textField = (JSObject) form.getMember("textField");
```

The first statement invokes `getMember()` for the `win` variable used to reference the current document window. The `"document"` string is passed as an argument. `getMember()` returns the JavaScript object corresponding to `window.document` and assigns it to the `doc` variable. The `doc`, `form`, and `textField` variables are all declared as class `JSObject` in the beginning of the definition of the `ReadForm` class.

In the second statement, `getMember()` is invoked for `doc` and returns the JavaScript object corresponding to `window.document.textForm`. This object is the form that was defined in Listing 27.4. It is assigned to the `form` variable.

The third statement invokes `getMember()` for the `form` variable. `getMember()` returns the JavaScript object `window.document.textForm.textField`. This object is assigned to the `textField` variable.

In the `actionPerformed()` method of Listing 27.9, the following statement is used to retrieve the value of an HTML text field and assign it to the Java `text` variable:

```
text= (String) textField.getMember("value");
```

Notice that in this statement, the value returned by `getMember()` is coerced into a value of the `String` class via the `(String)` type cast operator.

Using *eval()*

The eval() method of the JSObject class is used to invoke a method of a JavaScript object and make the value returned by the method available to a Java variable. It is used in the actionPerformed() method of Listing 27.9 to display the alert dialog box:

```
win.eval("alert(\"This alert comes from Java!\")");
```

Note that double quotes should be replaced by their escape character sequence \" when used as arguments to a method that is being evaluated.

Reading Values Entered in a Form

Now that you've covered the basics of Java-to-JavaScript communication, let's walk through the example provided by Listings 27.8 and 27.9.

Open use-app2.htm with your browser. It displays the web page shown in Figure 27.9. Type *Hello JavaScript!* in the form's text field and click the Display Text button. The Java applet generates the alert dialog box shown in Figure 27.10. After you've clicked OK, the applet uses JavaScript to read the text you typed into the HTML form and displays it in the applet area of the window, as shown in Figure 27.11. This small example shows how Java, JavaScript, and HTML can communicate to produce an interesting web page effect.

FIGURE 27.9:

Accessing JavaScript from an applet (Listing 27.8)

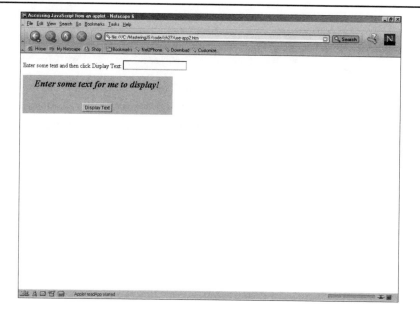

FIGURE 27.10:

Java generates a JavaScript
alert dialog box.
(Listing 27.8)

FIGURE 27.11:

Java uses JavaScript to read
the HTML form and dis-
plays its value in the
applet window area.
(Listing 27.8)

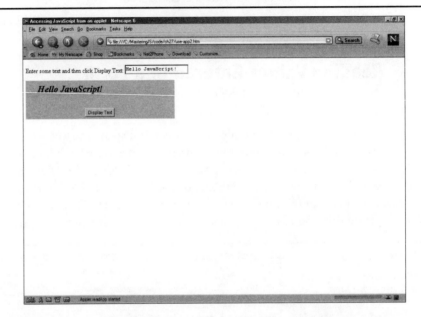

The HTML file shown earlier in Listing 27.8 combines a simple form with the ReadForm applet. No JavaScript code is used in the file. The applet shown in Listing 27.9 accesses the HTML form via the JavaScript objects that are automatically created by your browser. Note that the win, doc, form, and textField variables are declared as class JSObject. These variables are used with the getWindow() and getMember() methods to provide access to the text field of the form. The actionPerformed() method handles the clicking of the Display Text button and uses the eval() method to display the JavaScript alert dialog box.

Other *JSObject* Methods

The JSObject class provides other methods besides getWindow(), getMember(), and eval(). Table 27.1 contains a complete list of the JSObject methods.

TABLE 27.1: Methods of the JSObject Class

Method	Description
call(String, Object[])	Invokes the JavaScript method specified by String and passes it the arguments specified in Object[]
eval(String)	Invokes the JavaScript method specified by String
finalize()	Decrements the reference count on a JavaScript object
getMember(String)	Returns the object or value specified by String
getSlot(int)	Returns the object array element specified by int
getWindow(Applet)	Returns the window containing the specified Applet
removeMember(String)	Removes the object specified by String
setMember(String, Object)	Sets the object specified by String to the value specified by Object
setSlot(int,Object)	Sets the value of the object array element specified by int to the value specified by Object
toString()	Converts the JSObject to a String value

GraphIt!

JavaScript and Java provide complementary capabilities for web page development:

- JavaScript provides a way to control the entire browser window.

- Java provides a capability to execute advanced programs within a limited area of the browser window.

- LiveConnect and the Internet Explorer Object Model provide the capability to link events that occur in the larger JavaScript-controlled window area to the Java methods that control the applet's operation.

The example presented in this section shows how JavaScript can easily interface with and make use of Java components. This example creates a web application called *GraphIt!*, which allows a user to specify points to be plotted on a graph. The user types the coordinates of individual points he or she wishes to have included on the graph, and the applet draws line segments to connect the points. *GraphIt!* connects points according to their X coordinates, starting with the leftmost point and moving to the right. If two points have the same X coordinate, the applet connects to the lower point before drawing a line to the higher one. The user can also direct *GraphIt!* to remove a point from the graph; after it has done this, it redraws to show the new result.

The *GraphIt!* example illustrates the symbiosis between JavaScript and Java. The applet designer, on the one hand, is free to design the applet without having to develop an explicit control interface; all they have to do is provide methods for adding and deleting points of the graph. The web page designer, on the other hand, is able to use the applet without having to figure out the details of its operation; all they have to do is learn how to use the methods for adding and deleting points.

To see how the example works, open `graph.htm` (Listing 27.10) with your browser. The web page displayed by your browser should look like Figure 27.12. The drawing area shows the intersection of X and Y axes. Initially, the drawing area extends to +1 and -1 in each axis direction.

FIGURE 27.12:

The top portion of the initial graph display (`graph.htm`)

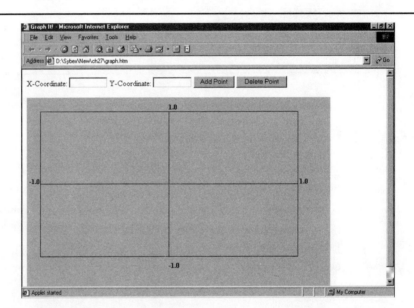

Perform the following steps to see *GraphIt!* in action:

1. For the first point on the graph, enter **2** in the X-Coordinate text field and **1** in the Y-Coordinate text field to indicate the point (2,1). Then, click the Add Point button. Because the graph contains only one point so far, no line is displayed, but the drawing area is automatically rescaled to accommodate this point. Refer to Figure 27.13.

FIGURE 27.13:

When you add a first point (2,1), the drawing area automatically rescales to include the point. (Listing 27.10)

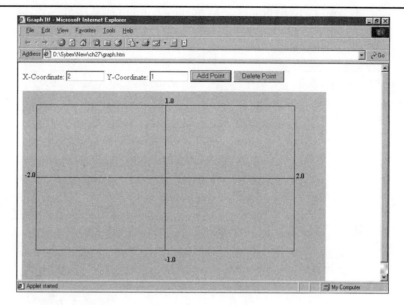

2. Now add a second point (-2,-3) by entering **-2** and **-3** in the text fields. Then, click Add Point. Notice how the drawing area is rescaled again to accommodate the greater value along the Y axis. Also, a line is drawn that connects the two points, as shown in Figure 27.14.

FIGURE 27.14:

The drawing area is rescaled again after adding (2,1) and (-2,-3). The graph begins to take shape, with a line drawn to connect the two points. (Listing 27.10)

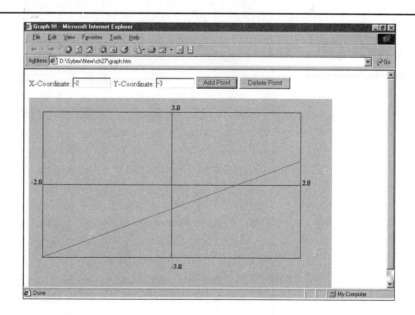

3. Add a third point (-1,1), as shown in Figure 27.15. Note how the graph is automatically updated to include this point. Because it connects the points in left-to-right, bottom-to-top order, it connects the point (-2,3) to (-1,1) and then connects (-1,1) to (2,1).

FIGURE 27.15:

The graph now connects all three points the user has entered: (2,1), (-2,-3), and (-1,1). (Listing 27.10)

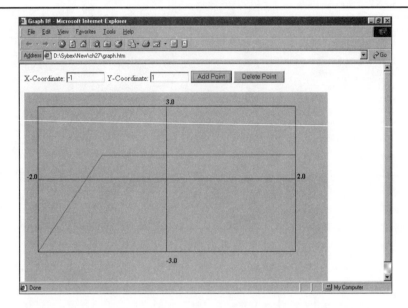

4. Now add the following points, one at a time: (3,-2), (4,2), (-4,1), (-6,-3), and (6,2). Your browser should look like that shown in Figure 27.16.

FIGURE 27.16:

The graph connecting (2,1), (-2,-3), (-1,1), (3,-2), (4,2), (-4,1), (-6,-3), and (6,2) (Listing 27.10)

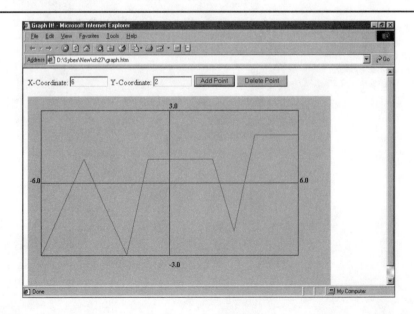

5. To see how the Delete Point feature works, delete the point (3,-2) by entering the coordinates in the text fields and clicking the Delete Point button. The results are shown in Figure 27.17. Compare this to the graph shown in Figure 27.16; notice how the graph was redrawn to eliminate the deleted point.

FIGURE 27.17:

The graph after deleting (3,-2) (Listing 27.10)

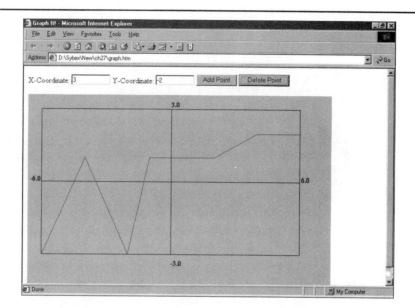

The graph.htm file is shown in Listing 27.10. It creates a simple form for specifying the points that are to be added and deleted from a graph. The addPoint() and deletePoint() functions handle the onClick events associated with the Add Point and Delete Point buttons. The addPoint() function reads the X and Y coordinates entered by the user, converts them to floating point, and passes them to the addPoint() method of the GraphApp class. The deletePoint() function interfaces with the deletePoint() method of the GraphApp class in a similar manner.

Listing 27.10:   A Graph Control Form (graph.htm)

```
<HTML>
<HEAD>
<TITLE>Graph It!</TITLE>
<SCRIPT LANGUAGE="JavaScript"><!--
function addPoint() {
 var x=parseFloat(window.document.xy.x.value)
 var y=parseFloat(window.document.xy.y.value)
 window.document.graph.addPoint(x,y)
}
```

```
function deletePoint() {
 var x=parseFloat(window.document.xy.x.value)
 var y=parseFloat(window.document.xy.y.value)
 window.document.graph.deletePoint(x,y)
}
// --></SCRIPT>
</HEAD>
<BODY>
<FORM NAME="xy">
X-Coordinate: <INPUT TYPE="text" NAME="x" SIZE="10">
Y-Coordinate: <INPUT TYPE="text" NAME="y" SIZE="10">
<INPUT TYPE="button" VALUE="Add Point"
 onClick="addPoint()">
<INPUT TYPE="button" VALUE="Delete Point"
 onClick="deletePoint()">
</FORM>
<APPLET CODE="GraphApp.class" NAME="graph" WIDTH=650 HEIGHT=400>
[Graph applet]
</APPLET>
</BODY>
</HTML>
```

The GraphApp.java file, shown in Listing 27.11, defines three classes: FloatPoint, PointSet, and GraphApp. The first one, FloatPoint, is used for storing two-dimensional floating-point coordinates. The second class, PointSet, is used for manipulating and graphing sets of points. (I'll present this class's functions below.) The third class, GraphApp, implements the basic applet code. It creates an object of class PointSet and uses addPoint() and deletePoint() for adding and deleting points to the PointSet object. The paint() method invokes the displayGraph() method of the PointSet class to draw the graph.

Listing 27.11: The Graphing Applet (GraphApp.java)

```
import java.applet.*;
import java.awt.*;
import java.util.*;

class FloatPoint {
 public float x;
 public float y;
 public FloatPoint(float x,float y) {
  this.x=x;
  this.y=y;
 }
 public String xVal() {
  return String.valueOf(x);
 }
 public String yVal() {
  return String.valueOf(y);
```

```
  }
}

class PointSet {
 Vector v = new Vector();
 int xUL, yUL, width, height, xOrig, yOrig, numPoints;
 float xMin, xMax, yMin, yMax, xDelta, yDelta;
 public void add(FloatPoint p) {
  for(int i=0;i<v.size();++i) {
   FloatPoint q=(FloatPoint) v.elementAt(i);
   if(q.x==p.x && q.y==p.y) return;
  }
  v.addElement(p);
 }
 public void delete(FloatPoint p) {
  for(int i=0;i<v.size();++i) {
   FloatPoint q=(FloatPoint) v.elementAt(i);
   if(q.x==p.x && q.y==p.y){
    v.removeElementAt(i);
    break;
   }
  }
 }
 public void displayGraph(Graphics g) {
  updateGraphParameters();
  drawGraphBox(g);
  drawAxes(g);
  labelAxes(g);
  drawPoints(g);
 }
 public void updateGraphParameters() {
  xUL=30;
  yUL=30;
  width=550;
  height=300;
  xOrig=xUL+(width/2);
  yOrig=yUL+(height/2);
  numPoints=v.size();
  if(numPoints==0){
   xMax=1;
   yMax=1;
  }else if(numPoints==1){
   FloatPoint p=(FloatPoint) v.firstElement();
   xMax=Math.abs(p.x);
   yMax=Math.abs(p.y);
  }else{
   FloatPoint p=(FloatPoint) v.firstElement();
   xMax=Math.abs(p.x);
   yMax=Math.abs(p.y);
   for(int i=0;i<numPoints;++i) {
    p=(FloatPoint) v.elementAt(i);
```

```
   if(Math.abs(p.x)>xMax) xMax=Math.abs(p.x);
   if(Math.abs(p.y)>yMax) yMax=Math.abs(p.y);
  }
 }
 xDelta=xMax*2;
 yDelta=yMax*2;
 xMin=-xMax;
 yMin=-yMax;
}
public void drawGraphBox(Graphics g) {
 g.drawRect(xUL-1,yUL-1,width+2,height+2);
}
public void drawAxes(Graphics g) {
 g.drawLine(xUL,yOrig,xUL+width,yOrig);
 g.drawLine(xOrig,yUL,xOrig,yUL+height);
}
public void labelAxes(Graphics g) {
 g.setFont(new Font("TimesRoman",Font.BOLD,14));
 int offset1=5;
 int offset2=25;
 g.drawString(String.valueOf(xMin),xUL-offset2,yOrig);
 g.drawString(String.valueOf(xMax),xUL+width+offset1,yOrig);
 g.drawString(String.valueOf(yMax),xOrig,yUL-offset1);
 g.drawString(String.valueOf(yMin),xOrig,yUL+height+offset2);
}
public void drawPoints(Graphics g) {
 sortPoints();
 Vector vTrans = new Vector();
 for(int i=0;i<numPoints;++i) {
  FloatPoint p = (FloatPoint) v.elementAt(i);
  int xTrans=xOrig;
  int yTrans=yOrig;
  xTrans+=Math.round(((float)width/2.0)*(p.x/xMax));
  yTrans-=Math.round(((float)height/2.0)*(p.y/yMax));
  vTrans.addElement(new Point(xTrans,yTrans));
 }
 Color currentColor = g.getColor();
 for(int i=0;i<numPoints-1;++i) {
  Point p1=(Point) vTrans.elementAt(i);
  Point p2=(Point) vTrans.elementAt(i+1);
  g.setColor(Color.red);
  g.drawLine(p1.x,p1.y,p2.x,p2.y);
 }
 g.setColor(currentColor);
}
public void sortPoints() {
 boolean again=true;
 while (again) {
  again=false;
  for(int i=0;i<numPoints-1;++i) {
   FloatPoint p1=(FloatPoint) v.elementAt(i);
```

```
    FloatPoint p2=(FloatPoint) v.elementAt(i+1);
    if(p2.x<p1.x || (p2.x==p1.x && p2.y<p1.y)){
     v.setElementAt(p2,i);
     v.setElementAt(p1,i+1);
     again=true;
    }
   }
  }
 }
}

public class GraphApp extends Applet {
 PointSet ps=new PointSet();
 public void paint(Graphics g) {
  ps.displayGraph(g);
 }
 public void addPoint(float x,float y) {
  FloatPoint p=new FloatPoint(x,y);
  ps.add(p);
  repaint();
 }
 public void deletePoint(float x,float y) {
  FloatPoint p=new FloatPoint(x,y);
  ps.delete(p);
  repaint();
 }
}
```

The variables and methods of the `PointSet` class are as follows:

The *v* variable   This variable is assigned a `Vector` object that is used to store the points added by the user.

The *xUL* and *yUL* variables   These variables specify the location of the upper-left corner of the graph with respect to the upper-left corner of the applet window.

The *width* and *height* variables   These variables identify the dimensions of the graph in pixels.

The *xOrig* and *yOrig* variables   These variables identify the location of the point (0,0) on the graph.

The *numPoints* variable   This variable identifies the number of points in the graph.

The *xMin, xMax, yMin*, and *yMax* variables   These variables identify the minimum and maximum coordinates of the points to be included in the graph. These values are used to rescale the graph to automatically accommodate newly added points.

The *xDelta* and *yDelta* variables   These variables identify the range of points that are to be included along each axis. (Note that X and Y axes are not of the same scale.)

The *add()* method   This method adds a point to v.

The *delete()* method   This method deletes a point from v.

The *displayGraph()* method   This method invokes the following five methods to display the graph:

UpdateGraphParameters()   This method sets the values of xUL, yUL, width, height, xOrig and yOrig. It then calculates the values of xMax, yMax, xMin, yMin, xDelta, and yDelta based upon the points entered by the user.

drawGraphBox()   This method draws the drawing area—the rectangle surrounding the graph area.

drawAxes()   This method draws X and Y axes.

labelAxes()   This method displays the values of the X and Y axes at their intersections with the graph boundary.

drawPoints()   This method invokes sortPoints() to sort v and then creates the vTrans vector to translate the absolute coordinates to points within the Graphics object on which the graph is to be displayed. It then draws a line between consecutive points of the vTrans vector.

The *sortPoints()* method   This method sorts the points contained in the v Vector object from left to right and bottom to top.

Summary

In this chapter, you were introduced to Java and learned about its capabilities. You covered the similarities and differences between Java and JavaScript, and you learned how to develop simple Java programs and applets. You also learned how to use JavaScript to communicate with Java applets and how to invoke JavaScript functions from within an applet. In the next chapter, you'll learn about ActiveX and how Internet Explorer supports communication between JavaScript, Java applets, and ActiveX components.

CHAPTER 28

Scripting ActiveX Components

- What is ActiveX?

- Using ActiveX components

- Accessing ActiveX components from within JScript

ActiveX is an approach to developing and using software components that is supported by Microsoft Windows. It is an extension of the Object Linking and Embedding (OLE) and Component Object Model (COM) technologies that were developed for Windows 3.1, and it enables these technologies to be used with web applications. In this chapter, you'll learn the basics of ActiveX, how to use ActiveX components in your web applications, and how to script ActiveX components using JScript. When you finish this chapter, you'll be able to integrate ActiveX components with your scripts.

WARNING   With a few minor exceptions, the use of ActiveX components is limited to Internet Explorer.

What Is ActiveX?

As I mentioned in this chapter's introduction, ActiveX is an extension of the OLE and COM technologies that were developed for Windows 3.1. To understand ActiveX, you must understand how it evolved from these earlier technologies. Microsoft developed OLE to simplify the process by which Windows programs could exchange information. OLE was created to enable objects that were developed in one program to be displayed and edited in others. For example, it enables an Excel spreadsheet to be pasted into a Word document and then displayed and edited from within the Word document.

This document-centric approach to object sharing is organized according to the program in which an object is embedded, called the *OLE container*, and the program that creates the embedded object, called the *OLE server*. In the example of the embedded Excel spreadsheet, Excel would be the OLE server, and Word would be the OLE container.

After having developed and deployed OLE in Windows 3.1, Microsoft realized that embedding objects within documents was only one aspect of the more general problem of how software components should interact in a client-server framework. Based on this realization, Microsoft developed COM, which enables software components to communicate and exchange services. Because of COM's power and flexibility, it quickly emerged as the foundation for Windows software components.

In 1996, ActiveX was introduced to attempt to transition COM-based software components from PC applications to Internet applications. Ideally, ActiveX would allow COM components to be used with web browsers, web servers, and other Internet-based software applications.

Microsoft portrayed ActiveX as a new technology, but essentially, it is just COM for the Internet. Since its introduction, ActiveX has been expanded to include a variety of related technologies including the following:

ActiveX components   COM components that can be used in Internet applications. ActiveX components that are GUI controls are referred to as ActiveX controls.

ActiveX scripting   The use of JScript, VBScript, and other scripting languages to integrate ActiveX controls in web applications.

Active Server Pages (ASP)   The extension of ActiveX components to web servers.

ActiveX data objects   Objects that enable databases to be accessed through the use of COM and OLE.

Active documents   An extension of OLE that allows documents to be more accessible within an ActiveX container, such as Internet Explorer.

ActiveX conferencing   ActiveX technologies, such as NetMeeting, that support conferencing over the Internet.

 In this chapter, I'll concentrate on the first two technologies: ActiveX components and ActiveX scripting. You'll learn how to use ActiveX controls in your web pages and how to script them using JScript. To learn more about ASP, see Chapter 34, "Scripting Microsoft Servers," on the companion CD.

NOTE   The term "ActiveX" is becoming more generic and is often used to refer to COM technologies in general, whether or not they are used in Internet applications.

Using ActiveX Components

Once you get the hang of it, ActiveX components are easy to insert and use in your web pages. There is somewhat of a learning curve, however, due to the arcane information required to include ActiveX components in your scripts. I'll start by showing you some scripted ActiveX components in action. After that, I'll show you the syntax required to include the components in a web page and access them from JScript.

NOTE   To run the examples in this chapter, you'll need Internet Explorer 5 or later. You'll also need the Windows Common Controls, which are available at `www.microsoft.com/officedev/prodinfo/odeandvb.htm`. Once you download the `comctl3zp.exe` file, extract it, and then install the controls using `regsvr32.exe comctl132.ocx`.

Open `axdemo.htm` (Listing 28.1) with Internet Explorer. It displays the web page shown in Figure 28.1. Note the two custom components displayed on the page. The top component is a progress bar. Its initial value is zero, so there is no progress. The bottom component is a slider. Its initial value is also set to zero. Both the slider and the progress bar are ActiveX components. Their interaction is scripted using JScript.

FIGURE 28.1:

Using some basic ActiveX
controls (Listing 28.1)

FIGURE 28.1:

Using some basic ActiveX
controls (Listing 28.1)

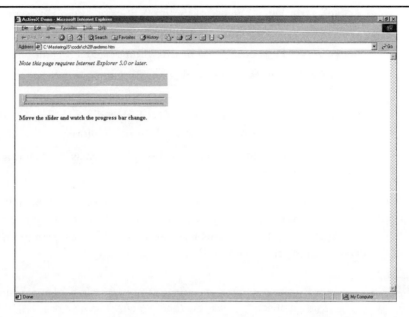

Move the slider to the right, you'll notice that the value of the progress bar changes to match the value of the slider (see Figure 28.2). Once you understand how the interaction between the slider and progress bar is implemented in JScript and how these components are inserted into a web page, you'll be well on the way to scripting ActiveX components.

FIGURE 28.2:

Moving the slider causes
the progress bar to change.
(Listing 28.1)

Listing 28.1:   Using ActiveX Components with JScript (axdemo.htm)

```
<HTML>
<HEAD>
<TITLE>ActiveX Demo</TITLE>
</HEAD>
<BODY>
<P><I>Note this page requires Internet Explorer 5.0 or later.</I></P>
    <OBJECT ID="ProgressBar1" WIDTH=400 HEIGHT=33
     CLASSID="CLSID:0713E8D2-850A-101B-AFC0-4210102A8DA7">
        <PARAM NAME="_ExtentX" VALUE="10583">
        <PARAM NAME="_ExtentY" VALUE="873">
        <PARAM NAME="_Version" VALUE="327682">
        <PARAM NAME="Appearance" VALUE="1">
    </OBJECT>
<P>
    <SCRIPT LANGUAGE="JavaScript" FOR="Slider1" EVENT="Change()">
<!--
ProgressBar1.value = Slider1.value
-->
    </SCRIPT>
    <OBJECT ID="Slider1" WIDTH=400 HEIGHT=33
     CLASSID="CLSID:373FF7F0-EB8B-11CD-8820-08002B2F4F5A">
        <PARAM NAME="_ExtentX" VALUE="10583">
        <PARAM NAME="_ExtentY" VALUE="873">
        <PARAM NAME="_Version" VALUE="327682">
        <PARAM NAME="Max" VALUE="100">
    </OBJECT>
<P><B>Move the slider and watch the progress bar change.</B></P>
</BODY>
</HTML>
```

The first thing that you should notice about Listing 28.1 is the use of the <OBJECT> tags. The two object tags are used to include the progress bar and slider. This is the typical way that ActiveX controls are included in a web page. You should also notice the script that is nestled in between the two <OBJECT> tags. This script is used to enable the interaction between the two ActiveX controls. We'll look at the <OBJECT> tags first and then come back to the controls.

The first object tag consists of the following:

```
<OBJECT ID="ProgressBar1" WIDTH=400 HEIGHT=33
    CLASSID="CLSID:0713E8D2-850A-101B-AFC0-4210102A8DA7">
        <PARAM NAME="_ExtentX" VALUE="10583">
        <PARAM NAME="_ExtentY" VALUE="873">
        <PARAM NAME="_Version" VALUE="327682">
        <PARAM NAME="Appearance" VALUE="1">
    </OBJECT>
```

The ID attribute provides an identifier for the control. You can use this identifier to access the control from your scripts. The WIDTH and HEIGHT attributes specify the control's dimensions in pixels. You can resize the progress bar by altering these values. The CLASSID attribute contains an alphanumeric value like none other; this monstrous value is used to uniquely identify the ActiveX object. Every COM object (and therefore every ActiveX component) is an instance of a class. The class identifier (specified by the CLASSID attribute) uniquely identifies the class to which a COM object belongs. This identifier is used to tell the COM library (a creator of COM objects) which class to use to create an object.

The <PARAM> tags are similar to the <PARAM> tags used with Java applets. They specify the names of ActiveX component parameters and the values of these parameters. The <PARAM> tags are also filled in by the ActiveX control pad.

The script that occurs between the two <OBJECT> tags consists of one line of code, shown here.

```
ProgressBar1.value = Slider1.value
```

It sets the value of the ProgressBar1 object to the value of the Slider1 object. The <SCRIPT> tag's FOR and EVENT attributes are used to connect events to scripts. The FOR attribute identifies the object for which the event occurs, and the EVENT attribute identifies the event. These attributes are used to identify the script as an event handler for the Change event of the Slider1 object.

Accessing ActiveX Components from within JScript

Now that you know the basics of using ActiveX components, let's take it one step further. Listing 28.2 shows an adaptation of Listing 28.1 that uses JScript to control both the slider and the progress bar. These controls are randomly updated as the result of the script's operation. Figure 28.3 provides a snapshot of the output it generates.

FIGURE 28.3:

FIGURE 28.3:

The script causes the slider and progress bar to be randomly updated .
(Listing 28.2)

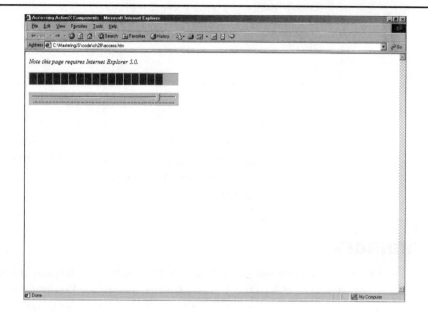

Listing 28.2:   Accessing ActiveX Controls (access.htm)

```
<HTML>
<HEAD>
<TITLE>Accessing ActiveX Components</TITLE>
<SCRIPT LANGUAGE="JavaScript">
function accessActiveX() {
 var newValue = (1000*Math.random()) % 101
 ProgressBar1.Value = newValue
 Slider1.Value = newValue
}
</SCRIPT>
</HEAD>
<BODY onLoad='setInterval("accessActiveX()",2000)'>
<P><I>Note this page requires Internet Explorer 5.0.</I></P>
    <OBJECT ID="ProgressBar1" WIDTH=400 HEIGHT=33
     CLASSID="CLSID:0713E8D2-850A-101B-AFC0-4210102A8DA7">
        <PARAM NAME="_ExtentX" VALUE="10583">
        <PARAM NAME="_ExtentY" VALUE="873">
        <PARAM NAME="_Version" VALUE="327682">
        <PARAM NAME="Appearance" VALUE="1">
    </OBJECT>
<P>
    <OBJECT ID="Slider1" WIDTH=400 HEIGHT=33
     CLASSID="CLSID:373FF7F0-EB8B-11CD-8820-08002B2F4F5A">
        <PARAM NAME="_ExtentX" VALUE="10583">
```

```
            <PARAM NAME="_ExtentY" VALUE="873">
            <PARAM NAME="_Version" VALUE="327682">
            <PARAM NAME="Max" VALUE="100">
        </OBJECT>
    </BODY>
    </HTML>
```

You should notice that the <OBJECT> tags are the same as in Listing 28.1. The only difference between access.htm and axdemo.htm is the script it contains in its head. The onLoad event handler of the <BODY> tag causes the accessActiveX() function to be invoked every two seconds. This function generates a random value between 0 and 100 and sets the value of the progress bar and slider to these values. As you can see from this example, ActiveX controls are easy to control with scripts.

Summary

In this chapter, you were introduced to ActiveX and you learned how to include ActiveX controls in your web pages. You also learned how to use JScript to access the properties, methods, and events of ActiveX controls. In the next chapter, you'll switch back to Navigator and learn how to access plug-ins from your scripts.

CHAPTER 29

Scripting Plug-Ins

- Popular plug-ins

- Working with MIME types

- Determining installed plug-ins

- Accessing plug-ins from within JavaScript

- Listing plug-in methods

- Synchronizing multiple plug-ins

Plug-ins provide the capability to extend your browser in a variety of ways. You can use a plug-in to listen to a radio broadcast, watch a video, or control another computer remotely. The potential applications for plug-ins are limitless. In this chapter, you'll learn all about plug-ins—how they work, how they are used, and how they interface with Netscape Navigator. You'll also access plug-ins from JavaScript.

NOTE   Although Netscape plug-ins are supported by Internet Explorer, Internet Explorer plug-ins are typically implemented as ActiveX components (see Chapter 28, "Scripting ActiveX Components"). This chapter shows how to use Navigator plug-ins from JavaScript with Netscape's LiveConnect. If you want to learn how to access an Internet Explorer plug-in from JScript, refer to Chapter 28.

TIP   The examples in this chapter work with Navigator 4, but many do not work with Navigator 6 or later. Neither Navigator 6 nor Navigator 6.1 provides the range of plug-in support provided by Navigator 4.

Popular Plug-Ins

Since Netscape first introduced them, a large variety of attractive and useful plug-ins has been developed. They range from inline viewers like the Adobe Acrobat viewer to complete browser-embedded applications, such as SCIENCE.ORG's transferRNA.

The following are a few of the most popular browser plug-ins:

LiveAudio   Netscape's LiveAudio plug-in comes standard with Netscape. It plays audio files in WAV, AU, AIFF, and MIDI formats. LiveAudio is LiveConnect-capable and may be accessed from JavaScript.

LiveVideo   The Netscape LiveVideo plug-in is LiveConnect-capable and can be accessed from JavaScript. It is used to display videos that are in the Windows AVI format.

Cosmo Player   Cosmo Player is a LiveConnect-capable Virtual Reality Modeling Language (VRML) plug-in that works with both Navigator and Internet Explorer. It is an excellent viewer for displaying the three-dimensional worlds of VRML. You can download it from www.sgi.com/software/cosmo/player.html.

QuickTime   The QuickTime plug-in displays QuickTime video files in an area of a browser window. The QuickTime plug-in was developed by Apple and is available at www.apple.com/quicktime/download/index.html.

Adobe Acrobat   Adobe's Acrobat plug-in allows you to display documents that are in Adobe's portable document format (PDF). PDF files have become a standard for distributing documents in electronic form. This plug-in is available from Adobe's home page at www.adobe.com.

PointCast   The PointCast Network plug-in allows up-to-the-minute news, weather, sports, and other information to be broadcast to your browser. It is available from the PointCast home page at www.pointcast.com.

Macromedia Shockwave   The Macromedia Shockwave plug-in displays animations, movies, and other multimedia presentations that are produced by the Macromedia Director. It is available from the Macromedia home page at www.macromedia.com.

The plug-ins listed above are some of the most useful and popular ones that are available. However, they represent only a small sample of what's available in plug-in technology. To find more information about what plug-ins are available for different applications, consult the BrowserWatch - Plug-In Plaza web page at browserwatch.internet.com/plug-in.html.

TIP   The Netscape Plug-In page provides links to many exciting and useful plug-ins. It is located at the URL home.netscape.com/plugins/.

Plug-Ins in Action

Plug-ins are independently developed software components that execute in the context of a browser window. They are compiled in the native executable code format of the operating system and computer in which they are run. Plug-ins are installed for use with Navigator by placing them in Navigator's Plugins directory and registering them for use with documents of a particular MIME type.

Plug-ins provide the capability to view documents of different MIME types. The documents can be viewed in *embedded mode* or in *full-page mode*. When a plug-in operates in embedded mode, it is assigned a dedicated part of a loaded HTML document in which to display information to the user and to respond to user-generated events, such as mouse and keyboard actions. When a plug-in operates in full-page mode, it is not displayed as part of a larger HTML document. Instead, it is given an entire browser window in which to operate.

Whether a plug-in document is viewed in embedded mode or full-page mode depends on how it is included in a document. If a plug-in document is inserted in an HTML document using the <embed> tag, then it is viewed in embedded mode. If a plug-in document is referenced as part of a URL, then it is displayed in full-page mode.

The following sections describe the uses of embedded and full-page mode.

WARNING Plug-ins, unlike HTML, JavaScript, and Java, are platform dependent. This means that some plug-ins do not exist for users of certain operating systems. Most plug-ins, however, support Windows and Macintosh platforms.

Embedded Plug-In Documents

Plug-in documents are inserted in a web page using the <embed> tag. The syntax of the <embed> tag is as follows:

```
<embed attributes>
```

An <embed> tag must contain either a SRC or a TYPE attribute. The SRC attribute, which identifies the document to be viewed by the plug-in, is used more often than the TYPE attribute. The TYPE attribute is used by plug-ins that aren't principally used as viewers, but rather are used to create browser-based applications that are not necessarily document-specific. This is discussed in the section, "Plug-Ins as Embedded Applications," later in this chapter.

There are numerous other attributes of the <embed> tag that can be included in addition to the SRC and TYPE attributes. For example, other important and frequently used attributes are the NAME attribute and the HEIGHT and WIDTH attributes. The NAME attribute is used in JavaScript to access the plug-in object by name. The HEIGHT and WIDTH attributes are used to specify the location of the window area that is assigned to the plug-in. These dimensions are important to the plug-in's appearance. The attributes of the <embed> tag are summarized in Table 29.1.

TABLE 29.1: The Attributes of the <embed> Tag

Attribute	Description
HEIGHT	Specifies the vertical dimension of the plug-in area.
HIDDEN	Specifies whether the plug-in is to be hidden or visible.
NAME	Associates a name with the plug-in instance.
PALETTE	Specifies the mode of the plug-in's color palette.
PLUGINSPAGE	Specifies a URL containing instructions for installing the plug-in. This helps you to assist the user in installing a plug-in needed for a particular MIME type.
SRC	Specifies the document to be displayed by the plug-in.
TYPE	Specifies the MIME type associated with the plug-in.
WIDTH	Specifies the horizontal dimension of the plug-in area.
UNITS	Specifies the units of measurement associated with the HEIGHT and WIDTH attributes. The default is pixels.

Plug-ins are free to define additional attributes besides those listed in Table 29.1. These are usually defined on the plug-in developer's website. The values of these plug-in–specific attributes are automatically passed to the plug-in by Navigator.

How the *SRC* Attribute Is Processed

When an <embed> tag contains a SRC attribute, the value of the attribute is a URL that identifies the location of a document to be viewed by a plug-in. For example, consider the following <embed> tag.

```
<embed SRC="movie.avi">
```

When your browser loads an HTML file containing the above tag, it asks the web server at the document's location what the document's MIME type is. When your browser receives the MIME type information from the web server, it checks in its MIME type table to see if there is a plug-in associated with that MIME type. If a registered plug-in is found, then the plug-in is loaded into memory and a specific instance of the plug-in is created.

After a plug-in instance is created, the document identified by the SRC attribute is retrieved from its web server by your browser. The contents of this document are then passed to the plug-in as a data stream. The plug-in reads the data stream and processes and displays the data in accordance with its MIME type. The plug-in is then free to interact with the user via its allocated window area (if it requires one). It may access other network resources by instructing the browser to get information at a specific URL or to post information to a URL.

When the page containing a plug-in document is no longer displayed in a browser window, the plug-in instance associated with the document is deleted. When all instances of a plug-in have been deleted, the plug-in is removed from memory.

Plug-In Documents Referenced as URLs

When a plug-in document is to be displayed in full-page mode, it is not referenced using an <embed> tag. Instead, it is referenced directly via a URL. For example, consider the following link:

```
<A HREF="manual.pdf">Link to a plug-in document.</A>
```

When you click the above link, your browser attempts to load the manual.pdf document. First, it queries the web server at the document's location to determine the document's MIME type. It then processes the MIME type information in the same way that it would for embedded plug-in documents. It looks in its table of registered MIME types to determine what plug-in (if any) is registered for that MIME type. If a registered plug-in is found, then the plug-in is loaded into memory and an instance of that plug-in is created.

The plug-in instance is given an entire Navigator window in which to interact with the user. This is the only difference between the ways that full-page and embedded plug-ins are handled. The plug-in instance is deleted either as the result of its window being closed or as the result of a different document being loaded into its window. The plug-in is removed from memory when all of its instances are deleted.

Plug-Ins as Embedded Applications

Back in the early days of the Web, separate helper programs, referred to as *external viewers*, were launched by a browser to display documents of those MIME types that could not be handled by the browser. These ancestors of modern plug-ins were cumbersome to install and work with.

Plug-ins were originally developed as *inline viewers*. This means they were used to integrate external viewers into the browser application. Most plug-ins still serve this purpose—they display plug-in documents in embedded or full-page mode. However, a new breed of plug-in is becoming popular: embedded *applications* that execute in the context of a browser window. These embedded applications might or might not display documents—their main purpose is to perform a service that is independent of a particular document. For example, SCIENCE .ORG's transferRNA plug-in is used to transfer files from one user to another. You can download this plug-in at `computers.science.org/transferRNA/`.

You may wonder how these plug-ins work if they aren't associated with a document of a specific MIME type. The answer is that they *are* associated with a MIME type but not with a specific document of that MIME type.

Embedded application plug-ins are identified using the TYPE attribute of an `<embed>` tag as opposed to the SRC attribute. Consider the following example:

```
<embed TYPE="application/x-transferRNA" HEIGHT="390" WIDTH="600"
ShowRecvPage="0">
```

The above `<embed>` tag may be used to include the transferRNA plug-in within your web page. When your browser encounters the above `<embed>` tag in a document, it uses the TYPE attribute to determine what MIME type is associated with the plug-in, and then it looks in its MIME type table to see what plug-in (if any) is registered for that MIME type. (In this case, the plug-in is the transferRNA plug-in. Note that the MIME type was named after the plug-in.) Your browser then loads the transferRNA plug-in.

Working with MIME Types

MIME types are fundamental to the operation of the Web. Browsers use MIME types to determine how to display files that are retrieved from web servers. Similarly, in order for you to use a plug-in, your browser must associate the files with a MIME type. The `mimeTypes` array, a property of the `navigator` object, describes all of the MIME types that are known to the browser.

The elements of the `mimeTypes` array are `mimeTypes` objects. Table 29.2 summarizes the properties of the `mimeTypes` object. These properties describe the MIME type and identify the plug-in that is installed and enabled to handle the MIME type. The `mimeTypes` object has no methods and is not associated with any events.

TABLE 29.2: Properties of the `mimeTypes` Object

Property	Description
type	The name of the MIME type.
description	A description of the MIME type.
enabledPlugin	The `plugins` object that is enabled to handle the MIME type. If no enabled plug-in is associated with the MIME type, then this value is `null`.
suffixes	A comma-separated list of the file extensions associated with the MIME type.

NOTE   The `plugins` object is covered in the next section.

Listing 29.1 shows how the `mimeTypes` array is used. Open `mime.htm` with your browser. It will display a list of the MIME types that your browser is familiar with. Figure 29.1 shows the MIME types that my browser displayed. Your browser may display a different list depending on the plug-ins you have installed.

Listing 29.1:   Using the *mimeTypes* Object (mime.htm)

```
<HTML>
<HEAD>
<TITLE>Determining how MIME types are handled</TITLE>
</HEAD>
<BODY>
<SCRIPT LANGUAGE="JavaScript"><!--
m=navigator.mimeTypes
for(var i=0;i<m.length;++i){
 with(document){
   writeln('<P><B>MIME type: </B>'+m[i].type+'</P>')
   writeln('<P><B>Description: </B>'+m[i].description+'</P>')
   writeln('<P><B>Suffixes: </B>'+m[i].suffixes+'</P>')
   writeln('<HR>')
 }
}
// --></SCRIPT>
</BODY>
</HTML>
```

FIGURE 29.1:

Displaying the MIME types that are familiar to your browser (Listing 29.1)

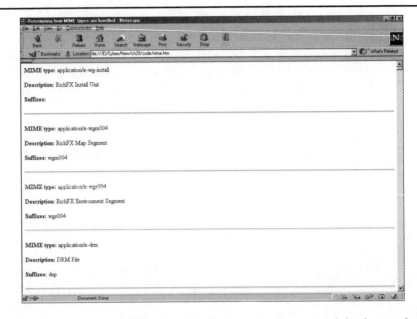

The script shown in Listing 29.1 iterates through the mimeTypes array and displays each mimeTypes object's type, description, and suffixes properties.

Determining Installed Plug-Ins

One of the first things that you'll want to do in order to use plug-ins is to determine which plug-ins are installed for a browser. JavaScript provides the plugins array for that purpose.

The plugins array is a property of the navigator object. It contains an entry for each plug-in that is installed for a browser. Each element of the array is a plugins object.

The plugins objects has the five properties described in Table 29.3. It does not have any methods, and it is not associated with any events. It does provide the capability to completely describe all plug-ins installed for a particular browser.

TABLE 29.3: Properties of the plugins Object

Property	Description
name	The name of the plug-in, as specified in the <embed> tag.
filename	The name of the file from which the plug-in is loaded.
description	The description of the plug-in provided by the plug-in's developer.

Continued on next page

TABLE 29.3 CONTINUED: Properties of the `plugins` Object

Property	Description
length	The number of MIME types supported by the plug-in.
[]	An array of the MIME types supported by the plug-in. Each element is a `mimeTypes` object.

Each `plugins` object is also an array of `mimeTypes` objects. This is confusing, so I'll summarize here how the `plugins` array and `plugins` object fit into the `navigator` object hierarchy:

- The `plugins` array is a property of the `navigator` object.

- Each element of the `plugins` array is a `plugins` object.

- The `plugins` object has five properties.

- One of those properties is an array of `mimeTypes` objects.

- The elements of this array are accessed by indexing the `plugins` object.

To clarify how the `plugins` array and the `plugins` object are used in a script, open plug-ins.htm (Listing 29.2) with your browser. Your browser will display a web page similar to the one shown in Figure 29.2. As you can see, the information provided by the `plugins` object is very comprehensive.

Listing 29.2:   Displaying Plug-In Information (plugins.htm)

```
<HTML>
<HEAD>
<TITLE>Determining Installed Plug-ins</TITLE>
</HEAD>
<BODY>
<SCRIPT LANGUAGE="JavaScript"><!--
p=navigator.plugins
for(var i=0;i<p.length;++i){
 with(document){
  writeln('<P><B>Plugin: </B>'+p[i].name+'</P>')
  writeln('<P><B>File name: </B>'+p[i].filename+'</P>')
  writeln('<P><B>Description: </B>'+p[i].description+'</P>')
  writeln('<P><B>MIME Types: </B>')
  for(var j=0;j<p[i].length;++j)
   writeln(p[i][j].type+'</BR>')
  writeln('</P><HR>')
 }
}
// --></SCRIPT>
</BODY>
</HTML>
```

FIGURE 29.2:

My browser's plug-in information (Listing 29.2)

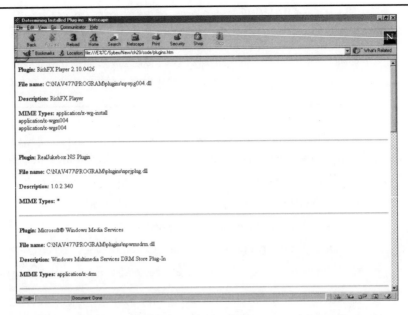

Listing 29.2 shows the contents of plugins.htm. A single script is included in the document's body. This script uses the p variable to refer to the plugins array. It then loops through each element of the plugins array and displays the name, filename, and description properties of each plugins object. The length property is used to determine how many MIME types are supported by the plugins object. The type property of each of the mime-Types objects referenced by each plugins object is printed.

NOTE   The way that Netscape designed the plugins object is very messy. It would have been much cleaner if Netscape had given the plugins object a mimeTypes property that consisted of an array of mimeTypes objects instead of defining each plugins object as an array of mimeTypes objects.

How About Plug-Ins Works

When you select Help ≻ About Plug-ins in Navigator, your browser displays a description of all plug-ins supported by your browser, in the format shown in Figure 29.3. If you select View ≻ Document Source, you'll see the HTML file shown in Listing 29.3. This file shows how the plugins and mimeTypes objects can be used together to list and describe all of the plugins known to a browser.

FIGURE 29.3:

The About Plug-ins display
(Listing 29.3)

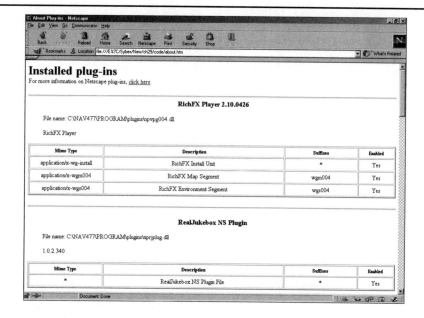

FIGURE 29.3:

The About Plug-ins display
(Listing 29.3)

Listing 29.3:   The About Plug-Ins Script (about.htm)

```
<HTML>
<HEAD>
<TITLE>About Plug-ins</TITLE>
</HEAD>
<BODY>
<SCRIPT language="javascript">
<!-- JavaScript to enumerate and display all installed
 plug-ins -->
numPlugins = navigator.plugins.length;
if (numPlugins > 0)
  document.writeln("<b><font size=+3>Installed plug-ins
   </font></b><br>");
else
 document.writeln("<b><font size=+2>No plug-ins are
  installed.</font></b><br>");
 document.writeln("For more information on Netscape
  plug-ins, <A HREF=http://home.netscape.com/comprod/
  products/navigator/version_2.0/plugins/index.html>
  click here</A>.<p><hr>");
for (i = 0; i < numPlugins; i++)
{
 plugin = navigator.plugins[i];
 document.write("<center><font size=+1><b>");
 document.write(plugin.name);
```

```
        document.writeln("</b></font></center><br>");
        document.writeln("<dl>");
        document.writeln("<dd>File name:");
        document.write(plugin.filename);
        document.write("<dd><br>");
        document.write(plugin.description);
        document.writeln("</dl>");
        document.writeln("<p>");
        document.writeln("<table width=100% border=2 cellpadding=5>");
        document.writeln("<tr>");
        document.writeln("<th width=20%><font size=-1>Mime Type</font>
         </th>");
        document.writeln("<th width=50%><font size=-1>Description
         </font></th>");
        document.writeln("<th width=20%><font size=-1>Suffixes</font>
         </th>");
        document.writeln("<th><font size=-1>Enabled</th>");
        document.writeln("</tr>");
        numTypes = plugin.length;
        for (j = 0; j < numTypes; j++)
        {
         mimetype = plugin[j];

         if (mimetype)
         {
          enabled = "No";
          enabledPlugin = mimetype.enabledPlugin;
          if (enabledPlugin && (enabledPlugin.name == plugin.name))
           enabled = "Yes";
          document.writeln("<tr align=center>");
          document.writeln("<td>");
          document.write(mimetype.type);
          document.writeln("</td>");
          document.writeln("<td>");
          document.write(mimetype.description);
          document.writeln("</td>");
          document.writeln("<td>");
          document.write(mimetype.suffixes);
          document.writeln("</td>");
          document.writeln("<td>");
          document.writeln(enabled);
          document.writeln("</td>");
          document.writeln("</tr>");
         }
        }

        document.write("</table>");
        document.write("<p><hr><p>");
       }
    </SCRIPT>
    </BODY>
    </HTML>
```

The `about.htm` file contains a single script in the document body. The `numPlugins` variable is set to the number of `plugins` objects contained in the `plugins` array. After displaying header information, the script loops through the `plugins` array and displays the `name`, `filename`, and `description` properties of each `plugins` object. The script then constructs a table to describe the `mimeTypes` objects associated with each `plugins` object. The table lists the `type`, `description`, and `suffixes` properties, and it contains a fourth column that identifies whether an enabled plug-in exists for the MIME type.

The `numTypes` property is set to the `length` property of each `plugins` object. The script then loops through the array of `mimeTypes` objects of each `plugins` object and displays the table data. The `enabledPlugin` variable is set to the value of the `mimeTypes` object's `enabledPlugin` property.

The `if` statement that follows this assignment checks if `enabledPlugin` is `true` (that is, not `null`) and that the `name` property of `enabledPlugin` is the same as that of the `plugins` object with which the `mimeTypes` object is associated. The reason for this check is that `enabledPlugin` could be null, indicating that no plug-in is enabled for the MIME type, or `enabledPlugin` could have its `name` property set to a different `plugins` object, indicating that another plug-in is enabled for the MIME type.

Detecting Plug-Ins

The `plugins` array may be indexed by the name of a plug-in, and the `mimeTypes` array may be indexed by the name of a MIME type. This feature provides a handy capability for determining whether a browser is capable of supporting a particular plug-in or MIME type. When the `plugins` or `mimeTypes` arrays are accessed with unsupported values, then a null value results.

Listing 29.4 (`detect.htm`) provides an example of using the `plugins` array and the `mimeTypes` array to determine whether or not a video should be displayed. Open `detect.htm` with your browser. If the LiveVideo plug-in is installed for your browser, then your browser will display the video as shown in Figure 29.4. If the LiveVideo plug-in is not installed for your browser, then a message will be displayed in lieu of the video.

NOTE   The AUTOSTART attribute can be set to TRUE or FALSE to specify whether or not LiveVideo should automatically start playing the video without the user clicking the Play button. Later in this chapter, in the sections "Plugging into LiveVideo" and "Listening to LiveAudio," I'll cover the Netscape documentation for LiveVideo and LiveAudio.

FIGURE 29.4:

The video is displayed.
(Listing 29.4)

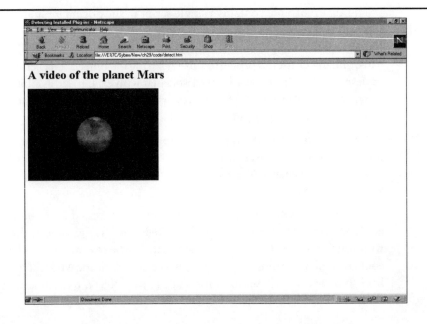

Listing 29.4:   Determining Whether the LiveVideo Plug-In Is Installed (detect.htm)

```
<HTML>
<HEAD>
<TITLE>Detecting Installed Plug-ins</TITLE>
</HEAD>
<BODY>
<H1>A video of the planet Mars</H1>
<SCRIPT LANGUAGE="JavaScript"><!--
plugins=navigator.plugins
if(plugins["NPAVI32 Dynamic Link Library"]){
 document.write('<EMBED SRC="mars.avi" AUTOSTART="TRUE"')
 document.writeln('WIDTH="350" HEIGHT="270">')
}else{
 document.write('Sorry. Your browser does not have ')
 document.writeln('LiveVideo installed.')
}
// --></SCRIPT>
</BODY>
</HTML>
```

NOTE   If your browser does not support LiveVideo, you should upgrade to a version that does. If you are using a non-Windows OS, then you'll have to follow along with the book. The reason I use LiveVideo and AVI files in this chapter is that LiveVideo provides full support of LiveConnect, and therefore, it allows plug-in methods to be accessed from JavaScript.

Accessing Plug-Ins from within JavaScript

With LiveConnect, accessing plug-ins is easy—you use the embeds array. The embeds array is a property of the document object. This array contains an entry for each of the document's <embed> tags. Each element of the embeds array is a plugin object.

The plugin object is different from the plugins object. The plugins objects are elements of the plugins array, which is a property of the navigator object. The plugin objects are elements of the embeds array, which is a property of the document object. Further, whereas the plugins object describes a plug-in, the plugin object provides access to the properties and methods of a plug-in.

Each plugin object is also a property of the document object. If an <embed> tag contains a NAME attribute, then the plugin object can be accessed by its name.

Listing 29.5 (access.htm) provides an example of how the plugin object may be used to access and control a plug-in. Open access.htm with your browser. After a few seconds, your browser loads and plays a Mars video, as shown in Figure 29.5. This is the same video as is shown in Figure 29.4 except for one difference: this time you are controlling it from within JavaScript. Click the Start button and the video is rewound to the beginning, as shown in Figure 29.6. Click the Play button and the video begins playing again. Click the Stop button to freeze the video on a particular frame. Use the Frame Forward and Frame Backward buttons to advance or rewind the video one frame at a time. Click the End button to go to the last frame of the video, as shown in Figure 29.7.

FIGURE 29.5:

The video automatically
plays when the page loads.
(Listing 29.5)

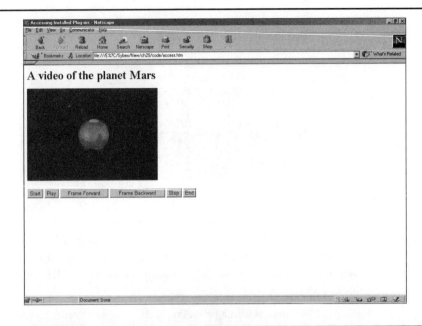

FIGURE 29.6:

Clicking the Start button
rewinds the video to the
beginning. (Listing 29.5)

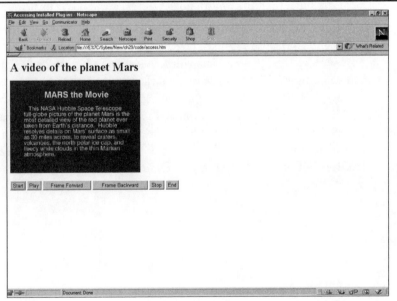

FIGURE 29.7:

Clicking the End button forwards the video to the end. (Listing 29.5)

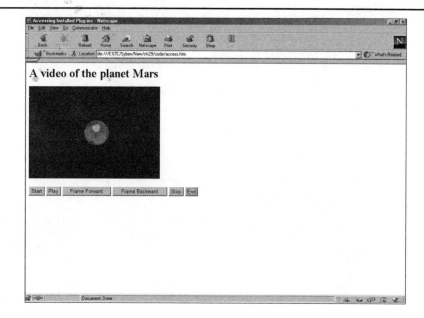

Listing 29.5:   Accessing a Plug-In (access.htm)

```
<HTML>
<HEAD>
<TITLE>Accessing Installed Plug-ins</TITLE>
<SCRIPT LANGUAGE="JavaScript"><!--
function playVideo() {
 window.document.mars.play()
}
function stopVideo() {
 window.document.mars.stop()
}
function rewindVideo() {
 window.document.mars.rewind()
}
function forwardVideo() {
 window.document.mars.forward()
}
function forward() {
 window.document.mars.frameBack()
}
function back() {
 window.document.mars.frameForward()
}
// --></SCRIPT>
</HEAD>
```

```
<BODY>
<H1>A video of the planet Mars</H1>
<SCRIPT LANGUAGE="JavaScript"><!--
plugins=navigator.plugins
if(plugins["NPAVI32 Dynamic Link Library"]){
 document.write('<EMBED SRC="mars.avi" NAME="mars" ')
 document.writeln('AUTOSTART="TRUE" WIDTH="350" HEIGHT="240">')
}else{
 document.write('Sorry. Your browser does not have ')
 document.writeln('LiveVideo installed.')
}
// --></SCRIPT>
<FORM>
<INPUT TYPE="BUTTON" VALUE="Start" onClick="rewindVideo()">
<INPUT TYPE="BUTTON" VALUE="Play" onClick="playVideo()">
<INPUT TYPE="BUTTON" VALUE="Frame Forward" onClick="forward()">
<INPUT TYPE="BUTTON" VALUE="Frame Backward" onClick="back()">
<INPUT TYPE="BUTTON" VALUE="Stop" onClick="stopVideo()">
<INPUT TYPE="BUTTON" VALUE="End" onClick="forwardVideo()">
</FORM>
</BODY>
</HTML>
```

Listing 29.5 shows how easy it is to access and control a plug-in from JavaScript. The onClick event handlers of the form's buttons are JavaScript functions that invoke the methods of the LiveVideo plug-in.

NOTE Note that the frameBack() and frameForward() methods of the LiveVideo plug-in work in an opposite manner than the one you might expect—frameBack() causes the video to move forward, and frameForward() causes the video to move back.

The script in the document body is similar to the one used in Listing 29.4. The only difference is that the <embed> tag is given a NAME attribute.

Netscape's Plug-In Documentation

When you worked with the LiveVideo example, you were probably wondering how I was able to determine what methods were supported by the LiveVideo plug-in. Part of the answer is that Netscape provides plug-in documentation at its website. This documentation includes the description of the netscape.plugin.Plugin Java class, which defines the minimal set of functions to be implemented by any LiveConnect-capable plug-in (and therefore the LiveVideo plug-in).

The other part of the answer is that LiveConnect lists all of the properties and methods of a plug-in as properties of whichever `plugin` object is associated with the plug-in. This lets you use the `for in` statement to list all of the plug-in's properties and methods.

The following subsections summarize the plug-in documentation provided by Netscape for LiveVideo and LiveAudio. Subsequent subsections describe the `netscape.plugin.Plugin` class and show how to use the `for in` statement to list all of a plug-in's properties and methods.

Plugging into LiveVideo

You've already used LiveVideo and are familiar with most of its methods. LiveVideo plays video files that are in the AVI format. Although LiveVideo is LiveConnect-capable, it is currently supported only on the Windows operating system platforms.

In this section, I'll summarize the LiveVideo documentation provided by JavaScript. In the later section, "Listing Plug-In Methods," you'll learn how to list all of the properties of a plug-in.

The LiveVideo plug-in supports three application-specific attributes: AUTOSTART, LOOP, and ALIGN. The AUTOSTART and LOOP attributes take on the values of TRUE or FALSE. Their default values are FALSE. The AUTOSTART attribute determines whether the plug-in should automatically play the movie when the page is loaded. The LOOP attribute determines whether the video should be played in a continuous loop. The ALIGN attribute controls text alignment around the video display area. It is used in the same way as the ALIGN attribute of the <img> tag.

The LiveVideo documentation identifies four methods that may be used with the Live-Video plug-in. These methods are described in Table 29.4. You'll learn additional methods in the section "Listing Plug-In Methods," later in this chapter.

TABLE 29.4: Documented LiveVideo Plug-In Methods

Method	Description
play()	Plays the video starting at the current frame
stop()	Stops playing the video at the current frame
rewind()	Sets the current frame to the first frame of the video
seek(n)	Sets the current frame to the frame specified by n

Listening to LiveAudio

LiveAudio is a very powerful LiveConnect-capable audio player that is capable of playing audio files that are in the WAV, AIFF, AU, and MIDI formats. You've used the Netscape LiveAudio plug-in in examples in previous chapters. You probably thought that it was awkward to work with. It *is* awkward to work with, at least in its default configuration. However, LiveAudio provides a number of configuration options that can be used to tailor the way it appears and behaves.

Table 29.5 describes attributes that can be used with the LiveAudio plug-in. They can be used to hide or change the appearance of the audio player or to customize the way that an audio file is played.

TABLE 29.5:   Attributes of the LiveAudio Plug-In

Attribute	Description
ALIGN	Controls the way text is displayed around the audio player's controls. It is used in the same manner here as it is used in the `<img>` tag.
AUTOSTART	When set to TRUE, the audio player begins playing the audio file when the web page is loaded. It is set to FALSE by default.
CONTROLS	May be set to CONSOLE, SMALLCONSOLE, PLAYBUTTON, PAUSEBUTTON, STOPBUTTON, or VOLUMELEVER to identify what type of audio control is to be displayed.
ENDTIME	Takes a `minutes:seconds` value that identifies where in the audio file the playback is to end.
HIDDEN	When set to TRUE, this attribute causes the audio controls to be hidden.
LOOP	Takes the values TRUE, FALSE, or an integer. If it is set to TRUE, it causes the audio file to be played in a continuous looping fashion. If it is set to FALSE, it turns off looping. If an integer value is supplied, then the audio file is repeatedly played the specified number of times.
MASTERSOUND	This attribute is used with the NAME attribute to identify which file contains the actual file to be played.
NAME	Rather than naming the plug-in so that it can be accessed from JavaScript, this attribute is used to name a group of controls that apply to a single sound.
STARTTIME	Takes a `minutes:seconds` value that identifies where in the audio file playback is to start.
VOLUME	Uses the values 0 to 100 to specify the percentage of the volume setting at which the audio file is to be played.

Table 29.6 identifies the LiveAudio methods supported by JavaScript. These methods provide all of the capabilities needed to implement custom audio controls.

TABLE 29.6:   Methods of the LiveAudio Plug-In

Method	Description
end_time(n)	Sets the end time n in seconds
fade_from_to(v1,v2)	Fades the volume level from v1 to v2
fade_to(v)	Fades the volume level to v
GetVolume()	Gets the current volume level
IsPaused()	Returns true if the audio player is currently paused
IsPlaying()	Returns true if the audio player is currently playing
IsReady()	Returns true if the audio player has been loaded
pause()	Causes the audio player to pause
play()	Causes the audio player to start playing
play(n,url)	Causes the audio player to start playing the first n seconds of the file located at the specified URL
setvol(v)	Sets the volume to the specified level
start_at_beginning()	Sets the start time to the beginning of the file
start_time(n)	Sets the start time to the specified number of seconds
stop()	Stops the playing of the audio file
stop_at_end()	Sets the end time to the end of the file

NOTE   Volume levels in LiveAudio methods are expressed as an integer in the range of 0 to 100.

The *netscape.plugin.Plugin* Class

The interface to LiveConnect-capable plug-ins is specified by the netscape.plugin.Plugin class. LiveConnect-capable plug-ins are subclasses of this class, and they add methods to it to enable the plug-ins to be accessed from Java and JavaScript. The netscape.plugin.Plugin class is of primary interest to plug-in developers, but as you'll see in the next section, it is good for you to know which methods it defines. This knowledge will help you to identify which methods are inherited from the Plugin class and which are specific to a particular plug-in. The methods of the netscape.plugin.Plugin class are described in Table 29.7.

TABLE 29.7:   Methods of the netscape.plugin.Plugin Class

Method	Description
Plugin()	The class constructor
destroy()	Automatically invoked when the plug-in is destroyed

Continued on next page

TABLE 29.7 CONTINUED: Methods of the `netscape.plugin.Plugin` Class

Method	Description
getPeer()	Returns the native object corresponding to the plug-in instance
getWindow()	Returns the JavaScript window in which the plug-in displays its results
init()	Automatically invoked to initialize a plug-in
isActive()	Determines whether the plug-in is active

Listing Plug-In Methods

The publicly accessible properties and methods of LiveConnect-capable plug-ins are accessible as the properties of `plugin` objects. Because the properties and methods are accessible as properties, you can use the `for in` statement to find all of the undocumented features of a plug-in. Listing 29.6 (`listprop.htm`) illustrates this technique. When you open `listprop.htm` with your browser, it displays a web page like that shown in Figure 29.8. Because I did not use the `WIDTH` and `HEIGHT` attributes in the `<embed>` tag, the video player display (the dark box at the top of the web page) is minimized. This is fine because we are more interested in LiveVideo's properties and methods than in watching the video.

FIGURE 29.8:

The properties of the
LiveVideo `plugin` object
(Listing 29.6)

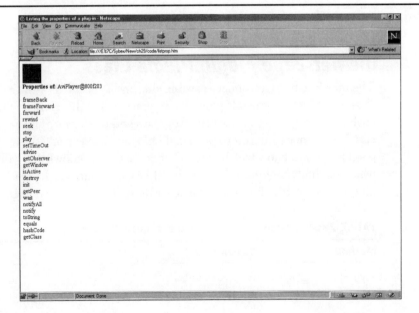

Listing 29.6:   Listing Plug-In Properties (listprop.htm)

```
<HTML>
<HEAD>
<TITLE>Listing the properties of a plug-in</TITLE>
<SCRIPT LANGUAGE="JavaScript"><!--
function listProperties(obj) {
 document.writeln("<B>Properties of: </B>"+obj+"<BR>")
 for(var p in obj)
   document.writeln(p+"<BR>")
}
// --></SCRIPT>
</HEAD>
<BODY>
<EMBED SRC="Mars.avi"><BR>
<SCRIPT LANGUAGE="JavaScript"><!--
listProperties(document.embeds[0])
// --></SCRIPT>
</BODY>
</HTML>
```

listprop.htm uses an <embed> tag to display the Mars.avi file. The script in the document's body invokes the listProperties() function with the LiveVideo plugin object passed as an argument.

listProperties() uses the for in statement to loop through and display the properties of the obj parameter.

listprop.htm may be easily adapted to display the properties of other plug-ins. Listing 29.7 shows the listaud.htm file that lists the properties of the LiveAudio plug-in. Figure 29.9 shows the web page it displays.

FIGURE 29.9:

The properties of the
LiveAudio plug in object
(Listing 29.7)

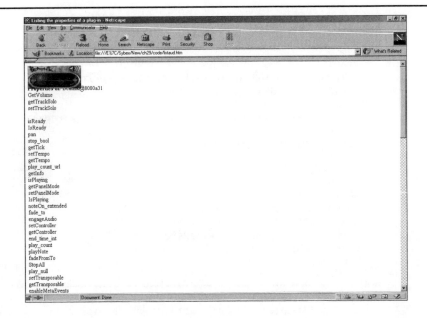

Listing 29.7:   **Tailoring** *listprop.htm* **(listaud.htm)**

```
<HTML>
<HEAD>
<TITLE>Listing the properties of a plug-in</TITLE>
<SCRIPT LANGUAGE="JavaScript"><!--
function listProperties(obj) {
 document.writeln("<B>Properties of: </B>"+obj+"<BR>")
 for(var p in obj)
  document.writeln(p+"<BR>")
}
// --></SCRIPT>
</HEAD>
<BODY>
<EMBED SRC="test.wav"><BR>
<SCRIPT LANGUAGE="JavaScript"><!--
listProperties(document.embeds[0])
// --></SCRIPT>
</BODY>
</HTML>
```

Synchronizing Multiple Plug-Ins

In some multimedia applications, you may wish to use two or more plug-ins. For example, the Mars.avi video that you used in this chapter was converted from a NASA MPEG video, and it does not contain any sound. If you're creating a multimedia application that uses the Mars.avi video, you may want to add an audio file to provide a narration for the video.

When you are using two or more plug-ins on the same web page, you may need to synchronize the plug-ins so that they start and stop together and display the correct information at the right time.

In general, most plug-ins do not provide synchronization primitives. To ensure that your plug-ins operate in tandem, you can provide synchronization at the user interface level. Listing 29.8 (synchro.htm) provides a simple example of this type of synchronization.

Open synchro.htm with your browser. It displays the web page shown in Figure 29.10. Click the Play button, and the video and audio files are played simultaneously. Click the Stop button, and the video and audio players stop at the same time. Click Play again, and they both play where they left off. The Start button "rewinds" the video and audio files, and the End button displays the last frame of the video file and stops the audio file.

FIGURE 29.10:

The initial script display (Listing 29.8)

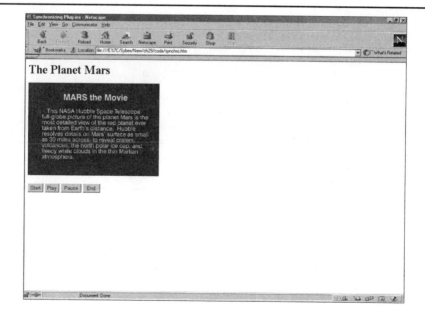

Listing 29.8:   Synchronizing Two Plug-Ins (synchro.htm)

```html
<HTML>
<HEAD>
<TITLE>Synchronizing Plug-ins</TITLE>
<SCRIPT LANGUAGE="JavaScript"><!--
function play() {
 window.document.embeds[0].play()
 window.document.embeds[1].play()
}
function stop() {
 window.document.embeds[0].stop()
 window.document.embeds[1].pause()
}
function start() {
 window.document.embeds[0].rewind()
 window.document.embeds[1].stop()
}
function end() {
 window.document.embeds[0].forward()
 window.document.embeds[1].stop()
}
// --></SCRIPT>
</HEAD>
<BODY onLoad="start()">
<H1>The Planet Mars</H1>
<EMBED SRC="mars.avi" NAME="video" AUTOSTART="TRUE"
 WIDTH="350" HEIGHT="240">
<EMBED SRC="mars.wav" HIDDEN="TRUE">
<FORM>
<INPUT TYPE="BUTTON" VALUE="Start" onClick="start()">
<INPUT TYPE="BUTTON" VALUE="Play" onClick="play()">
<INPUT TYPE="BUTTON" VALUE="Pause" onClick="stop()">
<INPUT TYPE="BUTTON" VALUE=" End " onClick="end()">
</FORM>
</BODY>
</HTML>
```

Listing 29.8 shows how the two plug-ins are synchronized. The document body loads the LiveVideo plug-in to display the mars.avi file. It then loads the LiveAudio plug-in to play the mars.wav file. The <body> tag's onClick event handler invokes the start() function to ensure that both files are rewound upon document loading. The four functions in the document header are used as follows:

The *play()* Function   This function invokes the play() method of both plug-ins to cause the plug-ins to begin playing at the same time. It handles the clicking of the Play button.

The *stop()* Function   This function invokes the stop() method of the LiveVideo plug-in and the pause() method of the LiveAudio plug-in to cause both plug-ins to stop playing at the current position within their respective files. It handles the clicking of the Stop button.

The *start()* Function   This function invokes the rewind() method of the LiveVideo plug-in and the stop() method of the LiveAudio plug-in to cause both plug-ins to rewind their respective files to their initial position. It handles the clicking of the Start button.

The *end()* Function   This function invokes the forward() method of the LiveVideo plug-in and the stop() method of the LiveAudio plug-in. This causes the LiveVideo plug-in to display its last frame and the LiveAudio plug-in to return to its start position. The end() function handles the clicking of the End button.

Summary

In this chapter, you learned how to use JavaScript to work with plug-ins. You learned how to use the plugins and mimetypes objects to detect available plug-ins and determine the MIME types associated with these plug-ins. You learned how to use LiveConnect to communicate with plug-ins and control their behavior. You learned how to work with multiple plug-ins and various approaches to synchronizing plug-ins. The following chapter introduces a platform-independent scripting environment, named Rhino, which was developed by the Mozilla project.

PART VI

Shell Programming

CHAPTER 30

Programming Rhino

- What is Rhino?

- Downloading and installing Rhino

- Running Rhino

- Creating simple Rhino scripts

- Using the JavaScript compiler

- Scripting Java

- Developing a presentation generator

In this chapter you'll work with an open source JavaScript implementation that is a result of the Mozilla project. You'll learn how to download and install Rhino and use it to script Java classes. You'll also create an example shell script that transforms structured text files into JavaScript slide show presentations. When you finish this chapter, you'll be able to add shell scripting to your JavaScript repertoire.

What Is Rhino?

Rhino is an open source implementation of JavaScript that was developed by the Mozilla project (the same project that developed the code base for Navigator 6). Rhino is written entirely in Java and, as a result, runs on every system that runs Java 1.1 or later. Rhino provides a complete implementation of JavaScript 1.5, which conforms to ECMAScript (ECMA 262) Edition 3.

Rhino can be used in a number of ways. It can be embedded in a product to add a scripting capability. JRun (see Chapter 35 on the CD) is an example of this usage of Rhino. Rhino can be used as a JavaScript compiler. You can compile JavaScript source files into Java .class byte-code files and distribute them as part of a Java application or applet. Rhino can also be used as a command-line JavaScript interpreter. You can create JavaScript source files and run them using the Rhino interpreter.

This chapter will focus on using Rhino as a JavaScript interpreter and compiler. You'll learn how to create small scripts that can be run from the command line. You'll also learn how to compile these scripts into Java applications.

NOTE   The Rhino home page is `www.mozilla.org/rhino/`.

Downloading and Installing Rhino

Rhino can be freely downloaded from the Mozilla FTP site at `ftp://ftp.mozilla.org/pub/js/`. Look for the latest version, which will be in a file of the form, `rhino*.zip`. At the time of this writing, the latest version was Rhino 1.5, which is available at `ftp://ftp.mozilla.org/pub/js/rhino15R1.zip`. You should also check out `www.mozilla.org/rhino/download.html`, which may contain additional information about the latest release.

You'll need a program, such as WinZip, that can unzip ZIP files. WinZip is available at `www.winzip.com`. On Windows systems, unzip the Rhino ZIP file into a directory, such as `C:\`. A directory named `rhino` will be created under the directory in which you unzip Rhino.

For the rest of this chapter, I'll assume that you are using Windows and that Rhino was unzipped under `C:\` to create `C:\rhino`.

Since Rhino runs under Java, you must download and install the Java Runtime Environment as a minimum. However, since you may want to use some of the Java development tools to supplement your scripts, I recommend that you install the full-blown Java 2 Software Development Kit, Standard Edition, version 1.3, which is available at `www.javasoft.com/j2se/1.3/`. Follow the installation instructions to download, install, and configure the software.

NOTE Chapter 27, "Communicating with Java Applets," covers the installation of the Java 2 SDK and the basics of the Java language.

Having installed and configured the Java 2 SDK and unzipped Rhino, you should add the `\rhino\js.jar` file to your CLASSPATH environment variable. The CLASSPATH environment variable tells the Java runtime system where to look for Java bytecode files. You can set the CLASSPATH by adding the following line to your AUTOEXEC.BAT file:

```
SET CLASSPATH=.;C:\rhino\js.jar;
  or by adding "C:\rhino\js.jar;" to the SET CLASSPATH statement if it already
  exists.
```

Restart your computer to make sure that all changes take effect.

To test your installation, open an MS-DOS window and run the following command:

```
java org.mozilla.javascript.tools.shell.Main
```

You should see the following Rhino prompt:

```
js>
```

If you don't get this prompt, recheck your CLASSPATH and Java installation.

Running Rhino

Running the Rhino interpreter is easy. Simply execute the following command from a MS-DOS command line:

```
java org.mozilla.javascript.tools.shell.Main
```

You can put the above command in a BAT file to avoid having to retype the command line. I put it in a file named `rhino.bat` in my `C:\Windows` directory. Go ahead and run Rhino as previously specified to get to the `js >` prompt. Then type in the `help()` command as follows:

```
js> help()
```

```
Command               Description
```

```
=======              ===========
help()               Display usage and help messages.
defineClass(className) Define an extension using the Java class
                     named with the string argument.
                     Uses ScriptableObject.defineClass().
load(["foo.js", ...]) Load JavaScript source files named by
                     string arguments.
loadClass(className) Load a class named by a string argument.
                     The class must be a script compiled to a
                     class file.
print([expr ...])    Evaluate and print expressions.
quit()               Quit the shell.
version([number])    Get or set the JavaScript version number.
```

The help() command lists the commands that are supported by the Rhino interpreter. The version() command is used to set (if an argument is supplied) or get (if no argument is supplied) the JavaScript version number. The defineClass() command is useful for extending the capabilities of Rhino with Java classes that you develop. The loadClass() command is used to load a compiled script. However, most of your initial programming will involve the print(), load(), and quit() commands.

The print() command takes a list of string arguments and displays them to the console window:

```
js> print("This","is","a test.")
This is a test.
```

The load() command loads and executes a script that is stored in a .js file. You'll see examples of its use in the next section. The quit() command ends the Rhino session and returns you to a command prompt. Go ahead and try it out.

Developing Simple Rhino Scripts

In this section, we'll develop a few simple scripts to give you a feel for Rhino's operation. We'll start with the standard Hello World! script, move on to a script that lists itself, and then create a script that lists arbitrary files.

Listing 30.1 contains a one-line script that uses Rhino's print command to print the Hello World! text. You run the script by opening a MS-DOS window, changing to the directory in which the file HelloWorld.js is located, starting Rhino, and running the load("HelloWorld.js") command. The following is an example of how to do this:

```
C:\WINDOWS>cd \mjscript\ch35
C:\mjscript\ch35>java org.mozilla.javascript.tools.shell.Main
js> load("HelloWorld.js")
```

```
Hello World!
js>
```

Listing 30.1:   The *HelloWorld.js* Script

```
print("Hello World!")
```
The script shown in Listing 30.2 reads and lists itself. Go ahead and run it as follows:
```
C:\mjscript\ch35>java org.mozilla.javascript.tools.shell.Main
js> load("ListIt.js")
reader = new java.io.FileReader("ListIt.js")
inFile = new java.io.BufferedReader(reader)
for(line = inFile.readLine(); line != null;
  line = inFile.readLine()) {
 print(line)
}
js>
```

Listing 30.2:   The *ListIt.js* Script

```
reader = new java.io.FileReader("ListIt.js")
inFile = new java.io.BufferedReader(reader)
for(line = inFile.readLine(); line != null;
  line = inFile.readLine()) {
 print(line)
}
```

Although the ListIt.js file is only six lines in length, it illustrates some important features of Rhino. The first line of the script creates a new FileReader object and assigns it to the reader variable. FileReader is a Java class that is defined in the java.io package. Java classes and interfaces are similar to JavaScript object types. A package is a collection of related classes and interfaces. The expression new java.io.FileReader("ListIt.js") creates a new FileReader object that reads the file ListIt.js. The capability to create and access Java objects is a valuable feature of Rhino.

In the second line of the script, the FileReader object referenced by reader is provided as an argument to the BufferedReader constructor. The BufferedReader class is defined in the java.io package. It provides the capability to read and buffer an entire line of input from a text file. The newly created BufferedReader object is assigned to the inFile variable.

The remaining four lines of the file are a `for` loop. The `for` statement begins with the following two lines:

```
for(line = inFile.readLine(); line != null;
   line = inFile.readLine()) {
```

The `readLine()` method of the `BufferedReader` object is invoked to read a line of input. The input (a `java.lang.String` object) is assigned to the `line` variable. The loop condition checks to see that `line != null`. When `line == null`, then the end of the file has been reached and the loop terminates. The next time the loop is executed, the third part of the `for` statement (`line = inFile.readLine()`) causes another line of input to be read and assigned to the `line` variable.

The statement `print(line)` simply displays the contents of the `line` variable.

NOTE   The Java 2 SDK version 1.3 API documentation is available online at `www.javasoft.com/j2se/1.3/docs/api/index.html`.

Invoking Scripts from the Command Line

While the `ListIt.js` script was able to list itself, it would be much more useful to enable it to list arbitrary files that are specified in a command line. To add this capability, we have to do two things:

- Modify `ListIt.js` to process command line arguments.

- Invoke a Rhino script from the command line and pass it command line arguments.

Listing 30.3 shows the `ListFile.js` script that upgrades `ListIt.js` to process command line arguments. It makes use of the arguments variable to access arguments that are passed through the command line. The following is the command line that you would use to invoke it:

```
java -jar C:\rhino\js.jar ListFile.js filename
```

For example, here is the output that it generates when I use it to list my `C:\config.sys` file:

```
C:\mjscript\ch35>java -jar C:\rhino\js.jar ListFile.js C:\config.sys
DEVICE=C:\WINDOWS\Panning.SYS
SHELL=C:\COMMAND.COM C:\ /E:8192 /P
```

Listing 30.3:   The *ListFile.js* Script

```
if(arguments.length == 0) {
 java.lang.System.out.println("Usage: java -jar C:\\rhino\\js.jar ListFile.js
filename")
 java.lang.System.exit(0)
}
reader = new java.io.FileReader(arguments[0])
```

```
inFile = new java.io.BufferedReader(reader)
for(line = inFile.readLine(); line != null;
  line = inFile.readLine()) {
  java.lang.System.out.println(line)
  }
```

If your `js.jar` file is installed in a location other than `C:\rhino`, substitute that location in the command line. The following is the general syntax for running JavaScript files from the command line:

```
java -jar locationOfjs.jar scriptName.js arguments
```

The arguments are optional and are separated by spaces.

NOTE   Note that in `ListFile.js` I substituted the `println()` method of the `out` variable of the `java.lang.System` class for the Rhino `print()` method. I prefer `println()` because it can be used with the JavaScript compiler, while the Rhino `print()` command cannot.

Using the JavaScript Compiler

I mentioned earlier in the chapter that Rhino provides the capability to compile JavaScript source files into executable Java bytecode files. In this section, I'll show you how it's done.

The JavaScript compiler is invoked using the following command line:

```
java org.mozilla.javascript.tools.jsc.Main [options] file1.js [file2.js...]
```

The compiler options are as follows:

-extends java-class-name Specifies that a Java class extending the Java class `java-class-name` should be generated from the incoming JavaScript source file. Each global function in the source file is made a method of the generated class, overriding any methods in the base class by the same name.

-implements java-intf-name   Specifies that a Java class implementing the Java interface `java-intf-name` should be generated from the incoming JavaScript source file. Each global function in the source file is made a method of the generated class, implementing any methods in the interface by the same name.

-debug or -g Specifies that debug information should be generated.

-nosource Does not save the source in the class file. Functions and scripts compiled this way cannot be decompiled. This option can be used to avoid distributing source or simply to save space in the resulting class file.

-o outputFile Writes the class file to the given file (which should end with `.class`).

-opt optLevel or **-O optLevel**   Optimizes at level *optLevel*, which must be an integer between -1 and 9. If *optLevel* is greater than zero, -debug may not be specified.

-package packageName   Specifies the name of the Java package to generate the class into.

-version versionNumber   Specifies the language version to compile with. The string versionNumber must be 100, 110, 120, 130, 140, or 150.

To show how the compiler works, let's compile `ListFile.js` to `ListFile.class`. The following command line shows how it's done:

```
java org.mozilla.javascript.tools.jsc.Main ListFile.js
```

When you execute this command line, you find that it produces the `ListFile.class` file. This file is the compiled Java code for the script. You can execute the compiled class using `java ListFile`. For example, the following command line lists my `C:\autoexec.bat` file:

```
C:\mjscript\ch35>java ListFile C:\autoexec.bat
```

Scripting Java

When using Rhino, you work with a much different object model than you do when writing scripts to run under Navigator or Internet Explorer. The Rhino object model consists of the classes and interfaces of the Java API. If you are a Java programmer, then you should have no trouble using Rhino. If you are not a Java programmer, then it will be well worth your while to take an introductory course in Java. Check `www.java.sun.com` for a list of free online Java courses.

> **NOTE**   You may want to refer back to Chapter 27 if you are new to Java programming.

Whether you are an experienced Java programmer or not, there is one issue that you'll have to deal with: Both Java and JavaScript define `String` objects. However, the methods supported by Java's and JavaScript's `String` objects differ. In many cases, your scripts will contain a mixture of Java and JavaScript `String` objects. Knowing whether an object is a JavaScript `String` object or a Java `String` object is key to keeping your scripts error-free.

Listings 30.4 and 30.5 illustrate this problem. The `StringTest1.js` script of Listing 30.4 is intended to display the length of each line of the file specified by its first argument. When I run `StringTest1.js` to display my `C:\autoexec.bat` file, I get the following strange output:

```
C:\mjscript\ch35>java -jar C:\rhino\js.jar StringTest1.js C:\autoexec.bat
org.mozilla.javascript.NativeJavaMethod@4b7453
org.mozilla.javascript.NativeJavaMethod@4b7453
org.mozilla.javascript.NativeJavaMethod@4b7453
org.mozilla.javascript.NativeJavaMethod@4b7453
```

```
org.mozilla.javascript.NativeJavaMethod@4b7453
org.mozilla.javascript.NativeJavaMethod@4b7453
```

The output is the result of the following line:

```
java.lang.System.out.println(line.length)
```

The length property of the JavaScript String object is used to determine the length of each line of the file that was read. However, the object referenced by line is a Java String object. Changing length to length() (i.e., the length() method of the Java String object) results in the correct output being generated.

Listing 30.5 shows a similar error. The StringTest2.js file is intended to display the length of the first argument. In this case, we confuse a JavaScript String object with a Java String object. Here is the output that it produces when I run it with Rhino as an argument:

```
C:\mjscript\ch35>java -jar C:\rhino\js.jar StringTest2.js Rhino
js: "StringTest2.js", line 2: uncaught JavaScript exception: TypeError: 5 is not
a function.
```

In this case, the following is the offending line:

```
java.lang.System.out.println(arguments[0].length())
```

The object referenced by arguments[0] is a JavaScript String object. The value of arguments[0].length is evaluated as 5 (the length of Rhino) and then the function 5() is invoked, which results in the error message being generated. The error is avoided by removing the parentheses.

A general rule for determining whether an object is a JavaScript String object or a Java String object is that if the object is the result of using a Java method or property, then it is probably a Java String object. Otherwise, the object is likely to be a JavaScript String object.

Listing 30.4:   The *StringTest1.js* Script

```
if(arguments.length > 0) {
  reader = new java.io.FileReader(arguments[0])
  inFile = new java.io.BufferedReader(reader)
  for(line = inFile.readLine(); line != null;
    line = inFile.readLine()) {
   java.lang.System.out.println(line.length)
  }
}
```

Listing 30.5:   The *StringTest2.js* Script

```
if(arguments.length > 0) {
  java.lang.System.out.println(arguments[0].length())
}
```

Using a Presentation Generator

Personally, I use Rhino a lot. I run it on my Windows and Linux computers. I even run it on my Windows CE handheld computer. One of my favorite applications is a script that quickly generates slide show presentations from a text file outline of the presentation. I'll introduce you to this script to give you a better idea of the capabilities that Rhino provides.

As a Java and JavaScript consultant, I wind up giving a lot of presentations. Not being much of a PowerPoint fan, I prefer to give presentations in HTML. However, it's a lot of work to put together the individual slides. So I developed a way to create the presentations in a shorthand text form and have them translated into HTML. I use Rhino and the present.js file, shown in Listing 30.6, to perform the translation.

The present.js script is executed using the following command line:

```
java -jar c:\rhino\js.jar present.js source.txt [directoryName [fileName]]
```

The directoryName and fileName arguments are optional. If fileName is supplied, then directoryName must also be supplied. The directoryName argument specifies the directory in which the presentation slides are created. The default value is the slides subdirectory of the current directory. The fileName argument specifies the name to be given to the generated slides. The slides are generated as fileName1.htm, fileName2.htm, and so on. The default value of fileName is slide. So the files that are generated are slide1.htm, slide2.htm, and so on. In addition to the slides, a CSS style sheet, named styles.css is also generated. You can edit styles.css to alter the style in which each slide is displayed.

The source.txt argument is the name of the text file containing the source text of the presentation. This file is line oriented. Each line of the file consists of one of the following:

A blank line   Blank lines are ignored.

A comment   Comments begin with the hash (#) character. Comments are also ignored.

A heading   Headings begin with zero or more asterisk (*) characters. The asterisk identifies the level of indenting of the heading in the presentation outline. A heading may also have a vertical bar (|) or a plus sign (+) as its first character. (The asterisks follow the | or +.) Both | and + indicate that the heading is the title of a new slide. The + indicates that heading should not be included in the next higher-level slide.

A start text marker   One or more asterisks followed by an opening brace ([) indicate the beginning of markup text. All lines following the start text marker up to (but not including the end text marker) are processed as HTML markup. The asterisks indicate the level of the markup in the briefing. A start text marker is only matched by an end text marker with the same number of asterisks.

An end text marker   One or more asterisks followed by a closing brace (]) indicate the ending of markup text.

Markup text   All text between a start text marker and the matching end text marker is processed as HTML markup.

The circumflex (^) character is used as an escape character. It is used to enable asterisks to appear in a heading or markup text. When it appears as the first character of a line, it is removed, and the rest of the line is processed as a heading or markup.

Listing 30.7 shows the present.txt file. This file contains the source of a slide show presentation of the workings of the present.js script. You can convert this source file into an HTML presentation by running the following command:

```
C:\mjscript\ch35>java -jar c:\rhino\js.jar present.js present.txt
present: A JavaScript presentation generator
Version 0.03

Processing present.txt ...

Generating slides ...

Slide 1: How present.js works
Slide 2: Main code
Slide 3: Global functions
Slide 4: generateHTML()
Slide 5: createDefaultStyles()
Slide 6: summarizeSlides()
Slide 7: displaySlides()
Slide 8: generateSlides()
Slide 9: getParentSlide(i)
Slide 10: parseSourceFile(sourceFile)
Slide 11: readFile(sourceFile)
Slide 12: parseStartEndText()
Slide 13: setLineDescProperties()
Slide 14: displayParseTable()
Slide 15: displayErrors()
Slide 16: exit()
Slide 17: Object types
Slide 18: LineDesc
Slide 19: Slide
Slide 20: SlideElement

Generating HTML ...

Generating default styles ...
```

The presentation is generated in the C:\mjscript\ch35\slides directory. Open up slide1.htm with your web browser to view the presentation that was generated.

Listing 30.6:   **The *present.js* Script**

```
// present.js
// A JavaScript presentation generator
//
// (c) Copyright 1999-2000 James Jaworski
// All rights reserved.
//
// Date      Version      Change/comment
// ----      -------      --------------
// 99-12-04  Version  0.01 Demo for Builder conference
// 00-04-25  Version  0.02 Added documentation
//                         Added processing of +
//                         Added support for dirName & fileName
// 00-05-16  Version  0.03 Simplified script for Rhino chapter

// Begin main code
print("present: A JavaScript presentation generator")
print("Version 0.03\n")
var sourceFile = null
var dirName = "slides"
var fileName = "slide"
if(arguments.length > 0) {
 sourceFile = arguments[0]
 if(arguments.length > 1) dirName = arguments[1]
 if(arguments.length > 2) fileName = arguments[2]
}else {
 var s = "Usage: java -jar js.jar present.js sourceFile [dirName [fileName]]"
 print(s)
 exit()
}
// Define data structures
// parseTable is an array that holds each input line as a LineDesc object
var parseTable = new Array()
var error = parseSourceFile(sourceFile)
if(error) exit()
var slides = new Array()
generateSlides()
summarizeSlides()
generateHTML()
exit()
// End main code

function generateHTML() {
 print("Generating HTML ...\n")
 // Create slide directory
 var dir = new java.io.File(dirName)
```

```
 dir.mkdir()
 // Create each slide
 var n = slides.length
 for(var i=0; i<n; ++i)
  slides[i].create(i,n)
 createDefaultStyles()
}

function createDefaultStyles() {
 print("Generating default styles ...")
 var f = new java.io.File(dirName+"/styles.css")
 f.createNewFile()
 var fw = new java.io.FileWriter(f)
 var out = new java.io.PrintWriter(fw)
 out.println("#BBUTTONS {")
 out.println("font-size: 10pt;")
 out.println("text-align: right;")
 out.println("}")
 out.println("#BPAGES {")
 out.println("font-size: 8pt;")
 out.println("text-align: right;")
 out.println("}")
 out.println("#BTITLE {")
 out.println("font-size: 24pt;")
 out.println("font-style: bold;")
 out.println("text-align: center;")
 out.println("}")
 out.println("#B0 {")
 out.println("font-size: 24pt;")
 out.println("font-style: bold;")
 out.println("text-decoration: underline;")
 out.println("text-align: center;")
 out.println("}")
 out.println("#B1 {")
 out.println("font-size: 20pt;")
 out.println("font-style: bold;")
 out.println("}")
 out.println("#B2 {")
 out.println("font-size: 18pt;")
 out.println("font-style: bold;")
 out.println("}")
 out.println("#B3 {")
 out.println("font-size: 14pt;")
 out.println("font-style: bold;")
 out.println("}")
 out.println("#B4 {")
 out.println("font-size: 12pt;")
 out.println("font-style: bold;")
 out.println("}")
 out.println("#B5 {")
 out.println("font-size: 10pt;")
```

```
  out.println("font-style: bold;")
  out.println("}")
  out.close()
}

function summarizeSlides() {
 for(var i=0; i<slides.length; ++i)
  slides[i].summarize(i)
 print("")
}

function displaySlides() {
 var n = slides.length
 for(var i=0; i<n; ++i) {
  print("\nSlide "+i+":")
  slides[i].display()
 }
 print("")
}

function generateSlides() {
 print("Generating slides ...\n")
 var slideCount = 0
 for(var i=0; i<parseTable.length; ++i) {
  var level = parseTable[i].level
  if(parseTable[i].type == "heading") {
   if(parseTable[i].newSlide) {
    if(level == 0) {
     slides[slideCount] = new Slide(parseTable[i].text, level)
     ++slideCount
    }else{
     if(parseTable[i].displayAsBullet) {
      var parentSlide = getParentSlide(i)
      var parentLevel = slides[parentSlide].level
      slides[parentSlide].addHeading(parseTable[i].text,level-
parentLevel,slideCount)
     }
     slides[slideCount] = new Slide(parseTable[i].text, level)
     ++slideCount
    }
   }else{
    var parentSlide = getParentSlide(i)
    var parentLevel = slides[parentSlide].level
    slides[parentSlide].addHeading(parseTable[i].text,level-parentLevel,-1)
   }
  }else if(parseTable[i].type == "text") {
   var parentSlide = getParentSlide(i)
   var parentLevel = slides[parentSlide].level
   slides[parentSlide].addText(parseTable[i].text,level-parentLevel)
  }
 }
```

```
}

function getParentSlide(i) {
 // Look back through slides to find a slide that's at a lower level
 var n = slides.length - 1
 for(var j=n; ;--j) {
  if(j == -1) {
   print(">>> Error: '" + parseTable[i].text + "' does not have a parent
heading.")
   exit()
  }
  if(slides[j].level < parseTable[i].level) return j
 }
}

function parseSourceFile(sourceFile) {
 print("Processing " + sourceFile + " ...\n")
 readFile(sourceFile)
 parseStartEndText()
 setLineDescProperties()
 return displayErrors()
}

// Read each line of input file into parseTable as
// LineDesc objects
function readFile(sourceFile) {
 var reader = new java.io.BufferedReader(new java.io.FileReader(sourceFile))
 // Read input file
 for(var i=0; ; ++i) {
  var line = reader.readLine()
  if(line == null) break
  parseTable[i] = new LineDesc(line)
 }
}

// Find lines of type startText and endText
// Everything between matching *[ and *] tags is set to be of type text
function parseStartEndText() {
 // Parse startText, text, and endText
 var state = "normal"
 var currentLevel = 0
 for(var i=0; i<parseTable.length; ++i) {
  if(state == "normal") {
   if(parseTable[i].isStartText()) {
    parseTable[i].type = "startText"
    currentLevel = parseTable[i].getLevel()
    parseTable[i].level = currentLevel
    state = "text"
   }
  }else{
   // Is this a matching endText?
```

```
    if(parseTable[i].isEndText() &&
       currentLevel == parseTable[i].getLevel()) {
     parseTable[i].type = "endText"
     state = "normal"
    }else{
     parseTable[i].type = "text"
     parseTable[i].text = parseTable[i].line
     if(parseTable[i].text.length() > 0 &&
        parseTable[i].text.substring(0,1).equals("^")) {
      parseTable[i].text = parseTable[i].text.substring(1)
     }
    }
    parseTable[i].level = currentLevel
   }
  }
}

// Completes the LineDesc object for each element of parseTable
function setLineDescProperties() {
 // Determine LineDesc properties
 for(var i=0; i<parseTable.length; ++i) {
  if(parseTable[i].type == "unknown") {
   if(parseTable[i].isComment()) parseTable[i].type = "comment"
   else if(parseTable[i].isBlank()) parseTable[i].type = "blank"
   else if(parseTable[i].isHeading()) {
    var l = parseTable[i].getLevel()
    parseTable[i].level = l
    var ch = new java.lang.String("")
    if(parseTable[i].line.length() > l)
     ch = parseTable[i].line.substring(l,l+1)
    if(ch.equals("|")) {
     parseTable[i].type = "heading"
     parseTable[i].newSlide = true
     if(parseTable[i].line.length() > l+1)
      parseTable[i].text = parseTable[i].line.substring(l+1)
     else
      parseTable[i].text = new java.lang.String("")
    }else if(ch.equals("+")) {
     parseTable[i].type = "heading"
     parseTable[i].newSlide = true
     parseTable[i].displayAsBullet = false
     if(parseTable[i].line.length() > l+1)
      parseTable[i].text = parseTable[i].line.substring(l+1)
     else
      parseTable[i].text = new java.lang.String("")
    }else{
     if(l == 0) {
      parseTable[i].type = "error"
      parseTable[i].text = "Must start a new slide."
     }else{
      parseTable[i].type = "heading"
```

```
        parseTable[i].newSlide = false
        if(parseTable[i].line.length() > 1) {
         var s = parseTable[i].line.substring(1)
         if(s.substring(0,1).equals("^")) {
          if(s.length() == 1) s = new java.lang.String("")
          else s = s.substring(1)
          }
         parseTable[i].text = s
        }else parseTable[i].text = new java.lang.String("")
       }
      }
    }else{
     parseTable[i].type = "error"
     parseTable[i].text = "Input type cannot be determined."
     }
    }
   }
  }
 }

function displayParseTable() {
 for(var i=0; i<parseTable.length; ++i) {
  parseTable[i].display()
 }
}

function displayErrors() {
 for(var i=0; i<parseTable.length; ++i) {
  if(parseTable[i].displayError(i)) return true
 }
 return false
}

function exit() {
 java.lang.System.exit(0)
}

// Begin object definitions

function LineDesc(line) {
 // Line from input file
 this.line = line
 // Valid types are heading, text, startText, endText, unknown, comment, blank,
and error
 // unknown: The default type until another type is found
 // startText, endText: lines of the form *[ and *]
 // text: between startText and endText
 // comment: begins with #
 // blank: whitespace
 // heading: presentation title or heading
 // error:
 this.type = "unknown"
```

```
// The level, based on *s
this.level = 0
// Display as a bullet on parent slide?
this.displayAsBullet = true
// Create a new slide for this heading?
this.newSlide = false
// The text of the line after stripping formatting characters
this.text = new java.lang.String("")
this.isStartText = LineDesc_isStartText
this.isEndText = LineDesc_isEndText
this.getLevel = LineDesc_getLevel
this.isComment = LineDesc_isComment
this.isBlank = LineDesc_isBlank
this.isHeading = LineDesc_isHeading
this.display = LineDesc_display
this.displayError = LineDesc_displayError
}

function LineDesc_display() {
 print("\ntype: " + this.type)
 print("level: " + this.level)
 print("line: " + this.line)
 print("text: " + this.text)
 print("newSlide: " + this.newSlide)
}

function LineDesc_displayError(i) {
 if(this.type == "error") {
  print("line " + i + ": " + this.line)
  print(">>> Error: " + this.text)
  return true
 }else return false
}

// Is it of the form *[ where there is one or more * chars
function LineDesc_isStartText() {
 var len = this.line.length()
 if(len < 2) return false
 for(var i=0; i<len-1; ++i)
  if(!this.line.substring(i,i+1).equals("*")) return false
 if(!this.line.substring(len-1).equals("[")) return false
 return true
}

// Is it of the form *] where there is one or more * chars
function LineDesc_isEndText() {
 var len = this.line.length()
 if(len < 2) return false
 for(var i=0; i<len-1; ++i)
  if(!this.line.substring(i,i+1).equals("*")) return false
 if(!this.line.substring(len-1).equals("]")) return false
```

```
 return true
}

// How many *s does this line begin with?
function LineDesc_getLevel() {
 var len = this.line.length()
 var count = 0
 for(var i=0; i<len; ++i)
  if(this.line.substring(i,i+1).equals("*")) ++count
  else return count
 return count
}

// A comment begins with # as the first character
function LineDesc_isComment() {
 var s = this.line
 if(s.length() == 0) return false
 if(s.substring(0,1).equals("#")) return true
 return false
}

// A line consisting of spaces
function LineDesc_isBlank() {
 var s = this.line
 if(s.length() == 0) return true
 for(var i=0; i<s.length(); ++i)
  if(!s.substring(i,i+1).equals(" ")) return false
 return true
}

// Begins with *, |, +
// + added in version 0.02 to keep a heading from being displayed as a bullet on
// a prior slide
function LineDesc_isHeading() {
 if(this.line.length() == 0) return false
 var ch = this.line.substring(0,1)
 if(ch.equals("|") || ch.equals("+") || ch.equals("*")) return true
 return false
}

function Slide(title, level) {
 this.title = title
 this.level = level
 this.elements = new Array()
 this.addHeading = Slide_addHeading
 this.addText = Slide_addText
 this.display = Slide_display
 this.summarize = Slide_summarize
 this.create = Slide_create
}
```

```
function Slide_create(n,max) {
 var f = new java.io.File(dirName+"/"+fileName+(n+1)+".htm")
 f.createNewFile()
 var fw = new java.io.FileWriter(f)
 var out = new java.io.PrintWriter(fw)
 out.println("<HTML><HEAD><TITLE>")
 out.println(this.title)
 out.println("</TITLE>")
 out.println("<LINK REL=\"STYLESHEET\" TYPE=\"text/css\" HREF=\"styles.css\">")
 out.println("</HEAD>")
 out.println("<BODY>")
 if(n==0) {
  out.println("<P ID=\"BPAGES\">1 of "+max+"</P>")
  out.println("<P ID=\"BPAGES\">")
  out.println("<A HREF=\""+fileName+"2.htm\">Next</A>")
  out.println("</P>")
  out.println("<DIV ID=\"BTITLE\">"+this.title+"</DIV>")
 }else{
  out.println("<P ID=\"BPAGES\">"+(n+1)+" of "+max+"</P>")
  out.println("<P ID=\"BPAGES\">")
  out.println("<A HREF=\""+fileName+"1.htm\">First</A>")
  out.println(" <A HREF=\""+fileName+n+".htm\">Previous</A>")
  if(n != max-1)
   out.println(" <A HREF=\""+fileName+(n+2)+".htm\">Next</A>")
  out.println("</P>")
  out.println("<DIV ID=\"B0\">"+this.title+"</DIV>")
 }
 for(var i=0; i<this.elements.length; ++i) {
  if(this.elements[i].type == "heading") {
   for(var j=0; j<this.elements[i].level; ++j) out.println("<UL>")
   out.println("<LI>")
   var k = this.elements[i].level
   if(k>5) k=5
   out.println("<DIV ID=\"B" + k + "\">")
   if(this.elements[i].link != -1)
    out.println("<A HREF=\"" + fileName + this.elements[i].link + ".htm\">")
   out.println(this.elements[i].text)
   if(this.elements[i].link != -1)
    out.println("</A>")
   out.println("</DIV>")
   out.println("</LI>")
   for(var j=0; j<this.elements[i].level; ++j) out.println("</UL>")
  }else{
   out.println(this.elements[i].text)
  }
 }
 out.println("</BODY></HTML>")
 out.close()
}

function Slide_summarize(i) {
```

```
   print("Slide "+(i+1)+": "+this.title)
}

function Slide_display() {
 print(this.title+" ("+this.level+")")
 var n = this.elements.length
 for(var i=0;i<n;++i) this.elements[i].display()
}

function Slide_addHeading(text, level, link) {
 var n = this.elements.length
 this.elements[n] = new SlideElement("heading", text, level, link)
}

function Slide_addText(text, level) {
 var n = this.elements.length
 this.elements[n] = new SlideElement("text", text, level, -1)
}

function SlideElement(type, text, level, link) {
 this.type = type
 this.text = text
 this.level = level
 this.link = link
 this.display = SlideElement_display
}

function SlideElement_display() {
 var s = ""
 for(var i=0; i<this.level; ++i) s += "."
 s += this.text + " (" + this.type + " " + this.link + ")"
 print(s)
}
```

Listing 30.7:   The *present.txt* Presentation Source File

```
|How present.js works
*|Main code
**Displays version/help information
**Processes arguments
**Defines and initializes global objects
**Generates slide objects and associated HTML
*|Global functions
**|generateHTML()
***Manages the HTML generation
***Creates the directory where the slides are to be generated
***Invokes the create() method of each slide to generate the HTML for that slide
***Invokes createDefaultStyles() to create the styles.css file
**|createDefaultStyles()
***Creates a default styles.css stylesheet file
```

***The styles.css file may be edited to change then display characteristics of
↳the entire presentation
**|summarizeSlides()
***Invokes the summarize() method of each slide
***Results in the slide number and title being displayed
**|displaySlides()
***Invokes the display() method of each slide
***Results in the title, level, and elements of the slide being displayed
***Used for debugging purposes
**|generateSlides()
***Converts the parsed source file data into an array of Slide objects
***Allocates headings and markup text to each slide
***Links the slides to each other
**|getParentSlide(i)
***Returns the parent of the ith slide
***The parent slide is the prior slide that introduces the slide's title heading
***Displays an error message of the parent cannot be found
**|parseSourceFile(sourceFile)
***Reads and parses the source presentation file
***Results in the development of the parseTable array
**|readFile(sourceFile)
***Reads each line of the source file and creates LineDesc objects that are
↳added to the parseTable array
***LineDesc objects describe the input lines that were read
**|parseStartEndText()
***Finds lines that contain start and end of markup tags
***Identifies markup text that belongs to those tags
**|setLineDescProperties()
***Completes input line parsing
***Specifies the properties of the LineDesc objects of parseTable
**|displayParseTable()
***Displays the LineDesc objects of parseTable
**|displayErrors()
***Displays errors idenified via the LineDesc objects of parseTable
**|exit()
***Terminates the script by invoking the exit() method of the java.lang.System
↳object
*|Object types
**|LineDesc
***Properties
****line
*****A copy of the line that was read from the presentation source file
****type
*****The type of line that was read
*****Valid types are heading, text, startText, endText, unknown, comment,
↳blank, and error
****level
*****The presentation indentation level associated with the line
****displayAsBullet
*****A boolean value that indicates whether the line should be displayed
↳with a bullet

```
****newSlide
*****A boolean value that indicates whether the line begins a new slide
****text
*****The parsed text of the line
***Methods
****isStartText()
*****Returns true if the line is a start of markup indicator
****isEndText()
*****Returns true if the line is a start of markup indicator
****getLevel()
*****Returns the level property
****isComment()
*****Returns true if the line is a comment
****isBlank()
*****Returns true if the line is blank
****isHeading()
*****Returns true if the line is a heading
****display()
*****Displays selected properties of the LineDesc object
****displayError()
*****Displays any errors associated with the line
**|Slide
***Properties
****title
*****The title of the slide
****level
*****The outline level of the slide
****elements
*****An array of SlideElement objects
***Methods
****addHeading(text, level, link)
*****Creates a new SlideElement object of type heading and adds it to the
⤷current slide
****addText(text, level)
*****Creates a new SlideElement object of type text and adds it to the
⤷current slide
****display()
*****Displays the slide's title, level, and elements
****summarize()
*****Displays the slide number and title
****create(n,max)
*****Creates slide n of max slides
*****Writes the slide's HTML to the file corresponding to the slide
**|SlideElement
***Properties
****type
*****The type of slide element: heading or text
****text
*****The text of the slide element
****level
*****The outline level of the slide element
```

```
****link
*****The slide in which the element is located
***Methods
****display()
*****Displays the properties of a SlideElement object
```

Summary

In this chapter you learned how to install and use the Rhino scripting tool. You created several small scripts and learned to use the Rhino interpreter and compiler. You examined some of the issues involved with scripting Java and then you worked through a Rhino slide show generator. In the next chapter, you'll learn about Microsoft's scripting environment called Windows Scripting Host.

Working with Windows Scripting Host

- Downloading and installing Windows Scripting Host

- Working with the Windows Scripting Host object model

- Accessing file system resources

- Using WSF files

Recognizing the value of JScript in both client and server web applications, Microsoft extended the use of JScript and other scripting languages to general desktop applications. This scripting technology is referred to as Windows Scripting Host (WSH) and is available for all 32-bit Windows platforms (Windows 95 and later). In this chapter, we'll focus on WSH scripting with JavaScript. We'll begin by downloading and installing WSH and the WSH documentation set. We'll run some sample scripts to give you a feel for what WSH is all about. We'll cover the WSH object model. We'll then develop a Windows application that takes advantage of WSH capabilities. By the time you finish this chapter, you'll be up to speed on WSH and the capabilities that it provides.

Introducing WSH

WSH is a scripting environment for 32-bit Windows platforms. It supports JScript, VBScript, Perl, and other scripting languages through the use of a language-independent scripting framework. WSH allows scripts to execute using windows or command-line text input and output. It provides a basic set of objects from which simple desktop applications may be constructed.

WSH's main use is in non-interactive scripting applications, such as logon scripting, batch command scripting, and the automation of repetitive tasks. It is simple to learn, easy to use, and depending upon your scripting needs, a handy tool to have in your scripting toolbox. I use it a lot for running common admin tasks, such as backing up critical files, setting environment variables, and updating network drive mappings.

WSH is documented at Microsoft's scripting website located at `http://msdn.microsoft.com/scripting/`.

Downloading and Installing WSH

WSH is easy to install. Simply go to `http://msdn.microsoft.com/scripting/` and follow the links to the WSH download section. Download the WSH setup files to your machine as well as the documentation, which is in a separate file.

When you have downloaded the WSH setup file, double-click it to install WSH on your system. Then double-click the documentation setup file to install the documentation. Make sure that you are still connected to the Internet when you open up the WSH documentation file (from the Windows Start menu) because it may need to download and install some supporting files. The documentation contains a tutorial and an object reference.

Running Sample WSH Scripts

Listing 31.1 provides an example of a WSH script. This script creates a WshShell object and assigns it to the shell variable. It then invokes the Popup() method of the shell to display a pop-up window with the "Hello from WSH" title and the "Hello World!" text. The pop-up window is displayed with a delay of 0 seconds.

> **NOTE** To run Listing 31.1, you'll need to have WSH installed on your system. You can check for wscript.exe in your \Windows directory. Simply double-click on wsh-hello.js to run the script.

FIGURE 31.1:

A simple WSH program that displays "Hello World!" (Listing 31.1)

Listing 31.1:   A WSH Script That Displays "Hello World!" (wsh-hello.js)

```
shell = WScript.CreateObject("WScript.Shell")
shell.Popup("Hello World!",0,"Hello from WSH")
```

Listing 31.2 provides another example of a WSH script (wsh-environ.js). This script is run from a command-line prompt using cscript.exe. The cscript.exe program is automatically installed with WSH. You can run wsh-environ.js as follows:

```
C:\WINDOWS\Desktop\wsh>cscript wsh-environ.js
Microsoft (R) Windows Script Host Version 5.1 for Windows
Copyright (C) Microsoft Corporation 1996-1999. All rights reserved.

Environment Settings:

PATH: C:\WINDOWS;C:\WINDOWS\COMMAND;C:\JDK1.3\BIN;;C:\ADABAS\BIN;C:\ADABAS\PGM;C
:\PROGRA~1\SSHCOM~1\SSHSEC~1

PROMPT: $p$g

WINDIR: C:\WINDOWS

TEMP: C:\WINDOWS\TEMP
```

```
TMP: C:\WINDOWS\TEMP
```

```
C:\WINDOWS\Desktop\wsh>
```

It displays the values of the PATH, PROMPT, WINDIR, TEMP, and TMP environment variables.

The wsh-environ.js script creates a WshShell object and assigns it to the shell variable. It then invokes the displayEnvironment() function to display selected environment variables.

The displayEnvironment() function creates a WshEnvironment object and assigns it to the environ variable. It then uses the object to access the PATH, PROMPT, WINDIR, TEMP, and TMP environment variables. The values of these variables are put into a string that is in the console window. A reference to the standard output stream object is obtained using WScript.StdOut. This object is assigned to the out variable. The WriteLine() method of the object is used to display the values of the environment variables.

NOTE   WSH runs GUI scripts using wscript.exe and console scripts via cscript.exe.

Listing 31.2:   A WSH Script That Displays Environment Variables (wsh-environ.js)

```
function displayEnvironment() {
// Obtain values of environment variables
var environ = shell.Environment("Process")
var edata = "PATH: "+environ("PATH")+"\n\n"
edata += "PROMPT: "+environ("PROMPT")+"\n\n"
edata += "WINDIR: "+environ("WINDIR")+"\n\n"
edata += "TEMP: "+environ("TEMP")+"\n\n"
edata += "TMP: "+environ("TMP")+"\n"
// Display to standard out
var out = WScript.StdOut
out.WriteLine("Environment Settings:\n")
out.WriteLine(edata)
}
displayEnvironment()
```

Working with the WSH Object Model

Having been exposed to WSH, you are probably wondering where all of these new objects came from. The answer is from the WSH object model. A WSH object reference is included in the WSH documentation. Here's a brief summary of these objects:

WScript   The basic object of a WSH application; provides access to other WSH objects.

WshArguments   Provides access to the arguments of a WSH application.

WshEnvironment Provides access to environment variables.

WshNetwork Provides access to network resources.

WshShell Provides access to pop-up windows, the system Registry, executable programs, and special system folders.

WshShortcut Encapsulates a shortcut to Windows' objects.

WshSpecialFolders Provides access to special windows directories, such as the desktop and Start menu.

WshURLShortcut Encapsulates a shortcut to objects that are accessed via a URL.

The WSH documentation contains a complete description of these objects, their properties and methods.

Accessing File System Resources

While WSH provides access to many of the objects that you need for Windows scripting, its I/O support is limited to the standard input, output, and error streams. This is not a problem, because access to file system resources may be obtained through the `FileSystemObject` object. This object is part of the core JScript objects that are supported for all Windows scripting (e.g., WSH, ASP, Internet Explorer, etc.).

A `FileSystemObject` is created using the ActiveX object constructor:

fso = new ActiveXObject("Scripting.FileSystemObject") The `FileSystemObject` can then be used to manipulate the available file system. Some useful `FileSystemObject` methods follow. Consult the JScript documentation for more information on the `FileSystemObject` object.

CopyFile(source, destination[, overwrite]) Copies a file from *source* to *destination*. The overwrite value (default `true`) specifies whether an existing file should be overwritten.

CopyFolder(source, destination[, overwrite]) Copies a folder from *source* to *destination*. The `overwrite` value (default `true`) specifies whether an existing folder should be overwritten.

CreateFolder(folderPathName) Creates the specified folder.

CreateTextFile(filename[, overwrite[, unicode]]) Creates the specified file. The `overwrite` value (default `true`) specifies whether an existing file should be overwritten. The `unicode` value (default false) specifies whether the file should be Unicode or ASCII.

DeleteFileDeleteFile(filespec[, force]) Deletes the specified file. The *filespec* may contain wild card characters. If *force* is `true` (`false` by default), read-only files are deleted.

DeleteFolder(filespec[, force])   Deletes the specified folder. The *filespec* may contain wild card characters. If *force* is `true` (`false` by default), read-only folders are deleted.

FileExists(filespec)   Returns a Boolean value that identifies whether the specified file exists.

FolderExists(filespec)   Returns a Boolean value that identifies whether the specified folder exists.

MoveFile(source, destination)   Moves the specified file from *source* to *destination*.

MoveFolder(source, destination)   Moves the specified folder from *source* to *destination*.

OpenTextFile(filename[, iomode[, create[, format]]])   Opens the specified file. The `iomode` parameter can be `ForReading`, `ForWriting`, or `ForAppending`. The `create` parameter (default `false`) specifies whether a file should be created if it does not exist. The format parameter may be `TristateTrue` (Unicode), `TristateFalse` (ASCII), or `TristateUseDefault` (use the system default).

Listing 31.3 provides an example of using the `FileSystemObject`. The script is a command-line script that copies a file to a file of a different name. You run the script as follows:

```
D:\Sybex\2001\ch36\code>cscript filecopy.js
Microsoft (R) Windows Script Host Version 5.1 for Windows
Copyright (C) Microsoft Corporation 1996-1999. All rights reserved.

Source file name: filecopy.js
Destination file name: filecopy2.js
filecopy.js was copied to filecopy2.js.

D:\Sybex\2001\ch36\code>
```

Enter the name of the file you want to copy when prompted for source. Enter the name of the copied file when prompted for destination. The `CopyFile()` method of the `FileSystemObject` is used to perform the file copying.

Listing 31.3:   Using the *FileSystemObject* to Copy Files (filecopy.js)

```
var input = WScript.StdIn
var output = WScript.StdOut
output.Write("Source file name: ")
var source = input.ReadLine();
output.Write("Destination file name: ")
var dest = input.ReadLine();
var fso = new ActiveXObject("Scripting.FileSystemObject")
fso.CopyFile(source, dest)
output.WriteLine(source + " was copied to " + dest + ".")
```

Using WSF Files

The easiest way to deploy WSH scripts is as JS files. However, Microsoft provides an alternative using WSF files. A WSF file is an XML file that allows you to store several scripts in the same file. Each script is associated with a unique job ID. Consult the WSH documentation for more information on WSF files.

Migrating *present.js* to WSH

In Chapter 30, "Programming Rhino," you created the application `present.js` using the capabilities provided by the Rhino scripting environment. Listing 31.4 provides a porting of `present.js` to WSH. The ported script (`wsh-present.js`) is a command-line script that provides equivalent functionality to the original `present.js`.

Only a few changes were needed to make the conversion. These are as follows:

WScript.Arguments   The Arguments collection of the WScript object is used to access command line arguments.

WScript.StdOut   The StdOut property of WScript is used to provide console output to the user. This replaces the Rhino print() method.

FileSystemObject   The FileSystemObject replaces the java.io package.

JavaScript *String* objects   Java String objects are replaced by JavaScript String objects.

Try running `wsh-present.js` with the `wsh-present.txt` file shown in Listing 31.5. You should get the following results:

```
D:\Sybex\2001\ch36\code>cscript wsh-present.js wsh-present.txt
Microsoft (R) Windows Script Host Version 5.1 for Windows
Copyright (C) Microsoft Corporation 1996-1999. All rights reserved.

wsh-present: A JavaScript presentation generator
Version 0.03

Processing wsh-present.txt ...

Generating slides ...

Slide 1: How wsh-present.js works
Slide 2: Main code
Slide 3: Global functions
Slide 4: generateHTML()
Slide 5: createDefaultStyles()
Slide 6: summarizeSlides()
```

```
Slide 7: displaySlides()
Slide 8: generateSlides()
Slide 9: getParentSlide(i)
Slide 10: parseSourceFile(sourceFile)
Slide 11: readFile(sourceFile)
Slide 12: parseStartEndText()
Slide 13: setLineDescProperties()
Slide 14: displayParseTable()
Slide 15: displayErrors()
Slide 16: exit()
Slide 17: Object types
Slide 18: LineDesc
Slide 19: Slide
Slide 20: SlideElement

Generating HTML ...

Generating default styles ...

D:\Sybex\2001\ch36\code>
```

The slides folder will be created in the directory where you run the script. It will contain a HTML presentation that documents the wsh-present.js script.

Listing 31.4:   A WSH Version of *present.js* (wsh-present.js)

```javascript
// wsh-present.js
// A JavaScript presentation generator
//

// Begin main code
shell = WScript.CreateObject("WScript.Shell")
output = WScript.StdOut
fso = new ActiveXObject("Scripting.FileSystemObject")
output.WriteLine("wsh-present: A JavaScript presentation generator")
output.WriteLine("Version 0.03\n")
var sourceFile = null
var dirName = "slides"
var fileName = "slide"
arguments = WScript.Arguments
if(arguments.length > 0) {
 sourceFile = arguments(0)
 if(arguments.length > 1) dirName = arguments(1)
 if(arguments.length > 2) fileName = arguments(2)
}else {
 var s = "Usage: cscript wsh-present.js sourceFile [dirName [fileName]]"
 output.WriteLine(s)
 exit()
}
```

```
// Define data structures
// parseTable is an array that holds each input line as a LineDesc object
var parseTable = new Array()
var error = parseSourceFile(sourceFile)
if(error) exit()
var slides = new Array()
generateSlides()
summarizeSlides()
generateHTML()
exit()
// End main code

function generateHTML() {
 output.WriteLine("Generating HTML ...\n")
 // Create slide directory
 if(!fso.FolderExists(dirName)) fso.CreateFolder(dirName)
 // Create each slide
 var n = slides.length
 for(var i=0; i<n; ++i)
  slides[i].create(i,n)
 createDefaultStyles()
}

function createDefaultStyles() {
 output.WriteLine("Generating default styles ...")
 var out = fso.OpenTextFile(dirName+"/styles.css", 2, true)
 out.WriteLine("#BBUTTONS {")
 out.WriteLine("font-size: 10pt;")
 out.WriteLine("text-align: right;")
 out.WriteLine("}")
 out.WriteLine("#BPAGES {")
 out.WriteLine("font-size: 8pt;")
 out.WriteLine("text-align: right;")
 out.WriteLine("}")
 out.WriteLine("#BTITLE {")
 out.WriteLine("font-size: 24pt;")
 out.WriteLine("font-style: bold;")
 out.WriteLine("text-align: center;")
 out.WriteLine("}")
 out.WriteLine("#B0 {")
 out.WriteLine("font-size: 24pt;")
 out.WriteLine("font-style: bold;")
 out.WriteLine("text-decoration: underline;")
 out.WriteLine("text-align: center;")
 out.WriteLine("}")
 out.WriteLine("#B1 {")
 out.WriteLine("font-size: 20pt;")
 out.WriteLine("font-style: bold;")
 out.WriteLine("}")
 out.WriteLine("#B2 {")
 out.WriteLine("font-size: 18pt;")
```

```
out.WriteLine("font-style: bold;")
out.WriteLine("}")
out.WriteLine("#B3 {")
out.WriteLine("font-size: 14pt;")
out.WriteLine("font-style: bold;")
out.WriteLine("}")
out.WriteLine("#B4 {")
out.WriteLine("font-size: 12pt;")
out.WriteLine("font-style: bold;")
out.WriteLine("}")
out.WriteLine("#B5 {")
out.WriteLine("font-size: 10pt;")
out.WriteLine("font-style: bold;")
out.WriteLine("}")
out.Close()
}

function summarizeSlides() {
 for(var i=0; i<slides.length; ++i)
  slides[i].summarize(i)
 output.WriteLine("")
}

function displaySlides() {
 var n = slides.length
 for(var i=0; i<n; ++i) {
  output.WriteLine("\nSlide "+i+":")
  slides[i].display()
 }
 output.WriteLine("")
}

function generateSlides() {
 output.WriteLine("Generating slides ...\n")
 var slideCount = 0
 for(var i=0; i<parseTable.length; ++i) {
  var level = parseTable[i].level
  if(parseTable[i].type == "heading") {
   if(parseTable[i].newSlide) {
    if(level == 0) {
     slides[slideCount] = new Slide(parseTable[i].text, level)
     ++slideCount
    }else{
     if(parseTable[i].displayAsBullet) {
      var parentSlide = getParentSlide(i)
      var parentLevel = slides[parentSlide].level
      slides[parentSlide].addHeading(parseTable[i].text,level-
parentLevel,slideCount)
     }
     slides[slideCount] = new Slide(parseTable[i].text, level)
     ++slideCount
```

```
      }
    }else{
      var parentSlide = getParentSlide(i)
      var parentLevel = slides[parentSlide].level
      slides[parentSlide].addHeading(parseTable[i].text,level-parentLevel,-1)
      }
  }else if(parseTable[i].type == "text") {
      var parentSlide = getParentSlide(i)
      var parentLevel = slides[parentSlide].level
      slides[parentSlide].addText(parseTable[i].text,level-parentLevel)
    }
  }
}

function getParentSlide(i) {
  // Look back through slides to find a slide that's at a lower level
  var n = slides.length-1
  for(var j=n; ;j = j-1) {
    if(j == -1) {
      output.WriteLine(">>> Error: '" + parseTable[i].text +
  ↳ "' does not have a parent heading.")
      exit()
    }
    if(slides[j].level < parseTable[i].level) return j
  }
}

function parseSourceFile(sourceFile) {
  output.WriteLine("Processing " + sourceFile + " ...\n")
  readFile(sourceFile)
  parseStartEndText()
  setLineDescProperties()
  return displayErrors()
}

// Read each line of input file into parseTable as
// LineDesc objects
function readFile(sourceFile) {
  var reader = fso.OpenTextFile(sourceFile, 1)
  // Read input file
  for(var i=0; ; ++i) {
    if(reader.AtEndOfStream) break
    var line = reader.ReadLine()
    parseTable[i] = new LineDesc(line)
  }
  reader.Close()
}

// Find lines of type startText and endText
// Everything between matching *[ and *] tags is set to be of type text
function parseStartEndText() {
```

```
// Parse startText, text, and endText
var state = "normal"
var currentLevel = 0
for(var i=0; i<parseTable.length; ++i) {
 if(state == "normal") {
  if(parseTable[i].isStartText()) {
   parseTable[i].type = "startText"
   currentLevel = parseTable[i].getLevel()
   parseTable[i].level = currentLevel
   state = "text"
  }
 }else{
  // Is this a matching endText?
  if(parseTable[i].isEndText() &&
     currentLevel == parseTable[i].getLevel()) {
   parseTable[i].type = "endText"
   state = "normal"
  }else{
   parseTable[i].type = "text"
   parseTable[i].text = parseTable[i].line
   if(parseTable[i].text.length > 0 &&
      parseTable[i].text.substring(0,1) == "^") {
    parseTable[i].text = parseTable[i].text.substring(1)
   }
  }
  parseTable[i].level = currentLevel
 }
}
}

// Completes the LineDesc object for each element of parseTable
function setLineDescProperties() {
 // Determine LineDesc properties
 for(var i=0; i<parseTable.length; ++i) {
  if(parseTable[i].type == "unknown") {
   if(parseTable[i].isComment()) parseTable[i].type = "comment"
   else if(parseTable[i].isBlank()) parseTable[i].type = "blank"
   else if(parseTable[i].isHeading()) {
    var l = parseTable[i].getLevel()
    parseTable[i].level = l
    var ch = ""
    if(parseTable[i].line.length > l)
     ch = parseTable[i].line.substring(l,l+1)
    if(ch == "|") {
     parseTable[i].type = "heading"
     parseTable[i].newSlide = true
     if(parseTable[i].line.length > l+1)
      parseTable[i].text = parseTable[i].line.substring(l+1)
     else
      parseTable[i].text = ""
    }else if(ch == "+") {
```

```
          parseTable[i].type = "heading"
          parseTable[i].newSlide = true
          parseTable[i].displayAsBullet = false
          if(parseTable[i].line.length > 1+1)
           parseTable[i].text = parseTable[i].line.substring(1+1)
          else
           parseTable[i].text = ""
        }else{
         if(1 == 0) {
          parseTable[i].type = "error"
          parseTable[i].text = "Must start a new slide."
         }else{
          parseTable[i].type = "heading"
          parseTable[i].newSlide = false
          if(parseTable[i].line.length > 1) {
           var s = parseTable[i].line.substring(1)
           if(s.substring(0,1) == "^") {
            if(s.length == 1) s = ""
            else s = s.substring(1)
           }
           parseTable[i].text = s
          }else parseTable[i].text = ""
         }
        }
      }else{
       parseTable[i].type = "error"
       parseTable[i].text = "Input type cannot be determined."
      }
     }
    }
}

function displayParseTable() {
 for(var i=0; i<parseTable.length; ++i) {
  parseTable[i].display()
 }
}

function displayErrors() {
 for(var i=0; i<parseTable.length; ++i) {
  if(parseTable[i].displayError(i)) return true
 }
 return false
}

function exit() {
 WScript.Quit()
}

// Begin object definitions
```

```
function LineDesc(line) {
 // Line from input file
 this.line = line
 // Valid types are heading, text, startText, endText, unknown,
 // comment, blank, and error
 // unknown: The default type until another type is found
 // startText, endText: lines of the form *[ and *]
 // text: between startText and endText
 // comment: begins with #
 // blank: whitespace
 // heading: presentation title or heading
 // error:
 this.type = "unknown"
 // The level, based on *s
 this.level = 0
 // Display as a bullet on parent slide?
 this.displayAsBullet = true
 // Create a new slide for this heading?
 this.newSlide = false
 // The text of the line after stripping formatting characters
 this.text = ""
 this.isStartText = LineDesc_isStartText
 this.isEndText = LineDesc_isEndText
 this.getLevel = LineDesc_getLevel
 this.isComment = LineDesc_isComment
 this.isBlank = LineDesc_isBlank
 this.isHeading = LineDesc_isHeading
 this.display = LineDesc_display
 this.displayError = LineDesc_displayError
}

function LineDesc_display() {
 output.Write("\ntype: " + this.type)
 output.Write(" level: " + this.level)
 output.WriteLine(" newSlide: " + this.newSlide)
 output.WriteLine("line: " + this.line)
 output.WriteLine("text: " + this.text)
}

function LineDesc_displayError(i) {
 if(this.type == "error") {
  output.WriteLine("line " + i + ": " + this.line)
  output.WriteLine(">>> Error: " + this.text)
  return true
 }else return false
}

// Is it of the form *[ where there is one or more * chars
function LineDesc_isStartText() {
 var len = this.line.length
 if(len < 2) return false
```

```
    for(var i=0; i<len-1; ++i)
     if(this.line.substring(i,i+1) != "*") return false
    if(this.line.substring(len-1) != "[") return false
    return true
}

// Is it of the form *] where there is one or more * chars
function LineDesc_isEndText() {
   var len = this.line.length
   if(len < 2) return false
   for(var i=0; i<len-1; ++i)
    if(this.line.substring(i,i+1) != "*") return false
   if(this.line.substring(len-1) != "]") return false
   return true
}

// How many *s does this line begin with?
function LineDesc_getLevel() {
   var len = this.line.length
   var count = 0
   for(var i=0; i<len; ++i)
    if(this.line.substring(i,i+1) == "*") ++count
    else return count
   return count
}

// A comment begins with # as the first character
function LineDesc_isComment() {
   var s = this.line
   if(s.length == 0) return false
   if(s.substring(0,1) == "#") return true
   return false
}

// A line consisting of spaces
function LineDesc_isBlank() {
   var s = this.line
   if(s.length == 0) return true
   for(var i=0; i<s.length; ++i)
    if(!s.substring(i,i+1) == " ") return false
   return true
}

// Begins with *, |, +
// + added in version 0.02 to keep a heading from being displayed as a bullet on
// a prior slide
function LineDesc_isHeading() {
   if(this.line.length == 0) return false
   var ch = this.line.substring(0,1)
   if(ch == "|" || ch == "+" || ch == "*") return true
   return false
```

```
    }

function Slide(title, level) {
 this.title = title
 this.level = level
 this.elements = new Array()
 this.addHeading = Slide_addHeading
 this.addText = Slide_addText
 this.display = Slide_display
 this.summarize = Slide_summarize
 this.create = Slide_create
}

function Slide_create(n,max) {
 var out = fso.OpenTextFile(dirName+"/"+fileName+(n+1)+".htm", 2, true)
 out.WriteLine("<HTML><HEAD><TITLE>")
 out.WriteLine(this.title)
 out.WriteLine("</TITLE>")
 out.WriteLine("<LINK REL=\"STYLESHEET\" TYPE=\"text/css\"
↳ HREF=\"styles.css\">")
 out.WriteLine("</HEAD>")
 out.WriteLine("<BODY>")
 if(n==0) {
  out.WriteLine("<P ID=\"BPAGES\">1 of "+max+"</P>")
  out.WriteLine("<P ID=\"BPAGES\">")
  out.WriteLine("<A HREF=\""+fileName+"2.htm\">Next</A>")
  out.WriteLine("</P>")
  out.WriteLine("<DIV ID=\"BTITLE\">"+this.title+"</DIV>")
 }else{
  out.WriteLine("<P ID=\"BPAGES\">"+(n+1)+" of "+max+"</P>")
  out.WriteLine("<P ID=\"BPAGES\">")
  out.WriteLine("<A HREF=\""+fileName+"1.htm\">First</A>")
  out.WriteLine(" <A HREF=\""+fileName+n+".htm\">Previous</A>")
  if(n != max-1)
   out.WriteLine(" <A HREF=\""+fileName+(n+2)+".htm\">Next</A>")
  out.WriteLine("</P>")
  out.WriteLine("<DIV ID=\"B0\">"+this.title+"</DIV>")
 }
 for(var i=0; i<this.elements.length; ++i) {
  if(this.elements[i].type == "heading") {
   for(var j=0; j<this.elements[i].level; ++j) out.WriteLine("<UL>")
   out.WriteLine("<LI>")
   var k = this.elements[i].level
   if(k>5) k=5
   out.WriteLine("<DIV ID=\"B" + k + "\">")
   if(this.elements[i].link != -1)
    out.WriteLine("<A HREF=\"" + fileName + this.elements[i].link + ".htm\">")
   out.WriteLine(this.elements[i].text)
   if(this.elements[i].link != -1)
    out.WriteLine("</A>")
   out.WriteLine("</DIV>")
```

```
    out.WriteLine("</LI>")
    for(var j=0; j<this.elements[i].level; ++j)
    out.WriteLine("</UL>")
  }else{
    out.WriteLine(this.elements[i].text)
  }
 }
 out.WriteLine("</BODY></HTML>")
 out.Close()
}

function Slide_summarize(i) {
 output.WriteLine("Slide "+(i+1)+": "+this.title)
}

function Slide_display() {
 output.WriteLine(this.title+" ("+this.level+")")
 var n = this.elements.length
 for(var i=0;i<n;++i) this.elements[i].display()
}

function Slide_addHeading(text, level, link) {
 var n = this.elements.length
 this.elements[n] = new SlideElement("heading", text, level, link)
}

function Slide_addText(text, level) {
 var n = this.elements.length
 this.elements[n] = new SlideElement("text", text, level, -1)
}

function SlideElement(type, text, level, link) {
 this.type = type
 this.text = text
 this.level = level
 this.link = link
 this.display = SlideElement_display
}

function SlideElement_display() {
 var s = ""
 for(var i=0; i<this.level; ++i) s += "."
 s += this.text + " (" + this.type + " " + this.link + ")"
 output.WriteLine(s)
}
```

⟳ **Listing 31.5:   A Sample Presentation File (wsh-present.txt)**

```
|How wsh-present.js works
*|Main code
```

```
**Displays version/help information
**Processes arguments
**Defines and initializes global objects
**Generates slide objects and associated HTML
*|Global functions
**|generateHTML()
***Manages the HTML generation
***Creates the directory where the slides are to be generated
***Invokes the create() method of each slide to generate the HTML for that slide
***Invokes createDefaultStyles() to create the styles.css file
**|createDefaultStyles()
***Creates a default styles.css stylesheet file
***The styles.css file may be edited to change then display
↳ characteristics of the entire presentation
**|summarizeSlides()
***Invokes the summarize() method of each slide
***Results in the slide number and title being displayed
**|displaySlides()
***Invokes the display() method of each slide
***Results in the title, level, and elements of the slide being displayed
***Used for debugging purposes
**|generateSlides()
***Converts the parsed source file data into an array of Slide objects
***Allocates headings and markup text to each slide
***Links the slides to each other
**|getParentSlide(i)
***Returns the parent of the ith slide
***The parent slide is the prior slide that introduces the slide's title heading
***Displays an error message of the parent cannot be found
**|parseSourceFile(sourceFile)
***Reads and parses the source presentation file
***Results in the development of the parseTable array
**|readFile(sourceFile)
***Reads each line of the source file and creates LineDesc objects
↳ that are added to the parseTable array
***LineDesc objects describe the input lines that were read
**|parseStartEndText()
***Finds lines that contain start and end of markup tags
***Identifies markup text that belongs to those tags
**|setLineDescProperties()
***Completes input line parsing
***Specifies the properties of the LineDesc objects of parseTable
**|displayParseTable()
***Displays the LineDesc objects of parseTable
**|displayErrors()
***Displays errors idenified via the LineDesc objects of parseTable
**|exit()
***Terminates the script by invoking the exit() method of the
↳java.lang.System object
*|Object types
**|LineDesc
```

```
***Properties
****line
*****A copy of the line that was read from the presentation source file
****type
*****The type of line that was read
*****Valid types are heading, text, startText, endText, unknown,
%comment, blank, and error
****level
*****The presentation indentation level associated with the line
****displayAsBullet
*****A boolean value that indicates whether the line should be
%displayed with a bullet
****newSlide
*****A boolean value that indicates whether the line begins a new slide
****text
*****The parsed text of the line
***Methods
****isStartText()
*****Returns true if the line is a start of markup indicator
****isEndText()
*****Returns true if the line is a start of markup indicator
****getLevel()
*****Returns the level property
****isComment()
*****Returns true if the line is a comment
****isBlank()
*****Returns true if the line is blank
****isHeading()
*****Returns true if the line is a heading
****display()
*****Displays selected properties of the LineDesc object
****displayError()
*****Displays any errors associated with the line
**|Slide
***Properties
****title
*****The title of the slide
****level
*****The outline level of the slide
****elements
*****An array of SlideElement objects
***Methods
****addHeading(text, level, link)
*****Creates a new SlideElement object of type heading and adds it
%to the current slide
****addText(text, level)
*****Creates a new SlideElement object of type text and adds it to
%the current slide
****display()
*****Displays the slide's title, level, and elements
****summarize()
```

```
*****Displays the slide number and title
****create(n,max)
*****Creates slide n of max slides
*****Writes the slide's HTML to the file corresponding to the slide
**|SlideElement
***Properties
****type
*****The type of slide element: heading or text
****text
*****The text of the slide element
****level
*****The outline level of the slide element
****link
*****The slide in which the element is located
***Methods
****display()
*****Displays the properties of a SlideElement object
```

Summary

In this chapter, you learned how to use the scripting capabilities of Microsoft's Windows Scripting Host. You learned about the WSH object model, how to develop and run WSH scripts, and how to use WSH to develop simple Windows applications. Congratulations on finishing the book! The following appendices provide valuable JavaScript reference information. Keep them on hand to look up objects, properties, and methods when you are developing your scripts.

Appendices

- Appendix A: Doing Math
- Appendix B: Working with Regular Expressions
- Appendix C: ECMAScript Object Reference
- Appendix D: DOM 0 Object Reference
- Appendix E: DOM 1 Object Reference
- Appendix F: Cascading Style Sheets

Doing Math

Almost every useful or entertaining program performs some sort of mathematical computation. Game programs use random number generators to shuffle cards, roll dice, or add variety to computer actions. Word processing programs use plenty of tedious arithmetic to determine how pages should be displayed or laid out in hard-copy form. Graphics programs use trigonometric functions to display different geometrical shapes. And so on.

Web programs have an equal affinity for math. The game programs that you developed in Chapter 20, "Programming Games," used a random number generator. Web sales forms calculate sales totals based on the prices of the products that a user selects. Search engines rank the search value of web pages based on a variety of formulae ranging from simple to complex.

In this appendix you'll learn about the extensive library of mathematical functions and constants that are provided by JavaScript's Math object. You'll learn how to use the Math object to perform simple computations, and you'll create a JavaScript calculator that illustrates the use of the constants and functions provided by Math. When you finish this appendix you'll have a thorough understanding of JavaScript's math capabilities.

Introducing the *Math* Object

The Math object is a predefined JavaScript object. It is a built-in object that is defined by the ECMAScript standard and supported by both Navigator and Internet Explorer. The Math object cannot be instantiated like Date and String to create specific object instances. Rather, it is available any time a JavaScript-capable browser is running. Think of Math as a library of mathematical constants and functions. The constants are properties of Math and the functions are its methods. Learning to use the Math object involves familiarizing yourself with these properties and methods.

Working with Mathematical Constants

For a scripting language, JavaScript provides a rich collection of mathematical constants—more than you'll need, even if you are a mathematician. These constants are described in Table A.1.

TABLE A.1: Math Constants Used in JavaScript

Constant	Description
E	Euler's constant. It is found everywhere in computational math and is the base for natural logarithms.
LN2	The natural logarithm of 2. This is a handy constant for converting between natural logarithms and base 2 logarithms.

Continued on next page

TABLE A.1 CONTINUED: Math Constants Used in JavaScript

Constant	Description
LN10	The natural logarithm of 10. Like LN2, it is used in logarithm conversions.
LOG2E	The base 2 logarithm of E. It is used in base 2 to base E logarithm conversions.
LOG10E	The base 10 logarithm of E. It is used in base 10 to base E logarithm conversions.
PI	Another famous mathematical constant, PI is the ratio of the circumference of a circle to its diameter.
SQRT1_2	The square root of ½ is used in many trigonometric calculations.
SQRT2	The square root of 2 is commonly used in algebraic formulas.

The mathematical constants are accessed as `Math.constant` where constant is one of the constants listed above. For example, pi times Euler's constant divided by the square root of two is written as follows:

```
Math.PI*Math.E/Math.SQRT2
```

Working with Mathematical Functions

The `Math` object provides 18 mathematical functions that cover the gamut from rounding to random number generation. These functions have been organized into the following categories:

- Rounding
- Comparison
- Algebraic
- Logarithmic and exponential
- Trigonometric
- Random number generation

To use any of the mathematical functions, invoke them as methods of the `Math` object. For example, the cosine of pi divided by 2 is written as follows:

```
Math.cos(Math.PI/2))
```

The categories of Math functions are described in the following paragraphs.

Rounding Functions

The `round()`, `floor()`, and `ceil()` functions are used to approximate floating-point numbers with integers. The `round()` function returns the closest integer to a floating-point number. The `floor()` function returns the greatest integer that is less than or equal to a floating-point number. Similarly, the ceil() function returns the least integer that is greater than or equal to a floating-point number.

Comparison Functions

The min() and max() functions are used to compare two numbers. The min() function returns the lesser of the two numbers, and the max() function returns the greater. These functions are often used in operations that rely on sorting.

Algebraic Functions

The abs() function calculates the absolute value of a number. It is very useful in calculating the distance between two numbers. It is also commonly found in solutions to algebraic problems. The sqrt() function calculates the square root of a number.

Logarithmic and Exponential Functions

JavaScript provides the natural logarithm function, log(). Base 2 or 10 logarithms can be calculated using the logarithm constants (LN2, LN10, LOG2E, LOG10E) to convert between different bases.

The power function, pow(), calculates a number raised to a power.

The exponential function, exp(), calculates Euler's constant raised to a power. The function exp(x) is the same as pow(Math.E,x).

Trigonometric Functions

JavaScript provides seven trigonometric function: cos(), sin(), tan(), acos(), asin(), atan(), and atan2(). Trig functions are used to calculate the position and relationship of points on circles, ellipses, waves, and other curved objects with respect to Cartesian coordinates. You probably won't use these functions unless you are involved in science or engineering.

Random Number Generation

The random() function generates a pseudo-random number between 0 and 1. You'll continue to use random() with many of the examples of this book—especially with games.

Using Math Functions in Scripts

When you use Math constants or functions in a script you must precede the constant or function reference with the keyword Math. However, this often brings clutter to your scripts. You can use the with statement to help eliminate this clutter in math-intensive scripts. For example, the following two statements are equivalent:

- Statement 1

```
with (Math) {
 y=sqrt(pow(cos(x),2)+pow(sin(x),2))
 }
```

- Statement 2

```
y=Math.sqrt(Math.pow(Math.cos(x),2)+ Math.pow(Math.sin(x),2))
```

Example Project—A JavaScript Calculator

Math can be a somewhat passionless subject. The same is true for the Math object. We've already covered all of JavaScript's mathematical constants and functions. To liven things up a bit, let's use these constants and functions to build an advanced scientific calculator.

Open math.htm with your browser. It displays the calculator shown in Figure A.1. This calculator is the same as most calculators that you've used before except that it has some of JavaScript's mathematical constants and functions attached to it. The purpose of the calculator is not to come up with a new calculator design but to illustrate the use of the JavaScript Math object. For example, click the e button. Your browser display should look like Figure A.2. Select log(x) from the Functions list, as shown in Figure A.3. Then click the Apply button to calculate the natural log of e. The answer is 1—just as you'd expect. Figure A.4 shows the result of this calculation. Play with the calculator to get a good feel for how it operates.

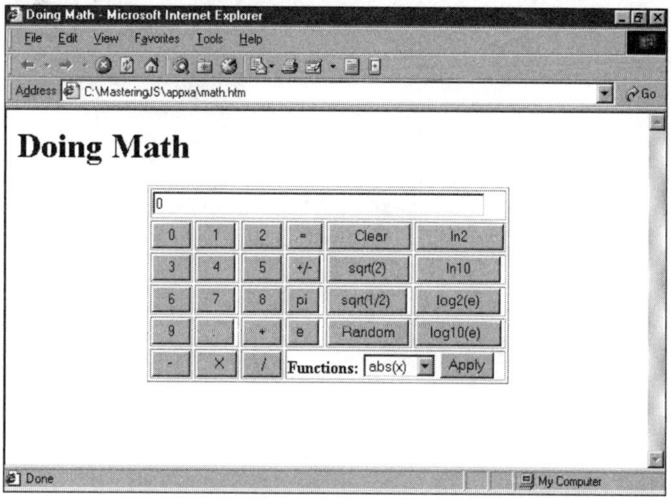

FIGURE A.1:

This calculator's keys are attached to JavaScript Math methods.
(Listing A.1)

FIGURE A.2:

Clicking the e button causes Euler's constant to be displayed. (Listing A.1)

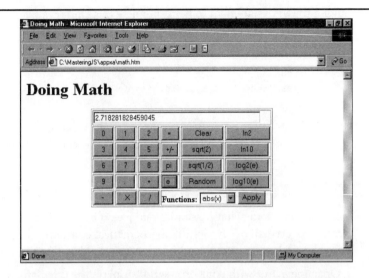

FIGURE A.3:

Selecting log(x) allows you to apply log(x) to e. (Listing A.1)

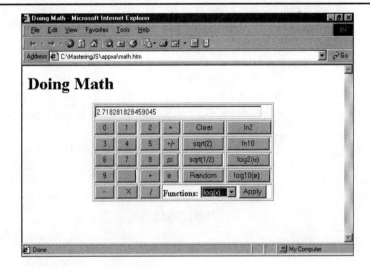

FIGURE A.4:

Applying $\log(x)$ to e results in an answer of 1. (Listing A.1)

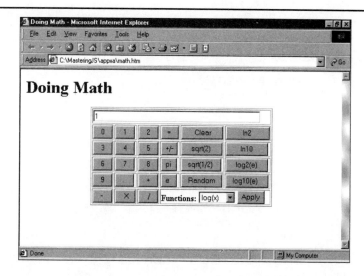

Listing A.1 shows the math.htm file that implements the calculator. This is a fairly long file and is about half HTML and half JavaScript. The HTML creates the nice-looking form used as the calculator. The JavaScript provides the computations behind the buttons.

NOTE   JavaScript's handling of floating point numbers can result in rounding anomalies. For example, The value of 100 − 89.01 is reported as 10.989999999999994 instead of 10.99. A detailed description of mathematical errors in JavaScript is provided by BugNet at www.bugnet.com/alerts/bugalert9298.html.

Listing A.1:   **A JavaScript Calculator (math.htm)**

```
<HTML>
<HEAD>
<TITLE>Doing Math</TITLE>
<SCRIPT LANGUAGE="JavaScript"><!--
r = new Array(2)
function setStartState(){
 state="start"
 r[0] = "0"
 r[1] = "0"
 operator=""
 ix=0
}
function addDigit(n){
 if(state=="gettingInteger" || state=="gettingFloat")
 r[ix]=appendDigit(r[ix],n)
 else{
```

```
  r[ix]=""+n
  state="gettingInteger"
 }
 display(r[ix])
}
function appendDigit(n1,n2){
 if(n1=="0") return ""+n2
 var s=""
 s+=n1
 s+=n2
 return s
}
function display(s){
 document.calculator.total.value=s
}
function addDecimalPoint(){
 if(state!="gettingFloat"){
  decimal=true
  r[ix]+="."
  if(state=="haveOperand" || state=="getOperand2") r[ix]="0."
  state="gettingFloat"
  display(r[ix])
 }
}
function clearDisplay(){
 setStartState()
 display(r[0])
}
function changeSign(){
 if(r[ix].charAt(0)=="-") r[ix]=r[ix].substring(1,r[ix].length)
 else if(parseFloat(r[ix])!=0) r[ix]="-"+r[ix]
 display(r[ix])
}
function setTo(n){
 r[ix]=""+n
 state="haveOperand"
 decimal=false
 display(r[ix])
}
function calc(){
 if(state=="gettingInteger" || state=="gettingFloat" ||
  state=="haveOperand"){
  if(ix==1){
   r[0]=calculateOperation(operator,r[0],r[1])
   ix=0
  }
 }else if(state=="getOperand2"){
  r[0]=calculateOperation(operator,r[0],r[0])
  ix=0
 }
 state="haveOperand"
```

```
 decimal=false
 display(r[ix])
}
function calculateOperation(op,x,y){
 var result=""
 if(op=="+"){
  result=""+(parseFloat(x)+parseFloat(y))
 }else if(op=="-"){
  result=""+(parseFloat(x)-parseFloat(y))
 }else if(op=="*"){
  result=""+(parseFloat(x)*parseFloat(y))
 }else if(op=="/"){
  if(parseFloat(y)==0){
   alert("Division by 0 not allowed.")
   result=0
  }else result=""+(parseFloat(x)/parseFloat(y))
 }
 return result
}
function performOp(op){
 if(state=="start"){
  ++ix
  operator=op
 }else if(state=="gettingInteger" || state=="gettingFloat" ||
  state=="haveOperand"){
  if(ix==0){
   ++ix
   operator=op
  }else{
   r[0]=calculateOperation(operator,r[0],r[1])
   display(r[0])
   operator=op
  }
 }
 state="getOperand2"
 decimal=false
}
function applyFunction(){
 var selectionList=document.calculator.functions
 var selIX=selectionList.selectedIndex
 var sel=selectionList.options[selIX].value
 if(sel=="abs") r[ix]=Math.abs(r[ix])
 else if(sel=="acos") r[ix]=Math.acos(r[ix])
 else if(sel=="asin") r[ix]=Math.asin(r[ix])
 else if(sel=="atan") r[ix]=Math.atan(r[ix])
 else if(sel=="ceil") r[ix]=Math.ceil(r[ix])
 else if(sel=="cos") r[ix]=Math.cos(r[ix])
 else if(sel=="exp") r[ix]=Math.exp(r[ix])
 else if(sel=="floor") r[ix]=Math.floor(r[ix])
 else if(sel=="log") r[ix]=Math.log(r[ix])
 else if(sel=="sin") r[ix]=Math.sin(r[ix])
```

```
    else if(sel=="sqrt") r[ix]=Math.sqrt(r[ix])
    else r[ix]=Math.tan(r[ix])
    decimal=false
    display(r[ix])
}
// --></SCRIPT>
</HEAD>
<BODY>
<SCRIPT LANGUAGE="JavaScript"><!--
setStartState()
// --></SCRIPT>
<H1>Doing Math</H1>
<FORM NAME="calculator">
<TABLE BORDER="BORDER" ALIGN="CENTER">
<TR>
<TD COLSPAN="6"><INPUT TYPE="TEXT" NAME="total" VALUE="0"
 SIZE="44"></TD></TR>
<TR>
<TD><INPUT TYPE="BUTTON" NAME="n0" VALUE="    0    "
 ONCLICK="addDigit(0)"></TD>
<TD><INPUT TYPE="BUTTON" NAME="n1" VALUE="    1    "
 ONCLICK="addDigit(1)"></TD>
<TD><INPUT TYPE="BUTTON" NAME="n2" VALUE="    2    "
 ONCLICK="addDigit(2)"></TD>
<TD><INPUT TYPE="BUTTON" NAME="equals" VALUE="    =    "
 ONCLICK="calc()"></TD>
<TD ROWSPAN="1"><INPUT
TYPE="BUTTON" NAME="clearField" VALUE="    Clear    "
 ONCLICK="clearDisplay()"></TD>
<TD COLSPAN="1"><INPUT
TYPE="BUTTON" NAME="ln2" VALUE="        ln2        "
 ONCLICK="setTo(Math.LN2)"></TD></TR>
<TR>
<TD><INPUT TYPE="BUTTON" NAME="n3" VALUE="    3    "
 ONCLICK="addDigit(3)"></TD>
<TD><INPUT TYPE="BUTTON" NAME="n4" VALUE="    4    "
 ONCLICK="addDigit(4)"></TD>
<TD><INPUT TYPE="BUTTON" NAME="n5" VALUE="    5    "
 ONCLICK="addDigit(5)"></TD>
<TD COLSPAN="1" ROWSPAN="1"><INPUT TYPE="BUTTON"
 NAME="sign" VALUE=" +/- " ONCLICK="changeSign()"></TD>
<TD ROWSPAN="1"><INPUT TYPE="BUTTON" NAME="sqrt2"
 VALUE="  sqrt(2)    " ONCLICK="setTo(Math.SQRT2)"></TD>
<TD COLSPAN="1" ROWSPAN="1"><INPUT TYPE="BUTTON" NAME="ln10"
 VALUE="        ln10        " ONCLICK="setTo(Math.LN10)"></TD></TR>
<TR>
<TD><INPUT TYPE="BUTTON" NAME="n6" VALUE="    6    "
 ONCLICK="addDigit(6)"></TD>
<TD><INPUT TYPE="BUTTON" NAME="n7" VALUE="    7    "
 ONCLICK="addDigit(7)"></TD>
<TD><INPUT TYPE="BUTTON" NAME="n8" VALUE="    8    "
 ONCLICK="addDigit(8)"></TD>
<TD COLSPAN="1" ROWSPAN="1"><INPUT
```

```html
TYPE="BUTTON" NAME="pi" VALUE=" pi    "
 ONCLICK="setTo(Math.PI)"></TD>
<TD COLSPAN="1" ROWSPAN="1"><INPUT
TYPE="BUTTON" NAME="sqrt12" VALUE="sqrt(1/2) "
 ONCLICK="setTo(Math.SQRT1_2)"></TD>
<TD COLSPAN="1" ROWSPAN="1"><INPUT
TYPE="BUTTON" NAME="log2e" VALUE="  log2(e)   "
 ONCLICK="setTo(Math.LOG2E)"></TD></TR>
<TR>
<TD><INPUT TYPE="BUTTON" NAME="n9" VALUE="   9    "
 ONCLICK="addDigit(9)"></TD>
<TD><INPUT TYPE="BUTTON" NAME="decimal" VALUE="    .    "
 ONCLICK="addDecimalPoint()"></TD>
<TD><INPUT TYPE="BUTTON" NAME="plus" VALUE="   +   "
 ONCLICK="performOp('+')"></TD>
<TD COLSPAN="1" ROWSPAN="1"><INPUT TYPE="BUTTON" NAME="e"
 VALUE="  e   " ONCLICK="setTo(Math.E)"></TD>
<TD COLSPAN="1" ROWSPAN="1"><INPUT TYPE="BUTTON"
 NAME="random" VALUE="Random"
 ONCLICK="setTo(Math.random())"></TD>
<TD COLSPAN="1" ROWSPAN="1"><INPUT TYPE="BUTTON" NAME="log10e"
 VALUE="log10(e)   " ONCLICK="setTo(Math.LOG10E)"></TD></TR>
<TR>
<TD><INPUT TYPE="BUTTON" NAME="minus" VALUE="   -    "
 ONCLICK="performOp('-')"></TD>
<TD><INPUT TYPE="BUTTON" NAME="multiply" VALUE="    X   "
 ONCLICK="performOp('*')"></TD>
<TD><INPUT TYPE="BUTTON" NAME="divide" VALUE="    /    "
 ONCLICK="performOp('/')"></TD>
<TD COLSPAN="3" ROWSPAN="1"><B>Functions: </B>
<SELECT NAME="functions" SIZE="1">
<OPTION VALUE="abs" SELECTED="SELECTED">abs(x)</OPTION>
<OPTION VALUE="acos">acos(x)</OPTION>
<OPTION VALUE="asin">asin(x)</OPTION>
<OPTION VALUE="atan">atan(x)</OPTION>
<OPTION VALUE="ceil">ceil(x)</OPTION>
<OPTION VALUE="cos">cos(x)</OPTION>
<OPTION VALUE="exp">exp(x)</OPTION>
<OPTION VALUE="floor">floor(x)</OPTION>
<OPTION VALUE="log">log(x)</OPTION>
<OPTION VALUE="sin">sin(x)</OPTION>
<OPTION VALUE="sqrt">sqrt(x)</OPTION>
<OPTION VALUE="tan">tan(x)</OPTION>
</SELECT>
<INPUT TYPE="BUTTON" NAME="apply" VALUE="Apply"
 onClick="applyFunction()"></TD></TR>
</TABLE>
</FORM>
</BODY>
</HTML>
```

The document contains two scripts: one in the head and one in the body. The script in the document's body invokes the setStartState() function to perform all necessary initializations. The script in the document's head defines the r array and 12 functions. A description of each of these follows.

The *r* Array

This array is used to hold two numbers, entered by the user, that are used as the operands of an arithmetic calculation.

The *setStartState()* Function

This function performs all variable initialization. It sets the state variable to start, the current operands to 0, the current operator to " " (null string), and the index of the current operand (ix) to 0.

The state variable may be set to any of the following states:

start   This state indicates the program has just loaded/reloaded or that the Clear button has been pressed.

gettingInteger   This state is entered when the user tries to enter an integer via the calculator's keypad.

gettingFloat   This state is entered when the user tries to enter a floating-point number and when the user clicks the decimal point button.

haveOperand   This state is entered when the user completes the entry of an integer or floating-point number by pressing = or a JavaScript constant or by selecting/applying a JavaScript function.

getOperand2   This state is entered when the user clicks an arithmetic operator (+, -, X, or /).

The *addDigit()* Function

This function handles the clicking of a digit (0 through 9). If the current state is gettingInteger or gettingFloat, then the digit is appended to the current operand. Otherwise, the current operand is initialized to the digit and the state is set to gettingInteger. The calculator's total field is then updated.

The *appendDigit()* Function

This function is invoked by addDigit() to append a digit to the current operand. If the value of the current operand is *0*, then the digit becomes the value of the current operand. Otherwise, it is appended to the current operand. Note that operands are maintained as string values.

The *display()* Function

This function displays a string (usually the current operand) in the total field of the calculator form.

The *addDecimalPoint()* Function

This function handles the clicking of the decimal point button. If the current state is gettingFloat, then the decimal point is ignored. Otherwise, it appends a decimal point to the current operand or creates a new operand equal to 0. (zero followed by a decimal point). It then sets the current state to gettingFloat and updates the value of the total field.

The *clearDisplay()* Function

This function invokes the setStartState() function to reinitialize the calculator and invokes display() to update the total field.

The *changeSign()* Function

This function handles the clicking of the change sign (+/-) button. It converts the current operand from negative to positive or vice versa. It then updates the calculator's total field.

The *setTo()* Function

This function handles the clicking of any of the JavaScript constants. It sets the value of the current operand to the constant and the current state to haveOperand. The decimal flag is set to false to indicate that a decimal point is not longer in effect. The calculator's total field is then updated with the value of the new operand.

The *calc()* Function

This function handles the clicking of the calculate (=) key. If the current state is getting-Integer, gettingFloat, or haveOperand, it checks ix to determine if the current operand is 1 or 0. If ix is 1, then the user has entered two operands and an operator. The calculate-Operation() function is invoked to calculate the result of applying the operator to the two operands. The resulting value is stored in the first operand and the number of operands (ix) is set to 0.

If the current state is getOperand2, then calculateOperation() is invoked to calculate the result of applying the current operator to the first operand and itself. The resultant value is stored in the first operand and the number of operands (ix) is set to 0.

After performing state-specific processing, the current state is set to haveOperand, the decimal flag is set to false, and the calculator's total field is updated.

The *calculateOperation()* Function

This function is invoked by `calc()` and `performOp()` to calculate the value of applying a binary operator to two operands. It handles addition, subtraction, multiplication, and division operations. It also checks for division by 0.

The *performOp()* Function

This function handles the clicking of a binary (two-value) operator, such as +, -, X, or /. If the current `state` is `start`, it increments the number of operands and sets the `operator` variable to the operator selected by the user.

If the current `state` is `gettingInteger`, `gettingFloat`, or `haveOperand`, then this function checks the number of operands in use (`ix`). If `ix` is 0, indicating that the current operand is the first operand, then it increments the number of operands and sets the `operator` variable to the operator selected by the user. If `ix` is 1, the `calculateOperation()` method is invoked to calculate the current operation entered by the user. The result is assigned to the first operand, and this operand is displayed in the calculator's `total` field. The `operator` variable is assigned the new operator.

The *applyFunction()* Function

This function responds to the clicking of the Apply button by applying the currently selected JavaScript function to the current operand. It then displays the new operand value in the calculator's `total` field.

Using Regular Expressions

This appendix describes regular expressions and shows how they are used to find and replace character patterns in strings.

What Are Regular Expressions?

Regular expressions were introduced in JavaScript 1.2. They are character-matching patterns that are used to find and replace character patterns in strings. Regular expressions were popularized by the Perl scripting language. JavaScript's support of regular expressions is based on that of Perl.

Regular expressions are somewhat complex when you first encounter them. This complexity is due to the efficient but somewhat arcane syntax they employ. However, after you have experimented with regular expressions in a few examples, you'll find them to be a powerful tool for string manipulation, parsing, and searching.

In JavaScript, regular expressions are implemented as RegExp objects and are created as follows:

```
re = new RegExp(pattern,modifiers)
```

The pattern is the pattern to be matched and the optional modifiers is a string containing g, i, m, or any combination of these. The g stands for global, the i stands for ignore case, and the m stands for multiline. You use g to perform a global search and replacement and i to ignore case when performing pattern matching. The m is used to treat a multiline string as multiple lines instead of one long line. The following creates a RegExp object with the pattern abc and uses all three modifiers:

```
myRE = new RegExp("abc","gim")
```

JavaScript provides a second way of creating RegExp objects using the Perl notation:

```
re = /pattern/modifers
```

For example, the RegExp object /abc/gim is equivalent to new RegExp("abc","gim").

NOTE   The multiline option is a new option that was introduced with JavaScript 1.5.

The Regular Expression Tester

Now that you know how to create RegExp objects, you can learn how to use them through a simple script that performs string search and replace operations using regular expressions. Listing B.1 shows the rextest.htm file. Open this file in your browser and it displays the window shown in Figure B.1.

FIGURE B.1:

The opening window of the
Regular Expression Tester
(Listing B.1)

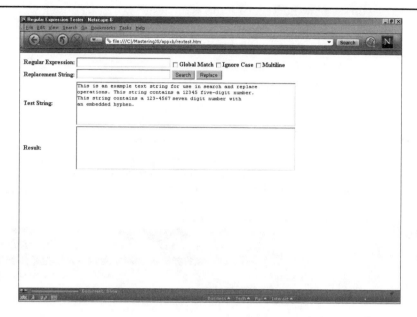

The Regular Expression Tester contains two text fields, two text area fields, three check boxes, and two buttons. These form fields are as follows:

Regular Expression   Enter the regular expression that you want tested in this field.

Global Match   Select this box if you want to perform a global replacement.

Ignore Case   Select this box if you want to ignore case when performing a search or replace operation.

Multiline   Select this box if you want multiline strings to be treated as multiple lines instead of as a single long line.

Replacement String   Enter the replacement text to be used in performing a replacement operation.

Search   Click this button to search for a regular expression in the test string.

Replace   Click this button to replace text in the test string that matches a regular expression with the text in the replacement string.

Test String   Use this text for your testing. Some sample text is provided. You can change this text if you like.

Result   This field displays the results of any search or replace operation.

To see how the Regular Expression Tester works, let's use it with a simple search operation. Enter `example` in the Regular Expression field and click the search button. The Regular Expression Tester displays the following output in the Result field (see Figure B.2):

```
/example/ found at position 11.
```

This indicates that the regular expression `/example/` was found in the test string at character position 11. Character positions begin at 0 and end at the length of the string minus 1.

NOTE   You should not surround the regular expression with / and / when you enter it in the Regular Expression field. The script creates the **RegExp** object using the **RegExp()** constructor. However, when the script displays the regular expression, it uses the shorter Perl-like syntax. Use this feature to see how regular expressions are written using the Perl notation.

FIGURE B.2:

Searching for `example`

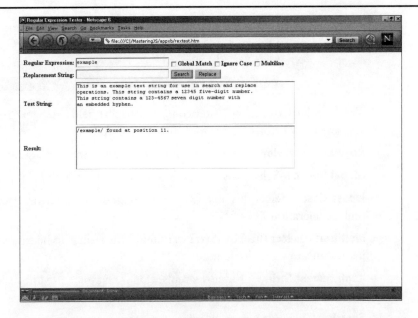

Now let's perform a search with and without the Ignore Case box selected. If you search for the regular expression `this` without having selected the Ignore Case box, the Regular Expression Tester displays the following output:

```
/this/ not found.
```

However, when Ignore Case is selected, it is able to find `this` at the beginning of the Test String:

```
/this/i found at position 0.
```

Now let's replace this with That. Enter this into the Regular Expression field, That into the Replacement String field, select the Ignore Case box, and click the Replace button. The Regular Expression Tester displays the following output (see Figure B.3):

```
That is an example text string for use in search and replace
operations. This string contains a 12345 five-digit number.
This string contains a 123-4567 seven-digit number with
an embedded hyphen.
```

FIGURE B.3:

Replacing this with That

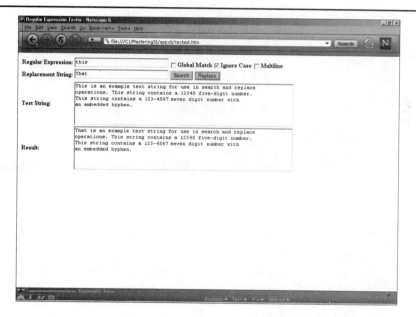

Note that the initial This of the first sentence was replaced with That. However, subsequent instances of this were not changed. To change all instances of this to That, select the Global Match box (see Figure B.4). The following are the results of the global change:

```
That is an example text string for use in search and replace
operations. That string contains a 12345 five-digit number.
That string contains a 123-4567 seven digit number with
an embedded hyphen.
```

FIGURE B.4:

Globally replacing this with That

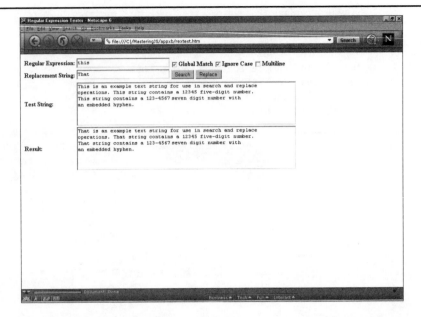

The ^ character is used to indicate the beginning of a line. Enter ^this into the Regular Expression field and That into the Replacement String field. Select the Global Match and Ignore Case check boxes, but not the Multiline check box (see Figure B.5). The results of the change are as follows:

```
That is an example text string for use in search and replace
operations. This string contains a 12345 five-digit number.
This string contains a 123-4567 seven digit number with
an embedded hyphen.
```

Notice that the first This was changed to a That but no others. If you select the Multiline box and rerun the replacement, you'll get the following output (refer to Figure B.6).

```
That is an example text string for use in search and replace
operations. This string contains a 12345 five-digit number.
That string contains a 123-4567 seven-digit number with
an embedded hyphen.
```

FIGURE B.5:

Replacing ^this
with That

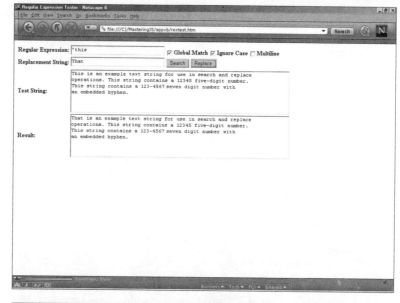

FIGURE B.6:

Replacing ^this with
That using the Multiline
modifier

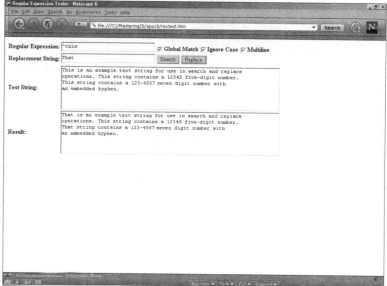

You get the previous result because the multiline modifier causes each line of the text area to be treated as a separate line instead of as one big line.

Listing B.1   The Regular Expression Tester (rextest.htm)

```
<HTML>
<HEAD>
<TITLE>Regular Expression Tester</TITLE>
<SCRIPT LANGUAGE="JavaScript"><!--
function accessFormElements() {
 flags = ""
 if(document.rexForm.global.checked) flags += "g"
 if(document.rexForm.ignore.checked) flags += "i"
 if(document.rexForm.multiline.checked) flags += "m"
 re = new RegExp(document.rexForm.rex.value,flags)
 rep = document.rexForm.replacement.value
 str = document.rexForm.testString.value
 res = document.rexForm.resultString
}
function searchExp() {
 accessFormElements()
 searchResult = str.search(re)
 if(searchResult==-1)
  res.value = re + " not found."
 else
  res.value = re + " found at position " + searchResult + "."
}
function replaceExp() {
 accessFormElements()
 res.value = str.replace(re,rep)
}
//--></SCRIPT>
</HEAD>
<BODY>
<FORM NAME="rexForm">
<TABLE BORDER="0">
<TR><TD><B>Regular Expression:</B></TD><TD>
<INPUT TYPE="TEXT" SIZE="30" NAME="rex">
<INPUT TYPE="CHECKBOX" NAME="global"><B>Global Match</B>
<INPUT TYPE="CHECKBOX" NAME="ignore"><B>Ignore Case</B>
<INPUT TYPE="CHECKBOX" NAME="multiline"><B>Multiline</B></TD></TR>
<TR><TD><B>Replacement String:</B></TD><TD>
<INPUT TYPE="TEXT" SIZE="30" NAME="replacement">
<INPUT TYPE="BUTTON" VALUE="Search" NAME="search"
 onClick="searchExp()">
<INPUT TYPE="BUTTON" VALUE="Replace" NAME="replace"
 onClick="replaceExp()"></TD></TR>
<TR><TD><B>Test String:</B></TD><TD>
<TEXTAREA ROWS="5" COLS="70" NAME="testString">
This is an example text string for use in search and replace
operations. This string contains a 12345 five-digit number.
```

```
This string contains a 123-4567 seven digit number with
an embedded hyphen.
</TEXTAREA></TD></TR>
<TR><TD><B>Result:</B></TD><TD>
<TEXTAREA ROWS="5" COLS="70" NAME="resultString">
</TEXTAREA></TD></TR>
</TABLE>
</FORM>
</BODY>
</HTML>
```

How the Regular Expression Tester Works

If you now think regular expressions are useful, hang in there, we've just begun. The section, "Regular Expression Syntax," later in this chapter provides an introduction to the syntax of regular expressions. But before going on, let's examine how the Regular Expression Tester works. The scripting consists of three functions that are defined in the document's head:

accessFormElements()   Invoked by both searchExp() and replaceExp() to access the form fields. Creates a RegExp object from the Regular Expression, Global Match, Ignore Case, and Multiline fields and assigns them to the re variable. Assigns the value of the Replacement String field to the rep variable and the value of the Test String field to the str variable. Allows res to be used to reference the Result field.

searchExp()   Invoked to handle the clicking of the Search button. Invokes the search() method of the test string assigned to str to search for the regular expression assigned to re. Assigns the result to searchResult. If searchResult is -1, indicating that the regular expression was not found, the value of the Result field (accessed via res) is updated accordingly. If searchResult is not -1, then it contains the position where the regular expression was found. The value of the Result field is updated to identify this position.

replaceExp()   Invoked to handle the clicking of the Search button. Invokes the replace() method of the test string (referenced by str), passing it the regular expression (re) and replacement string (rep) as arguments. The resulting string is stored in the Result field (res).

From this discussion you can see that the search() and replace() methods of the String object perform the core of the processing required to implement the Regular Expression Tester. These methods, as well as other regular expression methods of the String object, are covered in the next section.

String Methods That Use Regular Expressions

In the previous section, you were exposed to the search() and replace() methods of the String object. There are four String methods that are specifically designed to support regular expressions:

search(regularExpression)   Searches the string for an occurrence of the regular expression. If the regular expression is found, then its position within the string is returned. If it is not found, -1 is returned.

replace(regularExpression, replacementString)   Replaces occurrences of the regular expression with the replacement string. If the g option is specified in the regular expression, then all occurrences of the regular expression are replaced. Otherwise, only a single occurrence is replaced. The String object is not modified. Instead, a new String object is created and returned. The replacement string may contain regular expression properties. These properties are covered in the "Regular Expression Syntax" section later in this appendix.

match(regularExpression)   Matches the regular expression in the string and returns an array containing all occurrences of the match.

split(regularExpression, limit)   Splits the String object into an array of substrings and returns this array. The regular expression is used to identify the points at which the String object should be split. The limit identifies the maximum number of splits that should take place.

The array returned by the match() method has the following properties in addition to the length and prototype properties:

input   The original string against which the regular expression was matched.

index   The index of the match within the string.

Consult the API description of the Array object for more information on how to use these properties.

The RegExp() object also provides methods that can be used to perform pattern-matching functions. You'll learn about these methods in the "The Regular Expression Object" section later in this appendix.

Regular Expression Syntax

So far, the regular expressions that you have been using have been very primitive. Regular expressions support a rich (if cryptic) syntax that provides powerful pattern matching capabilities. This syntax uses the special characters shown in Table B.1.

TABLE B.1: Special Characters Used in Regular Expressions

Character	Description
^	Matches the beginning of a line
$	Matches the end of a line
*	Matches the preceding character zero or more times
+	Matches the preceding character one or more times
?	Matches the preceding character zero or one time
.	Matches any single character except the new line character
(x)	Matches x and remembers the matching value as a **RegExp** property
(?:x)	Matches x but does not remember the match
x(?=y)	Matches x only if x is followed by y
x(?!y)	Matches x only if x is not followed by y
x | y	Matches x or y
{n}	Matches exactly *n* occurrences of the preceding character
{n,}	Matches at least *n* occurrences of the preceding character
{n,m}	Matches at least *n* occurrences and at most *m* occurrences of the preceding character
[xyz]	Matches any of the enclosed characters: x, y, or z
[x-z]	Matches any character in the range x to z
[^xyz]	Matches any character except x, y, and z
[^x-z]	Matches any character except those in the range x to z
[\b]	Matches the backspace character
\b	Matches a word boundary
\B	Matches a non-word boundary
\cX	Matches the Control-X character
\d	Equivalent to [0–9]
\D	Equivalent to [^0–9]
\f	Matches a form feed
\n	Matches a linefeed
\r	Matches a carriage return
\s	Equivalent to [\f\n\r\t\v]
\S	Equivalent to [^\f\n\r\t\v]

Continued on next page

TABLE B.1 CONTINUED: Special Characters Used in Regular Expressions

Character	Description
\t	Matches a tab
\v	Matches a vertical tab
\w	Equivalent to [A–Za–z0–9_]
\W	Equivalent to [^A–Za–z0–9_]
\number	Matches a character with the specified numeric value
\0	Matches a NUL character
\xhex	Matches a character with the specified decimal value
\uhhhh	Matches the character whose value has the specified hexadecimal digits

As you can see from Table B.1, there are many special characters that can be used in regular expressions. The best way to learn them is to try them out using the regular expression tester. You should also check out some of the regular expression tutorials that are available via the Web, such as the one provided by Perl.com (www.perl.com).

Parentheses have two uses in regular expressions. The first use is to group matching characters into groups. For example, /Java(Script)/ matches Java or JavaScript. The second use of parentheses is to define subpatterns within the matching pattern. For example, in the regular expression /((ab)(cd))/i, the parentheses define three matching patterns (i.e., abcd, ab, cd). The expressions can be ordered according to the positions of their left parentheses. The character patterns that match the subpatterns are referred to by \n where n refers to the number of the left parenthesis of the subpattern. For example, \1 refers to the text that matches the first subpattern. Therefore, from the previous example, \1 would refer to a match of the pattern abcd, while \3 would refer to a match of cd.

The Regular Expression Object

The RegExp object is used to implement regular expressions in JavaScript. It is based on regular expressions as implemented in the Perl language. The properties of the RegExp object use Perl-like names. These properties are as follows:

constructor   Specifies the function that creates an object's prototype.

global   Indicates whether the g option is in effect.

ignoreCase   Indicates whether the i option is in effect.

lastIndex   The index at which to start the next match.

multiline   Indicates whether the m option is in effect.

prototype   Allows the addition of properties to all objects.

source   The regular expression source text without the slashes, g, or i.

The RegExp object also supports the following methods:

exec(string)   Executes the regular expression to find a match on the string. Returns an array of matches in the same manner as the match() method of the String object.

test(string)   Returns true or false depending on whether the regular expression is found in the string.

toString()   Converts the RegExp object into a string. The RegExp object is included in the ECMAScript specification.

ECMAScript (Rev 3) Object Reference

This appendix provides a summary of the objects, properties, and methods documented in revision 3 of the ECMAScript reference (ECMA Standard 262).

Array

The Array object represents a JavaScript array.

Browser Support

Supported by Navigator 3 and Internet Explorer 4.

Constructors

Arrays can be constructed in the following ways:

```
myArray = new Array(10)              // new Array(length)
myArray = new Array(100, 20, 40)     // new Array(element1, ..., elementN)
myArray = [2, 4, 6, 8]               // Assignment of array literal
```

In the first form, an array of length 10 is created. Its elements are initially undefined. In the second form, an array of length three is created. This array consists of the elements 100, 20, and 40. In the third form, the myArray variable is assigned an array literal that represents a four-element array consisting of the values 2, 4, 6, and 8.

If the constructor, new Array(n), where n is a positive integer, is used with Navigator 4 or later and the script's LANGUAGE attribute is set to JavaScript1.2, then the constructor creates a one-element array consisting of the value n. This is a quirk that was designed into JavaScript 1.2 by Netscape. This problem does not occur at all with Internet Explorer or with Navigator when the LANGUAGE attribute is not set to JavaScript1.2.

Properties

Name	Description
constructor	A reference to the object's constructor
length	The number of elements
prototype	Used to define additional properties

Methods

Name	Description
concat(array1, array2, ..., arrayN)	Returns a new Array object that is the original array concatenated with the arrays identified as the method's arguments.
join(separator)	Joins the elements of the array together as a string. The separator is placed between the joined elements.
pop()	Pops the last element off of the array (i.e., removes it) and returns it.
push(element1,..., elementN)	Adds the specified elements to the end of the array and returns the array's length. In JavaScript 1.2, push returned the last element added to the array.
reverse()	Reverses the elements of the array.
shift()	Removes and returns the first element of the array.
slice(begin, end)	Extracts and returns the array slice from begin (inclusive) to end (exclusive). If end is not supplied, then the slice continues to the end of the array.
sort(compareFunction)	Sorts the elements of the array using the specified compare function. If the compare function is omitted, then the elements are sorted in dictionary order. This method was updated to achieve ECMA 262 compliance in JavaScript 1.2.
splice(start, numRemove, [element1][, ..., elementN])	Removes numRemove elements starting at the index start. Then adds elements 1 through N. As of JavaScript 1.3, splice returns the elements that were removed.
toLocaleString()	Returns a string representation of the array in local format.
toString()	Returns a string representation of the array.
unshift(element1,..., elementN)	Adds the specified elements to the beginning of the array and returns the new length of the array.

Boolean

The Boolean object provides an object representation of the primitive boolean true and false values. Do not confuse Boolean objects with boolean primitive values. Boolean objects always evaluate to true when used in place of a boolean primitive value.

Browser Support

Supported by Navigator 3 and Internet Explorer 4.

Constructors

The Boolean constructor takes the following form:

```
new Boolean(value)
```

The *value* used in the constructor creates an object that represents false if *value* is false, 0, " ", NaN, null, or undefined, or if *value* is omitted. For any other *value*, an object is created that represents true.

Properties

Name	Description
constructor	A reference to the object's constructor
prototype	Used to define additional properties

Methods

Name	Description
toString()	Returns a string value of the object that is compatible with toSource()
valueOf()	Returns the object's primitive value

Date

The Date object provides access to basic date and time services.

Browser Support

Supported by Navigator 2 Internet Explorer 3.

Constructors

new Date()   Creates a Date object that represents the current (local) date and time.

new Date(dateString)   Creates a Date object based on the date specified by dateString. The string should have a value that is recognized by the parse method of Date.

new Date(milliseconds)   Creates a Date object that represents the time specified by the number of milliseconds since 12 a.m., 1 January 1970.

new Date(year, month, [date, hour, minute, second, millisecond])   Creates a Date object with the specified year, month (0–11), date (1–31), hour (0–23), minute (0–59), second (0–59), and millisecond (0–999) values.

Properties

Name	Description
constructor	A reference to the object's constructor
prototype	Used to define additional properties

Methods

Name	Description
getDate()	Returns the day of the month as an integer between 1 and 31
getDay()	Returns the day of the week as an integer between 0 (Sunday) and 6 (Saturday)
getFullYear()	Returns the full value of a year
getHours()	Returns the current hour (local time) between 0 and 23
getMilliseconds()	Returns the current milliseconds (local time) between 0 and 999
getMinutes()	Returns the current minutes (local time) between 0 and 59
getMonth()	Returns the current month (local time) between 0 and 11
getSeconds()	Returns the current seconds (local time) between 0 and 59
getTime()	Returns the number of milliseconds since 1 January 1970 00:00:00
getTimezoneOffset()	Returns the current time zone offset in minutes between local time and Greenwich Mean Time (GMT)

`getUTCDate()`	Returns the current day of the month in Universal Coordinated Time
`getUTCDay()`	Returns the current day of the week in Universal Coordinated Time
`getUTCFullYear()`	Returns the current year in Universal Coordinated Time
`getUTCHours()`	Returns the current hour in Universal Coordinated Time
`getUTCMilliseconds()`	Returns the current milliseconds in Universal Coordinated Time
`getUTCMinutes()`	Returns the current minutes in Universal Coordinated Time
`getUTCMonth()`	Returns the current month in Universal Coordinated Time
`getUTCSeconds()`	Returns the current seconds in Universal Coordinated Time
`setDate (dayOfMonth)`	Sets the day of the month (local time)
`setFullYear (year[,month, day])`	Sets the current year (local time)
`setHours(hour [,minutes, seconds, milliseconds])`	Sets the hour (local time)
`setMilliseconds (milliseconds)`	Sets the number of milliseconds (local time)
`setMinutes(minutes [,seconds, milliseconds])`	Sets the minutes (local time)
`setMonth(month[,day])`	Sets the month (local time)
`setSeconds(seconds [,milliseconds])`	Sets the seconds (local time)
`setTime(milliseconds)`	Sets the date/time as the number of milliseconds since 12 a.m., January 1, 1970 (local time)
`setUTCDate(dayOfMonth)`	Sets the day of the month (in Universal Coordinated Time)
`setUTCFullYear(year [,month,day])`	Sets the current year (in Universal Coordinated Time)

`setUTCHours(hours [, minutes, seconds, milliseconds])`	Sets the current hours (in Universal Coordinated Time)
`setUTCMilliseconds (milliseconds)`	Sets the number of milliseconds (in Universal Coordinated Time)
`setUTCMinutes (minutes[,seconds, milliseconds])`	Sets the number of minutes (in Universal Coordinated Time)
`setUTCMonth(month [,day])`	Sets the current month (in Universal Coordinated Time)
`setUTCSeconds (seconds [,milliseconds])`	Sets the seconds value (in Universal Coordinated Time)
`toDateString()`	Returns an implementation-dependent string that represents the date portion of the `Date` in the current time zone in a convenient, human-readable form
`toLocaleDateString()`	Returns an implementation-dependent string that represents the date portion of the `Date` in the current time zone in a convenient, human-readable form that corresponds to the conventions of the host environment's current locale
`toLocaleString()`	Converts the date to a string using locale conventions
`toLocaleTimeString()`	Returns an implementation-dependent string that represents the time portion of the `Date` in the current time zone in a convenient, human-readable form that corresponds to the conventions of the host environment's current locale
`toString()`	Converts the date to a string in local time
`toTimeString()`	Returns an implementation-dependent string that represents the time portion of the `Date` in the current time zone in a convenient, human-readable form
`toUTCString()`	Converts the date to a string in UTC
`valueOf()`	Returns the primitive value of the `Date` object, which is the number of milliseconds elapsed since 12 a.m., January 1, 1970

Error

Provides information about errors that occur during the execution of a script. Supported by the `try-catch-finally` statement. The following `Error` object subtypes are defined by ECMAScript version 3.

Error Object Type	Description
EvalError	Indicates that the global function `eval()` was used in a way that is incompatible with its definition.
RangeError	Indicates a numeric value has exceeded the allowable range.
ReferenceError	Indicate that an invalid reference value has been detected.
SyntaxError	Indicates that a parsing error has occurred.
TypeError	Indicates the actual type of an operand is different than the expected type.
URIError	Indicates that one of the global URI handling functions was used in a way that is incompatible with its definition.

Browser Support

Supported by Navigator 6 and Internet Explorer 5.

Constructors

new Error(message)   Creates a new `Error` object with the specified error message.

Properties

Name	Description
message	The error message
name	The name of the error object type

Methods

Name	Description
toString()	Converts the `Error` object to a string

Function

The Function object provides access to JavaScript functions as objects.

Browser Support

Supported by Navigator 3 and Internet Explorer 4.

Constructors

The following constructor is supported by the Function object:

```
new Function ([arg1[, arg2[, ... argN]],] functionBody)
```

This constructor creates a function that accepts arguments 1 through N with the specified function body (expressed as a string).

Properties

Name	Description
arguments	Identifies the arguments that are passed to a function
constructor	Identifies the object's constructor
length	Identifies the number of arguments expected by a function
prototype	Provides the capability to add new properties to the object

Methods

Name	Description
apply(argument [, argumentArray])	Allows a method to be applied to a different object
call(argument[, argument1 [,argument2 [, ...]]])	Allows a method to be called and used with a different object
toString()	Returns a string representing the source code of the function

Global

The Global object, as identified in ECMAScript, has been supported in Navigator and Internet Explorer since JavaScript 1.0 via "top-level" properties and methods. New properties and methods have been added since JavaScript 1.0.

Browser Support

Supported by Navigator 2 Internet Explorer 4.

Constructors

None.

Properties

Name	Description
Infinity	Is a value that represents infinity
NaN	Represents the value is not a number
undefined	Represents an undefined value

Methods

Name	Description
decodeURI(encodedURI)	Performs the opposite transformation of the encodeURI() function.
decodeURIComponent (encodedURIComponent)	Performs the opposite transformation of the encodeURIComponent() function.
encodeURI(uri)	Converts the URI into an encoded URI using UTF-8 encoding.
encodeURIComponent (uriComponent)	Converts the uriComponent into an encoded URI using UTF-8 encoding. Assumes that the argument is a component of a URI rather than a complete URI.
escape(string)	Returns the URL-encoding of string.
eval(string)	Evaluates the string as JavaScript code.
isFinite(number)	Returns a Boolean value indicating whether number is finite.
isNaN(value)	Returns a Boolean value indicating whether number is not a number.
parseFloat(string)	Converts a string to a floating-point number.
parseInt(string[, radix])	Converts a string to an integer.
unescape(string)	Converts the URL-encoded string to its value before encoding.

Math

The Math object is a core object that provides a set of static mathematical constants and functions.

Browser Support

Supported by Navigator 2 Internet Explorer 3.

Constructors

None.

Properties

Name	Description
E	Euler's constant
LN10	The natural log of 10
LN2	The natural log of 2
LOG10E	The base 10 log of e
LOG2E	The base 2 log of e
PI	The mathematical symbol pi
SQRT1_2	The square root of 1/2
SQRT2	The square root of 2

Methods

Name	Description
abs(x)	Returns the absolute value of x
acos(x)	Returns the arc cosine of x
asin(x)	Returns the arc sine of x
atan(x)	Returns the arc tangent of x
atan2(y,x)	Returns the arc tangent of y/x
ceil(x)	Returns the smallest integer that is greater than or equal to x
cos(x)	Returns the cosine of x
exp(x)	Returns e raised to the x power

`floor(x)`	Returns the largest integer that is less than or equal to x
`log(x)`	Returns the natural logarithm of x
`max(x1,..., xN)`	Returns the maximum value of the arguments
`min(x1,..., xN)`	Returns the minimum value of the arguments
`pow(x,y)`	Returns x raised to the y power
`random()`	Returns a random floating point number between 0 and 1
`round(x)`	Returns the value of x rounded to the nearest integer
`sin(x)`	Returns the sine of x
`sqrt(x)`	Returns the square root of x
`tan(x)`	Returns the tangent of x

Number

A core JavaScript object that is an object wrapper for number values.

Browser Support

Supported by Navigator 3 Internet Explorer 4.

Constructors

new Number(value)   Creates a number object with the specified value.

Properties

Name	Description
`constructor`	Identifies the object's constructor
`MAX_VALUE`	Identifies the largest number
`MIN_VALUE`	Identifies the smallest number
`NaN`	Used to identify values that are not a number
`NEGATIVE_INFINITY`	Represents negative infinity
`POSITIVE_INFINITY`	Represents positive infinity
`prototype`	Provides the capability to define additional properties

Methods

Name	Description
toExponential(fractionDigits)	Converts the number into an exponential string representation with the specified number of fraction digits.
toFixed(fractionDigits)	Converts the number into a string representation with the specified fixed number of fraction digits.
toLocaleString()	Returns a string representation of the number using the locale-specific formatting conventions.
toPrecision(precision)	Converts the number into a string representation with the specified numerical precision.
toString(radix)	Returns a string representation of the number. If the optional radix argument is supplied, the number is represented using the specified radix.
valueOf()	Returns the primitive value corresponding to the Number object.

Object

The core JavaScript object that defines properties and methods that are inherited by all other objects.

Browser Support

Supported by Navigator 2 Internet Explorer 4.

Constructors

new Object(value)   Constructs a new Object object based on the supplied value.

Properties

Name	Description
constructor	Refers to the object's constructor
prototype	Provides the capability to define additional properties

Methods

Name	Description
hasOwnProperty(propertyName)	Returns a Boolean value indicating whether the object has the specified property
isPrototypeOf(object)	Returns a Boolean value indicating whether the object is a prototype of the other object
propertyIsEnumerable(precision)	Returns a Boolean value indicating whether the object has the specified property and the property is enumerable
toLocaleString()	Returns a string representation of the object using locale-specific formatting conventions
toString()	Returns a string representation of the object
valueOf()	Returns the primitive value that is associated with the object

RegExp

A core object that encapsulates a regular expression and provides properties and methods for accessing the regular expression.

Browser Support

Supported by Navigator 4 Internet Explorer 4.

Constructors

/pattern/flags   Creates a RegExp object using the specified pattern and flags.

new RegExp("pattern"[, "flags"])   Creates a RegExp object using the specified pattern and flags.

Properties

Name	Description
constructor	Refers to the object's constructor
global	Identifies whether the regular expression is global

ignoreCase	Identifies whether case should be ignored when the regular expression is applied
lastIndex	Is the index at which to start the next match
multiline	Indicates whether to search across multiple lines
prototype	Provides the capability to define additional properties
source	Is the pattern to be matched

Methods

Name	Description
exec([string])	Executes the regular expression with the specified string
test([string])	Tests the regular expression with the specified string
toString()	Returns a string representation of the object

String

The String object is a core object that provides an object wrapper for string values.

Browser Support

Supported by Navigator 2 Internet Explorer 3.

Constructors

new String(string)   Constructs a String object from the string value.

Properties

Name	Description
constructor	References the constructor used to create the object
length	Identifies the length of the associated string
prototype	Provides the capability to define additional properties

Methods

Name	Description
charAt(index)	Returns the character at the specified index.

`charCodeAt([index])`	Returns a number corresponding to the Unicode character at the specified index.
`concat(string1[,...,stringN])`	Concatenates strings 1 through N to the current string.
`indexOf(searchValue[,index])`	Returns the index of the first occurrence of the search value.
`lastIndexOf (searchValue[,index])`	Returns the index of the last occurrence of the search value.
`localeCompare(s)`	Compares the string with the string s using a locale-specific comparison. It returns 0 if the strings are equivalent and a non-zero numeric value if the strings are not equivalent.
`match(regexp)`	Matches the regular expression against the string.
`replace(regexp, function)`	Matches the regular expression and replaces the matches with the result of invoking the function.
`replace(regexp, newSubstring)`	Matches the regular expression and replaces the matches with the new string.
`search(regexp)`	Searches the string for the regular expression.
`slice(beginslice[, endSlice])`	Returns a slice of the string.
`split([separator][, limit])`	Splits the string into an array of strings based on the specified separator.
`substr(start[, length])`	Returns a substring of the string.
`substring(indexA, indexB)`	Returns a substring of the string.
`toLocaleLowerCase()`	Returns a lowercase version of the string using locale-specific conventions.
`toLocaleUpperCase()`	Returns an uppercase version of the string formatted using locale-specific conventions.
`toLowerCase()`	Returns a lowercase version of the string.
`toString()`	Returns a string version of the object.
`toUpperCase()`	Returns an uppercase version of the string.
`valueOf()`	Returns the primitive value corresponding to the object.

DOM 0 Object Reference

This appendix provides a summary of the DOM Level 0 objects, properties, methods, and event handlers. DOM Level 0 is loosely defined as the browser objects supported by Navigator 3 and Internet Explorer 3. I've also added some objects, properties, methods, and event handlers that are supported by Navigator 4, Navigator 6, and Internet Explorer 4.

Anchor

The Anchor object represents a document-internal target of a hypertext link. An Anchor object is created for each A tag in the document that specifies a NAME attribute. These objects may be accessed from the anchors property of the document object. Under Navigator, an Anchor object may also be a Link object if the A tag specifies the HREF attribute in addition to the NAME attribute.

Browser Support

Supported by Navigator 2 and Internet Explorer 3.

Properties

Name	Description	Browser Support
name	The anchor's NAME attribute	Navigator 4, Internet Explorer 4

Methods

No DOM 0 methods are defined for this object.

Event Handlers

Name	Description	Browser Support
ondblclick	The object is double-clicked.	Navigator 4, Internet Explorer 4
onmouseout	The mouse is moved away from the object.	Navigator 3, Internet Explorer 4
onmouseover	The mouse is moved over the object.	Navigator 2, Internet Explorer 3

Applet

The Applet object represents a Java applet that is loaded with a document. The applets property of the document object provides access to an enumeration of the Applet objects that are associated with the document. An applet is accessible to JavaScript only if the MAYSCRIPT attribute is supplied in the applet's APPLET tag.

For example, the following APPLET tag loads an applet that is accessible from JavaScript:

```
<APPLET CODE="MyApplet.class" WIDTH=200 HEIGHT=300 NAME="MyApplet" MAYSCRIPT>
```

Because the following APPLET tag does not include the MAYSCRIPT attribute, it cannot be accessed from JavaScript:

```
<APPLET CODE="OtherApplet.class" WIDTH=200 HEIGHT=300 NAME="OtherApplet">
```

The Applet object inherits all of the public properties and methods of the applet.

Browser Support

Supported by Navigator 3 and Internet Explorer 4.

Properties

No DOM 0 properties are defined for this object.

Methods

No DOM 0 methods are defined for this object.

Event Handlers

No DOM 0 event handlers are defined for this object.

Area

The Area object defines an area of an image map. It is similar to a Link object in that it is associated with a URL. This URL is loaded when a user clicks on the area of the image map represented by the Area object.

Browser Support

Supported by Navigator 3 and Internet Explorer 4.

Properties

Name	Description	Browser Support
hash	The name of an anchor in the URL	Navigator 2, Internet Explorer 3
host	A hostname or IP address that represents the URL's host value.	Navigator 2, Internet Explorer 3
hostname	The host:port portion of the URL	Navigator 2, Internet Explorer 3
href	The text of the entire URL	Navigator 2, Internet Explorer 3
pathname	The pathname portion of the URL	Navigator 2, Internet Explorer 3
port	The port value of the URL	Navigator 2, Internet Explorer 3
protocol	The URL's protocol type	Navigator 2, Internet Explorer 3
search	The value of any query string that is included in the URL	Navigator 2, Internet Explorer 3
target	The value of the URL's TARGET attribute	Navigator 2, Internet Explorer 3

Methods

No DOM 0 methods are defined for this object.

Event Handlers

Name	Description	Browser Support
ondblclick	The object is double-clicked.	Navigator 2, Internet Explorer 3
onmouseout	The mouse is moved away from the object.	Navigator 3, Internet Explorer 4
onmouseover	The mouse is moved over the object.	Navigator 2, Internet Explorer 3

Button

The `Button` object provides access to the buttons of an HTML form.

Browser Support

Supported by Navigator 2 and Internet Explorer 3.

Properties

Name	Description	Browser Support
form	Provides a reference to the form object that contains the button	Navigator 2, Internet Explorer 3
name	The value of the button's NAME attribute	Navigator 2, Internet Explorer 3
type	The value of the button's TYPE attribute	Navigator 3, Internet Explorer 4
value	The value of the button's VALUE attribute	Navigator 2, Internet Explorer 3

Methods

Name	Description	Browser Support
blur()	Removes input focus from the button	Navigator 2, Internet Explorer 3
click()	Simulates clicking of the button	Navigator 2, Internet Explorer 3
focus()	Moves input focus to the button	Navigator 2, Internet Explorer 3

Event Handlers

Name	Description	Browser Support
onblur	Input focus is removed from the object.	Navigator 3, Internet Explorer 4
onclick	The object is clicked.	Navigator 2, Internet Explorer 3
onfocus	The object gains input focus.	Navigator 3, Internet Explorer 4

onmousedown	The mouse is pressed.	Navigator 2, Internet Explorer 3
onmouseup	The mouse is released.	Navigator 2, Internet Explorer 3

Checkbox

The Checkbox object provides access to the check boxes of an HTML form.

Browser Support

Supported by Navigator 2 and Internet Explorer 3.

Properties

Name	Description	Browser Support
checked	Provides the Boolean value of the check box's selection state	Navigator 2, Internet Explorer 3
defaultChecked	The value of the check box's CHECKED attribute	Navigator 2, Internet Explorer 3
form	Provides a reference to the form object that contains the check box	Navigator 2, Internet Explorer 3
name	The value of the check box's NAME attribute	Navigator 2, Internet Explorer 3
type	The value of the check box's TYPE attribute	Navigator 3, Internet Explorer 4
value	The value of the check box's VALUE attribute	Navigator 2, Internet Explorer 3

Methods

Name	Description	Browser Support
blur()	Removes input focus from the check box.	Navigator 2, Internet Explorer 3
click()	Simulates clicking of the check box.	Navigator 2, Internet Explorer 3
focus()	Moves input focus to the check box.	Navigator 2, Internet Explorer 3

Event Handlers

Name	Description	Browser Support
onblur	Input focus is removed from the object.	Navigator 3, Internet Explorer 4
onclick	The object is clicked.	Navigator 2, Internet Explorer 3
onfocus	The object gains input focus.	Navigator 3, Internet Explorer 4

Document

The document object is a fundamental object of client-side JavaScript. It provides access to a web page that is displayed in a browser window. It also provides properties and methods for accessing the objects that comprise the document.

Browser Support

Supported by Navigator 2 and Internet Explorer 3.

Properties

Name	Description	Browser Support
alinkColor	Specifies the color of an active link. That is, a link that has been clicked on (mouse down) before the mouse is released (mouse up)	Navigator 2, Internet Explorer 3
anchors	Provides access to the document's Anchor objects as an array. The array's elements are ordered according to how the objects appear in the document.	Navigator 2, Internet Explorer 3
applets	Provides access to the document's Applet objects as an array. The array's elements are ordered according to how the objects appear in the document.	Navigator 3, Internet Explorer 4

bgColor	Provides access to the document's background color.	Navigator 2, Internet Explorer 3
cookie	Provides access to the HTTP cookies that are associated with the document.	Navigator 2, Internet Explorer 3
embeds	Provides access to the document's Plugin objects as an array. The array's elements are ordered according to how the objects appear in the document.	Navigator 3, Internet Explorer 4
fgColor	Provides access to the document's foreground color.	Navigator 2, Internet Explorer 3
forms	Provides access to the document's Form objects as an array. The array's elements are ordered according to how the objects appear in the document.	Navigator 3, Internet Explorer 4
images	Provides access to the document's Image objects as an array. The array's elements are ordered according to how the objects appear in the document.	Navigator 3, Internet Explorer 4
lastModified	Identifies when the document was last modified based on information provided in its HTTP header.	Navigator 2, Internet Explorer 3
linkColor	Specifies the normal color of all links contained in the document.	Navigator 2, Internet Explorer 3
links	Provides access to the document's Link objects as an array. The array's elements are ordered according to how the objects appear in the document.	Navigator 2, Internet Explorer 3
plugins	Provides access to the document's Plugin objects as an array. The array's elements are ordered according to how the objects appear in the document.	Navigator 3, Internet Explorer 4

`referrer`	Identifies the URL of the document (if any) that provided the link to this document.	Navigator 2, Internet Explorer 3
`title`	Provides access to the document's title.	Navigator 2, Internet Explorer 3
`URL`	Provides access to the URL from which the document was loaded.	Navigator 2, Internet Explorer 3
`vlinkColor`	Specifies the color of visited links.	Navigator 2, Internet Explorer 3

Methods

Name	Description	Browser Support
`close()`	Closes output to the `document` object.	Navigator 2, Internet Explorer 3
`open([mimeType, [replace]])`	Creates and opens a new document of the specified MIME type. The `replace` argument specifies that the new document is to reuse the history entry of the previous document.	Navigator 2, Internet Explorer 3
`write(expr1 [, ...,exprN])`	Writes the HTML expressions to the current document object.	Navigator 2, Internet Explorer 3
`writeln(expr1 [, ...,exprN])`	Writes the HTML expressions to the current document object. A newline character is appended to the last expression.	Navigator 2, Internet Explorer 3

Event Handlers

Name	Description	Browser Support
`onclick`	The object is clicked.	Navigator 2, Internet Explorer 3
`ondblclick`	The object is double-clicked.	Navigator 4, Internet Explorer 4
`onkeydown`	A key is pressed.	Navigator 4, Internet Explorer 4
`onkeypress`	A key is pressed and released.	Navigator 4, Internet Explorer 4
`onkeyup`	A key is released.	Navigator 4, Internet Explorer 4
`onmousedown`	The mouse is pressed.	Navigator 4, Internet Explorer 4
`onmouseup`	The mouse is released.	Navigator 4, Internet Explorer 4

Event

The event object is used to encapsulate all events that can be handled by JavaScript. It is passed as an argument to an event handler, and contains properties that describe the event.

Browser Support

Supported by Navigator 4 and Internet Explorer 4.

Properties

Name	Description	Browser Support
screenX	Identifies the cursor's horizontal position (in pixels) relative to the screen.	Navigator 4, Internet Explorer 4
screenY	Identifies the cursor's vertical position (in pixels) relative to the screen.	Navigator 4, Internet Explorer 4
x	Identifies the horizontal position (in pixels) where the event occurred. When used with a resize event, it identifies the object's width.	Navigator 4, Internet Explorer 4
y	Identifies the vertical position (in pixels) where the event occurred. When used with a resize event, it identifies the object's height.	Navigator 4, Internct Explorer 4

Methods

No DOM 0 methods are defined for this object.

Event Handlers

No DOM 0 event handlers are defined for this object.

FileUpload

The FileUpload object provides access to the file upload objects of an HTML form. These objects are INPUT tags with their TYPE attribute set to FILE. They provide the user with the capability to upload a file to a web site.

Browser Support

Supported by Navigator 2 and Internet Explorer 4.

Properties

Name	Description	Browser Support
form	Provides a reference to the form object that contains the file upload element	Navigator 2, Internet Explorer 3
name	The value of the file upload's NAME attribute	Navigator 2, Internet Explorer 3
type	The value of the file upload's TYPE attribute	Navigator 3, Internet Explorer 4
value	The name of the file selected by the user	Navigator 2, Internet Explorer 3

Methods

Name	Description	Browser Support
blur()	Removes input focus from the file upload element	Navigator 2, Internet Explorer 3
focus()	Moves input focus to the file upload element	Navigator 2, Internet Explorer 3
select()	Selects (highlights) the input area of the file upload element	Navigator 2, Internet Explorer 3

Event Handlers

Name	Description	Browser Support
onblur	Input focus is removed from the object.	Navigator 3, Internet Explorer 4
onchange	The value of the object is updated.	Navigator 3, Internet Explorer 4
onfocus	The object gains input focus.	Navigator 3, Internet Explorer 4

Form

The Form object encapsulates an HTML form, and provides access to the elements contained in a form. It is used for handling user interactions with form elements and to perform form data validation prior to submission of form data to a web server.

Browser Support

Supported by Navigator 2 and Internet Explorer 3.

Properties

Name	Description	Browser Support
action	Identifies the form's ACTION attribute	Navigator 2, Internet Explorer 3
elements	An array containing all of the form's input elements in the order that they appear in the form	Navigator 2, Internet Explorer 3
encoding	Identifies the form's ENCTYPE attribute	Navigator 2, Internet Explorer 3
length	Identifies the number of elements contained in the form (the length of the elements array)	.Navigator 2, Internet Explorer 3
method	Identifies the form's METHOD attribute	Navigator 2, Internet Explorer 3
name	Identifies the form's NAME attribute	Navigator 2, Internet Explorer 3
target	Identifies the form's TARGET attribute	Navigator 2, Internet Explorer 3

Method

Name	Description	Browser Support
submit()	Submits the form's data	Navigator 2, Internet Explorer 3

Event Handlers

Name	Description	Browser Support
onreset	The contents of the form are reset.	Navigator 3, Internet Explorer 4
onsubmit	The contents of the form are submitted.	Navigator 2, Internet Explorer 3

Frame

The Frame object provides access to an HTML frame. It is equivalent to a window object. Refer to the window object for a description of frame.

Browser Support

Supported by Navigator 2 and Internet Explorer 3.

Hidden

Represents a hidden form field. Hidden form fields are INPUT tags with their TYPE attribute set to HIDDEN. They are used to store state information in forms.

Browser Support

Supported by Navigator 2 and Internet Explorer 3.

Properties

Name	Description	Browser Support
form	Provides a reference to the form object that contains the hidden field	Navigator 2, Internet Explorer 3
name	The value of the hidden field's NAME attribute	Navigator 2, Internet Explorer 3
type	The value of the hidden field's TYPE attribute	Navigator 3, Internet Explorer 4
value	The value stored in the hidden field	Navigator 2, Internet Explorer 3

Methods

No DOM 0 methods are defined for this object.

Event Handlers

No DOM 0 event handlers are defined for this object.

History

The History object maintains information on the URLs that the client has visited for a particular window.

Browser Support

Supported by Navigator 2 and Internet Explorer 3.

Property

Name	Description	Browser Support
length	Identifies the length of the history list	Navigator 2, Internet Explorer 3

Methods

Name	Description	Browser Support
back()	Loads the previous URL in the history list	Navigator 2, Internet Explorer 3
forward()	Loads the next URL in the history list	Navigator 2, Internet Explorer 3
go(delta)	Loads a URL from the relative position in the history list specified by delta	Navigator 2, Internet Explorer 3
go(location)	Loads a URL, based on the partial URL specified by location, by matching it with other URLs in the history list	Navigator 2, Internet Explorer 3

Event Handlers

No DOM 0 event handlers are defined for this object.

IMG (Image)

Represents an image that is loaded for the current document. The images property of the document object contains an array of all images loaded for that document.

Browser Support

Supported by Navigator 3 and Internet Explorer 4.

Properties

Name	Description	Browser Support
border	Identifies the value of the BORDER attribute	Navigator 3, Internet Explorer 4
complete	Identifies whether the image's loading has been completed	Navigator 3, Internet Explorer 4

height	Identifies the value of the HEIGHT attribute	Navigator 3, Internet Explorer 4
hspace	Identifies the value of the HSPACE attribute	Navigator 3, Internet Explorer 4
lowsrc	Identifies the value of the LOWSRC attribute	Navigator 3, Internet Explorer 4
name	Identifies the value of the NAME attribute	Navigator 3, Internet Explorer 4
src	Identifies the value of the SRC attribute	Navigator 3, Internet Explorer 4
vspace	Identifies the value of the VSPACE attribute	Navigator 3, Internet Explorer 4
width	Identifies the value of the WIDTH attribute	Navigator 3, Internet Explorer 4

Methods

No DOM 0 methods are defined for this object.

Event Handlers

Name	Description	Browser Support
onabort	The loading of the object was aborted.	Navigator 3, Internet Explorer 4
onerror	The loading of the object resulted in an error.	Navigator 3, Internet Explorer 4
onkeydown	A key is pressed.	Navigator 4, Internet Explorer 4
onkeypress	A key is pressed and released.	Navigator 4, Internet Explorer 4
onkeyup	A key is released.	Navigator 4, Internet Explorer 4
onload	The loading of the object was completed.	Navigator 3, Internet Explorer 4

Link (A)

The Link tag represents a hypertext link. A Link object is created for each A tag in the document that specifies an HREF attribute. These objects may be accessed from the links property of the document object.

Under Navigator, a Link object may also be an Anchor object if the A tag specifies the NAME attribute in addition to the HREF attribute.

Browser Support

Supported by Navigator 2 and Internet Explorer 3.

Properties

Name	Description	Browser Support
hash	The name of an anchor in the URL	Navigator 2, Internet Explorer 3
host	A hostname or IP address that represents the URL's host value	Navigator 2, Internet Explorer 3
hostname	The host:port portion of the URL	Navigator 2, Internet Explorer 3
href	The text of the entire URL	Navigator 2, Internet Explorer 3
pathname	The pathname portion of the URL	Navigator 2, Internet Explorer 3
port	The port value of the URL	Navigator 2, Internet Explorer 3
protocol	The URL's protocol type	Navigator 2, Internet Explorer 3
search	The value of any query string that is included in the URL	Navigator 2, Internet Explorer 3
target	The value of the URL's TARGET attribute	Navigator 2, Internet Explorer 3

Methods

No DOM 0 methods are defined for this object.

Event Handlers

Name	Description	Browser Support
onclick	The object is clicked.	Navigator 2, Internet Explorer 3
ondblclick	The object is double-clicked.	Navigator 4, Internet Explorer 4
onkeydown	A key is pressed.	Navigator 4, Internet Explorer 4
onkeypress	A key is pressed and released.	Navigator 4, Internet Explorer 4
onkeyup	A key is released.	Navigator 4, Internet Explorer 4
onmousedown	The mouse is pressed.	Navigator 4, Internet Explorer 4
onmouseout	The mouse is moved away from the object.	Navigator 3, Internet Explorer 4
onmouseover	The mouse is moved over the object.	Navigator 2, Internet Explorer 3
onmouseup	The mouse is released.	Navigator 4, Internet Explorer 4

Location

A Location object represents the URL of the document loaded into a window. The location property of the window object provides access to the window's Location object.

Browser Support

Supported by Navigator 2 and Internet Explorer 3.

Properties

Name	Description	Browser Support
hash	The name of an anchor in the URL	Navigator 2, Internet Explorer 3

host	A hostname or IP address that represents the URL's host value	Navigator 2, Internet Explorer 3
hostname	The host:port portion of the URL	Navigator 2, Internet Explorer 3
href	The text of the entire URL	Navigator 2, Internet Explorer 3
pathname	The pathname portion of the URL	Navigator 2, Internet Explorer 3
port	The port value of the URL	Navigator 2, Internet Explorer 3
protocol	The URL's protocol type	Navigator 2, Internet Explorer 3
search	The value of any query string that is included in the URL	Navigator 2, Internet Explorer 3

Methods

Name	Description	Browser Support
reload([force])	Reloads the current document. If the force argument is true, an HTTP GET is forced by the browser causing the document to be reloaded from the server instead of the browser's cache.	Navigator 3, Internet Explorer 4
replace(url)	Loads the specified URL over the current document.	Navigator 3, Internet Explorer 4

Event Handlers

No DOM 0 event handlers are defined for this object.

Navigator

The navigator object provides access to basic information about the browser that is executing the script.

Browser Support

Supported by Navigator 2 and Internet Explorer 3.

Properties

Name	Description	Browser Support
appCodeName	The browser's code name	Navigator 2, Internet Explorer 3
appName	The browser's name	Navigator 2, Internet Explorer 3
appVersion	The browser's version number	Navigator 2, Internet Explorer 3
mimeTypes	An array of MimeType objects supported by the browser	Navigator 3, Internet Explorer 4
plugins	An array of all Plugin objects supported by the browser	Navigator 3, Internet Explorer 4
userAgent	The user-agent header sent in the HTTP protocol by the browser to a web server	Navigator 2, Internet Explorer 3

Method

Name	Description	Browser Support
javaEnabled()	Returns true if Java is enabled by the browser	Navigator 3, Internet Explorer 4

Event Handlers

No DOM 0 event handlers are defined for this object.

Option

The Option object represents an option in the select field of a form.

Browser Support

Supported by Navigator 2 and Internet Explorer 3.

Properties

Name	Description	Browser Support
index	Identifies the index of the option in the options array of the corresponding Select object	Navigator 2, Internet Explorer 3
length	Identifies the length of the options array of the corresponding Select object	Navigator 2, Internet Explorer 3
selected	Identifies the option's current selection state	Navigator 2, Internet Explorer 3
text	Identifies the option's text	Navigator 2, Internet Explorer 3
value	Identifies the option's value	Navigator 2, Internet Explorer 3

Methods

No DOM 0 methods are defined for this object.

Event Handlers

No DOM 0 event handlers are defined for this object.

Password

A Password object represents a password field of an HTML form. Password fields are represented by INPUT tags with their TYPE attribute set to PASSWORD. Password objects allow a user to type in a password without its contents being displayed. However, the password values are not encrypted, and are transmitted in the clear from the user's browser to a web server via HTTP.

Browser Support

Supported by Navigator 2 and Internet Explorer 3.

Properties

Name	Description	Browser Support
defaultValue	The default value of the password field	Navigator 2, Internet Explorer 3

form	Provides a reference to the form object that contains the password field	Navigator 2, Internet Explorer 3
name	The value of the password field's NAME attribute	Navigator 2, Internet Explorer 3
type	The value of the password field's TYPE attribute	Navigator 3, Internet Explorer 4
value	The value entered by the user in the password field	Navigator 2, Internet Explorer 3

Methods

Name	Description	Browser Support
blur()	Removes input focus from the password field	Navigator 2, Internet Explorer 3
focus()	Moves input focus to the password field	Navigator 2, Internet Explorer 3
select()	Selects (highlights) the input area of the password field	Navigator 2, Internet Explorer 3

Event Handlers

Name	Description	Browser Support
onblur	Input focus is removed from the object.	Navigator 3, Internet Explorer 4
onfocus	The object gains input focus.	Navigator 3, Internet Explorer 4

Radio

Radio buttons are form fields that support the selection of exactly one choice from a set of one or more choices. They are INPUT elements that have their TYPE attribute set to RADIO. Radio buttons are grouped by setting their NAME attributes to the same values.

Browser Support

Supported by Navigator 2 and Internet Explorer 3.

Properties

Name	Description	Browser Support
checked	Identifies, via a Boolean value, whether the radio button is checked or unchecked	Navigator 2, Internet Explorer 3
defaultChecked	The value of the button's CHECKED attribute	Navigator 2, Internet Explorer 3
form	Provides a reference to the form object that contains the button	Navigator 2, Internet Explorer 3
name	The value of the button's NAME attribute	Navigator 2, Internet Explorer 3
type	The value of the button's TYPE attribute	Navigator 3, Internet Explorer 4
value	The value of the button's VALUE attribute	Navigator 2, Internet Explorer 3

Methods

Name	Description	Browser Support
blur()	Removes input focus from the button	Navigator 2, Internet Explorer 3
click()	Simulates clicking of the button	Navigator 2, Internet Explorer 3
focus()	Moves input focus to the button	Navigator 2, Internet Explorer 3

Event Handlers

Name	Description	Browser Support
onblur	Input focus is removed from the object.	Navigator 3, Internet Explorer 4
onclick	The object is clicked.	Navigator 2, Internet Explorer 3
onfocus	The object gains input focus.	Navigator 3, Internet Explorer 4

Reset

Reset buttons are form fields that reset form fields back to their original values. They are INPUT elements that have their TYPE attribute set to RESET.

Browser Support

Supported by Navigator 2 and Internet Explorer 3.

Properties

Name	Description	Browser Support
form	Provides a reference to the form object that contains the button	Navigator 2, Internet Explorer 3
name	The value of the button's NAME attribute	Navigator 2, Internet Explorer 3
type	The value of the button's TYPE attribute	Navigator 3, Internet Explorer 4
value	The value of the button's VALUE attribut.	Navigator 2, Internet Explorer 3

Methods

Name	Description	Browser Support
blur()	Removes input focus from the button	Navigator 2, Internet Explorer 3
click()	Simulates clicking of the button	Navigator 2, Internet Explorer 3
focus()	Moves input focus to the button	Navigator 2, Internet Explorer 3

Event Handlers

Name	Description	Browser Support
onblur	Input focus is removed from the object.	Navigator 3, Internet Explorer 4
onclick	The object is clicked.	Navigator 2, Internet Explorer 3
onfocus	The object gains input focus.	Navigator 3, Internet Explorer 4

Screen

Provides access to the parameters of the user's display monitor.

Browser Support

Supported by Navigator 4 and Internet Explorer 4

Properties

Name	Description	Browser Support
colorDepth	The number of colors supported by the current color palette	Navigator 4, Internet Explorer 4
height	The height of the screen	Navigator 4, Internet Explorer 4
width	The width of the screen	Navigator 4, Internet Explorer 4

Methods

No DOM 0 methods are defined for this object.

Event Handlers

No DOM 0 event handlers are defined for this object.

Select

A select field provides an HTML menu of choices to users. The SELECT tags enclose zero or more OPTION tags. The OPTION tags specify the menu choices, and are represented by OPTION objects in JavaScript.

Browser Support

Supported by Navigator 2 and Internet Explorer 3.

Properties

Name	Description	Browser Support
form	Provides a reference to the form object that contains the select field.	Navigator 2, Internet Explorer 3
length	Identifies the number of options.	Navigator 2, Internet Explorer 3
name	The value of the select field's NAME attribute.	Navigator 2, Internet Explorer 3
options	An array that identifies the Option objects of the select element. The objects appear in the same order that they do in the source HTML.	Navigator 2, Internet Explorer 3

| selectedIndex | Identifies (by index) the first selected option in the select element. This property is set to -1 if no options are selected. | Navigator 2, Internet Explorer 3 |
| type | If the select field's MULTIPLE attribute is set, type has the value select-multiple. Otherwise, it is set to select-one. | Navigator 3, Internet Explorer 4 |

Methods

Name	Description	Browser Support
blur()	Removes input focus from the select field	Navigator 2, Internet Explorer 3
focus()	Moves input focus to the select field	Navigator 2, Internet Explorer 3

Event Handlers

Name	Description	Browser Support
onblur	Input focus is removed from the object.	Navigator 2, Internet Explorer 3
onchange	The value of the object is updated.	Navigator 2, Internet Explorer 3
onfocus	The object gains input focus.	Navigator 2, Internet Explorer 3

Submit

A submit button is a form field that is used to submit form values to a web server for processing. A submit button is an INPUT element that has its TYPE attribute set to SUBMIT.

Browser Support

Supported by Navigator 2 and Internet Explorer 3.

Properties

Name	Description	Browser Support
form	Provides a reference to the form object that contains the button	Navigator 2, Internet Explorer 3

name	The value of the button's NAME attribute	Navigator 2, Internet Explorer 3
type	The value of the button's TYPE attribute	Navigator 3, Internet Explorer 4
value	The value of the button's VALUE attribute	Navigator 2, Internet Explorer 3

Methods

Name	Description	Browser Support
blur()	Removes input focus from the button	Navigator 2, Internet Explorer 3
click()	Simulates clicking of the button	Navigator 2, Internet Explorer 3
focus()	Moves input focus to the button	Navigator 2, Internet Explorer 3

Event Handlers

Name	Description	Browser Support
onblur	Input focus is removed from the object.	Navigator 3, Internet Explorer 4
onclick	The object is clicked.	Navigator 2, Internet Explorer 3
onfocus	The object gains input focus.	Navigator 3, Internet Explorer 4

Text

A text field is a form field that is used to obtain a single line of text from the user. A text field is an INPUT element that has its TYPE attribute set to TEXT.

Browser Support

Supported by Navigator 2 and Internet Explorer 3.

Properties

Name	Description	Browser Support
defaultValue	The value of the field's VALUE attribute	Navigator 2, Internet Explorer 3
form	Provides a reference to the form object that contains the field	Navigator 2, Internet Explorer 3

name	The value of the field's NAME attribute	Navigator 2, Internet Explorer 3
type	The value of the field's TYPE attribute	Navigator 3, Internet Explorer 4
value	The text string value currently contained in the field	Navigator 2, Internet Explorer 3

Methods

Name	Description	Browser Support
blur()	Removes input focus from the text field	Navigator 2, Internet Explorer 3
focus()	Moves input focus to the text field	Navigator 2, Internet Explorer 3
select()	Selects (highlights) the value of the text field	Navigator 2, Internet Explorer 3

Event Handlers

Name	Description	Browser Support
onblur	Input focus is removed from the object.	Navigator 2, Internet Explorer 3
onchange	The value of the object is updated.	Navigator 2, Internet Explorer 3
onfocus	The object gains input focus.	Navigator 2, Internet Explorer 3
onselect	The contents of the field are selected.	Navigator 2, Internet Explorer 3

Textarea

A text area field is a form field that is used to obtain multiple lines of text from the user. A text area field uses the TEXTAREA tags to surround lines of default text to be placed in the field.

Browser Support

Supported by Navigator 2 and Internet Explorer 3.

Properties

Name	Description	Browser Support
defaultValue	Identifies the default value of the text area field	Navigator 2, Internet Explorer 3
form	Provides a reference to the form object that contains the field	Navigator 2, Internet Explorer 3
name	The value of the field's NAME attribute	Navigator 2, Internet Explorer 3
type	The value of the field's TYPE attribute	Navigator 3, Internet Explorer 4
value	The text string value currently contained in the field	Navigator 2, Internet Explorer 3

Methods

Name	Description	Browser Support
blur()	Removes input focus from the text area field	Navigator 2, Internet Explorer 3
focus()	Moves input focus to the text area field	Navigator 2, Internet Explorer 3
select()	Selects (highlights) the value of the text area field	Navigator 2, Internet Explorer 3

Event Handlers

Name	Description	Browser Support
onblur	Input focus is removed from the object.	Navigator 2, Internet Explorer 3
onchange	The value of the object is updated.	Navigator 2, Internet Explorer 3
onfocus	The object gains input focus.	Navigator 2, Internet Explorer 3
onkeydown	A key is pressed.	Navigator 4, Internet Explorer 4

`onkeypress`	A key is pressed and released.	Navigator 4, Internet Explorer 4
`onkeyup`	A key is released.	Navigator 4, Internet Explorer 4
`onselect`	The contents of the field are selected.	Navigator 2, Internet Explorer 3

Window

The `window` object encapsulates a browser window and provides access to the objects that are contained in the window.

Browser Support

Supported by Navigator 2 and Internet Explorer 3.

Properties

Name	Description	Browser Support
`closed`	Identified whether the window is closed	Navigator 3, Internet Explorer 4
`defaultStatus`	The default status displayed in the bottom of the window	Navigator 2, Internet Explorer 3
`document`	The document that is loaded in the window	Navigator 2, Internet Explorer 3
`frames`	An array of frames that are contained in the current window	Navigator 2, Internet Explorer 3
`history`	Provides access to the `History` object associated with the window	Navigator 3, Internet Explorer 4
`length`	Identifies the length of the `frames` array property	Navigator 2, Internet Explorer 3
`location`	Provides access to the `Location` object associated with the window	Navigator 2, Internet Explorer 3
`name`	Identifies the window's name	Navigator 2, Internet Explorer 3

offscreenBuffering	Identifies whether offscreen buffering is turned on	Navigator 4, Internet Explorer 4
opener	Identifies the window object that caused the current window object to be opened	Navigator 3, Internet Explorer 4
parent	Identifies the window's parent window	Navigator 2, Internet Explorer 3
self	Refers to the current window	Navigator 2, Internet Explorer 3
status	Provides access to the window's status display area	Navigator 2, Internet Explorer 3
top	Provides access to the topmost browser window	Navigator 2, Internet Explorer 3
window	Refers to the current window	Navigator 2, Internet Explorer 3

Methods

Name	Description	Browser Support
alert(message)	Displays the alert message	Navigator 2, Internet Explorer 3
blur()	Removes focus from the window	Navigator 2, Internet Explorer 3
clearInterval (interval)	Clears the specified interval timer	Navigator 4, Internet Explorer 4
clearTimeout (timeout)	Clears the specified timeout	Navigator 2, Internet Explorer 3
close()	Closes the window	Navigator 2, Internet Explorer 3
confirm(string)	Displays a confirmation message	Navigator 2, Internet Explorer 3
focus()	Brings focus to the window	Navigator 3, Internet Explorer 4
open(url, name [, features])	Opens a window with the specified name and features	Navigator 2, Internet Explorer 3

prompt(string [,default])	Displays a prompt to the user	Navigator 2, Internet Explorer 3
setInterval (expression, milliseconds)	Sets an interval timer	Navigator 4, Internet Explorer 4
setInterval (function, milliseconds [, arg1 [, ..., argN]])	Sets an interval timer	Navigator 4, Internet Explorer 4
setTimeout (expression, milliseconds)	Sets a timeout	Navigator 2, Internet Explorer 3

Event Handlers

Name	Description	Browser Support
onblur	Input focus is removed from the object.	Navigator 3, Internet Explorer 4
onerror	The loading of the object resulted in an error.	Navigator 3, Internet Explorer 4
onfocus	The object gains input focus.	Navigator 3, Internet Explorer 4
onload	The loading of the object was completed.	Navigator 2, Internet Explorer 3
onresize	The object is resized.	Navigator 4, Internet Explorer 4
onunload	The contents of the object are unloaded.	Navigator 2, Internet Explorer 3

DOM 1 Object Reference

DOM1 XML Core Objects

Attr

Attr represents an XML/HTML attribute name/value pair, and extends the Node interface.

Properties

Name	Type	Access	Description
name	String	read-only	The name of the attribute.
value	String	read-write	The value of the attribute.
specified	Boolean	read-only	Whether or not the attribute was specified in the document.

CDATASection

Represents a CDATA section. CDATA sections are used to escape blocks of text containing characters that would otherwise be regarded as markup. CDATASection extends the Text interface.

CharacterData

The CharacterData interface extends Node with a set of attributes and methods for accessing character data in the DOM. This interface, like Node, is an abstract interface. No DOM objects correspond directly to CharacterData. It is extended by Text and other interfaces. It supports UTF-16 text characters. CharacterData extends the Node interface.

Properties

Name	Type	Access	Description
data	String	read-write	The character data of the node that implements this interface.
length	Number	read-only	The number of characters in the CharacterData.

Methods

substringData(offset, count)   Returns a count character substring starting at offset. The offset argument is of type Number. The count argument is of type Number. This method returns an object of type String. In the event of an error, this method throws an exception of type DOMException.

appendData(arg)   Appends the string to the end of the character data of the node. The `arg` argument is of type `String`. This method does not return a value. In the event of an error, this method throws an exception of type `DOMException`.

insertData(offset, arg)   Inserts the string at the specified `offset`. The `offset` argument is of type `Number`. The `arg` argument is of type `String`. This method does not return a value. In the event of an error, this method throws an exception of type `DOMException`.

deleteData(offset, count)   Deletes count characters starting at `offset`. The `offset` argument is of type `Number`. The `count` argument is of type `Number`. This method does not return a value. In the event of an error, this method throws an exception of type `DOMException`.

replaceData(offset, count, arg)   Replaces count characters starting at the specified `offset` with the specified string. The `offset` argument is of type `Number`. The `count` argument is of type `Number`. The `arg` argument is of type `String`. This method does not return a value. In the event of an error, this method throws an exception of type `DOMException`.

Comment

Represents the content of an XML or HTML comment. `Comment` extends the `CharacterData` interface.

Document

`Document` is the root node of the DOM document tree. It provides properties and methods by which the other document objects are accessed. It also provides methods for creating these objects. `Document` extends the `Node` interface.

Properties

Name	Type	Access	Description
doctype	DocumentType	read-only	Identifies the Document Type Declaration (DTD) associated with the document. Its value is `null` if the document does not have a DTD.
documentElement	Element	read-only	Provides direct access to the child node that is the root element of the document. For HTML documents, this is the element with the tag named "HTML".

`implementation`	`DOMImplementation`	read-only	Provides access to the `DOMImplementation` object associated with the document.

Methods

createElement(tagName)   Creates a new document element of the type specified by `tag-Name`. The `tagName` argument is of type `String`. This method returns an object of type `Element`. In the event of an error, this method throws an exception of type `DOMException`.

createDocumentFragment()   Creates a new `DocumentFragment` object. This method returns an object of type `DocumentFragment`.

createTextNode(data)   Creates a text node with the specified data. The `data` argument is of type `String`. This method returns an object of type `Text`.

createComment(data)   Creates a comment whose value is set by `data`. The `data` argument is of type `String`. This method returns an object of type `Comment`.

createCDATASection(data)   Creates a `CDATA` section whose value is set by `data`. The `data` argument is of type `String`. This method returns an object of type `CDATASection`. In the event of an error, this method throws an exception of type `DOMException`.

createProcessingInstruction(target, data)   Creates a processing instruction with the specified target and data. The `target` argument is of type `String`. The `data` argument is of type `String`. This method returns an object of type `ProcessingInstruction`. In the event of an error, this method throws an exception of type `DOMException`.

createAttribute(name)   Creates an attribute with the name specified by `tagName`. The attribute's value is set to the blank string. The `name` argument is of type `String`. This method returns an object of type `Attr`. In the event of an error, this method throws an exception of type `DOMException`.

createEntityReference(name)   Creates an entity reference with the name specified by `tagName`. The `name` argument is of type `String`. This method returns an object of type `EntityReference`. In the event of an error, this method throws an exception of type `DOMException`.

getElementsByTagName(tagname)   Returns a `NodeList` object of all the elements with the specified `tagName`. A `tagName` of "*" is used as a wildcard character and matches all tag names. The `tagname` argument is of type `String`. This method returns an object of type `NodeList`.

DocumentFragment

DocumentFragment is described as a "lightweight" or "minimal" Document object. It is used to create or access a fragment of a document. DocumentFragment extends Node, but does not define any additional properties or methods. DocumentFragment extends the Node interface.

DocumentType

Each Document has a doctype attribute whose value is either null or a DocumentType object. The DocumentType interface in the DOM Level 1 Core provides an interface to the list of entities that are defined for the document. DocumentType extends the Node interface.

Properties

Name	Type	Access	Description
name	String	read-only	The name of DTD; that is, the name immediately following the DOCTYPE keyword.
entities	NamedNodeMap	read-only	A NamedNodeMap containing the general entities, both external and internal, declared in the DTD.
notations	NamedNodeMap	read-only	A NamedNodeMap containing the notations declared in the DTD.

DOMException

DOMException is used to signal the fact that a particular operation cannot be performed because of an abnormal condition.

Property

Name	Type	Access	Description
code	short	read-write	The value of the code property is defined as follows.

Error Name	Value	Description
INDEX_SIZE_ERR	1	An index is out of range.
String_SIZE_ERR	2	The specified text is too large for a DOM string.
HIERARCHY_REQUEST_ERR	3	A node is inserted somewhere that it doesn't belong.

WRONG_DOCUMENT_ERR	4	A node is used in a document other than the one that created it, and this document doesn't support the node.
INVALID_CHARACTER_ERR	5	An invalid or illegal character was encountered.
NO_DATA_ALLOWED_ERR	6	A node that is not allowed to contain data is specified with data.
NO_MODIFICATION_ ALLOWED_ERR	7	An attempt was made to modify an object that is not allowed to be modified.
NOT_FOUND_ERR	8	A reference is made to a node that cannot be found.
NOT_SUPPORTED_ERR	9	The implementation does not support the type of object that was requested.
INUSE_ATTRIBUTE_ERR	10	An attempt was made to insert an attribute that is already in use.

DOMImplementation

Provides access to information about the underlying DOM implementation support.

Method

hasFeature(feature, version)

Returns a Boolean value that indicates whether or not the implementation supports the specified feature. The value of feature may be "HTML" (for DOM 1 HTML support) or "XML" (for DOM 1 XML Core support). The optional version may currently be "1.0". The feature argument is of type String. The version argument is of type String. This method returns an object of type Boolean.

Element

Represents an element of an XML or HTML document. Element extends the Node interface.

Property

Name	Type	Access	Description
tagName	String	read-only	The name of the tag of the element.

Methods

getAttribute(name)   Returns the value of the specified attribute. If the attribute does not exist, a blank string is returned. The `name` argument is of type `String`. This method returns an object of type `String`.

setAttribute(name, value)   Adds a new attribute if it does not exist. If an attribute with that name is already present in the element, its value is changed to be that of the `value` parameter. This value is a simple string; it is not parsed as it is being set. The `name` argument is of type `String`. The `value` argument is of type `String`. This method does not return a value. In the event of an error, this method throws an exception of type `DOMException`.

removeAttribute(name)   Removes the specified attribute. The `name` argument is of type `String`. This method does not return a value. In the event of an error, this method throws an exception of type `DOMException`. However, if `removeAttribute()` is invoked with a name that does not exist, no error is thrown.

getAttributeNode(name)   Returns the `Attr` object corresponding to the specified name. If the object does not exist, `null` is returned. The `name` argument is of type `String`. This method returns an object of type `Attr`.

setAttributeNode(newAttr)   Adds a new attribute node if it does not exist. If an attribute with that name is already present in the element, it is replaced by the new one. If the `newAttr` attribute replaces an existing attribute, the replaced `Attr` node is returned; otherwise, `null` is returned. The `newAttr` argument is of type `Attr`. This method returns an object of type `Attr`. In the event of an error, this method throws an exception of type `DOMException`.

removeAttributeNode(oldAttr   Removes the specified attribute and returns it. The `oldAttr` argument is of type `Attr`. This method returns an object of type `Attr`. In the event of an error, this method throws an exception of type `DOMException`.

getElementsByTagName(name)   Returns a `NodeList` of all descendant `Elements` with a given tag name. "*" is a wildcard that matches all tags. The `name` argument is of type `String`. This method returns an object of type `NodeList`.

normalize()   Normalizes all `Text` nodes in the subtree by combining adjacent `Text` nodes. This method does not return a value.

Entity

Represents an entity, either parsed or unparsed, in an XML document. Note that this models the entity itself, not the entity declaration. `Entity` extends the `Node` interface.

Properties

Name	Type	Access	Description
publicId	String	read-only	The public identifier of this entity. If the public identifier was not specified, this is null.
systemId	String	read-only	The system identifier of this entity. If the system identifier was not specified, this is null.
notationName	String	read-only	For unparsed entities, the name of the notation for the entity. For parsed entities, this is null.

EntityReference

Represents an entity reference in an XML or HTML document. Note that character references and references to predefined entities are considered to be expanded by the HTML or XML processor so that characters are represented by their Unicode equivalent rather than by an entity reference. Moreover, the XML processor may completely expand references to entities while building the structure model, instead of providing EntityReference objects. EntityReference extends the Node interface.

NamedNodeMap

Represents a collection of nodes that can be accessed by name.

Property

Name	Type	Access	Description
length	Number	read-only	The length of the NamedNodeMap.

Methods

getNamedItem(name)
Returns the named node of the NamedNodeMap. If the named node is not in the NamedNodeMap, it returns null. The name argument is of type String. This method returns an object of type Node.

item(index)
Returns the specified item of the NamedNodeMap or null if the index is not valid. The index argument is of type Number. This method returns an object of type Node.

setNamedItem(arg) Adds a node to the NamedNodeMap based on its nodeName property if it does not exist. If a node with that name is already present in this map, it is replaced by the new one. The arg argument is of type Node. This method returns an object of type Node. In the event of an error, this method throws an exception of type DOMException.

removeNamedItem(name) Removes the specified node and returns the node. Throws a DOMException if the node is not found. The name argument is of type String. This method returns an object of type Node. In the event of an error, this method throws an exception of type DOMException.

Node

Node interface is the primary interface type of the DOM. All document objects, including Document, extend Node. Therefore, the properties and methods of Node are available to all of these document objects.

Properties

Name	Type	Access	Description
nodeName	String	read-only	The name of the node, as described in the following table.
nodeValue	String	read-write	The value of the node, as described in the following table. Setting this property causes a DOMException to be thrown if its value is not null.
nodeType	short	read-only	An integer constant that identifies the type of the node, as defined in the following node type table.
parentNode	Node	read-only	The parent of this node, or null if this node doesn't have a parent.
childNodes	NodeList	read-only	A NodeList that contains all children of this node.
firstChild	Node	read-only	The first child of this node (if there is one), or null otherwise.
lastChild	Node	read-only	The last child of this node (if there is one), or null otherwise.
previous-Sibling	Node	read-only	The node immediately before this node (if there is one), or null otherwise.

nextSibling	Node	read-only	The node immediately after this node (if there is one), or null otherwise.
attributes	Named-NodeMap	read-only	Provides a NamedNodeMap containing the attributes of this node (if it is an Element), or null otherwise.
ownerDocument	Document	read-only	The Document object associated in which this node is contained. If this node is a Document, ownerDocument is null.

Node Type	Node Name	Node Value
Attr	Name of the attribute	Value of the attribute
CDATASection	#cdata-section	Contents of the CDATA section
Comment	#comment	Content of the comment
Document	#document	null
DocumentFragment	#document-fragment	null
DocumentType	Document type name	null
Element	Tag name	null
Entity	Entity name	null
EntityReference	Name of entity referenced	null
Notation	Notation name	null
Processing Instruction	Target	Entire content excluding the target
Text	#text	Content of the text node

Node Type	Node Type Constant
ELEMENT_NODE	1
ATTRIBUTE_NODE	2
TEXT_NODE	3
CDATA_SECTION_NODE	4
ENTITY_REFERENCE_NODE	5
ENTITY_NODE	6
PROCESSING_INSTRUCTION_NODE	7
COMMENT_NODE	8

DOCUMENT_NODE   9

DOCUMENT_TYPE_NODE   10

DOCUMENT_FRAGMENT_NODE   11

NOTATION_NODE   12

Methods

insertBefore(newChild, refChild)   Inserts the node newChild before the existing child node refChild. If refChild is null, inserts newChild at the end of the current list of children. If newChild is a DocumentFragment object, all its children are inserted, in the same order, before refChild. If newChild is already in the document, it is removed and then inserted. The new-Child argument is of type Node. The refChild argument is of type Node. This method returns an object of type Node. In the event of an error, this method throws an exception of type DOMException.

replaceChild(newChild, oldChild)   Replaces the child node oldChild with newChild in the list of children, and returns the oldChild node. If newChild is a DocumentFragment object, oldChild is replaced by all of the DocumentFragment children, which are inserted in the same order. If the newChild is already in the tree, it is first removed. The newChild argument is of type Node. The oldChild argument is of type Node. This method returns an object of type Node. In the event of an error, this method throws an exception of type DOMException.

removeChild(oldChild)   Removes the child node indicated by oldChild from the list of children, and returns it. The oldChild argument is of type Node. This method returns an object of type Node. In the event of an error, this method throws an exception of type DOMException.

appendChild(newChild)   Adds the node newChild to the end of the list of children of this node. If the newChild is already in the tree, it is first removed. The newChild argument is of type Node. This method returns an object of type Node. In the event of an error, this method throws an exception of type DOMException.

hasChildNodes()   Returns a Boolean value, indicating whether or not a node has any children. This method returns an object of type Boolean. In the event of an error, this method throws an exception of type DOMException.

cloneNode(deep)   Returns a duplicate copy of this node (including attributes). If deep is set to true, all contained nodes are copied. If deep is set to false, only this node is copied. The deep argument is of type Boolean. This method returns an object of type Node. In the event of an error, this method throws an exception of type DOMException.

NodeList

Defines an ordered collection of Node objects.

Property

Name	Type	Access	Description
length	long	read-only	The length of the NodeList.

Method

item(index)

Returns the specified Node in the NodeList, or null if the index is not valid. The index argument is of type Number. This method returns an object of type Node.

Notation

Represents a notation declared in the DTD. A notation either declares, by name, the format of an unparsed entity or is used for formal declaration of processing instruction targets. The nodeName attribute (inherited from Node) is set to the declared name of the notation. Notation extends the Node interface.

Properties

Name	Type	Access	Description
publicId	String	read-only	The public identifier of this notation. If the public identifier was not specified, this is null.
systemId	String	read-only	The system identifier of this notation. If the system identifier was not specified, this is null.

ProcessingInstruction

The ProcessingInstruction interface represents a "processing instruction", used in XML as a way to keep processor-specific information in the text of the document.

ProcessingInstruction extends the Node interface.

Properties

Name	Type	Access	Description
target	String	read-only	The target of this processing instruction. XML defines this as being the first token following the markup that begins the processing instruction.
data	String	read-write	The content of the processing instruction.

Text

Represents the textual content of an `Element` or `Attr`. `Text` extends the `CharacterData` interface.

Method

splitText(offset)

Breaks this node into two nodes at the specified offset, keeping both in the tree as siblings. The `offset` argument is of type `Number`. This method returns an object of type `Text`. In the event of an error, this method throws an exception of type `DOMException`.

DOM1 HTML Objects

HTMLAnchorElement

Represents an HTML A element. `HTMLAnchorElement` extends the `HTMLElement` interface.

Properties

Name	Type	Access	Description
accessKey	String	read-write	value of the ACCESSKEY attribute.
charset	String	read-write	value of the CHARSET attribute.
coords	String	read-write	value of the COORDS attribute.
href	String	read-write	value of the HREF attribute.
hreflang	String	read-write	value of the HREFLANG attribute.
name	String	read-write	value of the NAME attribute.
rel	String	read-write	value of the REL attribute.
rev	String	read-write	value of the REV attribute.
shape	String	read-write	value of the SHAPE attribute.
tabIndex	Number	read-write	value of the TABINDEX attribute.
target	String	read-write	value of the TARGET attribute.
type	String	read-write	value of the TYPE attribute.

Methods

blur()   Removes keyboard focus from this element. This method does not return a value.

focus()   Gives keyboard focus to this element. This method does not return a value.

HTMLAppletElement

Represents an HTML APPLET element. HTMLAppletElement extends the HTMLElement interface.

Properties

Name	Type	Access	Description
align	String	read-write	The value of the ALIGN attribute.
alt	String	read-write	The value of the ALT attribute.
archive	String	read-write	The value of the ARCHIVE attribute.
code	String	read-write	The value of the CODE attribute.
codeBase	String	read-write	The value of the CODEBASE attribute.
height	String	read-write	The value of the HEIGHT attribute.
hspace	String	read-write	The value of the HSPACE attribute.
name	String	read-write	The name of the applet. The value of the NAME attribute.
object	String	read-write	The value of the OBJECT attribute.
vspace	String	read-write	The value of the VSPACE attribute.
width	String	read-write	The value of the WIDTH attribute.

HTMLAreaElement

Represents an HTML AREA element. HTMLAreaElement extends the HTMLElement interface.

Properties

Name	Type	Access	Description
accessKey	String	read-write	value of the ACCESSKEY attribute.
alt	String	read-write	value of the ALT attribute.
coords	String	read-write	value of the COORDS attribute.
href	String	read-write	value of the HREF attribute.
noHref	Boolean	read-write	value of the NOHREF attribute.
shape	String	read-write	value of the SHAPE attribute.
tabIndex	Number	read-write	value of the TABINDEX attribute.
target	String	read-write	value of the TARGET attribute.

HTMLBaseElement

Represents an HTML BASE element. HTMLBaseElement extends the HTMLElement interface.

Properties

Name	Type	Access	Description
href	String	read-write	The base URI.
target	String	read-write	The default target frame.

HTMLBaseElement

Represents an HTML BASEFONT element. HTMLBaseFontElement extends the HTMLElement interface.

Properties

Name	Type	Access	Description
color	String	read-write	The value of the COLOR attribute.
face	String	read-write	The value of the FACE attribute.
size	String	read-write	The value of the SIZE attribute.

HTMLBodyElement

Represents an HTML BODY element. HTMLBodyElement extends the HTMLElement interface.

Properties

Name	Type	Access	Description
aLink	String	read-write	The value of the ALINK attribute.
background	String	read-write	The value of the BACKGROUND attribute.
bgColor	String	read-write	The value of the BGCOLOR attribute.
link	String	read-write	The value of the LINK attribute.
text	String	read-write	The value of the TEXT attribute.
vLink	String	read-write	The value of the VLINK attribute.

HTMLBRElement

Represents an HTML BR element. HTMLBRElement extends the HTMLElement interface.

Property

Name	Type	Access	Description
clear	String	read-write	The value of the CLEAR attribute.

HTMLButtonElement

Represents an HTML BUTTON element. HTMLButtonElement extends the HTMLElement interface.

Properties

Name	Type	Access	Description
form	HTMLForm Element	read-only	Returns the FORM element containing this control. Returns null if this control is not within the context of a form.
accessKey	String	read-write	A single character access key to give access to the form control.
disabled	Boolean	read-write	The value of the DISABLED attribute.
name	String	read-write	The value of the NAME attribute.
tabIndex	Number	read-write	The value of the TABINDEX attribute.
type	String	read-only	The type of this form control.
value	String	read-write	Represents the current contents of the corresponding form control.

HTMLCollection

An HTMLCollection is a list of nodes. An individual node may be accessed by either ordinal index or the node's name or id attributes.

Property

Name	Type	Access	Description
length	Number	read-only	The number of nodes in the collection.

Methods

item(index)   Returns the node identified by the index. A value of null is returned if the index is out of range. The index argument is of type Number. This method returns an object of type Node.

namedItem(name)

Returns the named node. A value of `null` is returned if the node cannot be found. The `name` argument is of type `String`. This method returns an object of type.

HTMLDirectoryElement

Represents an HTML `DIR` element. `HTMLDirectoryElement` extends the `HTMLElement` interface.

Property

Name	Type	Access	Description
compact	Boolean	read-write	Reduces spacing between list items. The value of the COMPACT attribute.

HTMLDivElement

Represents an HTML `DIV` element. `HTMLDivElement` extends the `HTMLElement` interface.

Property

Name	Type	Access	Description
align	String	read-write	Horizontal text alignment. The value of the ALIGN attribute.

HTMLDListElement

Represents an HTML `DL` element. `HTMLDListElement` extends the `HTMLElement` interface.

Property

Name	Type	Access	Description
compact	Boolean	read-write	Reduces spacing between list items. The value of the COMPACT attribute.

HTMLDocument

The root of the HTML hierarchy that holds the entire content of the document. Besides providing access to the hierarchy, it also provides some convenience methods for accessing certain sets of information from the document. `HTMLDocument` extends the `Document` interface.

Properties

Name	Type	Access	Description
title	String	read-write	The title of a document as specified by the TITLE element in the head of the document.
referrer	String	read-only	Returns the URI of the page that linked to this page. The value is an empty string if the user navigated to the page directly.
domain	String	read-only	The domain name of the server that served the document, or null if the server cannot be identified by a domain name.
URL	String	read-only	The complete URI of the document.
body	HTMLElement	read-write	The element that contains the content for the document. In documents with BODY contents, returns the BODY element. In frameset documents, this returns the outermost FRAMESET element.
images	HTMLCollection	read-only	A collection of all the IMG elements in a document. The behavior is limited to IMG elements for backward compatibility.
applets	HTMLCollection	read-only	A collection of all the OBJECT elements that include applets and APPLET elements in a document.
links	HTMLCollection	read-only	A collection of all AREA elements and anchor (A) elements in a document with a value for the href attribute.
forms	HTMLCollection	read-only	A collection of all the forms of a document.
anchors	HTMLCollection	read-only	A collection of all the anchor (A) elements in a document with a value for the name attribute. For reasons of backward compatibility, the returned set of anchors contains only those anchors created with the name attribute, not those created with the id attribute.

cookie	String	read-write	The cookies associated with this document. If there are none, the value is an empty string. Otherwise, the value is a string: a semicolon-delimited list of "name=value" pairs for all the cookies associated with the page.

Methods

open()   Opens a document stream for writing. If a document exists in the target, this method clears it. This method does not return a value.

close()   Closes a document stream opened by open(), and forces rendering. This method does not return a value.

write(text)   Writes a string of text to a document stream opened by open(). The text is parsed into the document's structure model. The text argument is of type String. This method does not return a value.

writeln(text)   Writes a string of text followed by a newline character to a document stream opened by open(). The text is parsed into the document's structure model. The text argument is of type String. This method does not return a value.

getElementById(elementId)   Returns the Element whose id is given by elementId. If no such element exists, returns null. Behavior is not defined if more than one element has this id. The elementId argument is of type String. This method returns an object of type Element.

getElementsByName(elementName)   Returns the (possibly empty) collection of elements whose name value is given by elementName. The elementName argument is of type String. This method returns an object of type NodeList.

HTMLElement

Base interface for defining all other HTML elements. The other HTML elements extend and inherit from this interface. HTMLElement extends the Element interface.

Properties

Name	Type	Access	Description
id	String	read-write	The element's identifier.
title	String	read-write	The element's advisory title.
lang	String	read-write	Language code defined in RFC 1766.

dir	String	read-write	Specifies the base direction of directionally neutral text and the directionality of tables.
className	String	read-write	The class attribute of the element.

HTMLFieldSetElement

Represents an HTML LEGEND element. HTMLFieldSetElement extends the HTMLElement interface.

Property

Name	Type	Access	Description
form	HTMLFormElement	read-only	Returns the FORM element containing this control. Returns null if this control is not within the context of a form.

HTMLFontElement

Represents an HTML FONT element. HTMLFontElement extends the HTMLElement interface.

Properties

Name	Type	Access	Description
color	String	read-write	The value of the COLOR attribute.
face	String	read-write	The value of the FACE attribute.
size	String	read-write	The value of the SIZE attribute.

HTMLFormElement

Represents an HTML FORM element. HTMLFormElement extends the HTMLElement interface.

Properties

Name	Type	Access	Description
elements	HTMLCollection	read-only	A collection of all control elements in the form.
length	Number	read-only	The number of controls in the form. Same as the length of elements.
name	String	read-write	Names the form.

acceptCharset	String	read-write	value of the ACCEPT-CHARSET attribute.
action	String	read-write	value of the ACTION attribute.
enctype	String	read-write	value of the ENCTYPE attribute.
method	String	read-write	value of the METHOD attribute.
target	String	read-write	value of the TARGET attribute.

Methods

submit()   Submits the form. It performs the same action as a submit button. This method does not return a value.

reset()   Restores a form element's default values. It performs the same action as a reset button. This method does not return a value.

HTMLFrameElement

Represents an HTML FRAME element. HTMLFrameElement extends the HTMLElement interface.

Properties

Name	Type	Access	Description
frameBorder	String	read-write	The value of the FRAMEBORDER attribute.
longDesc	String	read-write	URI designating a long description of this image or frame. The value of the LONGDESC attribute.
marginHeight	String	read-write	The value of the MARGINHEIGHT attribute.
marginWidth	String	read-write	The value of the MARGINWIDTH attribute.
name	String	read-write	The frame name (object of the target attribute).
noResize	Boolean	read-write	The value of the NORESIZE attribute.
scrolling	String	read-write	Specifies whether or not the frame should have scrollbars.
src	String	read-write	A URI designating the initial frame contents. The value of the SRC attribute.

HTMLFrameSetElement

Represents an HTML FRAMESET element. HTMLFrameSetElement extends the HTMLElement interface.

Properties

Name	Type	Access	Description
cols	String	read-write	The number of columns of frames in the frameset.
rows	String	read-write	The number of rows of frames in the frameset.

HTMLHeadElement

The HEAD element of an HTML document. HTMLHeadElement extends the HTMLElement interface.

Property

Name	Type	Access	Description
profile	String	read-write	URI designating a metadata profile.

HTMLHeadingElement

Represents an HTML heading (H1 through H6) element. HTMLHeadingElement extends the HTMLElement interface.

Property

Name	Type	Access	Description
align	String	read-write	Horizontal text alignment. The value of the ALIGN attribute.

HTMLHRElement

Represents an HTML HR element. HTMLHRElement extends the HTMLElement interface.

Properties

Name	Type	Access	Description
align	String	read-write	The value of the ALIGN attribute.
noShade	Boolean	read-write	The value of the NOSHADE attribute.
size	String	read-write	The value of the SIZE attribute.
width	String	read-write	The value of the WIDTH attribute.

Properties

Name	Type	Access	Description
lowSrc	String	read-write	URI designating the source of this image, for low-resolution output.
name	String	read-write	The name of the element.
align	String	read-write	value of the ALIGN attribute.
alt	String	read-write	value of the ALT attribute.
border	String	read-write	value of the BORDER attribute.
height	String	read-write	value of the HEIGHT attribute.
hspace	String	read-write	value of the HSPACE attribute.
isMap	Boolean	read-write	value of the ISMAP attribute.
longDesc	String	read-write	value of the LONGDESC attribute.
src	String	read-write	value of the SRC attribute.
useMap	String	read-write	value of the USEMAP attribute.
vspace	String	read-write	value of the VSPACE attribute.
width	String	read-write	value of the WIDTH attribute.

HTMLInputElement

Represents an HTML INPUT element. HTMLInputElement extends the HTMLElement interface.

Properties

Name	Type	Access	Description
defaultValue	String	read-write	When the type attribute of the element has the value "Text", "File", or "Password", this represents the HTML VALUE attribute of the element. The value of this attribute does not change if the contents of the corresponding form control, in an interactive user agent, changes. Changing this attribute, however, resets the contents of the form control.

defaultChecked	Boolean	read-write	When type has the value "Radio" or "Checkbox", this represents the HTML CHECKED attribute of the element. The value of this attribute does not change if the state of the corresponding form control, in an interactive user agent, changes. Changes to this attribute, however, reset the state of the form control.
form	HTMLForm Element	read-only	Returns the FORM element containing this control. Returns null if this control is not within the context of a form.
accept	String	read-write	A comma-separated list of content types that a server processing this form will handle correctly.
accessKey	String	read-write	A single character access key to give access to the form control.
align	String	read-write	Aligns this object (vertically or horizontally) with respect to its surrounding text.
alt	String	read-write	Alternate text for user agents not rendering the normal content of this element.
checked	Boolean	read-write	When the type attribute of the element has the value "Radio" or "Checkbox", this represents the current state of the form control in an interactive user agent. Changes to this attribute change the state of the form control, but do not change the value of the HTML value attribute of the element.
disabled	Boolean	read-write	The value of the DISABLED attribute.
maxLength	Number	read-write	Maximum number of characters for text fields, when type has the value "Text" or "Password".
name	String	read-write	Form control or object name when submitted with a form.

readOnly	Boolean	read-write	This control is read-only. Relevant only when type has the value "Text" or "Password".
size	String	read-write	Size information. The precise meaning is specific to each type of field.
src	String	read-write	When the type attribute has the value "Image", this attribute specifies the location of the image to be used to decorate the graphical submit button.
tabIndex	Number	read-write	Index that represents the element's position in the tabbing order.
type	String	read-only	The type of control created.
useMap	String	read-write	The value of the USEMAP attribute.
value	String	read-write	When the TYPE attribute of the element has the value "Text", "File" or "Password", this represents the current contents of the corresponding form control in an interactive user agent. Changing this attribute changes the contents of the form control, but does not change the value of the HTML VALUE attribute of the element. When the TYPE attribute of the element has the value "Button", "Hidden", "Submit", "Reset", "Image", "Checkbox", or "Radio", this represents the HTML VALUE attribute of the element.

Methods

blur()   Removes keyboard focus from this element. This method does not return a value.

focus()   Gives keyboard focus to this element. This method does not return a value.

select()   Selects the contents of the text area. For INPUT elements whose type attribute has one of the following values: "Text", "File", or "Password". This method does not return a value.

click()   Simulates a mouse-click. For INPUT elements whose type attribute has one of the following values: "Button", "Checkbox", "Radio", "Reset", or "Submit". This method does not return a value.

HTMLIsIndexElement

Represents an HTML ISINDEX element. HTMLIsIndexElement extends the HTMLElement interface.

Properties

Name	Type	Access	Description
form	HTMLFormElement	read-only	Returns the FORM element containing this control. Returns null if this control is not within the context of a form.
prompt	String	read-write	The prompt message.

HTMLLabelElement

Represents an HTML LABEL element. HTMLLabelElement extends the HTMLElement interface.

Properties

Name	Type	Access	Description
form	HTMLFormElement	read-only	Returns the FORM element containing this control. Returns null if this control is not within the context of a form.
accessKey	String	read-write	A single character access key to give access to the form control.
htmlFor	String	read-write	This attribute links this label with another form control by ID attribute.

HTMLLegendElement

Represents an HTML FIELDSET element. HTMLLegendElement extends the HTMLElement interface.

Properties

Name	Type	Access	Description
form	HTMLFormElement	read-only	Returns the FORM element containing this control. Returns null if this control is not within the context of a form.
accessKey	String	read-write	A single character access key to give access to the form control.
align	String	read-write	Text alignment relative to FIELDSET.

HTMLLIElement

Represents an HTML LI element. HTMLLIElement extends the HTMLElement interface.

Properties

Name	Type	Access	Description
type	String	read-write	List item bullet style. The value of the TYPE attribute.
value	Number	read-write	Resets sequence number when used in OL. The value of the VALUE attribute.

HTMLLinkElement

Represents an HTML LINK element. HTMLLinkElement extends the HTMLElement interface.

Properties

Name	Type	Access	Description
disabled	Boolean	read-write	Enables/disables the link. This is currently used only for style sheet links, and may be used to activate or deactivate style sheets.
charset	String	read-write	The character encoding of the resource being linked.
href	String	read-write	The URI of the linked resource.
hreflang	String	read-write	Language code of the linked resource.
media	String	read-write	The media attribute of the link.
rel	String	read-write	Identifies a forward link.
rev	String	read-write	Identifies a reverse link.
target	String	read-write	Frame to render the resource in.
type	String	read-write	Advisory content type.

HTMLMapElement

Represents an HTML MAP element. HTMLMapElement extends the HTMLElement interface.

Properties

Name	Type	Access	Description
areas	HTMLCollection	read-only	The list of areas defined for the image map.
name	String	read-write	Names the map (for use with USEMAP).

HTMLMenuElement

Represents an HTML MENU element. HTMLMenuElement extends the HTMLElement interface.

Property

Name	Type	Access	Description
compact	Boolean	read-write	Reduces spacing between list items. The value of the COMPACT attribute.

HTMLMetaElement

Represents an HTML META element. HTMLMetaElement extends the HTMLElement interface.

Properties

Name	Type	Access	Description
content	String	read-write	The value of the CONTENT attribute.
httpEquiv	String	read-write	The value of the HTTP-EQUIV attribute.
name	String	read-write	The value of the NAME attribute.
scheme	String	read-write	The value of the SCHEME attribute.

HTMLModElement

Represents the HTML INS and DEL elements. HTMLModElement extends the HTMLElement interface.

Properties

Name	Type	Access	Description
cite	String	read-write	The value of the CITE attribute.
dateTime	String	read-write	The value of the DATETIME attribute.

HTMLObjectElement

Represents an HTML OBJECT element. HTMLObjectElement extends the HTMLElement interface.

Properties

Name	Type	Access	Description
form	HTMLFormElement	read-only	Returns the FORM element containing this control. Returns null if this control is not within the context of a form.
code	String	read-write	The value of the CODE attribute.
align	String	read-write	The value of the ALIGN attribute.
archive	String	read-write	The value of the ARCHIVE attribute.
border	String	read-write	The value of the BORDER attribute.
codeBase	String	read-write	The value of the CODEBASE attribute.
codeType	String	read-write	The value of the CODETYPE attribute.
data	String	read-write	A URI specifying the location of the object's data. The value of the DATA attribute.
declare	Boolean	read-write	Declare (for future reference), but do not instantiate, this object. The value of the DECLARE attribute.
height	String	read-write	value of the HEIGHT attribute.
hspace	String	read-write	value of the HSPACE attribute.
name	String	read-write	The name of the element.
standby	String	read-write	Message to render while loading the object. The value of the STANDBY attribute.
tabIndex	Number	read-write	Index that represents the element's position in the tabbing order. The value of the TABINDEX attribute.
type	String	read-write	Content type for data downloaded via DATA attribute. The value of the TYPE attribute.
useMap	String	read-write	The value of the USEMAP attribute.
vspace	String	read-write	The value of the VSPACE attribute.
width	String	read-write	The value of the WIDTH attribute.

HTMLOListElement

Represents an HTML OL element. HTMLOListElement extends the HTMLElement interface.

Properties

Name	Type	Access	Description
compact	Boolean	read-write	Reduces spacing between list items. The value of the COMPACT attribute.
start	Number	read-write	Starting sequence number. The value of the START attribute.
type	String	read-write	Bullet style. The value of the TYPE attribute.

HTMLOptGroupElement

Represents an HTML OPTGROUP element. HTMLOptGroupElement extends the HTMLElement interface.

Properties

Name	Type	Access	Description
disabled	Boolean	read-write	The value of the DISABLED attribute.
label	String	read-write	The value of the LABEL attribute.

HTMLOptionElement

Represents an HTML OPTION element. HTMLOptionElement extends the HTMLElement interface.

Properties

Name	Type	Access	Description
form	HTMLFormElement	read-only	Returns the FORM element containing this control. Returns null if this control is not within the context of a form.
default Selected	Boolean	read-write	The value of the HTML SELECTED attribute.
text	String	read-only	The text contained within the OPTION element.

index	Number	read-only	The index of this OPTION in its parent SELECT, starting from 0.
disabled	Boolean	read-write	The value of the HTML DISABLED attribute.
label	String	read-write	The value of the HTML LABEL attribute.
selected	Boolean	read-write	Represents the current state of the corresponding form control in an interactive user agent. Changing this attribute changes the state of the form control, but does not change the value of the HTML SELECTED attribute of the element.
value	String	read-write	The value of the HTML VALUE attribute.

HTMLParagraphElement

Represents an HTML P element. HTMLParagraphElement extends the HTMLElement interface.

Property

Name	Type	Access	Description
align	String	read-write	Horizontal text alignment. The value of the ALIGN attribute.

HTMLParamElement

Represents an HTML PARAM element. HTMLParamElement extends the HTMLElement interface.

Properties

Name	Type	Access	Description
name	String	read-write	The name of a runtime parameter. The value of the NAME attribute.
type	String	read-write	Content type for the VALUE attribute when VALUE-TYPE has the value "ref".
value	String	read-write	The value of a runtime parameter. The value of the VALUE attribute.
valueType	String	read-write	Information about the meaning of the VALUE attribute value. The value of the VALUETYPE attribute.

HTMLPreElement

Represents an HTML PRE element. HTMLPreElement extends the HTMLElement interface.

Property

Name	Type	Access	Description
width	Number	read-write	The value of the WIDTH attribute.

HTMLQuoteElement

Represents the HTML BLOCKQUOTE and Q elements. HTMLQuoteElement extends the HTML-Element interface.

Property

Name	Type	Access	Description
cite	String	read-write	A URI designating a source document or message. The value of the CITE attribute.

HTMLScriptElement

Represents an HTML SCRIPT element. HTMLScriptElement extends the HTMLElement interface.

Properties

Name	Type	Access	Description
text	String	read-write	The script content of the element.
htmlFor	String	read-write	Reserved for future use.
event	String	read-write	Reserved for future use.
charset	String	read-write	The character encoding of the linked resource.
defer	Boolean	read-write	Indicates that the user agent can defer processing of the script.
src	String	read-write	URI designating an external script.
type	String	read-write	The content type of the script language.

HTMLSelectElement

Represents an HTML SELECT element. HTMLSelectElement extends the HTMLElement interface.

Properties

Name	Type	Access	Description
type	String	read-only	The type of this form control. This is the string "select-multiple" when the multiple attribute is true, and is the string "select-one" when false.
selectedIndex	Number	read-write	The ordinal index of the selected option, starting from 0. The value -1 is returned if no element is selected. If multiple options are selected, the index of the first selected option is returned.
value	String	read-write	The value of the VALUE attribute.
length	Number	read-only	The number of options in this SELECT element.
form	HTMLFormElement	read-only	Returns the FORM element containing this control. Returns null if this control is not within the context of a form.
options	HTMLCollection	read-only	The collection of OPTION elements contained by this element.
disabled	Boolean	read-write	The value of the DISABLED attribute.
multiple	Boolean	read-write	The value of the MULTIPLE attribute.
name	String	read-write	The value of the NAME attribute.
size	Number	read-write	The value of the SIZE attribute.
tabIndex	Number	read-write	The value of the TABINDEX attribute.

Methods

add(element, before)   Adds a new element to the collection of OPTION elements for this SELECT element. The element argument is of type HTMLElement. The before argument is of type HTMLElement. This method does not return a value. In the event of an error, this method throws an exception of type DOMException.

remove(index) Removes the specified element from the collection of OPTION elements for this SELECT element. Does nothing if no element has the given index. The index argument is of type Number. This method does not return a value.

blur() Removes keyboard focus from this element. This method does not return a value.

focus() Gives keyboard focus to this element. This method does not return a value.

HTMLStyleElement

Represents an HTML STYLE element. HTMLStyleElement extends the HTMLElement interface.

Properties

Name	Type	Access	Description
disabled	Boolean	read-write	Enables/disables the style sheet.
media	String	read-write	The MEDIA attribute of the style sheet.
type	String	read-write	The content type of the style sheet language.

HTMLTableCaptionElement

Represents an HTML CAPTION element. HTMLTableCaptionElement extends the HTMLElement interface.

Property

Name	Type	Access	Description
align	String	read-write	Caption alignment with respect to the table.

HTMLTableCellElement

Represents an HTML TD element. HTMLTableCellElement extends the HTMLElement interface.

Properties

Name	Type	Access	Description
cellIndex;	Number	read-only	The index of this cell in the row, starting from 0. This index is in document tree order, not in display order.
abbr	String	read-write	Abbreviation for header cells.
align	String	read-write	The value of the ALIGN attribute.
axis	String	read-write	Names group of related headers.

bgColor	String	read-write	The value of the BGCOLOR attribute.
ch	String	read-write	Alignment character for cells in a column.
chOff	String	read-write	Offset of the alignment character.
colSpan	Number	read-write	The value of the COLSPAN attribute.
headers	String	read-write	List of ID attribute values for header cells. The value of the HEADERS attribute.
height	String	read-write	The value of the HEIGHT attribute.
noWrap	Boolean	read-write	The value of the NOWRAP attribute.
rowSpan	Number	read-write	The value of the ROWSPAN attribute.
scope	String	read-write	Scope covered by header cells. The value of the SCOPE attribute.
vAlign	String	read-write	The value of the VALIGN attribute.
width	String	read-write	The value of the WIDTH attribute.

HTMLTableColElement

Represents an HTML COL element. HTMLTableColElement extends the HTMLElement interface.

Properties

Name	Type	Access	Description
align	String	read-write	Horizontal alignment of data within cells of this row.
ch	String	read-write	Alignment character for cells in a column.
chOff	String	read-write	Offset of alignment character.
span	Number	read-write	Identifies the number of columns in a group or affected by a grouping.
vAlign	String	read-write	Vertical alignment of cell data in column.
width	String	read-write	Default column width.

HTMLTableElement

Represents an HTML TABLE element. HTMLTableElement extends the HTMLElement interface.

Properties

Name	Type	Access	Description
caption	HTMLTableCaptionElement	read-write	Returns the table's CAPTION, or null if none exists.
tHead	HTMLTableSectionElement	read-write	Returns the table's THEAD, or null if none exists.
tFoot	HTMLTableSectionElement	read-write	Returns the table's TFOOT, or null if none exists.
rows	HTMLCollection	read-only	Returns a collection of all the rows in the table, including all in THEAD, TFOOT, and TBODY elements.
tBodies	HTMLCollection	read-only	Returns a collection of the defined table bodies.
align	String	read-write	value of the ALIGN attribute.
bgColor	String	read-write	value of the BGCOLOR attribute.
border	String	read-write	value of the BORDER attribute.
cellPadding	String	read-write	Specifies the horizontal and vertical space between cell content and cell borders.
cellSpacing	String	read-write	Specifies the horizontal and vertical separation between cells.
frame	String	read-write	Specifies which external table borders to render.
rules	String	read-write	Specifies which internal table borders to render.
summary	String	read-write	Description about the purpose or structure of a table.
width	String	read-write	Specifies the desired table width. Value of the WIDTH attribute.

Methods

createTHead()   Creates a table header row, or returns an existing one. This method returns an object of type HTMLElement.

deleteTHead()   Deletes the header from the table, if one exists. This method does not return a value.

createTFoot()   Creates a table footer row, or returns an existing one. This method returns an object of type HTMLElement.

deleteTFoot()   Deletes the footer from the table, if one exists. This method does not return a value.

createCaption()   Creates a new table caption object, or returns an existing one. This method returns an object of type HTMLElement.

deleteCaption()   Deletes the table caption, if one exists. This method does not return a value.

insertRow(index)   Inserts a new empty row in the table. The new row is inserted in the table immediately before and in the same section as the row with the specified index. If index is equal to the number of rows, the new row is appended. In addition, when the table is empty, the row is inserted into a TBODY, which is created and inserted into the table. The index argument is of type Number. This method returns an object of type HTMLElement. In the event of an error, this method throws an exception of type DOMException.

deleteRow(index)   Deletes a table row. The index argument is of type Number. This method does not return a value. In the event of an error, this method throws an exception of type DOMException.

HTMLTableRowElement

Represents an HTML TR element. HTMLTableRowElement extends the HTMLElement interface.

Properties

Name	Type	Access	Description
rowIndex	Number	read-only	The index of this row, relative to the entire table, starting from 0. This is in document tree order, not in display order. The rowIndex does not take into account sections (THEAD, TFOOT, or TBODY) within the table.

sectionRowIndex	Number	read-only	The index of this row, relative to the current section (THEAD, TFOOT, or TBODY), starting from 0.
cells	HTMLCollection	read-only	The collection of cells in this row.
align	String	read-write	value of the ALIGN attribute.
bgColor	String	read-write	value of the BGCOLOR attribute.
ch	String	read-write	Alignment character for cells in a column.
vAlign	String	read-write	Offset of alignment character.
vAlign	String	read-write	value of the VALIGN attribute.

Methods

insertCell(index)   Inserts an empty TD cell into this row. If index is equal to the number of cells, the new cell is appended. The index argument is of type Number. This method returns an object of type HTMLElement. In the event of an error, this method throws an exception of type DOMException.

deleteCell(index)   Deletes a cell from the current row. The index argument is of type Number. This method does not return a value. In the event of an error, this method throws an exception of type DOMException.

HTMLTableSectionElement

Represents the HTML THEAD, TFOOT, and TBODY elements. HTMLTableSectionElement extends the HTMLElement interface.

Properties

Name	Type	Access	Description
align	String	read-write	The value of the ALIGN attribute.
ch	String	read-write	Alignment character for cells in a column.
chOff	String	read-write	Offset of alignment character.
vAlign	String	read-write	The value of the VALIGN attribute.
rows	HTMLCollection	read-only	The collection of rows in this table section.

Methods

insertRow(index)   Inserts a row into this section. The new row is inserted in this section immediately before the row with the specified `index`. If `index` is equal to the number of rows in this section, the new row is appended. The `index` argument is of type `Number`. This method returns an object of type `HTMLElement`. In the event of an error, this method throws an exception of type `DOMException`.

deleteRow(index)   Deletes a row from this section. The `index` argument is of type `Number`. This method does not return a value. In the event of an error, this method throws an exception of type `DOMException`.

HTMLTextAreaElement

Represents an HTML `TEXTAREA` element. `HTMLTextAreaElement` extends the `HTMLElement` interface.

Properties

Name	Type	Access	Description
defaultValue	String	read-write	Represents the contents of the element.
form	HTMLFormElement	read-only	Returns the `FORM` element containing this control. Returns `null` if this control is not within the context of a form.
accessKey	String	read-write	A single character access key to give access to the form control.
cols	Number	read-write	Width of control (in characters).
disabled	Boolean	read-write	The value of the `DISABLED` attribute.
name	String	read-write	The value of the `NAME` attribute.
readOnly	Boolean	read-write	The value of the `READONLY` attribute.
rows	Number	read-write	The value of the `ROWS` attribute.
tabIndex	Number	read-write	The value of the `TABINDEX` attribute.
type	String	read-only	The type of this form control. This is the string "textarea".
value	String	read-write	Represents the current contents of the corresponding form control.

Methods

blur()   Removes keyboard focus from this element. This method does not return a value.

focus()   Gives keyboard focus to this element. This method does not return a value.

select()   Selects the contents of the TEXTAREA. This method does not return a value.

HTMLTitleElement

Represents an HTML TITLE element. HTMLTitleElement extends the HTMLElement interface.

Property

Name	Type	Access	Description
text	String	read-write	The specified title as a string.

HTMLUListElement

Represents an HTML UL element. HTMLUListElement extends the HTMLElement interface.

Properties

Name	Type	Access	Description
compact	Boolean	read-write	Reduces spacing between list items. The value of the COMPACT attribute.
type	String	read-write	Bullet style. The value of the TYPE attribute.

Cascading Style Sheets

This appendix summarizes the selectors, properties, and values defined by CSS1. For a more detailed description, refer to the CSS1 recommendation at www.w3.org/TR/REC-CSS1.

Selectors

The following subsections identify and describe the selectors that are defined for use with CSS1.

Tag Name

Tag names may be used as CSS selectors. They result in the style rules being applied to all tags within the document (unless they are overridden by another style rule). An example of their use follows:

```
h2 {
background-color: blue;
}
```

The preceding example sets the background color of all h2 tags to blue.

ID

ID attribute values may be used as CSS selectors. They result in the style rules being applied to all elements within the document that have the specified ID value. (Theoretically, each element should have a unique ID value. However, this is usually not enforced.) ID attribute values are preceded by a hash mark (#) when they are used as a selector. The following rule specifies that all elements with an ID of fineprint should be displayed with an x-small font.

```
#fineprint {
font-size: x-small;
}
```

Class

Class names may be used as CSS selectors. They result in the style rules being applied to all elements within the document that have the specified class name. Class names are preceded by a period (.) when they are used as a selector. A tag name may precede the period to limit the style rule to the tags of that tag. The following rule specifies that all paragraph elements with a class of secret should be displayed in red.

```
p.secret {
color: red;
}
```

Pseudo-Class

Pseudo-classes are used to select classes of elements that are not real HTML elements. CSS1 defines the following three pseudo-classes:

Pseudo-Class	Description
active	Specifies the style to be applied to a hyperlink when it is clicked.
link	Specifies the style to be applied to a hyperlink that has yet to be visited (that is, isn't in the browser's history list).
visited	Specifies the style to be applied to a hyperlink that has been visited.

The following example sets the background and text colors for hyperlinks based on whether they have or have not been visited.

```
:link {
background-color: red;
color: white;
}
:visited {
background-color: black;
color: white;
}
```

Pseudo-classes are preceded by a colon (:), and the colon may be preceded by another selector.

Pseudo-Element

Pseudo-elements are similar to pseudo-classes. Pseudo-elements are used to select parts of elements. CSS1 defines the following two pseudo-elements.

Pseudo-Element	Description
first-letter	Specifies the style to be applied to the first letter of an element.
first-line	Specifies the style to be applied to the first line of an element.

The following example sets the font-size for the first letter of each paragraph.

```
p:first-letter {
font-size: xx-large;
}
```

Pseudo-elements, like pseudo-classes, are preceded by a colon (:), and the colon may be preceded by another selector.

Properties

The following subsections identify and describe the properties that are defined for use with CSS1. Shorthand properties allow two or more properties of a group to be specified at once. Multiple values are separated by spaces. For example, you can specify all of the background properties of paragraphs using the following style definition:

```
p {
  background: fixed yellow url(image.gif) center no-repeat;
}
```

background

Shorthand property for properties beginning with 'background-'.

background-attachment

Specifies whether the background image scrolls with its associated element. Values are scroll (default) and fixed.

background-color

Identifies the element's background color. Colors may be specified by name, by color constant, or via the rgb(r, g, b) notation. The default value is transparent.

background-image

Specifies the URL of the element's background image using the url(value) notation.

background-position

Specifies the position of an element's background image using vertical and horizontal values. Values may be a percentage of the element; absolute offsets; or the names top, bottom, left, right, and center. By default, the image is positioned in the upper-left corner of the element.

background-repeat

Specifies how the background image should be repeated. Values are repeat, no-repeat, repeat-x, and repeat-y. The default value is repeat, which causes vertical and horizontal repeating of the background image.

border

A shorthand notation for specifying properties beginning with 'border-'.

border-bottom

A shorthand notation for specifying the width, style, and color of the bottom border.

border-bottom-width

Specifies the width of the bottom border. A numeric value may be supplied (with units) or the names thin, medium (default), and thick.

border-color

Shorthand notation for specifying the color of all four borders.

border-left

A shorthand notation for specifying the width, style, and color of the left border.

border-left-width

Specifies the width of the left border. A numeric value may be supplied (with units) or the names thin, medium (default), and thick.

border-right

A shorthand notation for specifying the width, style, and color of the right border.

border-right-width

Specifies the width of the right border. A numeric value may be supplied (with units) or the names thin, medium (default), and thick.

border-style

Shorthand notation for specifying the style of all four borders. Values are none (default), dotted, dashed, solid, double, groove, ridge, inset, and outset.

border-top

A shorthand notation for specifying the width, style, and color of the top border.

border-top-width

Specifies the width of the top border. A numeric value may be supplied (with units) or the names `thin`, `medium` (default), and `thick`.

border-width

Shorthand notation for specifying the width of all four borders.

clear

Specifies how floating images are to be positioned with respect to an element.

color

Specifies the foreground or text color of an element.

display

Used to specify how an element is to be displayed. Values are `block` (default), `inline`, `list-item`, and `none`.

float

Specifies the direction of float for an element. Floating specifies how the element (usually an image) is laid out with respect to text. Values are `left`, `right`, and `none` (default).

font

Shortcut for specifying properties that begin with 'font-'.

font-family

Specifies a font family to be used with an element. The default value is browser-specific.

font-size

Allows a font size to be specified in terms of a fixed point size, a percentage of the current point size, or via a font size name. The following font-size names may be used: `xx-small`, `x-small`, `small`, `medium` (default), `large`, `x-large`, `xx-large`, `larger`, and `smaller`.

font-style

Specifies the font style to be used with an element. Values are `normal` (default), `italic`, and `oblique`.

font-variant

Allows a variation on the font to be specified. Values are `normal` (default) and `small-caps`.

font-weight

Allows the weight of a font to be specified using the following names and values: `normal` (default), `bold`, `bolder`, `lighter`, 100, 200, 300, 400, 500, 600, 700, 800, and 900. The value of 400 is equivalent to `normal`.

height

Specifies the height of an element using a numeric unit or `auto` (default).

letter-spacing

Specifies the spacing between letters of an element. Values are `normal` (default) or a numeric unit.

line-height

Specifies the line-height of the element using a numeric value, a numeric unit, a percentage, or `normal` (default).

list-style

A shorthand for specifying styles that begin with 'list-style'.

list-style-image

Specifies an image to be used in bulleted lists. Values are a URL using the `url(value)` notation or `none` (default).

list-style-position

Specifies how an element is to be positioned in a list. Values are `inside` and `outside` (default).

list-style-type

Specifies how bullets are to be numbered (ordered lists) or displayed (unordered lists). Values are `disc` (default), `circle`, `square`, `decimal`, `lower-roman`, `upper-roman`, `lower-alpha`, `upper-alpha`, or `none`.

margin

Shorthand for specifying properties that begin with '`margin-`'.

margin-bottom

Specifies the bottom margin in terms of a numeric value, percentage, or `auto`. The margin is 0 by default.

margin-left

Specifies the left margin in terms of a numeric value, percentage, or `auto`. The margin is 0 by default.

margin-right

Specifies the right margin in terms of a numeric value, percentage, or `auto`. The margin is 0 by default.

margin-top

Specifies the top margin in terms of a numeric value, percentage, or `auto`. The margin is 0 by default.

padding

Shorthand for specifying properties that begin with '`padding-`'.

padding-bottom

Specifies the bottom padding in terms of a numeric value or a percentage. The default value is 0.

padding-left

Specifies the left padding in terms of a numeric value or a percentage. The default value is 0.

padding-right

Specifies the right padding in terms of a numeric value or a percentage. The default value is 0.

padding-top

Specifies the top padding in terms of a numeric value or a percentage. The default value is 0.

text-align

Specifies how text is to be aligned within an element. Values are left, right, center, and justify. The default value is browser-specific.

text-decoration

Specifies decorative effects for text. Values are none (default), underline, overline, line-through, and blink.

text-indent

Specifies how the first line of text of an element is to be indented. Values are a numeric unit or a percentage. The default value is 0.

text-transform

Specifies the use of capitalization. Values are none (default), capitalize, lowercase, and uppercase.

vertical-align

Specifies the vertical alignment of an element. Values are a percentage or baseline (default), sub, super, top, text-top, middle, bottom, and text-bottom.

white-space

Specifies how whitespace is rendered within an element. Values are normal (default), pre, and nowrap.

width

Specifies the width of an element using a numeric unit or auto (default).

word-spacing

Specifies the whitespace between words. Values are a numeric unit or normal (default).

INDEX

Note to the Reader: Throughout this index **boldfaced** page numbers indicate primary discussions of a topic. *Italicized* page numbers indicate illustrations.

SYMBOLS

& (ampersands)
  in assignment operators, 76
  in bit operators, 75
  character references for, 655
  for entities, 39, 656
  in logical operators, 74
  precedence of, 83
<> (angle brackets) in HTML, 7
* (asterisks)
  in assignment operators, 76
  for comments, 40, 387
  in DTDs, 657–658
  for multiplication, 73
  precedence of, 83
  in regular expressions, 955
  in source.txt, 894
\ (backslashes)
  in regular expressions, 955
  in string values, 53–54
{} (braces)
  for entities, 39
  for functions, 98
  for if statements, 87–88
  missing, **217**
  in regular expressions, 955
  for with statements, 105
^ (carets)
  in assignment operators, 76
  as bit operator, 75
  precedence of, 83
  in regular expressions, 950, 955
  in source.txt, 895
: (colons)
  in conditional expressions, 76
  precedence of, 83

in regular expressions, 955
in URLs, 335
, (comma) operator, 77
, (commas) for parameters, 175
$ (dollar signs)
  in names, 46
  in regular expressions, 955
"" (double quotes)
  for attributes, 121, 654
  for DOCTYPE declarations, 653
  for string values, 52–53
  syntax errors from, **218**
= (equal signs)
  in assignment operators, 76
  in comparison operators, 74–75
  precedence of, 83
! (exclamation points)
  for comments, 35
  for comparison operators, 74
  for DOCTYPE declarations, 653
  for logical operators, 74
  precedence of, 83
  for XML comments, 655
  for XML declarations, 653
/ (forward slashes)
  in assignment operators, 76
  for comments, 35, 40, 387
  for division, 73
  in HTML, 7
  precedence of, 83
  in URLs, 12–13, 335
> (greater than signs)
  in assignment operators, 76
  as bit operator, 75
  character references for, 655
  in comparison operators, 74
  for DOCTYPE declarations, 653
  precedence of, 83

A

D

F

H

I

J

JDK (Java Development Kit), 811, **817–818**, *818*
join() method, 184, 961
joining strings, 75
.jpe extension, 12
.jpeg extension, 12
JPEG files
    helper applications for, 10
    MIME type for, 12
.jpg extension, 12
JRE (Java Runtime Environment), 813
.js extension, 38
JScript language, 18, **852–854**, *853*
JScript LANGUAGE attribute, 33
JSException class, 832
JSObject class
    in Java, 832–834
    methods in, 836–837
JVM (Java Virtual Machine), 812–813

K

keycode property, 151
keywords
    in Java, 819
    in search scripts, **563–566**, *566–567*

L

label property
    in HTMLOptGroupElement, 1037
    in HTMLOptionElement, 1038
labelAxes() method, 844, 846
labels, **92**
    for break statements, 93
    for continue statements, 94
lang property, 430, 1025
LANGUAGE attribute, **31–34**, 74
lastChild property, 423, 1015
lastIndex property, 956, 973
lastIndexOf() method, 196, 974
lastModified property, 267, 982
layer tags, 501
layerX property, 150
layerY property, 150
layout documents, load events for, **128–129**
learning Java, **818**

left property, 404
left shift operator, 75
len variable, 294
length() method, 893
length of arrays, 65–67, *67*
length property
    in Array, 184, 960
    in CharacterData, 1008
    in Form, 281, 283, 287, 986
    in Function, 190, 967
    in History, 359, 988
    in HTMLCollection, 431, 1022
    in HTMLFormElement, 1026
    in HTMLSelectElement, 1040
    in NamedNodeMap, 425, 1014
    in NodeList, 425, 1018
    of objects, 69
    in Option, 994
    in plugins, 863–864, 867
    in Select, 998
    in String, 195, 973
    in Window, 247, 1003
less than signs (<)
    in assignment operators, 76
    as bit operator, 75
    character references for, 655
    in comparison operators, 74
    for DOCTYPE declarations, 653
    precedence of, 83
    for XML comments, 655
    for XML declarations, 653
letter-spacing property, 1055
letterSpacing property, 404
libraries, COM, 16
line-height property, 390–391, 1055
line parameter, 160
LineDesc_display() function
    in present.js, 902
    in wsh-present.js, 922
LineDesc_displayError() function
    in present.js, 902
    in wsh-present.js, 922
LineDesc() function
    in present.js, 901–902
    in wsh-present.js, 922
LineDesc_getLevel() function
    in present.js, 903
    in wsh-present.js, 923

O

P

S

X

Y

Z